KNOWLEDGE IS POWER

BE AS A QUIET WHISPER IN THE WIND

BY

ROY NOLAN

authorHOUSE™

1663 Liberty Drive, Suite 200
Bloomington, Indiana 47403
(800) 839-8640
www.AuthorHouse.com

First published by AuthorHouse 10/05/04

ISBN: 1-4184-8451-2 (sc)
ISBN: 1-4208-0208-9 (dj)

Printed in the United States of America
Bloomington, Indiana

This book is printed on acid-free paper.

DEDICATED TO :

EMERALD
DALLAS
JOSHUA.

BOOKS BY ROY NOLAN :-

[1] WISDOM : THE SECRETS OF SUCCESS IN LIFE MOUNT UP WITH WINGS AS EAGLE.

[2] WISDOM
KNOWLEDGE
UNDERSTANDING.

[IN ALL YOUR GETTING, GET IT]

[3] THE SWORD OF THE SPIRIT.

[IT BISECTS YOU INTO BITS AND PIECES]

[4] KNOWLEDGE
        IS
        POWER

HOW POWERFUL ARE YOU?   BE AS A QUIET WHISPER IN THE WIND.

ABOUT THIS BOOK :-

IT TELLS YOU ALL YOU NEED TO KNOW ABOUT THE BASICS IN THE ENGLISH LANGUAGE, SCIENCE,PHYSICS, CHEMISTRY, MATHEMATICS, GEOGRAPHY, HISTORY, ECONOMICS, COMMERCE, WORLD – FACTS, HUMAN BIOLOGY, GEOLOGY, OCEANOGRAPHY, SPORTS, AND A VAST ARRAY OF SUBJECTS MATTERS; TOPICS COVERED ARE SUCH AS THE CONTINENTS - NORTH AMERICA, EUROPE, AFRICA, SOUTH AMERICA, AUSTRALIA, ASIA, ANTARCTICA; ENGLAND, CANADA, COUNTRIES OF THE WORLD, RIVERS, OCEANS, LAKES, MOUNTAINS, DESERTS, WEST – INDIES CARIBBEAN, SOLAR SYSTEM; AND NUMEROUS OTHER SUBJECT MATTERS; TURN THE PAGES AND FIND OUT, YOU WILL BE GLAD YOU DID; BECOME POWERFUL; FOR KNOWLEDGE IS POWER. YOU CAN BE AS POWERFUL AS YOU WANT TO BE. IN THIS BOOK, YOU HAVE THE WORLD IN YOUR HANDS. BE SURE TO CHECK OUT THE QUESTIONS AND / WITH ANSWERS SECTIONS IT GIVES YOU ALL THE ANSWERS YOU NEED TO KNOW; SO YOU CAN ACCUMULATE THE WORLD OF KNOWLEDGE AND SO BECOME POWERFUL, AFTER ALL AS YOU KNOW, KNOWLEDGE IS POWER; SO HERE IS A GREAT OPPORTUNITY TO BECOME A POWERFUL PERSON WHO WOULD HAVE THE KNOWLEDGE OF THE WORLD IN YOUR HANDS. SEIZE THIS OPPORTUNITY AND TAKE IT! WILL YOU?

PREFACE :-

HEREIN LIES SKILLED AND ENTHUSIASTIC WRITINGS THAT WILL BE OF SUPPORT TO EVERYONE WHO USES THE ENGLISH LANGUAGE OR WANTS TO LEARN THE ENGLISH LANGUAGE. THIS TEXT IS DESIGNED TO BE A SELF–CONTAINED COURSE IN THE BASIC USE OF THE ENGLISH LANGUAGE; AS WELL AS GENERAL KNOWLEDGE IN ALL AREAS OF LIFE SUCH AS SCIENCE, PHYSICS, CHEMISTRY, MATHEMATICS, GEOGRAPHY, HISTORY, ECONOMICS, COMMERCE, WORLD FACTS, BUSINESS, GEOLOGY, OCEANOGRAPHY, HUMAN BIOLOGY, SPORTS AND MUCH, MUCH MORE. ALSO IT MIGHT SERVE AS A SELF – PACED INSTRUCTIONS OF LEARNING FOR CHILDREN AND PEOPLE OF ALL AGES; YOU WILL IMPROVE YOUR INTELLECTUAL SKILLS AND STUDY TECHNIQUES AND BECOME A POWERFUL PERSON AS YOU LEARN THE MATERIALS AT INDIVIDUAL SPEED. IT LOOKS AT THE BASICS IN THE ENGLISH LANGUAGE OBJECTIVELY, SO THAT ANYONE CAN TURN THE PAGES AND IMMEDIATELY LEARN AND BENEFIT FROM ITS VAST RESOURCES IN THE ENGLISH LANGUAGE AS WELL AS THE OTHER DIFFERENT SUBJECT AREAS IT COVERS.

THE TEST YOURSELF EXERCISES WITH ANSWERS SERVE AS A REVIEW GUIDE TO MAKE SURE YOU OBTAIN AND RETAIN THE KNOWLEDGE DISPENSED HEREIN.

THIS BOOK IS A POTENT TESTIMONY OF HOW EASY AND ACCESSIBLE THE ENGLISH LANGUAGE CAN BE TO ANYONE AND EVERYONE DESIROUS OF LEARNING THE BASICS OF THE ENGLISH LANGUAGE AND ALSO GAINING

GENERAL KNOWLEDGE AND BECOMING MORE CONFIDENT AND COMPETENT IN LIFE.

THIS BOOK SHOULD BE USED WHEREVER THE ENGLISH LANGUAGE IS SPOKEN OR TAUGHT; IT IS INVALUABLE AS A BASIC FOUNDATIONAL GUIDE IN THE ENGLISH LANGUAGE AND GENERAL WORLD KNOWLEDGE FOR PRACTICALLY EVERYONE; BOTH TO NATIVE ENGLISH SPEAKERS AND TO EVERYONE DESIROUS OF LEARNING THE ENGLISH LANGUAGE AND WANTING TO KNOW ABOUT THE DIFFERENT SUBJECT AREAS OF THE WORLD IN WHICH WE LIVE.

THE FACTUAL INFORMATION IT GIVES ON A VAST ARRAY OF SUBJECT MATTERS; WILL ENRICH YOUR LIFE BEYOND MEASURE; YOU WILL HAVE WORLD WIDE KNOWLEDGE AT YOUR FINGER TIPS; HERE IS YOUR OPPORTUNITY; TAKE IN AND ABSORB THIS KNOWLEDGE; FOR KNOWLEDGE IS POWER. IT WILL MAKE YOU AN INFORMED POWERFUL PERSON.

THERE ARE TWO KINDS OF PEOPLE; PEOPLE WHO SIT ON THE SIDE LINES AND WATCH OTHER PEOPLES' LIVES HAPPEN AND DEVELOP SUCCESSFULLY AND PEOPLE WHO GAIN KNOWLEDGE AND USE IT TO MAKE THEIR LIFE HAPPEN AND BECOME A SUCCESS IN LIFE. WHICH GROUP ARE YOU IN? COME ON, DON'T SIT ON THE SIDE LINES; GAIN THIS KNOWLEDGE, IT WILL HELP YOU TO MAKE YOUR LIFE HAPPEN AND HELP YOU TO BE SUCCESSFUL FOR NOW AND ALL ETERNITY. PEOPLE SUFFER FOR A LACK OF KNOWLEDGE; GAIN AND APPLY KNOWLEDGE IN YOUR LIFE SO YOU CAN BECOME A POWERFUL PERSON; MAKING YOUR LIFE MUCH BETTER SUCCESSFULLY FOR NOW AND ALL ETERNITY. BE A BLESSING AND BE BLESSED; LOVE AND BE LOVED; LIVE AND ENJOY A WONDERFUL LIFE WELL LIVED.

TABLE OF CONTENTS

INTRODUCTION :-

WE ARE LIVING IN A WORLD TODAY WHICH IN MANY ASPECTS IS DIFFERENT THAN THE WORLD OF THE PAST; HOWEVER, CERTAIN INFORMATION AND KNOWLEDGE ACQUIRED OVER THE YEARS ARE INDISPENSABLE IN LIVING IN THIS WORLD TODAY; THERE IS A POPULATION EXPLOSION WITH WHICH THE WORLD MUST COPE. WITH THE INCREASE OF POPULATION AND NEW AND IMPROVED RESEARCH AND DEVELOPMENT STRATEGIES AND TECHNIQUES; THIS GIVES RISE TO NEW AND MODERN TECHNOLOGY WITH WHICH COMES AN INCREASE OF KNOWLEDGE. ONE NEEDS TO TAKE UPON ONESELF TO SHED LIGHT UPON THE GREAT MYSTERY OF DARKNESS THAT SURROUNDS THE MASSES OF THE WORLD. ONE NEEDS TO UNDERSTAND DIVINE CONCEPTS AND MOVE INTO THE PATH OF DIVINE REALITIES. THIS BOOK "KNOWLEDGE IS POWER" CONFRONTS US WITH A COMPLETION OF TRUTHS OF LIFE. THIS BOOK OF KNOWLEDGE IS SELF – CONTAINED AND PRODUCES ALL THE INROADS AND HIGHWAYS LEADING TO ETERNAL TRUTHS OF THE KNOWLEDGE OF THE VARIOUS SUBJECT MATTERS OF THIS UNIVERSE IN WHICH WE LIVE; INSIGHTS ABOUT THE KNOWLEDGE OF LIFE ARE GIVEN AS TOWARDS THE WEALTH OF KNOWLEDGE ONE CAN GAIN. THIS IS THE WAY OF OBTAINING KNOWLEDGE, WALK IN IT, TAKE IT, ABSORB IT AND LIVE IT. WALK UPRIGHTLY AND ATTAIN TO THE PROMISED KNOWLEDGE OF THE UNIVERSE IN WHICH WE LIVE. HAVE YOUR HEARTS INDITED WITH THE STUDYING OF GOLDEN TRUTHS OF THIS WORLD; BENEFIT AND REJOICE

IN THE PROVIDENCE OF WISE KNOWLEDGE. FIND OUT THE FUNDAMENTAL TRUTH OF KNOWLEDGE AS IT RELATES TO LIVING A SUCCESSFULLY HAPPY, PEACEFUL AND SATISFIED LIFE. MAKE YOUR LIFE OF HIGH CALLING AND YOUR ASSURANCE OF SUCCESS SURE; EXPERIENCE THE VISIBLE AND GLORIFIED FEELING OF POWER THROUGH KNOWLEDGE. HAVE DOMINION OVER YOUR LIFE; INTERPRET AND APPLY YOURSELF IN A WAY SUCH AS THE WORLD HAS NEVER KNOWN; FOR THROUGH YOUR LIFE IS THE RESTITUTION OF ALL THINGS; UNTO PERFECTION OF HIGH CALLING; CONDITIONED UPON THE OBEDIENCE OF DISCIPLINE, SEEKING WISDOM THROUGH KNOWLEDGE. INVESTIGATING KNOWLEDGE CAN DO NO HARM AS LONG AS IT IS THE CORRECT REVELATION OF TRUTH. ACKNOWLEDGE TRUE KNOWLEDGE WHEN IT OCCURS AND PRESENTS ITSELF AND YOU STUMBLE UPON IT. PURSUE THIS BOOK "KNOWLEDGE IS POWER" SLOWLY AND PRAYERFULLY; UPON DERIVING SUBSTANTIAL GOOD, PASS IT ON, INFORM OTHERS, LET IT ALSO ENRICH OTHERS LIVES AS IT HAS DONE TO YOURS. I WAS PROMPTED, MOTIVATED AND INSPIRED TO PREPARE THIS BOOK. I SUBMIT ITS CONTENTS TO EVERYONE WITH THE FIRM CONVICTION THAT IT WILL CONTRIBUTE ITS SHARE OF KNOWLEDGE AND BLESSING TO YOUR LIFE; TO THE WELFARE OF HUMANITY AS A WHOLE. IN THIS WORLD, ONE CAN BECOME FED UP WITH THE SYSTEMS AND THINGS THAT FRUSTRATE THE GOVERNING OF ONE'S LIFE; WHERE YOU HAVE LESS AND LESS CONTROL OVER YOUR OWN LIVES; THEREFORE USE YOUR BRAINS – IMAGINATION, ACQUIRE AND ACCUMULATE GOODLY KNOWLEDGE WHICH WILL HELP YOU IN LIFE AND CAUSE YOU TO LIVE A LIFE OF LESS STRESS AND STRAIN; FREE FROM COMPLETE DESPAIR; HAVING GAINED KNOWLEDGE THAT CAN CHANGE YOUR LIFE; MAKING YOU A TRUE AND BETTER CITIZEN OF THIS WORLD; ONE WHO CAN BE SUCCESSFUL; BEING FINANCIALLY SOUND AND PERSONALLY SECURE; MOVING AWAY FROM THE ROUTINE PRESSURES OF OUR DAILY LIVES TO LIVE MORE KNOWLEDGEABLY RELAXED. GAIN KNOWLEDGE AND MAKE PROGRESS IN LIFE, SO YOU CAN LIVE WITHOUT STRESS, HASSLE, AND GRIEF THAT YOU HAVE HAD TO DEAL WITH IN YOUR CURRENT LIFE SITUATION. ACHIEVE A COMFORT FACTOR THAT WILL GIVE YOU

PERSONAL RIGHTS AND BENEFITS TO A SUCCESSFULLY MEANINGFUL LIFE. SO THEN THE CHOICE IS UP TO YOU, DO YOU WANT A GOOD LIVING AND A GOOD LIFE, GAIN KNOWLEDGE IT WILL CERTAINLY HELP YOU; MAKE YOUR LIFE A SENSATIONAL STORY, BE OVER ZEALOUS WITH INTELLIGENCE, IT'S YOUR PRIVILEGE IN LIFE. EXCHANGE YOUR PAST MEANINGLESS LIFE FOR A KNOWLEDGEABLE SUCCESSFUL LIFE. DO NOT LET YOUR LIFE BE AN APOLOGY BUT AN AUTHORITY. ESCAPE VINDICATION AND BE FREE FROM BLAME FOR THE STATE OF YOUR LIFE; DO NOT SETTLE FOR NOTHING LESS THAN THE BEST. GAIN KNOWLEDGE THAT CAN MAKE YOU INCREDIBLY AGGRESSIVE IN YOUR PURSUIT OF MEANINGFUL LIFE. BEING AWAKE FROM YOUR STUPOR TO BEING UNIQUELY SUITED AND GEARED FOR LIFE'S CHALLENGES. IMPROVE YOUR LIFESTYLE AND LIVE HEALTHIER LIVES; ELIMINATING ALL OF THE HEARTACHE AND GRIEF OF YOUR OLD WAY OF LIFE; OVERCOMING THE SOCIAL PROBLEMS THAT ENGULF THE WORLD. GAIN KNOWLEDGE, MAKE A CONCERTED EFFORT AT A NEW AND FRESH START IN LIFE, HAVE A NEW IDENTITY AND PERSONAL OUTLOOK OF LIFE. DON'T GIVE UP ON YOURSELF; DON'T BE A BRAINLESS BOZO; GAIN WORTHWHILE KNOWLEDGE AND DEFINE WHO AND WHAT YOU REALLY ARE. IT IS MY HOPE, THAT AFTER READING THIS BOOK, YOU WILL BE BETTER PREPARED IN EVERY FACET OF LIFE TO SUCCESSFULLY MAKE THE TRANSITION TO YOUR NEW LIFE IN YOUR NEW WORLD. IN THIS BOOK, YOU HAVE THE BEST INFORMATION YOU CAN POSSIBLY DREAM OF AND IT'S ALL AVAILABLE TO YOU FOR THE TAKING. SO CREATE A WHOLE NEW WAY OF LIVING YOUR LIFE, BREATHING KNOWLEDGE; GIVING YOURSELF A RENEWED PERSONALITY. IF YOU OBTAIN, LEARN AND RETAIN KNOWLEDGE; ALONG WITH LIVING A RIGHTFUL LIFE YOU WILL BE A RENEWED PERSON, SOMEONE YOU CAN BE PROUD AND PLEASE WITH HAVING SATISFACTION OUT OF LIFE AND BEING HAPPY TO ENJOY SPENDING THE REST OF YOUR LIFE ON THIS EARTH MEANINGFULLY FRUITFUL. KNOWLEDGE IS POWER. HOW POWERFUL YOU BECOME IN LIFE IS ALL UP TO YOU. SO THEN HOW POWERFUL ARE YOU? DON'T WASTE YOUR LIFE, ENJOY ALL GOD'S BLESSINGS. GAIN THE KNOWLEDGE DISPENSED IN THIS BOOK "KNOWLEDGE IS POWER" AND IN

YOUR LIFE YOU TOO CAN BECOME AS A QUIET WHISPER
IN THE WIND.

FLAGS OF THE WORLD

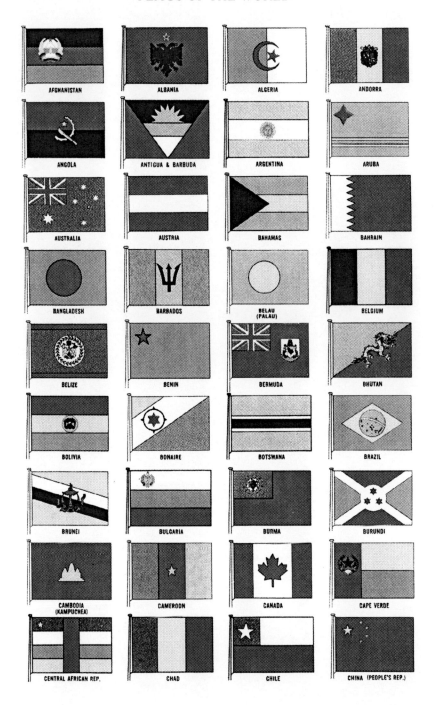

AFGHANISTAN • ALBANIA • ALGERIA • ANDORRA

ANGOLA • ANTIGUA & BARBUDA • ARGENTINA • ARUBA

AUSTRALIA • AUSTRIA • BAHAMAS • BAHRAIN

BANGLADESH • BARBADOS • BELAU (PALAU) • BELGIUM

BELIZE • BENIN • BERMUDA • BHUTAN

BOLIVIA • BONAIRE • BOTSWANA • BRAZIL

BRUNEI • BULGARIA • BURMA • BURUNDI

CAMBODIA (KAMPUCHEA) • CAMEROON • CANADA • CAPE VERDE

CENTRAL AFRICAN REP. • CHAD • CHILE • CHINA (PEOPLE'S REP.)

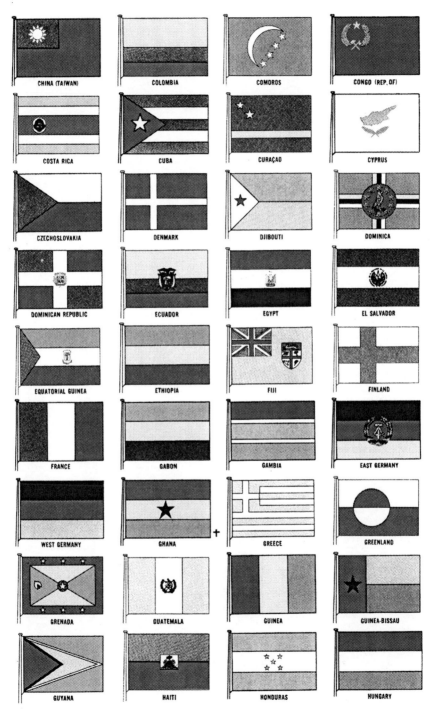

CHINA (TAIWAN) COLOMBIA COMOROS CONGO (REP. OF)

COSTA RICA CUBA CURAÇAO CYPRUS

CZECHOSLOVAKIA DENMARK DJIBOUTI DOMINICA

DOMINICAN REPUBLIC ECUADOR EGYPT EL SALVADOR

EQUATORIAL GUINEA ETHIOPIA FIJI FINLAND

FRANCE GABON GAMBIA EAST GERMANY

WEST GERMANY GHANA GREECE GREENLAND

GRENADA GUATEMALA GUINEA GUINEA-BISSAU

GUYANA HAITI HONDURAS HUNGARY

+ For flag of GREAT BRITAIN see UNITED KINGDOM

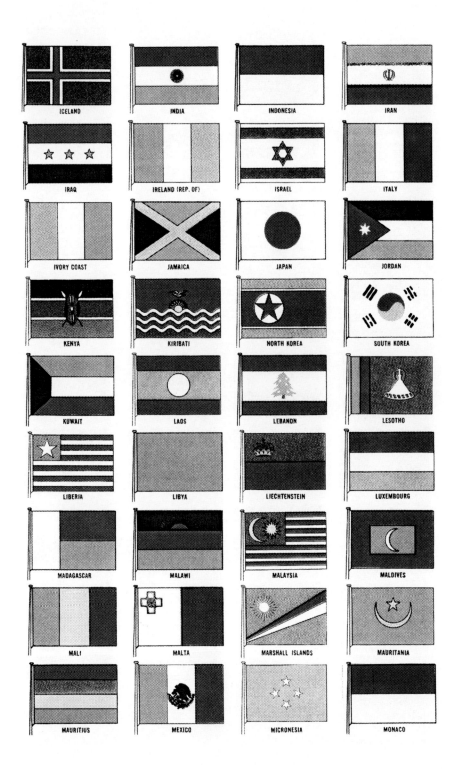

ICELAND   INDIA   INDONESIA   IRAN

IRAQ   IRELAND (REP. OF)   ISRAEL   ITALY

IVORY COAST   JAMAICA   JAPAN   JORDAN

KENYA   KIRIBATI   NORTH KOREA   SOUTH KOREA

KUWAIT   LAOS   LEBANON   LESOTHO

LIBERIA   LIBYA   LIECHTENSTEIN   LUXEMBOURG

MADAGASCAR   MALAWI   MALAYSIA   MALDIVES

MALI   MALTA   MARSHALL ISLANDS   MAURITANIA

MAURITIUS   MEXICO   MICRONESIA   MONACO

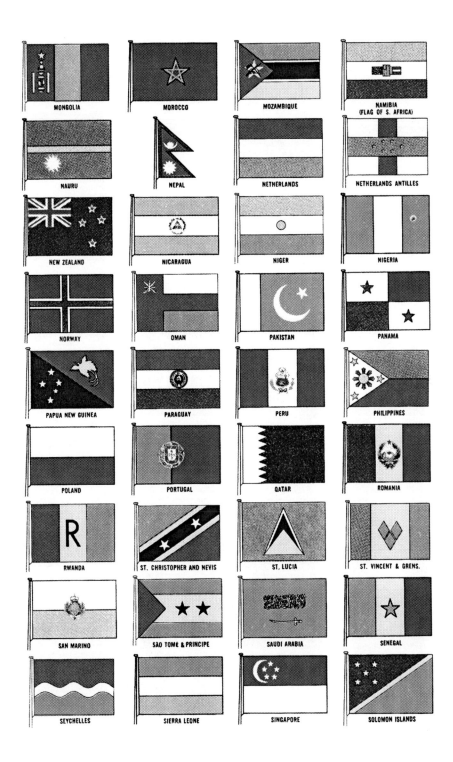

MONGOLIA

MOROCCO

MOZAMBIQUE

NAMIBIA
(FLAG OF S. AFRICA)

NAURU

NEPAL

NETHERLANDS

NETHERLANDS ANTILLES

NEW ZEALAND

NICARAGUA

NIGER

NIGERIA

NORWAY

OMAN

PAKISTAN

PANAMA

PAPUA NEW GUINEA

PARAGUAY

PERU

PHILIPPINES

POLAND

PORTUGAL

QATAR

ROMANIA

RWANDA

ST. CHRISTOPHER AND NEVIS

ST. LUCIA

ST. VINCENT & GRENS.

SAN MARINO

SÃO TOMÉ & PRINCIPE

SAUDI ARABIA

SENEGAL

SEYCHELLES

SIERRA LEONE

SINGAPORE

SOLOMON ISLANDS

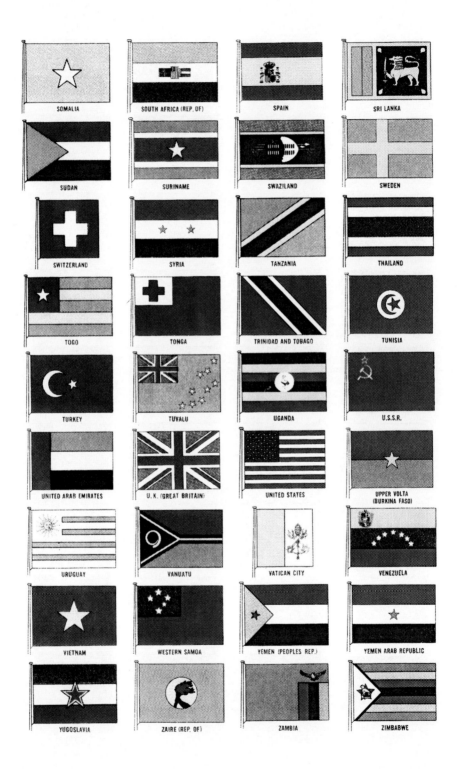

SOMALIA   SOUTH AFRICA (REP. OF)   SPAIN   SRI LANKA

SUDAN   SURINAME   SWAZILAND   SWEDEN

SWITZERLAND   SYRIA   TANZANIA   THAILAND

TOGO   TONGA   TRINIDAD AND TOBAGO   TUNISIA

TURKEY   TUVALU   UGANDA   U.S.S.R.

UNITED ARAB EMIRATES   U.K. (GREAT BRITAIN)   UNITED STATES   UPPER VOLTA (BURKINA FASO)

URUGUAY   VANUATU   VATICAN CITY   VENEZUELA

VIETNAM   WESTERN SAMOA   YEMEN (PEOPLES REP.)   YEMEN ARAB REPUBLIC

YUGOSLAVIA   ZAIRE (REP. OF)   ZAMBIA   ZIMBABWE

FLAGS OF THE STATES AND TERRITORIES OF THE UNITED STATES

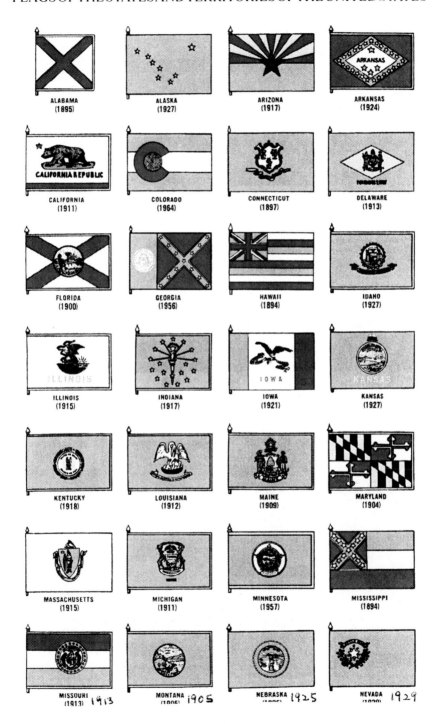

ALABAMA (1895)

ALASKA (1927)

ARIZONA (1917)

ARKANSAS (1924)

CALIFORNIA (1911)

COLORADO (1964)

CONNECTICUT (1897)

DELAWARE (1913)

FLORIDA (1900)

GEORGIA (1956)

HAWAII (1894)

IDAHO (1927)

ILLINOIS (1915)

INDIANA (1917)

IOWA (1921)

KANSAS (1927)

KENTUCKY (1918)

LOUISIANA (1912)

MAINE (1909)

MARYLAND (1904)

MASSACHUSETTS (1915)

MICHIGAN (1911)

MINNESOTA (1957)

MISSISSIPPI (1894)

MISSOURI (1913) 1913

MONTANA (1905) 1905

NEBRASKA (1925) 1925

NEVADA (1929) 1929

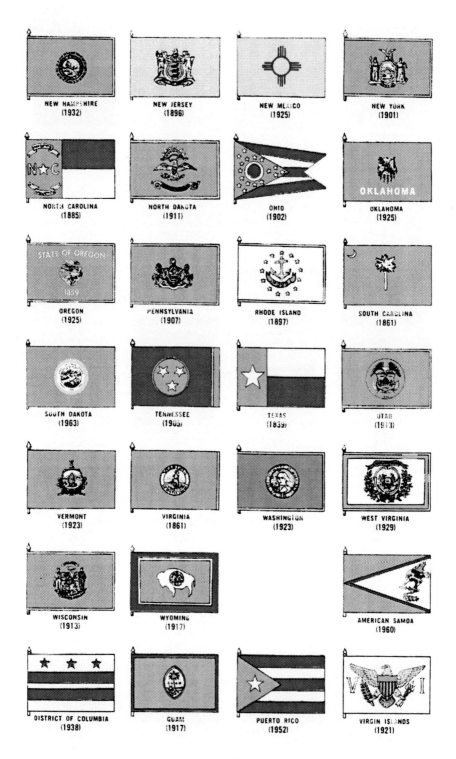

NEW HAMPSHIRE
(1932)

NEW JERSEY
(1896)

NEW MEXICO
(1925)

NEW YORK
(1901)

NORTH CAROLINA
(1885)

NORTH DAKOTA
(1911)

OHIO
(1902)

OKLAHOMA
(1925)

OREGON
(1925)

PENNSYLVANIA
(1907)

RHODE ISLAND
(1897)

SOUTH CAROLINA
(1861)

SOUTH DAKOTA
(1963)

TENNESSEE
(1905)

TEXAS
(1839)

UTAH
(1913)

VERMONT
(1923)

VIRGINIA
(1861)

WASHINGTON
(1923)

WEST VIRGINIA
(1929)

WISCONSIN
(1913)

WYOMING
(1917)

AMERICAN SAMOA
(1960)

DISTRICT OF COLUMBIA
(1938)

GUAM
(1917)

PUERTO RICO
(1952)

VIRGIN ISLANDS
(1921)

CHAPTER 1.

GENERAL WORLD KNOWLEDGE :-

CAPITAL LETTERS :

THE MAIN AND DIFFERENT USES OF CAPITAL LETTERS.

[1] THE FIRST WORD IN A SENTENCE.

[2] THE NAMES OF PERSONS.

[3] THE NAMES OF PARTICULAR PLACES.

[4] THE WORD I.

[5] THE FIRST WORD IN A DIRECT QUOTATION.

[6] THE NAMES OF THE DAYS OF THE WEEK.

[7] THE NAMES OF THE MONTHS OF THE YEAR.

[8] THE NAMES OF HOLIDAYS.

[9] THE NAMES OF ORGANIZATIONS, SUCH AS COMPANIES, CLUBS, RELIGIOUS GROUPS, ASSOCIATIONS, POLITICAL GROUPS ETC.

[10] NAMES OF TITLES OF BOOKS; STORIES, POEMS, MAGAZINES, NEWSPAPERS AND SUCH LIKE.

[11] NAMES OR TITLES OF TELEVISION SHOWS, SONGS, SKITS, FILMS AND THE LIKE.

[12] LANGUAGES.

[13] GEOGRAPHIC LOCATIONS.

[14] OPENING AND CLOSING OF A LETTER.

[15] TITLES OF PERSONS WHEN USED WITH THEIR NAMES.

[16] NAMES THAT SHOW FAMILY RELATIONSHIPS.

[17] SPECIFIC COURSES IN SCHOOL.

[18] TO BEGIN WORDS OF EXCLAMATION.

[19] TO BEGIN THE WORDS HE, HIM, HIS, IF THEY REFER TO GOD.

FIRST WORD IN A SENTENCE.

BEHOLD, HAPPY IS THE PERSON WHOM GOD CORRECTS.
CAPITALIZE THE B - IN BEHOLD, IT IS THE FIRST WORD IN THE SENTENCE.

G - IN THE WORD GOD IS ALWAYS CAPITALIZE.

PAUL AND MARY ARE GOING TO SCHOOL.
CAPITALIZE P - IN PAUL AND M - IN MARY; THEY ARE THE NAMES OF PERSONS.

PAUL AND MARY ARE GOING TO SCHOOL.
CAPITALIZE P - IN PAUL AND M - IN MARY; THEY ARE THE NAMES OF PERSONS.

PAUL AND MARY ARE GOING TO SCHOOL IN NEW YORK.

MARK AND ANN ARE VISITING THEIR RELATIVES AND FRIENDS IN FLORIDA.

IN ADDITION TO CAPITALIZING THE NAMES OF PERSONS; YOU ALSO CAPITALIZE NEW YORK AND FLORIDA; BECAUSE THEY ARE THE NAMES OF PARTICULAR PLACES.

YESTERDAY I MET JOHN AND PETAL AT THE PARK.

THE WORD I IS ALWAYS CAPITALIZED.

"DO YOU HAVE TIME TO GO TO THE STORE WITH ME?"

CAPITALIZE D - IN DO; BECAUSE IT IS THE FIRST WORD IN THE DIRECT QUOTATION.

NAMES OF THE DAYS OF THE WEEK ARE CAPITALIZED.
SUNDAY, MONDAY, TUESDAY, WEDNESDAY, THURSDAY, FRIDAY AND SATURDAY.

THERE ARE SEVEN DAYS IN THE WEEK; THE FIRST DAY BEING SUNDAY AND THE LAST DAY SATURDAY.

I GO TO SCHOOL ON MONDAY, TUESDAY, WEDNESDAY, THURSDAY, AND FRIDAY.

I WENT TO DANCE CLASSES ON SATURDAY.

ON SUNDAY WE VISITED THE ZOO.

THE NAMES OF THE MONTHS OF THE YEAR ARE CAPITALIZED.

JANUARY, FEBRUARY, MARCH, APRIL, MAY, JUNE, JULY, AUGUST, SEPTEMBER, OCTOBER, NOVEMBER AND DECEMBER.

THERE ARE TWELVE MONTHS IN THE YEAR; THE FIRST MONTH BEING JANUARY AND THE LAST MONTH DECEMBER.

SCHOOL CLOSES IN JUNE FOR THE SUMMER HOLIDAYS.

MY BIRTHDAY IS IN THE MONTH OF OCTOBER.

NAMES OF HOLIDAYS ARE CAPITALIZED : EXAMPLE, FOURTH OF JULY, LABOR DAY, CHRISTMAS, HONIKA, EED, PAGWAH ETC .

MY DAD TOOK ME TO THE BASKET BALL GAME ON LABOR DAY.

WE ALL WENT TO THE FOURTH OF JULY PARADE CELEBRATIONS.

NAMES OF ORGANIZATIONS ARE CAPITALIZED.

I WORK AT BARCLAYS BANK IN NEW AMSTERDAM.

I ATTEND THE Y M C A CLUB.

THE CATHOLICS AND PROTESTANTS AS WELL AS OTHER CHURCH GOERS ATTEND CHURCH ON SUNDAYS.

I AM A MEMBER OF THE LIBERTY FOR ALL - ASSOCIATION.

THE DEMOCRATIC AND REPUBLICAN PARTIES; ARE CONTESTING THE ELECTIONS FOR THE PRESIDENCY OF THE UNITED STATES OF AMERICA.

NAMES OF BOOKS, MAGAZINES AND SUCH LIKE ARE CAPITALIZED.

I READ THE BOOK TITLED. - WISDOM THE SECRETS OF SUCCESS IN LIFE BY ROY NOLAN.

I SUBSCRIBE TO SEVERAL MAGAZINES INCLUDING SPORTS, FORTUNE, MONEY AND PEOPLE.

I READ THE FOLLOWING NEWSPAPERS AMONG OTHERS. NEW YORK TIMES, CHIEF, NEWSDAY, DAILY NEWS AND WAVE CREST.

LANGUAGES.: -
HE KNOWS ENGLISH, SPANISH AND FRENCH; BUT HE SPEAKS ENGLISH FLUENTLY.

SHE READS AND WRITES SPANISH CLEARLY.

GEOGRAPHIC LOCATIONS.: -
JAMES AND SUSAN WERE BORN IN SOUTH AMERICA, THEY GREW UP IN AFRICA AND ARE NOW MARRIED AND LIVE IN THE UNITED STATES OF AMERICA.

ANDY GREW UP IN THE EAST, HE WORKED IN THE WEST FOR A NUMBER OF YEARS; AND THEN MOVED TO THE MIDWEST.

RACES, NATIONS, NATIONALITIES.: -
A CASE STUDY WAS DONE ON LOW - INCOME WEST INDIANS AND HIGH - INCOME AMERICANS.

THEY HAVE AMERICAN UTENSILS AND ITALIAN POTTERY IN THEIR HOME; AS WELL AS AFRICAN WOOD CARVING IN THE LIVING ROOM, ORIENTAL RUG IN THE BEDROOM AND GERMAN BICYCLES IN THE GARAGE.

OPENING AND CLOSING OF A LETTER.: -
DEAR MISS, DEAR SIR, DEAR MADAM.

TRULY YOURS, RESPECTFULLY YOURS, SINCERELY YOURS.

NOTE - CAPITALIZE ONLY THE FIRST WORD IN THE CLOSING OF A LETTER.

TITLES OF PERSONS WHEN USED WITH THEIR NAMES. –

I VISITED DR. ALAN'S OFFICE FOR MY REGULAR MEDICAL CHECKUP.

I WROTE TO PRESIDENT BUSH AND SENATOR KENNEDY WHO BOTH DIRECTED ME TO COUNCIL MAN JOSEPH.

NAMES THAT SHOW FAMILY RELATIONSHIPS. –

I WENT WITH GRANDMOTHER TO THE PARK.

MY AUNT AND UNCLE ALWAYS SEND ME CARDS ON HOLIDAYS.

SPECIFIC SCHOOL COURSES. –

I GOT AN A IN ENGLISH, B IN MATHEMATICS, BUT ONLY A C IN SCIENCE.

EXCLAMATION. –

"OH!" SHOUTED THE GIRL, "I FORGOT MY BOOK". "INDEED!" EXCLAIMED THE TEACHER, "YOU WILL HAVE TO ATTEND DETENTION FOR THAT".

REFERENCE TO GOD. –

AFTER GOD HAD WRITTEN THE TEN COMMANDMENTS; HE PROCEEDED TO GIVE THEM TO MOSES.

ACTIVITY EXERCISES. –

1. WRITE YOUR FULL NAME.
2. WRITE THE NAME OF YOUR MOTHER.
3. WRITE THE NAME OF YOUR FATHER.
4 WHERE DO YOU LIVE?
5 IN WHICH COUNTRY WERE YOU BORN?
6 NAME A STATE YOU WOULD LIKE TO VISIT.
7 NAME A COUNTRY YOU WOULD LIKE TO VISIT.
8 WHAT IS THE NAME OF YOUR SCHOOL?

9 NAME A SUPERMARKET YOUR MOTHER TOOK YOU TO?

10 NAME A SHOP OR STORE IN YOUR NEIGHBORHOOD?

11 WHAT DAYS OF THE WEEK ARE YOU HOME FROM SCHOOL?

12 WHAT DAYS OF THE WEEK DO YOU ATTEND SCHOOL?

13 NAME A COMPANY WHERE ONE OF YOUR RELATIVES WORKS.

14 WHERE DOES YOUR FATHER WORK?

15 WHICH DAY OF THE WEEK DO YOU LIKE BEST? WHY DO YOU LIKE THAT DAY BEST?

16 NAME FOUR OR FIVE HOLIDAYS THAT YOU KNOW.

17 WHICH HOLIDAY YOU LIKE BEST AND WHY?

18 WHAT IS THE FAVORITE JUICE YOU LIKE TO DRINK?

19 GIVE THE BRAND NAME OF A SODA YOU DRINK?

20 NAME A SONG YOU LIKE TO SING?

21 WHICH BOOK DO YOU LIKE TO READ?

22 WHAT IS THE NAME OF A CANDY YOU LIKE?

23 WHAT IS YOUR FAVORITE TELEVISION SHOW?

24 NAME A MOVIE THAT YOU SAW?

25 WHAT ARE THE NAMES OF THE NEWSPAPERS IN YOUR HOME AREA?

26 DO YOU KNOW THE NAMES OF ANY MAGAZINE?

27 ASK YOUR PARENTS WHO ARE THE POLITICAL REPRESENTATIVES IN YOUR CITY AND STATE AND COUNTRY.

HEADING :- PARTS OF SPEECH.

WHEN WE WISH TO EXPRESS A THOUGHT WE USE WORDS GROUPED TOGETHER IN A CERTAIN ORDER SO THAT WE CONVEY A SENSIBLE, DEFINITE AND CERTAIN MEANING. THIS COMBINATION OF WORDS IS TERMED A SENTENCE. IN WRITING OR CONVERSATION, YOUR THOUGHTS IN SENTENCES SHOULD ALWAYS BE USED IN ORDER THAT THE HEARER OR READER MAY WITHOUT DOUBT; UNDERSTAND THE MEANING.

THE WORDS OF THE ENGLISH LANGUAGE ARE CLASSIFIED AS PARTS OF SPEECH AND ARE NAMED ACCORDING TO THEIR FUNCTIONS. THIS MEANS THAT EVERY WORD, DEPENDENT ON ITS USE, FALLS INTO ONE OF THE FOLLOWING DIVISIONS. –

THE NOUN : -
A NOUN IS THE NAME OF A PERSON, PLACE, ANIMAL OR THING, E.G MARY, COLLEGE, DOG, BOOK.

THE VERB : -
A VERB IS SAID TO BE A DOING OR ACTION WORD, E.G WALK, WRITE, SING, PLAY.

THE PRONOUN : -
A PRONOUN IS A WORD WHICH TAKES THE PLACE OF A NOUN, E.G SHE, HE,IT.

THE ADJECTIVE : -
AN ADJECTIVE DESCRIBES A NOUN OR A PRONOUN, E.G BAD, HUMBLE, FAT, NICE.

THE ADVERB : -
AN ADVERB GENERALLY MODIFIES A VERB; MOST ADVERBS END IN - LY. E.G SLOWLY, QUIETLY, QUICKLY.

THE CONJUNCTION : -
A CONJUNCTION IS A WORD USED FOR JOINING WORDS AND CLAUSES, E.G BUT, AND.

THE PREPOSITION : -
A PREPOSITION SHOWS THE RELATIONSHIP BETWEEN ONE THING AND ANOTHER, E.G WITH, FOR.

THE EXCLAMATION : -
AN EXCLAMATION EXPRESSES SUDDEN EMOTION, E.G OH! HELLO! GO! COME HERE! STOP!

PUNCTUATION : -
BY CORRECT PUNCTUATION WE MEAN THE PROPER USE OF : -CAPITAL LETTERS, COMMA [,], PERIOD OR SOMETIMES

REFER TO AS FULL STOP [.], QUOTATION MARKS ["
"], EXCLAMATION MARK [!], QUESTION MARK [?], AND
APOSTROPHE ['].

THE APOSTROPHE IN CONTRACTIONS : -
WHEN THE APOSTROPHE IS USED TO ABBREVIATE
WORDS IT IS PLACED WHERE THE LETTERS HAVE BEEN
OMITTED, E.G -

ALL IS =ALL'S	OF THE CLOCK =O'CLOCK
CANNOT =CAN'T	OVER =O'ER
COULD NOT = COULDN'T	SHALL NOT =SHAN'T
ACROSS ='CROSS	SHE WILL =SHE'LL
DOES NOT =DOESN'T	SHOULD NOT = SHOULDN'T
HAS NOT = HASN'T	THAT IS = THAT'S
HE WOULD = HE'D	THERE IS = THERE'S
HE WILL = HE'LL	THEY WILL = THEY'LL
I AM = I'M	I HAVE = I'VE
I HAD = I'D	IT IS =IT'S
IS NOT = ISN'T	I WOULD = I'D
I WILL =I'LL	WHO IS = WHO'S
DO NOT = DON'T	DID NOT = DIDN'T
COULD NOT = COULDN'T	HAVE NOT = HAVEN'T
WE WILL =WE'LL	WOULD NOT = WOULDN'T
WE HAVE = WE'VE	YOU WILL = YOU'LL
WHATEVER = WHATE'ER	YOU ARE = YOU'RE
WHEREVER = WHERE'ER	IS NOT = ISN'T
WHOSOEVER = WHOSOE'ER	HE IS = HE'S
WHO HAVE = WHO'VE	WILL NOT = WON'T
THEY ARE = THEY'RE	WE ARE = WE'RE

APOSTROPHE TO SHOW POSSESSION OR OWNERSHIP. TO
SHOW POSSESSION, WE USE SUCH WORDS AS BELONGS TO,
OF, OWNED BY ETC .
EXAMPLE : -
THE HAT THAT BELONGS TO GARY. - GARY'S HAT.
THE STORE OWNED BY OUR COUSIN. - OUR COUSIN'S
STORE.
THE FOOD OF THE ANIMAL. - THE ANIMAL'S FOOD.

THE 'S GOES WITH THE OWNER OR POSSESSOR - IN THE EXAMPLES GIVEN GARY, COUSIN, ANIMAL. WHAT FOLLOWS IS THE PERSON OR THING POSSESSED - IN THE EXAMPLES GIVEN, HAT, STORE, FOOD ARE THE THINGS POSSESSED.

ABBREVIATIONS .: -

AN ABBREVIATION IS A HELPFUL TIME SAVER; YOU SHOULD AVOID MOST ABBREVIATIONS IN FORMAL WRITING. AN ABBREVIATION SHORTENS A WORD TO A FEW LETTERS. IT IS CUSTOMARY TO MARK ALL ABBREVIATIONS WITH A PERIOD OR FULL STOP. LISTED BELOW ARE ABBREVIATIONS THAT CAN ACCEPTABLY BE USED IN COMPOSITIONS AND OTHER FORMS OF WRITINGS.

A.A	-	ALCOHOLICS ANONYMOUS.
A.A.A.	-	AMERICAN AUTOMOBILE ASSOCIATION ANTIAIRCRAFT ARTILLERY.
A.B	-	ABLE - BODIED SEAMAN.
A.C	-	BEFORE CHRIST.
A.D	-	IN THE YEAR OF THE LORD.
A.L	-	AMERICAN LEGION.
A.L.A	-	AMERICAN LIBRARY ASSOCIATION.
A.M	-	BEFORE NOON.
A.W.O.L	-	ABSENT WITHOUT LEAVE.
Acct.	-	ACCOUNT.
Ave OR Av	_	AVENUE.
B.A	-	BACHELOR OF ARTS.
B.B.C	-	BRITISH BROADCASTING CORPORATION
B.C	-	BEFORE CHRIST.
B/L	-	BILL OF LADING.
B.L	-	BACHELOR OF LAW.
B.Sc	-	BACHELOR OF SCIENCE.
C.	-	CENTIGRADE.
C.A	-	CHARTERED ACCOUNTANT.
C.I.D	-	CRIMINAL INVESTIGATION DEPARTMENT.
Co.	-	COMPANY.
C.O.D	-	CASH ON DELIVERY.
Cr.	-	CREDIT.
C.S	-	CIVIL SERVICE.
C/O	-	IN CARE OF.

Deg.	-	DEGREE.
Dept	-	DEPARTMENT.
E.E.C	-	EUROPEAN ECONOMIC COMMUNITY.
e.g	-	FOR EXAMPLE.
E.S.I	-	EASTERN STANDARD TIME.
etc	-	AND THE OTHER THINGS.
F.	-	FAHRENHEIT.
F.B.I	-	FEDERAL BUREAU OF INVESTIGATION.
F.O.B	-	FREE ON BOARD.
G.A	-	GENERAL ASSEMBLY.
Govt	-	GOVERNMENT.
G.P.O	-	GENERAL POST OFFICE.
H.M	-	HER MAJESTY.
h.p	-	HORSE POWER.
I.E	-	THAT IS.
Inv	-	INVOICE.
I.Q	-	INTELLIGENCE QUOTIENT.
I.O.U	-	I OWE YOU.
J.P	-	JUSTICE OF THE PEACE.
K.g	-	KILOGRAM.
K.l	-	KILOLITER.
K.m	-	KILOMETER.
Kw	-	KILOWATT.
Lat.	-	LATITUDE.
Lb	-	LIBRA, A POUND.
Lieut or Lt	-	LIEUTENANT.
LL.B	-	BACHELOR OF LAWS.
Long	-	LONGITUDE.
L.t.d	-	LIMITED.
M.A	-	MASTER OF ARTS.
Mar	-	MARITIME, MARCH.
Math	-	MATHEMATICS.
Meas	-	MEASURE.
Mfg	-	MANUFACTURING.
Mi	-	MILE, MINUTE.
M.m	-	MILLIMETER.
M.s OR mss	-	MANUSCRIPT[S].
M.P	-	MEMBER OF PARLIAMENT.
M.t	-	MOUNTAIN, MOUNT.
N	-	NEUTER, NOUN.
N.A	-	NORTH AMERICA.

N.A.T.O	-	NORTH ATLANTIC TREATY ORGANIZATION
N.B	-	NOTE WELL OR TAKE NOTICE.
NO.	-	NUMBER.
N.P	-	NOTARY PUBLIC.
N.Y	-	NEW YORK.
N.Y.C	-	NEW YORK CITY.
O.K	-	ALL CORRECT.
P.O	-	POST OFFICE.
Pct.	-	PERCENT.
Pd.	-	PAID.
Pkg.	-	PACKAGE.
Pl.	-	PLURAL.
Pop.	-	POPULATION.
Pres.	-	PRESIDENT.
Prin.	-	PRINCIPAL.
Pub.	-	PUBLIC, PUBLISHER.
R.C	-	ROMAN CATHOLIC.
R.I.P	-	MAY HE OR SHE REST IN PEACE.
R.N	-	REGISTERED NURSE.
R.S.V.P	-	PLEASE ANSWER.
S.A	-	SALVATION ARMY, SOUTH AMERICA, SOUTH AFRICA.
Sr.	-	SENIOR.
Sq.	-	SQUARE.
Ter.	-	TERRITORY.
Tit.	-	TITLE.
Trig.	-	TRIGONOMETRY.
U	-	UNIVERSITY.
U.K	-	UNITED KINGDOM.
U.N	-	UNITED NATIONS.
U.S.A	-	UNITED STATES OF AMERICA.
V.	-	AGAINST.
VIZ.	-	NAMELY,
Wk.	-	WEEK.
Wt.	-	WEIGHT.
Xmas.	-	CHRISTMAS.
Y OR Yr.	-	YEAR.
Y.M.C.A	-	YOUNG MEN'S CHRISTIAN ASSOCIATION
Y.W.C.A	-	YOUNG WOMEN'S CHRISTIAN ASSOCIATION.

DR. MR. MRS.   -   WHEN   USED   WITH   PROPER NAMES.
EXAMPLE : -
DR. SMITH.
MR. TOM.
MRS. JENNY.

TIME REFERENCES : -
A.M   OR   a.m   P.M   OR   p.m   B.C   OR A.D.

FIRST OR MIDDLE NAME IN A SIGNATURE.
EXAMPLE : -
R. JOHN SMITH.
ROY N NOLAN.

ORGANIZATIONS, TECHNICAL WORDS AND TRADE NAMES KNOWN PRIMARILY BY THEIR INITIALS.
EXAMPLE : -
C.I.A   F.B.I   U.N   N.A.T.O   ETC.

A.M	BEFORE NOON.
D.R	DOCTOR.
LTD.	LIMITED.
MR.	MISTER.
MRS.	MISTRESS.
N.B	NOTE WELL.
P.M	AFTERNOON.
P.S	WRITTEN AFTER.
P.T.O	PLEASE TURN OVER.
R.S.V.P	REPLY IF YOU PLEASE.

CONTRACTIONS : -

AUTO	AUTOMOBILE.
EXAM	EXAMINATION.
GYM	GYMNASIUM
MAG	MAGAZINE.
PHONE	TELEPHONE.
PHOTO	PHOTOGRAPH.

PLANE	AEROPLANE.
PROM	PROMENADE.
SPECS	SPECTACLES.

NUMBERS : -

SPELL OUT NUMBERS THAT TAKE NO MORE THAN TWO WORDS. OTHER THAN THAT, USE NUMERALS - THE NUMBERS THEMSELVES.

THERE ARE FORTY - TWO CHILDREN IN THE CLASS.

THE TELEPHONE BILL WAS SEVENTY - SIX DOLLARS.

AT THE GARAGE SALE; I BOUGHT TWENTY - C.D RECORDS.

HOWEVER -
AT THE BEGINNING OF THE SCHOOL YEAR THERE WERE 341 CHILDREN ATTENDING THE SCHOOL.

THE COST FOR INSTALLING THE TELEPHONE LINES IS $285.

AT THE LIBRARY THE RECORD SHOWS THAT 101 PERSONS VISITED IT THIS WEEK.

USE NUMERALS TO SHOW DATES, TIMES, ADDRESSES, PERCENTAGES, AND PARTS OF A BOOK.

THE MEMO WAS DATED JANUARY 4, 1992.

MY APPOINTMENT WITH THE LAWYER IS AT 10:30 - HOWEVER, SPELL OUT NUMBERS BEFORE O'CLOCK. FOR EXAMPLE. MY LAST APPOINTMENT WITH THE DOCTOR WAS AT TEN O'CLOCK.

SHE LIVES AT 1029 BEACH 20 TH STREET.

ABOUT 50 PERCENT OF OUR CLASS ARE MEMBERS OF THE LIBRARY.

CHECK PAGE 204 IN CHAPTER 15 AND REVIEW THE ANSWERS FOR QUESTIONS 10 – 20.

BE CONSISTENT WHEN YOU USE A SERIES OF NUMBERS. IF SOME NUMBERS IN A SENTENCE OR PARAGRAPH REQUIRE MORE THAN TWO WORDS, THEN USE NUMERALS THROUGHOUT THE SELECTION.

EXAMPLE :-
DURING MY GRADUATION YEAR, I WENT TO 7 LIBRARIES, 16 COLLEGES, 49 WORK STUDY GROUPS, 124 COMPANIES - ORGANIZATIONS AND ATTENDED 292 LECTURES.

POSSESSIVE PRONOUNS : -

POSSESSIVE PRONOUNS INCLUDE HIS, HERS, ITS, YOURS, OURS, THEIRS DO NOT USE AN APOSTROPHE WITH POSSESSIVE PRONOUNS. THEY ALREADY SHOW OWNERSHIP.
EXAMPLE : -IT IS CORRECT TO SAY.

THE MONEY IS YOURS. NOT THE MONEY IS YOURS'.

HER TROUBLES ARE OURS, TOO. NOT HER TROUBLES ARE OURS', TOO.

HIS SKIN IS CLEARER THAN HERS. NOT HIS SKIN IS CLEARER THAN HERS'.

THE POSSESSIVE CASE OF A NOUN IS SHOWN BY A MARK ['] KNOWN AS AN APOSTROPHE. IN THE SINGULAR IT IS SHOWN BY 'S

EXAMPLE :-
MOM'S BAG, CAROL'S HAT, THE DOG'S FOOD   ETC.
IN THE PLURAL IT IS SHOWN IN TWO WAYS : -

[a] BY THE APOSTROPHE ONLY ['] WHEN THE PLURAL ENDS IN S OR ES
EXAMPLE :-
THE GIRLS' TOYS, THE LADIES' HATS.

[b] BY THE APOSTROPHE AND S ['S] WHEN THE PLURAL DOES NOT END IN S

EXAMPLE :-

THE MEN'S BOOKS, THE CHILDREN'S BICYCLES.

SINGULAR POSSESSIVE	PLURAL POSSESSIVE
THE BOY'S BOOK.	THE BOYS' BOOKS.
A DAY'S WORK.	TEN DAYS' WORK.
THE MAN'S SHIRT.	THE MEN'S SHIRTS.
THE GIRL'S SKIRT.	THE GIRLS' SKIRTS.
THE CHILD'S TOYS.	THE CHILDREN'S TOYS.

THE VERB : -

AS STATED EARLIER, THE VERB IS A SAID TO BE A DOING OR ACTION WORD.

IT IS USED TO MAKE A STATEMENT ABOUT A PERSON, PLACE, ANIMAL OR THING.

EXAMPLE :-

THE GIRL	CRIED.
THE DOG	BARKED.
THE AEROPLANE	FLIES.
THE APPLE	FALLS.

SOMETIMES WE USE TWO WORDS TO COMPLETE THE VERB E.G :-

THE DOG	WAS INJURED.
THE GIRL	WILL COME.
THE GLASSES	WERE BROKEN.

ACTIVITY EXERCISES :-
RECOGNIZING THE VERBS IN THE FOLLOWING SENTENCES :-

THE BAD DOG	SPRANG	AT THE MAN.
THE MOON	SHONE	BRIGHTLY IN THE NIGHT.
OUR FRIENDS	ARE HAVING	A PARTY.
THE CHOIR	SANG	A LOVELY SONG.
THE BABY	CREPT	SILENTLY OUT OF THE ROOM.
THE COUNTRIES	FOUGHT	AGAINST EACH OTHER.
THE CINEMA	WAS CROWDED	AT THE EVENING SHOW.
THE MAN	IS GOING	HOME FROM WORK.

THE PRONOUN : -

EXAMPLES OF PRONOUNS : -
I, YOU, THOU, WE, THEY.

RELATIVE PRONOUN :-
WHICH, WHO, WHOSE, THAT, WHAT.

PRONOUNS USED AS SUBJECTS MUST BE IN THE NOMINATIVE CASE, E.G :-

HE	CAUGHT A BIRD.
WE	SAW A BIG ELEPHANT.
THEY	SANG WITH JOY IN THEIR HEART.
SHE	RAN TO THE STORE.
YOU	WILL BE LATE FOR SCHOOL.
I	BOUGHT SOME FRUITS.
WHO	SAW THE DOG BIT THE MAN.

PRONOUNS USED AS OBJECTS MUST BE IN THE OBJECTIVE CASE,E.G :-

THE GAME BORED	ME.
THE PLAYERS PUSHED	YOU.
THE BOY WATCHED	HER.
THE VISITORS LEFT	US.
THE MEN WILL FOLLOW	HIM.
THE ANSWER WAS GIVEN BY	THEM.

PRONOUNS USED AS OBJECTS MUST BE IN THE OBJECTIVE CASE, E.G

WE KNOW SOMETHING	ABOUT	HIM.
THE BOY STARED	AT	ME.
THE SOLDIERS RAN	AFTER	THEM.
THE TEACHER WILL LISTEN	TO	YOU.
THE BIRDS GATHERED	ROUND	US.

ALL FORMS OF THE VERB "TO BE", WHEN USED BY THEMSELVES [AM, IS, ARE, WAS, WERE, HAVE, BEEN, WILL, BE ETC.], CONTROL THE FOLLOWING PRONOUNS.

IT IS I. [UNIVERSAL PRACTICE ALLOWS IT IS ME TO BE ACCEPTED].

IT IS SHE	NOT	IT IS HER.
IT IS WE	NOT	IT IS US.
IT IS HE	NOT	IT IS HIM.
IT IS THEY	NOT	IT IS THEM.

CORRECT FORMS : -

THAT WAS HE.
THOSE WERE THEY.
WHO ARE THEY?
WHO WAS SHE?
THE GIRL IS BELIEVED TO BE SHE   NOT   HER.
THE BOY IS BELIEVED TO BE HE   NOT   HIM.
THE WOMAN IS SAID TO BE SHE   NOT   HER.
THE BOY WHO WON THE RACE IS SUPPOSED TO BE HE   NOT   HIM.
AT THE PARK WE WERE THOUGHT TO BE THEY NOT THEM.

IT APPEARS TO BE HIM	NOT	HE.
IT APPEARS TO BE SHE	NOT	HER.
IT SEEMS TO BE THEY	NOT	THEM.

ERRORS WHICH ARE MADE IN EVERYDAY PRACTICE OF THE ENGLISH LANGUAGE.

WHO, WHICH, THAT.

1   WHO REFERS TO PERSONS.
2   WHICH REFERS TO ANIMALS, PLANTS AND THINGS.
3   THAT REFERS TO ANIMALS, PLANTS, THINGS OR PERSONS.

EXAMPLES OF CORRECT USAGE : -

THE MAN WHO   LIVES NEXT DOOR.
THE WOMAN   WHO   WEARS THE HAT.
THE CHILD   WHO   IS PLAYING IN THE PARK.

THE DOG WHICH   RAN AFTER THE BALL.
THE TREE   WHICH   IS IN THE FRONT OF THE YARD.
THE BAG WHICH   IS ON THE TABLE.

THE CAT   THAT   IS IN THE TREE.
THE FLOWER   THAT   IS IN THE VASE.
THE PEN   THAT   IS ON THE DESK.
THE LADY   THAT   IS IN THE YARD.

THE ADJECTIVE : -

ADJECTIVES MAY BE DIVIDED INTO THREE MAIN CLASSES.

1   ADJECTIVES OF DISTINCTION.

[a] DEMONSTRATIVE.
THESE, THOSE, THIS, THAT ETC.
E.G :-
THIS BALL WAS FOUND IN THE PARK.

[b] INTERROGATIVE.
WHOSE, WHICH, WHAT ETC.
E G :-
WHICH DRESS DO YOU WANT.

[c] DISTRIBUTIVE.

EVERY, EITHER, NEITHER,EACH ETC.
E G :-
SHE COULD GO TO SCHOOL BY EITHER BUS OR VAN.

2   ADJECTIVES OF QUANTITY.

[a] DEFINITE   [INCLUDING NUMERALS].
SECOND, BOTH, ONE, THIRTY, DOUBLE ETC.
E G :-
BOTH   GOALKEEPERS ALLOWED TWO GOALS   IN
THE   THIRD GAME.

[b] INDEFINITE.
MANY, FEW, ANY, MUCH,ALL, SOME ETC.
E G :-
WE MET ALL   THE FISHERMEN WHO HAD CAUGHT
SOME FISH.

3   DESCRIPTIVE ADJECTIVES.
YOUNG, OLD, GOOD, BAD, UGLY, RED,BLUE ETC .
E G :-
THE   YOUNG   MAN WORE A   RED   SHIRT.

THE ADVERB :-
IN ADDITION TO MODIFYING VERBS, AN ADVERB IS A
WORD THAT CAN ALSO ADD TO THE MEANING OF AN
ADJECTIVE OR ANOTHER ADVERB.

ADVERBS MAY BE DIVIDED, ACCORDING TO THEIR USE
INTO THE FOLLOWING CLASSES :-

[a] AFFIRMATION AND NEGATION :-
NO, NOT,YES,CERTAINLY ETC.
E G :-
I HAVE   NOT   SEEN THE MOVIE.
HE CAN   CERTAINLY   FIGHT.

[b] TIME :-
NOW,SINCE,BEFORE,THEN ETC.
E G :-
SHE MET HIM   BEFORE.

[c] QUESTIONING :-
WHERE, WHEN,HOW ETC.
E G :-
WHERE DID YOU SEE HIM?

[d] PLACE :-
HERE, THERE,EVERYWHERE ETC.
E G :-
THEY WENT   THEREYESTERDAY.

[e] NUMBER :-
ONCE, TWICE ETC.
E G :-
THEY RAN   TWICEAROUND THE PARK.

[f] MANNER :-
WELL, SLOWLY,EASILY ETC.
E G :-
THE GIRL WON THE RACE   EASILY.

[g] DEGREE :-
VERY,MUCH,ONLY,ALMOST ETC.
E G :-
THE OLD MAN CLIMBED THE STAIRS   VERY
SLOWLY.

THE CONJUNCTION :-

THERE ARE TWO MAIN KINDS OF CONJUNCTIONS.

[a] CONJUNCTIONS WHICH JOIN SIMILAR PARTS OF
SPEECH AND CLAUSES OF EQUAL VALUE.
E G :-
FOR, BUT, AND, BOTH, EITHER, OR ETC.
E G :-
THE MAN AND WOMAN DROVE HOME.
BOTH   HE   AND HIS   SISTER   WENT   TO   THE
LIBRARY.
HE WAS RICH   BUT   DISHONEST.

I GIVE HIM THE REWARD, FOR HE HAD EARNED IT.

EITHER MY BROTHER OR HIS FRIEND KNOWS THE PLACE.

[b] CONJUNCTIONS WHICH JOIN PRINCIPAL CLAUSES TO SUBORDINATE CLAUSES.

[A CLAUSE IS ONE PART OF A SENTENCE WITH A SUBJECT AND VERB].

IN ORDER TO LEARN MORE EASILY THE VARIOUS TYPES IN THIS CLASS, THE CONJUNCTIONS ARE PLACED UNDER CERTAIN HEADINGS.

PURPOSE :-

CONJUNCTIONS ARE :- IN ORDER THAT, LEST, SO THAT, THAT. ETC .

E G :-

1 THEY TRAINED HARD IN ORDER THAT THEY MIGHT WIN THE RACE.

2 TRAIN WELL, LEST YOU LOSE THE RACE.

3 I SENT HER A MEMO SO THAT SHE WOULD KNOW.

4 YOU COME TO THE LIBRARY THAT YOU MAY LEARN.

TIME :-

CONJUNCTIONS ARE :- WHEN, WHENEVER, WHILE, BEFORE, AFTER, SINCE, TILL, UNTIL, NOW, THAT, AS ETC.

E G :-

1 THE GIRLS WERE GOING HOME WHEN WE SAW THEM.

2 WHENEVER IT IS POSSIBLE WE SHALL SEE HIM.

3 WHILE THERE IS TIME, THERE IS HOPE.

4 THE LADY WENT TO THE MOVIES BEFORE SHE WENT HOME

5 AFTER THE MAN ENTERED THE CAR HE STARTED THE ENGINE.

6 SINCE I HAVE KNOWN HIM, WE NEVER GOT ALONG.

7 WE WILL WAIT HERE UNTIL THE NEXT BUS ARRIVES.

PLACE :-
CONJUNCTIONS ARE :- WHERE, WHEREVER ETC.
E G.:-
1 THE MONEY MUST BE FOUND   WHEREVER IT IS.
2 PUT IT WHERE   THE BABY CAN'T GET IT.

MANNER OR DEGREE :-
CONJUNCTIONS ARE :- SO AS, THAN, AS, AS IF, AS THOUGH
ETC.
E G.:-
1 JANE DOES NOT WRITE   SO   WELL AS
SUSAN.
2 SHE IS SHORTER   THAN I AM.
3 HE REMAINED IN THE ROOM   AS   HE   HAD
BEEN ORDERED
4 SHE ACTS   AS IF SHE KNOWS ABOUT IT.
5 I LAY   AS THOUGH I WERE DEAD.

CAUSE OR REASON :-
CONJUNCTIONS ARE :- BECAUSE, SINCE, AS ETC.
E G :-
1 WE KNOW SHE WAS THERE,   BECAUSE   S H E
SAID SO.
2 DO NOT SAY ANYTHING   SINCE SHE   DOESN'T
KNOW.
3 AS   SHE WAS IN A HURRY SHE FORGOT HER
BOOK.

CONDITION :-
CONJUNCTIONS ARE :- UNLESS, IF, EXCEPT – THAT ETC.
E G :-
1 HE WILL NOT DO HIS HOMEWORK   UNLESS
HIS PARENTS COMPEL HIM TO DO SO.
2 SEND ME WORD   IF   YOU HEAR FROM HER.
3 EXCEPT THAT SHE TRAINS POORLY, SHE IS A GOOD
ATHLETE.

CONCESSIONS :-
CONJUNCTIONS ARE :- WHILE, AS, ALTHOUGH, EVEN IF
ETC.
E G :-

1 WHILE WE SHOULD NOT CONDONE HIS ACTIONS, WE SHOULD APPLAUD HIS RESULTS.

2 SMART AS SHE WAS, SHE COULD NOT GET THE RIGHT ANSWERS.

3 ALTHOUGH I DON'T LIKE POLITICS, I STILL VOTED.

4 HE CANNOT WIN EVEN IF HE TRIES HIS BEST.

CONSEQUENCE :-
CONJUNCTIONS ARE :- SO - THAT, SO THAT ETC.
E G :-

1 THE LADY SHOUTED SO THAT SHE WAS HEARD.

2 HE IS SO SMART THAT HE CAN DO ALMOST ANYTHING.

PREPOSITION :-

THE PREPOSITION IS PLACED BEFORE A NOUN OR A PRONOUN. IT IS SOMEWHAT LIKE A CONJUNCTION AS IT SHOWS THE RELATIONSHIP BETWEEN NOUNS AND PRONOUNS IN THE SAME SENTENCE.

THE MOST COMMON PREPOSITIONS ARE :- ABOUT, ABOVE, ACROSS, AFTER, AGAINST, ALONG, AMONG, AROUND, AT, BEFORE, BEHIND, BELOW, BESIDE, BETWEEN, BY, DOWN, DURING, EXCEPT, FOR, FROM, IN, INTO, NEAR, ON, OFF, OF, OVER, SINCE, THROUGH, TO, TOWARDS, UNDER, UNTIL, UP, UPON, WITH, WITHIN, WITHOUT ETC.

HERE IS A LIST OF CORRECT PREPOSITIONS :-

OPPOSITE TO
PART FROM [SOMEBODY]
PART WITH [SOMETHING]
PROTEST AGAINST
REGARD FOR
RELY ON
SIMILAR TO
SUFFER FROM
TIRED WITH [ACTION]
TIRED OF [SOMETHING]
THIRST FOR

ACCORDING TO
AGREE TO [SOMETHING]
AGREE WITH [SOMEONE]
AIM AT
ANGRY WITH
VEXED AT [SOMETHING]
VEXED WITH [SOMEBODY]
VICTIM OF
ASHAMED OF
BLAME FOR
CHANGE WITH [SOMEBODY]
CHANGE FOR [SOMETHING]
WAIT FOR [PERSON OR THING]
WRITE ABOUT [SOMETHING]
WRITE TO [SOMEONE]
FULL OF
GOOD FOR
GUILTY OF
COMMENT ON
COMPLAIN OF
CONSCIOUS OF
DIE OF
INSPIRED BY
INTERFERE WITH
INVASION OF
DIFFER FROM [OPINION]
DIFFER WITH [SOMEBODY]
DISAGREE WITH
MEDDLE WITH
DISAPPOINTED IN [SOMETHING]
DISAPPOINTED WITH [SOMEONE]
DISLIKE FOR
DIVIDE AMONG [MANY]
DIVIDE BETWEEN [TWO]
EQUAL TO
FILLED WITH

QUOTATION MARKS :-

THE TWO MAIN USES OF QUOTATION MARKS ARE :-

1   TO INDICATE THE EXACT WORDS OF A WRITER OR SPEAKER.

2   TO SHOW THE TITLES OF SHORT WORKS.

USE QUOTATION MARKS WHEN YOU WANT TO SHOW THE EXACT WORDS OF A SPEAKER OR WRITER.

E G :-

1   "DO SOMETHING NICE TO ME,"SHOUTED ANN TO GARY.

[THE { " "} QUOTATION MARKS SET OFF THE EXACT WORDS ANN SPOKE TO GARY.]

2   ROY NOLAN ONCE WROTE, "THE MORE I KNOW ABOUT GOD, THE MORE I GAINED WISDOM."

[THE { " "} QUOTATION MARKS INDICATE THE EXACT WORDS THAT ROY NOLAN WROTE.]

3 "THE ONLY TRUE ANSWERS," THE TEACHER SAID, "IS THE ONE THAT GIVES FACTS."

[TWO PAIRS OF QUOTATION MARKS ARE USED TO ENCLOSE THE TEACHER'S EXACT WORDS.]

4   SHONDELL EXPLAINED, "I WORKED SO HARD AT UNIVERSITY. I SPENT FIVE YEARS IN CLASSES DOING NUMEROUS PAPERS ON DIFFERENT SUBJECT MATTERS. I FINALLY GRADUATED."

[PLACE QUOTATION MARKS BEFORE THE FIRST QUOTED WORD OF A SPEECH AND AFTER THE LAST QUOTED WORD. AS LONG AS NO INTERRUPTION OCCURS IN THE SPEECH, DO NOT USE QUOTATION MARKS FOR EACH NEW SENTENCE.]

IN THE EXAMPLES ABOVE, NOTICE THAT A COMMA SETS OFF THE QUOTED PART FROM THE REST OF THE SENTENCE. ALSO NOTE THAT COMMAS AND PERIODS OR FULL STOP AT THE END OF A QUOTATION ALWAYS GO INSIDE QUOTATION MARKS.

DIRECT AND INDIRECT QUOTATIONS.

AN INDIRECT QUOTATION IS A REWARDING OF SOMEONE ELSE'S COMMENTS, RATHER THAN A WORD - FOR - WORD DIRECT QUOTATION.

EXAMPLE :-

DIRECT QUOTATION :-
JENNY ASKED, "ANN, CAN I TURN ON THE MOVIE?"

INDIRECT QUOTATION :-
JENNY ASKED ANN IF SHE COULD TURN ON THE MOVIE.

DIRECT QUOTATION :-
ALAN SAID "THE WINDSHIELD ON MY JEEP IS CRACKED."
[ALAN'S EXACT SPOKEN WORDS ARE GIVEN SO QUOTATION MARKS ARE USED.]

INDIRECT QUOTATION :-
ALAN SAID THAT THE WINDSHIELD ON HIS JEEP WAS CRACKED.

DIRECT QUOTATION :-
RUBY'S MEMO TO ANDY READ, "I'LL BE LATE FOR DINNER. DON'T WAIT UP FOR ME."
[THE EXACT WORDS THAT RUBY WROTE IN THE MEMO ARE GIVEN, SO QUOTATION MARKS ARE USED.]

INDIRECT QUOTATION :-
RUBY LEFT A MEMO FOR ANDY THAT SAID SHE WOULD BE LATE FOR DINNER AND THAT HE SHOULD NOT WAIT UP FOR HER.

QUOTATION MARKS TO SET OFF THE TITLES OF SHORT WORKS :-
SHORT WORKS ARE USUALLY SET OFF BY QUOTATION MARKS. USE QUOTATION MARKS TO INDICATE THE TITLES OF SUCH SHORT WORKS AS ARTICLES IN BOOKS, CHAPTERS IN A BOOK, MAGAZINES OR NEWSPAPERS, SHORT STORIES, POEMS AND SONGS.

UNDERLINED :-
LONG WORKS ARE UNDERLINED; YOU SHOULD UNDERLINE THE TITLES OF BOOKS, PLAYS, MOVIES, RECORD ALBUMS, AND TELEVISION SHOWS.

OTHER USES OF QUOTATION MARKS :-
[a] TO MARK OFF A QUOTATION WITHIN A QUOTATION.

1 THE TEACHER SAID, "MAKE SURE YOU UNDERSTAND THE CHAPTER TITLED ` GET WISDOM ` IN KNOWLEDGE AND UNDERSTANDING IF YOU EXPECT TO GET GOOD GRADES IN THE TEST"

2 JACK SAID, "ONE OF MY IMPORTANT NURSERY RHYME LINES IS ` I WENT TO FETCH A PALE OF WATER, BUT I FELL. ` "

NOTE :- A QUOTATION WITHIN A QUOTATION IS INDICATED BY SINGLE QUOTATION MARKS.

COMMA :-
THE MAIN USES OF A COMMA :-
1 COMMAS OFTEN SIGNAL A PAUSE, IN A SENTENCE.
2 TO SEPARATE ITEMS IN A SERIES.
3 ON BOTH SIDES OF WORDS THAT INTERRUPT THE FLOW OF THOUGHT IN A SENTENCE.
4 TO INDICATE INTRODUCTORY MATERIAL.
5 BETWEEN TWO COMPLETE THOUGHTS CONNECTED BY AND, FOR, OR, BUT, YET, SO, NOR ETC.
6 FOR CERTAIN EVERYDAY MATERIAL.
7 TO SET OFF A DIRECT QUOTATION FROM THE REST OF THE SENTENCE.

USING COMMAS TO SEPARATE ITEMS IN A SERIES.
E G :-
1 I EAT GRAPES, APPLES, MANGOES, AND CHERRIES.
2 YESTERDAY THE DRIER BROKE DOWN, THE OVEN STOPPED WORKING, AND THE VACUUM GOT CLOGGED UP.
3 THE BASKETBALL GAME WAS SO FRUSTRATING THAT FRANK DID NOT KNOW WHETHER TO EAT, DRINK, OR THROW UP.
4 DALLAS ARRIVED HOME FROM A TIRED, IRRITATING DAY AT WORK

NOTES :-
THE FINAL COMMA IN A SERIES IS OPTIONAL, BUT OFTEN IT IS USED A COMMA IS USED BETWEEN TWO DESCRIPTIVE

WORDS IN A SERIES YOU CAN USE   AND   ONLY IF
AND   INSERTED BETWEEN THE WORDS SOUND NATURAL.

YOU COULD SAY :-
DALLAS ARRIVED HOME FROM A TIRED AND IRRITATING
DAY AT WORK.

HOWEVER, IN   THE   FOLLOWING   SENTENCE   THE
DESCRIPTIVE WORDS DO NOT SOUND NATURAL WHEN
AND   IS INSERTED BETWEEN   THEM. IN   SUCH   CASES, NO
AND OR COMMA IS USED.

YOUNG DROVE A DARK GREEN MERCEDES.
[A DARK AND GREEN MERCEDES   OR   A   DARK,
GREEN MERCEDES. DOESN'T SOUND RIGHT, SO NO   AND
OR   COMMA IS USED.

USE   COMMAS   ON   BOTH   SIDES   OF   WORDS   OR
PHRASES THAT INTERRUPT THE FLOW OF THOUGHT IN A
SENTENCE.
E G.: -
1   THE   CIRCUS   SHOW, AT   LONG   LAST, HAS   BEEN
SHOWN.
2 THE MAN USED THE OLD VAN, RUSTED FROM DISUSE,
AS A JUNKYARD PICKUP.
3 MY DAD, A SPORTS ENTHUSIAST, FOLLOWS ALL THE
DIFFERENT SPORTS PROGRAMS.
4 MARK   JONES, WHO   LIVES   IN   THE   NEIGHBORHOOD,
WON THE POOLS COMPETITION.

USUALLY   WORDS   THAT   ARE   INTERRUPTERS, CAN   BE
REMOVED FROM THE SENTENCE AND THE SENTENCE WOULD
STILL MAKE SENSE WITHOUT THE REMOVED WORDS. FROM
THIS   YOU   KNOW   THE   WORDS   ARE   INTERRUPTERS   AND
THE   INFORMATION   THEY   GIVE   IS   NONESSENTIAL. SUCH
NONESSENTIAL INFORMATION IS SET OFF WITH COMMAS;
AS IS THE CASE IN THE EXAMPLE NUMBER FOUR ABOVE.
THE   WORDS ' WHO   LIVES   IN   THE   NEIGHBORHOOD '
ARE EXTRA INFORMATION, NOT NEEDED TO IDENTIFY THE
SUBJECT OF THE SENTENCE, MARK JONES. PUT COMMAS
AROUND   SUCH   NONESSENTIAL   INFORMATION. HOWEVER,

ON THE OTHER HAND, THE MAN WHO LIVES IN THE NEIGHBORHOOD WON THE POOLS COMPETITION.

IN THIS CASE THE WORDS WHO LIVES IN THE NEIGHBORHOOD SUPPLY ESSENTIAL INFORMATION -- INFORMATION NEEDED FOR US TO IDENTIFY THE MAN BEING SPOKEN OF. IF THE WORDS WERE REMOVED FROM THE SENTENCE, WE WOULD NO LONGER KNOW WHO WON THE COMPETITION. COMMAS ARE NOT USED AROUND SUCH ESSENTIAL INFORMATION.

USE A COMMA TO SET OFF INTRODUCTORY MATERIAL.
E G. : -
1 LOOKING IN THE SWIMMING POOL, I SAW A MAN WHO WAS SWIMMING FASTER THAN A FISH.
2 IN ADDITION, HE HELD A SPADE IN HIS HAND.
3 ALSO, HE WORE A CRASH HELMET IN CASE A BASEBALL, SHOULD TRAVEL IN THE DIRECTION OF HIS HEAD.
4 AFTER PUNCHING THE WINDOW WITH HIS FIST, JOHN TURNED AROUND AND WALKED AWAY.

NOTE :-
IF THE INTRODUCTORY MATERIAL IS BRIEF, THE COMMA IS SOMETIMES OMITTED.

USE A COMMA BETWEEN TWO COMPLETE THOUGHTS CONNECTED BY AND, FOR, OR, BUT, YET, SO, NOR ETC.
E G :-
1 WE COULD ALWAYS TELL WHEN OUR FATHER FELT DISCOURAGED, FOR HIS CAR WOULD NOT BE PARKED PROPERLY.
2 MOM HAS TO WORK ON SUNDAY, SO SHE GOES TO CHURCH ON SATURDAY.
3   THE FLIGHT WAS SCHEDULED FOR SEVEN O ' CLOCK, BUT THEY CANCELLED IT AT FIVE

NOTES :-
[a] THE COMMA IS OPTIONAL WHEN THE COMPLETE THOUGHTS ARE SHORT.
E G :-

1 HER JUICE TURNED WATERY FOR THE ICE MELTED QUICKLY.

2 THE RAIN WAS FALLING SO THEY DIDN'T PLAY BASEBALL.

4 LORRAINE IS SHORT AND LEONARD IS TALL.

[b] BE CAREFUL NOT TO USE A COMMA IN SENTENCES HAVING ONE SUBJECT AND A DOUBLE VERB. THE COMMA IS USED ONLY IN SENTENCES MADE UP OF TWO COMPLETE THOUGHTS [TWO SUBJECTS AND TWO VERBS].

IN THE SENTENCE :-
DALLAS WILL GO PLAYING TONIGHT AND FORGET ALL ABOUT TOMORROW'S APPOINTMENT.

THERE IS ONLY ONE SUBJECT [DALLAS] AND A DOUBLE VERB [WILL GO AND FORGET]. NO COMMA IS NEEDED.

LIKEWISE IN THE FOLLOWING SENTENCE.:-
SAVITA WAS A CLEANER AT THE PENGUIN HOTEL LAST WINTER AND PROBABLY WILL WORK THERE THIS SUMMER.

THE ABOVE SENTENCE HAS ONLY ONE SUBJECT [SAVITA] AND A DOUBLE VERB [WAS AND WILL WORK]; THEREFORE, NO COMMA IS NEEDED.

USE A COMMA WITH CERTAIN EVERYDAY MATERIAL.

OPENING AND CLOSING OF LETTERS :-
DEAR JOSHUA,
DEAR SANDRA,
SINCERELY YOURS,
RESPECTFULLY YOURS,
TRULY YOURS,

PERSONS SPOKEN TO :-

ARNOLD, WHERE DID YOU PUT MY BALL?
ARE YOU GOING WITH US, KAMEEL?
GO TO BED, EMERALD, IF YOU ARE FEELING SLEEPY.

DATES :-

MARCH 11, 1989, IS WHEN SHARON GOT HER SECOND CHILD.

ADDRESSES :-

RODNEY'S PARENTS LIVE AT 1030 HEALY AVENUE, QUEENS, NEW YORK 11692

NOTE :-
[a] NO COMMA IS USED TO MARK OFF THE ZIP CODE.
[b] IN FORMAL LETTERS, A COLON IS USED AFTER THE OPENING :
E G :-
DEAR SIR :   DEAR MADAM :

NUMBERS :-

THE DISHONEST SALESMAN TURNED THE USED CAR'S ODOMETOR FROM 87,345 MILES TO 45, 345 MILES.

USE A COMMA TO SET OFF A DIRECT QUOTATION FROM THE REST OF A SENTENCE.
E G :-
1 HER MOTHER SCREAMED, "WHY DON'T YOU GO OUT AND GET MARRIED? "
2 "OUR WORLD TODAY, HAS LOST A SENSE OF SACREDNESS AND PURITY OF LIFE, "THE TEACHER SAID.
3 "YES "SAID BABY TO ALAN. "I WILL GO TO THE BOWLING ARENA WITH YOU."
4 "CAN YOU REMEMBER, "WROTE SUBRINA, "WHEN THE TIMES WERE NOT HARD AND FOOD NOT SCARCE?

NOTE :-
COMMAS AND PERIODS OR FULL STOPS AT THE END OF A QUOTATION GO INSIDE QUOTATION MARKS.

OTHER PUNCTUATION MARKS :-

DASH :- [--]

A DASH SHOWS A DEGREE OF PAUSE LONGER THAN A COMMA BUT NOT AS COMPLETE AS A PERIOD OR FULL STOP. USE A DASH TO SET OFF WORDS FOR DRAMATIC EFFECT.

E G :-

1 GORDON DIDN'T GO OUT WITH HER A SECOND TIME – ONCE WAS MORE THAN ENOUGH.

2 SOME OF YOU – AND YOU KNOW YOURSELVES – FAILED THE TEST.

3   IT WAS SO WINDY THAT THE BREEZE BLEW HIS HAT – AWAY.

NOTES :-

[a] BE CAREFUL NOT TO OVERUSE DASHES.

[b] THE DASH IS FORMED ON THE KEYBOARD OR TYPEWRITER BY STRIKING THE HYPHEN TWICE [--]. IN HANDWRITING, THE DASH IS AS LONG AS TWO LETTERS WOULD BE.

HYPHEN [--] :-

1 USE A HYPHEN TO DIVIDE A WORD AT THE END OF A LINE OF WRITING OR TYPING. WHEN YOU NEED TO DIVIDE A WORD AT THE END OF A LINE, DIVIDE IT BETWEEN SYLLABLES.

E G :-

WHEN PETAL LIFTED UP THE HOOD OF HER JEEP, SHE SAW THAT THE RADI—

ATOR COVER WAS OFF.

2 USE A HYPHEN WITH TWO OR MORE WORDS THAT ACT AS A SINGLE UNIT DESCRIBING A NOUN.

E G :-

[a] THE FAST—WALKING GIRL WAS SO GOOD THAT SHE WALKED TO SCHOOL.

[FAST AND WALKING COMBINE TO DESCRIBE THE GIRL.]

[b] I DISLIKE HIS WELL—ROUNDED ABILITY TO PLAY BALL.

[c] WHEN JACK REMOVED HIS DARK—TINTED SUNGLASSES, JILL SAW THE BLANKED—OUT LOOK IN HIS EYES.

NOTES :-
1 DO NOT DIVIDE A WORD IF YOU CAN AVOID DOING SO.
2 DO NOT DIVIDE WORDS OF ONE SYLLABLE.

COLON :-

USE THE COLON AT THE END OF A COMPLETE STATEMENT TO INTRODUCE A LIST, A LONG QUOTATION, OR AN EXPLANATION.

LIST :-
THE FOLLOWING WERE MY BEST JOBS : CLERK IN AN OFFICE, TEACHER IN A SCHOOL, AND PILOT AT AN AIRLINE COMPANY.

LONG QUOTATION :-
PAUL EXPLAINED TO JUDAS : "I WENT INTO THE WORLD BECAUSE I WISHED TO LIVE AND SHARE WITH OTHERS, THE ESSENTIAL FACTS OF LIFE, AND SEE IF I COULD NOT LEARN WHAT IT HAD TO TEACH, AND NOT, WHEN I BECOME OLD, REALIZE THAT I HAD NOT LIVED WELL."

EXPLANATION :-
THERE ARE TWO CRICKET LEAGUES IN OUR VILLAGE : THE FAST—BALL LEAGUE AND THE SOFT—BALL LEAGUE.

SEMICOLON :-
A SEMICOLON [;] IS MADE UP OF A PERIOD AND A COMMA. THE SEMICOLON SIGNALS MORE OF A PAUSE THAN A COMMA ALONE BUT NOT QUITE THE FULL PAUSE OF A PERIOD OR FULL STOP.

1 THE MAIN USE OF THE SEMICOLON IS TO MARK THE BREAK BETWEEN TWO COMPLETE THOUGHTS.

2 IT IS ALSO USED TO MARK OFF ITEMS IN A SERIES WHEN THE ITEMS THEMSELVES CONTAIN COMMAS.

3 A SEMICOLON IS ALSO SOMETIMES USED WITH A TRANSITIONAL – WORD AND A COMMA TO JOIN TWO COMPLETE THOUGHTS.

EXAMPLES OF NUMBER THREE.:-
[a] I HAD A BOOK TO WRITE; HOWEVER, MY BRAIN WAS NOT FUNCTIONING FOR A PERIOD OF TIME.

[b] I HAVE TO KEEP WRITING THE BOOK; OTHERWISE, I WILL NEVER FINISH IT.

[c] I DID NOT HAVE ENOUGH MONEY; THEREFORE, I DECIDED NOT TO GO TO THE BALL GAME.

LISTED BELOW ARE COMMON TRANSITIONAL WORDS; ALSO KNOWN AS ADVERBIAL CONJUNCTIONS.

THEREFORE, HOWEVER, OTHERWISE, INSTEAD, NEVERTHELESS, ON THE OTHER HAND, ALSO, AS A RESULT, INDEED, MEANWHILE ETC.

HERE ARE EXAMPLES OF NUMBER ONE SHOWING SENTENCES, WHERE A SEMICOLON, UNLIKE THE COMMA ALONE, CAN BE USED TO CONNECT THE TWO COMPLETE THOUGHTS IN EACH SENTENCE.

[a] A LOT OF MEN TODAY GET THEIR NAILS DONE; THEY USE PERFUME AND OTHER HERBS AS WELL.

[b] I CAN'T DO ANY WRITING THIS WEEKEND; MY MOTHER WANTS ME TO WORK WITH HER.

[c]SHE WAS AFRAID OF NOT DOING WELL IN THE RACE; SHE HAS ALWAYS HAD BAD LUCK ON THAT TRACK.

EXAMPLES OF NUMBER TWO :-

[a]THE FOLLOWING BOOKS MUST BE READ IN THE CLASS : THE SWORD OF THE SPIRIT, BY ROY NOLAN; AMAZING GRACE, BY PETAL DAWN; AND MAN'S SEARCH FOR TRUTH IN LIFE, BY SHONDELL SIMONE.

[b] WINNING PRIZES AT THE NATIONAL DOG SHOW WERE COLLETTE RICHARDS, NEW YORK, GREY HOUND; KIM JORDAN, NEW JERSEY, DOBERMAN; AND YOLAND BRUTUS, MIAMI, ALSTATION.

PARENTHESES [ ] .:-

PARENTHESES ARE USED TO SET OFF EXTRA OR INCIDENTAL INFORMATION FROM THE REST OF A SENTENCE.

E G.:-

[a] THE SECTION OF THE BIBLE ON THE REVELATION [PAGES 380 TO 405] IS SYMBOLIZED.

[b] THE OTHER DAY AT THE ZOO [MY FAVORITE PAST TIME PLACE], I MET THE ZOO KEEPER WHO LET ME HELP HIM FEED THE BIRDS

COMPOUND WORDS :-

A WORD IN ITS SIMPLEST FORM IS CALLED A PRIMARY WORD, E G. BALL, BLACK, GENTLE, MAN ETC.

IF WE COMBINE TWO PRIMARY WORDS TO FORM ONE WORD WE GET A COMPOUND WORD, USING THE EXAMPLES GIVEN WE CAN FORM WORDS SUCH AS BASKETBALL, BLACKBOARD, GENTLEMAN, MANSERVANT.

OTHER EXAMPLES ARE :-

DAY – TIME	=	DAYTIME
HEAD – ACHE	=	HEADACHE
TABLE – CLOTH	=	TABLECLOTH
FIRE – PLACE	=	FIREPLACE
GRAND – MASTER	=	GRANDMASTER

POST – MAN	=	POSTMAN
POST – OFFICE	=	POSTOFFICE
TEA – POT	=	TEAPOT
ROOM – MATE	=	ROOMMATE
TIME – ZONE	=	TIMEZONE
BACK – YARD	=	BACKYARD

HOMONYMS :- ARE SIMILAR SOUNDING WORDS.

E G.:-

ANT	AUNT	
BAIL	BALE	
BALL	BAWL	
BARE	BEAR	
BLEW	BLUE	
BOAR	BORE	
BOY	BUOY	
BY	BUY	BYE
CHECK	CHEQUE	
COURSE	COARSE	
DEAR	DEER	
DIE	DYE	
EWE	YOU	
FAIR	FARE	
FEAT	FEET	
FLOUR	FLOWER	
FORE	FOUR	
FOUL	FOWL	
GRATE	GREAT	
HAIL	HALE	
HAIR	HARE	
HIGHER	HIRE	
HOUR	OUR	
HIM	HYMN	
HOLE	WHOLE	
KNOWS	NOSE	
MADE	MAID	
MEET	MEAT	
PAIL	PALE	
PAIN	PANE	
PEAL	PEEL	
PLAIN	PLANE	

ROAD	RODE	ROWED
ROSE	ROWS	
SEA	SEE	
SON	SUN	
TAIL	TALE	
TIED	TIDE	
WAIT	WEIGHT	
WOULD	WOOD	
KNEW	NEW	
LOAN	LONE	
MAIL	MALE	
NONE	NUN	
PAIR	PARE	PEAR
PEACE	PIECE	
PICTURE	PITCHER	
REAL	REEL	
ROOT	ROUTE	
SAIL	SALE	
SOLE	SOUL	
STEAL	STEEL	
THEIR	THERE	
WAIST	WASTE	
WEEK	WEAK	

CHAPTER 2.

OUR FIVE SENSES :-

EVERY NORMAL PERSON IS BORN WITH FIVE SENSES BY WHICH HE OR SHE IS ABLE TO SEE, HEAR, SMELL, TASTE AND TOUCH.

SIGHT - IS THE ABILITY TO OBSERVE OR PERCEIVE BY THE EYE.
HEARING – IS THE ABILITY TO LISTEN OR PERCEIVE BY THE EAR.
SMELL – IS THE ABILITY TO DETECT ODORS OR PERCEIVE BY THE NOSE.

TASTE – IS THE ABILITY TO DETECT FLAVORS IN THE MOUTH OR PERCEIVE BY THE TONGUE.

TOUCH – IS THE ABILITY TO DETECT OBJECTS BY CONTACT OR PERCEIVE BY FEELING.

GENERAL KNOWLEDGE :-

IN THE FOLLOWING LIST MANY QUESTIONS CAN BE ANSWERED BY ONE WORD. WHEREVER AND WHENEVER POSSIBLE, DO SO.

A BOY WHO FRIGHTENS WEAKER BOYS.   BULLY
A NUMBER OF SOLDIERS.   ARMY

THE MEN WHO WORK ON A SHIP. CREW

CHILDREN IN A SCHOOL.   STUDENTS

A MAN WHO PROTECTS SHEEP.   SHEPHARD

A LOW GROUND BETWEEN TWO HILLS. VALLEY

A PLACE WHERE PUPILS ARE EDUCATED. UNIVERSITY.

A SHIP WHICH TRAVELS BELOW THE SURFACE OF THE
SEA. SUBMARINE.

A PLACE FOR STORING A MOTOR CAR.   GARAGE

A SMALL LEAF. LEAFLET

THE WOMAN IN CHARGE OF A HOSPITAL. MATRON

A FIELD IN WHICH FRUIT TREES GROW.. ORCHARD

AN INSTRUMENT FOR MEASURING TIME. CLOCK

FROM WHAT DO WE MAKE BUTTER?   MILK

A MAN WHO MAKES FURNITURE. JOINER

A FERTILE PLACE IN THE DESERT. OASIS

A HUNDRED YEARS. CENTURY

NAME INSTRUMENT FOR TELLING DIRECTION.
COMPASS

WHAT ARE THE STEPS OF A LADDER CALLED? RUNG

NAME TWO SPOTTED ANIMALS.   CAT   AND   TIGER

A DOCTOR WHO PERFORMS OPERATIONS. SURGEON

WHAT IS THE FRONT PART OF A SHIP CALLED? BOW

WHAT IS THE BACK PART OF A SHIP CALLED?   STERN

HEADGEAR WORN BY NATIVES OF INDIA. TURBAN

A PLACE WHERE BEER IS MADE.   BREWERY

WHAT IS DAYBREAK SOMETIMES TERMED?   DAWN

A MAN WHO DRAWS AND PAINTS. ARTIST

A SHALLOW CROSSING IN A RIVER.BAR

TWO CREATURES WHICH SEE WELL IN THE DARK.
OWL   AND   BAT

GIRL OR WOMAN WHO SERVES AT TABLE.MAID

WHAT DO WE CALL THE BREAKING OF A BONE.
FRACTURE

NAME TWO SHELLFISH.   CRAB, SHRIMP

WHAT IS THE FLESH OF A SHEEP CALLED.
MUTTON

THE FIRST MEAL OF THE DAY.   BREAKFAST

QUICKEST WAY OF SENDING MESSAGES. TELEPHONE

PLACE IN WHICH PHOTOGRAPHS ARE TAKEN.
STUDIO

A PLACE WHERE PEOPLE ARE BURIED.   CEMETERY

ANOTHER NAME FOR A POLICEMAN.   CONSTABLE OR OFFICER

NAME THE IMAGINARY LINE ROUND MIDDLE OF EARTH   EQUATOR

FROM WHAT DO WE MAKE CHEESE?   MILK

NAME THE FIVE HUMAN SENSES. SIGHT,   HEARING, SMELL, TASTE AND TOUCH.

WHAT LIGHTS MUST A SHIP SHOW AT NIGHTS? NAVIGATION LIGHTS

GOODS CARRIED OUT OF A COUNTRY.   EXPORT

GOODS TAKEN INTO A COUNTRY.   IMPORT

A PLACE WHERE BIRDS ARE KEPT. AVIARY

PERSON WHO GIVES LIFE IN A GOOD CAUSE.   HERO

THE AIR SURROUNDING THE EARTH.   ATMOSPHERE

A PERSON WHO SAVES AND HOARDS MONEY   MISER

A RELIGIOUS SONG.   HYMN

HOW DOES A FISH BREATHE IN WATER?   GILLS

WHAT IS THE SMALL TOP ROOM OF A HOUSE.   ATTIC

A THREE – SIDED FIGURE.   TRIANGLE

A PLACE WHERE AEROPLANES ARE KEPT. HANGAR

A VESSEL FOR HOLDING FLOWERS. VASE

A PERSON WHO CANNOT HEAR OR SPEAK.   MUTE

A ROOM ON BOARD A SHIP. CABIN

A SOLDIER WITH THREE STRIPES ON THE ARM. SERGEANT

A PERSON WHO TAKES THE PLACE OF ANOTHER. SUCCESSOR

HOW MANY LEGS HAS A FLY?   SIX

A MAN WHO DOES TRICKS WITH CARDS. TRICKSTER

WHAT IS THE FLESH OF A PIG CALLED.   PORK

A PLACE WHERE LEATHER IS MADE.   TANNERY

MACHINE WHICH MAKES ELECTRICITY.   GENERATOR

WHAT IS MILK – FAT CALLED?   CREAM

WHAT IS THE FLESH OF THE DEER CALLED? VENISON

NAME FOR SMUGGLED GOODS.   CONTRABAND

A PLACE WHERE CHICKENS ARE HATCHED. HATCHERY

WHAT ARE THE PRIMARY COLORS. BLACK AND WHITE

A PLACE WHERE FISH ARE KEPT? AQUARIUM

A PLACE WHERE YOU CAN LUNCH FOR PAYMENT.
RESTAURANT
WHAT IS CAPITAL PUNISHMENT?   DEATH
WHAT SIDE IS STARBOARD? RIGHT
WHAT SIDE IS PORT? LEFT
WHICH MONTH CONTAINS THE LONGEST DAY.   JUNE
WHAT IS A SONG FOR TWO CALLED?   DUET
WHAT IS A SONG FOR ONE CALLED?   SOLO
INSTRUMENT USED FOR DRAWING CIRCLES.
COMPASS
WHICH INSECT MAKES HONEY?   BEE
HOW MANY TEETH HAS AN ADULT PERSON?
THIRTY TWO
WHAT DO WE CALL WATER WHEN SOLID? ICE
AN INSTRUMENT FOR SEEING TINY OBJECTS.
MICROSCOPE
WHICH MONTH CONTAINS THE SHORTEST DAY?
JANUARY
WHICH ANIMAL IS CALLED THE "KING OF BEASTS "?
LION
THE NAME FOR A PERSON WHO FLIES A PLANE. PILOT
WHAT IS THE BED ON BOARD A SHIP CALLED? BUNK
WHICH ANIMAL COVERS GREAT DISTANCES WITHOUT
WATER?   CAMEL
NAME GAS WHICH SUPPORTS LIFE AND FLAME.
OXYGEN
NAME INSECT WHICH CARRIES MALARIA FEVER.
MOSQUITO
WHAT IS THE YELLOW PART OF AN EGG CALLED?
YOLK
NAME GIVEN TO A SAILOR'S MAP. CHART
WHAT IS THE SKIN OF THE ORANGE CALLED?   PEEL
NAME GIVEN TO A BARREL CORK. BUNG
ANOTHER WORD MEANING REMEDY.   CURE
SOLDIERS ON HORSEBACK. CALVIERY
WHAT IS MEANT BY A BIRD'S – EYE VIEW?
LOOKING FROM ABOVE
WHAT IS MEANT BY A WORM'S – EYE VIEW?
LOOKING FROM BELOW
WAY OUT SIGN ABOVE A DOOR.   EXIT
WHO IS A CLERGYMAN?   PRIEST

THE TOP OF A HILL OR MOUNTAIN.PEAK
NAME OF ROPE USED BY COWBOY. LASSO
WHAT IS MEANT BY WALKING IN INDIAN FILE?
WALKING SINGLE ONE BEHIND THE OTHER
ANOTHER NAME FOR A VILLAGE.   HAMLET
ANOTHER NAME FOR A HOTEL.   INN
WHAT IS THE WHITE OF AN EGG CALLED?
ALBUMEN
GIVE ANOTHER WORD MEANING MONEY. SALARY
NAME AN ANIMAL WHICH CHEWS THE CUD.   COW
WHICH LETTERS ARE VOWELS?   A,E,I, O,U
WHAT IS A CARNIVOROUS CREATURE?   F L E S H
EATING
WHAT IS THE MIDDLE PART OF AN APPLE CALLED?
CORE
A POCKET CASE FOR HOLDING MONEY AND
DOCUMENTS.PURSE

THE PRINCIPAL LANGUAGES OF THE WORLD ARE :-

ENGLISH, CHINESE, RUSSIAN, HINDI, SPANISH, GERMAN,
FRENCH, JAPANESE, PORTUGUESE AND ITALIAN.

THE LARGEST CITIES OF THE WORLD ARE :-

LONDON, NEW   YORK, TOKYO, BERLIN, CHICAGO,
SHANGHAI, PARIS AND MOSCOW.

THE LONGEST RIVERS ARE :-

MISSOURI – MISSISSIPPI, AMAZON, NILE, YANGTSE,
YENESEI, CONGO AND LENA.

PREFIXES AND SUFFIXES :-

A WORD MAY BE BUILT UP OR HAVE ITS MEANING CHANGED BY AN ADDITION AT EITHER END. THE ADDITION AT THE BEGINNING IS KNOWN AS A PREFIX, E G. FORE – TELL. THE ADDITION AT THE END IS KNOWN AS A SUFFIX, E G. CARE – LESS.

PREFIXES

PREFIX	MEANING	EXAMPLES
A	ON	AFLOAT, ALOFT, ASHORE.
A, AB, ABS	AWAY, FROM	AVERT, ABSOLVE, ABSTRACT.
AD, AC, AR	TO	ADHERE, ACCEPT, ARRIVE.
BI, BIS	TWO, TWICE	BICYCLE, BISECT, BISCUIT.
CIRCUM	ROUND	CIRCUMFERENCE, CIRCUIT.
COM	TOGETHER	COMPARISON, COMPETITION.
CONTRA	AGAINST	CONTRADICTION, CONTRARY, CONTRABAND
DE	DOWN	DEPRESS, DESCEND, DESCRIBE.
DIF, DIS,	APART, NOT	DIFFERENT, DISAPPEAR, DISAGREE.
EX	OUT OF	EXHALE, EXPORT, EXTRACT.
FORE	BEFORE	FORECAST, FORENOON, FORTELL, FORSEE.
IM, IN	IN, INTO	IMPORT, INCLUDE
IN	NOT	INCAPABLE, INHUMAN.
INTER	BETWEEN	INTERNATIONAL, INTERRUPT, INTERVAL
MIS	WRONG	MISDEED, MISJUDGE, MISTAKE.
OB	AGAINST	OBJECT, OBSTRUCTION.
POST	AFTER	POSTPONE, POSTSCRIPT, POST – WAR.
PRE	BEFORE	PREDICT, PREPARE, PRE – WAR.
PRO	FORTH	PROCEED, PRODUCE.
RE	BACK	RETAKE, RETURN, RETRACE.
SUB	UNDER	SUBMARINE, SUBWAY.
TRANS	ACROSS	TRANSFER, TRANSPORT, TRANSPOSE.
UN	NOT, WITHOUT	UNFIT, UNKNOWN, UNPAID, UNSAFE.
VICE	INSTEAD	VICE – CAPTAIN, VICEROY.

SUFFIXES

SUFFIX	MEANING	EXAMPLES
ABLE, IBLE	CAPABLE OF BEING	MOVABLE, EATABLE, INCREDIBLE
AIN, AN	ONE CONNECTED	CHAPLAIN, PUBLICAN
ANCE, ENCE	STATE OF	REPENTANCE, EXISTENCE
ANT	ONE WHO	ASSISTANT, SERVANT
EL, ET, ETTE	LITTLE	SATCHEL, LOCKET, CIGARETTE
ER, EER, IER	ONE WHO	BAKER, ENGINEER, FURRIER
ESS	THE FEMALE	GODDESS, PRINCESS, WAITRESS
FY	TO MAKE	GLORIFY, PURIFY, SIMPLIFY
ICLE, SEL	LITTLE	PARTICLE, MORSEL
LESS	WITHOUT	CARELESS, GUILTLESS, MERCILESS
LING	LITTLE	CODLING, GOSLING, DARLING
MENT	STATE OF BEING	MERRIMENT, ENJOYMENT
OON, ON	LARGE	SALOON, BALLOON, FLAGON
ORY	A PLACE FOR	DORMITORY, FACTORY
OUS	FULL OF	FAMOUS, GLORIOUS, MOMENTOUS

SYNONYMS :-

ARE WORDS SIMILAR IN MEANING.

EXAMPLES :-

ABANDON	LEAVE
ABODE	DWELLING
ABUNDANT	PLENTY
ACCUSED	BLAMED
ACUTE	SHARP
ADHERE	STICK
AFFECTIONATE	LOVING
AID	HELP
ALLY	FRIEND
ANCIENT	OLD
ASSEMBLE	GATHER
ASTONISH	SURPRISE
BLANK	EMPTY
BRIGHT	SHINING

BROAD	WIDE
CAUTION	CARE
CIRCULAR	ROUND
CLERGYMAN	MINISTER
COMMENCE	BEGIN
COMPREHEND	UNDERSTAND
CONCEAL	HIDE
CONVERSATION	TALK
COURAGE	BRAVERY
CUNNING	SLY
CUSTOM	HABIT
DECEIVE	CHEAT
DIFFICULT	HARD
ELUDE	ESCAPE
ENEMY	FOE
ENORMOUS	GIGANTIC
EXTERIOR	OUTSIDE
FALL	DROP
FEEBLE	WEAK
GAP	HOLE
GLANCE	LOOK
GROPE	FEEL
HALT	STOP
HEROIC	BRAVE
INTENTION	PURPOSE
INTERIOR	INSIDE
JOIN	UNITE
JUST	HONEST
LEAN	THIN
LOYAL	TRUE
MAD	INSANE
MARGIN	EDGE
MAXIMUM	MOST
MINIMUM	LEAST
MOAN	GROAN
MODERN	NEW
MUTE	DUMB
NOISY	ROWDY
ODOUR	SMELL
OPTION	CHOICE
PROFIT	GAIN

PROMPT	QUICK
POWERFUL	STRONG
PROTECT	GUARD
PURCHASE	BUY
QUANTITY	AMOUNT
RAPID	QUICK
REGRET	SORROW
REMEDY	CURE
REVEAL	SHOW
SLENDER	SLIM
SMALL	LITTLE
STUBBORN	OBSTINATE
STURDY	STRONG
SURRENDER	YIELD
TESTED	TRIED
TRANQUIL	PEACEFUL
TRANSPARENT	CLEAR
UNITE	JOIN
VACANT	EMPTY
VALOUR	BRAVERY
WEALTH	RICHES
WICKED	SINFUL
WITHDRAW	RETIRE
WRATH	ANGER
WRETCHED	MISERABLE
YEARLY	ANNUALLY

ANTONYMS :-

ARE WORDS OPPOSITE IN MEANING.

EXAMPLES :-

ADULT	CHILD
ALIVE	DEAD
ANCIENT	MODERN
ANSWER	QUESTION
ARRIVE	DEPART
ASLEEP	AWAKE
BACK	FRONT
BAD	GOOD
BARREN	FERTILE

BEAUTIFUL	UGLY
BIG	SMALL
BITTER	SWEET
BLACK	WHITE
BLESS	CURSE
BOTTOM	TOP
BROAD	NARROW
BUY	SELL
CHEAP	EXPENSIVE
CLEAN	DIRTY
COLD	HOT
COME	GO
CONCEAL	REVEAL
DIE	LIVE
DIFFICULT	EASY
DOWN	UP
DRUNK	SOBER
DRY	WET
EARLY	LATE
EAST	WEST
EASY	HARD
EBB	FLOOD
EMPTY	FULL
ENEMY	FRIEND
ENTRANCE	EXIT
EVENING	MORNING
EVER	NEVER
EVERYWHERE	NOWHERE
FALSE	TRUE
FAR	NEAR
FAT	THIN
FEW	MANY
FIRST	LAST
GO	COME
GOOD	BAD
HARD	EASY
HATE	LIKE
HEAVY	LIGHT
HERE	THERE
HERO	COWARD
HIGH	LOW

INNOCENT	GUILTY
LAND	SEA - WATER
LATE	EARLY
LIGHT	DARK
LONG	SHORT
LOST	FOUND
LOVE	HATE
NEW	OLD
NIGHT	DAY
NORTH	SOUTH
OPEN	CLOSE
OUT	IN
PAST	PRESENT
PEACE	WAR
PERMANENT	TEMPORARY
PLURAL	SINGLE
POOR	RICH
PRESENT	ABSENT
PRIVATE	PUBLIC
PURCHASE	SOLD
SMOOTH	ROUGH
SOFT	HARD
SOLID	LIQUID
SOUR	SWEET
STERN	BOW
STRAIGHT	BEND
STRONG	WEAK
SUCCESS	FAILURE
SUMMER	WINTER
SUPERIOR	INFERIOR
TAKE	GIVE
TALL	SHORT
TAME	WILD
TEMPORARY	PERMANENT
TINY	BIG
TOP	BOTTOM
TRUTH	LIE
UNITE	DIVIDE
VACANT	OCCUPIED
CORRECT	WRONG
DAMP	DRY

DARK	LIGHT
DAY	NIGHT
DEEP	SHALLOW
DEFEND	ATTACK
DEPART	ARRIVE
FOE	FRIEND
FOOLISH	WISE
FOREIGN	LOCAL
FOUND	LOST
FREEDOM	SLAVERY
FRONT	BACK
FULL	EMPTY
FUTURE	PAST
GENEROUS	STINGY
GIANT	DWARF
MAXIMUM	MINIMUM
MINORITY	MAJORITY
MOUNTAIN	VALLEY
MOVING	STATIONARY
MULTIPLY	DIVIDE
NARROW	WIDE
SADNESS	HAPPINESS
SENIOR	JUNIOR
SHALLOW	DEEP
SHORT	LONG
SHOW	HIDE
SHUT	OPEN
SLOW	FAST
VICTORY	DEFEAT
WEALTH	POOR
WEST	EAST
YOUNG	OLD

WORDS OPPOSITE IN MEANING BY ADDING PREFIX :-

DIS – ADVANTAGE
DIS – APPROVE
IN – AUDIBLE
UN – AWARE
MIS – BEHAVE
UN – COMFORTABLE
UN – COMMON
DIS – CONNECT
DIS – CONTENT
IN – CORRECT
IN – DIRECT
UN – ESSENTIAL
UN – FAIR
UN – HAPPY
IN – HUMAN
UN – JUST
UN – KIND
UN – KNOWN
IL – LEGAL
IL – LEGIBLE
DIS – LIKE
UN – LOCK
UN – LOYAL
IM – MORAL
UN – NECESSARY
UN – NOBLE
DIS – OBEY
DIS – ORDER
IM – PATIENT
IM – PERFECT
DIS – PLEASURE
IM – POLITE
IM – POSSIBLE
UN – PROPER
IM – PURE
IR – REGULAR
IR – RELEVANT
UN – SAFE
IN – SANE

UN – SCREW
UN – SELFISH
NON – SENSE
UN – TIDY
DIS – TRUST
UN – TWIST
IN – VISIBLE
UN – WISE

THE FOLLOWING MAY BE SAID TO BE OPPOSITES :-

HOST	GUEST
GUARDIAN	WARD
SHOPKEEPER	CUSTOMER
SPEAKER	LISTENER
TEACHER	STUDENT
GAMEKEEPER	POACHER
EMPLOYER	EMPLOYEE
DRIVER	CONDUCTOR
POLICEMAN	CRIMINAL
PARENT	CHILD
LEADER	FOLLOWER
DOCTOR	PATIENT
DETECTIVE	THIEF
AUTHOR	READER
KING	SUBJECT
LAWYER	CLIENT

SOUNDS :-

[MADE BY OBJECTS]

RUSTLING OF LEAVES
SCREECHING OF BRAKES
SHREIK OF A WHISTLE
SHUFFLING OF FEET
SIGHING OF THE WIND
SINGING OF THE KETTLE
SLAM OF A DOOR
SPLUTTER OF AN ENGINE
TICK OF A CLOCK

TINKLE OF A SMALL BELL
TINKLE OF GLASS
THROB OF AN ENGINE
THUNDER OF HOOFS
TRAMP OF FEET
TOOT OF A HORN
TWANG OF A BOW
WAIL OF A SIREN
WHACK OF A WHIP
BABBLE OF A STREAM
BANG OF A DOOR
BEAT OF A DRUM
BLARE OF A TRUMPET
BLAST OF AN EXPLOSION
BOOMING OF A GUN
BUBBLING OF WATER
BUZZ OF A SAW
PING OF A BULLET
POPPING OF CORKS
PURR OF AN ENGINE
RATTLING OF DISHES
REPORT OF A RIFLE
RING OF METAL
RINGING OF BELLS
RUMBLE OF A TRAIN
RING OF A TELEPHONE
CHIME OF A LARGE BELL
CHIME OF A CLOCK
CHUG OF AN ENGINE
CLANG OF A BELL
CLANKING OF CHAINS
CLATTER OF HOOFS
CLINK OF A COIN
CRACKLING OF WOOD
CRACK OF A WHIP
CREAK OF A HINGE
CRINKLE OF PAPER
PATTER OF RAIN
PATTER OF FEET
LASH OF A WHIP
LAPPING OF WATER

JINGLE OF COINS
JANGLING OF CHAINS
HOWLING OF THE WIND
HOOT OF A HORN
DRIPPING OF WATER

PROPER AND EFFECTIVE WORD CHOICE :-

BE EFFECTIVE AND EFFICIENT IN YOUR USE OF WORDS. CHOOSE YOUR WORDS CAREFULLY WHEN YOU SPEAK AND WRITE. ALWAYS TAKE THE TIME, PONDER OVER, THINK CAREFULLY ABOUT YOUR WORD CHOICES RATHER THAN SIMPLY USE THE FIRST WORD THAT COMES TO MIND. YOU WANT TO ENCOURAGE YOURSELF AND DEVELOP THE HABIT OF CHOOSING AND SELECTING WORDS THAT ARE APPROPRIATE, EFFECTIVE AND PROPER FOR YOUR PURPOSES. THE BEST WAY OF SHOWING AND DISPLAYING YOUR SENSITIVITY TO LANGUAGE IS BY AVOIDING WORDINESS, PRETENTIOUS WORDS, CLICHES AND SLANG.

WORDINESS :- USING MORE WORDS THAN NECESSARY TO EXPRESS A MEANING; IS A SIGN OF CARELESS TALKING AND WRITING. MAKE YOUR SPEECH AND WRITINGS DIRECT AND CONCISE; USING FEW WORDS TO EXPRESS A THOUGHT CLEARLY IS SOUND WISDOM.

EXAMPLES :-
[a] I WOULD LIKE TO SAY THAT MY SUBJECT IN THIS WRITING WILL BE THE KIND OF PEACE LOVING PEOPLE THAT THE AMERINDIANS WERE..
NOTE :- THIS CAN SIMPLY BE STATED :-
THE AMERINDIANS WERE A PEACE LOVING PEOPLE.

[b] ANGEL IS OF THE OPINION THAT BEING FOUND WITH A GUN SHOULD CARRY A PENALTY.
NOTE :- OMITTING NEEDLESS WORDS IMPROVES THE SENTENCES.
EXAMPLE OF THE ABOVE SENTENCE CAN BE STATED :-
ANGEL SUPPORTS THE HAVING A GUN PENALTY.
PRETENTIOUS WORDS :-

USING SIMPLE AND NATURAL WORDS IMPROVE THE UNDERSTANDING OF YOUR SPEECH AND WRITING. DO NOT USE WORDS THAT OBSCURES THE MEANING OF WHAT YOU INTEND TO PROJECT; COMMUNICATE CLEARLY AND MEANINGFULLY.

EXAMPLES :- OF UNNATURAL – SOUNDING SENTENCES.
[a] LAW ENFORCEMENT PERSONNEL DIRECTED TRAFFIC WHEN THE ACCIDENT OCCURRED.

[b] I AM A STRANGER TO EXCESSIVE ALCOHOL DRINKING.

[c] WHILE SITTING AND PARTAKING OF OUR EVENING MEAL; WE ENGAGED IN AN ANIMATED CONVERSATION.

THE SAME THOUGHTS CAN BE EXPRESSED MORE CLEARLY AND EFFECTIVELY BY USING, PLAIN, NATURAL LANGUAGE, AS BELOW :-
[a] POLICE OFFICERS DIRECTED TRAFFIC AT THE SCENE OF THE ACCIDENT.

[b] I HAVE NEVER DRUNK MUCH ALCOHOL.

[c] WHILE EATING SUPPER, WE HAD A LIVELY TALK.

CLICHES :-
A CLICHÉ IS AN EXPRESSION THAT HAS BEEN WORN OUT THROUGH CONSTANT USE. CLICHES ARE COMMON IN SPEECH BUT SHOULD BE USED SPARINGLY. CLICHES MAKE YOUR WRITING SEEM TIRED, WORN AND STALE. ALSO, THEY ARE OFTEN AN EVASION OF THE SPECIFIC DETAILS THAT YOU MUST WORK, TO PROVIDE IN YOUR WRITING. YOU SHOULD, THEN, AVOID CLICHES AND TRY TO EXPRESS YOURSELF IN MEANINGFUL, FRESH, ORIGINAL WAYS.

SOME TYPICAL CLICHES ARE :-

BREAK THE ICE
SAD BUT TRUE
TAKING A BIG CHANCE

PAIN IN THE NECK
KNOW THE ROPES
HOUR OF NEED
WORK LIKE A DOG
A SPOILED BRAT
SIGHT FOR SORE EYES
DROP IN THE BUCKET
WEAR YOURSELF OUT
COLD, CRUEL WORLD
AT A LOSS FOR WORDS
IT GOES WITHOUT SAYING
MANY HANDS MAKE LIGHT WORK
DON'T PUT OFF UNTIL TOMORROW WHAT YOU CAN DO TODAY
ANY FRIEND OF YOURS IS A FRIEND OF MINE
THERE'S NO PLACE LIKE HOME.
A CHAIN IS ONLY AS STRONG AS ITS WEAKEST LINK.
GIVE AND TAKE.
I SECOND THAT.
SEE EYE TO EYE.
YOU CAN SAY THAT AGAIN.
FOLLOWING IN HIS FOOTSTEPS.
LIKE FATHER, LIKE SON.
WHAT GOES AROUND, COMES AROUND.
WHAT'S GOOD FOR THE GOOSE IS GOOD FOR THE GANDER.
ALL IN DUE TIME.
AT THE LAST MINUTE.
BUSINESS AT HAND.
CALL IT A DAY.
IN THE NICK OF TIME.
JUST A MINUTE.
JUST A SECOND.
A STITCH IN TIME SAVES NINE.
TIME HEAL ALL WOUNDS.
RAINING CATS AND DOGS.
BONE CHILLING COLD.
ALL BENT OUT OF SHAPE.
DRIVING ME CRAZY.
FOR PETE'S SAKE.
I'VE HAD IT UP TO HERE.

EASY AS ABC.
EASY AS PIE.
CHILD'S PLAY.
A PIECE OF CAKE.
A COCK AND BULL STORY.
FAT AS A COW.
FAT AS A PIG.
ANOTHER DAY ANOTHER DOLLAR.
AS GOOD AS GOLD.
CLEAN BILL OF HEALTH.
MAKE ENDS MEET.
A PENNY FOR YOUR THOUGHTS.
TIME IS MONEY.
WORTH ITS WEIGHT IN GOLD.
BEAT THE STREET.
BOTTOM OUT.
GLIMMER OF HOPE.
GOD WILLING.
KEEP YOUR FINGERS CROSSED.
SHOOTING FOR THE MOON.
ALL'S WELL THAT ENDS WELL.
ASHES TO ASHES, DUST TO DUST.
SAY YOUR PRAYERS.

SLANG :-

WE USE SLANG EXPRESSIONS, BECAUSE THEY PAINT A COLORFUL PICTURE; HOWEVER, SLANG IS USUALLY OUT OF PLACE IN FORMAL WRITING. SLANG EXPRESSIONS HAVE A NUMBER OF DRAWBACKS; THEY GO OUT OF DATE AND BECOME TIRESOME IF USED EXCESSIVELY IN WRITING, AND THEY MAY COMMUNICATE CLEARLY TO SOME READERS, BUT BE UNCLEAR TO OTHERS. ALSO THE USE OF SLANG CAN BE AN EVASION OF THE SPECIFIC DETAILS THAT ARE OFTEN NEEDED TO MAKE ONE'S MEANING CLEAR IN WRITING. FOR EXAMPLE, IN "THE HUB CAPS ON MY JEEP MAKE IT LOOKS LIKE SOMETHING ELSE." THE WRITER HAS NOT PROVIDED THE SPECIFIC DETAILS ABOUT THE HUB CAPS NECESSARY FOR US TO UNDERSTAND THE STATEMENT CLEARLY. IN GENERAL, THEN YOU SHOULD AVOID THE USE OF SLANG IN YOUR WRITING.

EXAMPLE OF A SENTENCE WITH SLANG WORDS.

THE FOOTBALL GAME WAS A REAL BOMB S O WE CUT OUT EARLY.

THIS CAN BE WRITTEN :-

THE FOOTBALL GAME WAS TERRIBLE, SO WE LEFT EARLY.

THE BEST THING IN LIFE :-

KNOWLEDGE SAYS THE STUDENT
GOLD SAYS THE MISER
BUSINESS SAYS THE MERCHANT
HOME SAYS THE MOTHER
TRUTH SAYS THE SAGE
ORDER SAYS THE POLICEMAN
HONOR SAYS THE SOLDIER
FAME SAYS THE STATESMAN
REST SAYS THE TOILER
LOVE SAYS THE MAIDEN
FOOD SAYS THE GLUTTON
PLEASURE SAYS THE FOOL
ABUNDANCE SAYS THE FARMER
POWER SAYS THE ENGINEER
POWER SAYS THE POLITICIAN
HEALING SAYS THE DOCTOR
KINDNESS SAYS THE CHILD
SPORTS SAYS THE ATHLETE
BEAUTY SAYS THE ARTIST

RECEPTACLES :-
THE TYPES OF CONTAINERS USED TO HOLD AND CARRY FOODSTUFFS.EXAMPLE :-
BAG – COCOA, COFFEE, RICE, SAGO, SUGAR.
BARREL – APPLES, HERRING, OIL, POTATOES.
BOX – APPLES, BUTTER, CURRANTS, FISH.
CASK – BUTTER, MUSTARD.
CHEST – TEA, CLOVES.
SACK – FLOUR, POTATOES.

CERTAIN WORDS ARE USED IN IMITATION OF THE SOUNDS MADE BY CREATURES.

EXAMPLE :-

ASS, DONKEY	HEE – HAW
CAT	ME – OW
COCK	COCK – A – DOODLE – DO
COW	MOO
CUCKOO	CUCKOO
DOG	BOW – WOW
DUCK	QUACK
HEN	CLUCK
OWL	TU – WHOO
ROOK	CAW
SHEEP	BAA
SPARROW	TWEET – TWEET

THE FOLLOWING VERBS ARE OBTAINED FROM THE HABITS OF CREATURES :-

TO WOLF	TO EAT GREEDILY
TO RAM	TO DRIVE OR PUSH INTO
TO HOUND	TO FOLLOW OR CHASE
TO FOX	TO ACT CUNNINGLY
TO APE	TO IMITATE FOOLISHLY
TO BADGER	TO WORRY OR TEASE
TO CROW	TO BOAST OR SWAGGER
TO DOG	TO FOLLOW OR TRACK
TO DUCK	TO DIP OR PLUNGE
TO FERRET	TO SEARCH OUT

CHAPTER 3.

GROUP TERMS FOR COLLECTIONS OF PEOPLE.
EXAMPLES :-

AT A FOOTBALL MATCH	SPECTATORS
AT A DANCE	ASSEMBLY
AT A CONCERT	AUDIENCE
IN CHURCH	CONGREGATION
IN THE STREET	CROWD, THRONG
IN A RIOT	MOB
IN A ROWDY SCENE	RABBLE

COLLECTIONS OF OTHER THINGS :-
EXAMPLES :-
A PRIDE OF LIONS
A SKULK OF FOXES
A SLOTH OF BEARS
A STRING OF HORSES
A TRIBE OF GOATS
A TRUSS OF HAY
A SHOCK OF WHEAT
A SHEAF OF ARROWS
A PUNNET OF STRAWBERRIES
A PEAL OF BELLS
A NEST OF MACHINE GUNS
A BUNCH OF BANANAS
A GROUP OF ISLANDS
A GALAXY OF STARS
A POSSE OF POLICEMEN

A PADDLING OF DUCKS
A PACE OF ASSES
A NEST OF MICE
A LEAP OF LEOPARDS
A KINDLE OF KITTENS
A HOST OF SPARROWS
A HERD OF CRANES
A FLIGHT OF SWALLOWS
A FLIGHT OF DOVES
A FIELD OF RUNNERS
A BAREN OF MULES

ADULT   YOUNG

BEE	GRUB
BIRD	NESTLING
WASP	GRUB
TROUT	FRY
TOAD	TADPOLE
SALMON	PARR
MOTH	CATERPILLAR
BUTTERFLY	CATERPILLAR
FROG	TADPOLE

GROUP TERMS OR COLLECTIONS.

ANIMATE :-

A LITTER OF CUBS
A LITTER OF PUPS
A NEST OF RABBITS
A TROUPE OF DANCERS
A TROOP OF MONKEYS
A TROOP OF LIONS
A TRIBE OF NATIVES
A PACK OF WOLVES
A PARTY OF FRIENDS
A PLAGUE OF INSECTS
AN ARMY OF SOLDIERS
A BAND OF MUSICIANS
A SCHOOL OF WHALES

A SHOAL OF HERRING
A STAFF OF SERVANTS
A BENCH OF MAGISTRATES
A BEVY OF LADIES
A STAFF OF TEACHERS
A STUD OF HORSES
A BOARD OF DIRECTORS
A BROOD OF CHICKENS
A SWARM OF BEES
A SWARM OF INSECTS
A TEAM OF HORSES
A TEAM OF OXEN
A TEAM OF PLAYERS
A CHOIR OF SINGERS
A CLASS OF SCHOLARS
A COMPANY OF ACTORS
A CREW OF SAILORS
A DROVE OF CATTLE
A FLOCK OF BIRDS
A FLOCK OF SHEEP
A GANG OF LABORERS
A GANG OF THIEVES
A HERD OF CATTLE
A HOST OF ANGELS

INANIMATE :-

A TUFT OF GRASS
A FOREST OF TREES
A HAIL OF FIRE
A SUITE OF FURNITURE
A SUITE OF ROOMS
A HEDGE OF BUSHES
A SUIT OF CLOTHES
A LIBRARY OF BOOKS
A STRING OF BEADS
A STACK OF HAY
A PACK OF CARDS
A SHEAF OF CORN
A ROPE OF PEARLS
A SET OF CHINA

A SET OF TOOLS
A BALE OF COTTON
A BALE OF WOOL
A FLIGHT OF AEROPLANES
A FLIGHT OF STEPS
A BATCH OF BREAD
A BOUQUET OF FLOWERS
A FLEET OF MOTOR CARS
A FLEET OF SHIPS
A BUNCH OF GRAPES
A CRATE OF FRUIT
A COLLECTION OF PICTURES
A BUNDLE OF RAGS
A CLUTCH OF EGGS
A CLUSTER OF DIAMONDS
A CLUSTER OF STARS
A CHEST OF DRAWERS
A CLUMP OF TREES

CREATURES, SOUNDS AND MOTIONS

ALL CREATURES MAKE SOUNDS AND MOVE IN A FASHION PECULIAR TO THEIR SPECIES.

CREATURE	SOUND	MOTION
ASS	BRAYS	JOGS
APE	GIBBERS	SWINGS
BEE	HUMS	FLITS
BEAR	GROWLS	LUMBERS
BULL	BELLOWS	CHARGES
CAT	PURRS	STEALS
COW	LOWS	WANDERS
DOG	BARKS	RUNS
DEER	BELLS	BOUNDS
DONKEY	BRAYS	TROTS
ELEPHANT	TRUMPETS	AMBLES
HORSE	NEIGHS	GALLOPS
FROG	CROAKS	LEAPS
HYENA	SCREAMS	PROWLS
LAMB	BLEATS	FRISKS

LION	ROARS	PROWLS
MONKEY	CHATTERS	CLIMBS
MOUSE	SQUEAKS	SCAMPERS
PIG	GRUNTS	TROTS
PERSON	TALKS	WALKS
RABBIT	SQUEALS	LEAPS
SERPENT	HISSES	GLIDES
BIRD	WHISTLES	FLIES
WOLF	HOWLS	LOPES
COCK	CROWS	STRUTS
CROW	CAWS	FLAPS
DUCK	QUACKS	WADDLES
EAGLE	SCREAMS	SWOOPS
HEN	CACKLES	STRUTS
OWL	HOOTS	FLITS
SPARROW	CHIRPS	FLITS
SEAGULL	SCREAMS	GLIDES
PIGEON	COOS	FLUTTERS
PARROT	SCREECHES	FLITS
SWALLOW	TWITTERS	DIVES
TURKEY	GOBBLES	STRUTS
ROBIN	CHIRPS	HOPS
WREN	WARBLES	HOPS
ROOSTERS	CROW	
DOVES	COO	
CUCKOOS	CUCKOO	
GEESE	HONK	

USEFUL TERMS :-
AQUILINE -- LIKE AN EAGLE
ASININE -- LIKE AN ASS
BOVINE -- LIKE A COW OR OX
CANINE -- LIKE A DOG
CORVINE -- LIKE A CROW
ELEPHANTINE -- LIKE AN ELEPHANT
EQUINE -- LIKE A HORSE
FELINE -- LIKE A CAT
FERINE -- LIKE A WILD BEAST
LEONINE -- LIKE A LION
LUPINE -- LIKE A WOLF
OVINE -- LIKE A SHEEP

PISCINE -- LIKE A FISH
PORCINE -- LIKE A PIG
TIGRINE -- LIKE A TIGER
VULPINE -- LIKE A FOX

FAMILIES

PARENTS	YOUNG	
MALE	FEMALE	
FATHER	MOTHER	BABY OR CHILD
KING	QUEEN	PRINCE OR PRINCESS
MAN	WOMAN	BABY OR CHILD
UNCLE	AUNT	NEPHEW OR NIECE
INDIAN	SQUAW	PAPOOSE
BEAR	SHE BEAR	CUB
BILLY – GOAT	NANNY – GOAT	KID
BOAR [PIG]	SOW	PORKLING, PIGLET
BUCK [DEER]	HIND	FAWN
BUCK [HARE]	DOE	LEVERET
BUCK [RABBIT]	DOE	RACK
BULL [CATTLE]	COW	CALF
BULL [ELEPHANT]	COW	CALF
BULL [SEAL]	COW	CALF
BULL [WHALE]	COW	CALF
COB [SWAN]	PEN	CYGNET
COCK [FOWL]	HEN	CHICKEN
COCK [PIGEON]	HEN	SQUAB
DOG	BITCH	PUP
DOG [FOX]	VIXEN	CUB
DRAKE	DUCK	DUCKLING
EAGLE	EAGLE	EAGLET
GANDER	GOOSE	GOSLING
HAWK	BOWESS	BOWET
LEOPARD	LEOPARDESS	CUB
LION	LIONESS	CUB
OWL	OWL	OWLET
RAM [SHEEP]	EWE	LAMB
STALLION	MARE	FOAL
TIGER	TIGRESS	CUB

| TOM – CAT | QUEEN OR TABBY – CAT | KITTEN |
| WOLF | SHE – WOLF | CUB |

HOMES

PERSON	HOME
ARAB	DOWAR
CONVICT	PRISON
ESKIMO	IGLOO
GIPSY	CARAVAN
KING	PALACE
LUMBERMAN	LOG – CABIN
MAN	HOUSE
MONK	MONASTERY
NOBLE	CASTLE
NUN	CONVENT
PIONEER	WAGON
PRISONER	CELL
INDIAN	WIGWAM, TEPEE
SOLDIER	BARRACKS, CAMP
TINKER	TENT
VICAR	VICARAGE

CREATURE	HOME
APE	TREE – NEST
WASP	NEST
BADGER	EARTH, SETT
BEAR	DEN
TIGER	LAIR
SQUIRREL	DREY
BEAVER	LODGE
BEE	HIVE
SPIDER	WEB
SNAIL	SHELL
SHEEP	PEN, FOLD
BIRD	NEST
COW	BYRE
DOG	KENNEL
RABBIT	HUTCH, BURROW, WARREN

PIGEON	DOVE – COTE
PIG	STY
OWL	BARN, TREE
OTTER	HOLT
MOUSE	HOLE, NEST
MOLE	FORTRESS
LION	LAIR, DEN
HORSE	STABLE
HARE	FORM
FOX	EARTH, LAIR
FOWL	COOP
EAGLE	EYRIE

SIMILES

SIMILES COMPARE THINGS WHICH ARE ALIKE IN SOME RESPECT, ALTHOUGH THEY MAY BE DIFFERENT IN THEIR GENERAL NATURE.

[a] SIMILES SHOWING SPECIAL QUALITIES OF THINGS :-

AS EASY AS A. B.C.
AS EASY AS WINKING
AS LARGE AS LIFE
AS OPEN AS DAY
AS UGLY AS SIN
AS CHANGEABLE AS THE WEATHER
AS PALE AS DEATH
AS BITTER AS GALL
AS BLACK AS COAL
AS BOLD AS BRASS
AS BRIGHT AS A BUTTON
AS BRITTLE AS GLASS
AS WHITE AS SNOW
AS WEAK AS WATER
AS WARM AS WOOL
AS CLEAN AS A NEW PIN
AS CLEAR AS A BELL
AS CLEAR AS CRYSTAL
AS COLD AS ICE

AS TRUE AS STEEL
AS TRUE AS GOSPEL
AS TOUGH AS LEATHER
AS SWEET AS HONEY
AS COOL AS A CUCUMBER
AS DEAD AS A DOORNAIL
AS DEAF AS A DOORPOST
AS DRY AS A BONE
AS STURDY AS AN OAK
AS STRAIGHT AS AN ARROW
AS DRY AS A BONE
AS FAT AS BUTTER
AS FIT AS A FIDDLE
AS FLAT AS A PANCAKE
AS STEADY AS A ROCK
AS SOUR AS VINEGAR
AS SOFT AS PUTTY
AS SOFT AS BUTTER
AS SMOOTH AS GLASS
AS SILENT AS THE GRAVE
AS FRESH AS A DAISY
AS GOOD AS GOLD
AS GREEN AS GRASS
AS SHARP AS RAZOR
AS SHARP AS A NEEDLE
AS SAFE AS THE BANK
AS SAFE AS HOUSES
AS ROUND AS AN ORANGE
AS RIGHT AS RAIN
AS HARD AS IRON
AS HARD AS NAILS
AS HEAVY AS LEAD
AS HOT AS FIRE
AS LIGHT AS A FEATHER
AS LIKE AS TWO PEAS
AS OLD AS THE HILLS
AS QUICK AS LIGHTNING
AS REGULAR AS THE CLOCK

[b] SIMILES SHOWING DISTINCTIVE QUALITIES OF CREATURES :-

AS SOBER AS A JUDGE
AS STRONG AS A HORSE
AS STRONG AS AN OX
AS AGILE AS A MONKEY
AS BLIND AS A BAT
AS BRAVE AS A LION
AS BUSY AS AN ANT
AS BUSY AS A BEE
AS SURE – FOOTED AS A GOAT
AS SWIFT AS A DEER
AS SWIFT AS A HARE
AS SWIFT AS A HAWK
AS CALM AS A CAT
AS CRAFTY AS A FOX
AS CUNNING AS A FOX
AS TALL AS A GIANT
AS TENACIOUS AS A BULLDOG
AS TENDER AS A CHICKEN
AS DEVOTED AS A MOTHER
AS FAST AS A DEER
AS FAST AS A HARE
AS TENDER AS A SHEPHERD
AS THICK AS THIEVES
AS TIMID AS A MOUSE
AS TIMID AS A RABBIT
AS WISE AS AN OWL
AS WISE AS SOLOMON
AS WHITE AS A GHOST
AS FAT AS A PIG
AS MAD AS A HATTER
AS LOYAL AS AN APOSTLE
AS LIKE AS TWO HERRING
AS FEEBLE AS A CHILD
AS FIERCE AS A LION
AS INDUSTRIOUS AS A BEAVER
AS HUNGRY AS A WOLF
AS HUNGRY AS A HUNTER
AS HEAVY AS AN ELEPHANT

AS FLAT AS A FLOUNDER
AS FLEET AS A GAZELLE
AS FRISKY AS A LAMB
AS HARMLESS AS A DOVE
AS HAPPY AS A KING
AS HAIRY AS A GORILLA
AS GRACEFUL AS A SWAN
AS GENTLE AS A DOVE
AS GENTLE AS A LAMB

GENDER
GENDER IS THE DISTINCTION OF SEX. THERE ARE TWO SEXES, BUT GENDER IN GRAMMAR COMES UNDER FOUR HEADINGS :-

1 MASCULINE GENDER DENOTES THE MALE SEX.E.G. MAN, BOY
2 FEMININE GENDER DENOTES THE FEMALE SEX.E.G. WOMAN, GIRL.
3 COMMON GENDER DENOTES EITHER SEX.E.G OWNER, CHILD.
4 NEUTER GENDER DENOTES THINGS WITHOUT SEX. E.G TABLE, CHAIR

MASCULINE	FEMININE
NAMES	
JOHN	JOAN
JOSEPH	JOSEPHINE
OLIVER	OLIVE
ALEXANDER	ALEXANDRA
CECIL	CECILIA
PATRICK	PATRICIA
PAUL	PAULINE
CHARLES	CHARLOTTE
CHRISTIAN	CHRISTINA
CLARENCE	CLARA
ROBERT	ROBERTA
VICTOR	VICTORIA
GEORGE	GEORGINA

HENRY	HENRIETTA

PEOPLE

FATHER	MOTHER
GENTLEMAN	LADY
HE	SHE
HERO	HEROINE
HIM	HER
HUSBAND	WIFE
ACTOR	ACTRESS
AUTHOR	AUTHORESS
BARON	BARONESS
CONDUCTOR	CONDUCTRESS
KING	QUEEN
LAD	LASS
LORD	LADY
MALE	FEMALE
COUNT	COUNTESS
DEACON	DEACONESS
DUKE	DUCHESS
HEIR	HEIRESS
HOST	HOSTESS
INSTRUCTOR	INSTRUCTRESS
JEW	JEWESS
LION	LIONESS
MAN	WOMAN
MONK	NUN
MR.	MRS.
NEPHEW	NIECE
PAPA	MAMA
PROPRIETOR	PROPRIETRIX
MANAGER	MANAGERESS
MASTER	MISTRESS
MAYOR	MAYORESS
POET	POETESS
PRIEST	PRIESTESS
PRINCE	PRINCESS
SIR	MADAM
SON	DAUGHTER
UNCLE	AUNT

WIDOWER	WIDOW
WIZARD	WITCH
PROPHET	PROPHETESS
SHEPHERD	SHEPHERDESS
SORCERER	SORCERESS
STEWARD	STEWARDESS
TAILOR	TAILORESS
TIGER	TIGRESS
WAITER	WAITRESS
FATHER – IN – LAW	MOTHER – IN – LAW
GRANDFATHER	GRANDMOTHER
HEADMASTER	HEADMISTRESS
LANDLORD	LANDLADY
MALE – CHILD	FEMALE – CHILD
MANSERVANT	MAIDSERVANT
POSTMAN	POSTWOMAN
POSTMASTER	POSTMISTRESS
SON – IN – LAW	DAUGHTER – IN – LAW
BOY SCOUT	GIRL GUIDE

ANIMALS

BILLY – GOAT	NANNY – GOAT
BUCK – RABBIT	DOE – RABBIT
BULL – CALF	COW – CALF
COCK – SPARROW	HEN – SPARROW
HE – GOAT	SHE – GOAT
JACK – ASS	JENNY – ASS
BOAR	SOW
BUCK	DOE
BULL	COW
BULLOCK	HEIFER
COCK	HEN
COLT	FILLY
COB [SWAN]	PEN
DOG	BITCH
DRAKE	DUCK
GANDER	GOOSE
HART	HIND
RAM	EWE
STAG	HIND

STALLION	MARE
STEER	HEIFER

NUMBER

THE SINGULAR NUMBER DENOTES ONE AND THE PLURAL NUMBER DENOTES MORE THAN ONE.

IN MANY CASES, THE SINGULAR BECOMES PLURAL BY ADDING AN S OR ES . HOWEVER, THERE ARE EXCEPTIONS TO THE RULE.

SINGULAR	PLURAL
CHILD	CHILDREN
FOOT	FEET
GOOSE	GEESE
MAN	MEN
MOUSE	MICE
OX	OXEN
TOOTH	TEETH
WOMAN	WOMEN
BROTHER	BROTHERS, BRETHREN
CLOTH	CLOTHS, CLOTHES
DIE	DIES, DICE
FISH	FISHES, FISH
GENIUS	GENIUSES, GENII
PEAS	PEAS, PEASE
PENNY	PENNIES, PENCE
SHOT	SHOTS, SHOT
CANNON	CANNON
TROUT	TROUT
DEER	DEER
COD	COD
SALMON	SALMON
SWINE	SWINE
DOZEN	DOZEN
SHEEP	SHEEP

BROTHER – IN – LAW	BROTHERS – IN – LAW
BYE – LAW	BYE – LAWS
BY – WAY	BY – WAYS
CUPFUL	CUPFULS
MAID – OF – HONOR	MAIDS – OF – HONOR
SPOONFUL	SPOONFULS
SON – IN – LAW	SONS – IN – LAW
PASSER – BY	PASSERS – BY
MAN – OF – WAR	MEN – OF – WAR
ARMY	ARMIES
CITY	CITIES
FLY	FLIES
LADY	LADIES
CALF	CALVES
HALF	HALVES
KNIFE	KNIVES
LEAF	LEAVES
LIFE	LIVES
LOAF	LOAVES
SHELF	SHELVES
THIEF	THIEVES
WOLF	WOLVES
HOOF	HOOFS, HOOVES

THE FOLLOWING WORDS HAVE NO SINGULAR :-

BELLOWS
BILLIARDS
VICTUALS
TWEEZERS
GALLOWS
MEASLES
SCISSORS
PLIERS
PINCERS
SHEARS
TONGS
TIDINGS
THANKS
SPECTACLES

TROUSERS

SUBJECT – VERB AGREEMENT :-

THE BASIC BUILDING BLOCKS OF ENGLISH SENTENCES ARE SUBJECTS AND VERBS. UNDERSTANDING THEM IS AN IMPORTANT WAY OF MASTERING SENTENCE SKILLS.

EVERY SENTENCE HAS A SUBJECT AND A VERB. WHO OR WHAT THE SENTENCE SPEAKS ABOUT IS CALLED THE SUBJECT; WHAT THE SENTENCE SAYS ABOUT THE SUBJECT IS CALLED THE VERB.

EXAMPLES :-

THE   BOYS [SUBJECT]   PLAYED [VERB].

MOST   PUPILS [SUBJECT] FAILED [VERB] THE TEST.

THAT   WOMAN [SUBJECT] IS [VERB]   A THIEF.

SEVERAL CHAIRS [SUBJECT] FELL [VERB].

TO FIND A SUBJECT, ASK WHO OR WHAT THE SENTENCE IS ABOUT. AS SHOWN BELOW, YOUR ANSWER IS THE SUBJECT.

WHO IS THE FIRST SENTENCE ABOUT? BOYS.

WHO IS THE SECOND SENTENCE ABOUT? PUPILS.

WHO IS THE THIRD SENTENCE ABOUT? WOMAN.

WHAT IS THE FOURTH SENTENCE ABOUT? CHAIRS.

TO FIND A VERB, ASK WHAT THE SENTENCE SAYS ABOUT THE SUBJECT. AS SHOWN BELOW YOUR ANSWER IS THE VERB.

WHAT DOES THE FIRST SENTENCE SAY ABOUT THE BOY? THEY   PLAYED.

WHAT DOES THE SECOND SENTENCE SAY ABOUT THE PUPILS? THEY   FAILED.

WHAT DOES THE THIRD SENTENCE SAY ABOUT THE WOMAN? THE WOMAN   IS.

WHAT DOES THE FOURTH SENTENCE SAY ABOUT THE CHAIR? THE CHAIR FELL.

A SURE WAY TO KNOW THE VERB IS TO REMEMBER THAT MOST VERBS SHOW ACTION; IT'S A DOING WORD.

IN THE SENTENCES ALREADY CONSIDERED, THE THREE ACTION VERBS ARE PLAYED, FAILED AND FELL. CERTAIN OTHER VERBS, KNOWN AS LINKING VERBS, DO NOT SHOW ACTION. THEY DO HOWEVER, GIVE INFORMATION ABOUT THE SUBJECT. IN "THAT WOMAN IS A THIEF," THE LINKING VERB IS   TELLS US THAT THE WOMAN IS A THIEF OTHER COMMON LINKING VERBS INCLUDE AM, ARE, APPEAR, FEEL, LOOK, WAS, WERE, BECOME AND SEEM.

ANOTHER WAY TO FIND THE VERB IS TO PUT I, YOU, HE, SHE, IT OR THEY IN FRONT OF THE WORD YOU THINK IS A VERB. IF THE RESULT MAKES SENSE, YOU HAVE A VERB. FOR EXAMPLE, YOU COULD PUT THEY IN FRONT OF PLAYED IN THE FIRST SENTENCE ABOVE, WITH THE RESULT, THEY PLAYED, MAKING SENSE. THEREFORE YOU KNOW THAT PLAYED IS A VERB. YOU COULD USE THEY OR SHE TO TEST THE OTHER VERBS AS WELL.

A VERB MUST AGREE WITH ITS SUBJECT IN NUMBER. A SINGULAR SUBJECT [ONE PERSON OR THING] TAKES A SINGULAR VERB. A PLURAL SUBJECT [MORE THAN ONE PERSON OR THING] TAKES A PLURAL VERB. MISTAKES IN SUBJECT – VERB AGREEMENT ARE SOMETIMES MADE IN THE FOLLOWING SITUATIONS :-

1 WHEN A VERB COMES BEFORE A SUBJECT.
2 WITH COMPOUND SUBJECTS.
3 WITH INDEFINITE PRONOUNS
4 WHEN WORDS COME BETWEEN THE SUBJECT AND THE VERB.

1   A VERB AGREES WITH ITS SUBJECT EVEN WHEN THE VERB COMES BEFORE THE SUBJECT. WORDS THAT MAY PRECEDE THE SUBJECT INCLUDE HERE, THERE, AND IN QUESTIONS WHAT, WHO, WHICH, WHERE.

IF YOU ARE UNSURE OF THE SUBJECT, ASK WHO OR WHAT OF THE VERB.
EXAMPLES :-
HERE   IS [VERB]   YOUR BOOK [SUBJECT]
WHERE ARE [VERB] THEY [SUBJECT] GOING [VERB]

TO SHOP?

THERE ARE [VERB] MANY FAST FOOD PLACES [SUBJECT] IN OUR CITY.

ON DONNA'S PORCH WERE [VERB] THREE GIRL GUIDES [SUBJECT]

2 SUBJECTS JOINED BY AND GENERALLY TAKE A PLURAL VERB.

EXAMPLES :-

JACK [SUBJECT] AND JILL [SUBJECT] RUN [PLURAL VERB] UP THE HILL.

CHEESE [SUBJECT] AND EGGS [SUBJECT] TASTE [PLURAL VERB] NICE WITH BREAD.

SEEING [SUBJECT] AND HEARING [SUBJECT] HAVE [PLURAL VERB] A LOT TO DO WITH GOSSIP.

WHEN SUBJECTS ARE JOINED BY EITHER OR, NEITHER NOR, NOT ONLY   BUT ALSO, THE VERB AGREES WITH THE SUBJECT CLOSER TO THE VERB.

EXAMPLE :-

EITHER VANESSA WILLIAMS [SUBJECT] OR PAMELA ANDERSON [SUBJECT] DESERVES [SINGULAR VERB] THE AWARD FOR BEST ACTRESS OF THE YEAR.

NOTE :- THE NEAREST SUBJECT, PAMELA ANDERSON, IS SINGULAR, AND SO THE VERB – DESERVES IS SINGULAR.

3 INDEFINITE PRONOUNS :-

THE FOLLOWING WORDS KNOWN AS INDEFINITE PRONOUNS, ALWAYS TAKE SINGULAR VERBS.

EACH, EITHER, NEITHER.

[-- THING WORDS] :-

SOMETHING, NOTHING, ANYTHING, EVERYTHING.

[-- ONE WORDS] :-

ONE, SOMEONE, ANYONE, EVERYONE.

[--BODY WORDS] :-

ANYBODY, EVERYBODY, SOMEBODY, NOBODY.

NOTE :- BOTH   ALWAYS TAKES A PLURAL VERB.

4 WORDS THAT COME BETWEEN THE SUBJECT AND VERB DO NOT CHANGE SUBJECT – VERB AGREEMENT. IN THE SENTENCE.

THE MEAN DOGS NEXT DOOR GET LOUD WHEN BEING FED.

THE SUBJECT DOGS IS PLURAL AND SO THE VERB GET IS PLURAL. THE WORDS NEXT DOOR THAT COME BETWEEN THE SUBJECT AND VERB DO NOT AFFECT SUBJECT – VERB AGREEMENT.

MORE ABOUT SUBJECTS AND VERBS.

1 A PRONOUN [A WORD LIKE HE, SHE, IT, WE, YOU, OR THEY USED IN PLACE OF A NOUN] CAN SERVE AS THE SUBJECT OF A SENTENCE FOR EXAMPLE :-

SHE [SUBJECT] SEEMS [VERB] LIKE A NICE PERSON.

THEY [SUBJECT] BOTH LOVE [VERB] TO PLAY.

2 A SENTENCE MAY HAVE MORE THAN ONE VERB, MORE THAN ONE SUBJECT, OR SEVERAL SUBJECTS AND VERBS.

EXAMPLES :-

THE BAT [SUBJECT] AND BALL [SUBJECT] WERE [VERB] STOLEN [VERB] FROM THE LOCKER.

DAWN [SUBJECT] AND SIMONE [SUBJECT] PREPARED [VERB] THE REPORT TOGETHER AND PRESENTED [VERB] IT TO THE AUDIENCE.

3 THE SUBJECT OF A SENTENCE NEVER APPEARS WITHIN A PREPOSITIONAL PHRASE. A PREPOSITIONAL PHRASE IS A GROUP OF WORDS THAT BEGINS WITH A PREPOSITION.

FOLLOWING IS A LIST OF COMMON PREPOSITIONS :-

IN, BY, FOR, FROM, DURING, EXCEPT, OF, ON, OFF, ONTO, INTO, INSIDE, TO, OVER, WITH, THROUGH, UNDER, TOWARD, AT, ABOUT, ABOVE, ACROSS, AROUND, AMONG, BEFORE, BETWEEN, BEHIND, BELOW, BESIDE, BENEATH.

NOTE :- CROSS OUT PREPOSITIONAL PHRASES WHEN LOOKING FOR THE SUBJECT OF A SENTENCE.

EXAMPLES :-

THE COMIC PAGES [OF THE MAGAZINE]DISAPPEARED.

ONE [OF THE BAD DOGS   AT   THE HOUSE] BEGAN BARKING.

[IN SPITE OF WHAT WAS SAID,] DOLLY DID NOT GO TO THE DOCTOR

[DURING THE GAME], I SAT[IN MY FAVORITE SEAT]

4 MANY VERBS CONSIST OF MORE THAN ONE WORD. HERE, FOR EXAMPLE, ARE SOME OF THE MANY FORMS OF THE VERB   WALK :WALK, WALKS, DOES WALK, IS WALKING, ARE WAKING, WALKED, WERE WALKING, HAVE WALKED, HAD WALKED, HAD BEEN WALKING, SHOULD WALK, WILL BE WALKING, CAN WALK, COULD BE WALKING, MUST HAVE WALKED.

NOTES :-
[a] NO --ING WORD BY ITSELF IS EVER THE VERB OF A SENTENCE. [IT MAY BE PART OF THE VERB, BUT IT MUST HAVE A HELPING VERB IN FRONT OF IT]

THEY [LEAVING]EARLY FOR THE MOVIES.[NOT A SENTENCE, BECAUSE THE VERB IS NOT COMPLETE.]
THEY [ARE LEAVING] EARLY FOR THE MOVIES. [THE VERB ARE LEAVING IS COMPLETE, SO IT IS A SENTENCE.]

[b] NO VERB PRECEDED BY [TO] IS EVER THE VERB OF A SENTENCE.
EXAMPLES :-
MY DOG SUDDENLY BEGAN TO VOMIT ON THE ROADWAY.
I JUMPED TO AVOID HITTING THE BOY.

[c] WORDS LIKE ONLY, NOT, JUST, NEVER, AND ALWAYS ARE NOT PART OF THE VERB ALTHOUGH THEY MAY APPEAR WITHIN THE VERB.
EXAMPLES :-
JAMES [DID] NOT [FINISH] THE JOB BEFORE DARK.
THE HOUSE [WAS] JUST [COMPLETED] ONLY A MONTH AGO.

ANALOGIES

TABLE IS TO WOOD AS WINDOW IS TO GLASS
FOOD IS TO HUNGRY AS DRINK IS TO THIRSTY
STATUE IS TO SCULPTOR AS BOOK IS TO AUTHOR
NOSE IS TO SMELL AS MOUTH IS TO TASTE
WRIST IS TO CUFF AS NECK IS TO COLLAR
WALK IS TO LEGS AS FLY IS TO WINGS
KNIFE IS TO CUT AS GUN IS TO SHOOT
PICTURE IS TO WALL AS CARPET IS TO FLOOR
DESCEND IS TO DOWN AS ASCEND IS TO HEIGHT
WATER IS TO PIPES AS ELECTRICITY IS TO WIRES
TREE IS TO FOREST AS SHEEP IS TO FLOCK
SHELL IS TO EGG AS RIND IS TO ORANGE
CONSTABLE IS TO THIEF AS GAMEKEEPER IS TO
ANIMALS
WHISPER IS TO SHOUT AS WALK IS TO RUN
HEARING IS TO EAR AS SIGHT IS TO SEEING
WATER IS TO FISH AS AIR IS TO ANIMAL
PIG IS TO STY AS HORSE IS TO STABLE
STEAM IS TO HEAT AS SMOKE IS TO FIRE
EAT IS TO ATE AS GO IS TO WENT
DAY IS TO WEEK AS MONTH IS TO YEAR
HERE IS TO THERE AS THIS IS TO THAT
FLOCK IS TO SHEEP AS HERD IS TO CATTLE
SPIDER IS TO FLY AS CAT IS TO MILK
SHEEP IS TO MUTTON AS PIG IS TO PORK
BOY IS TO GIRL AS MAN IS TO WOMAN
RICH IS TO POOR AS ANCIENT IS TO MODERN
WING IS TO BIRD AS FIN IS TO FISH
BEE IS TO HIVE AS COW IS TO BYRE
SHOAL IS TO HERRING AS SCHOOL IS TO WHALES
ARTIST IS TO PAINT AS AUTHOR IS TO BOOK
FATHER IS TO SON AS MOTHER IS TO DAUGHTER
CAT IS TO KITTEN AS DOG IS TO PUP
JUNE IS TO JULY AS APRIL IS TO MAY
HIGH IS LOW AS UP IS TO DOWN
NORTH IS TO SOUTH AS EAST IS TO WEST
UNCLE IS TO NEPHEW AS AUNT IS TO NIECE
SOLDIER IS TO ARMY AS SAILOR IS TO NAVY
ARROW IS TO BOW AS BULLET IS TO RIFLE

WRIST IS TO ARM AS ANKLE IS TO LEG
BRAY IS TO DONKEY AS NEIGH IS TO HORSE
FINGER IS TO HAND AS TOE IS TO FOOT
TEAR IS TO SORROW AS SMILE IS TO HAPPINESS
FEATHERS ARE TO BIRDS AS SCALES ARE TO FISH

PARTS OF THE VERB

PRESENT TENSE	PAST TENSE	PAST PARTICIPLE
AM	WAS	BEEN
ARISE	AROSE	ARISEN
AWAKE	AWOKE	AWAKENED
BUY	BOUGHT	BOUGHT
BUILD	BUILT	BUILT
BEAR	BORE	BORNE
BEAT	BEAT	BEATEN
BEGIN	BEGAN	BEGUN
BRING	BROUGHT	BROUGHT
BREAK	BROKE	BROKEN
BLOW	BLEW	BLOWN
BLEED	BLED	BLED
BITE	BIT	BITTEN
BEND	BENT	BENT
CATCH	CAUGHT	CAUGHT
CHOOSE	CHOSE	CHOSEN
COME	CAME	COME
CUT	CUT	CUT
CREEP	CREPT	CREPT
DO	DID	DONE
DIG	DUG	DUG
DRIVE	DROVE	DRIVEN
DRINK	DRANK	DRUNK
DRAW	DREW	DRAWN
FEEL	FELT	FELT
FIGHT	FOUGHT	FOUGHT
FLY	FLEW	FLOWN
FORGET	FORGOT	FORGOTTEN
FREEZE	FROZE	FROZEN
GET	GOT	GOT
GROW	GREW	GROWN

GO	WENT	GONE
GIVE	GAVE	GIVEN
HEAR	HEARD	HEARD
HIDE	HID	HIDDEN
KEEP	KEPT	KEPT
KNEEL	KNELT	KNELT
KNOW	KNEW	KNOWN
LAY	LAID	LAID
LEAVE	LEFT	LEFT
LIE	LAY	LAIN
LOSE	LOST	LOST
MAKE	MADE	MADE
MEET	MET	MET
PAY	PAID	PAID
RIDE	RODE	RIDDEN
RING	RANG	RUNG
RUN	RAN	RUN
SELL	SOLD	SOLD
SAY	SAID	SAID
SEND	SENT	SENT
SHAKE	SHOOK	SHAKEN
SING	SANG	SUNG
SPEAK	SPOKE	SPOKEN
SWIM	SWAM	SWUM
TEAR	TORE	TORN
WRITE	WROTE	WRITTEN
HURT	HURT	HURT
EAT	ATE	EATEN

COMPARISON OF ADJECTIVES

THE POSITIVE IS USED WHEN SPEAKING OF OR DESCRIBING AN OBJECT, E.G. :-LONG, SMALL.

THE COMPARATIVE IS USED WHEN COMPARING TWO OBJECTS AND IS FORMED BY ADDING "ER "TO THE POSITIVE, E.G. :-LONGER, SMALLER.

THE SUPERLATIVE IS USED WHEN SPEAKING OF MORE THAN TWO OBJECTS AND IS FORMED BY ADDING "EST "TO THE POSITIVE, E.G :-LONGEST, SMALLEST.

POSITIVE	COMPARATIVE	SUPERLATIVE
MUCH	MORE	MOST
MANY	MORE	MOST
LITTLE	LESS	LEAST
BIG	BIGGER	BIGGEST
FAST	FASTER	FASTEST
GREAT	GREATER	GREATEST
LATE	LATER	LATEST
TALL	TALLER	TALLEST
BAD	WORSE	WORST
THIN	THINNER	THINNEST
FAR	FARTHER	FARTHEST
SHORT	SHORTER	SHORTEST
GOOD	BETTER	BEST

GENERALLY TO ADJECTIVES OF TWO OR MORE SYLLABLES MORE IS USED COMPARATIVELY, AND MOST IS USED SUPERLATIVELY, E.G :- BEAUTIFUL MORE BEAUTIFUL MOST BEAUTIFUL.

CAREFUL	MORE CAREFUL	MOST CAREFUL
IGNORANT	MORE IGNORANT	MOST IGNORANT
HANDSOME	MORE HANDSOME	MOST HANDSOME
BRILLIANT	MORE BRILLIANT	MOST BRILLIANT
CAUTIOUS	MORE CAUTIOUS	MOST CAUTIOUS
COMFORTABLE	MORE COMFORTABLE	MOST COMFORTABLE
GENEROUS	MORE GENEROUS	MOST GENEROUS
GRACIOUS	MORE GRACIOUS	MOST GRACIOUS

CHAPTER 4.

SIGHT SEEING WONDERS OF THE WORLD

THE SEVEN WONDERS :-
1 THE PYRAMIDS OF EGYPT.
2 THE PHAROS LIGHTHOUSE AT ALEXANDRIA.
3 THE STATUE OF JUPITER AT OLYMPUS.
4 THE HANGING GARDENS OF BABYLON.
5 THE COLOSSUS AT RHODES.
6 THE TOMB OF MAUSOLUS AT HALICARNASSUS.
7 THE TEMPLE OF DIANA AT EPHESUS.

OF THE SEVEN WONDERS AS THEY ARE REFERRED TO, THE GREAT PYRAMIDS OF EGYPT STILL STAND INTACT AND ARE VISITED ALL THE TIME BY VISITORS AND TOURISTS.

FORMERLY KNOWN WONDERS WHICH ARE FORGOTTEN TODAY :-
ABU SIMBEL TEMPLE IN EGYPT
ANGKOR WAT IN CAMBODIA
THE AZTEC TEMPLE IN TENOCHTITLAN – MEXICO CITY, MEXICO
THE BANAUE RICE TERRACES IN THE PHILIPPINES
BOROBUDUR TEMPLE IN INDONESIA
THE COLOSSEUM IN ROME, ITALY
THE GREAT WALL OF CHINA
THE INCA CITY OF MACHU PICCHU, PERU
THE LEANING TOWER OF PISA, ITALY

THE MAYAN TEMPLES OF TIKAL IN NORTHERN GUATEMALA

THE MOAI STATUES IN RAPA NUI [EASTER ISLAND], CHILE

MONT – SAINT – MICHEL IN NORMANDY, FRANCE

THE THRONE HALL OF PERSEPOLIS IN IRAN

THE PARTHENON IN ATHENS, GREECE

THE CATACOMBS OF ALEXANDRIA

PETRA, THE ROCK CARVED CITY IN JORDAN

THE SHWEDAGON PAGODA IN MYANMAR

STONEHENGE IN ENGLAND

TAJ MAHAL IN AGRA, INDIA

THE TEMPLE OF THE INSCRIPTIONS IN PALENQUE, MEXICO

SOME MODERN WONDERS RECOGNIZED TODAY ARE :-

THE CHANNEL TUNNEL

THE CLOCK TOWER [BIG BEN] IN LONDON, ENGLAND

THE CN TOWER IN TORONTO, CANADA

EIFFEL TOWER IN PARIS, FRANCE

THE EMPIRE STATE BUILDING IN NEW YORK, U.S.A

THE GATEWAY ARCH IN ST. LOUIS, U.S.A

THE GOLDEN GATE BRIDGE IN SAN FRANCISCO, U.S.A

THE HIGH DAM IN ASWAN, EGYPT

HOOVER DAM IN ARIZONA / NEVADA, U.S.A

ITAIPU DAM IN BRAZIL / PARAGUAY

MOUNT RUSHMORE NATIONAL MEMORIAL IN SOUTH DAKOTA, U.S.A

THE PANAMA CANAL

THE PETRONAS TOWERS OF KUALA LUMPUR, MALASIA

THE STATUE OF CRISTO REDENTOR IN RIO DE JANEIRO, BRAZIL

THE STATUE OF LIBERTY IN NEW YORK CITY, U.S.A

THE SUEZ CANAL IN EGYPT

THE SYDNEY OPERA HOUSE IN AUSTRALIA

SOME NATURAL WONDERS OF THE WORLD ARE :-

ANGEL FALLS IN VENEZUELA

KAIETURE FALLS IN GUYANA

THE BAY OF FUNDY IN NOVA SCOTIA, CANADA

THE GRAND CANYON IN ARIZONA, U.S.A

THE GREAT BARRIER REEF IN AUSTRALIA
IGUACU FALLS IN BRAZIL / ARGENTINA
KRAKATOA ISLAND IN INDONESIA
MOUNT EVEREST IN NEPAL
MOUNT FUJI IN JAPAN
MOUNT KILIMANJARO IN TANZANIA
NIAGARA FALLS IN ONTARIO, CANADA
PARICUTIN VOLCANO IN MEXICO
VICTORIA FALLS IN ZAMBIA / ZIMBABWE
THINGS THAT BEEN INVENTED THAT BOGGLES THE MIND ARE SUCH AS :-
[a] TELEPHONE.
[b] RADIO.
[c] TELEVISION.
[d] MOTORS.
[E] AIR TRANSPORTATION.
[F] SEA TRANSPORTATION.
[g] RAIL TRANSPORTATION.
[h] COMPASS.
[I] RADAR.
[j] MEDICINE.
[k]COMPUTER

INSTRUMENTS AND DEVISES USED FOR VARYING PURPOSES :-

A SAILOR'S MAP	CHART.
ATTRACTS IRON	MAGNET.
MACHINE USED FOR LETTER WRITING	K E Y B O A R D ,
TYPEWRITER	
INSTRUMENT FOR DRAWING CIRCLES	COMPASSES.
MEASURES ANGLES IN SURVEYING	THEODOLITE
GIVES DIRECTION	COMPASS
A SHIP WHICH TRAVELS BELOW WATER	SUBMARINE
MAKES ELECTRICITY	DYNAMO
A MACHINE FOR MEASURING TIME	CLOCK
TELLS IF A THING IS VERTICAL	PLUMB – LINE.
TELLS IF A THING IS HORIZONTAL	SPIRIT – LEVEL
HAND OR POCKET INSTRUMENT USED FOR TIME	
WATCH.	
TAKES PHOTOGRAPH THROUGH THE BODY	X – RAY.

TAKES PHOTOGRAPHS   CAMERA
MEASURES GAS OR ELECTRICITY USED   METER
HELPS THE VOICE TO CARRY   MEGAPHONE.
PICKS UP SOUND FOR SENDING OUT AGAIN
MICROPHONE.
CARRIES MESSAGES BY WIRE   TELEPHONE.
CARRIES SOUND WITHOUT THE USE OF WIRES
RADIO.
CARRIES MESSAGES BY WIRE ACROSS THE SEA
CABLE.
DOCTOR'S LISTENING INSTRUMENT   STETHOSCOPE.
MAGNIFIES TINY OBJECTS   MICROSCOPE.
MAKES DISTANT OBJECTS LOOK BIGGER   TELESCOPE.
MEASURES HEAT AND COLD   THERMOMETER.
INDICATES THE WEATHER   BAROMETER
GLASSES USED FOR BETTERING THE EYESIGHT
SPECTACLES.

COMPARISON OF ADVERBS :-

AS MOST ADVERBS ARE TWO – SYLLABLE WORDS THEY
GENERALLY FORM THE COMPARATIVE AND SUPERLATIVE BY
ADDING "MORE "AND "MOST "TO THE POSITIVE. HOWEVER,
THERE ARE EXCEPTIONS, FOR WHICH EXAMPLES ARE ALSO
GIVEN.

POSITIVE	COMPARATIVE	SUPERLATIVE
SOON	SOONER	SOONEST
FAST	FASTER	FASTEST
LONG	LONGER	LONGEST
EARLY	EARLIER	EARLIEST
BADLY	WORSE	WORST
WELL	BETTER	BEST
MUCH	MORE	MOST
FAR	FARTHER	FARTHEST
ILL	WORSE	WORST
LATE	LATER	LAST
SLOWLY	MORE SLOWLY	MOST SLOWLY

QUICKLY	MORE QUICKLY	MOST QUICKLY
BRAVELY	MORE BRAVELY	MOST BRAVELY
CAREFULLY	MORE CAREFULLY	MOST CAREFULLY
CLEARLY	MORE CLEARLY	MOST CLEARLY
LOUDLY	MORE LOUDLY	MOST LOUDLY
HAPPILY	MORE HAPPILY	MOST HAPPILY
BITTERLY	MORE BITTERLY	MOST BITTERLY
CRUELLY	MORE CRUELLY	MOST CRUELLY
EASILY	MORE EASILY	MOST EASILY
GREEDILY	MORE GREEDILY	MOST GREEDILY
FREELY	MORE FREELY	MOST FREELY

CONCORD :-

CONCORD IS AGREEMENT WITH OR IN HARMONY OF EACH OTHER. IN GRAMMAR WE APPLY THIS WORD AS MEANING PERFECT AGREEMENT BETWEEN SUBJECT AND VERB. THIS IS SHOWN BY THE SUBJECT AND VERB HAVING THE SAME PERSON AND NUMBER.

[a] WHEN THE SUBJECT IS SINGULAR THE VERB IS SINGULAR.
    E.G :-

THE MAN	PLAYS
THE BABY	SLEEPS
SHE	WALKS
HE	FIGHTS
THE WOMAN	COOKS

[b] WHEN THE SUBJECT IS PLURAL THE VERB IS PLURAL.
    E.G :-

THE MEN	PLAY
THE BABIES	SLEEP
WE	WALK
THEY	FIGHT
THE WOMEN	COOK

[c] USING EXPRESSIONS SUCH AS "EACH OF ", "ONE OF ", "NEITHER OF ", "EVERYONE OF ", "NOT ONE OF "AND WORDS SUCH AS "EACH ", "EVERY ", "NONE ", "ANYBODY

", "EVERYBODY "AND "NOBODY "MUST BE FOLLOWED BY VERBS IN THE SINGULAR.

EXAMPLE :-

[1] EACH OF THE GIRLS HAS A DOLL.

[2] ONE OF THE GIRLS IS A MODEL.

[3] NEITHER OF THE SISTERS WAS IN SCHOOL.

[4] EVERY ONE OF US KNOWS THAT IT IS THE RIGHT THING TO DO.

[5] NOT ONE OF THE BOYS HAS A BASKETBALL.

[6] EACH BOY WAS SELECTED.

[7] EVERY WOMAN HAS A SECRET OF GETTING MARRIED.

[8] ANYBODY IS ADMITTED TO THE MOVIES.

[9] EVERYBODY WAS DELIGHTED WITH THE GAME.

[10] NOBODY IS HAPPY WITH THEIR GIFTS.

[d] A SINGULAR SUBJECT WITH ATTACHED PHRASES INTRODUCED BY "AS WELL AS ", "WITH "OR "LIKE "IS FOLLOWED BY A SINGULAR VERB.

EXAMPLE :-

JOSHUA, AS WELL AS EMERALD, SLEEPS LATE AT NIGHT.

THE GIRL, WITH SEVERAL OTHERS, WAS EARLY FOR GYM.

DALLAS, LIKE TEDDY, IS SHORT FOR THEIR SIZE.

[e] WHEN A VERB HAS TWO SINGULAR SUBJECTS CONNECTED BY "AND ", THE VERB IS PLURAL.

EXAMPLE :-

THE MAN AND HIS WIFE ARE GOOD FRIENDS.

THE CAT AND THE WERE ALWAYS FIGHTING.

TOM AND JERRY ARE GOOD FRIENDS.

[f] WHEN A VERB HAS ONE OR MORE PLURAL SUBJECTS CONNECTED BY "AND "THE VERB IS PLURAL.

EXAMPLE :-

THE MAJOR AND HIS MEN WERE FIGHTING THE WAR.

THE BROTHERS AND THE SISTERS ARE SURE OF THEIR FRIENDSHIP.

THE BOY AND GIRL ARE SURE OF THEIR LOVE.

[g] TWO SINGULAR SUBJECTS SEPARATED BY "EITHER OR ", "NEITHER NOR "TAKE A SINGULAR VERB.

EXAMPLE :-

EITHER   ONE   OR   THE OTHER HAS TROUBLE.

EITHER   SHE   OR   HE IS WRONG.

NEITHER   ANN   NOR   JENNY KNOWS THE ANSWER.

NEITHER   HE   NOR   SHE SPELLS WELL.

[h] SUBJECTS SEPARATED BY "EITHER [PLURAL] OR ", "NEITHER [PLURAL] NOR ", "BOTH AND ", ALSO "ALL BUT ", TAKE A PLURAL VERB.

EXAMPLE :-

EITHER THE MEN OR THE WOMEN ARE TO BE BLAMED.

NEITHER THE MARINES NOR THE NAVY WERE AFRAID OF FIGHTING.

BOTH NIGEL AND GAIL WERE PLAYING.

ALL BUT ALAN ARE GOING TO THE PARK.

ALL OF THEM BUT ANDY ARE WRONG.

HOMONYMS :-

HOMONYMS ARE COMMONLY CONFUSED WORDS. THEY HAVE THE SAME OR SIMILAR SOUNDS BUT DIFFERENT MEANINGS AND SPELLINGS.

EXAMPLES :-

ITS -- BELONGING TO IT.

IT'S - THE SHORTENED FORM OF "IT IS "OR "IT HAS ".

THE TRUCK BLEW ITS TIRE. [THE TIRE BELONGING TO IT, THE TRUCK].

IT'S [IT HAS] BEEN SNOWING ALL WINTER AND IT'S [IT IS] SNOWING NOW.

YOUR - BELONGING TO YOU.

YOU'RE - THE SHORTENED FORM OF "YOU ARE "

YOU'RE [YOU ARE] NOT GOING TO THE MOVIES UNLESS YOUR HUSBAND [THE HUSBAND BELONGING TO YOU] GOES WITH YOU.

THEIR - BELONGING TO THEM.

THERE - AT THAT PLACE, OVER THERE   A   NEUTRAL WORD USED WITH VERBS LIKE IS, WAS, WERE, ARE, HAD, HAVE ETC.

THEY'RE - THE SHORTENED FORM OF "THEY ARE ".

EXAMPLES :-

1 THREE PERSONS OWN THAT HORSE OVER THERE [AT THAT PLACE] THEIR HORSE [THE HORSE BELONGING TO THEM] IS GOING TO ENTER THE RACE; THEY'RE [THEY ARE] GOING TO BET ON IT.

2 THEY [THEY ARE] NOT GOING TO INVITE US TO THEIR HOUSE [THE HOUSE BELONGING TO THEM] BECAUSE THERE [AT THAT PLACE] IS NO ROOM FOR US TO SLEEP.

TO - A VERB PART, AS IN TO WALK.

TOO - OVERLY, AS IN "THE FOOD WAS TOO HOT "AS IN "THE SODA WAS COLD, TOO "

TWO - THE NUMBER 2.

EXAMPLES :-

1 ROXANNE WALKED TO THE MALL TO SHOP WITH AUDREY.

2 ANGEL'S JACKET IS TOO SMALL; HER HAT IS TIGHT, TOO.

3 YOU NEED TWO HANDS TO COUNT THE MONEY.

NO - A NEGATIVE ANSWER.

KNOW - TO UNDERSTAND SOMETHING.

EXAMPLES :-

1 "THERE'S NO ONE THING THE PLAYERS HAVE ALIKE ".

2 "I KNOW OF NO WAY OF TELLING WHETHER HE IS TELLING THE TRUTH OR NOT ".

3 "NO, I AM NOT GOING TO THE ZOO ".

4 "DO YOU KNOW WHY HE ASKS THAT QUESTION? "

KNEW - PAST TENSE OF KNOW.

NEW - NOT OLD, NEVER USED.

EXAMPLES :-

1 I WORE A NEW TIE TO CHURCH.

2 I KNEW SOMETHING WAS WRONG; FROM THE MOMENT I SAW HER CRYING.

3 TOM KNEW THAT GETTING HIS FACIAL DONE WOULD GIVE HIS FACE A NEW LOOK.

HEAR - PERCEIVE WITH THE EAR.
HERE - IN THIS PLACE, RIGHT HERE.
EXAMPLES :-
1 "DID YOU HEAR ABOUT THE CORRUPT POLITICIAN WHO IS CAMPAIGNING FOR ELECTION RIGHT HERE IN THIS CITY? "
2 "THE PLAYERS ACT AS THOUGH THEY DON'T SEE OR HEAR ME; EVEN THOUGH I HAVE BEEN WITH THIS TEAM HERE FOR MONTHS NOW ".

COARSE - ROUGH, TOUGH.
COURSE - A SUBJECT IN SCHOOL, DIRECTION ETC .
E.G. :-
EMERALD FELT THE DANCE INSTRUCTOR'S WAY OF DOING THINGS WAS TOO COARSE FOR HER LIKING, AND WAS GLAD WHEN SHE FINISHED THE COURSE.

HOLE - AN EMPTY SPOT.
WHOLE - ENTIRE, ALL.
E.G. :-
THE WHOLE TIME I WAS AT THE HOSPITAL; I TRIED TO HIDE THE HOLE IN MY FOOT FROM THE DOCTOR.

PASSED - WENT BY, HANDED OVER TO.
PAST - A TIME BEFORE THE PRESENT; ALSO WHEN YOU PAST BY SOMETHING.
E.G. :-
LYN PASSED HIM A PLATE OF FOOD; IT WAS HIS WAY OF FORGETTING HIS UNHAPPY PAST DAY AT WORK.

EXAMPLES OF OTHERS ARE :-

BRAKE - STOP. COME TO A FULL STOP.
BREAK - COME APART, PULL ASUNDER.

PEACE - CALM, QUIET.
PIECE - A PART OF SOMETHING.

PLAIN - A FLAT AREA.
PLANE - AN AIRCRAFT.

WRITE - IS WHAT YOU DO WITH PEN AND PAPER.
RIGHT - CORRECT, OPPOSITE TO LEFT.

THAN - USED IN COMPARISONS.
THEN - AT THAT TIME.

WHERE - IN WHAT PLACE.
WEAR - TO HAVE ON, WEARING OF CLOTHES AND OTHER THINGS.

WEATHER - ATMOSPHERIC CONDITION.
WHETHER - IN CASE, IF ETC .

WHOSE - BELONGING TO WHOM.
WHO'S - THE SHORTENED FORM FOR "WHO IS "AND "WHO HAS ".

THROUGH - FINISHED, FROM ONE SIDE TO THE OTHER.
THREW - THE PAST TENSE OF THROW.

CORRECT USAGE OF THE ENGLISH LANGUAGE :-

A, AN - BOTH A AND AN ARE USED BEFORE OTHER WORDS TO MEAN "ONE ". GENERALLY YOU SHOULD USE "AN "BEFORE WORDS STARTING WITH A VOWEL [A, E,I,O U,].
E.G. :-
AN APPLE, AN EGG, AN ANT, AN ACHE, AN EXPERIENCE, AN ELEPHANT.
GENERALLY YOU SHOULD USE "A "BEFORE WORDS STARTING WITH A CONSONANT [ALL OTHER LETTERS OF THE ALPHABET APART FROM THE FIVE VOWELS]
E.G. :-
A MAN, A DRINK, A GAME, A RADIO, A STOVE, A BOOK.

AMONG - IMPLIES THREE OR MORE.
BETWEEN - SIGNIFIES ONLY TWO.
E.G. :-

ROY NOLAN

1 THEY HAD TO CHOOSE FROM AMONG 145 DIFFERENT KINDS OF WALL PAPER BUT BETWEEN ONLY TWO HOUSES.

2 THE SELECTORS HAD TO CHOOSE BETWEEN THE TWO BASKETBALL PLAYERS TO PLAY AMONG THE WORLD CUP TEAMS

BESIDE - ALONG THE SIDE OF.
BESIDES - IN ADDITION TO.

DESSERT - LAST PART OF A MEAL.
DESERT - TO ABANDON ONE'S DUTY, ALSO A STRETCH OF DRY LAND

MADE - TO MAKE.
MAID - AN UNMARRIED YOUNG WOMAN; A SERVANT GIRL.

SAIL - CANVAS SHEET TO CATCH THE WIND AND MOVE A VESSEL.
SALE - SPECIAL SELLING OF GOODS AT REDUCED PRICES.

THOUGHT - PAST TENSE OF THINK.
THOUGH - DESPITE THE FACT THAT.

ACCEPT - RECEIVE.
EXCEPT - EXCLUDE.

LESS - REFERS TO VALUE, AMOUNT, DEGREE.
FEWER - USED WITH THINGS THAT CAN BE COUNTED.

ADVICE - A NOUN MEANING AN OPINION.
ADVISE - A VERB MEANING TO GIVE ADVICE.

AFFECT - A VERB MEANING TO INFLUENCE.
EFFECT - A VERB MEANING TO BRING ABOUT SOMETHING.
EFFECT - A NOUN MEANING RESULT.

LOSE - FAIL TO WIN, MISPLACED.

LOOSE - NOT FASTENED, NOT TIGHT FITTING.

QUITE - REALLY, RATHER, ENTIRELY.
QUIET - PEACEFUL, TRANQUIL.

LEAD - DIRECT OR GUIDE AS BY GOING BEFORE.
LEAD - HEAVY, SOFT METAL, A CHEMICAL ELEMENT.

LEAN - BEND OR SLANT.
LEAN - LITTLE OR NO FAT.

SEA - THE OCEAN.
SEE - HAVE THE POWER OF SIGHT.

WAIT - ACT OR TIME OF WAITING.
WEIGHT - UNIT OF HEAVINESS, BURDEN.

BEAN - EDIBLE SEED OF SOME PLANTS.
BEEN - OF TO BE.
BEING - EXISTENCE, LIFE.
BLUE - COLOR OF THE CLEAR SKY.
BLEW - OF TO BLOW.

CLOSE - CONFINED, CLOSE TOGETHER.
CLOTHES - CLOTHING, PUT CLOTHES ON.

DEAR - MUCH LOVED.
DEER - HOOFED, CUD – CHEWING ANIMAL.
DARE - HAVE THE COURAGE.

FLOWER - PETALS AND PISTIL OF A PLANT.
FLOUR - POWDERY SUBSTANCE GROUND FROM GRAIN.

GUESS - ESTIMATE, SURMISE, JUDGE, SUPPOSE.
GUEST - ONE ENTERTAINED AT ANOTHER'S HOME.

HOARSE - SOUNDING ROUGH AND HUSKY.
HORSE - LARGE ANIMAL.

NIECE - DAUGHTER OF ONE'S SISTER OR BROTHER.
NICE - PLEASANT, KIND, GOOD.

NOT - IN NO MANNER, DEGREE.
KNOT - TYING TOGETHER OF STRING.

PAIN - HURT FELT IN BODY OR MIND.
PANE - SHEET OF GLASS.

PEAR - SOFT, JUICY FRUIT.
PAIR - TWO THINGS, MATCHED TO MAKE A UNIT.

SUIT - COAT AND TROUSERS.
SUITE - GROUP OF CONNECTED ROOMS. SET OF MATCHED FURNITURE

THREE - A NUMBER, ONE MORE THAN TWO.
TREE - LARGE, WOODY PLANT.

WAIST - BODY PART BETWEEN THE RIBS AND THE HIPS.
WASTE - WASTED MATTER, REFUSE.

WARE - THING FOR SALE; POTTERY.
WEAR - HAVE ON THE BODY AS CLOTHES.

WEEK - PERIOD OF SEVEN DAYS.
WEAK - LACKING STRENGTH, POWER ETC .

CHAPTER 5.

IMPROVING SPELLING :-

IN UNDERSTANDING BASIC SPELLING RULES.
HERE'S HOW YOU CAN IMPROVE YOUR SPELLING.

1 FINAL SILENT E. DROP A FINAL E BEFORE AN ENDING
THAT STARTS WITH A VOWEL [THE VOWELS ARE A,E,I, O,U
].
E.G. :-
WRITE + ING =WRITING.
DEBATE +ABLE =DEBATABLE.

2 CHANGE Y TO I. WHEN A WORD ENDS IN A CONSONANT
PLUS Y, CHANGE Y TO I WHEN YOU ADD AN ENDING.
E.G :-
WORRY + ED =WORRIED.
TERRIFY + ED =TERRIFIED.

3 KEEP THE FINAL E BEFORE AN ENDING THAT STARTS
WITH A CONSONANT.
E.G. :-
CARE + FUL =CAREFUL.
LEISURE + LY =LEISURELY.

4 DOUBLING A FINAL CONSONANT. DOUBLE THE FINAL
CONSONANT OF A WORD WHEN THE FOLLOWING ARE
TRUE OR OCCUR.

[a] THE ENDING YOU ARE ADDING STARTS WITH A VOWEL.

[b] THE WORD ENDS IN A SINGLE CONSONANT PRECEDED BY A SINGLE VOWEL.

[c] THE WORD IS ONE SYLLABLE OR IS ACCENTED ON THE LAST SYLLABLE.

E.G. :-

BEGIN + ING =BEGINNING.

RUN + ING =RUNNING.

CONTROL + ED =CONTROLLED.

IMPROVING SPELLING :-
SPELLING LISTS OF BASIC WORDS COMMONLY USED.

IN REFERRING TO PEOPLE :-
AMERICAN
FOREIGNER
BROTHER
SISTER
CITIZEN
ADULT
YOUTH
AUNT
WIDOWER
WIDOW
BABIES
STUDENT
TEACHER
DAUGHTER
SON
MOTHER
CHILDREN
COUSIN
FATHER
FRIEND
GUEST
DOCTOR
DENTIST
TEACHER
LECTURER
HOSTESS

HOST
MAIDEN
NEPHEW
NIECE
FAMILY
HUSBAND
WIFE
MAID
SERVANT
ORPHAN
PARENTS
RELATIVES
UNCLE
VISITOR
GARDENER
BUTLER
COOK
CHEF
GRANDFATHER
GRANDMOTHER
PERSON
POLICEMAN
SOLDIER
PRESIDENT
MINISTER
SENATOR
ACTOR
ACTRESS
AUTHOR
WOMAN
MAN

WORDS REFERRING TO THE HUMAN BODY :-
BACK
HEAD
NOSE
EYES
EARS
MOUTH
TEETH
WRIST

ANKLES
FOREHEAD
HEART
BUTTOCKS
BREAST
CHEEK
HAND
KNEES
KNUCKLES
LIMBS
LUNGS
VEINS
MUSCLES
NOSTRILS
SHOULDER
TONGUE
FOOT
FINGERS
TOES
TONGUE
THROAT
THIGH
SKELETON
SKULL
STOMACH
NAILS
WAIST
HIP
TORSO

WORDS REFERRING TO THINGS OF THE HOME :-
TABLE
CHAIR
BOOKS
ATTIC
CELLAR
CLOTHING
FLOWER
VASE
CURTAINS
CUSHION

KITCHEN
LOBBY
MATTRESS
RADIO
TELEVISION
CLOCK
LIGHTS
METER
MIRROR
BED
PILLOW
DOOR
STEPS
WALL
SHOWER
TOILET
BATH
CHIMNEY
ROOMS
SINK
CUPBOARDS
WINDOWS
DECORATIONS

WORDS REFERRING TO FOODSTUFF IN THE KITCHEN :-
OVALTINE
BEEF
PORK
CHICKEN
FISH
BACON
SUGAR
VENISON
BISCUITS
BREAD
BUTTER
CHEESE
SALT
PEPPER
ONION
GARLIC

CHOCOLATE
COFFEE
COCOA
STEAK
SAUSAGES
POTATOES
MARGARINE
SALMON
MUTTON
LAMB
PORRIDGE
PUDDING
SAGO
FLOUR

WORDS ASSOCIATED WITH JOBS -- PROFESSIONS :-
DESIGNER
PHARMACIST
SURVEYOR
TAILOR
SEAMSTRESS
BUTCHER
CARPENTER
SHIPWRIGHT
SCULPTOR
PLUMBER
CHEMIST
DOCTOR
ENGINEER
BOOK – KEEPER
LAWYER
MASON
GROCER
JOURNALIST
MANAGER
MECHANIC
CAPTAIN
PILOT

SPELLING LIST OF WORDS OF ANIMALS.
DOG

APE
BAT
WHALE
ZEBRA
BEAR
BEAVER
TIGER
WALRUS
BULL
BUFFALO
MULE
MOUSE
SQUIRREL
SHEEP
LION
LEOPARD
MONGOOSE
MONKEY
KANGAROO
JAGUAR
HORSE
ELEPHANT
GIRAFFE
GAZELLE
FOX
DONKEY
DEER
CAT
COW
CAMEL
HIPPOPOTAMUS
GOAT
HEDGEHOG
GORILLA
HARE
OX
PANTHER
PIG
RABBIT
RAT
PORCUPINE

SEAL

SPELLING LIST OF NAMES OF DOGS.:-
BULLDOG
COLLIE
BLOODHOUND
ALSATIAN
DALMATIAN
GREYHOUND
POODLE
RETRIEVER
SHEEPDOG
SPANIEL
TERRIER
SETTER
POMERANIAN
POINTER
PEKINESE
BOXER
DOBERMAN PINSCHER
MASTIFF
ROTTWEILER
COLLIE
GERMAN SHEPHERD
TERRIER
SPANIEL
MALTESE
PUG
AMERICAN FOXHOUND
BLOODHOUND
POINTER
SETTER
RETRIEVER
LABRADOR
SPANIEL

SPELLING LIST OF NAMES OF FAMILIAR BIRDS.:-
HAWK
KINGFISHER
ROBIN
SANDPIPER

ROOK
HERON
JACKDAW
ALBATROSS
BLACKBIRD
CANARY
CRANE
LAPWING
MOORHEN
SPARROW
NIGHTINGALE
SEAGULL
SKYLARK
CROW
OWL
STARLING
STORK
CUCKOO
PARROT
SWALLOW
DIPPER
PARTRIDGE
SWAN
DUCK
SWIFT
EAGLE
PELICAN
FALCON
PENGUIN
TURKEY
PHEASANT
FLAMINGO
PIGEON
VULTURE
GANNET
WAGTAIL
GOOSE
WOODPECKER
WREN
RAVEN

REGULAR BASIC WORDS DEALING WITH THE SEA -
WATERWAYS.
SEA
RIVER
OCEAN
LAKE
LAGOON
FIORD
INLET
TRIBUTARY
WAVES
CREST
TROUGH
TORRENT
HARBOR
CHANNEL
BILLOWS
BREAKERS

REGULAR WORDS ASSOCIATED WITH LAND - MASSES :-
COUNTRY
CONTINENT
MOUNTAIN
VALLEY
ISLAND
PLAIN
PRAIRIE
SUMMIT
PRECIPICE
CLIFF
CAPE
HILL
MARSH
TUNDRA
PENINSULA

NORMAL WORDS SIGNIFICANT TO THE SKY :-
SKY
ASTRONOMY
ATMOSPHERE
CLOUDS

ECLIPSE
HEAVENS
HORIZON
PLANET
SOLAR
ALTITUDE
COMET
CRESCENT
DAWN
SUNSET
TWILIGHT
ZENITH
UNIVERSE

WORDS OF THINGS RELATING TO THE SCHOOL ENVIRONMENT :-
PUPIL
STUDENT
SCHOLAR
TEACHER
LECTURER
BOOKS
PENCILS
PENS
SHARPENER
ERASERS
CHALK
SUBJECTS
ENGLISH
MATHEMATICS
BIOLOGY
HISTORY
SCIENCE
GENERAL KNOWLEDGE
COMPOSITION
WRITING
SPELLING
GRAMMAR
POETRY
DICTATION
DETENTION

COPIES
CUPBOARD
PICTURE

THINGS THAT HAVE TO DO WITH THE MEDICAL FIELD
:-

DOCTOR
NURSE
SURGEON
MEDICINE
DISEASE
FEVER
ACCIDENT
INFECTION
CASUALTY
OPERATION
OINTMENT
PHYSICIAN
STERILISE
THERMOMETER
WARD
HOSPITAL

WORDS DEALING WITH THE TRAVEL INDUSTRY :-
CAR
BUS
VAN
TRUCK
BICYCLE
MOTORCYCLE
AEROPLANE
SHIP
CARRIAGE
COACH
CRUISE
EXPRESS
ENGINE
FARES
LUGGAGE
PARCEL
PIER

PASSENGERS
PURSER
SIGNAL
SKIS
SLEDGE
SLEIGH
TOURIST
TRAVELLER
TUNNEL
VEHICLES

WORDS OF THINGS ASSOCIATED WITH PLANTS :-
BEAN
CABBAGE
CARROT
APPLE
BANANA
PLUM
TOMATO
RASPBERRY
STRAWBERRY
SPROUT
ASH
BEECH
BIRCH
CARNATION
BLUEBELL
VIOLET
BUTTERCUP
FIR
CEDAR
ELM
CROCUS
DAFFODIL
CHERRY
CURRANT
GRAPE
LEMON
TULIP
MELON
ORANGE

CELERY
THISTLE
GARLIC
CUCUMBER
LETTUCE
DAHLIA
DAISY
LARCH
LIME
MAPLE
DANDELION
ONION
PARSLEY
PEA
SUNFLOWER
PEACH
PEAR
FORGET - ME - NOT
GERANIUM
OAK
OLIVE
PALM
POTATO
RADISH
PINEAPPLE
ROSE
PLUM
HONEYSUCKLE
HYACINTH
PINE
POPLAR
SYCAMORE
IRIS
LILY
ORCHID
PANSY

WORDS REFERRING TO LIQUID SUBSTANCES :-
MILK
OIL
WATER

TEA
COFFEE
COCOA
ALCOHOL
BEER
SODA
PETROL
ACID
CIDER
BRINE
LEMONADE
PARAFFIN
WINE
VINEGAR

WORDS OF MINERALS FOUND THROUGHOUT THE WORLD
:-

GOLD
DIAMOND
BRONZE
BRASS
ALUMINIUM
COAL
COPPER
IRON
GRANITE
MARBLE
MERCURY
LEAD
PLATINUM
NICKEL
SILVER
RADIUM
STEEL
TIN
ZINC
SLATE
SULPHUR

WORDS OF NAMES OF INSECTS THAT GOVERN THE WORLD :-
FLY
MOSQUITO
FLEA
ANT
BUG
CRICKET
BEE
DRAGON FLY
BEETLE
CENTIPEDE
GRASSHOPPER
LOCUST
MOTH
LOUSE
WASP
BUTTERFLY

COMMON WORDS USED IN DESCRIBING PEOPLE :-
ARGUMENTATIVE
SOFTHEARTED
ENERGETIC
PATIENT
RELIABLE
INDEPENDENT
STUBBORN
FLIRTATIOUS
IRRESPONSIBLE
STINGY
GOOD – HUMORED
COOPERATIVE
DISCIPLINED
SENTIMENTAL
DEFENSIVE
HONEST
BAD – TEMPERED
AMBITIOUS
BIGOTED
CONSIDERATE
HARDWORKING

SUPPORTIVE
SUSPICIOUS
OPEN – MINDED
LAZY
JEALOUS
MATERIALISTIC
SARCASTIC
SELF – CENTERED
GENEROUS
PERSISTENT
SHY
SLOPPY
TRUSTWORTHY
AGGRESSIVE
COURAGEOUS
COMPULSIVE
DISHONEST
INSENSITIVE
UNPRETENTIOUS
NEAT

EVERYDAY BASIC WORDS USED IN COMMUNICATION :-
ACCEPT
ACHE
ACCIDENT
ADDRESS
ADVICE
AGAIN
AGAINST
AFTER
AGREE
ALMOST
ALL RIGHT
ALSO
ALREADY
ALWAYS
ALTHOUGH
AMOUNT
AMONG
ANSWER
ANIMAL

ANOTHER
ANXIOUS
APPETITE
APPLY
APPROVE
AROUND
ARGUE
ATTEMPT
ATTENTION
AVENUE
BEEN
BECAUSE
BECOME
BEAUTIFUL
BACK
BEGIN
BEFORE
BELIEVE
BLACK
BLUE
BETWEEN
BICYCLE
BOTTLE
BORROW
BOARD
BRAKE
BOTTOM
BRILLIANT
BREAST
BREATHE
BUILDING
BROTHER
BUSINESS
CARELESS
CAREFUL
CAREFREE
COME
CAME
CAN'T
CERTAIN
CEREAL

CHAIR
CHEAP
CHARITY
CHANGE
CHEAT
CHICKEN
CHILDREN
CITY
CIGARETTE
CHOOSE
CHURCH
CITIZEN
COFFEE
CLOTHING
CLOTHES
CLOTH
COLOR
COLLEGE
COLLECT
COPY
COMPANY
CONVERSATION
CONDITION
DEAR
DAY
DAYBREAK
DAILY
DANGER
DEAD
DEATH
DEED
DECIDE
DIED
DID
DENTIST
DEPOSIT
DESCRIBE
DIRECTION
DINNER
DIFFERENT
DISTANCE

DISCOVER
DISEASE
DOLLAR
DOCTOR
DOES
DURING
DOZEN
DOWN
DOUBT
EASY
EIGHT
EDUCATION
EACH
EARLY
EASY
EARTH
EMPTY
EVENING
ENGLISH
ENTRANCE
ENOUGH
EXERCISE
EVERYTHING
EXCEPT
EXPECT
EXIT
FAMILY
FACTORY
FEW
FIFTEEN
FAR
FEBRUARY
FOREIGN
FOREHEAD
FIGHT
FLOWER
FORTY
FOURTEEN
FIFTEEN
FRIDAY
FROM

FRIEND
GET
GARDEN
GENERAL
GREAT
GOOD
GRAMMAR
GUESS
GROW
HAND
HALF
HEAD
HAPPY
HAVING
HEARD
HIGH
HIMSELF
HOLIDAY
HOME
HOUSE
HOSPITAL
HOW
HUNDRED
HUSBAND
INTELLIGENCE
INTO
IRON
ITSELF
INTEREST
JANUARY
JUNE
JULY
KITCHEN
KNOWLEDGE
LANGUAGE
LAST
LEARN
LAUGH
LEFT
LEAD
LETTER

LENGTH
LESSON
LITTLE
LIFE
LISTEN
LIGHT
LONG
LOSE
MADE
MUCH
MANY
MATTER
MARCH
MATCH
MARRY
MAY
MEN
MEASURE
MEDICINE
MIDDLE
MIGHT
MILLION
MINUTE
MISTAKE
MONEY
MONTH
MOTHER
MORNING
MORE
MOUNTAIN
MOUTH
MUCH
NEAR
NEVER
NEEDLE
NEITHER
NEVER
NEWSPAPER
NIECE
NIGHT
NINETY

NOT
NONE
NOISE
NOVEMBER
NOTHING
NUMBER
NOW
O'CLOCK
OCTOBER
OFTEN
OLD
ONLY
ONCE
ONE
OPPORTUNITY
OPINION
ORIGINAL
OPTIMIST
PAPER
PEACE
PART
PENCIL
PEOPLE
PERFECT
PERSONAL
PICTURE
PILLOW
PIECE
PLEASE
PLAIN
PLANE
PLEASE
POLICEMAN
POSSIBLE
POTATO
POWER
PRESIDENT
PRETTY
PROBABLY
PUBLIC
PROMISE

PUT
QUIET
QUICK
QUARTER
QUITE
QUIZ
READ
READY
REALLY
REASON
RECEIVE
RELIGION
RECOGNIZE
REMEMBER
REPEAT
RESOURCE
RESTAURANT
RIGHT
RIDICULOUS
SAME
SATURDAY
SANDWICH
SCHOOL
SCISSORS
SEASON
SENTENCE
SEPTEMBER
SEVENTEEN
SERVICE
SEVERAL
SHOES
SHOULD
SINCE
SIGHT
SISTER
SIXTEEN
SLEEP
SOAP
SOLDIER
SOMETIMES
SOMETHING

SOUL
SOUTH
STAMP
STATE
STOCKINGS
STREET
STUDYING
STUDENT
STRONG
SUCH
SUGAR
SUIT
SUNDAY
SUMMER
SUPPER
SWEET
TELEPHONE
TELEGRAM
TENANT
TENTH
THAN
THAT
THEM
THEIR
THERE
THEY
THING
THIS
THIRTEEN
THOUGH
THOUGHT
THROUGH
THREE
TREE
THOUSAND
THURSDAY
TODAY
TIME
TIRED
TOMORROW
TOGETHER

TONIGHT
TONGUE
TOWARD
TOUCH
TROUBLE
TRAVEL
TWELVE
TRULY
UNDER
UNDERSTAND
UNCLE
UNTIL
USED
USUAL
VALUE
VALLEY
VEGETABLE
VISITOR
VERY
VIEW
VISITOR
VOICE
VOTE
WAIST
WAIT
WALK
WAKE
WARNING
WARM
WATER
WEATHER
WEDNESDAY
WEEK
WELCOME
WERE
WENT
WELL
WHETHER
WHAT
WHICH
WHILE

WHOLE
WHOSE
WIDOW
WIDOWER
WIFE
WINDOW
WINTER
WITHOUT
WOMAN
WORK
WORLD
WOULD
WRITE
WRITING
YEAR
YESTERDAY
YOUNG
ZEBRA
ZOO

THE VERB :-

THE VERB ENDING --S 0R --ES IS NEEDED WITH A REGULAR VERB IN THE PRESENT TENSE WHEN THE SUBJECT IS HE, SHE, IT OR ONE PERSON OR ONE THING.
EXAMPLE :-

HE	SHOUT[S].
SHE	RUN[S] AWAY.
SHE	BRUSH[ES] HER HAIR.
IT	REALLY BOTHER[S] ME.
ONE PERSON	THEIR DAUGHTER LEAVE[S] THE HOME.
ONE THING	THE BUS RUMBLE[S] ON THE ROAD.

THE STANDARD FORMS OF REGULAR VERBS ARE AS FOLLOWS :-
EXAMPLE :-

PRESENT TENSE	PAST TENSE
WALK	
I WALK	I WALKED
YOU WALK	YOU WALKED
HE, SHE, IT WALKS	HE, SHE, IT WALKED

WE WALK	WE WALKED
YOU WALK	YOU WALKED
THEY WALK	THEY WALKED

JUMP

I JUMP	I JUMPED
YOU JUMP	YOU JUMPED
HE, SHE, IT JUMPS	HE, SHE, IT JUMPED
WE JUMP	WE JUMPED
YOU JUMP	YOU JUMPED
THEY JUMP	THEY JUMPED

THE STANDARD REGULAR FORMS OF THE COMMON IRREGULAR VERBS BE,DO,HAVE

BE

PRESENT TENSE	PAST TENSE
I AM	I WAS
YOU ARE	YOU WERE
HE, SHE, IT IS	HE, SHE, IT WAS
WE ARE	WE WERE
YOU ARE	YOU WERE
THEY ARE	THEY WERE

DO

I DO	I DID
YOU DO	YOU DID
HE, SHE, IT DOES	HE, SHE, IT DID
WE DO	WE DID
YOU DO	YOU DID
THEY DO	THEY DID

HAVE

I HAVE	I HAD
YOU HAVE	YOU HAD
HE, SHE, IT HAS	HE, SHE, IT HAD
WE HAVE	WE HAD
YOU HAVE	YOU HAD
THEY HAVE	THEY HAD

IRREGULAR VERBS HAVE IRREGULAR FORMS IN THE PAST TENSE AND PAST PARTICIPLE.

NOTE :- THE PRESENT PARTICIPLE IS FORMED BY SIMPLY ADDING [--ING] TO THE BASE FORM OF THE VERB.

HERE ARE SOME IRREGULAR VERBS THAT YOU WILL NEED TO BECOME FAMILIAR WITH :-

PRESENT	PAST	PAST PARTICIPLE
BE [AM, ARE, IS]	WAS	BEEN
BECOME	BECAME	BECOME
BEGIN	BEGAN	BEGUN
BITE	BIT	BITTEN
BLOW	BLEW	BLOWN
BREAK	BROKE	BROKEN
CHOOSE	CHOSE	CHOSEN
COST	COST	COST
DO [DOES]	DID	DONE
DRAW	DREW	DRAWN
DRINK	DRANK	DRUNK
DRIVE	DROVE	DRIVEN
EAT	ATE	EATEN
FALL	FELL	FALLEN
FLY	FLEW	FLOWN
FREEZE	FROZE	FROZEN
GO [GOES]	WENT	GONE
GROW	GREW	GROWN
HIDE	HID	HIDDEN
KNOW	KNEW	KNOWN
LET	LET	LET
LIE	LAY	LAIN
RIDE	RODE	RIDDEN
RING	RANG	RUNG
SEE	SAW	SEEN
SHAKE	SHOOK	SHAKEN
SING	SANG	SUNG
SPEAK	SPOKE	SPOKEN
SWEAR	SWORE	SWORN
SWIM	SWAM	SWUM
TAKE	TOOK	TAKEN

TEAR	TORE	TORN
WRITE	WROTE	WRITTEN

PRONOUN AGREEMENT :-PRONOUNS ARE WORDS THAT TAKE THE PLACE OF NOUNS [PERSONS, PLACES, OR THING]. THE WORD PRONOUN MEANS "FOR A NOUN ". PRONOUNS ARE USED AS SHORT CUTS THAT KEEP YOU FROM UNNECESSARILY REPEATING WORDS.

EXAMPLE :-

WHEN THE THREE LITTLE CHILDREN SAW THE CLOWN, THEY CRIED. [THEY IS A PRONOUN THAT TAKES THE PLACE OF CHILDREN].

HARRY PUT SO MUCH PRESSURE ON THE BAT, THAT IT BROKE. [IT IS A PRONOUN THAT REPLACES BAT].

IN USING PRONOUNS FOLLOW THESE SIMPLE WAYS :-

[a] A PRONOUN MUST REFER CLEARLY TO THE WORD IT REPLACES.

[b] PRONOUNS SHOULD NOT SHIFT UNNECESSARILY IN POINT OF VIEW.

[c] A PRONOUN MUST AGREE IN NUMBER WITH THE WORD OR WORDS IT REPLACES.

A PRONOUN MUST AGREE IN NUMBER WITH THE WORD OR WORDS IT REPLACES. IF THE WORD A PRONOUN REFERS TO IS SINGULAR, THE PRONOUN MUST BE SINGULAR, IF THE WORD IS PLURAL, THE PRONOUN MUST BE PLURAL.

EXAMPLE :-

1 [LORRAINE] DECIDED TO GIVE ME [HER] NEW TELEVISION SET.

2 [PEOPLE] GOING TO THE RALLY MUST WATCH [THEIR] BACKS BECAUSE OF RIOTS.

IN THE FIRST EXAMPLE, THE PRONOUN HER REFERS TO THE SINGULAR WORD LORRAINE; WHEREAS IN THE SECOND EXAMPLE, THE PRONOUN THEIR REFERS TO THE PLURAL WORD PEOPLE.

NOTE :- THE FOLLOWING WORDS KNOWN AS INDEFINITE PRONOUNS, ARE ALWAYS SINGULAR.[--ONE   WORDS   ]

SUCH AS SOMEONE, EVERYONE. [BODY WORDS] SUCH AS EVERYBODY, SOMEBODY.

EXAMPLES :-

[a] [NOBODY] FEELS WORSE THAN [SHE] DOES ABOUT THE EXAMINATION RESULTS.

[b] [ONE] OF THE PLAYERS COULD NOT FIND [HIS] BAT.

TYPE OF PRONOUNS SINGULAR PLURAL

FIRST PERSON PRONOUNS I [MY, MINE, ME] WE [OUR, US].

SECOND PERSON PRONOUNS YOU [YOUR] YOU [YOUR].

THIRD PERSON PRONOUNS HE [HIS, HIM] THEY [THEIR, THEM].

SHE [HER]

IT [ITS]

NOTE :-ANY PERSON, PLACE, OR THING, AS WELL AS ANY INDEFINITE PRONOUN LIKE ONE, SOMEONE AND SO ON IS A THIRD PERSON WORD.

CHAPTER 6.

THE MODEL FAMILY :-
HAVING GOOD FAMILY PRINCIPLES AND VALUES ARE IMPORTANT AND NECESSARY FOR A UNITED AND STRONG FAMILY UNION. REMEMBER UNITED WE STAND DIVIDED WE FALL.

THINGS MUST HAVE RIGHT PRIORITIES.
[a] THE FAMILY NEEDS TO EXHIBIT A STRONG AND HEALTHY RELATIONSHIP BETWEEN THE PARENTS. MOMS AND DADS ARE TO COMPLIMENT, RATHER THAN DOMINATE EACH OTHER.
[b] CHILDREN ARE TO LISTEN AND OBEY THEIR PARENTS AND ALWAYS ENDEAVOR TO KEEP THEIR PARENTS UNITED IN LOVE FOR THE EXISTENCE OF A STRONG AND VIBRANT FAMILY STRUCTURE.
[c] CHILDREN SHOULD BE INFLUENCED BY THEIR PARENTS AND OTHERS OF GOOD CHARACTER; SO THEIR LIVES CAN BE FRUITFUL AND MEANINGFUL IN SOCIETY.
[d] FAMILY MEMBERS ARE TO LISTEN AND RESPOND TO EACH OTHER NEEDS AS THE CIRCUMSTANCE AND SITUATION DICTATE.
[e] THE FAMILY NEEDS TO RECOGNIZE UNSPOKEN MESSAGES; FOR COMMUNICATION OF FEELINGS CAN BE NON VERBAL AND NEEDS TO BE ADDRESSED.
[f] FAMILY MEMBERS ARE TO BE SUPPORTIVE AND ENCOURAGE INDIVIDUAL THINKING FOR A PROGRESSIVE FUTURE.

[g] THE FAMILY SHOULD AVOID TURN – OFF WORDS AND PUT – DOWN PHRASES, BUT LIFT UP, ENCOURAGE ONE TO SEEK HIGHER HEIGHTS IN LIFE.

[h] FAMILY MEMBERS ARE TO BE IN CONTROL OF THEIR LIVES; LEARN HOW TO REACT AND RESPOND POSITIVELY TO CHANGES IN LIFE.

[I] ALWAYS FORGIVE A FAMILY MEMBER, FORGET WHAT THEY DID WRONG, AND LOOK FORWARD TO A HEALTHY, PRODUCTIVE AND PROSPEROUS FUTURE

[j] THE FAMILY MUST ALWAYS BE OPEN TO CONVERSATION; ALWAYS WILLING TO WORK ALONG WITH EACH OTHER FOR THE GOOD OF ALL.

COMPETENT WRITING :-
THE TWO MOST IMPORTANT STEPS IN COMPETENT WRITING ARE :-
[a] MAKING A POINT OF VIEW.
[b] SUPPORTING THAT POINT OF VIEW WITH SPECIFIC EVIDENCE.

THE POINT THAT OPENS A PARAGRAPH IS CALLED A TOPIC SENTENCE. WHEN YOU LOOK CLOSELY AT A POINT OF VIEW, OR TOPIC SENTENCE, YOU CAN SEE THAT IT IS MADE UP OF TWO PARTS
1 THE LIMITED TOPIC.
2 THE WRITER'S IDEA ABOUT THE TOPIC.
EXAMPLES :-
[a] MY [MOTHER] IS [VERY WISE].
HERE MOTHER IS THE LIMITED TOPIC, AND VERY WISE IS THE IDEA ABOUT THE TOPIC.
[b] MY [FORD JEEP] IS THE [MOST DEPENDABLE] VEHICLE I HAVE.

IN THIS CASE FORD JEEP IS THE LIMITED TOPIC AND MOST DEPENDABLE IS THE IDEA ABOUT THE TOPIC.

TO BE AN EFFECTIVE WRITER, USE SPECIFIC, RATHER THAN GENERAL, WORDS. SPECIFIC WORDS GIVE A CLEAR PICTURE IN THE READER'S MIND. THEY CAPTURE INTEREST, CREATE A GOOD IMPRESSION AND MAKE YOUR MEANING CLEAR.

PRACTICE NOT USING VAGUE, INDEFINITE WRITING; BUT LIVELY, IMAGE – FILLED WRITING, THAT CAPTURES YOUR READER'S INTEREST AND MAKES YOUR MEANING CLEAR.

EXAMPLES :-

COMPARE THE FOLLOWING SENTENCES.

1 THE MAN CAME DOWN THE AVENUE.[GENERAL]

GARY WALKED DOWN HEALY AVENUE.[SPECIFIC]

2 HE STOPPED THE TRUCK.[GENERAL]

ANDY SLAMMED ON THE BRAKES OF HIS FORD TRUCK.[SPECIFIC]

3 A BIRD WAS SEEN IN THE YARD.[GENERAL]

A SWALLOW SWOOPED DOWN ON THE GREEN-GRASS COVERED FRONT LAWN.[SPECIFIC]

THE SPECIFIC SENTENCES CREATE CLEAR PICTURES IN YOUR READER'S MIND. THE DETAILS SHOW READERS EXACTLY WHAT HAS HAPPENED.

HERE ARE WAYS TO MAKE YOUR WRITINGS SPECIFIC.

[a] USE EXACT NAMES.

HE LOVES HIS VEHICLE.

LEONARD LOVES HIS TOYOTA JEEP.

[b] USE DESCRIPTIVE WORDS BEFORE NOUNS.

A BOY CAME OUT DOORS.

A TALL, SLIM BOY CAME OUT OF THE OLD WHITE HOUSE.

[c]USE LIVELY VERBS.

THE TRACTOR WENT DOWN THE AVENUE.

THE OLD TRACTOR RUMBLED DOWN PARK AVENUE.

[d] USE WORDS THAT RELATE TO THE FIVE SENSES.- SIGHT, TASTE, HEARING, SMELL AND TOUCH.

EXAMPLES :-

1 THE MAN IS A SOCCER PLAYER.

THE SLIM, ATHLETIC MAN IS AN EXPERT SOCCER PLAYER.[SIGHT]

2 ANN OFFERED ME A MANGO.

ANN OFFERED ME A RIPE, JUICY MANGO.[TASTE]

3 WHEN THE VACUUM STOPPED, A SIGNAL SOUNDED.

WHEN THE CLANKING VACUUM STOPPED, A LOUD BUZZER SOUNDED.[HEARING]

4 THE COOK OPENED THE OVEN.

THE COOK OPENED THE OVEN DOOR AND BAKED TURKEY FILLED THE AIR.[SMELL]

5 I PULLED THE SHEET AROUND ME TO FIGHT OFF THE COLD.

I PULLED THE WOOLEN SHEET AROUND ME TO FIGHT OFF THE CHILLING WIND.[TOUCH]

AN EFFECTIVE PARAGRAPH DOES TWO ESSENTIAL THINGS.

[a] IT MAKES A POINT.

[b] IT PROVIDES SPECIFIC DETAILS TO SUPPORT THAT POINT.

THE FOUR ESSENTIAL POINTS IN WRITING IN AN EFFECTIVE WAY ARE

UNITY, SUPPORT, COHERENCE,SENTENCE SKILLS.

1 MAKE ONE POINT AND STICK TO THAT POINT; YOU WILL HAVE UNITY IN YOUR WRITING.

2 IF YOU SUPPORT THE POINT WITH SPECIFIC EVIDENCE; YOU WILL HAVE SUPPORT IN YOUR WRITING.

3 IF YOU ORGANIZE AND CONNECT THE SPECIFIC EVIDENCE; YOU WILL HAVE COHERENCE IN YOUR WRITING.

4 IF YOU WRITE CLEAR, ERROR FREE SENTENCES, YOU WILL HAVE EFFECTIVE SENTENCE SKILLS IN YOUR WRITING.

THE THREE MOST COMMON PURPOSES OF SPEAKING AND WRITING ARE TO INFORM, TO ENTERTAIN, AND TO PERSUADE.

IN HANDLING ANY SUBJECT MATTER, GENERATE IDEAS AND DETAILS BY ASKING ALL THE QUESTIONS YOU CAN THINK OF ABOUT YOUR SUBJECT. SUCH QUESTIONS INCLUDE, WHAT? WHEN? WHO? WHY? HOW? WHERE?

ONE KEY TO EFFECTIVE WRITING IS THE ABILITY TO DISTINGUISH BETWEEN MAJOR IDEAS AND THE DETAILS THAT FIT UNDER THOSE IDEAS.

E.G :-

MAJOR IDEA -- HEADING   MEDICINE.

DETAILS   COUGH SYRUP, TYLENOL, CAPSULES, TABLETS, TONIC, MILK - OF – MAGNESIA ETC .

LISTED ARE THE FIVE DIFFERENT STAGES IN THE COMPOSING AND WRITING A PAPER TO IT'S CONCLUSION.

1 PREWRITING – LISTING SUBJECTS, TOPICS.

2 PREWRITING – LISTING AND OUTLINE.

3 FIRST DRAFT – WRITING WITHOUT CORRECTING MISTAKES.

4 SECOND DRAFT – CORRECTING MISTAKES.

5 FINAL DRAFT – CHECKING TO MAKE SURE EVERYTHING IS IN ORDER – COMPLETION.

TRADITIONALLY, ALL WRITING HAS BEEN DIVIDED INTO FOUR MAJOR FORMS. THEY ARE AS FOLLOWS :-

[a] EXPOSITION.

[b] DESCRIPTION.

[c] NARRATION.

[d] PERSUASION OR ARGUMENTATION.

COLLOQUIALISMS :-

COLLOQUIALISMS ARE EXPRESSIONS USED IN COMMON CONVERSATION.

EXAMPLES :-

A ROUGH DIAMOND   A WELL – LIKED PERSON OF ROUGH MANNERS

SILVER TONGUED	ELOQUENT AND PLAUSIBLE
GOLDEN VOICED	PLEASING TO HEAR
PURSE – PROUD	CONCEITED ABOUT MONEY
THE APPLE OF ONE'S	EYE SOMEBODY SPECIALLY

DEAR

OUT OF SORTS	NOT WELL
ARMED TO THE TEETH	COMPLETELY ARMED
A WET BLANKET	A DISCOURAGING PERSON
ON THE SQUARE	HONEST
DEAD BEAT	EXHAUSTED

STUCK UP	CONCEITED
THICK IN THE HEAD	STUPID
IN THE SAME BOAT	IN THE SAME CIRCUMSTANCES
BESIDE ONESELF	ANGRY
HEAVY EYED	SLEEPY
CARRIED AWAY	HIGHLY EXCITED
A CHIP OF THE OLD BLOCK	VERY MUCH LIKE FATHER
UNDER A CLOUD	IN TROUBLE
DOWN IN THE MOUTH	IN LOW SPIRITS
ALL EARS	PAYING CLOSE ATTENTION
AT A LOOSE END	NOTHING TO DO
A QUEER FISH	AN ODD PERSON
GOOD FOR NOTHING	USELESS
A SON OF A GUN	A RASCAL
HARD OF HEARING	ALMOST DEAF
HARD UP	SHORT OF MONEY
HARD HIT	SERIOUSLY TROUBLED
IN EVIL CASE	POOR
ILL – USED	BADLY TREATED
LION HEARTED	OF GREAT COURAGE
AT LOGGERHEADS	QUARRELING
THE MAN IN THE STREET	AN ORDINARY MAN
UP TO THE MARK	GOOD ENOUGH
AN OLD SALT	AN EXPERIENCED SAILOR
AT REST	DEAD
A PEPPERY INDIVIDUAL	A HOT TEMPERED PERSON

MAKING USE OF "COLOR "WORDS IN EVERYDAY SPEECH.

EXAMPLE :-

[a] HE HAS BLUE BLOOD IN HIS VEINS.

HE IS OF ARISTOCRATIC DESCENT.

[b] I AM IN HIS BLACK BOOKS.

HE IS DISPLEASED WITH ME.

[c] HIS BROTHER WAS A BLUE JACKET.

HIS BROTHER WAS A SEAMAN IN THE NAVY.

[d] HE WAS A GREENHORN AT THE GAME.

HE WAS INEXPERIENCED AT THE GAME.

[e] I SAW IT IN BLACK AND WHITE.

I SAW IT IN WRITING OR PRINT.

[f] THE MAN WAS YELLOW AT HEART.

THE MAN WAS A COWARD.

[g] HE WAS THE BLACK SHEEP OF THE FAMILY.

HE DISGRACED HIS FAMILY.

[h] THE GREEN – EYED MONSTER CAUSED HIM TO STRIKE HIS FATHER

JEALOUSY CAUSED HIM TO STRIKE HIS FATHER.

[I] THE GIRL LOOKED BLUE.

THE GIRL LOOKED AS IF SHE WAS DEPRESSED IN SPIRITS.

[j] SHE WAS IN BLUE FUNK.

SHE WAS IN GREAT TERROR.

[k] "DO YOU SEE ANY GREEN IN MY EYE? "

"DO I LOOK AS IF I COULD BE EASILY IMPOSED UPON?
"

GENERAL COLLOQUIAL EXPRESSIONS :-

TO   TO

DRAW THE LONG BOW TELL INCREDIBLE STORIES

MAKE A CLEAN BREAST OF CONFESS

WEIGH ANCHOR LIFT THE ANCHOR

BURY THE HATCHET MAKE PEACE

KEEP UP APPEARANCES HAVE OUTWARD SHOW

HAVE ONE'S HEART IN ONE'S MOUTH BE FRIGHTENED

HAVE ONE'S HEART IN ONE'S BOOTS BE VERY DESPONDENT

PUT ONE'S BEST FOOT FORWARD DO THE BEST POSSIBLE

SWEEP THE BOARD TAKE ALL

BURN THE CANDLE AT BOTH ENDS OVERDO WORK AND PLAY

MAKE NO BONES ABOUT IT BE PLAIN AND OUTSPOKEN

HAVE A FEATHER IN ONE'S CAP HAVE SOMETHING TO BE PROUD OF

TAKE A RISE OUT OF FOOL

RUB THE WRONG WAY IRRITATE BY OPPOSING

THROW DUST IN THE EYES DECEIVE

KEEP ONE'S POWDER DRY BE READY AND PREPARED

GET INTO HOT WATER GET INTO TROUBLE
DRAW THE LINE FIX THE LIMIT
THROW UP THE SPONGE GIVE UP
THROW IN THE CARDS GIVE UP
SHOW A CLEAN PAIR OF HEELS ESCAPE BY RUNNING
LEAD A DOG'S LIFE HAVE A WRETCHED LIFE
PULL UP SHORT STOP SUDDENLY
KEEP ONE'S DISTANCE STAY ALOOF
KEEP A THING DARK HIDE SOMETHING
WAIT TILL THE CLOUDS ROLL BY AWAIT A SUITABLE TIME
TURN ONE'S COAT CHANGE ONE'S PRINCIPLES
LEAD UP THE GARDEN DECEIVE BY HIDING REAL INTENTION
LEAD A DANCE DELUDE
GIVE THE COLD SHOULDER SHOW INDIFFERENCE OR IGNORE
THROW COLD WATER ON DISCOURAGE
CUT A DASH BE VERY SHOWY
HAVE A CROW TO PLUCK WITH HAVE SOMETHING TO SETTLE
TURN THE TABLES REVERSE A RESULT
SMELL A RAT BE SUSPICIOUS
MAKE BOTH ENDS MEET MANAGE FINANCIALLY
FACE THE MUSIC MEET THE WORSE
RAISE THE WIND OBTAIN MONEY
MIND YOUR P'S AND Q'S BE CAREFUL ABOUT YOUR BEHAVIOR
SIT ON THE FENCE AVOID TAKING SIDES
PUT ONE'S FOOT IN IT TO SPOIL SOMETHING
FALL FOUL OF COME AGAINST
GET INTO HOT WATER GET INTO TROUBLE
RAIN CATS AND DOGS RAIN VERY HEAVILY
KEEP THE POT BOILING KEEP GOING
TAKE FRENCH LEAVE GO WITHOUT PERMISSION
PLAY THE GAME ACT FAIRLY
HIT BELOW THE BELT ACT UNFAIRLY
PAD THE HOOF WALK
SEND ONE PACKING DISMISS QUICKLY
NIP IN THE BUD CUT OFF
HOLD ONE'S TONGUE KEEP SILENT

BLOW ONE'S TRUMPET TO BOAST
SLING MUD SLANDER
MAKE THE MOUTH WATER CAUSE TO DESIRE
HIT THE NAIL ON THE HEAD BE RIGHT
KICK UP A DUST CREATE A ROW
PUT THE CART BEFORE THE HORSE START AT THE WRONG END
BITE THE DUST FALL TO THE GROUND
KNOCK ON THE HEAD STOP SUDDENLY
GO THROUGH THE MILL UNDERGO SUFFERING
TELL IT TO THE MARINES EXPRESS DISBELIEF
TURN OVER A NEW LEAF CONDUCT ONESELF BETTER
PULL ONE'S LEG HOAX
BACK CHAT BE RUDE
GO ON ALL FOURS TRAVEL ON HANDS AND KNEES
BLAZE THE TRAIL LEAD THE WAY
RIDE THE HIGH HORSE BE SNOBBISH
LET THE CAT OUT THE BAG TELL WHAT SHOULD BE KEPT SECRET
SWING THE LEAD AVOID WORK PURPOSELY
PLAY WITH FIRE TEMPT SERIOUS TROUBLE
TURN UP ONE'S NOSE SCORN DELIBERATELY
HAUL OVER THE COALS TO PUNISH OR SCOLD
TAKE THE BULL BY THE HORNS ACT DESPITE RISK
HANG ONE'S HEAD FEEL ASHAMED
LIVE FROM HAND TO MOUTH LIVE IN HARDSHIP
STRIKE WHILE THE IRON IS HOT ACT WITHOUT DELAY
ACT THE GOAT BEHAVE FOOLISHLY
CHEW THE FAT ARGUE
TAKE FORTY WINKS SLEEP

DOUBLE WORDS :-
USED IN SPEECH TO GIVE GREATER EMPHASIS AND BETTER MEANING
1 BY WORDS OF SIMILAR SOUND :-
EXAMPLES :-
WEAR AND TEAR, OUT AND ABOUT, HIGH AND DRY, FAIR AND SQUARE.
2 BY RELATED WORDS :-
EXAMPLES :-

LOCK AND KEY, HEAD AND SHOULDERS, HAND AND FOOT, BODY AND SOUL, HEART AND SOUL, ROOT AND BRANCH.

3 BY REPETITION OF ACTUAL WORDS :-

EXAMPLES :-

OVER AND OVER, BY AND BY, SUCH AND SUCH, SO AND SO,ROUND AND ROUND, AGAIN AND AGAIN.

4 BY REPETITION OF MEANING :-

EXAMPLES :-

NULL AND VOID, ODDS AND ENDS, OUT AND AWAY, FAR AND AWAY, BECK AND CALL, WAY AND MEANS, HUE AND CRY.

5 BY OPPOSITES :-

EXAMPLES :-

COME AND GO, ON AND OFF, GREAT AND SMALL, GIVE AND TAKE, ONE AND ALL, UPS AND DOWNS, IN AND OUT, THIS AND THAT.

6 BY ALLITERATION [WORDS BEGINNING WITH THE SAME LETTER] :-

EXAMPLES :-

KITH AND KIN, PART AND PARCEL, SAFE AND SOUND, SPICK AND SPAN, TIME AND TIDE, ONE AND ONLY, ROUGH AND READY.

7 SOME MORE EXAMPLES ARE :-

HARD AND FAST, ROUGH AND TUMBLE, OVER AND ABOVE, TOUCH AND GO, TIME AND AGAIN, ALL AND SUNDRY, FREE AND EASY.

CULTURE :-

COUNTRY	PEOPLE	LANGUAGE
UNITED STATES	AMERICAN	ENGLISH
NEW ZEALAND	NEW ZEALANDERS	ENGLISH
MAORIS	MAORI	
ITALY	ITALIAN	ITALIAN
AUSTRALIA	AUSTRALIAN	ENGLISH
BELGIUM	BELGIAN	FLEMISH, FRENCH
GUYANA	GUYANESE	ENGLISH
CANADA	CANADIAN	ENGLISH, FRENCH
CHINA	CHINESE	CHINESE
ARABIA	ARABIAN	ARABIC
DENMARK	DANES	DANISH

BULGARIA	BULGARIAN	BULGARIAN
EGYPT	EGYPTIAN	ARABIC
ENGLAND	ENGLISH	ENGLISH
WALES	WELSH	ENGLISH, CYMRIC
SPAIN	SPANISH	SPANISH
SWITZERLAND	SWISS	FRENCH, GERMAN
TURKEY	TURKS	TURKISH
SOUTH AFRICA	SOUTH AFRICANS	E N G L I S H , AFRIKAANS
FINLAND	FINNS	FINNISH
FRANCE	FRENCH	FRENCH
GERMANY	GERMAN	GERMAN
SCOTLAND	SCOTTISH	ENGLISH, GAELIC
PORTUGAL	PORTUGUESE	PORTUGUESE
HOLLAND	DUTCH	DUTCH
GREENLAND	ESKIMO	ESKIMO
POLAND	POLES	POLISH
GREECE	GREEK	GREEK
HUNGARY	HUNGARIAN	MAGYAR
INDIA	INDIAN	H I N D U S T A N I , ENGLISH
JAPAN	JAPANESE	JAPANESE
MEXICO	MEXICAN	SPANISH
NIGERIA	NIGERIAN	YORUBA, HAUSA, IBO,ENGLISH
SIAM	SIAMESE	SIAMESE
ISRAEL	JEWS, ARABS	HEBREW, ARABIC
TRINIDAD	TRINIDADIAN	ENGLISH
BARBADOS	BARBADIAN	ENGLISH
CUBA	CUBANS	SPANISH
BRAZIL	BRAZILIAN	SPANISH

HERE ARE SOME DESCRIPTIVE WORDS THAT CAN BE APPLIED TO PEOPLE :-

GENEROUS
TRUSTWORTHY
HONEST
DISHONEST
INSENSITIVE
AGGRESSIVE
PERSISTENT

COURAGEOUS
SHY
NEAT
SLOPPY
COMPULSIVE
JEALOUS
HARDWORKING
EASYGOING
BAD – TEMPERED
SUPPORTIVE
MATERIALISTIC
SARCASTIC
AMBITIOUS
SUSPICIOUS
OPEN – MINDED
SELF – CENTERED
LAZY
CONSIDERATE
GOOD – HUMORED
INDEPENDENT
DEPENDENT
ARGUMENTATIVE
STUBBORN
COOPERATIVE
SOFTHEARTED
ENERGETIC
DISCIPLINED
DEFENSIVE
RELIABLE
DEPENDABLE
STINGY
PATIENT
IMPATIENT
RESPONSIBLE
IRRESPONSIBLE
SENTIMENTAL
HARSH
RUDE
MANNERLY

EXAMPLES OF USING DESCRIPTIVE WORDS :-
[a] HE LOST HIS SCHOOL BOOK   IRRESPONSIBLE.
[b] SHE HELPED THE OLD MAN CROSS THE ROAD
CONSIDERATE [c] HE LIKES TO DO HIS HOMEWORK
ALONE   CAPABLE, INDEPENDENT.

THE DESCRIPTIVE WORDS SHOW THE QUALITY OF THE
PERSON.

READING ASSIGNMENTS :-
READ UP ABOUT THE FOLLOWING AND LEARN TO DO
THEM THE BEST WAY YOU CAN. GET HELP FROM FAMILY
AND OTHERS AS YOU LEARN TO DO THEM. IT BUILDS SELF
– CONFIDENCE AND INDEPENDENCE.
[a] HOW TO BATHE A PET SUCH AS A DOG, A CAT ETC
.

[b] HOW TO PLAY GAMES THAT INTEREST YOU BOTH
OUTDOORS AND INDOORS SUCH AS BASEBALL, BASKETBALL,
CHECKERS, MONOPOLY ETC .
[c] HOW TO LOAD A CAR TRUNK.
[d] HOW TO PACK – PUT THINGS IN THE FRIDGE.
[e] HOW TO PACK FOODSTUFFS IN A CUPBOARD.
[f] MAKE A TIMETABLE TO DO EFFECTIVE AND EFFICIENT
STUDIES.
[g] HOW TO LEARN A SONG AND SING IT.
[h] HOW TO USE YOUR MONEY ALLOWANCE SENSIBLY.
[I] HOW TO PLANT A KITCHEN OR FLOWER GARDEN.
[j] HOW TO WATER AND TAKE CARE OF PLANTS.
[k] HOW TO DO SIMPLE SCIENCE PROJECTS E.G. FIND
OUT HOW THE MAGNET WORKS.
[l] HOW TO DO LAUNDRY.
[m] LEARN TO WASH DISHES WELL.
[n] LEARN TO CLEAN A BATHROOM.
[o] LEARN TO PACK AND PUT AWAY YOUR CLOTHES IN
THE RESPECTIVE DRAWERS.
[p] HOW TO BE CONSIDERATE AND MAKE PEOPLE
HAPPY.
[q] HOW TO GO ABOUT GREETING AND MEETING
PEOPLE.
[r] HOW TO LIVE A DISCIPLINED LIFE.

[s] LEARNING NOT TO PROCRASTINATE; BUT TO HAVE PRIORITIES AND GET THINGS ACCOMPLISHED.

[t] HOW TO WRITE A POEM AND LEARN IT.

HAVE LOTS OF FUN LEARNING, STAY FOCUSED, CONCENTRATE AND LEARN. YOUR FUTURE DEPENDS ON IT.

COMPARING AND CONTRASTING :-

COMPARISON AND CONTRAST ARE TWO THOUGHT PROCESSES WE CONSTANTLY PERFORM IN EVERYDAY LIFE. IN COMPARING TWO THINGS WE SHOW HOW THEY ARE SIMILAR; WHEN WE CONTRAST TWO THINGS WE SHOW HOW THEY ARE DIFFERENT. THE PURPOSE OF COMPARING OR CONTRASTING IS TO UNDERSTAND EACH OF THE TWO THINGS MORE CLEARLY AND, AT TIMES, TO MAKE JUDGEMENTS AND DECISIONS ABOUT THEM.

EXAMPLES OF COMPARING AND CONTRASTING :-

[a] TWO TELEVISION SHOWS; WHEEL OF FORTUNE AND THE PRICE IS RIGHT.

[b] TWO MAKES OF CARS; HONDA AND TOYOTA.

[c] TWO KINDS OF FRUITS; BANANA AND APPLE.

[d] YOUR FATHER AND YOUR MOTHER.

[e] THE BENEFITS OF MILK AND ORANGE JUICE TO THE HUMAN BODY

WRITING ASSIGNMENTS :-

WRITE A COMPARISON OR CONTRASTING PARAGRAPH ON EACH OF THE FOLLOWING.

[a] TWO PARENTS.

[b] TWO FRIENDS.

[c] TWO RELATIVES.

[d] TWO TEACHERS.

[e] TWO SINGERS.

[f] TWO ACTORS.

[g] TWO PETS.

[h] TWO WAYS OF STUDYING.

[I] TWO CARS.

[j] TWO BOOKS.

EXAMPLE :-

MY MOM IS SHORT AND FAT; SHE IS VERY LOVING AND NICE TO ME

MY DAD IS TALL AND THIN; HE IS VERY ATHLETIC AND SERIOUS; HE DISCIPLINES ME.

DEFINITIONS OF THE FOLLOWING :-

1 ALPHABET -- LETTERS OF A LANGUAGE; IN THE REGULAR ORDER.

2 PHRASE -- GROUP OF WORDS, NOT A CLAUSE OR SENTENCE, CONVEYING A SINGLE IDEA.

3 CLAUSE -- PART OF A SENTENCE, WITH A SUBJECT AND VERB.

4 SENTENCE -- GROUP OF WORDS STATING SOMETHING.

5 PARAGRAPH - DISTINCT SECTION OF A PIECE OF WRITING, BEGUN ON A NEW LINE AND OFTEN INDENTED.

6 ESSAY -- IS A PAPER OF SEVERAL PARAGRAPHS.

7 MANUSCRIPT -- WRITTEN OR TYPED BOOK.

8 BOOK -- A BOUND, PRINTED WORK.

9 BIOGRAPHY -- ONE'S LIFE STORY WRITTEN BY ANOTHER.

10 COMPOSITION - TO WRITE AND COMBINE IN PROPER FORM; A SONG, POEM ETC .

11 PRECIS - TO GIVE A SUMMARY.

CHAPTER 7.

THE NAMES OF SOME TYPE OF PERSONS :-
ATHLETE
ACTOR
ACTRESS
BABY
CHIEF
COOK
STUDENT
PUPIL
TEACHER
LECTURER
PHOTOGRAPHER
CAMPER
GRANDPARENT
MUSICIAN
HUNTER
MUSICIAN
OUTDOORS PERSON
DRUG ADDICT
FOOTBALL PLAYER
BASEBALL PLAYER
BASKETBALL PLAYER
TENNIS PLAYER
WRESTLER
PAINTER
ARTIST
CHEERLEADER

CARPENTER
PASTOR
RABBI
WORLD TRAVELER
ROLLER SCATER
ALCHOLIC
CLOWN
PRIEST
PRINCIPAL

THE NAMES OF SOME TYPES OF PLACES :-
GYMNASIUM
SCHOOL
COLLEGE
UNIVERSITY
RESTAURANT
LADIES' ROOM
MEN'S ROOM
MOVIE THEATER
RECORD STUDIO
HOUSE
PALACE
GARAGE
HAIR SALON
DOCTOR'S OFFICE
DENTIST'S OFFICE
BANK
POLICE STATION
DRESSING ROOM
ATTIC
CELLAR
BASEMENT
MARKET
STORE
SHOP

INTERESTING TYPES OF PEOPLE :-
DANCER
SINGER
ACTOR
ACTRESS

TEACHER
LECTURER
POLICE OFFICER
SOLDIER
CLERGYMAN
MANAGER
JOKER
BARTENDER
MOVIE PERSONALITY
TELEVISION PERSONALITY

AN EMOTIONAL PREDOMINANT CONDITION :-
HAPPINESS
ANGER
HATE
PRIDE
FEAR
JEALOUSY
SATISFACTION
DISAPPOINTMENT
EMBARRASSMENT
SYMPATHY
SHYNESS
BITTERNESS
NOSTALGIA
SURPRISE
VIOLENCE
SILLINESS
ENVY
FRUSTRATION
SHOCK
LOVE
SADNESS
RELIEF
TERROR
LOSS

THE PRESENT PARTICIPLE IS FOUND BY ADDING "-ING "TO THE PRESENT TENSE.

PRESENT TENSE PRESENT PARTICIPLE

GIVE	GIVING
THROW	THROWING
BEGIN	BEGINNING
FALL	FALLING
LEAVE	LEAVING
MAKE	MAKING
SELL	SELLING
BEAT	BEATING
CHEAT	CHEATING
KICK	KICKING
RUN	RUNNING
EAT	EATING
BUY	BUYING
BLOW	BLOWING
MAKE	MAKING
RIDE	RIDING

NOTE :- IN MOST CASES THE "-E "IS DROPPED BEFORE ADDING "-ING ".

THE PRESENT INFINITIVE IS FOUND BY PLACING "TO "BEFORE THE PRESENT TENSE.

PRESENT TENSE	PRESENT INFINITIVE
EAT	TO EAT
DRINK	TO DRINK
RUN	TO RUN
PLAY	TO PLAY
DANCE	TO DANCE

WORDS THAT ARE PRONOUNCED ALIKE BUT DIFFER IN MEANING :-

[a] A FLIGHT OF STEPS	STAIRS.
TO LOOK FIXEDLY	STARE.
[b] IN THAT PLACE	THERE.
BELONGING TO THEM	THEIR.
[c] BELONGING TO US	OUR.
SIXTY MINUTES	HOUR.
[d] BRANCH OF TREE	BOUGH.
FRONT OF SHIP	BOW.
[e] PLACE FOR GOLF	COURSE.

ROUGH	COARSE.
[f] NO	NAY.
CRY OF A HORSE	NEIGH.
[g] A KIND OF METAL	LEAD.
GUIDED BY SOMEONE	LED.

USE THE CORRECT PARTS OF THE VERBS IN THE BLANK SPACES :-

[a] [DREAM] THE GIRL WAS DREAMING ABOUT SCHOOL

[b] [AWAKE] THE OLD MAN WAS AWAKEN BY THE NOISE.

[c] [SEE] SHE SAW HER UNCLE YESTERDAY.

[d] [GO] THE OLD LADY HAD GONE FOR A DRIVE.

[e] [FALL] THE BABY FELL ASLEEP IN THE CRIB.

FILL IN EACH SPACE CORRECTLY WITH ONE OF THESE WORDS :-

RISEN, RAISED, ROSE, RAISE, RISE.

[a] THE MOON HAD RISEN IN THE SKY.

[b] HE TRIED TO RAISE THE COVER OF THE POT.

[c] I SAW HER RISE FROM HER SEAT.

[d] YESTERDAY THE MAN ROSE AT SEVEN O'CLOCK FOR WORK.

[e] WHEN HE SAW THE QUEEN HE RAISED HIS HAT.

VALUED POSSESSIONS :-
HOUSE
FURNITURE
COMPUTER
CAMERA
PHOTOGRAPH ALBUM
CLOTHING
RADIO
TELEVISION SET
JEWELRY
CAR
JEEP
BUS
VAN
TRUCK

APPLIANCES
STEREO SYSTEM
EXERCISE EQUIPTMENT
TELEPHONE
MONEY

ON READING AND WRITING :-
IT'S IMPORTANT TO KNOW HOW TO READ AND WRITE. ILLITERACY IS A SERIOUS AND COSTLY PROBLEM IN THE WORLD. THE CONSEQUENCES OF NOT KNOWING TO READ AND WRITE ARE IMMEASURABLE. KNOWING TO READ AND WRITE WELL; THAT IS TO HAVE KNOWLEDGE GIVES US THE BEST OPPORTUNITIES IN LIFE. YOUR EDUCATION IS YOUR BEST ASSET; IT IS WHAT TAKES YOU THROUGH LIFE SUCCESSFULLY.

ALWAYS ENDEAVOR TO IMPROVE UPON YOUR KNOWLEDGE; USE YOUR GIFTS, TALENTS AND ABILITIES TO BENEFIT YOUR LIFE. USE YOUR TIME WISELY, MAKE SURE YOU ALWAYS HAVE TIME TO READ, DEVELOP YOUR READING SKILLS, READING BOOKS IS USEFUL, SENSIBLE AND PRACTICAL. THE RESULTS OF NOT READING ARE GRAVE; YOU BECOME STAGNANT IN LIFE, YOUR SOCIAL CONSCIENCE LIES DORMANT, AND WE LOSE OUR BEST OPPORTUNITY TO EXPLORE OUR INNER SELVES AND LEARN ABOUT THIS UNIVERSE IN WHICH WE LIVE. READING IS FOR YOUR OWN BEST INTEREST; MAKE READING ONE OF YOUR HOBBIES, YOU WILL BE GLAD YOU DID.

HERE IS A LIST OF NORMAL-REGULAR JOB OPPORTUNITIES - CAREERS SORT FOR :-

TAXI DRIVERS
TRUCK DRIVERS
BUS DRIVERS
CLERKS
SALES WORKERS
CASHIERS
RETAIL ASSISTANTS
ACCOUNTANTS
AUDITORS
LAWYERS

DOCTORS
MACHINE OPERATORS
SWITCHBOARD OPERATORS
SECRETARY
COSMETOLOGISTS
CIVIL ENGINEERS
MECHANICAL ENGINEERS
WAITER
WAITRESS
COOKS
CHEFS
SECURITY GUARDS
NURSING ATTENDANTS
NURSING AIDS
LICENSED PRACTICAL NURSES
REGISTERED NURSES
TEACHERS
BARTENDERS
DANCERS
CARPENTERS
ELECTRICIANS
ELECTRONICS TECHNICIANS
COMPUTER OPERATORS
COMPUTER PROGRAMMERS
AUTO MECHANICS
HAIR DRESSER

CHAPTER 8.

COUNTRIES AND THEIR CAPITALS :-

COUNTRY	CAPITAL
ARGENTINE	BUENOS AIRES
AUSTRALIA	CANBERRA
AFGHANISTAN	KABUL
ALBANIA	TIRANA
ALGERIA	ALGIERS
ANDORRA	ANDORRA LA VELLA
ANGOLA	LUANDA
ANTIGUA AND BARBUDA	ST. JOHN'S
ARMENIA	YEREVAN
AUSTRIA	VIENNA
AZERBAIJAN	BAKU
BAHAMAS	NASSAU
BAHRAIN	MANAMA
BANGLADESH	DHAKA
BARBADOS	BRIDGETOWN
BELARUS	MINSK
BELIZE	BELMOPAN
BENIN	PORTO – NOVO
BHUTAN	THIMBU
BOLIVIA	SUCRE, LA PAZ
BOSNIA AND HERCEGOVINA	SARAJEVO
BOTSWANA	GABORONE
BRUNEI	BANDAR SERI BEGAWAN
BULGARIA	SOFIA
BURKINA FASO	OUAGADOUGOU

BURMA [MYANMAR]	RANGOON [YANGON]
BURUNDI	BUJUMBURA
BELGIUM	BRUSSELS
BRAZIL	BRASILIA
CANADA	OTTAWA
CAMBODIA	PHNOM PENH
CAMEROON	YAOUNDE
CAPE VERDE	PRAIA
CENTRAL AFRICAN REPUBLIC	BANGUI
CHAD	N'DJAMENA
CHILE	SANTIAGO
CHINA	BEIJING
COLUMBIA	BOGOTA
COMOROS	MORONI
CONGO	BRAZZAVILLE
COSTA RICA	SAN JOSE
CROATIA	ZAGREB
CUBA	HAVANA
CYPRUS	LEFKOSIA
CZECH REPUBLIC	PRAGUE
CZECHOSLOVKIA	PRAGUE
DENMARK	COPENHAGEN
DJIBOUTI	DJIBOUTI
DOMINICA	ROSEAU
DOMINICAN REPUBLIC	SANTO DOMINGO
ECUADOR	QUITO
EGYPT	CAIRO
EL SALVADOR	SAN SALVADOR
EQUATORIAL GUINEA	MALABO
ERITREA	ASMARA
ESTONIA	TALLINN
ETHIOPIA	ADDIS ABABA
FIJI	SUVA
FINLAND	HELSINKI
GABON	LIBREVILLE
GAMBIA	BANJUI
GEORGIA	TBILISI
GERMANY	BERLIN
GHANA	ACCRA
GRENADA	ST. GEORGE
GUATEMALA	GUATEMALA CITY

GUINEA	CONAKRY
GUINEA – BISSAU	BISSAU
GUYANA	GEORGETOWN
JAMAICA	KINGSTON
TRINIDAD AND TOBAGO	PORT OF SPAIN
ENGLAND	LONDON
FRANCE	PARIS
GREECE	ATHENS
HAITI	PORT – AU – PRINCE
HONDURAS	TEGUCIGALPA
HOLLAND	AMSTERDAM
HUNGARY	BUDAPEST
ICELAND	REYKJAVIK
INDIA	NEW DELHI
INDONESIA	JAKARTA
IRAN	TEHRAN
IRAQ	BAGHDAD
IRELAND	DUBLIN
ISRAEL	JERUSALEM
IVORY COAST	YAMOUSSOUKRO
ITALY	ROME
JAPAN	TOKYO
JORDAN	AMMAN
KAZAKHSTAN	AKMOLA
KENYA	NAIROBI
KIRIBATI	TARAWA
KOREA	PYONGYANG
KUWAIT	KUWAIT CITY
KYRGYZSTAN	BISHKEK
LAOS	VIENTIANE
LATVIA	RIGA
LEBANON	BEIRUT
LESOTHO	MASERU
LIBERIA	MONROVIA
LIBYA	TRIPOLI
LIECHTENSTEIN	VADUZ
LITHUANIA	VILNIUS
LUXEMBOURG	LUXEMBOURG
MACEDONIA	SKOPJE
MADAGASCAR	ANTANANARIVO
MALAWI	LILONGWE

MALAYSIA	KUALA LUMPUR
MALDIVES	MALE
MALI	BAMAKO
MALTA	VALLETTA
MARSHALL ISLANDS	DALAP – ULIGA – DARRIT
MAURITANIA	NOUAKCHOTT
MAURITIUS	PORT LOUIS
MEXICO	MEXICO CITY
MICRONESIA	PALIKIR
MOLDOVA	CHISINAU
MONGOLIA	ULAN BATOR
MOROCCO	RABAT
MOZAMBIQUE	MAPUTO
NAMIBIA	WINDHOEK
NAURU	YAREN
NEPAL	KATMANDU
NEW ZEALAND	WELLINGTON
NIGERIA	ABUJA
NETHERLANDS	AMSTERDAM
NICARAGUA	MANAGUA
NIGER	NIAMEY
NORWAY	OSLO
OMAN	MUSCAT
PALAU	KOROR
PANAMA	PANAMA CITY
PAPUA NEW GUINEA	PORT MORESBY
PARAGUAY	ASUNCION
PERU	LIMA
PHILIPPINES	MANILA
PAKISTAN	ISLAMABAD
SCOTLAND	EDINBURGH
POLAND	WARSAW
RUMANIA	BUCHAREST
PORTUGAL	LISBON
QATAR	DOHA
ROMANIA	BUCHAREST
RUSSIA	MOSCOW
RWANDA	KIGALI
ST KITTS AND NEVIS	BASSETERRE
ST LUCIA	CASTRIES
ST VINCENT AND THE	

GRENADINES	KINGSTON
SAN MARINO	SAN MARINO
SAO TOME AND PRINCIPE	SAO TOME
SAUDI ARABIA	RIYADH
SENEGAL	DAKAR
SEYCHELLES	VICTORIA
SIERRA LEONE	FREETOWN
SINGAPORE	SINGAPORE
SLOVAKIA	BRATISLAVA
SLOVENIA	LJUBLJANA
SOLOMON ISLANDS	HONIARA
SOMALIA	MOGADISHU
SOUTH AFRICA	PRETORIA
SPAIN	MADRID
SRI LANKA	COLOMBO
SWEDEN	STOCKHOLM
SWITZERLAND	BERNE
SUDAN	KHARTOUM
SURINAME	PARAMARIBO
SWAZILAND	MBABANE
SYRIA	DAMASCUS
TAIWAN	TAIPEI
TAJIKISTAN	DUSHANBE
TANZANIA	DODOMA
THAILAND	BANGKOK
TOGO	LOME
TONGA	NUKU' ALOFA
TUNISIA	TUNIS
TURKEY	ANKARA
TURKMENISTAN	ASHGABAT
TUVALU	FUNAFUTI
UGANDA	KAMPALA
UKRAINE	KIEV
UNITED ARAB EMIRATES	ABU DHABI
UNITED STATES OF AMERICA	WASHINGTON, DC
URUGUAY	MONTEVIDEO
UZBEKISTAN	TASHKENT
VANUATU	VILA
VENEZUELA	CARACAS
VIETNAM	HANOI
WESTERN SAMOA	APIA

YEMEN	SANA
YUGOSLAVIA	BELGRADE
ZAIRE	KINSHASA
ZAMBIA	LUSAKA
ZIMBABWE	HARARE

DIMINUTIVES :- THIS REFERS TO THINGS IN THEIR SMALLEST FORM -- TINY.

EXAMPLES :-
STREAMLET
LOCKET
ROSETTE
DAMSEL
OWLET
STATUETTE
MORSEL
CIRCLET
POCKET
WAGGONETTE
NAPKIN
CODLING
DUCKLING
GOSLING
PORKLING
SEEDLING
NESTLING
GLOBULE
MOLECULE
BOOKLET
CHICKEN
BRACELET
CYGNET
KITTEN
GOBLET
EAGLET
CIGARETTE
LEAFLET
ISLET
CUBICLE
RINGLET
KITCHENETTE

RIVULET
PARTICLE
HILLOCK

CURRENCIES OF VARIOUS COUNTRIES :-

UNITED STATES	DOLLAR, CENT.
NEW ZEALAND	DOLLAR, CENT.
AUSTRALIA	DOLLAR, CENT.
BARBADOS	DOLLAR, CENT.
CANADA	DOLLAR, CENT.
JAMAICA	DOLLAR, CENT.
TRINIDAD AND TOBAGO	DOLLAR, CENT.
GUYANA	DOLLAR, CENT.
ITALY	LIRA, CENTESIMI.
INDIA	RUPEE, PAISE.
JAPAN	YEN
MEXICO	PESO, CENTAVO.
ARGENTINA	PESO, CENTAVO.
BELGIUM	FRANC, CENTIME.
CHINA	YUAN
DENMARK	KRONE, ORE.
EGYPT	POUND, PIASTRE.
FRANCE	FRANC, CENTIME.
GERMANY	DEUTSCHE MARK.
HOLLAND	GUILDER, CENT.
GREECE	DRACHMA, LEPTON.
NIGERIA	NAIRA, KOBO.
POLAND	ZLOTY, GROSZ.
PORTUGAL	ESCUDO, CENTAVO
SPAIN	PESETA, CENTIMO
AUSTRIA	SCHILLING
BAHAMAS	DOLLAR
BANGLADESH	TAKA
BELARUS	RUBLE
BOLIVIA	BOLIVIANO
BOTSWANA	PULA
BRAZIL	REAL
BULGARIA	LEV
BURMA	KYAT
CAMBODIA	RIEL

CHILE	PESO
COLOMBIA	PESO
CUBA	PESO
CROATIA	KUNA
COSTA RICA	COLON
ECUADOR	SUCRE
EL SALVADOR	COLON
ETHIOPIA	BIRR
FIJI	DOLLAR
FINLAND	MARKKA
HAITI	GOURDE
HONDURAS	LEMPIRA
HONG KONG	DOLLAR
HUNGARY	FORINT
ICELAND	KRONA
INDONESIA	RUPIAH
IRAN	RIAL
IRAQ	DINAR
IRELAND	POUND
ISRAEL	NEW SHEKEL
KENYA	SHILLING
KOREA	WON
KUWAIT	DINAR
LAOS	KIP
LEBANON	POUND
LIBERIA	DOLLAR
LIBYA	DINAR
MADAGASCAR	FRANC
MALAYSIA	RINGGIT
MALTA	LIRA
MONACO	FRENCH FRANC
MOROCCO	DIRHAM
MOZAMBIQUE	METICAL
NAMIBIA	RAND
NEPAL	RUPEE
NETHERLANDS	GUILDER
NORWAY	KRONE
PAKISTAN	RUPEE
PANAMA	BALBOA
PAPUA NEW GUINEA	KINA
PERU	NEW SOL

PHILIPPINES	PESO
POLAND	ZLOTY
PORTUGAL	ESCUDO
ROMANIA	LEU
SAUDI ARABIA	RIYAL
SINGAPORE	DOLLAR
SOUTH AFRICA	RAND
SPAIN	PESETA
SRI LANKA	RUPEE
SUDAN	DINAR
SURINAME	GUILDER
SWAZILAND	LILANGENI
SWEDEN	KRONA
SWITZERLAND	FRANC
TAIWAN	DOLLAR
TANZANIA	SHILLING
THAILAND	BAHT
TURKEY	LIRA
UGANDA	SHILLING
URUGUAY	PESO URUGUAYO
VENEZUELA	BOLIVAR
VIETNAM	DONG
YEMEN	RIAL
YUGOSLAVIA	NEW DINAR
ZAIRE	NEW ZAIRE
ZAMBIA	KWACHA
ZIMBABWE	DOLLAR

NOTE :-THERE HAS BEEN A GROUPING OF SEVERAL EUROPEAN COUNTRIES WHICH NOW USE THE COMMON CURRENCY CALLED THE - EURO. ACTUALLY THE EURO IS THE CURRENCY OF TWELVE EUROPEAN UNION COUNTRIES NAMELY :-

BELGIUM
GERMANY
GREECE
SPAIN
FRANCE
IRELAND
ITALY
LUXEMBOURG

NETHERLANDS
AUSTRIA
PORTUGAL
FINLAND

AN ADVERB ADDS TO THE MEANING OF A VERB.
SOME REGULARLY USED VERBS WITH SUITABLE
ADVERBS :-

VERBS	ADVERBS
FELL	HEAVILY, SUDDENLY.
DECIDED	IMMEDIATELY, CAREFULLY.
CREPT	SLOWLY, SILENTLY, STEALTHILY, QUIETLY.
ACTED	WONDERFULLY, WARILY.
EXPLAINED	CLEARLY, CONCISELY, BRIEFLY.
CHARGED	DESPERATELY, FURIOUSLY, BRAVELY, BOLDLY.
ATE	HUNGRILY, GREEDILY, WARILY.
BLED	OPENLY, PROFUSELY, SLIGHTLY, FREELY.
FOUGHT	BRAVELY, FURIOUSLY, COWARDLY.
LEFT	HURRIEDLY, SUDDENLY, QUIETLY, QUICKLY.
LISTENED	ATTENTIVELY, ANXIOUSLY, CAREFULLY.
ANSWERED	IMMEDIATELY, CORRECTLY, WRONGLY.
LOST	TERRIBLY, BADLY, HEAVILY, SPORTINGLY.
FROWNED	SULKILY, DISGUSTINGLY, WORRIEDLY.
MUMBLED	INAUDIBLY, INDISTINCTLY.
RAN	HURRIEDLY, QUICKLY, SLOWLY.
PONDERED	THOUGHTFULLY, CAREFULLY, SERIOUSLY.
SANG	LUSTILY, SWEETLY, SOFTLY, TUNEFULLY.
REMEMBERED	DISTINCTLY, CLEARLY, VIVIDLY, FAINTLY.
SLEPT	SOUNDLY, QUIETLY, LIGHTLY.
SHONE	BRIGHTLY, CLEARLY, BRILLIANTLY.
TREMBLED	VISIBLY, FEARFULLY, TERRIBLY.
WALKED	SLOWLY, QUICKLY, SMARTLY, SLOUCHINGLY.
WEPT	SADLY, TOUCHINGLY, BITTERLY.
SPOKE	PLAINLY, CLEARLY, LOUDLY, QUIETLY.
SPENT	FOOLISHLY, SPARINGLY, FREELY.
WAITED	ANXIOUSLY, PATIENTLY, LONGINGLY.
SPRANG	SUDDENLY, QUICKLY, HURRIEDLY.

SMILED   OPENLY, HAPPILY, BROADLY.
WHISPERED QUIETLY, WEAKLY, AUDIBLY, SOFTLY.

ALWAYS TRY TO AVOID USING THE WORD "GOT ". THERE IS USUALLY ANOTHER WORD THAT CAN BE USED TO BETTER EFFECT.
SUBSTITUTE A BETTER WORD IN EACH OF THE FOLLOWING SENTENCES.
[a] SHE GOT A BAD COLD YESTERDAY. CAUGHT.
[b] HE GOT TO THE BUS STATION IN TIME. REACHED
[c] HE GOT HIS LUNCH EARLY. HAD.
[d] SHE GOT A DOLLAR FROM HER FATHER. RECEIVED.
[e] THE WOMAN GOT UP AT TEN O'CLOCK. WOKE.

WORDS ENDING IN "– ABLE ":-
[a] A TELEGRAM FROM OVERSEAS. CABLE.
[b] A HORSE'S HOME.   STABLE.
[c] A PIECE OF FURNITURE.   TABLE.
[d] DIAMONDS ARE   VALUABLE.
[e] A CARROT   VEGETABLE.
[f] GLASS THINGS ARE   BREAKABLE.

A SINGLE WORD FOR EACH OF THE FOLLOWING :-
[a] TO GO OUT   EXIT.
[b] TO GO INTO   ENTER.
[c] TO GO QUICKLY   RAPIDLY.
[d] TO GO BACK   RETREAT.
[e] TO GO AWAY   LEAVE.
[f] TO GO DOWN   DESCEND.
[g] TO GO UP   ASCEND.
[h] TO GO FORWARD   ADVANCE.

PROVERBS :-
PROVERBS ARE REGULAR, POPULAR SAYINGS EXPRESSED IN A PRECISE, CLEVER AND BRIEF MANNER.
EXAMPLES :-
HABIT IS SECOND NATURE.
HALF A LOAF IS BETTER THAN NONE.
HE LAUGHS BEST WHO LAUGHS LAST.
HE GOES A – SORROWING WHO GOES A – BORROWING.
IN FOR A PENNY IN FOR A POUND.

LEAVE WELL ALONE.
LET NOT THE POT CALL THE KETTLE BLACK.
LET SLEEPING DOGS LIE.
GREAT OAKS FROM LITTLE ACORNS GROW.
GREAT MINDS THINK ALIKE.
FORTUNE KNOCKS ONCE AT EVERY MAN'S DOOR.
FIRST COME FIRST SERVED.
FIRE IS A GOOD SERVANT BUT A BAD MASTER.
A FAINT HEART NEVER WON A FAIR LADY.
FAR FROM COURT FAR FROM CARE.
EXPERIENCE TEACHES FOOLS.
EXCHANGE IS NO ROBBERY.
EVERY TIDE HAS ITS EBB.
LITTLE BOYS SHOULD BE SEEN AND NOT HEARD.
LOOK AFTER THE CENTS AND THE DOLLARS WILL TAKE CARE OF THEMSELVES.
LOOK BEFORE YOU LEAP.
MAKE HAY WHILE THE SUN SHINES.
A BAD WORKMAN QUARRELS WITH HIS TOOLS.
A DROWNING MAN WILL CLUTCH AT A STRAW.
ABSENCE MAKES THE HEART GROW FONDER.
A FOOL AND HIS MONEY ARE SOON PARTED.
A BIRD IN THE HAND IS WORTH TWO IN THE BUSH.
A FRIEND IN NEED IS A FRIEND INDEED.
A HUNGRY MAN IS AN ANGRY MAN.
A MISS IS AS GOOD AS A MILE.
AN APPLE A DAY KEEPS THE DOCTOR AWAY.
ALL'S WELL THAT ENDS WELL.
A PENNY SAVED IS A PENNY GAINED.
A STITCH IN TIME SAVES NINE.
A ROLLING STONE GATHERS NO MOSS.
A SMALL LEAK WILL SINK A GREAT SHIP.
BETTER HALF A LOAF THAN NO BREAD.
AS YOU MAKE YOUR BED SO YOU MUST LIE ON IT.
BETTER LATE THAN NEVER.
AS THE TWIG IS BENT SO IS THE TREE INCLINED.
CHARITY BEGINS AT HOME.
BIRDS OF A FEATHER FLOCK TOGETHER.
CUT YOUR COAT ACCORDING TO YOUR CLOTH.
EARLY TO BED, EARLY TO RISE.
DON'T CARRY ALL YOUR EGGS IN ONE BASKET.

DON'T COUNT YOUR CHICKENS BEFORE THEY ARE HATCHED.

DISCRETION IS THE BETTER PART OF VALOR.

EVERY DOG HAS ITS DAY.

EMPTY VESSELS MAKE THE MOST SOUND.

ENOUGH IS AS GOOD AS A FEAST.

EVERY CLOUD HAS A SILVER LINING.

SILENCE GIVES CONSENT.

MISERY MAKES STRANGE BEDFELLOWS.

NECESSITY IS THE MOTHER OF INVENTION.

MORE HASTE, LESS SPEED.

NO CROSS NO CROWN.

NO NEWS IS GOOD NEWS.

NEW BROOMS SWEEP CLEAN.

NO SMOKE WITHOUT FIRE.

OUT OF SIGHT, OUT OF MIND.

ONE MAN'S MEAT IS ANOTHER MAN'S POISON.

ONCE BITTEN TWICE SHY.

ONE GOOD TURN DESERVES ANOTHER.

PENNY WISE POUND FOOLISH.

PRIDE GOES BEFORE A FALL.

OUT OF THE FRYING PAN INTO THE FIRE.

ROBBING PETER TO PAY PAUL.

SET A THIEF TO CATCH A THIEF.

STILL WATERS RUN DEEP.

SPARE THE ROD AND SPOIL THE CHILD.

SPEECH IS SILVER, SILENCE GOLDEN.

THE EARLY BIRD CATCHES THE WORM.

THE LEAST SAID THE SOONEST MENDED.

TWO HEADS ARE BETTER THAN ONE.

TOO MANY COOKS SPOIL THE BROTH.

WHEN THE CAT'S AWAY THE MICE WILL PLAY.

WE NEVER MISS THE WATER TILL THE WELL RUNS DRY.

UNION IS STRENGTH.

WHERE THERE'S A WILL THERE'S A WAY.

USEFUL INFORMATION :-

ABRASIVES :- SUBSTANCES USED FOR GRINDING OR POLISHING.

THE MOHS SCALE LISTS MINERALS IN THE ORDER OF THEIR HARDNESS [FROM SOFTEST TO HARDEST] SHOWS THEIR RELATIVE EFFECTIVENESS AS ABRASIVES.

1 TALC.
2 GYPSUM
3 CALCITE
4 FLUORITE
5 APATITE
6 FELDSPAR
7 QUARTZ
8 TOPAZ
9 CORUNDUM
10 DIAMOND

ABERRATION -IN OPTICS, A CONDITION THAT CAUSES A BLURRING AND LOSS OF CLEARNESS IN THE IMAGES PRODUCED BY LENSES OR MIRRORS.

ACADEMY -A GROUP OF PEOPLE VOLUNTARILY ASSOCIATED TO DISCUSS ART, SCIENCE OR LITERATURE.

ACCESSORY -IN LAW, A PERSON WHO IS NOT THE CHIEF ACTOR IN AN OFFENCE AND IS NOT PRESENT WHEN IT IS COMMITTED, BUT WHO STILL IS CONNECTED WITH IT IN SOME OTHER WAY.

ACETIC ACID -AN ORGANIC ACID BELONGING TO THE FATTY ACID SERIES. IN ITS DILUTE STATE IT IS KNOWN AS VINEGAR.

ACETYLENE -A COLORLESS GAS. IT IS USED AS A FUEL AND AS A RAW MATERIAL TO PRODUCE NUMEROUS VALUABLE SUBSTANCES INCLUDING ACETIC ACID, VARIOUS VINYL PLASTICS, AND SYNTHETIC RUBBER.

ACLINIC LINE OR MAGNETIC EQUATOR, AN IMAGINARY, IRREGULAR LINE CIRCLING THE EARTH NEAR THE GEOGRAPHICAL EQUATOR. THE ATTRACTION OF THE NORTH AND SOUTH MAGNETIC POLES IS EQUAL AT ALL POINTS ON THIS LINE. FOR THIS REASON A COMPASS NEEDLE IS

NEUTRALIZED AND WILL NOT DIP WHEN IT IS ON THE ACLINIC LINE.

ACT -A STATUTE OR LAW PASSED BY A CONGRESS, PARLIAMENT, OR OTHER LEGISLATIVE BODY.

ACT OF GOD -A LEGAL EXPRESSION USED TO COVER NATURAL AND ACCIDENTAL DISASTERS BEYOND THE CONTROL OF MAN. CYCLONES, HAILSTORMS, STROKES OF LIGHTNING, AND STORMS AT SEA ARE ACTS OF GOD IN A LEGAL SENSE.

ACTOR OR ACTRESS -A PERSON WHO TAKES THE PART OF A CHARACTER IN A PLAY. AN ACTOR MAY PERFORM ON THE STAGE, OR IN MOTION PICTURES, RADIO, OR TELEVISION.

VITAL SIGNS :- IS A TERM USED IN DIAGNOSTIC MEDICINE TO INCLUDE FOUR OBSERVABLE PHENOMENA IN PATIENTS : TEMPERATURE, PULSE, RESPIRATION RATE, AND BLOOD PRESSURE.

CHAPTER 9.

THE UNITED STATES AND CAPITALS :-

STATES	CAPITAL
ALABAMA	MONTGOMERY
ALASKA	JUNEAU
ARIZONA	PHOENIX
ARKANSAS	LITTLE ROCK
CALIFORNIA	SACRAMENTO
COLORADO	DENVER
CONNECTICUT	HARTFORD
DELAWARE	DOVER
DISTRICT OF COLUMBIA	
FLORIDA	TALLAHASSEE
GEORGIA	ATLANTA
HAWAII	HONOLULU
IDAHO	BOISE
ILLINOIS	SPRINGFIELD
INDIANA	INDIANAPOLIS
IOWA	DES MOINES
KANSAS	TOPEKA
KENTUCKY	FRANKFORT
LOUISIANA	BATON ROUGE
MAINE	AUGUSTA
MARYLAND	ANNAPOLIS
MASSACHUSETTS	BOSTON
MICHIGAN	LANSING
MINNESOTA	ST. PAUL

MISSISSIPPI	JACKSON
MISSOURI	JEFFERSON CITY
MONTANA	HELENA
NEBRASKA	LINCOLN
NEVADA	CARSON CITY
NEW HAMPSHIRE	CONCORD
NEW JERSEY	TRENTON
NEW MEXICO	SANTA FE
NEW YORK	ALBANY
NORTH CAROLINA	RALEIGH
NORTH DAKOTA	BISMARCK
OHIO	COLUMBUS
OKLAHOMA	OKLAHOMA CITY
OREGON	SALEM
PENNSYLVANIA	HARRISBURG
RHODE ISLAND	PROVIDENCE
SOUTH CAROLINA	COLUMBIA
SOUTH DAKOTA	PIERRE
TENNESSEE	NASHVILLE
TEXAS	AUSTIN
UTAH	SALT LAKE CITY
VERMONT	MONTPELIER
VIRGINIA	RICHMOND
WASHINGTON	OLYMPIA
WEST VIRGINIA	CHARLESTON
WISCONSIN	MADISON
WYOMING	CHEYENNE

OUTLYING AREAS OF THE UNITED STATES OF AMERICA.:-

COUNTRY	CAPITAL
AMERICAN SAMOA	PAGO PAGO
GUAM	AGANA
NORTHERN MARIANA ISLANDS	SAIPAN
PUERTO RICO	SAN JUAN
VIRGIN ISLANDS	CHARLOTTE AMALIE

UNITED NATIONS :- THE PURPOSE OF THE UNITED NATIONS IS TO HELP CONFLICT PREVENTION; KEEPING THE PEACE AMONG NATIONS OF THE WORLD BEFORE AS WELL

AS AFTER POST CONFLICT; INTERNATIONAL JUSTICE AND OTHER ORGANIZATIONAL ACTIVITIES.

THE UNITED NATIONS SYSTEM OF ORGANIZATIONAL ACTIVITIES COMPRISES OF :-

ACC :-ADMINISTRATIVE COMMITTEE ON COORDINATION.

CEB :-ECONOMIC COMMISSION FOR AFRICA IN ETHIOPIA

ECE :-ECONOMIC COMMISSION FOR EUROPE IN GENEVA, SWITZERLAND

ECLAC :-ECONOMIC COMMISSION FOR LATIN AMERICA AND THE CARIBBEAN IN SANTIAGO, CHILE

ESCAS :-ECONOMIC AND SOCIAL COMMISSION FOR ASIA AND THE PACIFIC IN BANGKOK, THAILAND

ESCWA :-ECONOMIC AND SOCIAL COMMISSION FOR WESTERN ASIA IN BEIRUT, LEBANON

UNDOF :-UN DISENGAGEMENT OBSERVER FORCE.

UNFICYP :-UN PEACE – KEEPING FORCE IN CYPRUS

UNIFIL :-UN INTERIM FORCE IN LEBANON

UNMOGIP :-UN MILITARY OBSERVER GROUP IN INDIA AND PAKISTAN.

UNTSO :-UN TRUCE SUPERVISION ORGANIZATION IN PALESTINE.

INSTRAW :-INTERNATIONAL RESEARCH AND TRAINING INSTITUTE FOR THE ADVANCEMENT OF WOMEN.[SANTO DOMINGO]

UNICEF :-UN CHILDREN'S FUND.[NEW YORK]

UNCTAD :-UN CONFERENCE ON TRADE AND DEVELOPMENT.[GENEVA]

UNHCR :-UN HIGH COMMISSIONER FOR REFUGEES.[GENEVA]

UNITAR :-UN INSTITUTE FOR TRAINING AND RESEARCH.[NEW YORK]

WFP :-UN/FAO WORLD FOOD PROGRAM.[ROME]

UNDP :-UN DEVELOPMENT PROGRAM.[NEW YORK]

UNIDO :-UN INDUSTRIAL DEVELOPMENT ORGANIZATION.[VIENNA]

UNEP :-UN ENVIRONMENT PROGRAM.[NAIROBI]

UNC :-UN UNIVERSITY.[TOKYO]

WFC :-WORLD FOOD COUNCIL.[ROME]

UNCHS :-UN CENTER FOR HUMAN SETTLEMENTS.[NAIROBI]

UNFPA :-UN FUND FOR POPULATION ACTIVITIES.[NEW YORK]

IAEA :-INTERNATIONAL ATOMIC ENERGY AGENCY.[VIENNA]

GATT :-GENERAL AGREEMENT ON TARIFFS AND TRADE.[GENEVA]

ILO :-INTERNATIONAL LABOR ORGANIZATION.[GENEVA]

FAO :-UN FOOD AND AGRICULTURE ORGANIZATION.[ROME]

UNESCO :-UN EDUCATIONAL, SCIENTIFIC, AND CULTURAL ORGANIZATION.[PARIS]

WHO :-WORLD HEALTH ORGANIZATION.[GENEVA]

IMF INTERNATIONAL MONETARY FUND.[WASHINGTON]

IBRD :-INTERNATIONAL BANK FOR RECONSTRUCTION AND DEVELOPMENT.[WASHINGTON]

IDA :-INTERNATIONAL DEVELOPMENT ASSOCIATION.[WASHINGTON]

IFC :-INTERNATIONAL FINANCE CORPORATION.[WASHINGTON]

ICAO :-INTERNATIONAL CIVIL AVIATION ORGANIZATION.[MONTREAL]

UPU :-UNIVERSAL POSTAL UNION.[BERN]

ITU :-INTERNATIONAL TELECOMMUNICATION UNION.[GENEVA]

WMO :-WORLD METEOROLOGICAL ORGANIZATION.[GENEVA]

IMO :-INTERNATIONAL MARITIME ORGANIZATION.[LONDON]

WIPO :-WORLD INTELLECTUAL PROPERTY ORGANIZATION.[GENEVA]

IFAD :-INTERNATIONAL FUND FOR AGRICULTURAL DEVELOPMENT [ROME]

HLCM :-HIGH LEVEL COMMITTEE ON MANAGEMENT IN GENEVA.

IANWGE :-INTER – AGENCY NETWORK ON WOMEN AND GENDER EQUALITY IN NEW YORK

ICJ :-INTERNATIONAL COURT OF JUSTICE THE HAGUE, NETHERLANDS

IFAD :-INTERNATIONAL FUND FOR AGRICULTURAL DEVELOPMENT IN ROME, ITALY

WTO :-WORLD TRADE ORGANIZATION IN GENEVA, SWITZERLAND

WORLD TOURISM ORGANIZATION IN MADRID, SPAIN

UNITED NATIONS CHILDREN'S FUND IN NEW YORK, U.S.A

OFFICE FOR OUTER SPACE

MEDIA AND PEACE INSTITUTE IN PARIS, FRANCE.

AMONG OTHERS.

THE UNITED NATIONS ESTABLISHES ITS HEADQUARTERS IN THE UNITED STATES OF AMERICA IN THE STATE OF NEW YORK.

THE MEMBER COUNTRIES OF THE UNITED NATIONS ARE :-

AFGHANISTAN

ALBANIA

ALGERIA

ANDORRA

ANGOLA

ANTIGUA AND BARBUDA

ARGENTINA

ARMENIA

AUSTRALIA

AUSTRIA

AZERBAIJAN

BAHAMAS

BAHRAIN

BANGLADESH

BARBADOS

BELARUS

BELGIUM

BELIZE

BENIN

BHUTAN

BOLIVIA

BOSNIA AND HERZEGOVINA

BOTSWANA

BRAZIL
BRUNEI DARUSSALAM
BULGARIA
BURKINA FASO
BURUNDI
CAMBODIA
CAMEROON
CANADA
CAPE VERDE
CENTRAL AFRICAN REPUBLIC
CHAD
CHILE
CHINA
COLOMBIA
COMOROS
CONGO
COSTA RICA
COTE D'LVOIRE
CROATIA
CUBA
CYPRUS
CZECH REPUBLIC
DEMOCRATIC PEOPLE REPUBLIC OF KOREA
DEMOCRATIC REPUBLIC OF THE CONGO
DENMARK
DJIBOUTI
DOMINICA
DOMINICAN REPUBLIC
ECUADOR
EGYPT
EL SALVADOR
EQUATORIAL GUINEA
ERITREA
ESTONIA
ETHIOPIA
FIJI
FINLAND
FRANCE
GABON
GAMBIA
GEORGIA

GERMANY
GHANA
GREECE
GRENADA
GUATEMALA
GUINEA
GUINEA BISSAN
GUYANA
HAITI
HONDURAS
ICELAND
INDIA
INDONESIA
IRAN
IRAQ
IRELAND
ISRAEL
ITALY
JAMAICA
JAPAN
JORDAN
KAZAKHSTAN
KENYA
KIRIBATI
KUWAIT
KYRGYZSTAN
LAO PEOPLE'S DEMOCRATIC REPUBLIC
LATVIA
LEBANON
LESOTHO
LIBERIA
LIBYAN ARAB JAMAHIRIYA
LIECHTENSTEIN
LITHUANIA
LUXEMBOURG
MADAGASCAR
MALAWI
MALAYSIA
MALDIVES
MALI
MALTA

MARSHALL ISLANDS
MAURITANIA
MAURITUS
MEXICO
MICRONESIA
MONACO
MONGOLIA
MOROCCO
MOZAMBIQUE
MYANMAR
NAMIBIA
NAURU
NEPAL
NETHERLANDS
NEW ZEALAND
NICARAGUA
NIGER
NIGERIA
NORWAY
OMAN
PAKISTAN
PALAU
PANAMA
PAPAU NEW GUINEA
PARAGUAY
PERU
PHILIPPINES
POLAND
PORTUGAL
QATAR
REPUBLIC OF KOREA
REPUBLIC OF MOLDOVA
ROMANIA
RUSSIAN FEDERATION
RWANDA
ST. KITTS AND NEVIS
ST. LUCIA
ST. VINCENT AND THE GRENADINES
SAMOA
SAN MARINO
SAO TOME AND PRINCIPE

SAUDI ARABIA
SENEGAL
SERBIA AND MONTENEGRO
SEYCHELLES
SIERRA LEONE
SINGAPORE
SLOVAKIA
SLOVENIA
SOLOMON ISLAND
SOMALIA
SOUTH AFRICA
SPAIN
SRI LANKA
SUDAN
SURINAME
SWAZILAND
SWEDEN
SWITZERLAND
SYRIAN ARAB REPUBLIC
TAJIKISTAN
THAILAND
THE FORMER YUGOSLAVIA REPUBLIC OF MACEDONIA
TIMOR – LESTE
TOGO
TONGA
TRINIDAD AND TOBAGO
TUNISIA
TURKEY
TURKMENISTAN
TUVALU
UGANDA
UKRAINE
UNITED ARAB EMIRATES
UNITED KINGDOM OF GREAT BRITAIN AND NORTHERN
IRELAND
UNITED REPUBLIC OF TANZANIA
UNITED STATES OF AMERICA
URUGUAY
UZBERKISTAN
VANUAKU
VENEZUELA

VIETNAM
YEMEN
ZAMBIA
ZIMBABWE

THE PRESIDENTS OF THE UNITED STATES OF AMERICA

YEAR	PRESIDENT ELECTED.
1789	GEORGE WASHINGTON
1792	GEORGE WASHINGTON
1796	JOHN ADAMS
1800	THOMAS JEFFERSON
1808	JAMES MADISON
1812	JAMES MADISON
1816	JAMES MONROE
1820	JAMES MONROE
1824	JOHN QUINCY ADAMS
1828	ANDREW JACKSON
1832	ANDREW JACKSON
1836	MARTIN VAN BUREN
1840	WILLIAM H HARRISON
1844	JAMES K POLK
1848	ZACHARY TAYLOR
1852	FRANKLIN PIERCE
1856	JAMES C BUCHANAN
1860	ABRAHAM LINCOLN
1864	ABRAHAM LINCOLN
1868	ULYSSES S GRANT
1872	ULYSSES S GRANT
1876	RUTHERFORD B HAYES
1880	JAMES A GARFIELD
1884	GROVER CLEVELAND
1888	BENJAMIN HARRISON
1892	GROVER CLEVELAND
1896	WILLIAM McKINLEY
1900	WILLIAM McKINLEY
1904	THEODORE ROOSEVELT
1908	WILLIAM H TAFT
1912	WOODROW WILSON
1916	WOODROW WILSON
1920	WARREN G HARDING

1924	CALVIN COOLIDGE
1928	HERBERT HOOVER
1932	FRANKLIN D ROOSEVELT
1936	FRANKLIN D ROOSEVELT
1940	FRANKLIN D ROOSEVELT
1944	FRANKLIN D ROOSEVELT
1948	HARRY S TRUMAN
1952	DWIGHT D EISENHOWER
1956	DWIGHT D EISENHOWER
1960	JOHN F KENNEDY
1964	LYNDON B JOHNSON
1968	RICHARD M NIXON
1972	RICHARD M NIXON
1976	JIMMY CARTER
1980	RONALD W REGAN
1984	RONALD W REGAN
1988	GEORGE H W BUSH
1992	BILL CLINTON
1996	BILL CLINTON
2000	GEORGE BUSH

MIDDLE EASTERN COUNTRIES :-
ALGERIA
BAHRAIN
CYPRUS
EGYPT
IRAN
IRAQ
ISRAEL
JORDAN
KUWAIT
LEBANON
LIBYA
MOROCCO
OMAN
QATAR
SAUDI ARABIA
SUDAN
SYRIA
TUNISIA
TURKEY

UNITED ARAB EMIRATES
YEMEN

MAJOR ETHNIC GROUPS OF THE MIDDLE EAST :-

[a] ARABS -THE OVERWHELMING MAJORITY OF PEOPLE IN THE MIDDLE EAST, ARE DESCENDED FROM ANCIENT PEOPLE OF THE ARABIAN PENINSULA AND ARE BOUND BY THE COMMON LANGUAGE OF ARABIC.

[b] JEWS -TRACE THEIR LINEAGE TO AN ANCIENT MIDDLE EASTERN PEOPLE CALLED HEBREWS.

[c] PERSIANS -MAKE UP THE MAJORITY OF IRAN'S POPULATION AND FORM SMALLER GROUPS IN OTHER COUNTRIES. THEY ARE DESCENDED FROM AN ANCIENT ASIAN PEOPLE CALLED ARYANS.

[d] TURKS -ARE DESCENDANTS OF AN ANCIENT PEOPLE THAT LIVED IN CENTRAL ASIA AND MAKE UP THE MAJORITY OF THE POPULATION IN TURKEY.

[e] KURDS -ARE PEOPLE OF A MOUNTAINOUS REGION IN SOUTHWEST ASIA THAT EXTENDS OVER PARTS OF ARMENIA, IRAN, IRAQ, SYRIA, AND TURKEY.

[f] BERBERS -LIVE IN NORTHWEST AFRICA AND THE SAHARA REGION AND SPEAK A WIDE VARIETY OF BERBER DIALECTS.

[g] NUBIANS -ARE PEOPLE OF MIXED AFRICAN, ARAB, AND MEDITERRANEAN ANCESTRY. THEY LIVE ALONG THE NILE RIVER IN SOUTHERN EGYPT AND IN SUDAN.

COUNTRIES OF LATIN AMERICA :-
ANTIGUA AND BARBUDA
ARGENTINA
BAHAMAS
BARBADOS
BELIZE
BOLIVIA
BRAZIL
CHILE
COLOMBIA
COSTA RICA
CUBA
DOMINICA
DOMINICAN REPUBLIC

ECUADOR
EL SALVADOR
GRENADA
GUATEMALA
GUYANA
HAITI
HONDURAS
JAMAICA
MEXICO
NICARAGUA
PANAMA
PARAGUAY
PERU
PUERTO RICO
ST. KITTS AND NEVIS
ST. LUCIA
ST. VINCENT AND THE GRENADINES
SURINAME
TRINIDAD AND TOBAGO
URUGUAY
VENEZUELA

CHAPTER 10.

ELEMENTS COMPOSING THE HUMAN BODY.
[THE FIGURE SHOWN ARE APPROXIMATE PERCENTAGES BY WEIGHT]

OXYGEN	65.00
CARBON	18.00
HYDROGEN	10.00
NITROGEN	3.00
CALCIUM	2.00
PHOSPHORUS	1.00
POTASSIUM	0.35
SULFUR	0.25
CHLORINE	0.15
SODIUM	0.15
MAGNESIUM	0.05
ALL OTHER	0.05

MAMMALS :- EXAMPLES OF LIVING ORDERS.

[a] PRIMATES, MAMMALS WITH THE MOST HIGHLY DEVELOPED BRAIN MAN, MONKEY.

[b] CARNIVORA, THE FLESH EATERS DOG, LION.

[c] ARTIODACTYLA, EVEN – TOED MAMMALS WITH HOOFS   SHEEP

[d] CETACEA,MAMMALS COMPLETELY ADAPTED TO LIFE IN WATER   WHALE.

[e] CHIROPTERA, FLYING MAMMALS BAT.

[f] DERMOPTERA, GLIDING MAMMALS. THERE ARE ONLY TWO SPECIES   FLYING LEMUR.

[g] EDENTATA, A PRIMITIVE GROUP LIVING IN CENTRAL AND SOUTH AMERICA, AND IN THE SOUTHWESTERN UNITED STATES   ANTEATER, ARMADILLO, GROUND   SLOTH; SLOTH.

[h] HYRACOIDEA, FROM ASIA AND AFRICA CONIES.

[I]   INSECTIVORA, PRIMITIVE, INSECT – EATING MAMMALS   MOLE.

[j] LAGOMORPHA, SMALL, LEAPING MAMMALS   PIKA, RABBITS, HARES.

[k] MARSUPIALIA, MAMMALS THAT CARRY THEIR YOUNG IN A POUCH KANGAROO.

[l] PERISSODACTYLA, HOOFED MAMMALS WITH AN ODD NUMBER OF TOES HORSE.

[m] PHOLIDOTA, OF ASIA AND AFRICA   PANGOLINS, OR SCALY ANTEATERS.

[n]   PROBOSCIDEA, HOOFED   MAMMALS   WITH PROBOSCISES   ELEPHANT.

[o]   RODENTIA, GNAWING   MAMMALS. THIS   IS   THE LARGEST ORDER OF MAMMALS RODENT, BEAVER.

[p] SIRENIA,   MANATEE – SEA COWS.

[q] TUBULIDENTATA, FOUND ONLY IN AFRICA AARDVARK.

[r] MONOTREMATA   PLATYPUS – DUCKBILL.

BRANCHES OF MATHEMATICS :-
[a] ARITHMETIC.
[b] ALGEBRA.
[c] GEOMETRY.
[d] TRIGONOMETRY.
[e] THE CALCULUS.
[f] STATISTICS.
[g] SYMBOLIC LOGIC.
[h] TOPOLOGY.
[I] THEORY OF GAMES.

EXAMPLES OF MINERALS AND ROCKS :-
[a] GOLD
[b] COPPER.
[c] QUARTZ.
[d] GRANITE
[e] GRAPHITE.

[f] BERYL.
[g] AGATE.
[h] ASBESTOS.
[I] CORUNDUM.
[j] FELDSPAR.
[k] FLINT.
[l] GARNET.
[m] HEMATITE.
[n] JADE.
[o] MICA.
[p] OBSIDIAN.
[q] SOAPSTONE.
[r] SLATE.

PLANTS BELONGING TO THE MINT FAMILY.
[a] THYME.
[b] BALM.
[c] LAVENDER.
[d] BASIL.
[e] BERGAMOT.
[f] CATNIP.
[g] HOREHOUND.
[h] HYSSOP.
[I] MARJORAM.
[j] OSWEGO TEA.
[k] PENNYROYAL.
[l] ROSEMARY.
[m] SAVORY.
[n] SPEARMINT.
[o] PEPPERMINT.
[p] SAGE.

THE WORLD'S HIGHEST MOUNTAINS :-
CONTINENT   ELEVATION
FEET   METERS

NORTH AMERICA
MOUNT McKINLEY [ALASKA RANGE] U.S.A 20,320 6,194
MOUNT LOGAN [St.ELIAS Mts.] CANADA 19,850 6,050
ORIZABA OR CITLALTEPETL. MEXICO 18,700 5,700

MOUNT St.ELIAS [St.ELIAS Mts.] CANADA – U.S.A 18,008 5,489

EUROPE
ELBRUS [CAUCASUS Mts.] SOVIET UNION 18,510 5,642
MOUNT KAZBEK [CAUCASUS Mts.] SOVIET UNION 16,558 5,047
MONT BLANC [ALPS] FRANCE 15,771 4,807
MONTE ROSA [ALPS] SWITZERLAND – ITALY 15,203 4,634

SOUTH AMERICA
ACONCAGUA [ANDES] ARGENTINA 22,834 6,960
BONETE [ANDES] ARGENTINA 22,546 6,872
OJOS DEL SALADO [ANDES] ARGENTINA – CHILE 22,539 6,870
TUPUNGATO [ANDES] ARGENTINA – CHILE 22,310 6,800

AFRICA
KILIMANJARO TANZANIA 19,340 5,895
MOUNT KENYA KENYA 17,058 5,199
MOUNT STANLEY [RUWENZORI] UNGANDA – CONGO 16,763 5,109
RAS DASHAN ETHIOPIA 15,158 4,620

ASIA
MOUNT EVEREST [HIMALAYAS] NEPAL – CHINA 29,028 8,848
MOUNT GODWIN AUSTEN OR K2 [KARAKORAM RANGE] KASHMIR – CHINA 28,250 8,611
KANCHENJUNGA [HIMALAYAS] NEPAL – INDIA 28,208 8,598
MAKALU [HIMALAYAS] NEPAL – CHINA 27,824 8,481

AUSTRALIA
MOUNT KOSCIUSKO [AUSTRALIAN ALPS] 7,310 2,228

ANTARCTICA
VINSON MASSIF [ELLSWORTH Mts.] 16,860 5,139
MOUNT TYREE [ELLSWORTH Mts.] 16,290 4,965

IN GREEK MYTHOLOGY, THE NINE GODDESSES WHO PRESIDED WERE :

CALLIOPE	MUSIC AND EPIC POETRY.
CLIO	HISTORY
ERATO	LOVE POETRY.
EUTERPE	LYRIC POETRY.
MELPOMENE	TRAGEDY
POLYHYMNIA	SACRED POETRY
TERPSICHORE	DANCE AND SONG.
THALIA	COMEDY AND PASTORAL POETRY.
URANIA	ASTRONOMY.

CHAPTER 11.

MUSICAL INSTRUMENT :- A DEVICE THAT PRODUCES MUSICAL SOUNDS. INSTRUMENTS ARE TRADITIONALLY DIVIDED INTO THREE BROAD CLASSES -PERCUSSION, STRING, AND WIND.

PERCUSSION :-

BELL.
CASTANETS
CELESTA
CHIME
CYMBAL
DRUM
GLOCKENSPIEL
GONG
MARIMBA
TAMBOURINE
TRIANGLE
XYLOPHONE

STRING :-

AEOLIAN HARP
BALALAIKA
BANJO
BASS VIOL
CELLO

CLAVICHORD
CONTRABASS
DULCIMER
GUITAR
HARP
HARPSICHORD
HURDY – GURDY
LUTE
LYRE
MANDOLIN
PIANO
SITAR
UKULELE
VIOL
VIOLA
VIOLIN
VIRGINAL
ZITHER

WIND :-

BRASS INSTRUMENT
REED INSTRUMENT
WIND INSTRUMENT
WOODWIND INSTRUMENT

ALSO :-

MECHANICAL :-
CARILLON
HAND ORGAN
MUSIC BOX

ELECTRONIC :-
GUITAR
VIBRAPHONE
ORGANS

ADOLESCENCE :-THE PERIOD OF LIFE BETWEEN CHILDHOOD AND ADULTHOOD. IT STARTS WITH PUBERTY, THE PHYSICAL BEGINNING OF WOMANHOOD AND MANHOOD,

AT ABOUT THE AGE OF TWELVE IN GIRLS AND FOURTEEN IN BOYS. IT EXTENDS TO MATURITY, ABOUT THE AGE OF EIGHTEEN TO TWENTY ONE.

GOALS OF ADOLESCENCE :-

AS THEY DEVELOP FROM THE DEPENDENCE OF CHILDHOOD INTO THE INDEPENDENCE OF ADULTHOOD, ADOLESCENCE FACE SEVERAL TASKS OR GOALS.

EACH MUST LEARN TO :-

1 ACCEPT ONE'S BODY AND APPEARANCE AND ONE'S MASCULINE OR FEMININE ROLE.

2 ACHIEVE EMOTIONAL INDEPENDENCE OF PARENTS AND OTHER ADULTS.

3 ACCEPT ONE'S RESPONSIBILITIES TO THE COMMUNITY AND SOCIETY

4 DEVELOP WAYS OF GETTING ALONG WITH OTHERS OF THE SAME AGE OF BOTH SEXES.

5 BUILD STANDARDS OF MORAL AND RELIGIOUS VALUES.

6 SELECT AND PREPARE FOR AN OCCUPATION.

7 PREPARE FOR MARRIAGE AND FAMILY LIFE.

ACHIEVEMENT OF THESE IS IMPORTANT IF THE TASKS AN ADOLESCENT WILL FACE AS AN ADULT ARE TO BE ACCOMPLISHED SUCCESSFULLY. PARENTS AND TEACHERS CAN HELP BY UNDERSTANDING EACH TASK WITH WHICH AN ADOLESCENT IS STRUGGLING AT ANY PARTICULAR TIME.

FABLE :-BRIEF TALE HAVING A MORAL STORY.
EXAMPLES OF SAYINGS FROM FABLES ARE :-
[a] UNITED WE STAND, DIVIDED WE FALL.
[b] FAMILIARITY BREEDS CONTEMPT.
[c] PUT YOUR SHOULDER TO THE WHEEL.
[d] THE GOD HELP THOSE THAT HELP THEMSELVES.
[e] PLEASE ALL AND YOU WILL PLEASE NONE.
[f] IT IS ADVISABLE TO LET WELL ENOUGH ALONE.
[g] IT IS EASY TO BE BRAVE FROM A SAFE DISTANCE.
[h] I AM SURE THE GRAPES ARE SOUR.
[I] IT IS EASY TO DESPISE WHAT YOU CANNOT GET.

THE COUNTRIES AND CAPITALS OF AFRICA :-

COUNTRIES	CAPITALS
ALGERIA	ALGIERS
ANGOLA	LUANDA
BASUTOLAND	MASERU
BECHUANALAND PROTECTORATE	MAFEKING
BURUNDI	BUJUMBURA
CAMEROUN	YAOUNDE
CANARY ISLANDS	SANTA CRUZ DE TENERIFE
CAPE VERDE ISLANDS	PRAIA
CENTRAL AFRICAN REPUBLIC	BANGUI
CHAD	Ft.LAMY
COMORO ARCHIPELAGO, OR COMORES [ISLANDS]	DZAOUNDZI
CONGO	BRAZZAVILLE
CONGO REPUBLIC	LEOPOLDVILLE
DAHOMEY	PORTO NOVO
EGYPT	CAIRO
ETHIOPIA	ADDIS ABABA
GABON	LIBREVILLE
GAMBIA	BATHURST
GHANA	ACCRA
GUINEA	CONAKRY
IFNI	SIDI IFNI
IVORY COAST	ABIDJAN
KENYA	NAIROBI
LIBERIA	MONROVIA
LIBYA	TRIPOLI
MADAGASCAR OR MALAGASY REPUBLIC	TANANARIVE
MADEIRA ISLANDS	FUNCHAL
MALAWI	ZOMBA
MALI	BAMAKO
MAURITANIA	NOUAKCHOTT
MAURITIUS	PORT LOUIS
MOROCCO	RABAT
MOZAMBIQUE	LOURENCO MARQUES
NIGER	NIAMEY

NIGERIA	LAGOS
PORTUGUESE GUINEA	BISSAU
RHODESIA	SALISBURY
RWANDA	KIGALI
SAO TOME E PRINCIPE [ISLANDS]	SAO TOME
St.HELENA ISLAND	JAMESTOWN
SENEGAL	DAKAR
SEYCHELLES [ISLANDS]	VICTORIA
SIERRA LEONE	FREETOWN
SOMALIA	MOGADISCIO
SOMALILAND	DJIBOUTI
SOUTH AFRICA	PRETORIA , CAPETOWN
SOUTH WEST AFRICA	WINDHOEK
SPANISH GUINEA	SANTA ISABEL
SPANISH SAHARA	AIUN
SUDAN	KHARTOUM
SWAZILAND	MBABANE
TANZANIA	DAR ES SALAAM
TOGO	LOME
TUNISIA	TUNIS
UGANDA	KAMPALA
UPPER VOLTA	OUAGADOUGOU
ZAMBIA	LUSAKA

AIR IS VERY IMPORTANT AND ESSENTIAL IN THIS WORLD.:-

AIR IS A MIXTURE OF NITROGEN [ABOUT SEVENTY – EIGHT PERCENT], OXYGEN [ABOUT TWENTY – ONE PERCENT AT SEA LEVEL], CARBON DIOXIDE, WATER VAPOR, ARGON, AND OTHER GASES.

[a] HUMAN BEINGS BREATHE IN OXYGEN AND BREATHE OUT CARBON DIOXIDE.

[b] WITHOUT AIR, THERE WOULD BE NO SOUND, BECAUSE SOUND IS CAUSED BY AIR WAVES STRIKING THE AIR DRUM.

[c] PLANT LEAVES BREATHE IN CARBON DIOXIDE FROM AIR. THE PLANTS ABSORBS THE CARBON. THE LEAVES GIVE OFF OXYGEN TO THE AIR.

[d] NODULES ON THE ROOTS OF SUCH PLANTS AS ALFALFA AND CLOVER ENRICH THE SOIL BY TAKING NITROGEN FROM THE AIR AND ADDING IT TO THE EARTH.

[e]AIRPLANES, PARACHUTES, AND BALLOONS ARE SUPPORTED BY THE WEIGHT OF AIR.

[f] ARTIFICIAL AIR CURRENTS ARE CREATED BY MAN FOR COOLING, DRYING, AND CLEANING.

[g] EVEN FISHES MUST HAVE AIR. MOST HAVE AIR SACS.

[h] NATURAL AIR CURRENTS DRIVE SAILING VESSELS, TURN WINDMILLS, AND DO OTHER JOBS FOR MAN.

[I] AIR CAN BE COMPRESSED TO DRIVE MACHINES LIKE PAINT SPRAYERS AND PAVEMENT – BREAKERS.

[j] THE IRON LUNG AND OTHER MACHINES OPERATED BY AIR PUMP, ALLOWS A PARALYZED PERSON TO BREATHE.

[k] AIR – FILLED TIRES SUPPORT VEHICLES INCLUDING CARS, BUSES AND TRUCKS.

ALCOHOL HAS IMPORTANT USES IN THIS WORLD.
DIRECT USES OF ALCOHOL.
[a] MOTOR FUEL.
[b] ANTI – FREEZE
[c] SOURCE OF HEAT AND LIGHT.
[d] DISINFECTANTS AND SEDATIVES.
PRODUCTS CONTAINING ALCOHOL.
[a] SYNTHETIC CHEMICALS.
[b] SYNTHETIC RUBBER.
[c] LIQUOR.
[d] EXPLOSIVES.
[e] ANESTHETIC.
[f] CLEANING FLUID.
[g] FLAVORING EXTRACT.
[h] ACETIC ACID.
[I] PRESERVATIVE.
ALCOHOL IS USED IN THE MANUFACTURE OF :-
[a] PAINT AND LACQUER.
[b] SOAP.
[c] INKS.
[d] CELLULOID.
[e] PERFUMES.
[f] DYES.

[g] DRUGS.
[h] FILM.

AN ALLOY IS METAL MIXTURE.
PRINCIPAL ALLOYS.
1 BRONZES.
2 ALUMINUM.
3 IRON.
4 BRASSES.
5 FUSIBLE ALLOYS.
6 AMALGAMS.
7 LEAD.
8 MAGNESIUM.
9 ZINC.
10 NICKEL.
11 TIN.
12 PRECIOUS METALS.

GOLD IS OFTEN ALLOYED WITH COPPER TO GIVE IT STRENGTH. PURE GOLD IS CALLED TWENTY – FOUR CARAT; EIGHTEEN CARAT GOLD WOULD BE EIGHTEEN PARTS GOLD AND SIX PARTS COPPER.

SILVER IS USUALLY ALLOYED WITH COPPER.
PLATINUM IS COMMONLY ALLOYED WITH IRIDIUM.

ANGLE :-
IN PLANE GEOMETRY, A FIGURE FORMED BY TWO RAYS [PORTIONS OF STRAIGHT LINES] THAT START FROM THE SAME POINT. THE TWO RAYS ARE THE SIDES OF THE ANGLE, AND THE POINT WHERE THEY MEET IS CALLED THE VERTEX.

TYPES OF ANGLES.
1 ACUTE.
2 OBTUSE.
3 RIGHT.
4 STRAIGHT.
5 REFLEX
6 COMPLEMENTARY.
7 SUPPLEMENTARY.

THE STUDY OF ANIMALS IS DONE AS IT RELATES TO :-
1 AGRICULTURE.
2 ECOLOGY.
3 ANIMAL HUSBANDRY.
4 BIOLOGY.
5 ZOOLOGY.
6 PALEONTOLOGY.
7 ACCLIMATIZATION
8 ADAPTATION
9 ANIMAL WORSHIP.
10 CELL.
11 EVOLUTION
12 HEREDITY.
13 HIBERNATION.
14 INSECTICIDE.
15 INSTINCT.
16 OSMOSIS.
17 PARASITE
18 VETERINARY MEDICINE.

CLASSIFICATION OF ANIMALS :-
THE ANIMAL KINGDOM IS DIVIDED INTO TWO BROAD GROUPS -THE INVERTEBRATES [ANIMALS WITHOUT BACKBONES] AND THE VERTEBRATES [ANIMALS WITH BACKBONES]

THE INVERTEBRATES ARE COMPLICATED AND ARE DIVIDED INTO A NUMBER OF MAJOR GROUPS, EACH KNOWN AS A PHYLUM. THE PHYLUM IS IN TURN DIVIDED IN THIS MANNER   CLASS, ORDER, FAMILY, GENUS, SPECIES. THE DOMESTIC CAT FOR EXAMPLE BELONGS TO THE PHYLUM CHORDATA, CLASS MAMMALIA, ORDER CARNIVORA, FAMILY FELIDAE, GENUS FELIS, SPECIES DOMESTICUS.

THE CLASSIFICATION OF ANIMALS AND PLANTS IS CALLED TAXONOMY.

VERTEBRATE ANIMALS ARE :-
[a] BIRDS.
[b] MAMMALS.

[c] AMPHIBIANS.
[d] REPTILES.
[e] FISHES.

CHAPTER 12.

MAN'S QUEST TO REACH THE NORTH POLE.

THE FOLLOWING TABLE SHOWS HOW EXPLORERS GRADUALLY GOT NEARER TO THE NORTH POLE [90 DEGREES LATITUDE] UNTIL ROBERT E PEARY FINALLY REACHED THAT GOAL APRIL 6, 1909.

YEAR	EXPLORER	LATITUDE
1588	JOHN DAVIS [ENGLISH]	72 DEGREES 12 MINUTES.
1594	WILLIAM BARENTS [DUTCH]	77 DEGREES 20 MINUTES.
1607	HENRY HUDSON [ENGLISH]	80 DEGREES 23 MINUTES.
1806	WILLIAM SCORESBY [ENGLISH]	81 DEGREES 30 MINUTES.
1827	SIR WILLIAM PARRY [ENGLISH]	82 DEGREES 45 MINUTES.
1876	SIR GEORGE NARES [ENGLISH]	83 DEGREES 20 MINUTES.
1882	A. W. GREELY [U. S. A.]	83 DEGREES 24 MINUTES.
1896	FRIDTJOF NANSEN [NORWEGIAN]	86 DEGREES 14 MINUTES.
1897	DUKE OF THE ABRUZZI [ITALIAN]	86 DEGREES 33 MINUTES.
1906	ROBERT E PEARY [U. S. A.]	87 DEGREES 06 MINUTES.
1909	ROBERT E PEARY [U. S. A.]	90 DEGREES.

ASTRONOMY :-THE SCIENCE OF HEAVENLY BODIES.

THE PLANETS :-
1 EARTH
2 MARS
3 PLUTO
4 VENUS
5 MERCURY
6 JUPITER
7 SATURN
8 URANUS
9 NEPTUNE

THE ZODIAC :-A BELT OF TWELVE CONSTELLATIONS.
1 ARIES
2 PISCES
3 AQUARIUS
4 CAPRICORNUS
5 SAGITTARIUS
6 SCORPIO
7 LIBRA
8 TAURUS
9 GEMINI
10 CANCER
11 LEO
12 VIRGO

CONSTELLATION	ENGLISH NAME
ANDROMEDIA	ANDROMEDIA
AQUARIUS	WATER CARRIER
ARIES	RAM
CANCER	CRAB
CANIS MAJOR	GREATER DOG
CANIS MINOR	LESSER DOG
CAPRICORNUS	GOAT
CASSIOPEIA	CASSIOPEIA
CENTAURUS	CENTAUR
CEPHEUS	CEPHEUS
CETUS	WHALE
COMA BERENICES	BERENICE'S HAIR

CORVUS	CROW
CRUX	SOUTHERN CROSS
CYGNUS	SWAN
DRACO	DRAGON
EQUULEUS	LITTLE HORSE
ERIDANUS	RIVER
GEMINI	TWINS
HERCULES	HERCULES
HYDRA	WATER SNAKE
LEO	LION
LEO MINOR	LESSER LION
LIBRA	SCALES
LYRA	LYRE
ORION	ORION
PEGASUS	PEGASUS
PERSEUS	PERSEUS
PISCES	FISHES
SAGITTARIUS	ARCHER
SCORPIUS	SCORPION
TAURUS	BULL
URSA MAJOR	GREAT BEAR
URSA MINOR	LITTLE BEAR
VIRGO	VIRGIN

PHASES OF THE MOON AS SEEN FROM THE EARTH.
1 NEW
2 CRESENT
3 QUARTER
4 GIBBOUS
5 FULL

STAR :-A LARGE BALL OF GAS THAT CREATES AND EMITS ITS OWN RADIATION.

STARS :-THERE ARE SOME 100,000,000,000 STARS IN OUR OWN GALAXY

STAR CLUSTER :-A BUNCH OF STARS [RANGING IN NUMBER FROM A FEW TO HUNDREDS OF THOUSANDS] WHICH ARE BOUND TO EACH OTHER BY THEIR MUTUAL GRAVITATIONAL ATTRACTION.

STELLAR CLASSIFICATION :-STARS ARE GIVEN A DESIGNATION CONSISTING OF A LETTER AND A NUMBER

ACCORDING TO THE NATURE OF THEIR SPECTRAL LINES WHICH CORRESPONDS ROUGHLY TO SURFACE TEMPERATURE. THE SUN IS DESIGNATED G 2

NORTH STAR, ALSO CALLED THE POLE STAR OR POLARIS, IS THE STAR THE EARTH'S AXIS POINTS TOWARD IN THE NORTHERN SKY. THE NORTH STAR HAS BEEN USED AS A NAVIGATION AID AND TO CHART NAVIGATIONAL MAPS. IT HAS ALSO BEEN USED TO MEASURE ASTRONOMICAL LATITUDE; SINCE WE MAP LATITUDES TO THE EQUIVALENT SKY POSITIONS. THE NORTH POLE EQUATES TO + 90 DEGREES LATITUDE ON EARTH AS DOES ITS PROJECTION INTO THE SKY.

THE SOUTHERN CROSS CONSTELLATION IS EAGERLY SOUGHT BY TRAVELERS FROM THE NORTH, VISITING THE SOUTHERN HEMISPHERE. THE CROSS HAS FOUR MAIN STARS MAKING THE TIPS; ALPHA, BETA, GAMMA, AND DELTA. THE TWO BRIGHT STARS, ALPHA AND BETA CENTAURI, ARE POINTERS TO THE HEAD OF THE CROSS. THE ALPHA CENTAURI IS A TRIPLE STAR. IT HAS 1 AND 2 A CLOSE DOUBLE STAR; PLUS 3, A DISTANT, FAINT RED STAR CALLED PROXIMA CENTAURI; WHICH IS THE CLOSEST STAR TO OUR SOLAR SYSTEM.

SUN :-IS A HUGE, GLOWING BALL AT THE CENTER OF OUR SOLAR SYSTEM. THE SUN PROVIDES LIGHT, HEAT, AND OTHER ENERGY TO EARTH. THE SUN IS MADE UP ENTIRELY OF GAS. EARTH TRAVELS AROUND THE SUN AT AN AVERAGE DISTANCE OF ABOUT 92,960,000 MILES FROM IT. THE SUN IS ONE OF OVER 100 BILLION STARS IN THE MILKY WAY GALAXY.

COLORS OF THE STARS :-
1 BLUE - WHITE
2 WHITE
3 YELLOWISH - WHITE
4 YELLOW
5 ORANGE
6 RED

COMET :-IS A NEBULOUS CELESTIAL BODY REVOLVING AROUND THE SUN. A COMET IS CHARACTERIZED BY A LONG, LUMINOUS TAIL, BUT ONLY IN THE SEGMENT OF

THE COMET'S ORBIT WHEN IT PASSES CLOSEST TO THE SUN.

IMPORTANT SPACE MISSIONS :-
NAME   YEAR MISSION HIGHLIGHTS
[a] CASSINI 2004 CLOSE UP STUDY OF SATURN AND ITS MOONS AND RINGS. IT WILL ALSO LAND A PROBE ON TITAN.

[b] SPIRIT AND OPPORTUNITY ROVERS 2004 IMAGES AND DATA FROM MARTIAN SURFACE.

[c] ICESat / CHIPSat JANUARY 2003

[d] SORCE JANUARY 2003

[e] GALEX APRIL 2003

[f] MARS EXPLORATION ROVER OPPORTUNITY JULY 2003

[g] SPACE INFRARED TELESCOPE FACILITY AUGUST 2003

[h] CHANDRA X – RAY OBSERVATORY JULY 1999

[I] INTERNATIONAL SPACE STATION BUILDING STARTED IN 1998

[j] MARS PATHFINDER 1997 LANDED A ROBOTIC ROVER ON MARS

[k] MARS GLOBAL SURVEYOR 1997 ORBITS MARS SENDING BACK DETAILED IMAGES OF SURFACE.

[l] MARS GLOBAL SURVEYOR NOVEMBER 1996

[m] NEAR EARTH ASTEROID RENDEZVOUS [NEAR] FEBRUARY 1996

[n] SOHO DECEMBER 1995

[o] GALILEO 1995 CLOSE UP STUDY OF JUPITER AND ITS MOONS

[p] ULYSSES OCTOBER 1990

[q] MAGELLAN 1990 ORBITED VENUS SENDING BACK DETAILED RADAR MAPS OF SURFACE.

[R] MIR SPACE STATION FEBRUARY 1986

[s] VENERA 15 AND 16 1983

[t] SPACE SHUTTLES FIRST FLIGHT 1981

[u] VOYAGER 2 1979 FLYBYS OF URANUS AND NEPTUNE

[v] VOTAGER 1 1979 – 1980 FLYBYS OF JUPITER AND SATURN

[w] VIKING 1976 ORBITING AND LANDING ON MARS.

ASTRONAUT :-TRAVELER IN OUTER SPACE.

ASTRONAUTICS :-IS THE SCIENCE OF SPACECRAFT AND SPACE TRAVEL.

ASTRONOMY :-IS THE SCIENCE OF THE STARS, PLANETS, ETC.

THE NAMES OF SOME ASTRONAUTS WHO HAVE TRAVELED TO SPACE ARE :-
NEIL ARMSTRONG
ROBERTA BONDAR
FRANK BORMAN
DAVID M BROWN
SCOTT CARPENTER
EUGENE A CERMAN
KALPANA CHAWIA
LAUREL B S CLARK
EILEEN COLLINS
MICHAEL COLLINS
YURI GAGARIN
MARC GARNEAU
JOHN GLENN
RICK D HUSBAND
YANG LIWEL
EDWARD LU
WILLIAM C McCOOL
BARBARA MORGAN
ELLEN OCHOA
SALLY RIDE
ALAN SHEPHERD
AL WORDEN
JOHN W YOUNG

OBSERVATORIES :-ARE BUILDINGS FOR ASTRONOMICAL RESEARCH. SOME OBSERVATORIES IN THE WORLD ARE :-
ANGLO – AUSTRALIAN OBSERVATORY [AAO]
APACHE POINT OBSERVATORY
ASTRONOMICAL INSTITUTE AND NATIONAL OBSERVATORY OF ATHENS

ASTRONOMY IN LATIVA
BEIJING ASTRONOMICAL OBSERVATORY [BAO]
BIG SKY PROJECT
ESTACION ASTRONOMICA RIO GRANDE ARGENTINA
KOPEMIK SPACE EDUCATION CENTER
LEIDEN   OBSERVATORY   LEIDEN   UNIVERSITY
NETHERLANDS
MT. GRAHAM INTERNATIONAL OBSERVATORY [MGIO]
NOAO CERRO TOLOLO INTERAMERICAN OBSERVATORY
NORMAN LOCKYER OBSERVATORY AND PLANETARIUM
OBSERVATORIO   ASTRONOMICO   NACIONAL   DE
COLOMBIA
OBSERVATORIO NACIONAL BRAZIL
ROYAL OBSERVATORY OF BELGIUM
ROYAL OBSERVATORY, EDINBURGH
SOUTH AFRICAN ASTRONOMICAL OBSERVATORY
SOUTH   EASTERN   ASSOCIATION   FOR   RESEARCH   IN
ASTRONOMY
SOUTHERN SKY OBSERVATORY
VATICAN OBSERVATORY VATICAN CITY
WORTH HILL OBSERVATORY WORTH MATRAVERS, U.K

MAJOR OBSERVATORIES IN SPACE ARE :-
HUBBLE SPACE TELESCOPE
HIGH ENERGY TRANSIENT EXPLORER
CHANDRA X – RAY OBSERVATION
FAR ULTRAVIOLET SPECTROSCOPIC EXPLORER
SPACED INFRARED TELESCOPE FACILITY
MICROWAVE ANISOTROPY PROBE

RADIO TELESCOPES :-
ARECIBO IN PUERTO RICO
VERY LARGE ARRAY NEAR SOCORRO IN NEW MEXICO

LARGE OPTICAL TELESCOPES :-
HALE ON MOUNT PALOMAR IN SOUTHERN CALIFORNIA
KECK ON MANUA KEA IN HAWAII
HOBBY – EBERLY ON MOUNT LOCKE IN TEXAS
VERY LARGE TELESCOPE ON CERRO PARANAL IN
CHILE
GEMINI NORTH ON MAUNA KEA IN HAWAII

GEMINI SOUTH ON CERRO PACHON IN CHILE.

TIME ZONES :-TIMES OF COUNTRIES OF THE WORLD ARE RECKONED FROM GREENWICH MEAN TIME [GMT] IN UNITED KINGDOM. THE GEOGRAPHICAL LOCATION IS 51 DEGREES 28 MINUTES NORTH. A CHART TO EXPLAIN THIS FOLLOWS :-

PLACE	DATE	TIME	
GMT	FRIDAY 16 APRIL,2004	12:00 PM	
ATHENS		3:00 PM DAYLIGHT SAVING TIME [DST]	
BANGKOK		7:00 PM	
BERLIN		2:00 PM	DST
CAIRO		2:00 PM	
DUBLIN		1:00 PM	DST
HONG KONG		8:00 PM	
JERUSALEM		3:00 PM	DST
LONDON		1:00 PM	DST
LOS ANGLES		5:00 AM	DST
MELBOURNE		10:00 PM	
MOSCOW		4:05 PM	DST
NEW YORK		8:05 AM	DST
PARIS		2:05 PM	DST
ROME		2:05 PM	
SEOUL		9:05 PM	
WELLINGTON		12:05 AM	
VANCOVER		5:05 AM	
TOKOYO		9:05 PM	

CHAPTER 13.

FACTS ABOUT ASIA :-

SIZE :-PROBABLY ABOUT 16, 900,000 SQUARE MILES, ALTHOUGH ESTIMATES RANGE FROM 16, 500, 000 TO 18, 500, 000 SQUARE MILES. IT IS THE LARGEST OF THE CONTINENTS; MORE THAN FIVE TIMES AS LARGE AS THE UNITED STATES; ONE – THIRD OF LAND AREA OF THE GLOBE [THE EARTH]

MOUNT EVEREST :-MAY BE 29, 610 FEET HIGH, BUT OFFICIAL FIGURE GIVEN IS 29, 028 FEET [HIGHEST MOUNTAIN IN THE WORLD] LOCATED ON THE NEPAL – TIBET FRONTIER.

YANGTZE KIANG -3, 430 MILES LONG. FLOWS ACROSS THE ENTIRE WIDTH OF CHINA. LONGEST RIVER IN ASIA.

GOBI DESERT -500, 000 SQUARE MILES [ONE OF THE LARGEST IN THE WORLD] MOSTLY IN MONGOLIA.

LAKE BAIKAL -12,000 TO 13, 000 SQUARE MILES IN AREA AND MORE THAN ONE MILE DEEP IN CENTRAL SECTION. [LARGEST AND DEEPEST FRESHWATER BASIN IN EURASIA] LOCATED IN THE SOUTHEASTERN PART OF THE SOVIET UNION.

FACTS ABOUT AUSTRALIA :-

NAME -FROM THE LATIN AUSTRALIS, MEANING SOUTHERN. THE NICKNAME "DOWN UNDER "REFERS TO ITS

POSITION ON THE GLOBE IN RELATION TO GREAT BRITAIN [ENGLAND]

SIZE -2,974,581 SQUARE MILES INCLUDING TASMANIA [ABOUT FIVE – SIXTHS AS LARGE AS THE UNITED STATES OF AMERICA.

HIGHEST MOUNTAIN -MOUNT KOSCIUSKO [7,316 FEET]

LONGEST RIVER -THE MURRAY, 1,600 MILES.

DESERTS -MORE THAN 35 % OF AUSTRALIA'S INTERIOR INTERIOR IS CLASSIFIED AS DESERT.

A DESERT IS AN ARID, SANDY REGION.

LAKE EYRE -A LARGE, SHALLOW SALT LAKE [3,700 SQUARE MILES] ABOUT 40 FEET BELOW SEA LEVEL.

GREATEST LENGTH - 2,000 MILES [NORTH TO SOUTH].

GREATEST WIDTH - 2,400 MILES [EAST TO WEST].

GREAT INVENTIONS AND DISCOVERIES.
UNDER THE FOLLOWING HEADINGS :-
INVENTION OR DISCOVERY INVENTOR OR DISCOVERER DATE NATIONALITY.

TELESCOPE HANS LIPPERSHEY 1608 DUTCH
BAROMETER EVANGELISTA TORRICELLI 1643 ITALIAN
STEAM ENGINE THOMAS NEWCOMEN 1705 BRITISH
PIANO BARTOLOMEO CRISTOFORI 1710 ITALIAN
MARINE CHRONOMETER JOHN HARRISON 1759 BRITISH
AUTOMOBILE NICOLAS JOSEPH CUGNOT 1770 FRENCH
BALLOON JOSEPH M MONTGOLFIER AND JACQUES E MONTGOLFIER
1783 FRENCH
POWER LOOM EDMUND CARTWRIGHT 1785 BRITISH
STEAMBOAT JOHN FITCH 1786 AMERICAN
GAS TURBINE JOHN BARBER 1791 BRITISH
SMALLPOX VACCINATION EDWARD JENNER 1796 BRITISH
ELECTRIC BATTERY COUNT ALESSANDRO VOLTA 1800 ITALIAN
STEAM LOCOMOTIVE RICHARD TREVITHICK 1804 BRITISH
FOOD PRESERVATION FRANCOIS APPERT 1810 FRENCH

RAILROAD LOCOMOTIVE GEORGE STEPHENSON 1814 BRITISH

SAFETY LAMP SIR HUMPHRY DAVY 1815 BRITISH

STETHOSCOPE RENE T H LAENNEC 1819 FRENCH

ELECTRIC MOTOR MICHAEL FARADAY 1821 BRITISH

SEWING MACHINE BARTHELEMY THIMONNIER 1830 FRENCH

PISTOL SAMUEL COLT 1835 AMERICAN

TELEGRAPH SAMUEL F B MORSE 1837 AMERICAN

SIR CHARLES WHEATSTONE BRITISH

PHOTOGRAPHY LOUIS J M DAGUERRE AND JOSEPH N NIEPCE FRENCH

WILLIAM H F TALBOT 1839 BRITISH

VULCANIZED RUBBER CHARLES GOODYEAR 1839 AMERICAN

BICYCLE KIRKPATRICK MACMILLAN 1840 BRITISH

SAFETY PIN WALTER HUNT 1849 AMERICAN

WATER TURBINE JAMES B FRANCIS 1849 AMERICAN

ELEVATOR ELISHA G OTIS 1852 AMERICAN

GYROSCOPE JEAN B L FOUCAULT 1852 FRENCH

SAFETY MATCHES J LUNDSTROM 1855 SWEDISH

GAS BURNER ROBERT W BUNSEN 1855 GERMAN

SPECTROSCOPE GUSTAV R KIRCHOFF AND 1859 GERMAN

ROBERT W BUNSEN

MACHINE GUN RICHARD J GATLING 1861 AMERICAN

PAPER BENJAMIN C TILGHMAN 1866 AMERICAN

DYNAMITE ALFRED B NOBEL 1866 SWEDISH

TYPEWRITER CARLOS GLIDDEN AND 1868 AMERICAN CHRISTOPHER L SHOLES

AIR BRAKE GEORGE WESTINGHOUSE 1868 AMERICAN

TELEPHONE ALEXANDER GRAHAM BELL 1876 AMERICAN

MICROPHONE EMILE BERLINER 1877 AMERICAN

ELECTRIC WELDING ELIHU THOMSON 1877 AMERICAN

CASH REGISTER JAMES J RITTY 1879 AMERICAN

FOUNTAIN PEN LEWIS E WATERMAN 1884 AMERICAN

GRAPHOPHONE CHICHESTER A BELL AND 1885 AMERICAN

CHARLES S TAINTER

AC TRANSFORMER WILLIAM STANLEY 1885 AMERICAN

ADDING MACHINE WILLIAM S BURROUGHS 1888 AMERICAN

KODAK CAMERA GEORGE EASTMAN 1888 AMERICAN

SYNTHETIC RUBBER SIR WILLIAM A TILDEN 1891 BRITISH

AC MOTOR NIKOLA TESIA 1892 AMERICAN

DIESEL ENGINE RUDOLF DIESEL 1893 GERMAN

GASOLINE AUTOMOBILE CHARLES E DURYEA AND 1893 AMERICAN

J FRANK DURYEA

MOTION PICTURE MACHINE THOMAS A EDISON 1893 AMERICAN

MOTION PICTURE PROJECTION LOUIS J LUMIERE AND 1894 FRENCH

AUGUSTE M LUMIERE

EXPERIMENTAL AIRPLANE SAMUEL P LANGLEY 1896 AMERICAN

WIRELESS TELEGRAPH MARCHESE G MARCONI 1896 ITALIAN

RADIO TELEPHONE VALDEMAR POULSEN 1902 DANISH

REGINALD A FESSENDEN AMERICAN

AIRPLANE WILBUR WRIGHT AND ORVILLE WRIGHT 1903 AMERICAN

GYROCOMPASS HERMANN ANSCHUTZ – KAMPFE 1906 GERMAN

VITAMINS CASIMIR FUNK 1911 POLISH

CELLOPHANE JACQUES EDWIN BRANDENBERGER 1911 SWISS

CRACKED GASOLINE WILLIAM M BURTON 1913 AMERICAN

X-RAY TUBE WILLIAM D COOLIDGE 1916 AMERICAN

INSULIN SIR FREDERICK GRANT BANTING 1922 CANADIAN

TELEVISION ICONOSCOPE VLADIMIR K ZWORYKIN 1923 AMERICAN

TELEVISION IMAGE DISSECTOR TUBE PHILO FARNSWORTH1925 AMERICAN

PENICILLIN SIR ALEXANDER FLEMING 1928 BRITISH

NYLON WALLACE H CAROTHERS 1930 AMERICAN

MODERN GAS TURBINE ENGINE SIR FRANK WHITTLE 1930 BRITISH

RADAR SIR ROBERT WATSON – WATT 1935 BRITISH

ELECTRON MICROSCOPE GERMAN SCIENTISTS 1935 GERMAN

TWIN ROTOR HELICOPTER HEINRICH FOCKE 1936 GERMAN

TURBOJET AIRCRAFT ENGINE SIR FRANK WHITTLE 1941 BRITISH

ATOMIC BOMB U.S GOVERNMENT SCIENTISTS 1945 AMERICAN

ELECTRONIC DIGITAL COMPUTER JOHN P ECKERT JR. 1946 AMERICAN

AND JOHN W MAUCHLY

POLAROID LAND CAMERA EDWIN H LAND 1947 AMERICAN

TRANSISTOR JOHN BARDEEN, WALTER H BRATTAIN 1948 AMERICAN

AND WILLIAM SHOCKLEY

HYDROGEN BOMB U.S GOVERNMENT SCIENTISTS 1952 AMERICAN

SOLAR BATTERY LABORATORY SCIENTISTS 1954 AMERICAN

SYNTHETIC DIAMONDS G.E. SCIENTISTS 1955 AMERICAN

ARTIFICIAL EARTH SATELLITE U.S.S.R SCIENTISTS 1957 SOVIET

COMMUNICATIONS SATELLITE U.S SCIENTISTS 1958 AMERICAN

LASER CHARLES H TOWNES, ARTHUR L SCHAWLOW 1960 AMERICAN

AND GORDON GOULD

CHLOROPHYLL SYNTHESIZED ROBERT B WOODWARD 1960 AMERICAN

BIRTH CONTROL PILL GREGORY PINCUS, JOHN ROCK 1960 AMERICAN

AND MIN – CHUEH CHANG

ARTIFICIAL HEART MICHAEL E DEBAKEY 1966 AMERICAN

HUMAN HEART TRANSPLANT CHRISTIAAN N BARNARD 1967

SOUTH AFRICAN

FIRST COMPLETE SYNTHESIS OF A GENE HAR G KHORANA 1970

AMERICAN

SYNTHESIS OF HUMAN INSULIN GENES ROBERT CREA 1978 AMERICAN

TADAAKI HIROSE, ADAM KRASZEWSKI, KEIICHI ITAKURA

MAMMAL TO MAMMAL GENE TRANSPLANTS PAUL BERG 1978 AMERICAN

RICHARD MULLIGAN, AND BRUCE HOWARD

KNOWLEDGE :-

CHAPTER 14.

LAW :-ANY OF THE RULES OF CONDUCT MADE BY A GOVERNMENT.

LAWYER OR ATTORNEY:-IS A PERSON LICENSED TO PRACTICE LAW.

SOME AREAS OF LAW ARE :-

ARBITRATION AND MEDIATION

BANKRUPTCY LAW

BUSINESS LAW

CLASS ACTION LAWSUITS

CATASTROPHIC INJURIES CASES

CONSUMER LAW

CRIMINAL LAW

ELDER ABUSE CASES

EMPLOYMENT LAW

FAMILY LAW

IMMIGRATION LAW

INSURANCE LAW

INTELLECTUAL PROPERTY LAW

JUVENILE LAW

LABOR LAW

LANDLORD - TENANT LAW

MALPRACTICE LAW

REAL PROPERTY – ESTATE LAW

SECURITIES LAW

SERIOUS PERSONAL INJURY CASES

SOCIAL SECURITY LAW

TAX LAW

TORT LAW
TOXIC MOLD CASES
TRAFFIC TICKETS / DMV ISSUES
WILLS AND ESTATE PLANNING LAW
WORKERS COMPENSATION LAW
ADMIRALITY LAW
ANTITRUST LAW
ASBESTOS LAW
BANKING LAW
CIVIL RIGHTS LAW
COMMUNICATIONS LAW
CONSTITUTIONAL LAW
CONTRACT LAW
CORPORATION LAW
DISPUTE RESOLUTION
DIVORCE LAW
EDUCATION LAW
ENTERTAINMENT LAW
INCORPORATION LAW
INTERNET LAW
MEDICAL MALPRACTICE
MILITARY LAW

A TYPICAL COURT SYSTEM :-
DISTRICT COURTS
TERRITORIAL COURTS
TAX COURT
CLAIMS COURT
INTERNATIONAL TRADES COURT
COURTS OF APPEALS
SUPREME COURT

THE INTERNATIONAL COURT OF JUSTICE IS IN THE NETHERLANDS. DISPUTES INVOLVING NATIONS ARE HANDLED AND DEALT WITH THERE.

CRIMINOLOGY :-IS THE SOCIAL SCIENCE DEALING WITH THE NATURE, CAUSES AND EXTENT OF CRIME; THE CHARACTERISTICS OF CRIMINALS AND THEIR ORGANIZATIONS; THE PROBLEMS OF APPREHENDING AND CONVICTING OFFENDERS; THE OPERATIONS OF

CORRECTIONAL INSTITUTIONS AND PRISONS; THE REHABILITATION OF CONVICTS BOTH IN AND OUT OF PRISON; AND THE PREVENTION OF CRIME.

THE OSCILLOSCOPE AIDS IN CRIME DETECTION BY PROVIDING ADVANCED METHODS OF RECOGNIZING AND IDENTIFYING FINGERPRINTS. FINGERPRINTING IS THE METHOD OF IDENTIFICATION USING THE IMPRESSIONS MADE BY THE FINGERS IN HUMANS. NO TWO PERSONS HAVE EXACTLY THE SAME ARRANGEMENTS OF PATTERNS OF FINGERPRINTS; AND THESE PATTERNS OF FINGERPRINTS OF ANY ONE INDIVIDUAL REMAIN UNCHANGED THROUGH LIFE. IT IS AN IDENTIFICATION SYSTEM THAT IS ALMOST INFALLIBLE.

DNA [DEOXYRIBONUCLEIC ACID] IS THE GENETIC BLUEPRINT OF LIFE. SAMPLES ARE OBTAINED FROM PEOPLE FROM SUCH SUBSTANCES AS SALIVA, BLOOD, SEMEN, HAIR ROOTS. COMPARING THE UNIQUE DNA PATTERNS OF INDIVIDUALS HELPS CONVICTS RAPISTS, ESTABLISH PATERNITY OR MATERNITY, AND ALSO HELPS WITH IDENTIFYING MISSING PEOPLE. IT IS A VERY RELIABLE AND ACCURATE WAY OF IDENTIFICATION PROCESS.

QUANTITIES ARE GOVERNED OR MEASURED UNDER HEADINGS SUCH AS :-
LENGTH
MASS
TIME
PLANE ANGLE
SOLID ANGLE
VOLUME
AREA
VELOCITY
ACCELERATION
FREQUENCY
FORCE
DENSITY
MAGNETIC FIELD STRENGTH
LUMINANCE
PRESSURE

STRESS
LUMINOUS INTENSITY
CONDUCTANCE
ELECTRIC CURRENT
THERMODYNAMIC TEMPERATURE

SOME INTERESTING FIELDS OF STUDIES :-
ART
MATHEMATICS
BIOLOGY
GEOSCIENCE
CHEMISTRY
PHYSICS
ENGLISH LANGUAGE
MODERN LANGUAGES
COMPUTER SCIENCE
LITERATURE
ECONOMICS
POLITICAL SCIENCE
PHILOSOPHY
LAW
MEDICINE
RELIGIOUS STUDIES
PSYCHOLOGY
MUSIC
HISTORY
GEOGRAPHY
PHYSICAL EDUCATION
CLASSICS
ANTHROPOLOGY
SOCIOLOGY
BUSINESS
COMMERCE
ARCHAEOLOGY
GEOLOGY
OCEANOGRAPHY
SPACE SCIENCE
WEATHER
ZOOLOGY
HEALTH AND DISEASE
BEHAVIORAL SCIENCES

BOTANY

AGRICULTURE :-IS THE ART, SCIENCE, AND INDUSTRY OF MANAGING THE GROWTH OF PLANTS AND ANIMALS FOR HUMAN USE.
THE AGRICULTURE OF THE WORLD CONSISTS OF :-
LIVESTOCK RANCHING AND HERDING.
DAIRY FARMING
LIVESTOCK FARMING
GENERAL FARMING
MIXED FARMING
SPECIAL CROPS
CEREALS
CASH CROPS
DIVERSIFIED TROPICAL CROPS
DIVERSIFIED SUBTROPICAL CROPS
FORESTS EXPLORATION
FISH FARMING

CHEMICAL ELEMENTS -ARE SUBSTANCES THAT CANNOT BE DECOMPOSED, OR BROKEN DOWN INTO MORE ELEMENTARY SUBSTANCES BY ORDINARY MEANS. OVER A HUNDRED CHEMICAL ELEMENTS ARE KNOWN TO EXIST IN THE UNIVERSE AND ARE CLASSIFIED AS METALS AND NONMETALS.
SOME WELL KNOWN CHEMICAL ELEMENTS ARE AS FOLLOWS :-
ALUMINUM
CALCIUM
CARBON
CHLORINE
COBALT
COPPER
GOLD
HELIUM
HYDROGEN
IODINE
IRON
LEAD
MANGANESE
MERCURY

NEON
NICKEL
NITROGEN
OXYGEN
POTASSIUM
RADIUM
SILVER
SODIUM
SULFUR
TIN
URANIUM
ZINC

MINERALS :-A MINERAL IS A NATURALLY OCCURING, CRYSTALLINE SOLID, HAVING A DISTINCT INORGANIC CHEMICAL COMPOSITION; IT IS ORE, ROCK ETC. FOUND NATURALLY IN THE EARTH.
SOME THINGS THAT ARE CLASSIFIED AS MINERALS ARE :-

COPPER
LEAD
ZINC
NICKEL
CHROMIUM
COBALT
MOLYBDENUM
MANGANESE
VANADIUM
TUNGSTEN
SILVER
GOLD
IRON ORE
COAL
NATURAL GAS
PETROLEUM
ATOMIC MINERALS
LIMESTONE
MARL
BAUXITE
DIAMOND
AGATE

AMBER
AQUAMARINE
CHALK
CRYOLITE
EMERALD
FLUORITE
GARNET
GYPSUM
JASPER
MAGNESIA
ONYX
OPAL
QUARTZ
RUBY
SAPPHIRE
SOAPSTONE
TALC
TALCUM
TOPAZ
URANINITE
ZINCITE

COUNTRIES OF EUROPE :-
ALBANIA
ANDORRA
AUSTRIA
BELGIUM
BULGARIA
CHANNEL ISLANDS
CZECHOSLOVAKIA
DENMARK
FAEROE ISLANDS
FINLAND
FRANCE
GERMANY
GIBRALTAR
GREAT BRITAIN [ENGLAND]
GREECE
HUNGARY
ICELAND
IRELAND

ISLE OF MAN
ITALY
LIECHTENSTEIN
LUXEMBOURG
MALTA
MONACO
NETHERLANDS
NORWAY
POLAND
PORTUGAL
ROMANIA
SAN MARINO
SPAIN
SVALBARD AND JAN MAYEN
SWEDEN
SWITZERLAND
UNION OF SOVIET SOCIALIST REPUBLICS [U.S.S.R]
ARMENIAN
AZERBAIJAN
BELORUSSIAN
ESTONIAN
GEORGIAN
LATVIAN
LITHUANIAN
MOLDAVIAN
UKRAINIAN
YUGOSLAVIA

A HIERARCHICAL SYSTEM OF THE MAKE UP OF THE WORLD; FROM THE SMALLEST TO THE LARGEST ENTITIES. STARTING WITH ELEMENTARY PARTICLES WHICH MAKE UP ATOMS; ATOMS COMBINE TO FORM MOLECULES; AND SO ON.

ELEMENTARY PARTICLES
ATOMS
MOLECULES
CRYSTALS
CELLS
ORGANISMS
POPULATIONS
ECOSYSTEMS

EARTH
SOLAR SYSTEM
STARS
GALAXIES
UNIVERSE

AIR POLLUTION :- IS THE CONTAMINATION OF THE ATMOSPHERE BY GASEOUS, SOLID OR LIQUID WASTES OR BYPRODUCTS THAT CAN ENDANGER HUMAN HEALTH AND THE HEALTH AND WELFARE OF ANIMALS AND PLANTS.
SOME AIR POLLUTANTS ARE :-
LEAD
CARBON DIOXIDE
CARBON MONOXIDE
SULFUR DIOXIDE
NITROGEN OXIDES
PHOTOCHEMICAL OXIDANTS
ETHANE
ETHYLENE
PROPANE
BUTANES
ACETYLENE
OZONE
SUSPENDED PARTICLE MATTER

SOURCES OF ENERGY FOR COMMERCIAL USE :-
[a] GAS
[b] ELECTRICITY
[c] SOLID FUELS
[d] LIQUID FUELS

TYPES OF GASES :-
HELIUM
HYDROGEN
NITROGEN
OXYGEN
CARBON DIOXIDE
AMMONIA
STEAM – WATER

THE COUNTIES OF ENGLAND :-

AVON
BEDFORDSHIRE
BERKSHIRE
BUCKINGHAMSHIRE
CHESHIRE
CLEVELAND
CORNWALL AND ISLES OF SCILLY
CUMBRIA
DERBYSHIRE
DEVON
DORSET
DURHAM
ESSEX
GLOUCESTERSHIRE
HAMPSHIRE
HEREFORD AND WORCESTER
HERTFORDSHIRE
HUMBERSIDE
KENT
LANCASHIRE
LEICESTERSHIRE
LINCOLNSHIRE
MANCHESTER
MERSEYSIDE
MIDLANDS
NORFOLK
NORTHAMPTONSHIRE
NORTHUMBERLAND
NOTTINGHAMSHIRE
OXFORDSHIRE
SHROPSHIRE
SOMERSET
STAFFORDSHIRE
SUFFOLK
SURREY
SUSSEX
TYNE AND WEAR
WARWICKSHIRE
WIGHT ISLE OF
WILTSHIRE
YORKSHIRE

COMMONWEALTH :-IS A BODY OF PEOPLE IN A POLITICALLY ORGANIZED COMMUNITY THAT SEEKS TO BE INDEPENDENT, AND IN WHICH THE GOVERNMENT FUNCTIONS BY THE COMMON CONSENT OF THE PEOPLE.

COMMONWEALTH OF NATIONS :-

WESTERN HEMISPHERE

GUYANA
JAMAICA
TRINIDAD AND TOBAGO
BARBADOS
BELIZE
BERMUDA
CANADA
ANGUILLA
ANTIGUA AND BARBUDA
BAHAMAS
BRITISH ANTARCTIC TERRITORY
CAYMAN ISLANDS
DOMINICA
FALKLAND ISLAND AND DEPENDENCIES
GRENADA
MONTSERRAT
SAINT CHRISTOPHER AND NEVIS
SAINT LUCIA
SAINT VINCENT AND THE GRENADINES
TURKS AND CAICOS ISLANDS
BRITISH VIRGIN ISLANDS

ASIA
HONG KONG
INDIA
SRI LANKA
BANGLADESH
CYPRUS
BRUNEI
MALAYSIA
MALDIVES
SINGAPORE

EUROPE

GREAT BRITAIN [ENGLAND]
IRELAND
GIBRALTAR
CHANNEL ISLANDS
MALTA
ISLE OF MAN

AUSTRALIA AND OCEANIA
AUSTRALIA AND DEPENDENCIES.
NEW ZEALAND AND DEPENDENCIES
FIJI
KIRIBATI
NAURU
SOLOMON ISLANDS
TONGA
PAPUA NEW GUINEA
PITCAIRN ISLAND
TUVALU
VANUATU
WESTERN SAMOA

AFRICA
GHANA
KENYA
NIGERIA
ZAMBIA
BOTSWANA
GAMBIA
BRITISH INDIAN OCEAN TERRITORY
LESOTHO
MALAWI
MAURITIUS
SAINT HELENA
SWAZILAND
SEYCHELLES
SIERRA LEONE
TANZANIA
UGANDA
ZIMBABWE

CHAPTER 15.

CIGARETTE SMOKING CAUSES OR MAY RESULT IN YOU HAVING :-
LUNG CANCER
HEART DISEASE
EMPHYSEMA
PREGNANCY – FETAL INJURY
PREMATURE BIRTH
LOW BIRTH WEIGHT

CIGARETTE SMOKE CONTAINS CARBON MONOXIDE.

ILLEGAL DRUGS :-
IS DANGEROUS AND HARMFUL TO THE HEALTH AND WELL BEING OF PEOPLE GENERALLY. IT IS SAID THAT PEER PRESSURE AND LACK OF PARENTAL AND OTHERS IN SUPERVISORY POSITION LACK OF PROPER AND EFFECTIVE SUPERVISION AND EDUCATION OF THE YOUNG ONES ARE WHAT LURE THEM INTO TRYING DRUGS AND THEN THEY EVENTUALLY BECOME HOOKED ON DRUGS AND ULTIMATELY DESTROY THEIR LIVES. ADVISE TO EVERYONE IS TO AVOID ILLEGAL DRUGS; IT DOES YOU NO GOOD.

TELEVISION :- A WAY OF SENDING PICTURES THROUGH SPACE BY RADIO RAVES TO A RECEIVING SET.
SEPARATING THE TRUTH FROM UNTRUTH ON COMMON QUESTIONS CONCERNING TELEVISION AND YOUR HEALTH.

1 TELEVISION CARRIES ALL MANNER OF SUBJECT MATTERS. IT IS FOR YOU TO DECIPHER AND SELECT THE PROGRAMS THAT ARE IN YOUR BEST INTEREST. LIMITED USE SHOULD BE ADHERED TO USING THE TELEVISION, FOR ONE CAN BECOME ADDICTED TO THE TELEVISION, AND END UP SPENDING VALUABLE TIME SITTING AND GAZING ONE'S LIFE AWAY. DON'T AIMLESSLY USE THE REMOTE, BE WISE TURN OFF THE TELEVISION AND USE YOUR TIME IN LIFE TO FULL EFFECT; ALWAYS HAVE TIME FOR COMMUNICATION WITH FAMILY AND ACQUAINTANCES.

2 RADIATION IS NOT A DANGER :-YOU HAVE BEEN MADE TO SIT BACK SEVERAL FEET FROM THE TELEVISION SCREEN, TO AVOID THE EFFECTS OF WHATEVER THE TELEVISION PUT OUT THAT MIGHT BE HARMFUL TO YOU. HOWEVER SUCH CONCERN AND PRECAUTION IS ENTIRELY NEEDLESS, FOR MODERN RECEIVERS ARE BUILT EFFICIENTLY; USING LOWER VOLTAGES AND BETTER SHIELDING. NO MATTER HOW CLOSE YOU SIT TO THE TELEVISION SET YOU ARE NOT AFFECTED BY ANY FORM OF RADIATION OR WHATEVER YOU MIGHT FEEL THE TELEVISION PUT OUT.

3 NO, LOOKING AT TELEVISION DOES NOT DAMAGE YOUR VISION [EYES] THE CONTRAST BETWEEN A BRIGHT TELEVISION SET AND A DARK ROOM MAY TEMPORARILY TIRE YOUR EYES, AS DOES THE REFLECTIVE GLARE OFF THE SCREEN OF A POORLY PLACED LAMP [LIGHT] BUT NEITHER SITUATION WILL LEAD TO LONG TERM DAMAGE OF THE EYES.

4 WILL TELEVISION MAKE ME GAIN WEIGHT :- NO NOT DIRECTLY, BUT INDIRECTLY IT CAN, IF YOU DO A LOT OF EATING, BUILDING UP THE CALORIES WHILE YOU ARE WATCHING TELEVISION. BE CAREFUL DON'T BE A COUCH POTATO.

ALCOHOL :-INTOXICATING LIQUID OBTAINED FROM FERMENTED GRAIN, FRUIT ETC .

ALCOHOLIC :-IS ONE WHO IS ADDICTED TO ALCOHOL.

ALCOHOLISM IS A SIGNIFICANT SOCIAL AND MEDICAL PROBLEM. IT IS IMPORTANT THAT PEOPLE

[a] LEARN THE FULL EXTENT OF THE DANGERS OF ALCOHOL CONSUMPTION.

[b] FIND HEALTHFUL WAYS OF DEALING WITH LIFE'S PROBLEMS AND DISAPPOINTMENTS; BY FACING THEM RATHER THAN TRYING TO DRINK THEM AWAY.

[c] IF UNFORTUNATE TO BE ENSNARED BY ALCOHOLISM SEEK HELP FROM PHYSICIANS AND GROUPS LIKE THE ALCOHOLICS ANONYMOUS [A.A].

ALCOHOLISM IS A DISORDER IN WHICH A PERSON REPEATEDLY DRINKS EXCESSIVE AMOUNTS OF ALCOHOL BEVERAGES, WITH RESULTING HARM TO HEALTH, RELATIONS WITH OTHER PEOPLE, AND WORK AND LIVING PERFORMANCE. DO NOT ALLOW YOURSELF TO BECOME PHYSICALLY AS WELL AS PSYCHOLOGICALLY DEPENDENT ON ALCOHOL. ALCOHOLICS SUFFER FROM SYMPTOMS SUCH AS HALLUCINATIONS, TREMORS, FEVER, STRESS, CONVULSIONS OR SEIZURES.

SUGGESTED REASONS WHY PEOPLE BECOME ALCOHOLICS ARE BECAUSE OF BEING SHY, LONELY, IMMATURE, HAVING A DEPENDANT PERSONALITY. STRESSFUL, POOR SELF IMAGE, INFERIORITY COMPLEX. HAVING FAMILY DISTURBANCES ETC . IN SHORT ALCOHOL IS HARMFUL AND HE WHO IS WISE AVOIDS IT.

SATELLITE :- IS A SMALL PLANET REVOLVING AROUND A LARGER ONE.

ARTIFICIAL SATELLITE :-IS ANY OF THE OBJECTS PLACED INTO ORBIT AROUND THE EARTH AND USED FOR A VARIETY OF TECHNOLOGICAL AND SCIENTIFIC PURPOSES; SUCH AS WEATHER PREDICTIONS, GLOBAL COMMUNICATIONS AND NAVIGATIONAL.

FIELDS OF SCIENCE :-
PHYSICS
CHEMISTRY
ZOOLOGY
METEOROLOGY
BOTANY
GEOLOGY
MECHANICS
OPTICS
ARITHMETIC
GEOMETRY

MUSIC
ASTRONOMY
COSMOLOGY
PHYSIOLOGY
EMBRYOLOGY
ANATOMY
GENETICS
ECOLOGY

THE SOIL OF THE EARTH OF THE WORLD IS MADE UP OF DIFFERENT TYPES :-
VERTISOL
INCEPTISOL
ENTISOL
MOLLISOL
ARIDISOL
ALFISOL
SPODOSOL
ULTISOL
HISTOSOL
OXISOL

SOUTH AMERICA :-IS THE FOURTH LARGEST CONTINENT.
THE COUNTRIES OF SOUTH AMERICA.
BRAZIL
VENEZUELA
COLOMBIA
ECUADOR
PERU
BOLIVIA
ARGENTINA
PARAGUAY
URUGUAY
CHILE
SURINAME
FRENCH GUIANA
GUYANA

LANGUAGES :-

SPANISH IS SPOKEN AS THE OFFICIAL LANGUAGE OF NINE OF THE SOUTH AMERICAN COUNTRIES. VENEZUELA, COLOMBIA, ECUADOR, PERU, BOLIVIA, CHILE, ARGENTINA, PARAGUAY AND URUGUAY; THEY ALL SPEAK SPANISH.

PORTUGUESE IS THE OFFICIAL LANGUAGE OF BRAZIL.

DUTCH IS THE OFFICIAL LANGUAGE OF SURINAME.

FRENCH IS THE OFFICIAL LANGUAGE OF FRENCH GUIANA.

GUYANA HAS THE DISTINCTION OF BEING THE ONLY ENGLISH SPEAKING COUNTRY IN SOUTH AMERICA.

SWIMMING :-IS THE ART OF SELF SUPPORT OR SELF MOVEMENT, BY MEANS OF HANDS AND FEET, IN OR ON THE WATER. SWIMMING IS DONE IN SALT OR FRESH WATER. THE CHIEF OBSTACLE IN LEARNING TO SWIM IS FEAR OF THE WATER OR EXTREME NERVOUSNESS, WHICH PRODUCES MUSCULAR TENSION.

FIVE RECOGNIZED STROKES OF SWIMMING ARE IN USE, THEY ARE :-

[a] FREESTYLE WHICH IS ALSO CALLED THE CRAWL OR OVERHAND STROKE.

[b] BREASTSTROKE.

[c] BACKSTROKE.

[d] BUTTERFLY.

[e] SIDESTROKE.

WORLD RECORDS ARE ONLY RECOGNIZED AS SET IN FIFTY METERS POOL. IN INTERNATIONAL COMPETITION, THE LENGTH OF RACES RANGE FROM ONE HUNDRED TO FIFTEEN HUNDRED METERS. SWIMMING COMPETITION GOES WAY BACK TO THE FIRST MODERN OLYMPIC GAMES, HELD AT ATHENS IN 1896.

TAXATION :-IS A SYSTEM OF COMPULSORY CONTRIBUTIONS LEVIED BY A GOVERNMENT ON PERSONS, PROPERTY, AND CORPORATIONS, PRIMARILY AS A SOURCE OF REVENUE FOR GOVERNMENT EXPENSES AND OTHER PUBLIC PURPOSES. IN DESIGNING TAX SYSTEMS, GOVERNMENTS USUALLY CONSIDER THREE BASIC INDICATORS OF TAXPAYER WEALTH OR ABILITY TO PAY; WHAT PEOPLE OWN, WHAT THEY SPEND, AND WHAT THEY EARN.

EXAMPLES OF TAXATION ARE :-
PROPERTY TAX
TAXES ON SALE OR TRANSFER OF GOODS.
IMPORT DUTIES
EXCISES TAXES.
LUXURY TAXES.
INCOME TAXES.

TEETH :-ARE HARD CALCIFIED STRUCTURES, ATTACHED TO THE UPPER AND LOWER JAWS OF VERTEBRATES AND A FEW LOWER ANIMALS, AND USED PRIMARILY FOR CHEWING. HUMAN TEETH CONSIST OF AN EXTERNAL PORTION, CALLED THE CROWN, AND A ROOT THAT IS EMBEDDED WITHIN THE JAW. IN HUMANS, ONE SET OF TWENTY TEETH IS PRODUCED FOR USE DURING EARLY JAW DEVELOPMENT; THESE ARE CALLED THE DECIDUOUS TEETH OR, MORE COMMONLY, THE BABY TEETH. A SECOND SET OF THIRTY TWO LARGER PERMANENT TEETH REPLACES THE DECIDUOUS TEETH AS THE JAW MATURES.

THE PERMANENT TEETH OF BOTH THE UPPER AND LOWER JAWS ARE FROM FRONT TO BACK :-
CENTRAL INCISORS
LATERAL INCISORS
CUSPIDS
FIRST BICUSPIDS
SECOND BICUSPIDS
FIRST MOLARS
SECOND MOLARS
THIRD MOLARS

TOPOGRAPHY :-IN GEOGRAPHY AND SURVEYING, IS THE LAYOUT OF NATURAL AND ARTIFICIAL FEATURES ON THE SURFACE OF THE EARTH, AND THE SCIENCE OF THEIR DETAILED, GRAPHIC REPRESENTATIONS ON MAPS AND CHARTS.

THERMOMETER :-IS AN INSTRUMENT USED TO MEASURE TEMPERATURE. THE DEGREE OF HOTNESS OR COLDNESS; FEVER.

SPORTS :-

WORLD TRACK AND FIELD EVENTS :-
MEN'S RUNNING
100 METERS
200 M
400 M
800 M
1000 M
1500 M
1 MILE
2000 METER
3000 M
5000 M
10, 000 M
20, 000 M
25, 000 M
30, 000 M
3000 METER STEEPLECHASE

HURDLES
110 METER
400 M

RELAY RACES FOR MEN AND WOMEN
400 METER [4 X 100]
800 M [4 X 200]
1600 M [4 X 400]
3200 M [4X 800]

WOMEN'S RUNNING
100 METER
200 M
400 M
800 M
1500 M
1 MILE
3000 METER
5000 M
10, 000 M

HURDLES
100 METER

400 M

FIELD EVENTS FOR MEN AND WOMEN
HIGH JUMP
LONG JUMP
TRIPLE JUMP
SHOT PUT
DISCUS THROW
JAVELIN THROW
HAMMER THROW
POLE VAULT
DECATHION
BIATHLON

OTHER SPORTING EVENTS RECOGNIZED IN THE WORLD
ARE SUCH AS
AUTOMOBILE RACING
BASEBALL
BASKETBALL
BOXING
FOOTBALL
SOCCER
GOLF
HORSE RACING
HARNESS RACING
HOCKEY
ICE HOCKEY
SKIING
SWIMMING
TENNIS
WINTER OLYMPICS
SUMMER OLYMPICS
WRESTLING
FIGURE SKATING
BOBSLEDDING
LUGE
SPEED SKATING
CYCLING
BOWLING
GYMNASTICS
WEIGHT LIFTING

BODY BUILDING
ICE SKATING
YACHTING
BOATING
CRICKET
FENCING
MARTIAL ARTS
KARATE
JUDO
KICK BOXING
SQUASH
NET BALL
RODEO
SURFING
LACROSSE
JUTITSO

GAME SHOWS
DOG SHOWS
CIRCUS
AMUSEMENT PARKS

INDOORS SPORTS SUCH AS :-
CARDS
MONOPOLY
BINGO
POOLS
SKITTLES
SCRABBLE
DOMINOES

CHESS :- A POPULAR GAME OF SKILL BETWEEN TWO PLAYERS, INVOLVING INTENSE INTELLECTUAL COMPETITION, WITH ALMOST NO ELEMENT OF CHANCE.EACH PLAYER HAS SIXTEEN CHESS PIECES, ONE SET CALLED WHITE, THE OTHER BLACK. EACH SET CONSISTS OF A KING, A QUEEN, TWO BISHOPS, TWO KNIGHTS, TWO ROOKS, AND EIGHT PAWNS. THE OBJECT OF THE GAME, WHICH SYMBOLIZES WARFARE IS TO CAPTURE THAT IS CHECKMATE THE OPPOSING KING.

THIS IS A VERY INTERESTING AND CHALLENGING GAME MAYBE YOU WOULD WANT TO TRY IT SOMETIME.

RED CROSS :-IS AN INTERNATIONAL HUMANITARIAN SOCIETY DEDICATED, IN TIME OF WAR, TO ALLEVIATING THE SUFFERINGS OF WOUNDED SOLDIERS, CIVILIANS, AND PRISONERS OF WAR. IN TIME OF PEACE, IT RENDERS MEDICAL AID AND OTHER HELP TO PERSONS AFFLICTED BY MAJOR DISASTERS SUCH AS FLOODS, TORNADO, EARTHQUAKES, FAMINES AND EPIDEMICS AND ALSO CARRIES OUT OTHER PUBLIC SERVICE FUNCTIONS.

CHAPTER 16.

SOME IMPORTANT AND NOTABLE EXPLORATIONS THAT MARKED HISTORY IN NO UNCERTAIN WAY.

[a] ALEXANDER THE GREAT FROM THE COUNTRY OF MACEDONIA BETWEEN THE YEARS OF 334 – 323 BC CONQUERED AND EXPLORED SYRIA, PALESTINE, PERSIA, EGYPT, AND A PART OF INDIA.

[b] GAIUS JULIUS CAESAR FROM ROME IN THE YEARS 58 – 52 BC CONQUERED AND EXPLORED MOST OF W EUROPE AND PART OF BRITAIN.

[c] ERIC THE RED OF NORWAY IN THE YEARS 982 – 86 AD DISCOVERED, EXPLORED AND COLONIZED SW COAST OF GREENLAND.

[d] MARCO POLO FROM VENICE BETWEEN THE YEARS OF 1271 – 95 BC TRAVELED THROUGH CENTRAL ASIA, INDIA, CHINA, MALAY ARCHIPELAGO, AND TIBET.

[e] IBN BATUTA OF MOROCCO BETWEEN THE YEARS OF 1325 – 49 BC TRAVELED IN AFRICA, THE MIDDLE EAST, INDIA, CHINA, THE STEPPES OF CENTRAL ASIA, CEYLON, AND INDONESIA.

[f] BARTOLOMEU DIAS FROM PORTUGAL IN THE YEAR 1488 BC EXPLORED ALGOA AND MOSSEL BAYS IN S AFRICA, OBSERVING AND NAMING CAPE OF STORMS WHICH HAS BEEN RENAMED CAPE OF GOOD HOPE.

[g] CHRISTOPHER COLUMBUS OF ITALY BETWEEN THE YEARS OF 1492 – 1504 BC MADE SEVERAL DISCOVERIES IN AMERICA DURING FOUR VOYAGES IN THE WORLD.

[h] JOHN CABOT OF ITALY BETWEEN 1497 – 1498 BC MADE TWO VOYAGES IN THE WORLD AND DISCOVERED NOVA SCOTIA, CAPE BRETON ISLAND AND EXPLORED THE E AND W COASTS OF GREENLAND, E COAST OF LABRADOR, W COAST OF BAFFIN ISLAND, AND A PART OF THE S COAST OF NEWFOUNDLAND.

[I] VASCO DA GAMA OF PORTUGAL BETWEEN 1497 –98 BC SAILED AROUND CAPE OF GOOD HOPE TO MALINDI ON E COAST OF AFRICA, AND THEN ACROSS THE INDIAN OCEAN TO CALICUT, INDIA.

[j] AMERIGO VESPUCCI OF ITALY BETWEEN THE YEARS 1497 –1502 BC SAILED THROUGH THE CARIBBEAN ALONG THE COAST OF SOUTH AMERICA.

[k] ALONSO DE OJEDA OF SPAIN IN 1499 – 1500 BC EXPLORED N COAST OF SOUTH AMERICA.

[l] SEBASTIAN CABOT OF ITALY BETWEEN THE YEARS OF 1508 –1509 BC AND BETWEEN 1553 – 1556 BC VOYAGED TO LABRADOR WHILE SEARCHING FOR THE NORTH WEST PASSAGE, AND SAILED AS FAR AS THE HUDSON BAY. HE DISCOVERED THE WHITE SEA AND THE SEA ROUTE TO RUSSIA.

[m] FERDINAND MAGELLAN OF PORTUGAL BETWEEN THE YEARS 1519 –21 BC EXPLORED ESTUARY OF RIO DE LA PLATA, SAILED S, PROCEEDING THROUGH STRAIT THAT BEARS HIS NAME, AND TRAVERSED PACIFIC OCEAN TO PHILIPPINE ISLANDS, WHERE HE WAS KILLED. HE WAS THE FIRST PERSON TO SAIL WEST AROUND THE GLOBE TO A LONGITUDE PREVIOUSLY REACHED ON AN EAST VOYAGE.

[n] GIOVANNI DA VERRAZANO OF ITALY IN THE YEAR 1524 BC EXPLORED EAST COAST OF NORTH AMERICA NORTH TO NEW FOUNDLAND, DISCOVERING NEW YORK AND NARRAGANSETT BAYS.

[o] FRANSCISCO DE ORELLANA OF SPAIN DURING 1540 - 1541 BC TRACED THE AMAZON RIVER FROM ITS HEAD WATERS IN THE ANDES TO ITS OUTLET IN THE ATLANTIC OCEAN.

[p] SIR WALTER RALEIGH OF ENGLAND IN 1595 AD EXPLORED GUYANA, THE COAST OF TRINIDAD, AND ORINOCO RIVER.

[q] JOHN SMITH OF ENGLAND IN THE YEAR 1607 AD EXPLORED THE EAST COAST OF NORTH AMERICA.

[r] HENRY HUDSON OF ENGLAND BETWEEN 1609 – 10 AD EXPLORED HUDSON RIVER, HUDSON STRAIT, AND HUDSON BAY.

[s] JOHN AND RICHARD LANDER OF ENGLAND DURING 1830 –31 AD TRACED DOWNSTREAM NIGER RIVER OF WEST AFRICA, ESTABLISHING ITS COURSE AND OUTLET.

[t] EDWARD JOHN EYRE OF ENGLAND BETWEEN THE YEARS OF 1839 – 44 AD EXPLORED AUSTRALIA; AUSTRALIA'S LARGEST LAKE BEARS HIS NAME.

FISHES :-THEY EXHIBIT DIVERSE MEANS OF PRODUCING YOUNG FISHES. OVIPAROUS FISHES ARE THOSE THAT LAY EGGS THAT ARE FERTILIZED OUTSIDE THE FEMALE'S BODY. IN SUCH SPECIES, DEVELOPMENT OF THE YOUNG IS ALSO EXTERNAL. SOME SPECIES OF FISH PRODUCE EGGS IN VERY LARGE QUANTITIES AND SCATTER THE EGGS IN OPEN WATERS; TAKE THE COD FOR EXAMPLE, ONE SINGLE COD MAY PRODUCE OVER THREE MILLION EGGS. THE PACIFIC SALMON IS ANOTHER EXAMPLE THAT MAY UNDERTAKE REMARKABLE HOMING MIGRATIONS IN ORDER TO CARRY OUT THEIR SPAWNING ACTIVITY. ON THE OTHER HAND VIVIPAROUS FISHES HAVE INTERNAL FERTILIZATION AND BRING FORTH THE YOUNG FISHES IN AN ADVANCED STATE OF DEVELOPMENT. EXAMPLES OF SUCH FISHES ARE THE SHARK, THE COELACANTH; AND AQUARIUM FISHES LIKE THE GUPPY AND MOLLIE. FISHES OCCUPY ALMOST EVERY CONCEIVABLE AQUATIC HABITAT; BOTH FRESH [SWEET] WATER AND SALT WATER. CLASSIFICATION OF FISHES ARE VERY COMPLEX; FISHES ARE DIVIDED INTO MORE THAN ONE HUNDRED ORDERS AND SUB ORDERS. FISHES BREATHE THROUGH GILLS AND USE THEIR FINS FOR SWIMMING MOVEMENTS. FISH IS ONE OF THE MOST IMPORTANT SOURCE OF PROTEIN FOR HUMANS, AND MOST FISHES ARE USED AS FOOD. SUBSIDIARY USES OF FISH AND FISH PRODUCTS INCLUDE THE MANUFACTURE OF FERTILIZERS, EXTRACTIONS OF FISH LIVER – OILS AS A SOURCE OF VITAMIN D; FISH SCALES ARE USED IN MAKING ARTIFICIAL PEARLS AND GLUE IS MADE FROM FISH OFFAL [REFUSE]. THERE ARE OVER 25,000 DIFFERENT KINDS OF FISHES ALL OVER THE WORLD. SOME FISH CAN LIVE FOR OVER 100 YEARS. SOME FISH ARE NAMED FOR OTHER ANIMALS LIKE

THE HOGFISH, COWFISH, LIZARDFISH, FROGFISH, DOGFISH, CATFISH, SNAKE EEL, LIONFISH, ZEBRAFISH, SEA HORSE. THE NAMES OF SOME OTHER FISHES ARE :-

BARRACUDA
JELLY FISH
STING RAYS
DOLPHINS
SNAPPER
WHITING
BASS
FLOUNDER
GROUPER
MULLET
SALMON
MACKEREL
SHARK
CROAKER
COD
EEL
SEABASS
TROUT
KINGFISH
BANGA MARY
CUFUM
TALAPA
HOURI
SUNFISH
PATWA
HASSAR
AMONG OTHERS :-

BIRDS :-ARE WARM BLOODED VERTEBRATE WITH FEATHERS AND WINGS. BIRDS INHABIT EVERY CONTINENT AND ALMOST EVERY ISLAND IN THE WORLD AND ARE ADAPTED TO VIRTUALLY EVERY ECOLOGICAL ENVIRONMENT. CERTAIN SPECIES AND TYPES OF BIRDS LIVE SEEMINGLY ANYWHERE; IN JUNGLES, ON MOUNTAINS, IN SWAMPS, IN MARSHES, ON ROCKY AND SANDY COASTS, IN FIELDS AND FORESTS, IN DESERTS, IN THE COLD EVEN ANTARCTICA AS WELL AS IN CITIES OF THE WORLD.

HERE IS A TABLE OF BIRDS ORDERS; THAT IS THE GROUPINGS OF BIRDS AND THE NAME GIVEN TO THEM.

ANSERIFORMES SUCH AS GEESE, DUCKS, SWANS.

APODIFORMES -HUMMING BIRDS, SWIFTS.

APTERYGIFORMES -KIWIS.

CASUARIIFORMES -EMUS, CASSOWARIES.

CHARADRIIFORMES -GULLS, JACANAS, SKUAS, SKIMMERS,TERNS.

CICONIIFORMES -STORKS, HERONS, FLAMINGOS, IBIS, BITTERNS.

COLUMBIFORMES -PIGEONS.

CORACIIFORMES -BEE–EATERS, HORNBILLS, KINGFISHERS, ROLLERS.

CUCULIFORMES -ROADRUNNERS, CUCKOOS, ANIS.

FALCONIFORMES -HAWKS, VULTURES.

GALLIFORMES -TURKEYS, QUAILS, GROUSE, PHEASANTS.

GRUIFORMES -CRANES, COOTS, RAILS, GALLINULES.

PASSERIFORMES -CROWS, WRENS, SPARROWS, BLACKBIRDS, SWALLOWS, FLYCATCHERS, LARKS.

PELECANIFORMES -DARTERS, GANNETS, PELICANS.

PICIFORMES -WOODPECKERS.

PROCELLARIIFORMES -SHEARWATERS, ALBATROSSES.

PSITTACIFORMES -PARROTS.

SPHENISCIFORMES -PENGUINS.

STRIGIFORMES -OWLS.

STRUTHIONIFORMES -OSTRICHES.

TINAMIFORMES -TINAMOUS.

ECOLOGY :-IS THE SCIENCE DEALING WITH ORGANISMS IN THEIR ENVIRONMENT OR SURROUNDINGS.

HELICOPTER :-DOES NOT DERIVE ITS LIFT FROM FIXED WINGS LIKE CONVENTIONAL AIRCRAFTS; BUT IT USES POWER DRIVEN ROTOR OR ROTORS REVOLVING ON A VERTICAL AXIS ABOVE THE FUSELAGE. HELICOPTERS CAN RISE OR DESCEND VERTICALLY, HOVER IN POSITION, AND MOVE FORWARD, BACKWARD, OR SIDEWAYS. THE HELICOPTER HAS TWO PRINCIPAL ADVANTAGES OVER CONVENTIONAL AIRCRAFT; THE ABILITY TO FLY SLOWLY OR HOVER; AND THE ABILITY TO TAKE OFF AND LAND IN A RESTRICTED SPACE.

AIRPLANE :-IS A MOTOR DRIVEN OR JET – PROPELLED AIRCRAFT. AN AIRPLANE IN FLIGHT IS THE CENTER OF A CONTINUOUS TUG OF WAR BETWEEN FOUR FORCES; LIFT, GRAVITY – FORCE OR WEIGHT, THRUST, AND DRAG ARE CONSIDERED AERODYNAMIC FORCES BECAUSE THEY EXIST DUE TO THE MOVEMENT OF THE AIRCRAFT THROUGH THE AIR. IN LEVEL FLIGHT AT CONSTANT SPEED, THRUST EXACTLY EQUALS DRAG AND LIFT EXACTLY EQUALS THE WEIGHT OR GRAVITY FORCE, FOR LANDINGS, THRUST MUST BE REDUCED BELOW THE LEVEL OF DRAG AND LIFT BELOW THE LEVEL OF THE GRAVITY FORCE OR WEIGHT. GRAVITY IS THE PULL ON THE PLANE TOWARDS EARTH. THRUST IS FORCE CREATED BY A POWER SOURCE WHICH GIVES AN AIRPLANE FORWARD MOTION. IT CAN EITHER PULL OR PUSH AN AIRPLANE FORWARD. THRUST IS THAT FORCE WHICH OVERCOMES DRAG. CONVENTIONAL AIRPLANES UTILIZE ENGINES AS WELL AS PROPELLERS TO OBTAIN THRUST. DRAG IS THE FORCE WHICH DELAYS OR SLOWS THE FORWARD MOVEMENT OF AN AIRPLANE THROUGH THE AIR WHEN THE AIRFLOW DIRECTION IS OPPOSITE TO THE DIRECTION OF MOTION OF THE AIRPLANE. IT IS THE FRICTION OF THE AIR AS IT MEETS AND PASSES OVER AND ABOUT AN AIRPLANE AND ITS COMPONENTS. THE MORE SURFACE AREA EXPOSED TO RUSHING AIR, THE GREATER THE DRAG. AN AIRPLANE'S STREAMLINED SHAPE HELPS IT PASS THROUGH THE AIR MORE EASILY.

HOLIDAYS :-THE PRINCIPAL HOLIDAYS OBSERVED IN THE UNITED STATES OF AMERICA; SOME OF WHICH ARE OBSERVED INTERNATIONALLY.

SUNDAY	
CHRISTMAS	DECEMBER 25
NEW YEAR'S DAY	JANUARY 1
MARTIN LUTHER KING JR'S BIRTHDAY	THIRD MONDAY IN JANUARY
LINCOLN'S BIRTHDAY	FEBRUARY 12
WASHINGTON'S BIRTHDAY	FEBRUARY 22
GOOD FRIDAY	FRIDAY IMMEDIATELY PRECEDING EASTER.

MEMORIAL DAY	MAY 30
INDEPENDENCE DAY	JULY 4
LABOR DAY	FIRST MONDAY OF SEPTEMBER.
COLUMBUS DAY	OCTOBER 12

ELECTION DAY FIRST TUESDAY AFTER THE FIRST MONDAY OF NOVEMBER

VETERANS DAY	NOVEMBER 11

THANKSGIVING DAY FOURTH OR LAST THURSDAY OF NOVEMBER.

AMERICAN INDIAN DAY	FOURTH FRIDAY IN SEPTEMBER.
ARMED FORCES DAY	THIRD SATURDAY IN MAY.
FATHER'S DAY	THIRD SUNDAY IN JUNE.
MOTHER'S DAY	SECOND SUNDAY IN MAY.
FLAG DAY	JUNE 14
ST. PATRICK'S DAY	MARCH 17
ST. VALENTINE'S DAY	FEBRUARY 14
HALLOWEEN	OCTOBER 31

IN HUMAN BEINGS :-HUMANISM - PHILOSOPHY OR THE STUDY OF ULTIMATE REALITY, ETHICS, IS DETERMINING THE ATTITUDE THAT EMPHASIZES THE DIGNITY AND WORTH OF AN INDIVIDUAL. A RATIONALITY FOR THE CAPACITY OF TRUTH AND GOODNESS. THE TERM HUMANISM IS MOST OFTEN USED TO DESCRIBE A LITERARY AND CULTURAL MOVEMENT OF A BODY OF PEOPLE.

NOBEL PRIZES :-ARE AWARDS GRANTED ANNUALLY TO PERSONS OR INSTITUTIONS FOR OUTSTANDING CONTRIBUTIONS DURING THE PREVIOUS YEAR IN THE FIELDS OF PHYSICS, INTERNATIONAL PEACE, PHYSIOLOGY OR MEDICINE, CHEMISTRY, LITERATURE AND ECONOMICS. THE YEARLY PRIZES ARE AWARDED FROM THE INTEREST ACCRUING FROM A TRUST FUND PROVIDED BY THE TESTAMENT OF THE SWEDISH INVENTOR AND PHILANTHROPIST [ONE WHO DOES SOMETHING TO HELP MANKIND] ALFRED BERNHARD NOBEL. SOME NOTABLY NAMES WHO HAVE RECEIVED THE PEACE PRIZE OVER THE YEARS ARE :-

INSTITUTE OF INTERNATIONAL LAW IN 1904

INTERNATIONAL PEACE BUREAU IN 1910

WILSON WOODROW [U.S.A] IN 1919

SIR JOSEPH A CHAMBERLAIN [GREAT BRITAIN] IN 1925

INTERNATIONAL COMMITTEE OF THE RED CROSS IN 1944.

UNITED NATIONS HIGH COMMISSIONER FOR REFUGEES IN 1954.

INTERNATIONAL COMMITTEE OF RED CROSS IN 1963.

MARTIN LUTHER KING JR [U.S.A] IN 1964.

UNITED NATIONS CHILDREN'S FUND IN 1965

INTERNATIONAL LABOR ORGANIZATION IN 1969

HENRY A KISSENGER [U.S.A] IN 1973

AMNESTY INTERNATIONAL IN 1977

ANWAR SADAT [EGYPT] IN 1978

MOTHER TERESA [INDIA] IN 1979

OFFICE OF THE U.N HIGH COMMISSIONER FOR REFUGEES IN 1981

DESMOND TUTU [SOUTH AFRICA] IN 1984

INTERNATIONAL PHYSICIANS FOR THE PREVENTION OF NUCLEAR WAR [U.S.S.R AND U.S.A]

UNITED NATIONS PEACE KEEPING FORCES IN 1988

DALAI LAMA [TIBET] IN 1989

GORBACHEV S MIKHAIL [U.S.S.R] IN 1990

AUNG SANSUKYI 1991

RIGOBERTA MENCHU TUM 1992

NELSON MANDELA AND FREDRIK WILLEM DE KLERK 1993

YASSER ARAFAT, SHIMON PERES,AND YITZHAK RABIN 1994

JOSEPH ROTBLAT 1995

CARLOS FELIPE XIMENES BELO AND JOSE RAMOS – HORTA 1996

JODY WILLIAMS 1997

INTERNATIONAL CAMPAIGN TO BAN LAND MINES [ICBL] 1997

JOHN HUME AND DAVID TRIMBLE 1998

DOCTORS WITHOUT BORDERS - BRUSSELS, BELGIUM

KIM DAE JUNG 2000

KOFI AMMAN 2001

UNITED NATIONS 2001

JIMMY CARTER JR. 2002
SHIRIN EBADI 2003

PULITZER PRIZES - AWARDS FOR OUTSTANDING
ACHIEVEMENTS IN LETTERS AND JOURNALISM; ESTABLISHED
BY THE WILL OF JOSEPH PULITZER, PUBLISHER OF
THE NEW YORK WORLD. THEY HAVE BEEN PRESENTED
ANNUALLY SINCE 1917 BY COLUMBIA UNIVERSITY ON
RECOMMENDATION OF THE ADVISORY BOARD OF THE
SCHOOL OF JOURNALISM. THE AWARD IS AWARDED IN THE
FOLLOWING AREAS.
BIOGRAPHY
AUTOBIOGRAPHY
CARTOONS
COMMENTARY
CRITICISM
DRAMA
EDITORIAL WRITING
FICTION
GENERAL NONFICTION
HISTORY
MERITORIOUS PUBLIC SERVICE
MUSIC
PHOTOGRAPHY
REPORTING
POETRY
SPECIAL CITATIONS

NUMERALS AND NUMBERS :-

ARABIC	ROMAN	NAME
0	ZERO, NAUGHT	
1	I	ONE
2	II	TWO
3	III	THREE
4	IIII OR IV	FOUR
5	V	FIVE
6	VI	SIX
7	VII	SEVEN
8	VIII	EIGHT
9	VIIII OR IX	NINE
10	X	TEN

11	XI	ELEVEN
12	XII	TWELVE
13	XIII	THIRTEEN
14	XIIII OR XIV	FOURTEEN
15	XV	FIFTEEN
16	XVI	SIXTEEN
17	XVII	SEVENTEEN
18	XVIII	EIGHTEEN
19	XVIIII OR XIX	NINETEEN
20	XX	TWENTY
21	XXI	TWENTY – ONE
22	XXII	TWENTY – TWO
23	XXIII	TWENTY – THREE
24	XXIIII OR XXIV	TWENTY – FOUR
25	XXV	TWENTY – FIVE
26	XXVI	TWENTY – SIX
27	XXVII	TWENTY – SEVEN
28	XXVIII	TWENTY – EIGHT
29	XXVIIII OR XXIX	TWENTY – NINE
30	XXX	THIRTY
40	XXXX OR XL	FORTY
50	L	FIFTY
60	LX	SIXTY
70	LXX	SEVENTY
80	LXXX	EIGHTY
90	LXXXX OR XC	NINETY
100	C	ONE HUNDRED
200	CC	TWO HUNDRED
300	CCC	THREE HUNDRED
400	CCCC OR CD	FOUR HUNDRED
500	D	FIVE HUNDRED
600	DC	SIX HUNDRED
1000	M	ONE THOUSAND
2000	MM	TWO THOUSAND
3000	MMM	THREE THOUSAND
10,000	$\overline{X}$	TEN THOUSAND

20,000	$\overline{XX}$	TWENTY THOUSAND
100,000	$\overline{C}$	ONE HUNDRED THOUSAND
1,000,000	$\overline{M}$	ONE MILLION
1,000,000,000	$\overline{\overline{M}}$	ONE BILLION
1,000,000,000,000	$\overline{\overline{\overline{M}}}$	ONE TRILLION

CHAPTER 17.

OCEAN -BODY OF SALT WATER COVERING MUCH OF THE EARTH.
THE OCEANS OF THE WORLD ARE :-
OCEANS AREA GREATEST DEPTH PLACE WITH GREATEST DEPTH

PACIFIC OCEAN 155,557,000 SQ.KM 11.033 M MARINA TRENCH
ATLANTIC OCEAN 76,762,000 SQ.KM 9,219 M PUERTO RICO TRENCH
INDIAN OCEAN 68,556,000 SQ KM 7,455 M SUNDA TRENCH
ANTARCTIC OR SOUTHERN OCEAN 20,327,000 SQ.KM 7,235 M
SOUTH SANDWIC TRENCH
ARCTIC OCEAN 14,056,000 SQ KM 5,625 M 77 DEGREES 45 MINUTES N
175 DEGREES W

THE PACIFIC OCEAN :-IS THE LARGEST AND DEEPEST OF THE WORLD'S OCEANS, COVERING OVER A THIRD OF THE EARTH'S SURFACE AND CONTAINING MORE THAN HALF OF ITS FREE WATER. NORTH OF THE EQUATOR IT IS CALLED THE NORTH PACIFIC AND SOUTH OF THE EQUATOR IT IS REFERRED TO AS THE SOUTH PACIFIC THE NAME PACIFIC WAS GIVEN TO IT BY THE PORTUGUESE NAVIGATOR FERDINAND MAGELLAN IN 1520. PACIFIC

MEANS PEACEFUL. THE PACIFIC OCEAN CONTAINS MORE THAN 30,000 ISLANDS; THEIR TOTAL LAND AREA, HOWEVER, AMOUNTS TO ONLY ONE – QUARTER OF ONE PERCENT OF THE OCEAN'S SURFACE AREA.

THE LARGEST ISLANDS, IN THE WEST REGION, FORM VOLCANIC ISLAND ARCS THAT RISE FROM THE BROAD CONTINENTAL SHELF ALONG THE EASTERN EDGE OF THE EURASIAN PLATE, THESE ARE CALLED OCEANIC ISLANDS; COLLECTIVELY CALLED OCEANIA.

COUNTRIES FORMING OCEANIA ARE AMONG OTHERS :-
TAIWAN
JAPAN
INDONESIA
PHILIPPINES
NEW GUINEA
NEW ZEALAND

OCEANOGRAPHY -THE STUDY OF THE OCEAN ENVIRONMENT.

OCEAN AND OCEANOGRAPHY IN MORE DETAIL-GREAT BODY OF SALT WATER COMPRISING ALL THE OCEANS AND SEAS THAT COVER NEARLY THREE – FOURTHS OF THE SURFACE OF THE EARTH, AND THE SCIENTIFIC STUDY OF THE PHYSICAL, CHEMICAL, AND BIOLOGICAL ASPECTS OF THE WORLD OCEANS. THE STUDY OF OCEANOGRAPHY IS TO UNDERSTAND THE GEOLOGIC AND GEOCHEMICAL PROCESSES INVOLVED IN THE EVOLUTION AND ALTERATION OF THE OCEANS, TO EVALUATE THE INTERACTION OF THE OCEANS AND THE ATMOSPHERE SO THAT GREATER KNOWLEDGE OF CLIMATIC VARIATIONS CAN BE ATTAINED, AND TO DESCRIBE HOW THE BIOLOGICAL PRODUCTIVITY IN THE SEA IS CONTROLLED.

THE WORLD OCEANS COVER APPROXIMATELY SEVENTY – ONE PERCENT OF THE EARTH'S SURFACE, OR ABOUT THREE HUNDRED AND SIXTY ONE MILLION SQUARE KILOMETERS, WHICH IS ONE HUNDRED AND FORTY MILLION SQUARE MILES. ITS AVERAGE DEPTH IS FIVE THOUSAND METER,

WHICH IS SIXTEEN THOUSAND FEET; AND ITS TOTAL VOLUME IS ABOUT 1,347,000,000 CU KM.

WATER :-IS THE COLORLESS LIQUID OF RIVERS, LAKES ETC .
TIDE :-IS THE RISE AND FALL OF THE OCEAN WATER EVERYDAY.
CURRENT :-IS THE FLOW OF WATER, AIR, ELECTRICITY, ETC .

THE DRIVING FORCE FOR OCEAN CURRENTS ARE THE EARTH'S ROTATION, WIND FRICTION AT THE SURFACE OF THE WATER, AND DIFFERENCES IN TEMPERATURE AND SALINITY. THE INTERACTION BETWEEN WIND AND CURRENT HAS A MAJOR EFFECT ON CLIMATE AND IS STUDIED FOR WEATHER PREDICTIONS AND FOR SEA TRAVEL.

THE LARGEST SEAS OF THE WORLD :-
NAME AREA GREATEST DEPTH PLACE OF GREATEST DEPTH
MEDITERRANEAN SEA 2,965,800 SQKM 4,632M OFF CAPE MATAPAN GREECE
CARIBBEAN SEA 2,718,200 SQ KM 6,946 M OFF CAYMAN ISLANDS
SOUTH CHINA SEA 2,319,000 SQ KM 5,016 M WEST OF LUZON
BERING SEA 2,291,900 SQ KM 4,773 M OFF BULDI ISLAND
GULF OF MEXICO 1,592,800 SQ KM 3,787 M SIGSBEE DEEP
OKHOTSK SEA 1,589,700 SQ KM 3,658 M 146 DEGREES 10 MINUTES E
46 DEGREE 50 MINUTES N
EAST CHINA SEA 1,249,200 SQ KM 2,782 M 25 DEGREES 16 MINUTES N
125 DEGREES E
HUDSON BAY 1,232,300 SQ KM 183 M NEAR ENTRANCE
JAPAN SEA 1,007,800 SQ KM 3,742 M CENTRAL BASIN
ANDAMAN SEA 797,799 SQ KM 3,777 M OFF CAR NICOBAR ISLAND
NORTH SEA 575,200 SQ KM 660 M SKAGERRA

RED SEA 438,000 SQ KM 2,211 M OFF PORT SUDAN
BALTIC SEA 422,200 SQ KM 421 M OFF GOTLAND

LARGEST LAKES OF THE WORLD :-
NAME AND LOCATION AREA LENGTH MAXIMUM
DEPTH
CASPIAN SEA [RUSSIA – IRAN] 152,239 SQ MI 745 MI 3,104
FT
SUPERIOR [U.S – CANADA] 31,820 SO MI 383 MI 1,333 FT
VICTORIA [TANZANIA – UGANDA] 26,828 SQ MI 200 MI 270
FT
HURON [U.S – CANADA] 23,010 SQ MI 247 MI 750 FT
MICHIGAN [U.S] 22,400 SQ MI 321 MI 923 FT
ARAL [KAZAKHSTAN –UZBEKISTAN] 13,000 SQ MI 266 MI
223 FT
TANGANYIKA [TANZANIA – CONGO] 12,700 SQ MI 420 MI
4,708 FT
BAIKAL [RUSSIA] 12,162 SQ MI 395 MI 5,712 FT
GREAT BEAR [CANADA] 12,000 SQ MI 232 MI 270 FT
NYASA [MALAWI – MOZAMBIQUE – TANZANIA]11,600 SQ MI
360 MI 2,316 FT
GREAT SLAVE [CANADA] 11,170 SQ MI 298 MI 2,015 FT
CHAD [CHAD – NIGER – NIGER] 9,946 SQ MI NOT GIVEN 23
FT
ERIE [U.S – CANADA] 9,930 SQ MI 241 MI 210 FT
WINNIPEG [CANADA] 9,094 SQ MI 264 MI 204 FT
ONTARIO [U.S – CANADA] 7,520 SQ MI 193 MI 778 FT
BALKHASH [KAZAKHSTAN] 7,115 SQ MI 376 MI 87 FT
LADOGA [RUSSIA] 7,000 SQ MI 124 MI 738 FT
ONEGA [RUSSIA] 3,819 SQ MI 154 MI 361 FT
TITICACA [BOLIVIA – PERU] 3,141 SQ MI 110 MI 1,214 FT
NICARAGUA [NICARAGUA] 3,089 SQ MI 110 MI 230 FT
ATHABASKA [CANADA] 3,058 SQ MI 208 MI 407 FT
RUDOLF [KENYA]2,473 SQ MI 154 MI NOT GIVEN
REINDEER [CANADA] 2,444 SQ MI 152 MI NOT GIVEN
EYRE [AUSTRALIA] 2,400 CUBIC MILES 130 MI VARIES
ISSYK-KUL [KYRGYZSTAN] 2,394 SQ MI 113 MI 2,297 FT
URMIA [IRAN] 2,317 SQ MI 81 MI 49 FT
TORRENS [AUSTRALIA] 2,200 SQ MI 130 MI NOT GIVEN
VANEM [SWEDEN] 2,141 SQ MI 87 MI 322 FT
WINNIPEGOSIS [CANADA] 2,086 SQ MI 152 MI 59 FT

MOBUTU SESE SEKO [UGANDA] 2,046 SQ MI 100 MI 180 FT

NETTILLING, BAFFIN ISLAND [CANADA] 1,950 SQ MI 79 MI NOT GIVEN

NIPIGON [CANADA] 1,870 SQ MI 72 MI NOT GIVEN

MANITOBA [CANADA] 1,817 SQ MI 140 MI 22 FT

GREAT SALT [U.S] 1,800 SQ MI 75 MI 25 FT

KIOGA [UGANDA]1,700 SQ MI 50 MI 30 FT

GEOGRAPHY :-SCIENCE OF THE EARTH'S SURFACE, CLIMATES, PLANTS, ANIMALS ETC .

GEOPHYSICS :-SCIENCE OF THE EFFECTS OF WEATHER, TIDES, ETC. ON THE EARTH.

KNOTS :-IS THE ART OF JOINING TOGETHER PIECES OF SUCH FLEXIBLE MATERIAL AS ROPE, AND OF FORMING LOOPS OR DESIGNS IN ROPES, STRING AND FIBERS INCLUDING WIRE ROPE. IT IS ONE OF THE OLDEST HUMAN SKILLS. IT SERVES BOTH UTILITARIAN AND DECORATIVE PURPOSES; IN SOME CASES KNOTTING HAS HAD RELIGIOUS AND MAGICAL SIGNIFICANCE.;IT IS LEARNT BY BOYS SCOUTS AND SEAMEN. IT IS PARTICULARLY ESSENTIAL TO USE ON BOARD SHIPS AND VESSELS OF ALL KINDS AND DESCRIPTION.

HERE ARE SOME COMMON AND POPULAR KNOTS MAYBE YOU CAN LEARN TO MAKE THEM.

OVERHAND KNOT

SHEET BEND

RUNNING KNOT

FIGURE OF EIGHT KNOT

SQUARE KNOT

BOWLINE

CATSPAW

DOUBLE SHEET BEND

CLOVE HITCH

OUTSIDE CLINCH

FISHERMAN'S BEND

TWO HALF HITCHES

HALF HITCH

SHEEPSHANK

TIMBER HITCH
BOWLINE ON THE BIGHT
REEFKNOT

ALSO SPLICES WHICH SAILORS MUST KNOW IN ORDER TO PERFORM THEIR FUNCTIONS ON BOARD SHIPS EFFICIENTLY AND EFFECTIVELY. ON BOTH ROPE AND WIRE.
EYE SPLICE
LONG SPLICE
CUT SPLICE
SHORT SPLICE

LANGUAGE :-COMMUNICATION AMONG HUMAN BEINGS THAT IS CHARACTERIZED BY THE USE OF SPOKEN OR WRITTEN SYMBOLS WITH AGREED UPON MEANING. LANGUAGE IS A MEANS OF COMMUNICATION OR EXPRESSION AND NECESSARILY INCLUDES GESTURES AND SOUNDS. HUMAN LANGUAGE IS LEARNED BY CHILDREN FROM ADULTS AND IS PASSED DOWN THROUGH THE GENERATIONS. LANGUAGE IS THE CONCERN OF PEOPLE IN MANY FIELDS, AMONG THEM COMMUNICATIONS, SPEECH AND RHETORIC, LITERATURE, SOCIOLOGY, PSYCHOLOGY, AND POLITICAL SCIENCE.
LINGUIST :- IS ONE WHO IS ADEPT IN SEVERAL LANGUAGES.
LINGUISTICS :- IS THE SCIENCE OF LANGUAGE.
LEARNING AND SPEAKING MORE THAN ONE LANGUAGE CAN BE WONDERFUL EXPERIENCES BOTH CHALLENGING AND REWARDING.

SOME OF THE LANGUAGES SPOKEN IN THE WORLD ARE :-
AFRIKAANS
ALURIAN
ARABIC
ARKIAN
ASSYRIAN
ASTURIAN
BENGALI
BERBER
BRAZILIAN PORTUGESE

BUHI
BULGARIAN
CATALAN
CHICHEWA
DUTCH
FRENCH
GREEK
HINDI
HAWAIIAN
HMONG
IRISH
ITALIAN
JAMELD
JAPANESE
MALAT
OCCITAN
PORTUGUES
PUNJABI
QUECHUA
RUSSIAN
SANSKRIT
SLOVENE
SPANISH
TENGWAR
TURKISH
URDU
VOGU
YIDDISH
ENGLISH
GERMAN
CHINESE

FUR :-THE TERM FUR REFERS TO ANY ANIMAL SKIN OR PART THAT HAS HAIR, FLEECE OR FUR FIBERS ATTACHED, EITHER IN A RAW OR PROCESSED STATE. SKINS OF FUR BEARING ANIMALS ARE ALSO CALLED PELTRIES.

FUR INDUSTRY :-AREA OF COMMERCE THAT ENCOMPASSES FARMING AND TRAPPING CERTAIN FUR BEARING ANIMALS AND PROCESSING THEIR SKINS FOR SALE IN THE MARKETING WORLD OF FUR GARMENTS.

HERE ARE THE MOST KNOWN COMMERCIALLY VALUABLE FURS.

[a] CARNIVORA MUSTELIDAE GOTTEN FROM ANIMALS SUCH AS THE MINK, WEASEL, WOLVERINE, OTTER, SKUNK, FITCH, BADGER, SABLE ETC .

[b] CARNIVORA FELIDAE GOTTEN FROM ANIMALS SUCH AS THE LEOPARD, JACQUAR, LYNX, OCELOT ETC .

[c] MARSUPIALIA FROM ANIMALS SUCH AS THE KANGAROO, OPOSSUM, WALLABY ETC .

[d] PRIMATES SUCH AS THE MONKEY.

[e] PINNIPEDIA SUCH AS THE VARIOUS KINDS OF SEALS.

[f] UNGULATA ANIMALS SUCH AS THE GOAT, LAMB, PONY, SHEEP, ANTELOPE ETC .

[g] RODENTIA FROM ANIMALS SUCH AS THE BEAVER, CHIPMUNK, HARE, RABBIT, SQUIRREL, CHINCHILLA, MARMOT ETC .

FUR FARMING, OR RAISING ANIMALS UNDER CONTROLLED CONDITIONS, STARTED WAY BACK IN 1887.

GEM :-IS A PRECIOUS STONE. GEMSTONES ARE BEAUTIFUL, RARE AND VALUABLE CREATIONS OF NATURE. GEMSTONES ARE CLASSIFIED ACCORDING TO THEIR CHEMICAL AND PHYSICAL PROPERTIES.

A LIST OF SOME COMMON GEMS ARE :-
EMERALDS
RUBIES
SAPPHIRES
AMETHYSTS
DIAMONDS
SPINELS
GARNETS
BERYL
TOPAZ
AGATE
ONYX
RED TOURMALINE
GREEN TOURMALINE
JACINTH

OPAL
JASPER
JADE
JARGON
COLOR CHANGE GARNET
COLOR CHANGE SAPPHIRE
DINOSAUR BONE
FLUORITE
FRESH WATER PEARLS
MOONSTONE
QUARTZ
SUNSTONE
ZIRCON

JEWELRY :-FOR THOUSANDS OF YEARS, ROCKS, GEMS, AND MINERALS HAVE BEEN USED AS JEWELRY FOR PERSONAL ADORNMENT; EARRINGS, PENDANTS, CHAINS, NECKLACES, BRACELETS ETC .

BIRTHSTONES AS SPECIFIED BY THE JEWEL INDUSTRY.

BIRTHSTONE	MONTH	SYMBOLIZING
GARNET	JANUARY	CONSTANCY
AMETHYST	FEBRUARY	SINCERITY
AQUAMARINE, BLOODSTONE	MARCH	COURAGE
DIAMOND	APRIL	INNOCENCE
EMERALD	MAY	LOVE, SUCCESS
PEARL, MOONSTONE	JUNE	H E A L T H , LONGEVITY
RUBY	JULY	CONTENTMENT
SARDONYX, PERIDOT	AUGUST	MARRIED HAPPINESS
SAPPHIRE	SEPTEMBER	CLEAR THINKING
OPAL, TOURMALINE	OCTOBER	HOPE
TOPAZ	NOVEMBER	FIDELITY
ZIRCON, TURQUOISE	DECEMBER	PROSPERITY

GEOCHEMISTRY :-THE APPLICATION OF CHEMICAL PRINCIPLES AND TECHNIQUES TO GEOLOGIC STUDIES, TO UNDERSTAND HOW CHEMICAL ELEMENTS ARE DISTRIBUTED IN THE CRUST, MANTLE AND CORE OF THE EARTH.

ENVIRONMENTAL GEOCHEMISTRY, DEALS WITH AND FOCUSES DIRECTLY ON PUBLIC HEALTH ISSUES RELATING TO THE ENVIRONMENT. TRACE ELEMENTS, NORMALLY PRESENT IN MINUTE AMOUNTS IN ROCKS, SOIL, AND WATER, ARE A MAJOR INFLUENCE ON HEALTH. SOME ARE ESSENTIAL TO GROWTH AND METABOLISM, OTHERS ARE TOXIC; SOME ARE BENEFICIAL IN MINUTE QUANTITIES BUT TOXIC IF CONCENTRATED.

GEOLOGY :-INCLUDES THE STUDIES OF INTERACTIONS BETWEEN THE EARTH'S ROCKS, SOILS, WATERS, ATMOSPHERE AND LIFE FORMS .

GEOLOGY IS DIVIDED INTO SEVERAL FIELDS OF STUDIES INCLUDING :

PHYSICAL GEOLOGY
GEOPHYSICS
GEOCHEMISTRY
PETROLOGY
MINERALOGY
STRUCTURAL GEOLOGY
SEDIMENTOLOGY
PALEONTOLOGY
GEOMORPHOLOGY
ECONOMIC GEOLOGY
ENGINEERING GEOLOGY
ENVIRONMENTAL GEOLOGY

VIRUS :-IS ANY INFECTIVE AGENT THAT CAUSES DISEASE.
BACTERIA :-MICROORGANISMS CAUSING DISEASES.

VIRUS IS ANY OF A NUMBER OF ORGANIC ENTITIES CONSISTING OF GENETIC MATERIAL SURROUNDED BY A PROTECTIVE COAT. BY ITSELF A VIRUS IS A LIFELESS FORM, BUT WITHIN LIVING CELLS IT CAN REPLICATE MANY TIMES AND HARM ITS HOST IN THE PROCESS. HUNDREDS OF VIRUSES ARE KNOWN WHICH CAUSE A WIDE RANGE OF DISEASES IN HUMANS, ANIMALS, PLANTS, AND INSECTS.

INCLUDED AMONG VIRUS CAUSING DISEASES ARE :-
COLD
FEVERS
YELLOW FEVER
MEASLES
MUMPS
INFLUENZA
DIARRHEA
BLISTERS
WARTS
RESPIRATORY DISEASES
CHICKEN POX
SHINGLES

HYDROLOGY :-OR NATURAL WATER CYCLE IS THE SCIENCE CONCERNED WITH THE DISTRIBUTION OF WATER ON THE EARTH, ITS PHYSICAL AND CHEMICAL REACTION WITH OTHER NATURALLY OCCURRING SUBSTANCES, AND ITS RELATION TO LIFE ON EARTH; THE CONTINUOUS MOVEMENT OF WATER BETWEEN THE EARTH AND THE ATMOSPHERE IS KNOWN AS THE HYDROLOGICAL CYCLE. UNDER CERTAIN CIRCUMSTANCES AND INFLUENCES, OF WHICH HEAT IS PREDOMINANT, WATER IS EVAPORATED FROM BOTH WATER AND LAND SURFACES AND IS TRANSPIRED FROM LIVING CELLS. THIS VAPOR CIRCULATES THROUGH THE ATMOSPHERE AND IS PRECIPITATED IN THE FORM OF RAIN AND SNOW. IT'S A CONTINUOUS PROCESS OF MOVEMENT OF WATER BETWEEN THE EARTH AND THE ATMOSPHERE.

WEIGHTS AND MEASURES
THE ENGLISH SYSTEM :-
LINEAR MEASURE [LENGTH]
1000 MILS = 1 INCH [IN]
12 INCHES = 1 FOOT [FT]
3 FEET = 1 YARD [YD]
5.5 YARDS = 1 ROD [RD]
40 RODS = 1 FURLONG [FUR]
8 FURLONGS = 1 MILE [MI]
5280 FEET = 1 MILE.

63360 INCHES = 1 MILE.
3 MILES = 1 LEAGUE [L]

SQUARE MEASURE [AREA]
144 SQUARE INCHES [SQ IN] = 1 SQUARE FOOT [SQ FT].
9 SQUARE FEET =1 SQUARE YARD [SQ YD].
30.25 SQUARE YARDS = 1 SQUARE ROD [SQ RD].
160 SQUARE RODS = 1 ACRE
640 ACRES = 1 SQUARE MILE [SQ MI].

CUBIC MEASURE [VOLUME]
1728 CUBIC INCHES [CU IN] = 1 CUBIC FOOT [CU FT]
27 CUBIC FEET = 1 CUBIC YARD [CU YD]
231 CUBIC INCHES = 1 U.S GALLON [GAL]
277.27 CUBIC INCHES = 1 BRITISH IMPERIAL GALLON.
2150.42 CUBIC INCHES = 1 U.S BUSHEL [BU]
2219.36 CUBIC INCHES = 1 BRITISH IMPERIAL BUSHEL.

LIQUID MEASURE [CAPACITY]
4 FLUID OUNCES [FL OZ] = 1 GILL [GI]
4 GILLS = 1 PINT [PT]
2 PINTS = 1 QUART [QT]
4 QUARTS = 1 GALLON

DRY MEASURE [CAPACITY]
2 PINTS = 1 QUART
8 QUARTS = 1 PECK [PK]
4 PECKS = 1 BUSHEL

WEIGHT [AVOIRDUPOIS]
27.3438 GRAINS = 1 DRAM [DR]
16 DRAMS = 1 OUNCE [OZ]
16 OUNCES = 1 POUND [LB]
14 POUNDS = 1 STONE
100 POUNDS = 1 HUNDREDWEIGHT [CWT]
8 STONES = 1 LONG HUNDREDWEIGHT [1 CWT]
2000 POUNDS = 1 SHORT TON [ST]
2240 POUNDS = 1 LONG TON [LT] OR 20 L CWT

WEIGHT [TROY]

24 GRAINS = 1 PENNYWEIGHT [DWT]
20 PENNYWEIGHTS 1 OUNCE [OZ T]
12 OUNCES =1 POUND [LB T]

WEIGHT [APOTHECARIES]
20 GRAINS = 1 SCRUPLE [S AP]
3 SCRUPLES = 1 1 DRAM [DR AP]
8 DRAMS = 1 OUNCE [OZ AP]
12 OUNCES =1 POUND [LB AP]

SURVEYORS' MEASURE
7.92 INCHES = 1 LINK [LI]
100 LINKS = 1 1 CHAIN [CH]
66 FEET = 1 CHAIN
80 CHAINS = 1 MILE

MARINERS' [SEAMEN] MEASURE
6 FEET = 1 FATHOM [FATH]
120 FATHOMS = 1 CABLE'S LENGTH [U.S NAVY]
1852 METERS = 1 NAUTICAL MILE [N MI]
1 NAUTICAL MILE PER HOUR [N MPH] = 1 KNOT [K]

PAPER MEASURE
25 SHEETS = 1 QUIRE [QR]
20 QUIRES = 1 STANDARD REAM [RM]
516 SHEETS = 1 PRINTERS' REAM
2 REAMS = 1 BUNDLE [BDL]
4 BUNDLES = 1 CASE [C]

PRINTERS' MEASURE [TYPOGRAPHY]
0.013837 INCHES = 1 POINT
12 POINTS = 1 PICA

WOOD MEASURE
144 CUBIC INCHES [1X1X1] = 1 BOARD FOOT [FBM]
16 CUBIC FEET [4X4X1] = 1 CORD FOOT [CD FT]
8 CORD FEET = 1 CORD [CD]

CIRCULAR OR ANGULAR MEASURE
60 SECONDS = 1 MINUTE [MIN]
60 MINUTES = 1 DEGREE

30 DEGREES = 1 ZODIAC SIGN
57.2958 DEGREES = 1 RADIAN
90 DEGREES = 1 QUADRANT OR RIGHT ANGLE
360 DEGREES = 1 CIRCLE

METRIC SYSTEM OF WEIGHTS AND MEASURES :-
LINEAR MEASURE [LENGTH]
1/10 METER [M] = 1 DECIMETER [DM]
1/10 DECIMETER = 1 CENTIMETER [CM]
1/10 CENTIMETER = 1 MILLIMETER [MM]
1/1000 MILLIMETER = 1 MICROMETER [UM]
1/1000 MICROMETER = 1 NANOMETER [NM]
100 METERS = 1 HECTOMETER [HM]
10 HECTOMETERS =1 KILOMETER [KM]
1000 KILOMETERS =1 MEGAMETER.

SQUARE MEASURE [AREA]
1 ARE = 1 SQUARE DECAMETER [SQ DAM]
1 HECTARE = 1 SQUARE HECTOMETER [SQ HM]

CUBIC MEASURE [VOLUME OR CAPACITY]
1/10 LITER = 1 DECILITER [DL]
1/1000 LITER = 1 MILLILITER [ML]
1000 LITERS = 1 CUBIC METER [CU M]

WEIGHT
1/1000 GRAM = 1 MILLIGRAM [MG]
1/1000 MILLIGRAM = 1 MICROGRAM [UG]
1000 GRAMS = 1 KILOGRAM [KG]
1000 KILOGRAMS = 1 METRIC TON OR MEGAGRAM
TONNE [T]

CHAPTER 18.

WEST INDIES :-
A CHAIN OF ISLANDS IN THE NORTH PART OF THE WESTERN HEMISPHERE, SEPARATING THE CARIBBEAN SEA FROM THE ATLANTIC OCEAN. DISCOVERED AND CALLED THE INDIES BY CHRISTOPHER COLUMBUS, IT WAS SUBSEQUENTLY CALLED THE WEST INDIES TO DISTINGUISH IT FROM THE EAST INDIES CHAIN OF ISLANDS.

COUNTRIES OF THE WEST INDIES :-
MARTINIQUE
GUADELOUPE
MONTSERRAT
NETHERLANDS ANTILLES
PUERTO RICO
ST. LUCIA
ST. KITTS – NEVIS
ST VINCENT AND THE GRENADINES
TURKS AND CAICOS ISLANDS
TRINIDAD AND TOBAGO
BRITISH VIRGIN ISLANDS
U.S VIRGIN ISLANDS
GREATER ANTILLES
LESSER ANTILLES
AVES ISLAND
LEEWARD ISLANDS
WINDWARD ISLANDS
ANGUILLA

ANTIGUA AND BARBUDA
ARUBA
BAHAMAS
JAMAICA
BARBADOS
BERMUDA
CUBA
CAYMAN ISLANDS
HAITI
DOMINICA
DOMINICAN REPUBLIC
GRENADA

CARIBBEAN :-IS THE REGION INCLUDING THE CARIBBEAN ISLANDS; IT'S AN ARM OF THE ATLANTIC OCEAN BETWEEN NORTH AND SOUTH AMERICA.
COUNTRIES OF THE CARIBBEAN :-
ANTIGUA AND BARBUDA
ARUBA
BAHAMAS
BARBADOS
CAYMAN ISLANDS
CUBA
DOMINICA
DOMINICAN REPUBLIC
GRENADA
GUADELOPE
HAITI
JAMAICA
MARTINIQUE
PUERTO RICO
ST. KITTS AND NEVIS
ST. LUCIA
ST. VINCENT AND THE GRENADINES
TRINIDAD AND TOBAGO
TURKS AND CAICOS ISLANDS
VIRGIN ISLANDS

SOME CARIBBEAN REGIONAL RESOURCES GROUP :-
AFRICAN, CARIBBEAN AND PACIFIC GROUP OF STATES.

THE AGRICULTURAL, SCIENCE AND TECHNOLOGY SYSTEM OF THE CARIBBEAN.
ASSOCIATION OF CARIBBEAN STATES
CARIBBEAN AGRICULTURAL RESEARCH AND DEVELOPMENT INSTITUTE
CARIBBEAN AMERINDIAN CENTER
CARIBBEAN ASSOCIATION OF INDUSTRY AND COMMERCE
CARIBBEAN BANANA EXPORTERS ASSOCIATION
CARIBBEAN CONFERENCE OF CHURCHES
THE CARIBBEAN DEVELOPMENT BANK
CARIBBEAN DISASTER EMERGENCY RESPONSE AGENCY
CARIBBEAN COMMUNITY SECRETARIAT
CARIBBEAN CONSERVATION ASSOCIATION
CARIBBEAN ENVIRONMENTAL HEALTH INSTITUTE
CARIBBEAN EXPORT DEVELOPMENT AGENCY
CARIBBEAN HALL OF FAME
CARIBBEAN NEWS AGENCY
CARIBBEAN STUDIES ASSOCIATION
CARIBBEAN TOURISM ORGANIZATION
CARIBNATION TELEVISION
U.N ECONOMIC COMMISSION FOR LATIN AMERICA AND THE CARIBBEAN.

THE CARIBBEAN COMMUNITY SECRETARIAT [CARICOM]
CARICOM MEMBER STATES :-
ANTIGUA AND BARBUDA
THE BAHAMAS
BARBADOS
BELIZE
DOMINICA
GRENADA
GUYANA
HAITI
JAMAICA
MONTSERRAT
ST. LUCIA
ST. KITTS AND NEVIS
ST. VINCENT AND THE GRENADINES
SURINAME
TRINIDAD AND TOGAGO

CARICOM ASSOCIATE MEMBERS ARE :-
CAYMAN ISLANDS
TURKS AND CAICOS ISLANDS
BRITISH VIRGIN ISLANDS
ANGUILLA
BERMUDA

THE LARGEST COUNTRIES OF THE WORLD :-

RUSSIA	6.6 MILLION SQUARE MILES
CANADA	3.9 MILLION SQUARE MILES
CHINA	3.7 MILLION SQUARE MILES
UNITED STATES	3.7 MILLION SQUARE MILES
BRAZIL	3.3 MILLION SQUARE MILES
AUSTRALIA	3 MILLION SQUARE MILES
INDIA	1.2 MILLION SQUARE MILES
ARGENTINA	1.1 MILLION SQUARE MILES
KAZAKHSTAN	1,050,000 SQUARE MILES
SUDAN	966,000 SQUARE MILES

THE LARGEST ISLANDS IN THE WORLD :-

GREENLAND	NORTHERN ATLANTIC
NEW GUINEA	SOUTHWEST PACIFIC
BORNEO	SOUTHWEST PACIFIC
MADAGASCAR	WESTERN INDIAN
BAFFIN ISLAND	NORTHERN ATLANTIC

WIND AND CURRENT :-
WIND IS AIR IN MOTION; APPLIES TO THE NATURAL HORIZONTAL MOTION OF THE ATMOSPHERE.

CURRENT :-MOTION IN A VERTICAL DIRECTION IS CALLED A CURRENT.

WINDS ARE PRODUCED BY DIFFERENCES IN ATMOSPHERIC PRESSURE, WHICH ARE PRIMARILY ATTRIBUTABLE TO DIFFERENCES IN TEMPERATURE. VARIATIONS IN THE DISTRIBUTION OF PRESSURE AND TEMPERATURE ARE CAUSED LARGELY BY UNEQUAL DISTRIBUTION OF HEAT FROM THE SUN, TOGETHER WITH DIFFERENCES IN THE THERMAL PROPERTIES OF OCEAN AND LAND SURFACES.

THE BEAUFORT WIND SCALE IS USED BY MARINERS AND METEOROLOGISTS TO INDICATE WIND VELOCITY. IT

WAS INVENTED IN 1805 BY THE IRISH HYDROGRAPHER FRANCIS BEAUFORT.

BEAUFORT SCALE   WIND SPEED M A R I N E R ' S DESCRIPTION

[KM / HR]		[MPH]	
0	BELOW 1	BELOW 1	CALM
1	1 - 5	1 - 3	LIGHT AIR
2	6 -11	4 - 7	LIGHT BREEZE
3	12 - 19	8 - 12	GENTLE BREEZE
4	20 - 28	13 - 18	MODERATE BREEZE
5	29 - 38	19 - 24	FRESH BREEZE
6	39 - 49	25 - 31	STRONG BREEZE
7	50 - 61	32 - 38	MODERATE GALE
8	62 - 74	39 - 46	FRESH GALE
9	75 - 88	47 - 54	STRONG GALE
10	89 - 102	55 - 63	WHOLE GALE
11	103 - 117	64 - 75	STORM
12	ABOVE 117	ABOVE 75	HURRICANE

PEST :-IS SOMETHING THAT CAUSES TROUBLE.

PEST CONTROL IS PRACTICED; IT IS A WIDE RANGE OF ENVIRONMENTAL INTERVENTIONS THAT HAVE AS THEIR OBJECTIVE THE REDUCTION TO ACCEPTABLE LEVELS OF INSECT PESTS, PLANT PATHOGENS, AND WEED POPULATIONS. CONTROL METHODS INCLUDE CHEMICAL, PHYSICAL, AND BIOLOGICAL MECHANISMS. DESPITE ALL THE STEPS TAKEN TO CONTROL PESTS. ANNUALLY ABOUT THIRTY FIVE PERCENT OF ALL CROPS WORLDWIDE ARE DESTROYED BY PESTS. AFTER FOOD IS HARVESTED, BIRDS, INSECTS, RODENTS, AND MICROORGANISMS DAMAGE OR DESTROY A FURTHER TEN TO TWENTY PERCENT LOSS; BRINGING THE TOTAL DESTRUCTION TO ANYWHERE BETWEEN FORTY OR FIFTY PERCENT.

THE CHEMICAL AGENTS CALLED PESTICIDES INCLUDE INSECTICIDES, HERBICIDES, AND FUNGICIDES. TODAY, INTEGRATED PEST MANAGEMENT [IPM] IS A DEVELOPED TECHNOLOGY FOR PEST CONTROL THAT IS AIMED AT ACHIEVING THE DESIRED RESULTS OF CONTROL WHILE REDUCING THE USE OF PESTICIDES. TO ACHIEVE THIS,

VARIOUS COMBINATIONS OF CHEMICAL, BIOLOGICAL, AND PHYSICAL CONTROLS ARE EMPLOYED.

HERE ARE A FEW OF THE MORE KNOWN PESTS OF THE MANY THOUSANDS OF SPECIES OF PESTS THAT AFFECT THE HEALTH AND ECONOMY OF HUMANS IN EVERYDAY LIFE.

HOUSEFLY
DRAIN FLY
COCKROACH
CRICKET
FLEA
MOSQUITO
WEEVIL
TICK
SANDFLY
BOOKLOUSE
CENTIPEDE
EARWIG
MITE
LOUSE
MILLIPEDE
TERMITE
CRAB LOUSE
BODY LOUSE

PESTILENCE :-IS A CONTAGIOUS DISEASE.

PET :-IS A DOMESTICATED ANIMAL TREATED FONDLY.

BRIDGE :-IS A STRUCTURE PROVIDING CONTINUOUS PASSAGE OVER A BODY OF WATER SUCH AS A RIVER, ROADWAY, VALLEY ETC .BRIDGES CARRY PATHWAYS, ROADS, RAILROADS AS WELL AS PIPELINES, POWER – TRANSMISSION LINES ETC .

A BRIDGE BUILT OVER DRY LAND OR A VALLEY IS CALLED A VIADUCT. OVERPASS IS REFERRED TO SHORT BRIDGES CROSSING HIGHWAYS AND RAILROADS. A LOW BRIDGE OVER A LAKE OR BAY IS REFERRED TO AS A

CAUSEWAY. BRIDGES THAT CARRY CANALS OR WATER CONDUITS ARE CALLED AQUEDUCTS.

CANAL :-IS AN ARTIFICIAL WATERWAY CONSTRUCTED FOR PURPOSES OF NAVIGATION, IRRIGATION, DRAINAGE, OR IN CONNECTION WITH A HYDROELECTRIC DAM.

SOME MAJOR CANALS OF THE WORLD ARE AS FOLLOWS :-

NAME	LOCATION	LENGTH IN MILES	YEAR IN USE
PANAMA	PANAMA	50.72	1914
SUEZ	EGYPT	100.76	1869
SAULT STE MARIE	CANADA	1.30	1895
BALTIC WHITE SEA	U.S.S.R	141.00	1933
ALBERT	BELGIUM	81.00	1939
AMSTERDAM – RHINE	NETHERLANDS	39.00	1947
CAPE COD	U.S	17.50	1914
LAKE WASHINGTON SHIP	U.S	8.00	1916
HOUSTON SHIP	U.S	50.00	1914
CHICAGO SHIP	U.S	30.00	1900
GOTA	SWEDEN	54.00	1832
MANCHESTER SHIP	ENGLAND	35.50	1894
NORD OSTSEE	GERMANY	60.00	1895

OTHER IMPORTANT CANALS :-
   ERIE CANALS
   THE CHESAPEAKE – DELAWARE CANAL
   THE CORINTH CANAL
   THE WELLAND SHIP CANAL
   THE KARA KUM CANAL
   IRELAND'S GRAND CANAL
   CHINA'S GRAND CANAL
   THE CALEDONIAN CANAL
   THE FORTH & CLYDE CANAL
   THE SHINNECOCK CANAL

THE MOSCOW CANAL

THE WORLD'S LONGEST MAN – MADE CANAL WATERWAY IS CHINA'S GRAND CANAL.

CANADA :-

PROVINCE	CAPITAL
NORTHWEST TERRITORIES	YELLOWKNIFE
NOVA SCOTIA	HALIFAX
ONTARIO	TORONTO
PRINCE EDWARD ISLAND	CHARLOTTETOWN
QUEBEC	QUEBEC
SASKATCHEWAN	REGINA
YUKON TERRITORY	WHITEHORSE
ALBERTA	EDMONTON
MANITOBA	WINNIPEG
NEW FOUNDLAND AND LABRADOR	SAINT JOHN'S
BRITISH COLUMBIA	VICTORIA
NEW BRUNSWICK	FREDERICTON

RAINBOW :-IS AN ARCH OF LIGHT EXHIBITING THE SPECTRUM COLORS IN THEIR ORDER, CAUSED BY DROPS OF WATER FALLING THROUGH THE AIR. IT CAN BE SEEN IN THE SKY OPPOSITE TO THE SUN AT THE END OF A SHOWER OF RAINFALL AND ALSO IN THE SPRAY OF WATERFALLS. THE COLOR ARRANGED FROM THE OUTER EDGE TO INNER EDGE ARE AS FOLLOWS :-

RED
ORANGE
YELLOW
GREEN
BLUE
INDIGO
VIOLET

BASIC KNOWLEDGE :-

CHAPTER 19.

ANATOMY :-IS THE BRANCH OF SCIENCE THAT DEALS WITH THE STRUCTURAL ORGANIZATION OF LIVING THINGS. THE NATURE OF ANATOMY CAN BE DIVIDED AND CLASSIFIED AS ANIMAL ANATOMY AND PLANT ANATOMY.

UNDER HUMAN ANATOMY WE HAVE SEVERAL SYSTEMS

[a] NERVOUS SYSTEM - THE NERVOUS SYSTEM HAS TWO DIVISIONS; THE AUTONOMIC, WHICH IS INVOLUNTARY AND CONTROLS CARDIAC – OF THE HEART AND SMOOTH MUSCLE AND GLANDS. ALSO THERE IS THE SOMATIC DIVISION WHICH ALLOWS VOLUNTARY CONTROL OVER SKELETAL MUSCLES. VOLUNTARY MOVEMENT OF PARTS OF THE BODY SUCH AS THE HEAD AND LIMBS IS CAUSED BY NERVE IMPULSES ARISING IN THE MOTOR AREA OF THE CORTEX OF THE BRAIN AND CARRIED BY CRANIAL NERVES OR BY THOSE THAT EMERGE FROM THE SPINAL CORD TO REACH SKELETAL MUSCLES.

[b] SKELETAL OR MUSCULOSKELETAL SYSTEM :-THE HUMAN SKELETAL SYSTEM HAVE MORE THAN TWO HUNDRED BONES BOUND TOGETHER BY TOUGH AND RELATIVELY INELASTIC CONNECTIVE TISSUES CALLED LIGAMENTS. BODY PARTS ARE DIFFERENT AND DIFFER IN THEIR AMOUNT OF MOVEMENTS FOR EXAMPLE THE MOVEMENTS OF INDIVIDUAL VERTEBRAE [ANY SINGLE

BONE OF THE SPINAL COLUMN] ARE VERY LIMITED; THE BONES COMPOSING THE SKULL ARE IMMOVABLE. ON THE OTHER HAND THE BONES – JOINT AT THE ARM OF THE SHOULDER IS VERY MOVABLE. WHEREAS THE KNEE JOINT IS LIMITED IN MOVEMENT. MOVEMENTS OF BONES OF THE SKELETON ARE EFFECTED BY CONTRACTIONS OF THE SKELETAL MUSCLES, TO WHICH THE BONES ARE ATTACHED BY TENDONS. THESE MUSCULAR CONTRACTIONS ARE CONTROLLED BY THE NERVOUS SYSTEM.

[c] CIRCULATORY SYSTEM :-THIS SYSTEM DEALS WITH CIRCULATION OF THE BLOOD THROUGH OUT THE BODY. IT STARTS IN THE HEART; BLOOD PUMPED BY THE HEART FLOWS THROUGH THE RIGHT CHAMBERS OF THE HEART, THROUGH THE LUNGS WHERE IT PICKS UP OXYGEN AND RETURNS TO THE LEFT CHAMBERS OF THE HEART; THE BLOOD IS THEN PUMPED INTO THE MAIN ARTERY THE AORTA, WHICH BRANCHES INTO SMALLER ARTERIES, UNTIL IT PASSES THROUGH THE SMALLEST KNOWN AS ARTERIOLES; THEN THE BLOOD PASSES THROUGH WHAT IS CALLED CAPILLARIES. HERE THE BLOOD GIVES UP ITS OXYGEN AND NUTRIENTS TO THE BODY TISSUES AND TAKE IN FROM THEM CARBON DIOXIDE AND OTHER WASTE PRODUCTS OF METABOLISM. THE BLOOD THEN RETURNS TO THE HEART THROUGH THE VEINS ARRANGEMENT, UNTIL THE BLOOD REACHES THE LARGEST VEINS THE INFERIOR AND SUPERIOR VENAE CAVAE, WHICH THEN RETURNS THE BLOOD TO THE RIGHT SIDE OF THE HEART. BLOOD IS DRIVEN INTO CIRCULATION BY THE CONTRACTIONS OF THE HEART.

[d] IMMUNE SYSTEM :-THE BODY DEFENDS ITSELF AGAINST FOREIGN BODIES AND INFECTIOUS MICROORGANISMS BY MEANS OF TWO WAY SYSTEM THAT DEPENDS ON RECOGNIZING THE INVADER. THE TWO PARTS OF THE SYSTEM ARE TERMED CELLULAR IMMUNITY, IN WHICH LYMPHOCYTES THROUGH THE LYMPHATIC SYSTEM ARE THE EFFECTIVE AGENT, AND HUMORAL IMMUNITY, BASED ON THE ACTION OF ANTIBODY MOLECULES.

[e] DIGESTIVE SYSTEM :-ENERGY IS REQUIRED FOR MAINTENANCE AND GOOD AND PROPER FUNCTIONING OF THE HUMAN BODY. THIS ENERGY IS GOTTEN FROM FOOD EATEN. DIGESTION STARTS FROM CHEWING OF THE FOOD UNTIL FINALLY ABSORPTION OF NUTRIENTS WHICH OCCURS MAINLY IN THE SMALL INTESTINES.

[f] EXCRETORY SYSTEM :-THE BODY GETS RID OF WASTE PRODUCTS THAT ARE NOT NEEDED AND WHICH CAN BE HARMFUL TO THE BODY. WATER, SALTS AND WASTE PRODUCTS ARE EXPELLED FROM THE BODY IN THE FORM OF SWEAT, URINE AND FECES.

[g] ENDOCRINE SYSTEM :-CONTROL OF VARIOUS BODY FUNCTION IS CARRIED OUT BY ENDOCRINE GLANDS WHICH FORM THE ENDOCRINE SYSTEM IMPORTANT PARTS OF THIS SYSTEM ARE SUCH AS THE PITUITARY WHICH LIES AT THE BASE OF THE BRAIN; THE PANCREAS AND THE PARATHYROID; THEY SECRETE HORMONES THAT REGULATE CERTAIN FUNCTIONS WITHIN THE HUMAN BODY; FOR EXAMPLE THE POSTERIOR LOBE OF THE PITUITARY SECRETS VASOPRESSIN, WHICH ACTS ON THE KIDNEY TO CONTROL THE VOLUME OF URINE; A LACK OF VASOPRESSIN CAUSES DIABETES INSIPIDUS, WHICH RESULTS IN PASSING OF LARGE VOLUMES OF URINE.

[h] THE REPRODUCTIVE SYSTEM :-IS WHAT IS RESPONSIBLE FOR PRODUCING OFFSPRING. REPRODUCTION IS ACCOMPLISHED BY THE UNION OF THE MALE SPERM AND THE FEMALE OVUM. DURING SEXUAL INTERCOURSE THE MALE ORGAN EJACULATES MORE THAN TWO HUNDRED AND FIFTY MILLION SPERMS INTO THE VAGINA. WHEN AN EGG FROM THE FEMALE AND A SPERM FROM THE MALE MERGES, PREGNANCY OCCURS. OVULATION, THE RELEASE OF AN EGG INTO THE UTERUS OCCURS ABOUT EVERY TWENTY EIGHT DAYS; THIS IS WHAT LEADS TO MENSTRUATION. THE DURATION OF PREGNANCY IS ABOUT TWO HUNDRED AND EIGHTY DAYS.

LYMPHATIC SYSTEM :-COMMON NAME FOR THE CIRCULATORY VESSELS OR DUCTS IN WHICH FLUIDS

BATHING THE TISSUE CELLS OR VERTEBRATES IS COLLECTED AND CARRIED TO JOIN THE BLOOD STREAM. THIS SYSTEM IS OF PRIMARY IMPORTANCE IN TRANSPORTING DIGESTED FAT FROM THE INTESTINE TO THE BLOOD STREAM; IN REMOVING AND DESTROYING TOXIC SUBSTANCES; AND IN RESISTING THE SPREAD OF DISEASE THROUGHOUT THE BODY.

THERE ARE ALSO OTHER SYSTEMS SUCH AS THE ARTICULAR, MUSCULAR, RESPIRATORY, URINARY, AND INTEGUMENTARY. ANATOMY, IS DIVIDED INTO SEVERAL BROAD FIELDS AND SPECIFIC ORGANS; THESE ARE DEALT WITH IN A LATER CHAPTER OF THIS BOOK, WHERE ILLUSTRATIONS - PICTURES ARE SHOWN EXPLAINING THE IMPORTANT ANATOMY STRUCTURE ORGANIZATION OF THE HUMAN BODY.

BRAIN :-IS A MASS OF NERVE TISSUE IN THE HEAD. IT IS THAT PORTION OF THE CENTRAL NERVOUS SYSTEM WITHIN THE SKULL. IN HUMANS IT IS THREE POUNDS OF A MASS OF PINKISH – GRAY TISSUE COMPOSED OF SOME TEN BILLION NERVE CELLS, EACH LINKED TO ANOTHER AND TOGETHER RESPONSIBLE FOR ALL MENTAL FUNCTIONS. IN ADDITION TO NERVE CELLS CALLED NEURONS, THE BRAIN CONTAINS GLIAL CELLS, BLOOD VESSELS, AND SECRETORY ORGANS. THE BRAIN IS THE CONTROL CENTER FOR VIRTUALLY EVERY VITAL ACTIVITY NECESSARY FOR SURVIVAL IN LIFE SUCH AS SLEEP, MOVEMENTS, HUNGER ETC . ALL HUMAN EMOTIONS SUCH AS LOVE, HATE, HAPPINESS, SADNESS, FEAR ETC ARE CONTROLLED BY THE BRAIN. IT ALSO RECEIVES AND INTERPRETS THE NUMBERLESS SIGNALS THAT ARE SENT TO IT FROM OTHER PARTS OF THE BODY AND FROM THE EXTERNAL ENVIRONMENT. THE BRAIN CONTROLS THE MIND SYSTEM AND IS RESPONSIBLE FOR YOUR INTELLIGENCE IQ,VOCABULARY, VISUAL APTITUDE, AND EVERY AREA OF MENTAL ABILITY INCLUDING CREATIVE AND INVENTIVE ABILITIES.

THE SPINAL CORD :-IS THE MAIN PATHWAY FOR INFORMATION CONNECTING THE BRAIN AND PERIPHERAL NERVOUS SYSTEM. THE HUMAN SPINAL CORD IS PROTECTED

BY THE BONY SPINAL COLUMN; WHICH IS MADE UP OF BONES CALLED VERTEBRAE.

SKIN :-THE SKIN IS AN ORGAN OF DOUBLE LAYERED TISSUE STRETCHED OVER THE SURFACE OF THE BODY AND PROTECTS IT FROM DRYING OR LOSING FLUID; FROM HARMFUL EXTERNAL SUBSTANCES, AND FROM EXTREMES OF TEMPERATURE. THE SWEAT GLANDS EXCRETE WASTE AND COOL THE BODY THROUGH EVAPORATION OF FLUID DROPLETS.

CANCER:-IS DEFINED AS A MALIGNANT TUMOR; NEW GROWTH OF TISSUE RESULTING FROM A CONTINUOS RAPID INCREASE OF ABNORMAL CELLS THAT HAVE THE ABILITY TO INVADE AND DESTROY OTHER TISSUES. CANCER MAY ARISE FROM ANY TYPE OF CELL AND IN ANY BODY TISSUE. CANCER IS NOT A SINGLE DISEASE; BUT A LARGE NUMBER OF DISEASES CLASSIFIED ACCORDING TO THE TISSUE AND TYPE OF CELL OF ORIGIN. SEVERAL HUNDREDS OF SUCH CLASSES EXIST; AND ARE DIVIDED INTO THREE MAJOR SUBTYPES.

[a] LEUKEMIAS AND LYMPHOMAS INCLUDE THE CANCERS THAT INVOLVE BLOOD FORMING TISSUE AND SHOWN BY THE ENLARGEMENT OF THE LYMPH NODES, THE INVASION OF THE SPLEEN AND BONE MARROW, AND THE OVERPRODUCTION OF IMMATURE WHITE CELLS.

[b] SARCOMAS ARISE FROM CONNECTIVE AND SUPPORTIVE TISSUE, SUCH AS NERVE, BLOOD VESSEL, BONE, CARTILAGE, MUSCLE, AND FAT.

[c] CARCINOMAS, WHICH INCLUDE THE MOST FREQUENTLY OCCURRING FORMS OF HUMAN CANCER, ARISE FROM TISSUE SUCH AS THE SKIN, THE LINING OF THE BODY CAVITIES AND ORGANS, AS WELL AS THE TISSUE OF THE BREAST AND PROSTATE.

ALMOST ALL CANCERS FORM TUMORS, BUT NOT ALL TUMORS ARE CANCEROUS, OR MALIGNANT; THE GREATEST NUMBER ARE BENIGN. BENIGN CANCER TUMORS ARE

CHARACTERIZED BY ENTIRELY LOCALIZED GROWTH AND ARE USUALLY SEPARATED FROM CLOSE BY TISSUE BY A SURROUNDING CAPSULE. BENIGN CANCER TUMORS GENERALLY GROW SLOWLY; IN SOME CASES THEY AFFECT AND ENDANGER THE PATIENT BY OBSTRUCTING, COMPRESSING, OR DISPLACING NEIGHBORING STRUCTURES; AS IN THE BRAIN FOR EXAMPLE. THE MOST SIGNIFICANT ATTRIBUTES OF MALIGNANT CANCER TUMORS IS THEIR ABILITY TO INVADE AND SPREAD BEYOND THE PLACE IN THE BODY OF THEIR ORIGIN. CANCERS MAY INVADE OTHER TISSUE BY DIRECT EXTENSION OR INFILTRATION OR MAY DISSEMINATE TO DISTANT SITES, FORMING SECONDARY GROWTHS KNOWN AS METASTASES.

A NUMBER OF FACTORS PRODUCE CANCER IN INDIVIDUALS; AMONG THEM BEING VIRUSES, RADIATION, CHEMICALS, HEREDITY, AND ALTERATIONS IN THE IMMUNE SYSTEM. OTHER SUPPOSEDLY CAUSES OF CANCER IN AN INDIRECT OR DIRECT MANNER ARE ATTRIBUTED TO ABNORMALITIES IN THE FOLLOWING AREAS :-
TOBACCO
ALCOHOL
DIET
POLLUTION
REPRODUCTION
MEDICINE
MEDICAL PROCEDURES
INFECTION
FOOD ADDITIVES
SEXUAL BEHAVIOR
OCCUPATION
GEOPHYSICAL FACTORS
INDUSTRIAL PRODUCTS

AREAS OF THE BODY COMMONLY DISTURBED BY CANCEROUS ATTACKS ARE :-
PROSTATE GLAND
COLON
STOMACH
LIVER
LUNG
SKIN

TESTIS
KIDNEY
BRAIN AND NERVOUS SYSTEM
URINARY BLADDER
PANCREAS
LARYNX
BREAST
OVARY
THYROID GLAND
RECTUM
ESOPHAGUS

DOCTOR :-IS A PHYSICIAN OR SURGEON WITH A HIGH DEGREE IN THE FIELD OF MEDICINES; WHO TREATS MEDICAL ILLNESS OR RELATED ILLNESS.

THERE ARE DOCTORS IN VARYING FIELDS SUCH AS :-
CARDIOLOGY
BIOTECHNOLOGY
DENTISTRY
DERMATOLOGY
GENERAL MEDICINE
INFECTIOUS DISEASES
NEPHROLOGY
NEUROLOGY
OPHTHALMOLOGY
PATHOLOGY
PEDIATRICS
GERIATRICS
PHARMACEUTICS
PHARMACOLOGY
PSYCHIATRY
SURGEON
PODIATRIST

A FEW DEADLY DISEASES THAT PEOPLE SUFFER FROM ARE :-
STROKE
CANCER
HEART DISEASES
AIDS

VARIOUS SEXUAL DISEASES
DIABETES
ARTHRITIS
OSTEOPOROSIS
AUTO – IMMUNE
ALZHEIMER'S
MENTAL

SCIENCES :- ARE BROADLY CATEGORIZED AS :-
PURE SCIENCE
APPLIED SCIENCE
EXACT SCIENCE
DESCRIPTIVE SCIENCE
NATURAL SCIENCES
SOCIAL SCIENCES ARE ECONOMICS, PSYCHOLOGY
PHYSICAL SCIENCES -ASTRONOMY
PALEONTOLOGY
BIOLOGY :-IS THE SCIENCE OF LIFE IN ANIMALS AND PLANTS.

CHAPTER 20.

CONTINENT :-A CONTINENT IS A LARGE LAND MASS. THE SEVEN CONTINENTS OF THE WORLD ARE :-

ANTARCTICA
ASIA
EUROPE
AFRICA
SOUTH AMERICA
NORTH AMERICA
AUSTRALIA

ANTARCTICA :-IS THE FIFTH LARGEST CONTINENT, LOCATED ALMOST ENTIRELY SOUTH OF LATITUDE 66 DEGREES 30 MINUTES SOUTH. IT'S REFERRED TO AS THE ANTARCTIC CIRCLE. IT IS MOSTLY CIRCULAR IN SHAPE WITH A LONG ARM REFERRED TO AS THE ANTARCTIC PENINSULA— REACHING OUT TOWARDS SOUTH AMERICA. ITS TOTAL AREA IS ABOUT 5.5 MILLION SQUARE MILES IN SUMMER. DURING THE WINTER ANTARCTICA DOUBLES IN SIZE BECAUSE OF THE LARGE AMOUNT OF SEA ICE THAT FORMS AT ITS OUTER BOUNDARIES. THE TRUE BOUNDARY OF ANTARCTICA IS NOT THE COASTLINE OF THE CONTINENT ITSELF BUT THE ANTARCTIC CONVERGENCE, WHICH IS A DEFINED ZONE IN THE SOUTH EXTREMITIES OF THE ATLANTIC, INDIAN, AND PACIFIC OCEANS BETWEEN ABOUT LATITUDE 48 DEGREES SOUTH AND LATITUDE 60 DEGREES SOUTH. AT THIS POINT THE COLDER WATERS FLOWING NORTH FROM ANTARCTICA MIX WITH THE WARMER WATERS FLOWING

SOUTH. THE ANTARCTIC CONVERGENCE MARKS A DEFINITE PHYSICAL DIFFERENCE IN THE OCEANS; BECAUSE OF THIS THE WATER SURROUNDING THE ANTARCTIC CONTINENT IS CONSIDERED AN OCEAN IN ITSELF KNOWN AS THE ANTARCTIC OCEAN. ANTARCTICA IS MORE THAN 95 % ICE COVERED AND CONTAINS ABOUT 90 % OF THE WORLD'S FRESH WATER. IT IS THE HIGHEST OF ALL CONTINENTS. ANTARCTICA HAS NO NATIVE POPULATION, ITS RESIDENTS ARE SCIENTISTS AND SUPPORTING CAST MEMBERS. SEVEN NATIONS; NORWAY, FRANCE, AUSTRALIA, NEW ZEALAND, CHILE, GREAT BRITAIN, AND ARGENTINA HAVE OVER THE YEARS ANNOUNCED TERRITORIAL CLAIMS TO PARTS OF ANTARCTICA. IT IS INTERESTING TO NOTE THAT U.S NOR U.S.S.R HAS NOT MADE A CLAIM TO ANTARCTICA. HOWEVER, THEY DO NOT RECOGNIZE THE CLAIMS TO ANTARCTICA BY THE OTHER SEVEN COUNTRIES. SINCE THE ANTARCTIC TREATY OF 1961 COUNTRIES CLAIM TO ANTARCTICA HAVE BEEN PUT ASIDE IN THE INTEREST OF INTERNATIONAL COOPERATION IN SCIENTIFIC RESEARCH.

THE ARCTIC :-IS LARGE COLD REGIONS AROUND THE NORTH POLE. THE ARCTIC IS NOT A CLEARLY DEFINED AREA; IT INCLUDES THE ARCTIC OCEAN, MANY ISLANDS, AND PARTS OF THE MAINLANDS OF ASIA, EUROPE, AND NORTH AMERICA. THE LARGEST ARCTIC LAND AREAS ARE IN CANADA, THE U.S.S.R, GREENLAND, SCANDINAVIA, ICELAND, ALASKA, AND OTHER ISLANDS. HERE THE PLACE IS INHABITED BY PEOPLE INCLUDING THE ESKIMOS AS WELL AS PLANT AND ANIMAL LIFE SUCH AS THE POLAR BEAR, FOX,WOLF ETC . ANIMAL LIFE IS ABUNDANT BOTH ON LAND AND IN THE SEA.

ASIA :-IS THE LARGEST OF THE EARTH'S SEVEN CONTINENTS. IT COVERS APPROXIMATELY 17,350,000 SQUARE MILES, WHICH IS ABOUT ONE – THIRD OF THE WORLD'S TOTAL LAND AREA. ITS PEOPLE ACCOUNTS FOR ABOUT THREE – FIFTHS OF THE WORLDS POPULATION.ASIA HAS AN INTERIOR THAT CONSISTS OF MOUNTAINS, PLATEAUS, AND INTERVENING STRUCTURAL BASINS.

THE COUNTRIES OF ASIA :-

AFGHANISTAN
BAHRAIN
BANGLADESH
BHUTAN
BRUNEI
BURMA
CAMBODIA
CHINA
TAIWAN
CYPRUS
HONG KONG
INDIA
INDONESIA
IRAN
IRAQ
ISRAEL
JAPAN
JORDAN
KOREA NORTH AND SOUTH
KUWAIT
LAOS
LEBANON
MACAU
MALAYSIA
MALDIVES
MONGOLIAN
NEPAL
OMAN
PAKISTAN
PHILIPPINES
QATAR
SAUDI ARABIA
SINGAPORE
SRI LANKA
SYRIA
THAILAND
TURKEY
U.S.S.R
UNITED ARAB EMIRATES
VIETNAM
YEMEN

CENTRAL AMERICA :-IS A REGION OF THE WESTERN HEMISPHERE ACTUALLY IT IS A LONG TAPERING ISTHMUS THAT FORMS A BRIDGE BETWEEN NORTH AND SOUTH AMERICA. THE COUNTRIES OF CENTRAL AMERICA ARE :-
GUATEMALA
COSTA RICA
BELIZE
PANAMA
EL SALVADOR
HONDURAS
NICARAGUA

LOGIC :-IS THE SCIENCE OF REASONING. IT IS IMPORTANT TO TEST OPINIONS FOR LOGICAL CONSISTENCY, BE CAREFUL NOT TO LET YOUR REASONING IN LIFE LEAD FROM TRUE PREMISES TO FALSE CONCLUSIONS. DEDUCE YOUR POSITION IN LIFE FROM PRINCIPLES, EXPERIENCE AND PRECISE OBSERVATION.

LOGISTICS :-IS THE MILITARY SCIENCE OF MOVING AND SUPPLYING TROOPS.

ETHICS :-MORAL STANDARDS OR VALUES IN LIFE. CONCEPTS OF HUMAN NATURE AND SELF REALIZATION. HUMAN NATURE CERTAINLY INVOLVES FOR EVERYONE, A CAPACITY FOR FORMING HABITS; BUT THE HABITS THAT A PARTICULAR INDIVIDUAL FORMS DEPEND ON THAT INDIVIDUAL'S TRADITIONAL BACKGROUND, CULTURE, INFLUENCES, AND REPEATED PERSONAL CHOICES IN LIFE. ALL HUMAN BEINGS INNATE CAPACITIES IS TO SEEK AND STRIVE FOR HAPPINESS IN LIFE.

UNDERSTANDING ART AND SCIENCE :-ARTIST AND SCIENTIST TRY TO CREATE ORDER OUT OF THE SEEMINGLY RANDOM AND MULTIFARIOUS EXPERIENCES OF THE WORLD. ART AS WELL AS SCIENCE REQUIRE TECHNICAL SKILLS; BOTH TRY TO UNDERSTAND AND APPRECIATE THE WORLD FOR WHAT IT IS AND TO CONVEY THEIR EXPERIENCES TO OTHERS. AN ESSENTIAL DIFFERENCE, HOWEVER, EXISTS; THE ARTIST SELECTS QUALITATIVE PERCEPTIONS AND

ARRANGES THEM TO EXPRESS PERSONAL UNDERSTANDING. THE SCIENTIST STUDIES QUANTITATIVE SENSE PERCEPTIONS IN ORDER TO DISCOVER LAWS OR CONCEPTS THAT ARE UNIVERSALLY TRUE. WHEREAS FURTHER INVESTIGATION MAY CAUSE A SCIENTIFIC LAW TO BE INVALIDATED, A WORK OF ART, DESPITE CHANGES IN THE ARTIST'S VIEW OR THE PUBLIC ACCEPTANCE, HAS PERMANENT VALIDITY AS AN AESTHETIC STATEMENT AT A PARTICULAR TIME AND PLACE.

ART FORGERY :-IS IN ORDER TO DECEIVE IN MOST CASES FOR FINANCIAL GAIN, BY TRYING TO PRESENT SOMETHING IN THIS CASE AN ART OBJECT AS REPRESENTING SOMETHING OTHER THAN WHAT IT IS. ART FORGERY HAS MANY SUBDIVISIONS, SUCH AS THE DELIBERATE IMITATION OFFERED AS AN ORIGINAL. COPIES OF ART NOT INITIALLY INTENDED TO DECEIVE BUT LATER PASSED OFF AS ORIGINALS; WORKSHOP ARTIFACTS [ANY OBJECT MADE BY HUMAN WORK]ATTRIBUTED TO THE MASTER AS WELL AS OTHER AREAS OF FORGERY.

ART GALLERY :-A ROOM, HALL OR BUILDING USED FOR THE EXHIBITION OF ART OBJECTS. AN ART GALLERY IS ALSO A PRIVATE COMMERCIAL ESTABLISHMENT OFFERING WORKS OF ART FOR SALE. MANY ARTISTS HAVE FORMAL ARRANGEMENTS WITH GALLERIES THAT ACT AS THEIR AGENTS OR DEALERS, SHOWING THEIR ART WORKS AND TAKING A PERCENTAGE OF THE SELLING PRICE.

ARCHITECTURE :-IS THE SCIENCE OF DESIGNING AND CONSTRUCTING BUILDINGS. THE ARCHITECTURAL HISTORY OF THE WORLD IS OF INTEREST FOR SOME HAVE SOUGHT TO PRESERVE SOME HISTORICAL STRUCTURES INTACT; HAVING THEM DISPLAYED AS NATIONAL MONUMENTS AND DESIGNATED LANDMARKS SUCH AS MUSEUMS FOR TOURISTS ATTRACTION, AND TO OFFER AN HISTORIC SETTING IN THE VARIOUS COUNTRIES.

U.S.S.R :-UNION OF SOVIET SOCIALIST REPUBLICS DISINTEGRATION CAME ABOUT IN 1991. THE BREAKUP OF THE SOVIET UNION SAW A FORMATION OF FIFTEEN STATES

CREATING A COMMONWEALTH OF INDEPENDENT STATES. WHAT WAS FORMERLY THE SOVIET UNION IS NOW THE FOLLOWING STATES :-

RUSSIA
LATVIA
ESTONIA
LITHUANIA
BELARUS
MOLDOVA
UKRAINE
GEORGIA
ARMENIA
AZERBAIJAN
TURKMENISTAN
UZBEKISTAN
TAJIKISTAN
KYRGYZSTAN
KAZAKHSTAN

CABINET OF THE UNITED STATES :-
VICE PRESIDENT
SECRETARY OF STATE
SECRETARY OF THE TREASURY
SECRETARY OF DEFENSE
SECRETARY OF AGRICULTURE
SECRETARY OF THE INTERIOR
SECRETARY OF COMMERCE
SECRETARY OF LABOR
SECRETARY OF HEALTH
SECRETARY OF HUMAN SERVICES
SECRETARY OF HOUSING
SECRETARY OF URBAN DEVELOPMENT
SECRETARY OF TRANSPORTATION
SECRETARY OF ENERGY
SECRETARY OF EDUCATION
SECRETARY OF VETERANS AFFAIRS
ATTORNEY GENERAL
CHIEF OF STAFF

DEGREES GRANTED AND THEIR ABBREVIATIONS FOR CERTAIN AREAS OF STUDIES :-

B.A	BACHELOR OF ARTS
M.A	MASTER OF ARTS
B.C.L	BACHELOR OF CIVIL LAW
B.B.S	BACHELOR OF BUSINESS SCIENCE
B.D	BACHELOR OF DIVINITY
B.Lit	BACHELOR OF LETTERS OR LITERATURE
B.Sc OR B.S	BACHELOR OF SCIENCE
LL.B	BACHELOR OF LAWS
C.E	CIVIL ENGINEER
Ch.E	CHEMICAL ENGINEER
D.C.L	DOCTOR OF CIVIL LAW
D.D	DOCTOR OF DIVINITY
D.D.S	DOCTOR OF DENTAL SURGERY
D.LiTT	DOCTOR OF LETTERS OR LITERATURE
D.M.D	DOCTOR OF DENTAL MEDICINE
D.Sc	DOCTOR OF SCIENCE
D.V.M	DOCTOR OF VETERINARY MEDICINE
E.E	ELECTRICAL ENGINEER
J.D	DOCTOR OF LAW
L.H.D	DOCTOR OF HUMANITIES
LLD	DOCTOR OF LAWS
M.B.A	MASTER OF BUSINESS ADMINISTRATION
M.C.E	MASTER OF CIVIL ENGINEER
M.D	DOCTOR OF MEDICINE
M.E	MECHANICAL ENGINEER
Mus.B	BACHELOR OF MUSIC
Mus.D	DOCTOR OF MUSIC
Ph.D	DOCTOR OF PHILOSOPHY
Ph.G	GRADUATE IN PHARMACY
S.T.B	BACHELOR OF SACRED THEOLOGY
V.S	VETERINARY SURGEON

A DESERT IS AN ARID, SANDY REGION. DESERTS COVER ABOUT ONE FIFTH OF THE EARTH'S SURFACE AND OCCUR WHERE RAINFALL IS LESS THAN FIFTY CENTIMETERS A YEAR. THERE ARE FOUR MAJOR TYPES OF DESERTS; HOT AND DRY, SEMIARID, COASTAL, AND COLD.

DESERT REGIONS OF THE WORLD :-
DESERTS LOCATION APPROXIMATE AREA

SAHARA NORTHERN AFRICA 3.5 MILLION SQUARE MILES
GOBI MONGOLIA, NORTH – CENTRAL CHINA 500,000 SQUARE MILES
AUSTRALIAN DESERT AUSTRALIA 1.3 MILLION SQUARE MILES
ARABIAN PENINSULA ARABIAN PENINSULA 1 MILLION SQUARE MILES
TURKESTAN SOVIET CENTRAL ASIA 750,000 SQUARE MILES
NORTH AMERICAN DESERT S.W UNITED STATE 500,000 SQUARE MILES
NORTHERN MEXICO
PATAGONIA SOUTHERN ARGENTINA 260,000 SQUARE MILES
THAR DESERT PAKISTAN, N.W INDIA 230,000 SQUARE MILES
KALAHARI DESERT SOUTH WESTERN AFRICA 220,000 SQUARE MILES
TAKLA MAKAN NORTH WESTERN CHINA 185,000 SQUARE MILES
ATACAMA DESERT NORTHERN CHILE 140,000 SQUARE MILES
SOUTHERN PERU

THE EARTH :-THE PLANET WE LIVE ON. IT IS ONE OF THE PLANETS IN THE SOLAR SYSTEM; IT IS THE FIFTH LARGEST OF THE PLANETS IN DIAMETER AND THE THIRD IN DISTANCE FROM THE SUN. THE MEAN DISTANCE OF THE EARTH FROM THE SUN IS 149,503,000 KM OR 92,897,000 MI. IT IS THE ONLY PLANET KNOWN TO SUPPORT LIFE. A SURVEY OF THE EARTH SHOWS THE FOLLOWING DIMENSIONS.

TOTAL SURFACE AREA 510,100,000 SQ KM OR 196,950,000 SQ MI

VOLUME 1,083,230,000,000 CU KM OR 259,880,000,000 CU MI

APPROXIMATE MASS 5,980,000,000,000,000,000,000 METRIC TONS

AVERAGE DENSITY 5.52

EQUATORIAL DIAMETER 12,756.34 KM OR 7926.42 MI

EQUATORIAL CIRCUMFERENCE 40,076.5 KM OR 24,902.4 MI

POLAR CIRCUMFERENCE 40,008.6 KM OR 24,860.2 MI

POLAR DIAMETER 12,713.54 KM OR 7899.83 MI

EQUATOR :-IS AN IMAGINARY CIRCLE AROUND THE EARTH, EQUIDISTANT FROM THE NORTH AND SOUTH POLES. THE EARTH IS DIVIDED BY THE EQUATOR INTO TWO HEMISPHERES, THE NORTHERN HEMISPHERE AND THE SOUTHERN HEMISPHERE.

POLE :-END OF AN AXIS, AS OF THE EARTH.

POLAR :-HAVING OPPOSITE MAGNETIC POLES; NORTH AND SOUTH POLES OF THE EARTH.

NORTH :-DIRECTION TO THE RIGHT OF ONE FACING THE SUNSET.

SOUTH :-DIRECTION TO THE LEFT OF ONE FACING THE SUNSET.

EAST :-DIRECTION IN WHICH SUNRISE OCCURS.

WEST :-DIRECTION IN WHICH SUNSET OCCURS.

ANALYSIS :-IS THE SEPARATION OF A WHOLE INTO ITS PARTS TO FIND OUT THEIR NATURE.

SOME KINDS OF SPECIALIZED ANALYSIS :-

TYPES OF ANALYSIS MATERIALS OR ASPECT ANALYZED

OCEANOGRAPHIC SEAWATER AND THE OCEAN FLOOR

ORGANIC COMPOUNDS CONTAINING ELEMENTS SUCH AS CARBON AND HYDROGEN

INORGANIC COMPOUNDS IN WHICH CARBON COMBINED WITH HYDROGEN OR OXYGEN IS NOT THE MAIN INGREDIENT

CLINICAL IN MEDICINE, SUCH AS BLOOD COMPONENTS

PETROLEUM OIL AND PETROLEUM PRODUCTS

POLLUTION TOXIC SUBSTANCES

PHARMACEUTICAL DRUGS

FORENSIC EVIDENCE IN THE STUDY OF CRIME

GEOCHEMICAL ROCKS AND MINERALS

SURFACE ANALYSIS OF A SAMPLE'S SKIN AS OPPOSED TO ITS INTERIOR

TRACE VERY SMALL QUANTITIES.

LIBRARY IS A PLACE FOR COLLECTION OF BOOKS; A REPOSITORY FOR VARIOUS FORMS OF RECORDED INFORMATION. THERE ARE VARIOUS TYPES OF LIBRARIES SUCH AS :-

PUBLIC LIBRARIES

NATIONAL LIBRARIES
RESEARCH LIBRARIES
SCHOOL LIBRARIES
ACADEMIC LIBRARIES
SPECIAL LIBRARIES
ANTIQUITY LIBRARIES
NATIONAL ARCHIVES
AGRICULTURAL LIBRARIES
TECHNICAL LIBRARIES
BUSINESS LIBRARIES
SCIENCE LIBRARIES
CHURCH LIBRARIES
STATE LIBRARIES

LIBRARIES ARE FOUND ALL OVER THE WORLD. SOME LIBRARIES OF VARYING COUNTRIES OF THE WORLD ARE :-

AL AKHAWAYN UNIVERSITY, MOROCCO
ALASKA STATE LIBRARY
ARIZONA DEPARTMENT OF LIBRARY, ARCHIVES AND PUBLIC RECORDS
ASIAN INSTITUTE OF TECHNOLOGY, THAILAND
AUSTRALIAN NATIONAL UNIVERSITY, CANBERRA
AUSTRIAN NATIONAL LIBRARY, VIENNA
GUYANA PUBLIC LIBRARY, GUYANA
BIBLIOTECA ELECTRONICA CRISTIANA, PERU
BIRMINGHAM PUBLIC LIBRARY
CAMBRIDGESHIRE COUNTY LIBRARIES
CANTERBURY PUBLIC LIBRARY, CHRISTCHURCH
CENTRAL AND REGIONAL LIBRARY OF BERLIN
CENTER FOR MATHEMATICS AND COMPUTER SCIENCE, AMSTERDAM
COMMONWEALTH SCIENTIFIC AND INDUSTRIAL RESEARCH ORGANIZATION [CSIRO] LIBRARY NETWORK, CANBERRA
COPAC, UNION CATALOGUE OF THE U.K CONSORTIUN OF UNIVERSITY RESEARCH LIBRARIES [CURL]
GERMAN LIBRARY INSTITUTE, BERLIN
HAMPSHIRE COUNTY LIBRARIES
HOSEI UNIVERSITY, OHARA INSTITUTE FOR SOCIAL RESEARCH, TOKYO

IIT BOMBAY
LIBRARY AND INFORMATION SERVICE OF WESTERN AUSTRALIA [LISWA] PERTH
LONDON LIBRARY
NATIONAL AND UNIVERSITY LIBRARY OF ICELAND
NATIONAL ARCHIVES OF AUSTRALIA, CANBERRA
NATIONAL ART LIBRARY
NATIONAL CENTRAL LIBRARY, TAIPEI
NATIONAL LIBRARY OF CHINA
NATIONAL LIBRARY OF LIBYA
NATIONAL LIBRARY OF NEW ZEALAND, WELLINGTON
NATIONAL LIBRARY OF POLAND, WARSAW
NATIONAL LIBRARY OF PORTUGAL, LISBON
NATIONAL LIBRARY OF SCOTLAND
NATIONAL LIBRARY OF SWITZERLAND, BERNE
NATIONAL LIBRARY OF THE NETHERLANDS, THE HAGUE
PEKING UNIVERSITY LIBRARY
ROYAL LIBRARY OF BELGIUM, BRUSSELS
RUDJER BOSKOVIC INSTITUTE, CROATIA
SOUTH AFRICAN LIBRARY, CAPE TOWN
NATIONAL LIBRARY OF SOUTH AFRICA
STATE LIBRARY OF BERLIN
STATE RESEARCH LIBRARY OF CESKE BUDEJOVICE, CZECH REPUBLIC
TRADE DEVELOPMENT COUNCIL BUSINESS LIBRARY, HONG KONG
TSINGHUA UNIVERSITY LIBRARY, CHINA
WASHINGTON STATE LIBRARY
WESTMINISTER LIBRARIES AND ARCHIVES
WORLD BANK AND IMF LIBRARIES.

LIBRARY OF KNOWLEDGE CLASSIFICATION :-LIBRARY SCIENCE IS A METHOD OF CLASSIFYING KNOWLEDGE FOR THE PURPOSE OF CATALOGING BOOKS AND OTHER LIBRARY MATERIALS. IN THE LIBRARY OF CONGRESS SYSTEM FOR EXAMPLE ALL KNOWLEDGE IS DIVIDED INTO TWENTY ONE LARGE CLASSES, INDICATED BY CAPITAL LETTERS AS FOLLOWS.

A   GENERAL WORKS
B   RELIGION, PHILOSOPHY

C	AUXILIARY SCIENCE, HISTORY
D	UNIVERSAL HISTORY
E F	AMERICAN HISTORY
G	GEOGRAPHY, ANTHROPOLOGY
H	SOCIAL SCIENCES
J	POLITICAL SCIENCE
K	LAW
L	EDUCATION
M	MUSIC
N	FINE ARTS
P	LANGUAGE AND LITERATURE
Q	SCIENCE
R	MEDICINE
S	AGRICULTURE
T	TECHNOLOGY
U	MILITARY SCIENCE
V	NAVAL SCIENCE
Z	BIBLIOGRAPHY AND LIBRARY SCIENCE.

MAP :-IS THE REPRESENTATION OF A GEOGRAPHIC AREA; A PORTION OF THE EARTH'S SURFACE, DRAWN ON A FLAT SURFACE. IT USUALLY CONTAINS A NUMBER OF GENERALLY ACCEPTED SYMBOLS, WHICH INDICATE THE VARIOUS NATURAL, ARTIFICIAL, AND CULTURAL FEATURES OF THE AREA IT COVERS.

CHART :-IS A MAP USED FOR NAVIGATION.

GRAPH :-IS A DIAGRAM THAT SHOWS CHANGES IN VALUE.

ATLAS :-IS A BOOK OF MAPS.

LUMBER ;-WOOD SAWED INTO BOARDS, BEAMS, PLANKS, SHINGLES ETC .
LUMBER INDUSTRY DEALS WITH HARVESTING AND PRODUCING OF TIMBER – WOOD FOR CONSTRUCTION PURPOSES SUCH AS HOME BUILDING, FURNITURE MANUFACTURE, CABINET – WORK; ETC .LUMBER IS PRODUCED IN MANY COUNTRIES INCLUDING U.S.A, CANADA, JAPAN, SWEDEN, GERMANY, GUYANA, POLAND,

FRANCE, FINLAND AND BRAZIL. MANY TYPES OF TIMBER, SUCH AS MAHOGANY

GREENHEART

EBONY

ROSEWOOD

BOCOTE

BRAZILIAN CHERRY

COCOBOLO

GONCALO ALVES

IDIGBO

IPE OR LAPACHO

MADERO NEGRO

NARGUSTA

PEROBA ROSA

PRIMAVERA

PURPLEHEART

ROBLE

SANTA MARIA

TEAK

TREBOL

WILD TAMBRAN

PULPWOOD IS PRODUCED FOR THE MAKING OF PULP AND PAPER.

CHAMBER OF COMMERCE :-IS A LOCAL, NATIONAL OR INTERNATIONAL ASSOCIATION OF BUSINESS PEOPLE; ESTABLISHED TO PROMOTE COMMERCIAL AND OTHER ENTERPRISES. CHAMBERS OF COMMERCE ARE ENGAGED IN VARIOUS SURVEYS SUCH AS HOUSING, POPULATION, SCHOOL, SAFETY, LAWS AND OTHER THINGS THAT DETERMINE THE ATTRACTION AND PROMOTION OF BUSINESSES IN THEIR SPHERE OF INTERESTS. CHAMBERS OF COMMERCE ARE PARTICULARITY CONCERNED WITH PROBLEMS OF DOMESTIC AND FOREIGN TRADE AND WITH GOVERNMENTAL POLICIES AND POLITICAL EVENTS AFFECTING TRADE AND BUSINESS.

SOME CHAMBER OF COMMERCE AROUND THE WORLD ARE :-

ADDIS ABABA CHAMBER OF COMMERCE

ATHLONE CHAMBER OF COMMERCE AND INDUSTRY, IRELAND

ATHENS CHAMBER OF COMMERCE, GREECE
BERMUDA CHAMBER OF COMMERCE
BRITISH CHAMBER OF COMMERCE
CHAMBER OF COMMERCE AND INDUSTRY, FRANKFURT AM MAIN
CHAMBER DE COMMERCE ET D'INDUSTRIE DE PARIS
CHAMBER OF COMMERCE AND INDUSTRY OF ROMANIA AND BUCHAREST
CHAMBER OF COMMERCE OF CENTRAL SWEDEN
EAST JAVA CHAMBER OF COMMERCE AND INDUSTRY, INDONESIA
FEDERATION OF INDIAN CHAMBERS OF COMMERCE AND INDUSTRY
ONTARIO CHAMBER OF COMMERCE, CANADA
PIETERMARITZBURG CHAMBER OF COMMERCE AND INDUSTRY, JOHANNESBURG
SINGAPORE INDIAN CHAMBER OF COMMERCE AND INDUSTRY
SINGAPORE INTERNATIONAL CHAMBER OF COMMERCE
SOUTH TRINIDAD CHAMBER OF INDUSTRY AND COMMERCE INC.
GUYANA CHAMBER OF COMMERCE.
STOCKHOLM CHAMBER OF COMMERCE
THE AMERICAN CHAMBER OF COMMERCE IN HUNGARY
TRINIDAD AND TOBAGO CHAMBER OF INDUSTRY AND COMMERCE

ECONOMICS :-IS THE SCIENCE THAT DEALS WITH THE PRODUCTION, DISTRIBUTION, AND USE OF WEALTH.
ECONOMIC :- THE MANAGEMENT OF INCOME.

MONEY :-IS WEALTH; ANY MEDIUM OF EXCHANGE THAT IS WIDELY ACCEPTED FOR GOODS AND SERVICES AND IN SETTLEMENT OF DEBTS. THE NUMBER OF UNITS OF MONEY REQUIRED TO BUY AN ITEM IS THE PRICE OF THE ITEM. MONEY SERVES AS A STANDARD OF VALUE FOR MEASURING THE RELATIVE WEALTH AND WORTH OF GOODS AND SERVICES. THE FUNCTIONS OF MONEY AS A MEDIUM OF EXCHANGE AND A MEASURE OF VALUE GREATLY FACILITATE THE EXCHANGE OF GOODS AND SERVICES AND

THE SPECIALIZATION OF PRODUCTION AND DISTRIBUTION. WITHOUT THE USE OF MONEY TRADE WOULD REMAIN IN A BARTER SYSTEM OR THE DIRECT EXCHANGE OF ONE COMMODITY FOR ANOTHER; THIS WAS THE MEANS USED IN ANCIENT DAYS, AND IS STILL PRACTICED IN SOME PARTS OF THE WORLD ESPECIALLY IN REMOTE AREAS SUCH AS THE IN THE JUNGLES AND MOUNTAINOUS REGIONS. MONEY AS MEANS OF TRADE IS ESSENTIAL AND NECESSARY AS A MEANS OF TRANSACTING BUSINESS, AND A USEFUL WAY OF MANAGING MODERN ECONOMIC LIFE. SOME MEANS OF TRANSACTION AND EXCHANGE USED OVER THE YEARS AND IN VARYING PARTS OF THE WORLD HAVE BEEN :-

LIVESTOCK
SKINS OF ANIMALS
FURS
ELEPHANT TUSKS
SHELLS
BEADS
IRON
BRONZE
COPPER
DIAMOND
GOLD
SILVER
COINS
PAPER MONEY

THE REAL VALUE OF MONEY IS DETERMINED BY ITS PURCHASING POWER; WHICH REFLECT THE DEMAND AND SUPPLY OF GOODS AND SERVICES.

RELIGION :-IS THE BELIEF IN GOD AND SYSTEM OF WORSHIP. SOME PRACTICED RELIGIONS OF THE WORLD ARE AS FOLLOWS :-

CHRISTIANITY
ROMAN CATHOLIC CHURCH
ORTHODOX CHURCH
ANGLICANS
PROTESTANTISM
EVANGELICALISM
PENTECOSTAL
MISSIONARY

DENOMINATION
LUTHERAN
NAZARINE
CHURCH OF LATER DAY SAINTS – MORMONISM
CHURCH OF JESUS CHRIST
CHURCH OF GOD
SEVEN DAYS ADVENTIST
JEHOVAH'S WITNESSES
BAPTIST
AMERINDIANS RELIGIONS
AFRICIAN RELIGIONS
JUDAISM - JEWISH
ISLAM - MUSLIMS
HINDUISM
HARE RAMA HARE CHRISTNA
SIKH
BUDDHISM
ASSEMBLIES OF GOD
BAHAI FAITH
BULGARIAN ORTHODOX CHURCH
RUSSIAN ORTHODOX CHURCH
SCIENTOLOGY
SHINTO
SHIRDI SAI BABA
UNITED METHODIST CHURCH
PRESBETARIAN

EARTHQUAKE :-IS A SHAKING OF THE CRUST OF THE EARTH.

THE WORLD LARGEST EARTHQUAKE SINCE 1900 OCCURRED AS FOLLOWS :-

YEAR LOCATION

RICHTER MAGNITUDE SCALE

1905	NORTHERN MONGOLIA	8.5
1906	NORTHWESTERN MONGOLIA	8.4
1906	PACIFIC OCEAN FLOOR, NEAR ECUADOR	8.8
1906	CENTRAL CHILE	8.2
1917	WESTERN SAMOA	8.5
1920	CENTRAL CHINA	8.3
1922	CENTRAL CHILE	8.5
1923	KAMCHATKA PENINSULA, RUSSIA	8.5
1924	MACQUARIE ISLAND, AUSTRALIA	8.3
1933	PACIFIC OCEAN FLOOR, NEAR JAPAN	8.4
1938	BANDA SEA FLOOR, NEAR INDONESIA	8.5
1938	PACIFIC SEA FLOOR, NEAR ALASKA PENINSULA	8.2
1950	ARUNACHAL PRADESH, INDIA	8.6
1952	KAMCHATKA PENINSULA, RUSSIA	9.0
1957	ALENTIAN ISLAND	9.1
1957	NORTHERN MONGOLIA	8.1
1958	KURIL ISLAND	8.7
1960	SOUTHERN CHILE	9.5
1963	KURIL ISLAND	8.6
1964	SOUTHERN ALASKA	9.2
1965	ALENTIAN ISLAND	8.7
1966	WESTERN PERU	8.2
1968	PACIFIC OCEAN FLOOR, NEAR JAPAN	8.3
1977	SUMBAWA ISLAND, INDONESIA	8.2
1979	NORTHWESTERN ECUADOR	8.3
1989	SOUTH PACIFIC OCEAN FLOOR, NEAR MACQUARIE ISLAND AUSTRALIA	8.2
1994	KURIL ISLAND	8.3
1994	NORTHWESTERN BOLIVIA	8.2
2000	PAPAU NEW GUINEA	8.0
2001	WESTERN PERU	8.4

AIRPORT :-IS AN AIRFIELD WHERE AIRPLANES LAND AND TAKE OFF; AS WELL AS HAVING FACILITIES FOR REPAIRS ETC .

SOME OF THE WORLD BIGGEST AIRPORTS ARE :-

NAME OF AIRPORT	LOCATION	
CHARLES		
KINGSFORD – SMITH	SYDNEY	AUSTRALIA
MCDONALD / CARTIER	OTTAWA	CANADA
JOHN DIEFENBAKER	SASKATOON	CANADA
LESTER B PEARSON	TORONTO	CANADA
BILLY BISHOP	LOWENSOUND	CANADA
RAYMOND COLLISHAW	NANAIMO	CANADA
KONRAD ADENAUER	COLOGNE	GERMANY
ROGER DE SAINT EXUPERY	LYON	FRANCE
CHARLES DE GAULLE	FRANCE	
ELEFTHERIOS VENIZELOS	ATHENS	GREECE
INDIRA GHANDI	DELHI	INDIA
BEN GURION	TEL AVIV	ISRAEL
LEONARDO DA VINCI	ROME	ITALY
CHRISTOPHER COLUMBUS	GENOA	ITALY
SADDAM HUSSIEN	BAGHDAD	IRAQ
NORMAN MANLEY	KINGSTON	JAMAICA
JOMO KENYATTA	NAIROBI	KENYA
NINOY AQUINO	MANILA	PHILIPPINES
QUEEN SOFIA	TENERIFE	SPAIN
LOUIS BOTHA	DURBAN	SOUTH AFRICA
KING ABDUL	JEDDAH	SAUDI ARABIA
KING KHALID	RAYADH	SAUDI ARABIA
PRINCE MOHAMMAD	MEDINAH	SAUDI ARABIA
CHIANG KAI SHEK	TAIPEI	TAIWAN
SOCKARNO	JAKARTA	INDONESIA
SIMON BOLIVAR	CARACAS VENEZUELA	
JOHN LENNON	LIVERPOOL UNITED KINGDOM	
FIORELLO LANGUARDIA	NEW YORK	U.S.A.
GERALD FORD	GRAND RAPIDS	U.S.A.
GEORGE BUSH	HOUSTON	U.S.A.
JOHN KENNEDY	NEW YORK	U.S.A.
RONALD REGAN	WASHINGTON,	

	DC	U.S.A
JOHN FOSTER DULLES	WASHINGTON, DC	U.S.A
WILL ROGERS	OKLAHOMIA CITY	U.S.A
LOUIS ARMSTRONG	NEW ORLEANS	U.S.A
JOHN WAYNE	IRVINE	U. S. A
CHARLES LINDBERGH	SAN DIEGO	U.S.A
CHUCK YEAGER	CHARLESTON	U.S. A
EDWARD O' HARE	CHICAGO	U.S.A

VOLCANO :-MOUNTAIN FORMED BY ERUPTING MOLTEN ROCK.

GEOLOGISTS GENERALLY GROUP VOLCANOES INTO FOUR MAIN KINDS

CINDER CONES

COMPOSITE VOLCANOES

SHIELD VOLCANOES

LAVA DOMES

THERE ARE MORE THAN FIVE HUNDRED ACTIVE VOLCANOES; FIFTY OF WHICH ARE IN THE UNITED STATES [HAWAII, ALASKA, WASHINGTON, OREGON, AND CALIFORNIA] MORE THAN HALF THE NUMBER OF VOLCANOES EN CIRCLE THE PACIFIC OCEAN. VOLCANOES ARE ALSO IN THE MEDITERRANEAN SEA, MOUNT ETNA IN SICILY – ITALY. VOLCANOES TEND TO CLUSTER ALONG NARROW MOUNTAINS BELTS. VOLCANOES BOTH HARASS AND HELP MANKIND. THE DRAMATIC CATASTROPHIC ERUPTION OF MOUNT ST. HELENA ON MAY 1980 AND PINATUBO IN JUNE 1991; WRECK HAVOC AND DEVASTED THE PLACE. HOWEVER, VOLCANIC MATERIALS ULTIMATELY BREAK DOWN TO FORM SOME OF THE MOST FERTILE SOILS OF THE EARTH. PEOPLE ALSO USE VOLCANIC PRODUCTS AS CONSTRUCTION MATERIALS, AS ABRASIVE AND CLEANING AGENTS AND AS RAW MATERIALS FOR MANY CHEMICAL AND INDUSTRIAL USES.

STORMS :-ARE GIVEN NAMES WHEN SUSTAINED WIND REACHES THIRTY NINE MILES PER HOUR. THEY BECOME HURRICANE IF THE SPEED INCREASES TO SEVENTY FOUR MILES PER HOUR.

CYCLONE :-IS A STORM WITH HEAVY RAIN AND WHIRLING WINDS.

TORNADO :-IS THE MOST VIOLENT OF ALL STORMS. A TORNADO SOMETIMES CALLED A TWISTER, CONSISTS OF A RAPIDLY ROTATING COLUMN OF AIR THAT FORMS UNDER A THUNDERCLOUD. TORNADO WINDS SWIRL AT SPEEDS THAT MAY EXCEED THREE HUNDRED MILES PER HOUR OR FOUR HUNDRED AND EIGHTY KILOMETERS PER HOUR. A POWERFUL TORNADO CAN LIFT ANIMALS, VEHICLES, AND EVEN HOMES IN THE AIR AND DESTROY ALMOST EVERYTHING IN ITS PATH

THE FUJITA SCALE IS USED FOR ESTIMATING THE SPEED IN MILES PER HOUR OR KILOMETERS PER HOUR FOR TORNADOES AND OTHER VIOLENT WINDS BASED ON THE DAMAGES CAUSED.

FUJITA SCALE	DAMAGE	WIND SPEED MPH	KPH
F O	LIGHT	40 – 72	64 – 116
F 1	MODERATE	73 – 112	117 – 180
F 2	CONSIDERABLE	113 – 157	181 – 253
F 3	SEVERE	158 – 206	254 – 332
F 4	DEVASTATING	207 – 260	333 – 419
F 5	INCREDIBLE	261 – 318	420 – 512
F 6	INCONCEIVABLE	319 – 379	

HURRICANE :-TROPICAL CYCLONE IN WHICH WINDS ATTAIN SPEEDS GREATER THAN 74 MI OR 119 KM PER HOUR. WIND SPEEDS REACH OVER 190 MI OR 289 KM PER HOUR IN SOME HURRICANES. HURRICANES HAVE A LIFE SPAN OF 1 TO 30 DAYS; THEY RAPIDLY DECAY AFTER MOVING OVER LAND AREAS.

THE TOP TEN DEADLIEST HURRICANES :-

GALVESTON	TEXAS	1900
FLORIDA	1928	
FLORIDA AND TEXAS	1919	
NEW ENGLAND	1938	
FLORIDA KEYS	1935	
HURRICANE AUDREY	1957	
NORTHEASTERN UNITED STATES	1944	

LOUISIANA   1909
LOUISIANA   1915
GALVESTON TEXAS   1915

THE TOP TEN MOST INTENSE HURRICANES :-
FLORIDA KEYS   1935
HURRICANE CAMILLE
HURRICANE ANDREW
FLORIDA AND TEXAS   1919
LAKE OKEECHOBEE   1928
HURRICANE DONNA
GALVESTON TEXAS   1900
GRAND ISLE HURRICANE
LOUISIANA   1915
HURRICANE CARLA

THE TOP TEN MOST EXPENSIVE HURRICANES :-
HURRICANE ANDREW
HURRICANE HUGO
HURRICANE FLOYD
HURRICANE FRAN
HURRICANE OPAL
HURRICANE FREDERIC
HURRICANE AGNES
HURRICANE ALICIA
HURRICANE BOB
HURRICANE JUAN

SCALE :-IS DETERMINED BY A SERIES OF GRADATIONS OR DEGREES; ALSO IT'S A BALANCE OR WEIGHING MACHINE.
SOME TYPES OF SCALES AND MONITORING MACHINES ARE :-
ELECTRONIC SCALES
MECHANICAL SCALES
POCKET SCALES
BABY SCALES
BATHROOM SCALES
BLOOD PRESSURE MONITORS
BODY FAT MONITORS
COUNTING SCALES
CRANE SCALES

EDUCATION SCALES
FLOOR SCALES
FOOD / DELI SCALES
HEART RATE MONITORS
HEIGHT MEASUREMENT
INDUSTRIAL SCALES
JEWELRY SCALES
KITCHEN SCALES
MEDICAL SCALES
RETAIL SCALES
SHIPPING SCALES
LAB / ANALYTICAL SCALES
FISH / GAME SCALES
FORCE MEASUREMENT
LIVESTOCK SCALES
PALLET SCALES
PORTABLE SPRING GAUGES

CHEMISTRY :-IS THE SCIENCE DEALING WITH THE COMPOSITION, REACTIONS, ETC. OF SUBSTANCES.

CHEMISTRY IS DIVIDED INTO MANY FIELDS AND CATEGORIES SUCH AS :-
ATMOSPHERIC CHEMISTRY
BIOCHEMISTRY
CHEMICAL AND BIOLOGICAL WEAPONS
CHEMICAL ENGINEERING
CHEMICAL PHYSICS
CHEMISTS
COMPUTATIONAL CHEMISTRY
ELECTROCHEMISTRY
GEOCHEMISTRY
ORGANIC CHEMISTRY
PHILOSOPHY OF CHEMISTRY
PHYSICAL CHEMISTRY
SONOCHEMISTRY
THEORETICAL CHEMISTRY
VIRTUAL CHEMISTRY
CYBER CHEMISTRY
GENERAL CHEMISTRY
HARZARDOUS CHEMICAL

PHYSICS :-IS THE SCIENCE THAT DEALS WITH MATTER AND ENERGY.

PHYSICS IS DIVIDED INTO MANY FIELDS AND CATEGORIES SUCH AS :-

AMUSEMENT PARK RIDE PHYSICS
ASTROPHYSICS
ATOMIC PHYSICS
BIOPHYSICS
CHEMICAL PHYSICS
HIGH ENERGY AND PARTICLE PHYSICS
PHILOSOPHY OF PHYSICS
PHYSICISTS
PLASMA PHYSICS
THEORETICAL PHYSICS
MATHEMATICAL PHYSICS

COMPUTER :-IS AN ELECTRONIC MACHINE THAT RAPIDLY CALCULATES AND CORRELATES DATA INFORMATION.

THE COMPUTER IS MADE UP OF HARDWARE AND SOFTWARE.

HARDWARE :-IS THE ELECTRONIC EQUIPMENT AND INCLUDES ALL EXTERNAL EQUIPMENT; TERMINAL MONITOR, SCANNER, PRINTER, MOUSE, KEYBOARD, ETC .

SOFTWARE :-IS THE VARIOUS PROGRAMS ETC FOR A COMPUTER SUCH AS WORD, EXCEL, OFFICE, GRAPHICS AND PUBLISHING ETC .

IN USING THE COMPUTER ONE NEEDS TO GUARD AGAINST :-

INTERNET FRAUD
INTERNET SCAM
CHAIN LETTERS
BE SELECTIVE AND SURE OF THE CHAT ROOMS YOU NEED TO BE INVOLVED WITH.
VIRUS HOAX WARNINGS
ONE SHOULD ALSO BE CONSCIOUS OF TEEN SAFETY ON THE INFORMATION HIGHWAY - THE INTERNET.

AS WELL AS THERE SHOULD BE KIDS – CHILDREN RULES IN PLACE FOR CHILDREN ONLINE SAFETY.

CHAPTER 21.

SOME IMPORTANT INTERNATIONAL ORGANIZATIONS
ARE :-
AFRICAN UNION [AU]
AGENCE DE LA FRANCOPHONIE [ACCT]
ARCTIC COUNCIL
AUSTRALIAN SISTER CITIES ASSOCIATION INC
BALTIC SEA STATES SUPPORT GROUP
BANK FOR INTERNATIONAL SETTLEMENTS [BIS]
CARICOM
CLIMATE TECHNOLOGY INITIATIVE [CTI]
COMMONWEALTH
COMUNIDAD ANDINA
COUNCIL OF EUROPE
COUNCIL OF EUROPEAN MUNICIPALITIES AND REGIONS
DELEGATIONS OF THE EUROPEAN COMMISSION
ECONOMIC COOPERATION ORGANIZATION [ECO]
EUROPEAN UNION
FOUNDATION FOR DEMOCRACY IN AFRICA
G – 20
G 8 SUMMITS
GLOBAL LEGISLATORS ORGANIZATION FOR A BALANCED
ENVIRONMENT [GLOBE INTERNATIONAL]
INTER – AMERICAN DEFENSE BOARD
THE INTER – AMERICAN DIALOGUE
INTERNATIONAL COUNCIL ON SOCIAL WELFARE
INTERNATIONAL FEDERATION OF INVESTORS'
ASSOCIATIONS [IFIA]

INTERNATIONAL JOINT COMMISSION
INTERNATIONAL PARLIAMENT FOR SAFETY AND PEACE
JEWISH INSTITUTE FOR NATIONAL SECURITY AFFAIRS
METROPOLIS – WORLD ASSOCIATION OF THE MAJOR METROPOLISES
MS – NEPAL : DANISH ASSOCIATION FOR INTERNATIONAL COOPERATION
MULTINATIONAL FORCE AND OBSERVERS [MFO]
NATIONAL ENDOWMENT FOR DEMOCRACY
NON – ALIGNED MOVEMENT [NAM]
ORGANIZATION OF AMERICAN STATES [OAS]
ORGANIZATION OF WORLD HERITAGE CITIES [OWHC]
SECRETARIAT OF THE PACIFIC COMMUNITY
SISTER CITIES INTERNATIONAL
SOVEREIGNTY INTERNATIONAL
TRANSPARENCY INTERNATIONAL
UNITED NATIONS [UN]
UNION OF INTERNATIONAL ASSOCIATIONS [UIA]
WESTMINISTER FOUNDATION FOR DEMOCRACY
WORLD BANK
WORLD CUSTOMS ORGANIZATION [WCO]
WORLD TRADE ORGANIZATION
WORLD HEALTH ORGANIZATION [WHO]
ACADEMY OF EUROPEAN LAW
ASIAN AID ORGANIZATION
BRITISH COUNCIL
CARE INTERNATIONAL
CHILDREACH
COUNCIL OF EUROPE
DIRECT RELIEF INTERNATIONAL
EUROPEAN UNION
FORD FOUNDATION
GLOBAL MARKETS
GREENPEACE INTERNATIONAL
HERITAGE FOUNDATION
INTER PARLIAMENTARY UNION [IPU]
INTERGOVERNMENTAL OCEANOGRAPHIC COMMISSION [IOC]
INTERNATIONAL BUREAU OF CHAMBERS OF COMMERCE [IBCC]
INTERNATIONAL DEVELOPMENT ASSOCIATION [IDA]

INTERNATIONAL INDIAN ECONOMIC ASSOCIATION
INTERNATIONAL LABOR ORGANIZATION [ILO]
INTERNATIONAL MONETARY FUND [IMF]
INTERNATIONAL ORGANIZATION FOR MIGRATION [IOM]
INTERNATIONAL ORGANIZATION FOR STANDARDIZATION [ISO]
INTERNATIONAL YOUTH FOUNDATION
NOBEL FOUNDATION
NORTH ATLANTIC TREATY ORGANIZATION [NATO]
NUCLEAR AGE PEACE FOUNDATION
OVERSEAS PRIVATE INVESTMENT CORPORATION
PARIS COMMISSION
POPULATION COUNCIL
SOIL AND WATER CONSERVATION SOCIETY
TECHNOLOGY AND ACTION FOR RURAL ADVANCEMENT [TARA]
UNION OF INTERNATIONAL ASSOCIATIONS
URBAN AND REGIONAL INFORMATION SYSTEMS ASSOCIATIONS [URISA]
WATER FOR PEOPLE
WORLD BANK
WORLD CITIZEN FOUNDATION
WORLD ECONOMIC FORUM
WORLD FOOD PROGRAMME
WORLD TRADE ORGANIZATION
WORLD WILDLIFE FUND

SOME OF THE HIGHEST WATERFALLS OF THE WORLD ARE :-

NAME	COUNTRY	SOURCE / RIVER	HEIGHT	
			FEET	METERS
ANGEL	VENEZULA	RIO CARONI	3,212	979
TUGELA	S O U T H AFRICA	T U G E L A RIVER	2,800	850
UTIGORD	NORWAY	G L A C I E R FED	2,625	800
MONGE	NORWAY	MONGE BECK	2,540	774
MUTARAZI	ZIMBABWE	M U T A R A Z I RIVER	2,499	762
YOSEMITE	CALIFORNIA U.S.A	Y O S E M I T E CREEK	2,425	739
PIEMAN	V I C T O R I A AUSTRALIA	P I E M A N ' S CREEK	2,346	715
ESPELANDS	NORWAY	OPO RIVER	2,307	703
LOWER MAR VALLEY	NORWAY	M A R D A L S STREAM	2,151	655
TYSSEST RENGENE	NORWAY	T Y S S A RIVER	2,123	647
CUQUENAN	VENEZUELA	CUQUENAN RIVER	2,000	610
DUDHSAGAR	INDIA	KHANDEPAR RIVER	1,969	600
SUTHER LAND	N E W ZEALAND	A R T H U R RIVER	1,904	580
KJELL	NORWAY	GUDVA NGEN	1,841	561
KAHIWA	HAWAII	U.S.A	1,750	533
TAKKAKAW	B.C. CANADA	TAKKAKAW CREEK	1,650	503
RIBBON	CALIFORNIA	U.S.A RIBBON STREAM	1,612	491
K I N G GEORGE VI	GUYANA	COURAN TYNE RIVER	1,600	488

KAIETEUR	GUYANA	POTARO	ESSEQ UIBO RIVER	740	
KALAMBO	TANZANIA / ZAMBIA	KALAMBO RIVER	726	221
WOLLOM OMBI	AUSTRALIA	WOLLO MOMBI	722	220
FEIGUM	NORWAY	FEIGUMELVI	715	218

TRANSPORTATION IS THE MEANS OF GETTING FROM ONE PLACE TO ANOTHER. THE SAFETY, EFFICIENCY, AND COST OF ALL MODES OF TRANSPORTATION AND THEIR IMPACT ON THE ENVIRONMENT ARE HIGH ON THE LIST OF MAJOR CONCERNS IN EVERY COUNTRY AROUND THE WORLD. FREEDOM TO TRAVEL BINDS THE NATIONS TOGETHER AND LINK US TO THE REST OF THE WORLD.

MODE OF TRANSPORTATION :-
WALK
CYCLE
BUS
CAR
SHIP
TRAIN
AIRPLANE
SKI
TRUCK
VAN
TAXI
HELICOPTER
SEDAN CHAIRS
DONKEY AND CART
HORSE
CAMEL
RICKSHAWS
HORSE AND CARRIAGE

A FEW OF THE TOP AND IMPORTANT UNIVERSITIES OF THE WORLD :-

UNIVERSITY	COUNTRY
OXFORD	UNITED KINGDOM

HARVARD	UNITED STATES OF AMERICA
YALE	UNITED STATES OF AMERICA
UNIVERSITY OF THE WEST INDIES	TRINIDAD AND TOGAGO
UNIVERSITY OF GUYANA	GUYANA
AMERICAN INTERCONTINENTAL UNIVERSITY	U.S.A
BRIGHAM YOUNG UNIVERSITY	U.S.A
UNIVERSITY OF NEW MEXICO	U.S.A
STANFORD UNIVERSITY	U.S.A
EMORY UNIVERSITY	U.S.A
PRINCETON UNIVERSITY	U.S.A
UNIVERSITY OF RICHMOND	U.S.A
VANDERBILT UNIVERSITY	U.S.A
CALIFORNIA STATE UNIVERSITY	U.S.A
COLUMBIA UNIVERSITY	U.S.A
TOKYO UNIVERSITY	JAPAN
UNIVERSITY COLL LONDON	UNITED KINGDOM
UNIVERSITY MICHIGAN	U.S.A
UNIVERSITY TORONTO	CANADA
KYOTO UNIVERSITY	JAPAN
DUKE UNIVERSITY	U.S.A
UNIVERSITY BRITISH COLUMBIA	CANADA
KAROLINSKA INST. STOCKHOLM	SWEDEN
UNIVERSITY UTRECHT	NETHERLANDS
UNIVERSITY EDINBURG	UNITED KINGDOM
UNIVERSITY ZURICH	SWITZERLAND
UNIVERSITY MUNICH	GERMANY
AUSTRALIAN NATL. UNIVERSITY	AUSTRALIA

COLLEGE :-SCHOOL OF HIGHER LEARNING OR SPECIAL INSTRUCTION.

UNIVERSITY :-SCHOOL MADE UP OF COLLEGE AND, OFTEN, GRADUATE SCHOOLS.

THE WORLDS TALLEST BUILDINGS – STRUCTURES ARE :-

RANK BUILDING CITY YEAR STORIES HEIGHT METERS FEET
1 TAIPEI 101,TAIPEI TAIWAN UC04 101 508 1,667 2 PETRONAS TOWER 1 KAULA LUMPUR 1998 88 452 1483

MALAYSIA

3 PETRONAS TOWER 2 KAULA LUMPUR 1998 88 452 1483

MALAYSIA

4 SEARS TOWER CHICAGO 1974 110 442 1450

5 JIN MAO BUILDING SHANGHAI 1999 88 421 1381

6 TWO INTERNATIONAL FINANCE CENTER UC03 88 412 1352

HONG KONG

7 CITIC PLAZA, GUANGZHOU, CHINA 1996 80 391 1283

8 SHUN HING SQUARE, SHENZHEN, CHINA 1996 69 384 1260

9 EMPIRE STATE BUILDING NEW YORK U.S.A 1931 102 381 1250

10 CENTRAL PLAZA HONG KONG 1992 78 374 1227

THERE ARE MANY OTHER TALL BUILDINGS IN THE WORLD SUCH AS :

PARK TOWER CHICAGO U.S.A 2000 67 257 844

RINKU GATE TOWER, OSAKA JAPAN 1996 56 256 840

MESSETURM FRANKFURT GERMANY 1990 70 257 843

TOWER :-IS A HIGH STRUCTURE; OFTEN PART OF ANOTHER BUILDING

THE WORLD TALLEST TOWERS ARE :-

RANK TOWER CITY YEAR HEIGHT

METERS FEET

1 CANADIAN NATIONAL TOWER 1975 553 1815

TORONTO, CANADA

2 OSTANKINO TOWER 1967 537 1762

MOSCOW, RUSSIA

3 ORIENTAL PEARL TOWER 1995 468 1535

SHANGHAI, CHINA

4 MENARA KUALA LUMPUR 1996 421 1403

KUALA LUMPUR, MALAYSIA

5 CENTRAL RADIO AND T.V TOWER 1992 417 1369

BEIJING, CHINA

6 TIANJIN T.V TOWER 1991 415 1362

TIANJIN, CHINA

7 LORAN – C TOWER PORT CLARENCE 1962 411 1350

ALASKA, U.S.A

8 TASHKENT TOWER 1985 375 1230
TASHKENT, UZBEKISTAN
9 LIBERATION TOWER 1996 370 1214
KUWAIT CITY, KUWAIT
10 FERNSEHTURM TOWER 1996 365 1198
BERLIN, GERMANY

BILLIONAIRES :-OF ABOUT 500 BILLIONAIRES AS THE WORLD'S RICHEST PEOPLE; ONLY ABOUT 40 0R 8 % ARE WOMEN.
THE TOP RICHEST PEOPLE ARE :-
WILLIAM GATES U.S.A
WARREN BUFFETT U.S.A
PAUL GARDENER ALLEN U.S.A
LAWRENCE JOSEPH ELLISON U.S.A
THEO ALBRECHT AND KARL GERMANY
PRINCE ALWALEED BIN TALAL ALSAUD SAUDI ARABIA
THE WALTON FAMILY, HELEN, JIM C, JOHN T, ROBSON S, ALICE L.U.S.A
JOHANNA QUANDT
STEPHEN ANTHONY BALLMER U.S.A
LILIANE BETTENCOURT FRANCE
KEMUTH THOMSON AND FAMILY CANADA
INGVER KAMPRAD
CARLOS SLIM HELU LATIN AMERICA
MICHAEL S DELL U.S.A
KIRSTEN RANSING AND FAMILY UNITED KINGDOM
JOHN W KLUGE
KARL AND THEO ALBRECHT

MICHAEL BLOOMBURG U.S.A IS ALSO A BILLIONAIRE

THE WORLD'S RICHEST WOMEN :-
RANK NAME COUNTRY ORIGIN – SOURCE OF WEALTH
8 ALICE L WALTON U.S.A WAL – MART
10 HELEN R WALTON U.S.A WAL – MART
12 JOHANNA QUANDT AND FAMILY GERMANY B M W
13 LILIANE BETTENCOURT FRANCE L'OREAL
19 KIRSTEN RANSING AND FAMILY SWEDEN PACKAGING
21 ANNE COX CHAMBERS U.S.A MEDIA

26 JACQUELINE BADGER MARS U.S.A CANDY

29 ABIGAIL JOHNSON U.S.A FIDELITY

76 CHARLENE DE CARVALHO NETHERLANDS HEINEKEN

112 ARISON DORSMAN SHARI ISRAEL CRUISES

144 LAURIE NANCY WALTON U.S.A WAL – MART

157 SUSAN THOMPSON BUFFETT U.S.A BERKSHIRE HATHAWAY

168 NINA WANG HONG KONG REAL ESTATE

168 BARBARA PIASECKA JOHNSON U.S.A JOHNSON AND JOHNSON

208 ANNELIESE BROST AND FAMILY GERMANY NEWSPAPER

208 KROC JOHN B AND FAMILY U.S.A McDONALD'S

225 LEONA HEMSLEY U.S.A REAL ESTATE

258 MARY ALICE DORRANCE MALONE U.S.A CAMPBELL SOUP

293 MARIA A ARAMBURUZABALA AND FAMILY MEXICO BEER

293 DORIS F FISHER U.S.A GAP

327 BARBARA C GAGE AND FAMILY U.S.A TRAVEL SERVICES

327 MARLYN N CARLSON AND FAMILY U.S.A TRAVEL SERVICES

351 ALICIA KOPLOWITZ SPAIN INVESTMENTS

378 RONDA E STRYKER U.S.A INHERITANCE

413 CHARLOTTE C WEBER U.S.A CAMPBELL SOUP

413 MIUCCIA PRADA AND FAMILY ITALY PRADA

445 ANTONIA JOHNSON SWEDEN DIVERSIFIED

446 ESTER KOPLOWITZ SPAIN CONSTRUCTION

447 HOPE HILL VAN BUEREN U.S.A CAMPBELL SOUP

448 LILY SAFRA BRAZIL INHERITED

449 FRIEDE SPRINGER GERMANY PUBLISHING

450 MARGUERITE HARBERT U.S.A CONSTRUCTION

OPRAH WINFREY U.S.A IS ALSO A BILLIONAIRE

SOME OF THE MOST POWERFUL WOMEN IN THE WORLD ARE :-

NAME OF WOMAN	COMPANY ASSOCIATED WITH
CARLY FIORINA	HEWLETT – PACKARD
MEG WHITMAN	EBAY
ANDREA JUNG	AVON PRODUCTS

ANNE MULCAHY	XEROX
MARJORIE MAGNER	CITIGROUP
KAREN KATEN	PFIZER
OPRAH WINFREY	HARPO INC.
INDRA NOOYI	PEPSI CO
PAT WOERTZ	CHEVRON TEXACO
BETSY HOLDEN	KRAFT FOODS
ABIGAIL JOHNSON	FIDELITY MANAGEMENT AND RESEARCH
BETSY BERNARD	AT&T
ANN MOORE	AOL – TIME WARNER
SALLIE KRAWCHECK	CITIGROUP
JUDY MCGRATH	VIACOM
SHELLY LAZARUS	WPP
DOREEN TOBEN	VERIZON
STACEY SNIDER	VIVENDI UNIVERSAL
COLLEEN BARRETT	SOUTHWEST AIRLINES
SHERRY LANSING	VIACOM
PAT RUSSO	LUCENT TECHNOLOGIES
AMY BRINKLEY	BANK OF AMERICA
JUDY LEWENT	MERCK
ANN LIVERMORE	HEWLETT – PACKARD
GAIL BERMAN	NEWS CORP
CATHLEEN BLACK	HEARST MAGAZINE
CHRISTINE POON	JOHNSON & JOHNSON
LINDA DILLMAN	WAL – MART STORES
MYRTLE POTTER	GENENTECH
SUSAN DESMOND HELLMAN	GENENTECH
SUSAN ARNOLD	PROCTER & GAMBLE
LOIS JULIBER	COLGATE – PALMOLIVE
DINA DUBLON	J. P MORGAN CHASE
DEB HENRETTA	PROCTER & GAMBLE
ANNE SWEENEY	WALT DISNEY
NANCY PERETSMAN	ALLEN & CO
MARY SAMMONS	RITE AID
AMY PASCAL	SONY
MARIA ELENA LAGOMASINO	J. P.MORGAN CHASE
VIVIAN BANTA	PRUDENTIAL FINANCIAL
VANESSA CASTAGNA	J. C.PENNEY

JENNY MING	GAP
LOIS QUAM	UNITED HEALTH GROUP
URSULA BURNS	XEROX
MARILYN CARLSON NELSON	CARLSON COS
ANN FUDGE	WPP
LOUSIE FRANCESCONI	RAYTHEON
JANET ROBINSON	NEW YORK TIMES CO
CHRISTINA GOLD	FIRST DATA
DAWN HUDSON	PEPSI CO

50 COMPANIES FOR WHICH MINORITIES MAKE UP A LARGE PERCENTAGE OF THE WORK FORCE :-

McDONALDS
FANNIE MAE
DENNEY'S
UNION BANK OF CALIFORNIA
SEMPRA ENERGY
SOUTHERN CALIFORNIA EDISON
SBC COMMUNICATIONS
FREDDIE Mac
PEPSICO
PNM RESOURCES
U.S POSTAL SERVICE
WYNDHAM INTERNATIONAL
XEROX
APPLIED MATERIALS
J.P.MORGAN CHASE CO
COLGATE – PALMOLIVE
SOLECTRON
HYATT
SAFEWAY
HILTON HOTELS
LUCENT TECHNOLOGIES
MARRIOTT INTERNATIONAL
PG&E CORP
VERIZON COMMUNICATIONS
COCA – COLA
UNITED PARCEL SERVICE
DTE ENERGY
DARDEN RESTAURANTS

CONSOLIDATED EDISON
WASHINGTON MUTUAL
MGM MIRAGE
SILICON GRAPHICS
NORDSTROM
EASTMAN KODAK
BELLSOUTH
AFLAC
LEVI STRAUSS
PROCTER & GAMBLE
PEP BOYS
FEDEX
CITIGROUP
CUMMINS
BANK OF AMERICA CORP
AT&T
AVON PRODUCTS
PRUDENTIAL FINANCIAL
ABBOTT LABORATORIES
TIAA – CREF
S.C JOHNSON & SON

SOME OF THE LARGEST MUTUAL FUNDS ARE :-

FUND	TOTAL NET ASSETS IN BILLIONS
FIDELITY MAGELLAN FUND	71. 5
VANGUARD INDEX 500	60. 8
WASHINGTON MUTUAL	45. 7
INVESTMENT CO. OF AMERICA	43. 9
FIDELITY GRO & INC	43. 5
FIDELITY CONTRAFUND	33. 5
VANGUARD WINDSOR	29. 8
AMER CENT TC ULTRA; INV	25. 5
VANGUARD WELLINGTON FUND	24. 6
FIDELITY PURITAN	24. 6

THE COUNTRIES WHICH HAVE THE MOST BILLIONAIRES ARE :-

UNITED STATES OF AMERICA	270
JAPAN	29
GERMANY	28

ITALY	17
CANADA	16
SWITZERLAND	15
FRANCE	15
HONG KONG	14
MEXICO	13
UNITED KINGDOM	12
RUSSIA	8
SAUDI ARABIA	8

NOTE THE RANKINGS AND AMOUNT OF MONEY THEY HAVE ARE CONSTANTLY CHANGING

FOREST :-IS A TRACT OF LAND COVERED WITH TREES
FORESTRY :-IS THE SCIENCE OF THE CARE OF FORESTS
THERE ARE THREE MAJOR TYPES OF FORESTS CLASSED ACCORDING TO LATITUDE; THAT IS THE REGION IN WHICH THEY ARE FOUND. THE THREE TYPES OF FORESTS ARE TROPICAL, TEMPERATE, AND BOREAL [TAIGA].

TROPICAL FORESTS ARE CHARACTERIZED BY THE GREATEST DIVERSITY OF SPECIES. THEY OCCUR NEAR THE EQUATOR, WITHIN THE AREA BOUNDED BY LATITUDES 23.5 DEGREES NORTH AND 23.5 DEGREES SOUTH. ONLY TWO SEASONS ARE PRESENT RAINY AND DRY. THE LENGTH OF DAYLIGHT IS ABOUT TWELVE HOURS. TEMPERATURE IS ON AVERAGE 20 - 25 DEGREES CENTIGRADE.
FLORA IS HIGHLY DIVERSE, AND FAUNA INCLUDE NUMEROUS BIRDS, BATS, SMALL MAMMALS, AND INSECTS.

TEMPERATE FORESTS OCCUR IN EASTERN NORTH AMERICA, NORTHEASTERN ASIA AND WESTERN AND CENTRAL EUROPE. WELL DEFINED SEASONS WITH A DISTINCT WINTER CHARACTERIZE THIS FOREST. TEMPERATURES VARIES FROM MINUS 30 TO 30 DEGREES CENTIGRADE. THE SOIL IS FERTILE, CANOPY IS MODERATELY DENSE AND ALLOWS LIGHT TO PENETRATE. IT HAS RICH VEGETATION AND STRATIFICATION OF ANIMALS.
FLORA IS GOVERNED BY MANY TREE SPECIES, AND FAUNA IS REPRESENTED BY SQUIRRELS, RABBITS, SKUNKS,

BIRDS, DEER, MOUNTAIN LION, BOB CAT, TIMBER WOLF, FOX, BLACK BEAR AMONG OTHERS.

THE BOREAL FORESTS REPRESENT THE LARGEST TERRESTRIAL BIRONE. OCCURING BETWEEN 50 AND 60 DEGREES NORTH LATITUDE; BOREAL FORESTS CAN BE FOUND IN THE BROAD BELT OF EURASIA AND NORTH AMERICA, TWO – THIRDS IN SIBERIA, WITH THE REST IN SCANDINAVIA, ALASKA AND CANADA. SEASONS ARE DIVIDED INTO SHORT, MOIST AND MODERATELY WARM SUMMERS AND LONG, COLD AND DRY WINTERS.

FLORA CONSISTS MOSTLY OF COLD – TOLERANT EVERGREEN CONIFERS WITH NEEDLE LIKE LEAVES, SUCH AS PINE, FIR AND SPRUCE. FAUNA INCLUDE HAWKS, WOODPECKERS, MOOSE, BEAR, WEASEL, LYNX, FOX, WOLF, DEER, HARES, CHIPMUNKS, SHREWS, AND BATS AMONG OTHERS. THERE IS EXTENSIVE LOGGING IN BOREAL FORESTS.

FLORA :-IS THE PLANTS OF A REGION.

FAUNA :-IS THE ANIMALS OF A CERTAIN REGION.

TERRESTRIAL :-HAS TO DO WITH THINGS OF THE EARTH.

CELESTIAL :-HAS TO DO WITH THINGS OF THE HEAVENS.

LATITUDE :-IS THE DISTANCE IN DEGREES FROM THE EQUATOR.

LONGITUDE :-IS THE DISTANCE IN DEGREES, EAST OR WEST OF A LINE THROUGH GREENWICH, ENGLAND.

TUNDRA :-IS THE COLDEST OF ALL THE BIOMES THAT IS THE WORLD'S MAJOR COMMUNITIES; ITS NOT SO BARREN A LAND; A TREELESS PLAIN; IT IS NOTED FOR ITS FROST – MOLDED LANDSCAPES, LOW TEMPERATURE, POOR NUTRIENTS AND SHORT GROWING SEASON.

THE CHARACTERISTS OF TUNDRA ARE :-

EXTREMELY COLD CLIMATE
LOW BIOTIC DIVERSITY
SIMPLE VEGETATION STRUCTURE
LIMITATION OF DRAINAGE
SHORT SEASON OF GROWTH AND REPRODUCTION
ENERGY AND NUTRIENTS IN THE FORM OF DEAD ORGANIC MATERIAL
LARGE POPULATION OSCILLATIONS

THERE ARE FIVE MAJOR TYPES OF BIOMES [WORLD'S MAJOR COMMUNITIES]
AQUATIC
DESERTS
FORESTS
GRASSLANDS
TUNDRA

GRASSLANDS :-ARE CHARACTERIZED AS LANDS DOMINATED BY GRASSES RATHER THAN SHRUBS OR TREES. THERE ARE TWO MAIN DIVISIONS OF GRASSLANDS.
TROPICAL GRASSLANDS CALLED SAVANAS
TEMPERATE GRASSLANDS

FRESHWATER :-REGIONS IS DEFINED AS HAVING A LOW SALT CONCENTRATION USUALLY LESS THAN 1 %. DIFFERENT TYPES OF FRESHWATER REGIONS ARE PONDS, LAKES, STREAMS, RIVERS, WETLANDS.

CORAL REEFS :-ARE WIDELY DISTRIBUTED IN WARM SHALLOW WATERS. THEY CAN BE FOUND AS BARRIERS ALONG CONTINENTS. E.G THE GREAT BARRIER REEF OFF AUSTRALIA, FRINGING ISLANDS, AND ATOLLS. THE DOMINANT ORGANISMS IN CORAL REEFS ARE CORALS. THERE ARE ABOUT 60 DIFFERENT KINDS OF CORALS IN THE CARIBBEAN SEA. EXAMPLES OF CORALS ARE ELK HORN, BRAIN, LETTUCE, FIRE. THERE ARE ABOUT 700 DIFFERENT KINDS [SPECIES] OF CORALS UNDERWATER AROUND THE WORLD. CORAL IS A HARD MASS OF SEA ANIMALS SKELETONS; THEY ARE YELLOWISH RED IN COLOR.

ESTUARIES :-ARE AREAS WHERE FRESHWATER STREAMS OR RIVERS MERGE WITH THE OCEAN.

THE WORLD REGIONS ARE :-
AFRICA
MIDDLE EAST
EUROPE
ASIA
NORTH AMERICA
CENTRAL AMERICA
THE CARIBBEAN
SOUTH AMERICA
OCEANIA

THE RICHEST COUNTRIES OF THE WORLD ARE :-
RANK   COUNTRY   G.D.P PER   CAPITA [GROSS DOMESTIC PRODUCT -   THE AVERAGE INCOME]

RANK	COUNTRY	G.D.P PER CAPITA
1	LUXEMBOURG	$ 44,000
2	UNITED STATES	$ 37,600
3	BERMUDA	$ 35,200
4	CAYMAN ISLAND	$ 35,000
5	SAN MARINO	$ 34,600
6	NORWAY	$ 31,800
7	SWITZERLAND	$ 31,700
8	IRELAND	$ 30,500
9	CANADA	$ 29,400
10	DENMARK	$ 29,000
11	BELGIUM	$ 29,000
12	ARUBA	$ 28,000
13	JAPAN	$ 28,000
14	AUSTRIA	$ 27,700
15	AUSTRALIA	$ 27,000
16	MONACO	$ 27,000
17	NETHERLANDS	$ 26,900
18	SINGAPORE	$ 26,500
19	GERMANY	$ 26,500
20	FINLAND	$ 26,200
21	HONG KONG	$ 26,000
22	JERSEY	$ 24,800
23	FRANCE	$ 24,400
24	LIECHSTENSTEIN	$ 23,500

THE POOREST COUNTRIES OF THE WORLD ARE :-

RANK	COUNTRY	G.D.P PER CAPITA
1	EAST TUMOR	$ 500
2	SOMALIA	$ 550
3	SIERRA LEONE	$ 580
4	GAZA STRIP	$ 600
5	MAYOTTE	$ 600
6	BURUNDI	$ 600
7	CONGO	$ 610
8	TANZANIA	$ 630
9	RWANDA	$ 720
10	COMOROS	$ 725
11	ERITREA	$ 750
12	YEMEN	$ 750
13	ETHIOPIA	$ 750
14	MADAGASCAR	$ 780
15	AFGHANISTAN	$ 800
16	TUVALU	$ 800
17	MALI	$ 820
18	KIRIBATI	$ 860
19	ZAMBIA	$ 880
20	GUINEA BISSAU	$ 900
21	MALAWI	$ 940
22	SUDAN	$ 940
23	NIGERIA	$ 970

NOTE WELL :-THESE FIGURES ARE CONSTANTLY BEING CHANGED.

SOME BUSINESS INDUSTRIES ARE :-
ADVERTISING
AEROSPACE
AIRLINES
AUTO MANUFACTURING
AUTO PARTS AND TIRES
BANKS
BEVERAGE
BIOTECHNOLOGY
BROADCASTING
BUILDING MATERIALS

CHEMICALS
COMMUNICATIONS
CONSUMER SERVICES
CONTAINERS AND PACKAGING
COSMETICS
DIVERSIFIED FINANCIAL
ELECTRIC
ELECTRIC COMPONENTS AND EQUIPTMENT
ENERGY
ENTERTAINMENT
FIXED LINE COMMUNICATIONS
FOOD
FOOD RETAILERS
FOREST PRODUCTS
GAS
HEALTHCARE PRODUCTS
HEAVY CONSTRUCTION
HOME CONSTRUCTION AND FURNISHINGS
HOUSEHOLD PRODUCTS
INDUSTRIAL EQUIPMENT
INDUSTRIAL SERVICES
INDUSTRIAL TRANSPORTATION
INDUSTRIAL DIVERSIFIED
INSURANCE
LEISURE GOODS
MEDICAL PRODUCTS
MINING AND METAL
PHARMACEUTICAL
PUBLISHING
REAL ESTATE
RETAILERS
SECURITIES BROKERS
SEMICONDUCTORS
SOFTWARE
TECHNOLOGY HARDWARE AND EQUIPMENT
TECHNOLOGY SERVICES
TEXTILE AND APPARAL
TOBACCO
WATER
WIRELESS COMMUNICATIONS

THE TOP BUSINESS COMPANIES OF THE WORLD IN RANKING ORDER :-

WAL – MART STORES
GENERAL MOTORS
EXXON MOBIL
ROYAL DUTCH / SHELL GROUP
BP
FORD MOTOR
DAIMLER CHRYSLER
TOYOTA MOTOR
GENERAL ELECTRIC
MITSUBISHI
MITSUI
ALLIANZ
CITIGROUP
TOTAL
CHEVRON TEXACO
NIPPON TELEGRAPH AND TELEPHONE
ING GROUP
ITOCHU
INTL. BUSINESS MACHINES   I B M
VOLKSWAGEN
SIEMENS
SUMITOMO
MARUBENI
VERIZON COMMUNICATIONS
AMERICAN INTL. GROUP
HITACHI
U.S. POSTAL SERVICE
HONDA MOTOR
CARREFOUR
ALTRIA GROUP
AXA
SONY
NIPPON LIFE INSURANCE
MATSUSHITA ELECTRIC INDUSTRIAL
ROYAL AHOLD
CONOCO PHILLIPS
HOME DEPOT
NESTLE
McKESSON

HEWLETT – PACKARD
NISSAN MOTOR
VIVENDI UNIVERSAL
BOEING
ASSICURAZIONI GENERALI
FANNIE MAE
FIAT
DEUTSCHE BANK
CREDIT SUISSE
MUNICH RE GROUP
MERCK
KROGER
PEUGEOT
CARDINAL HEALTH
BNP PARIBAS
DEUTSCHE TELEKOM
STATE FARM INSURANCE COS
AVIVA
METRO
SAMSUNG ELECTRONICS
VODAFONE
AT&T
TOSHIBA
ENI
BANK OF AMERICA CORP
ELECTRICITE DE FRANCE
UNILEVER
AMERISOURCE BERGEN
E.ON
CHINA NATIONAL PETROLEUM
SINOPEC
FRANCE TELECOM
TARGET
FORTIS
SUEZ
J.P MORGAN CHASE & CO
SBC COMMUNICATIONS
DAI – ICHI MUTUAL LIFE INSURANCE
BERKSHIRE HATHAWAY
UBS
TIME WARNER

SEARS ROEBUCK
RWE
ZURICH FINANCIAL SERVICES
TESCO
TOKYO ELECTRIC POWER
PROCTER & GAMBLE
BMW
DEUTSCHE POST
HSBC HOLDINGS
FREDDIE MAC
TYCO INTERNATIONAL
COSTCO WHOLESALE
NEC
HYUNDAI MOTOR
PEMEX
NISSHO IWAI
FUJITSU
CREDIT AGRICOLE
HYPO VEREINSBANK
SUMITOMO LIFE INSURANCE

NOTE :-THE RANKINGS OF THE COMPANIES CHANGE CONSTANTLY.

THE MOST ADMIRED COMPANIES IN THE WORLD ARE :-

WAL – MART STORES	U.S.A	
GENERAL ELECTRIC	U.S.A	
MICROSOFT	U.S.A	
JOHNSON & JOHNSON	U.S.A	
BERKSHIRE HATHAWAY	U.S.A	
DELL	U.S.A	
IBM	U.S.A	
TOYOTA MOTOR	JAPAN	
PROCTER & GAMBLE	U.S.A	
FEDEX	U.S.A	
COCA – COLA	U.S.A	
CITIGROUP	U.S.A	
UNITED PARCEL SERVICE	UPS	U.S.A
PFIZER	U.S.A	
BMW	GERMANY	

SONY	JAPAN
INTEL	U.S.A
WALT DISNEY	U.S.A
NOKIA	FINLAND
HOME DEPOT	U.S.A
NESTLE	SWITZERLAND
PEPSI CO	U.S.A
ANHEUSER – BUSCH	U.S.A
HONDA MOTOR	JAPAN
LOWE'S	U.S.A
TARGET	U.S.A
BP	BRITISH PETROLEUM
BRITAIN	
CISCO SYSTEMS	U.S.A
COLGATE – PALMOLIVE	U.S.A
MERCK	U.S.A
AMERICAN INTERNATIONAL	
GROUP	U.S.A
EXXON MOBIL	U.S.A
SINGAPORE AIRLINES	SINGAPORE
CANON	JAPAN
L'OREAL	FRANCE
DUPONT	U.S.A
COSTCO WHOLESALE	U.S.A
ROYAL DUTCH / SHELL	
GROUP	BRITAIN / NETHERLANDS
VERIZON	
COMMUNICATIONS	U.S.A
WALGREEN	U.S.A
CATERPILLAR	U.S.A
NORTHWESTERN MUTUAL	U.S.A
UNILEVER	U.S.A
ELI LILLY	U.S.A
CONTINENTAL AIRLINES	U.S.A
GILLETTE	U.S.A
VODAFONE	BRITAIN
BANK OF AMERICA	U.S.A
KELLOGG	U.S.A
GLAXO SMITH KLINE	BRITAIN

THE TOP OIL PRODUCING COUNTRIES OF THE WORLD
ARE :-

SAUDI ARABIA
UNITED STATES
RUSSIA
MEXICO
CHINA
IRAN
NORWAY
VENEZUELA
CANADA
UNITED KINGDOM
UNITED ARAB EMIRATES
IRAQ
NIGERIA
KUWAIT
ALGERIA
BRAZIL
LIBYA
INDONESIA
KAZAKHSTAN
ANGOLA
OMAN
MALAYSIA
ARGENTINA
INDIA
QATAR
EGYPT
AUSTRALIA
COLOMBIA
SYRIA
YEMEN
ECUADOR
DENMARK
VIETNAM
AZERBAIJAN
GABON
EQUATORIAL GUINEA
SUDAN
BRUNEI
THAILAND

TURKMENISTAN
UZBEKISTAN
TRINIDAD AND TOBAGO
ROMANIA
ITALY
PERU
TUNISIA
CAMEROON
PAPUA NEW GUINEA

CHAPTER 22.

SOME INTERESTING FACTS ABOUT THE WORLD ARE AS FOLLOWS :-

1 THE UNITED STATES HAS MORE PERSONAL COMPUTERS THAN THE NEXT SEVEN COUNTRIES COMBINED.

2 LUXEMBOURGERS, THE WORLD'S RICHEST PEOPLE, ARE ALSO THE MOST GENEROUS.

3 ANDORRA HAS NO UNEMPLOYMENT WHICH IS JUST AS WELL BECAUSE THEY HAVE NO BROADCAST CHANNELS EITHER.

4 ANDORRANS LIVE THE LONGEST, FOUR YEARS LONGER THAN IN NEIGHBORING FRANCE AND SPAIN.

5 CHINA HAS THE MOST WORKERS; THEY ALSO HAVE LOTS OF TELEVISION SETS

6 CHINA'S LABOR FORCE STANDS AT NEARLY 710 MILLION PEOPLE, ALMOST 3 TIMES THAT OF EUROPE, AND 2 TIMES THAT OF NORTH AND SOUTH AMERICA COMBINED.

7 CHIPPERTON ISLAND IS THE WORLD'S MOST UNUSUAL LOOKING COUNTRY.

8 EAST INDIANS GO TO THE MOVIES 3 BILLION TIMES A YEAR.

9 AMERICANS AND ICELANDERS GO TO THE MOVIES ON AVERAGE 5 TIMES A YEAR, WHILE JAPANESE ONLY ONCE.

10 ISRAEL ENJOYS A G.D.P PER CAPITA 21 TIMES THAT OF THE PALESTINIAN WEST BANK AND 33 TIMES THAT OF GAZA STRIP. ITS MILITARY SPENDING PER CAPITA TOPS THE WORLD.

11 NORTH KOREA SPENDS MOST OF ITS G.D.P ON ITS MILITARY.

12 THE CZECH REPUBLIC HAS MORE INTERNET SERVICE PROVIDERS THAN ANY OTHER NON – ENGLISH SPEAKING COUNTRY.

13 THE U.S.A SPENDS MORE MONEY ON ITS MILITARY THAN THE NEXT 12 NATIONS COMBINED.

14 HALF THE POPULATION OF UGANDA IS UNDER 15 YEARS OLD.

15 MOST PEOPLE LIVE IN POVERTY IN MOST AFRICAN COUNTRIES.

16 ONLY TWO COUNTRIES IN THE WORLD ARE LANDLOCKED; LIECHTENSTEIN AND UZBEKISTAN.

17 IN RUSSIA THERE IS TWO OVER 65 WOMEN FOR EVERY MAN.

18 IN GREENLAND THERE'S 38 SQUARE KILOMETERS PER PERSON.

19 THE VIRGIN ISLANDS HAS 5 WOMEN TO EVERY 4 MEN.

20 THE U.S.A HAS THE MOST MONEY, POWER, AIRPORTS, CELL PHONES, INTERNET SERVICE PROVIDERS, AND RADIOS IN THE ENTIRE WORLD.

21 SOUTH KOREA IS THE HELIPORT CAPITAL OF THE WORLD.

22 THE U.S.A CONSUMES MORE ENERGY THAN INDIA, THE MIDDLE EAST, SOUTH AMERICA, AFRICA, SOUTH EAST ASIA AND OCEANIA COMBINED.

23 THE WORLD'S SMALLEST COUNTRY, CORAL SEA ISLANDS IS ONE OF 13 STATES CONSIDERED TO HAVE NO ECONOMIC ACTIVITY.

24 YOU ARE 66 TIMES MORE LIKELY TO BE PROSECUTED IN THE U.S.A THAN IN FRANCE.

25 NEARLY 1 % OF MONTSERRATIONS ARE POLICE.

26 MOST ZAMBIANS DON'T LIVE TO SEE THE 40 TH BIRTHDAY.

27 NORWAY HAS THE HIGHEST SCHOOL ATTENDANCE.

28 MEXICO HAS THE MOST JEHOVAL'S WITNESSES PER CAPITA IN THE OECD.

29 GUINEA HAS THE WETTEST CAPITAL ON EARTH WITH 3.7 METERS OF RAIN A YEAR.

30 QATARIS HAS LOTS OF GAS.

31 GUATAMALAN WOMEN WORK 11.5 HRS A DAY WHILE SOUTH AFRICAN MEN ONLY WORK 4.5 HRS A DAY.

32 KENYAN WOMEN WORK 35% LONGER THAN THEIR MENFOLK.

33 ETHOPIANS ARE BY FAR THE MOST AGRICULTURAL PEOPLE ON EARTH.

34 HALF OF THE CZECH AND SLOVAK MEN WORK IN FACTORIES.

35 BELGIUM IS THE ONLY COUNTRY IN THE WORLD WHERE WOMEN DOMINATE THE MINISTRY.

36 SWEDES AND NORWEIGANS RANK TOP 5 FOR BOTH PROVIDING AID AND EXPORTING WEAPONS.

37 FORMER ENEMIES, U.S.A AND RUSSIA NOW TOGETHER LEAD THE WORLD IN LOCKING PEOPLE UP.

38 JAPANESE AND SOUTH KOREAN CHILDREN ARE THE BEST AT SCIENCE AND MATHEMATICS.

39 AMERICAN ADULTS HAVE BEEN EDUCATED THE LONGEST.

40 JAPAN HAS 52 NUCLEAR REACTORS AND IS PLANNING TO BUILD MORE.

41 AROUND 1992, SAUDI ARABIA OVERTOOK THE U.S.A AS THE WORLD'S LARGEST OIL PRODUCER.

42 DANISH WORKERS STRIKE 150 TIMES MORE THAN THEIR GERMAN NEIGHBORS.

43 MANY AMERICANS LIVE ALONE, LEADING THE WORLD IN ONE PERSON HOUSEHOLDS.

44 HUNGARIANS DIE OF CANCER THE MOST AND FINNS THE LEAST.

45 LIBYA IS THE ONLY COUNTRY WITH A SINGLE – COLORED FLAG.

46 EVERY COUNTRY IN THE WORLD HAS A RECTANGLE FLAG EXCEPT NEPAL.

OECD :-IS AN ORGANIZATION OF ECONOMIC COOPERATION AND DEVELOPMENT. THE COUNTRIES THAT MAKE UP THE OECD ARE :-

AUSTRALIA
AUSTRIA
BELGIUM
CANADA
DENMARK

IRELAND
CZECH REPUBLIC
FINLAND
FRANCE
GERMANY
GREECE
HUNGARY
ICELAND
ITALY
JAPAN
SOUTH KOREA
SLOVAKIA
LUXEMBOURG
MEXICO
NETHERLANDS
NORWAY
NEW ZEALAND
POLAND
PORTUGAL
SPAIN
SWEDEN
SWITZERLAND
TURKEY
UNITED KINGDOM
UNITED STATES OF AMERICA

INTERESTING FACTS :-

MUSEUM :- IS A PLACE FOR DISPLAYING ARTISTIC, HISTORICAL OR SCIENTIFIC OBJECTS. SOME INTERESTING MUSEUMS OF THE WORLD ARE :-
ADELSON GALLERIES
AFINS ART
AIR FORCE MUSEUM   MONINO, RUSSIA
AMERICAN AIRPOWER MUSEUM
AMERICAN COMPUTER MUSEUM, MONTANA
AMERICAN MUSEUM OF NATURAL HISTORY
ANCIENT GHETTO OF VENICE
ART GALLERY OF NEW SOUTH WALES
ART GALLERY OF NOVA SCOTIA
ART GALLERY OF ONTARIO

BLOOMFIELD SCIENCE MUSEUM   JERUSALEM
BIRMINGHAM AND MIDLAND MUSEUM OF TRANSPORT
BRITISH MUSEUM
CADBURY WORLD
CIRCUS WORLD MUSEUM, WISCONSIN
CHILDREN'S MUSEUM OF MANHATTAN, NEW YORK,
U.S.A
COPENHAGEN ART GALLERY DENMARK
CUBAN ORIGINAL ART GALLERY, FLORIDA
CURIOUS KIDS MUSEUM
GALLERY OF PHOTOGRAPHY, IRELAND
IDAHO BLACK HISTORY MUSEUM
ISRAEL MUSEUM, JERUSALEM
JEWISH MUSEUM, NEW YORK, U.S.A
KANSAS COSMOSPHERE AND SPACE CENTRE
LISBON UNIVERSITY MUSEUM OF SCIENCE, PORTUGAL
MARITIME MUSEUM, SAN DIEGO
MODERN ART, OXFORD
MOKA BUDDHIST MUSEUM
MUSEO DE LA CIUDAD DE MEXICO
MUSEO DEL PRADO, SPAIN
MUSEUM FOR TEXTILES
MUSEUM OF ANTIQUITIES
NATIONAL MUSEUM OF WOMENS' HISTORY
ORIENTAL INSTITUTE MUSEUM
PACIFIC SPACE CENTER, CANADA
PRINCE OF WALES MUSEUM OF WESTERN INDIA,
MUMBAI
PUSHLIN MUSEUM OF FINE ARTS, RUSSIA
SURFWORLD, AUSTRALIA
THE CENTER OF CONTEMPORARY ART, NEW ZEALAND
THE COSTUME MUSEUM OF CANADA
THE DICKENS HOUSE MUSEUM, LONDON
STOCK EXCHANGE :-IS AN EXCHANGE ON WHICH STOCKS
AND COMMON STOCKS EQUIVALENTS ARE BOUGHT AND
SOLD, INCLUDING, BONDS, OPTIONS, FUTURES, COMMODITIES
ETC .

A LIST OF SOME OF THE IMPORTANT STOCK EXCHANGES
IN THE WORLD ARE :-
AMERICAN STOCK EXCHANGE

NEW YORK STOCK EXCHANGE
AMSTERDAM STOCK EXCHANGE
ATHENS STOCK EXCHANGE
AUSTRALIAN STOCK EXCHANGE
BAHRAIN STOCK EXCHANGE
BARCELONA STOCK EXCHANGE
BEIRUT STOCK EXCHANGE
BERMUDA STOCK EXCHANGE
BOMBAY STOCK EXCHANGE
BOSTON STOCK EXCHANGE
BOURSE DE PARIS
BUDAPEST STOCK EXCHANGE
BULGARIAN STOCK EXCHANGE
CHICAGO STOCK EXCHANGE
COLOMBO STOCK EXCHANGE
CYPRUS STOCK EXCHANGE
DHAKA STOCK EXCHANGE
GHANA STOCK EXCHANGE
NIGERIA STOCK EXCHANGE
ITALIAN STOCK EXCHANGE
JAMAICA STOCK EXCHANGE
JOHANNESBURG STOCK EXCHANGE
KOREA STOCK EXCHANGE
KUALA LUMPUR STOCK EXCHANGE
LAHORE STOCK EXCHANGE
LONDON STOCK EXCHANGE
LISBON STOCK EXCHANGE
LUXEMBOURG STOCK EXCHANGE
MADRID STOCK EXCHANGE
MEXICAN STOCK EXCHANGE
MONTREAL EXCHANGE
MOSCOW CENTRAL STOCK EXCHANGE
NAMIBIAN STOCK EXCHANGE
NATIONAL STOCK EXCHANGE OF INDIA
NATIONAL STOCK EXCHANGE OF LITHUANIA
NEW ZEALAND STOCK EXCHANGE
PACIFIC EXCHANGE
PARIS STOCK EXCHANGE
PHILADELPHIA STOCK EXCHANGE
PRAGUE STOCK EXCHANGE
RUSSIAN STOCK EXCHANGE

STOCK EXCHANGE OF HONG KONG
STOCK EXCHANGE OF SINGAPORE
STOCK EXCHANGE OF THAILAND
TAIWAN STOCK EXCHANGE
TEHRAN STOCK EXCHANGE
TEL AVIV STOCK EXCHANGE
TORONTO STOCK EXCHANGE
TOKYO STOCK EXCHANGE
VENEZUELA ELECTRONIC STOCK EXCHANGE
VIENNA STOCK EXCHANGE
WINNIPEG STOCK EXCHANGE

SHIPS :-IS A LARGE WATER CRAFT. THE REASON A SHIP FLOATS;IS BECAUSE A SHIP WILL FLOAT WHEN THE WEIGHT OF THE WATER IT DISPLACES EQUALS THE WEIGHT OF THE SHIP. BECAUSE OF THE PRINCIPLE OF BUOYANCY A SHIP OR ANYTHING WILL FLOAT IF IT IS SHAPED TO DISPLACE ITS OWN WEIGHT OF WATER BEFORE IT REACHES THE POINT WHERE IT WILL SUBMERGE. YOU CAN LOOK AT IT THIS WAY, A SHIP THAT IS LAUNCHED SINKS INTO THE SEA UNTIL THE WEIGHT OF THE WATER IT DISPLACES IS EQUAL TO ITS OWN WEIGHT. AS THE SHIP IS LOADED, IT SINKS DEEPER, DISPLACING MORE WATER, AND SO THE MAGNITUDE OF THE BUOYANT FORCE CONTINUOUSLY MATCHES THE WEIGHT OF THE SHIP AND ITS CARGO. THE CENTER OF BUOYANCY IN A FLOATING SHIP IS THE POINT IN WHICH ALL THE BODY PARTS EXACTLY BALANCE EACH OTHER AND MAKE EACH OTHER FLOAT. IN OTHER WORDS, THE METACENTER REMAINS DIRECTLY ABOVE THE CENTER OF BUOYANCY REGARDLESS OF THE LIST OF THE FLOATING SHIP. WHEN A SHIP LISTS [TILT], ONE SIDE DISPLACES MORE WATER THAN THE OTHER SIDE, AND THE CENTER OF BUOYANCY MOVES AND IS NO LONGER DIRECTLY UNDER THE CENTER OF GRAVITY; BUT REGARDLESS OF THE AMOUNT OF THE LIST, THE CENTER OF BUOYANCY REMAINS DIRECTLY BELOW THE METACENTER. IF THE METACENTER IS ABOVE THE CENTER OF GRAVITY, BUOYANCY RESTORES STABILITY WHEN THE SHIP LISTS. IF THE METACENTER IS BELOW THE CENTER OF GRAVITY, THE BOAT OR SHIP BECOMES UNSTABLE AND A DANGEROUS SITUATION EXISTS WHICH CAN CAUSE THE SHIP OR BOAT TO CAPSIZE.

SEAPORTS :-PORTS FOR OCEAN SHIPS. HERE ARE SOME SEAPORTS OF THE WORLD :-

PORT OF AABENRAA   DENMARK
PORT OF ANTWERP   BELGIUM
PORT OF BORDEAUX   FRANCE
PORT OF GEORGETOWN   GUYANA
PORT OF EDEN AUSTRALIA
PORT OF GLADSTONE
PORT OF KALUNDBORG   DENMARK
PORT OF KAWASAKI   JAPAN
PORT OF KITAKYUSHU JAPAN
MARSEILLES PORT SERVICES
PORT OF MONTREAL   CANADA
PORT OF OOSTENDE   BELGIUM
PORT OF OSAKA JAPAN
PORT OF HAMBURG
PORT OF PUSAN KOREA
PORT OF QUEBEC   CANADA
PORT OF REYKJAVIK   ICELAND
PORT OF ROSTOCK   GERMANY
PORT OF SANTOS   BRAZIL
PORT OF VANCOUVER CANADA
PORT OF YAMBA   AUSTRALIA
PORT OF ZEEBRUGGE BELGIUM

WORLD TREATIES :-AGREEMENTS BETWEEN NATIONS. SOME TREATIES INVOLVING NATION – COUNTRIES OF THE WORLD ARE :-

CTBT
GATT [GENERAL AGREEMENT ON TARIFFS AND TRADES]
MAI [MULTILATERAL AGREEMENT ON INVESTMENT]
NAFTA [NORTH AMERICAN FREE TRADE AGREEMENT]
NON – PROLIFERATION TREATY
NORTH ATLANTIC TREATY ORGANISATION
PATENT COOPERATION TREATY

WAR :-COMES ABOUT WHEN THERE IS A CONFLICT BETWEEN TWO PARTIES; AFTER A BREAKDOWN IN

COMMUNICATION. HERE ARE SOME IMPORTANT WARS THAT
HAVE OCCURRED IN THE WORLD OVER THE YEARS.

AMERICAN CIVIL WAR
ARAB – ISRAELI WARS
AROOSTOOK WAR
BANGLADESH WAR OF LIBERATION
BOER WAR
BOXER REBELLION
CRIMEAN WAR
CUBAN REVOLUTION
FALKLANDS WAR
FRENCH REVOLUTION
GREEK WAR OF INDEPENDENCE
GULF WAR
HAITIAN REVOLUTION
INDIA – PAKISTAN WAR – 1971
IRANIAN REVOLUTION
KOREAN WAR
MEXICAN REVOLUTION
NANJING MASSACRE
NAPOLEONIC WAR
OPIUM WARS
PHILIPPINE – AMERICAN WAR
PUNIC WARS
RUSSIAN REVOLUTION
SECOND SINO – JAPANESE WAR
SOMALIAN CIVIL WAR
SPANISH – AMERICAN WAR
SPANISH CIVIL WAR
U.S. - MEXICAN WAR
VIETMAN WAR
WAR OF 1812 – 1814
WORLD WAR 1
WORLD WAR 2

ARCHAEOLOGY :-IS THE STUDY OF ANCIENT PEOPLES;
AS BY EXCAVATION OF RUINS. SOME ARCHAEOLOGY
ASSOCIATIONS IN THE WORLD ARE AS FOLLOWS :-
AMERICAN CULTURAL RESOURCES ASSOCIATION
APPLIED ANTHROPOLOGY COMPUTER NETWORK [
ANTHAP]

ANTHROPOLOGICAL SOCIETY OF NIPPON
ARBUCKLE'S FORT ARCHAEOLOGY EXCAVATION
ARCHAEOLOGICAL INSTITUTE OF AMERICA
ARCHAEOLOGICAL AND ANTHROPOLOGY – THEORY AND
PRACTICE
ARCHAEOLOGICAL SURVEY ASSOCIATION [A.S.A]
ASSOCIATION OF SOCIAL ANTHROPOLOGY IN OCEANIA
[ASAO]
ARCHAEOLOGICAL SURVEY ASSOCIATION [ASA]
ASSOCIATION OF HISTORICAL ARCHAEOLOGISTS OF THE
PACIFIC NORTH WEST [AHAPN]
ASSOCIATION FOR ENVIRONMENTAL ARCHAEOLOGY [
AEA]
CANADIAN   SOCIOLOGY   AND   ANTHROPOLOGY
ASSOCIATION
CENTRAL GULF COAST ARCHAEOLOGICAL SOCIETY [
CGCAS]
COUNCIL FOR BRITISH ARCHAEOLOLGY [CBA]
CLASSICS AND MEDITERRANEAN ARCHAEOLOGY
NAUTICAL ARCHAEOLOGY AT TEXAS A&M
NEVADA ARCHAEOLOGICAL ASSOCIATION [NAA]
ONLINE RESOURCES FOR CANADIAN HERITAGE
ONTARIO ARCHAEOLOGICAL SOCIETY [OAS]
SOCIETY OF ANTHROPOLOGY OF EUROPE
THE   MIDDLE   ATLANTIC   ARCHAEOLOGICAL
CONFERENCE
THE SOCIETY FOR LATIN AMERICAN ANTHROPOLOGY [
SLAA]
THE WENNER GREN FOUNDATION
UNDERWATER ARCHAEOLOGICAL SOCIETY OF BRITISH
COLUMBIA

POPULATION :-THE TOTAL NUMBER OF INHABITANTS.
COUNTRIES WITH THE MOST POPULATION – NUMBER OF
PEOPLE IN ORDER OF RANK :-
1 CHINA
2 INDIA
3 UNITED STATES
4 INDONESIA
5 BRAZIL
6 PAKISTAN

7 RUSSIA
8 BANGLADESH
9 NIGERIA
10 JAPAN
11 MEXICO
12 PHILIPPINES
13 GERMANY
14 VIETNAM
15 EGYPT
16 IRAN
17 TURKEY
18 ETHIOPIA
19 THAILAND
20 FRANCE
21 UNITED KINGDOM
22 ITALY
23 CONGO
24 SOUTH KOREA
25 UKRAINE
26 SOUTH AFRICA
27 BURMA
28 COLOMBIA
29 SPAIN
30 ARGENTINA
31 POLAND
32 SUDAN
33 TANZANIA
34 ALGERIA
35 CANADA
36 MOROCCO
37 KENYA
38 AFGHANISTAN
39 PERU
40 NEPAL
41 UZBEKISTAN
42 UGANDA
43 IRAQ
44 VENEZUELA
45 SAUDI ARABIA
46 MALAYSIA
47 TAIWAN

48 NORTH KOREA
49 ROMANIA
50 GHANA

THE VATICAN CITY :-IS ABOUT AS LARGE AS AN AVERAGE CITY PARK. IT LIES ON VATICAN HILL IN NORTH WESTERN ROME, JUST WEST OF THE TIBER RIVER. HIGH STONE WALLS SURROUND MOST OF THE CITY. THE IRREGULARLY SHAPED AREA WITHIN THESE WALLS CONTAINS PICTURESQUE BUILDINGS IN SEVERAL ARCHITECTURAL STYLES. IT ALSO CONTAINS MANY COURTYARDS, LANDSCAPED GARDENS AND QUIET STREETS. THE HUGE ST. PETER'S BASILICA – CHURCH, WITH ITS GIANT DOME, DOMINATES THE ENTIRE CITY. IT HAS LIBRARY, MUSEUM, PALACE AMONG OTHER BUILDINGS. IT'S A PRIVATE CITY; WHERE THE ROMAN CATHOLIC – POPE LIVES. IT ATTRACTS MANY VISITORS.

THE TELEPHONE :-IS CONSIDERED ONE OF THE MOST MARVELOUS INVENTIONS OF THE COMMUNICATIONS ERA. PHYSICAL DISTANCE IS CONQUERED INSTANTLY, AND ANY TELEPHONE IN THE WORLD CAN BE REACHED THROUGH A VAST COMMUNICATION NETWORK THAT SPANS OCEANS AND CONTINENTS. THIS FORM OF COMMUNICATION IS BOTH NATURAL AND UNIQUE, NAMELY HUMAN SPEECH. THE TELEPHONE WAS INVENTED BY ALEXANDER GRAHAM BELL.

RADIO :-IT IS INCREDIBLY EASY TO TRANSMIT WITH STATIC. ALL RADIOS TODAY, USE CONTINUOUS SINE WAVES TO TRANSMIT INFORMATION [AUDIO, VIDEO, DATA ETC.] THE REASON THAT WE USE CONTINUOUS SINE WAVES TODAY IS BECAUSE THERE ARE SO MANY DIFFERENT PEOPLE AND DEVICES THAT WANT TO USE RADIO WAVES AT THE SAME TIME. IF YOU HAD SOME WAY TO SEE THEM, YOU WOULD FIND THAT THERE ARE LITERALLY THOUSANDS OF DIFFERENT RADIO WAVES – IN THE FORM OF SINE WAVES AROUND YOU RIGHT NOW; TELEVISION BROADCASTS, AM AND FM RADIO BROADCASTS, POLICE AND FIRE RADIOS, SATELLITE T.V TRANSMISSIONS, CELL PHONE CONVERSATIONS, VARIOUS SIGNALS AND SO ON. IT IS AMAZING HOW MANY USES THERE ARE FOR RADIO

WAVES TODAY. EACH DIFFERENT RADIO SIGNAL USES A DIFFERENT SINE WAVE FREQUENCY, AND THAT IS HOW THEY ARE ALL SEPARATED. ANY RADIO SET UP HAS TWO PARTS; THE TRANSMITTER AND THE RECEIVER.

THE TRANSMITTER TAKES SOME SORT OF MESSAGE, IT COULD BE THE SOUND OF SOMEONE'S VOICE, PICTURES FOR A T.V SET, DATA FOR A RADIO MODEM OR WHATEVER. IT ENCODES IT ONTO A SINE WAVE AND TRANSMITS IT WITH RADIO WAVES. THE RECEIVER RECEIVES THE RADIO WAVES AND DECODES THE MESSAGE FROM THE SINE WAVE IT RECEIVES. BOTH THE TRANSMITTER AND RECEIVER USE ANTENNAS TO RADIATE AND CAPTURE THE RADIO SIGNAL.

THE RADIO WAS INVENTED BY GUZLICLMO MARCONI OF ITALY.

NUCLEAR AND HAZARDOUS WASTE :-IS WASTE THAT POSE SUBSTANTIAL OR POTENTIAL THREATS TO PUBLIC HEALTH OR THE ENVIRONMENT; THE WASTE EXHIBIT ONE OR MORE OF THE CHARACTERISTICS OF HAZARDOUS WASTE SUCH AS IGNITABILITY, CORROSIVITY, REACTIVITY, AND / OR TOXICITY.

NUCLEAR AND HAZARDOUS WASTE ARE GOVERNED UNDER SEVERAL HEADINGS SUCH AS :-
HAZARDOUS WASTE MANAGEMENT
WASTE DISPOSAL POLICIES
THE INTERNATIONAL TRAFFIC IN HAZARDOUS WASTE
GLOBAL DUMPING GROUND FOR HAZARDOUS WASTE
HAZARDOUS WASTE TREATMENT FACILITIES
THE HAZARDOUS WASTE TRADE
NUCLEAR SITES
INTERNATIONAL MANAGEMENT OF HAZARDOUS WASTE

PRESERVING ENDANGERED SPECIES OF ANIMALS AND PLANTS :-
IN ORDER TO PREVENT THE EXTINCTION OF ANIMALS AND PLANTS AS WELL AS FISH FROM THIS WORLD, THERE ARE NUMEROUS ORGANIZATIONS THAT WORK TOWARDS THIS INTEREST. SOME OF THESE ORGANIZATIONS ARE AS FOLLOWS :-

PLANTS AND ANIMALS CONVENTION ON NATURE PROTECTION AND WILD LIFE PRESERVATION W O R L D TUFTS UNIVERSITY

PLANTS AND ANIMALS INTERNATIONAL CONVENTION FOR THE REGULATION OF WHALING WORLD TUFTS UNIVERSITY

PLANTS AND ANIMALS AGREEMENT FOR THE ESTABLISHMENT OF A GENERAL FISHERIES COUNCIL WORLD TUFTS UNIVERSITY

PLANTS AND ANIMALS CONVENTION ON INTERNATIONAL TRADE ON ENDANGERED SPECIES WORLD TUFTS UNIVERSITY

PLANTS, FORESTS, TREES, ENDANGERED, INTERNATIONAL, TROPICAL, TIMBER AGREEMENT WORLD INTERNATIONAL TROPICAL TIMBER AGREEMENT.

PLANTS AND ANIMALS LIST OF WORLD HERITAGE IN ENDANGERED DANGER UNESCO

PLANTS AND ANIMALS WORLD CONSERVATION MONITORING CENTER WORLD CONSERVATION MONITORING CENTER U.K

PLANTS AND ANIMALS ENDANGERED, WILD FLORA AND FAUNA LIST. WORLD CONSERVATION MONITORING CENTER.

LIGHTNING AND THUNDER :-

THUNDER AND LIGHTNING OCCUR TOGETHER; THE LIGHT REACHES YOU AT ONCE, SOUND TAKES SOME TIME TO REACH YOU. USUALLY YOU SEE THE LIGHTNING STROKE BEFORE YOU HEAR THE THUNDER. AS SOON AS YOU SEE THE LIGHTNING, LETS SAY IT TOOK 5 SECONDS UNTIL YOU HEAR THE THUNDER, THE LIGHTNING WAS ABOUT A MILE AWAY SOUND TRAVELS ABOUT 1000 FEET A SECOND. IF YOU SEE THE LIGHTNING AND HEAR THUNDER AT JUST ABOUT THE SAME TIME; THE STORM IS RIGHT ABOVE YOU. ON A HOT DAY, CUMULUS CLOUDS BUILD UP; THEY GROW LARGER, TOWERING HIGHER AND HIGHER, THEY DARKEN. THE TOP OF THE CLOUDS MAY BE SPREAD OUT BY WINDS AT HIGH ALTITUDES. AS CLOUDS DEVELOP, PARTICLES IN THE CLOUDS BECOME CHARGED WITH ELECTRICITY. WHEN THE CHARGES OVERFLOW, THEY MAKE A LIGHTNING FLASH WITH A THUNDERING NOISE. LIGHTNING MAY GO FROM

ONE PART OF A CLOUD TO ANOTHER, OR FROM CLOUD TO CLOUD. IT MAY GO FROM A CLOUD TO THE EARTH. LIGHTNING TAKES THE SHORT PATH; SO, IT HITS THE HIGH OBJECTS – A TOWER, A TALL TREE OR A PERSON STANDING ALONE IN A FLAT FIELD.

CLOUDS :-THERE ARE THREE GENERAL TYPES OF CLOUDS.
STRATUS
CUMULUS
CIRRUS
CLOUDS ARE USUALLY A COMBINATION AND VARIATIONS OF THE THREE GENERAL TYPES.
SOME VARIATIONS OF THE THREE GENERAL TYPES ARE :-
ALTO STRATUS
ALTO CUMULUS

GREENHOUSE EFFECT :-
THE ATMOSPHERE OF THE EARTH BEHAVES LIKE A BLANKET, RETAINING A PORTION OF THE HEAT GENERATED BY SOLAR ENERGY. THIS GREENHOUSE EFFECT, KEEPS THE AVERAGE TEMPERATURE OF THE EARTH ABOUT 30 DEGREES C OR 86 DEGREES F ;THAT'S WARMER THAN IT WOULD BE WITHOUT ATMOSPHERIC CLOUDS AND CERTAIN ATMOSPHERIC GASSES SUCH AS WATER VAPOR, AND CARBON DIOXIDE, THEREBY PROVIDING THIS WARMING EFFECT.

SOME WORLD LEADERS - HEADS OF STATES :-

U.S.A	PRESIDENT	GEORGE W BUSH
U.K	PRIME MINISTER	TONY BLAIR
AUSTRALIA	PRIME MINISTER	JOHN HOWARD
REPUBLIC OF		
SLOVENIA	PRESIDENT	JANEZ DRNOVSEK
ETHIOPIA	PRESIDENT	GIRMA WOLDE GIORGIS
DEMOCRATIC		
REPUBLIC OF TIMOR - LESTE	PRESIDENT	
KAY RALA XANANA GUSMAO		
REPUBLIC OF BERIN		GENERAL MATHIEU KERE KON

NEPAL	KING GYANENDRA BIR BIKRAM SHAH DEV	
THAILAND	PRIME MINISTER	THAKSIN SHINAWATRA
ALBANIA	PRIME MINISTER	FATOS NANO
ANTIGUA AND BARBUDA	PRIME MINISTER	LESTER BIRD
ARGENTINA	PRESENDENTE	DR. CARLOS SAUL MENEM
BARBADOS	PRIME MINISTER	OWEN ARTHUR
CANADA	PRIME MINISTER	JEAN CHRETIEN
DENMARK	PRIME MINISTER	POUL NYRUP RASMUSSEN
EGYPT	PRESIDENT	MOHAMMED HOSNI MUBAREK
FINLAND	PRESIDENT	MARTII AHTISAARI
FRANCE	PRESIDENT	JACQUES CHIRAC
GHANA	PRESIDENT	JERRY RAWLINGS
GERMANY	CHANCELLOR	GERHARD SCHOEDER
GREECE	PRESIDENT	CONSTANTINOS STEPHANOPOULOS
HUNGARY	PRIME MINISTER	VIKTOR ORBAN
IRAN	PRESIDENT	SEYED MOHAMMAD KHATAMI
JAPAN	PRIME MINISTER	KEIZO OBUCHI
GUYANA	PRESIDENT	BHARRAT JADGEO
TRINIDAD AND TOBAGO	PRESIDENT	A.N.R.ROBINSON
SWEDEN	PRIME MINISTER	GORAN PERSSON
SURINAME	PRESIDENT	JULES WIJDENBOSCH
ST. LUCIA	PRIME MINISTER	KENNY ANTHONY
PAKISTAN	PRIME MINISTER	MIAN MUHAMMAD NAWAZ SHARIF
NORWAY	PRIME MINISTER	KJELL MAGNE BONDEVIK
NEW ZEALAND	PRIME MINISTER	JENNY SHIPLEY

LUXEMBOURG   PRIME MINISTER   JEAN   –   CLAUDE JUNCKER

JORDAN	KING HUSSAIN BIN TALAL
ALBANIA	PRESIDENT REXHEP MEJDANI
ARMENIA	PRESIDENT ROBERT KOCHARIAN
AUSTRIA	PRESIDENT GEIDAR ALIYEV
BELARUS	PRESIDENT ALEKSANDR LUKASHENKO
BELGIUM	PRIME MINISTER M. JEAN - LUE DEHAENE
BRAZIL	PRESIDENT FERNANDO HENRIQUE CARDOSO
BULGARIA	PRESIDENT PETAR STOYANOV
CAMEROON	PRESIDENT PAUL BIYA
CHILE	PRESIDENT EDUARDO FREI RUIZ – TAGLE
COLOMBIA	PRESIDENT PRESIDENT ANDRES PASTRANA ARANGO
CROATIA	PRESIDENT DR. FRANJO TUDJMAN
CZECH REPUBLIC	PRESIDENT VACLAV HAVEL
DOMINICA	PRESIDENT CRISPIN ANSELM SORHAINDO
DOMINICAN REPUBLIC	PRESIDENT LEONEL FERNANDEZ REYNA
ECUADOR	PRESIDENT JAMIL MAHUAD WITT
EL SALVADOR	PRESIDENT ARMANDO CALDERON SOL
ESTONIA	PRESIDENT LENNART MERI
FIJI	PRESIDENT KAMISESE MARA
GABON	PRESIDENT EL HAJD OMAR BONGO
GEORGIA	CHAIRMAN, STATE COUNCIL EDUARD SHEVARDNADZE
GUATEMALA	PRESIDENT ALVARN ARZN
IRELAND	PRESIDENT MARY MCALEESE
ISRAEL	PRIME MINISTER BENJAMIN NETANYAHU
JAMAICA	PRIME MINISTER PERCIVAL JOHN PATTERSON
LATIVA	PRESIDENT GUNTIS ULMANIS
LEBANON	PRIME MINISTER SELIM AHMED HOSS
LITHUANIA	PRESIDENT VALDAS ADAMKUS

MALAYSIA PRIME MINISTER DR. DATO SERI MAHATHIR MOHAMAD

MALDIVES	PRESIDENT MAUMOON ABDUL GAYOOM
MAURITIUS	PRESIDENT CASSAM UTEEM

MICRONESIA	PRESIDENT JACOB NENA
MONGOLIA	PRESIDENT NATSAGIYN BAGABANDI
NAMBIA	PRESIDENT SAM NIYOMA
PANAMA	PRESIDENT ERNESTO PEREZ BALLADARES
POLAND	PRESIDENT ALEKSANDER KWASNIEWSKI
PORTUGAL	PRIME MINISTER ANTONIO GUTERRES
ROMANIA	PRESIDENT EMILE CONSTANTINESCU
SOUTH KOREA	PRESIDENT KIM DAE JONG
SRI LANKA	PRESIDENT CHANDRIKA BANDARANAIKE KUMARATUNGA
SWAZILAND	PRIME MINISTER DR. BARNABAS SIBUSISO DLAMINI
TOGO	PRESIDENT ETIENNE GUASSINGLE EYADEMA
TURKEY	PRESIDENT SULEYMAN DEMIREL
UGANDA	PRESIDENT YOWERI KAGUTA MUSEVENI
UKRAINE	PRESIDENT LEONID KUCHMA
URUGUAY	PRESIDENT JULIO MARIA SANGUINETTI
UZBEKISTAN	PRESIDENT ISLAM KARIMOV
YUGOSLAVIA	FEDERAL PRESIDENT SLOBODAN MILOSEVIC
ZAMBIA	PRESIDENT FREDERICK CHILUBA

NOTE :-FROM TIME TO TIME FOR VARIOUS REASONS SUCH AS ELECTIONS, HEADS OF COUNTRIES ARE CHANGED.

TIME RECKONING :-
60 SECONDS MAKE 1 MINUTE
60 MINUTES MAKE 1 HOUR
24 HOURS MAKE 1 DAY
7 DAYS MAKE 1 WEEK
SUNDAY
MONDAY
TUESDAY
WEDNESDAY
THURSDAY
FRIDAY
SATURDAY
12 MONTHS MAKE 1 YEAR
JANUARY

FEBRUARY
MARCH
APRIL
MAY
JUNE
JULY
AUGUST
SEPTEMBER
OCTOBER
NOVEMBER
DECEMBER
365 DAYS MAKE ONE YEAR
366 DAYS MAKE ONE LEAP YEAR
ALL THE MONTHS HAVE 31 DAYS EXCEPT APRIL, JUNE, SEPTEMBER, AND NOVEMBER WHICH HAVE 30 DAYS EACH; ALSO FEBRUARY HAS 28 DAYS; HOWEVER IN A LEAP YEAR WHICH OCCURS EVERY 4 YEARS, FEBRUARY HAS 29 DAYS.

GENERATION :-IS ABOUT 30 YEARS.

CENTURY :-IS 100 YEARS.

CHAPTER 23.

SOME FAMOUS AND POPULAR ACTORS AND ACTRESSES :-

CLINT EASTWOOD OF SAN FRANCISCO CALIFORNIA, ACADEMY AWARD FOR BEST DIRECTOR 1992 UNFORGIVEN.

JULIA ROBERTS OF SMYRNA GEORGIA MOVIES INCLUDE PRETTY WOMAN.

BARBARA JOAN STREISAND OF BROOKLYN, NEW YORK ACADEMY AWARD FOR BEST ACTRESS 1968 IN FUNNY GIRL

MARILYN MONROE OF LOS ANGELES, CALIFORNIA MOVIES INCLUDE ALL ABOUT EVE.

CHARLES BRONSON OF EHRENFIELD, PA   MARRIED TO ACTRESS JILL IRELAND MOVIES INCLUDE DEATH WISH.

ROBERT CHARLES REDFORD JR. OF SANTA MONICA CALIFORNIA MOVIES INCLUDE THE STING AND ALL THE PRESIDENT'S MEN

KEVIN COSTNER OF LOS ANGELES CALIFORNIA ACADEMY AWARD BEST DIRECTOR 1990 DANCES WITH WOLVES.

FRANK ALBERT SINATRA HOBOKEN NEW JERSEY ACADEMY AWARD BEST SUPPORTING ACTOR 1953 IN FROM HERE TO ETERNITY

EDDIE MURPHY OF BROOKLYN NEW YORK MOVIES INCLUDE COMING TO AMERICA AND 48 HOURS.

ARNOLD SCHWARZENEGGER OF GRAZ AUSTRIA MOVIES INCLUDE THE TERMINATOR AND PREDATOR.

AL PACINO OF NEW YORK, N.Y ACADEMY AWARD BEST ACTOR 1992 IN SCENT OF A WOMAN

TOM CRUISE OF SYRACUSE NEW YORK MARRIED TO NICOLE KIDMAN MOVIES INCLUDE A FEW GOOD MEN AND THE LAST SAMURI

FAYE DOROTHY DUNAWAY OF BASCOM FLORIDA ACADEMY AWARD BEST ACTRESS 1976 IN NETWORK

CLARK WILLIAM GABLE OF CADIZ OH ACADEMY AWARD BEST ACTOR 1935 IN IT HAPPENED ONE NIGHT

FRED ASTAIRE OF OMAHA, NE MOVIES INCLUDE THE SKY'S THE LIMIT AND YOU'LL NEVER GET RICH

BRUCE LEE OF SAN FRANCISCO CALIFORNIA MOVIES INCLUDE THE BIG BOSS AND ENTER THE DRAGON

JACK NICHOLSON OF NEPTUNE NEW JERSEY ACADEMY AWARDS BEST ACTOR 1975 IN ONE FLEW OVER THE CUCKOO'S NEST AND BEST SUPPORTING ACTOR 1983 IN TERMS OF ENDEARMENT

CARY GRANT OF BRISTOL ENGLAND MOVIES INCLUDE THE PHILADELPHIA STORY AND WALK, DON'T RUN

ELIZABETH TAYLOR OF LONDON ENGLAND ACADEMY AWARDS BEST ACTRESS 1960 IN BUTTERFIELD 8; BEST ACTRESS 1966 IN WHO'S AFRAID OF VIRGINA WOOLF

SOPHIA LOREN OF ROME ITALY ACADEMY AWARD 1961 IN TWO WOMEN

PAUL LEONARD NEWMAN OF CLEVELAND OHIO ACADEMY AWARD 1986 IN THE COLOR OF MONEY

PETER SEAMUS O'TOOLE OF CONNEMARA REGION IRELAND MOVIES INCLUDE WHAT'S NEW PUSSYCAT AND THE LAST EMPEROR

OMAR SHARIF OF ALEXANDRIA, EGYPT MOVIES INCLUDE LAWRENCE OF ARABIA AND THE NIGHT OF THE GENERALS

KIRK DOUGLAS OF AMSTERDAM NEW YORK MOVIES INCLUDE I WALK ALONE AND THE BIG SKY

ROBERT DE NIRO OF NEW YORK N.Y ACADEMY AWARDS 1974 BEST SUPPORTING ACTOR IN THE GODFATHER, PART 2; BEST ACTOR 1981 IN RAGING BULL

INGRID BERGMAN OF STOCKHOLM SWEDEN ACADEMY AWARDS BEST ACTRESS 1944 IN GASLIGHT; BEST ACTRESS 1957 IN ANASTASIA; BEST SUPPORTING ACTRESS 1974 IN MURDER ON THE ORIENT EXPRESS

JOHN WAYNE OF WINTERSET IA ACADEMY AWARD BEST ACTOR 1969 IN TRUE GRIT

KIM BASINGER OF ATHENS GA MOVIES INCLUDE BATMAN AND FINAL ANALYSIS

AVA GARDNER OF SMITHFIELD NC MOVIES INCLUDE THE BLUE BIRD AND THE SUN ALSO RISES

DENZEL WASHINGTON OF MOUNT VERNON N.Y ACADEMY AWARD BEST SUPPORTING ACTOR 1990 IN GLORY

KATHARINE HEPBURN OF HARTFORD CT OSCARS BEST ACTRESS 1933 IN MORNING GLORY BEST ACTRESS 1967 IN GUESS WHO'S COMING TO DINNER BEST ACTRESS 1968 IN THE LION IN WINTER BEST ACTRESS 1981 IN ON GOLDEN POND

RICHARD GERE OF PHILADELPHIA PA MOVIES INCLUDE PRETTY WOMAN AND AN OFFICER AND A GENTLEMAN

ELVIS PRESLEY OF TUPELO MS MOVIES INCLUDE LOVE ME TENDER AND GI BLUES

MERYL STREEP OF SUMMIT NJ ACADEMY AWARDS BEST ACTRESS 1979 KRAMER VS KRAMER, BEST ACTRESS 1982 IN SOPHIE'S CHOICE

JODIE FOSTER OF LOS ANGELES CA ACADEMY AWARDS BEST ACTRESS 1988 THE ACCUSED, BEST ACTRESS 1991 SILENCE OF THE LAMBS.

NICK NOLTE OF OMAHA NE MOVIES INCLUDE NEW YORK STORIES AND 48 HOURS.

LAUREN BACALL OF NEW YORK NY MOVIES INCLUDE THE BIG SLEEP AND FLAME OVER INDIA

RITA HAYWORTH OF NEW YORK NY MOVIES INCLUDE SEPARATE TABLES AND AFFAIR IN TRINIDAD

MARLENE DIETRICH OF BERLIN GERMANY MOVIES INCLUDE WITNESS FOR THE PROSECUTION AND DESIRE

JAMES DEAN OF MARION IN MOVIES INCLUDE EAST OF EDEN AND REBEL WITHOUT A CAUSE

WARREN BEATTY OF RICHMOND VA ACADEMY AWARD BEST DIRECTOR 1981 FOR REDS

GINA LOLLOBRIGIDA OF SUBIACO ITALY MOVIES INCLUDE STRANGE BEDFELLOWS AND THE WAYWARD WIFE.

GLENDA JACKSON OF BIRKENHEAD ENGLAND ACADEMY AWARDS BEST ACTRESS 1970 IN WOMAN IN LOVE, BEST ACTRESS 1973 IN A TOUCH OF CLASS

THEDA BARA CINCINNATI, OH MOVIES INCLUDE THE SHE – DEVIL AND THE DEVIL'S DAUGHTER

JON VOIGHT OF YONKERS NY ACADEMY AWARD BEST ACTOR 1977 IN COMING HOME

NATALIE WOOD OF SAN FRANCISCO CA MOVIES INCLUDE BRAINSTORM AND SPLENDOR IN THE GRASS

WALTER BRENNAN OF SWAMPSCOTT MA ACADEMY AWARDS BEST SUPPORTING ACTOR 1936 IN COME AND GET IT; BEST SUPPORTING ACTOR 1938 IN KENTUCKY; BEST SUPPORTING ACTOR 1940 IN THE WESTERNER

ANTHONY PERKINS OF NEW YORK NY MOVIES INCLUDE PSYCHO 3 AND PSYCHO

GRACE KELLY OF PHILADELPHIA PA ACADEMY AWARD BEST ACTRESS 1954 IN THE COUNTRY GIRL

URSULA ANDRESS OF BERN SWITZERLAND MOVIES INCLUDE CLASH OF THE TITANS AND CASINO ROYALE

JESSICA LANGE OF CLOQUET MN ACADEMY AWARD BEST SUPPORTING ACTRESS 1982 IN TOOTSIE

GENE KELLY OF PITTSBURGH PA ACADEMY AWARD HONORARY AWARD FOR ACHIEVEMENTS IN THE ART OF CHOREOGRAPHY 1951

JUDY GARLAND OF GRAND RAPIDS MN MOVIES INCLUDE A STAR IS BORN AND THE WIZARD OF OZ

VIVIEN LEIGH OF DARJEELING INDIA ACADEMY AWARDS BEST ACTRESS 1939 IN GONE WITH THE WIND, BEST ACTRESS 1951 IN A STREETCAR NAMED DESIRE.

GLENN GLOSE OF GREENWICH CT MOVIES INCLUDE MEETING VENUS AND FATAL ATTRACTION

MICKEY ROURKE OF SCHENECTADY, NY MOVIES INCLUDE WILD ORCHID AND ANGEL HEART

ERROL FLYNN OF TASMANIA AUSTRALIA MOVIES INCLUDE THE ROOTS OF HEAVEN AND TOO MUCH TOO SOON

MARLEE MATLIN OF MORTON GROVE IL ACADEMY AWARD BEST ACTRESS 1986 IN CHILDREN OF A LESSER GOD

DEBBIE ALLEN OF HOUSTON TX MOVIES INCLUDE RAGTIME AND ROOTS THE NEXT GENERATION

THE ACADEMY AWARDS AFFECTIONATELY KNOWN AS THE OSCARS ARE THE OLDEST, BEST KNOWN, MOST

INFLUENTIAL, MOST PRESTIGIOUS, AND FAMOUS OF FILM AWARDS. THE AWARDS ARE GOLD – PLATED STATUETTES, WHICH HAVE BEEN PRESENTED SINCE 1927; HOWEVER, THE FIRST ANNUAL ACADEMY – OSCAR AWARDS PRESENTATION HAS BEEN HELD SINCE 1929.

WINNERS OF THESE AWARDS SINCE 1990, HAVE BEEN AMONG OTHERS

KEVIN KOSTNER
ROBERT DE NIRO
RICHARD HARRIS
KATHY BATES
JULIA ROBERTS
MERYL STREEP
JOANNE WOODWARD
ANDY GARCIA
GRAHAM GREENE
WHOOPI GOLDBERG
WARREN BEATTY
ROBIN WILLIAMS
JACK PALANCE
TOMMY LEE JONES
CLINT EASTWOOD
DENZEL WASHINGTON
GENE HACKMAN
TOM HANKS
HOLLY HUNTER
JOHN TRAVOLTA
NICOLAS CAGE
MEL GIBSON
TOM CRUISE
JACK NICHOLSON
DUSTIN HOFFMAN
KIM BASINGER
JAMES CAMERON
JAMES COBURN
ROBERT DUVALL
KEVIN SPACEY
MICHAEL CAINE
ANGELINA JOLIE
SAM MENDES
RUSSELL CROWE

LAURA LINNEY
HALLE BERRY
ADRIEN BRODY
SEAN PENN
BEN KINGSLEY
JUDE LAW
BILL MURRAY
CHARLIZE THERON
TIM ROBBINS
RENEE ZELLWEGER
PATRICIA CLARKSON
MARCIA GAY HARDEN
PETER JACKSON

SOME FAMOUS AND POPULAR INDIAN MOVIE STARS
OVER THE YEARS ARE :-
AMITABH BACHCHAN
ANIL KAPOOR
AJAY DEVGAN
ASHUTOSH RANA
BONEY KAPOOR
DEVANAND
DHARMENDRA
GULSHAN KUMAR
JACKIE SHROFF
NASIR KHAN
RAJ KAPOOR
RAJESH KHANNA
RAKESH ROSHAN
RISHI KAPOOR
SANJAY DUTT
SANJAY KAPOOR
VINOD MEHRA
JEETENDRA
MEHMOOD
AAYESHA
AMRITA SINGH
ANTRA MALLI
DIMPLE KAPADIA
DIVYA DUTTA
ESHA

HEMA MALINI
JUHI CHAWLA
NAZIA HASSAN
PREETA
RAMBHA
REKHA
SAKSHI
SHABANA AZMI
KIM SHARMA
MOHINI SHARMA
MUMTAZ
SHARMILA TAGORE
SUSHMITA SEN
TWINKLE KHANNA
ZEENAT AMAN

WORLD MUSIC AWARDS :-
WORLD'S BEST ARTIST 50 CENT
WORLD'S BEST POP FEMALE ARTIST NORAH JONES
WORLD'S BEST POP MALE ARTIST 50 CENT
WORLD'S BEST POP GROUP T.A.T.U
WORLD'S BEST DUO T.A.T.U
WORLD'S BEST POP / ROCK ARTIST EMINEM
WORLD'S BEST POP / ROCK GROUP DIXIE CHICKS
WORLD'S BEST ROCK ARTIST GROUP LINKIN PARK
WORLD'S BEST DANCE ARTIST JUSTIN TIMBERLAKE
WORLD'S BEST DANCE GROUP T.A.T.U
WORLD'S BEST ADULT CONTEMPORARY ARTIST NORAH JONES
WORLD'S BEST CLASSICAL ARTIST ANDREA BOCELLI
WORLD'S BEST R & B ARTIST 50 CENT
WORLD'S BEST RAP / HIP – HOP ARTIST 50 CENT
WORLD'S BEST LATIN FEMALE ARTIST SHAKIRA
WORLD'S BEST LATIN MALE ARTIST DAVID BISBAL
WORLD'S BEST NEW ARTIST 50 CENT
WORLD'S BEST NEW GROUP EVANESCENCE

NOTE AWARDS SUCH AS THESE ARE GIVEN OUT ANNUALLY.

SOME OF THE BEST MALE SINGERS OVER THE YEARS
HAVE BEEN :-
HARRY BELAFONTE
JAMES BROWN
NAT KING COLE
LUTHER VANDROSS
STEVIE WONDER
CHUCK BERRY
SAMMY DAVIS JR.
MICHAEL JACKSON
QUINCY JONES
PRINCE
LL COOL J
WILL SMITH
JAY – Z
FRANK SINATRA
ELTON JOHN
BILLY HOLIDAY
TEDDY PENDERGRASS
DAVID BISBAL
NELLY

SOME OF THE BEST FEMALE SINGERS OVER THE YEARS
HAVE BEEN :
MADONNA
ELLA FITZGERALD
ARETHA FRANKLIN
GLADYS KNIGHT
ANITA BAKER
TONI BRAXTON
WHITNEY HOUSTON
JANET JACKSON
QUEEN LATIFAH
DIANA ROSS
TINA TURNER
CHER
BRANDY
BRITNEY SPEARS
BARBARA STREISAND
DONNA SUMMER
DIONNE WARRICK

JULIE ANDREWS
DOLLY PARTON
LATA MANGESHKAR
ASHA BHOSLE
JOAN SEBASTIAN
BEYONCE
JENNIFER LOPEZ
ASHANTI

MALE SINGING GROUPS OF PROMINENCE :-
THE BEATLES
BOYS II MEN
THE COMMODORES
THE JACKSON 5
THE TEMPTATIONS

FEMALE SINGING GROUPS OF PROMINENCE :-
EN VOGUE
THE SUPREMES
TLC

RENOWNED FEMALE GOSPEL ARTISTS ARE :-
YOLANDA ADAMS
SHIRLEY CAESAR
MALE GOSPEL SINGERS SUCH AS :-
RANDY TRAVIS
DONNIE MC CLURKIN
KIRK FRANKLIN

DANCING AS A PROFESSION ATTRACT A LARGE
NUMBER OF ARTISTS ONE CENSOR GIVES THE NUMBER
OF REGISTERED DANCERS ENTRIES AS NEARLY 4400; WITH
SOME 2800 BEING WOMEN AND ABOUT 1600 BEING MEN.
THE TOP COUNTRIES FROM WHICH ARE DRAWN DANCERS
TO THE PROFESSION ARE :-
U.S.A
U.K
SWITZERLAND
SWEDEN
AUSTRALIA
GERMANY

CANADA
FRANCE
INDIA
CHINA

THE TOP STATES FROM WHICH DANCERS ARE DRAWN
IN THE U.S.A ARE :-
CALIFORNIA
NEW YORK
TEXAS
WASHINGTON
MICHIGAN

SOME INTERNATIONAL AWARDS ARE PRESENTED IN THE
FOLLOWING AREAS :-
CHAPTER AWARDS
FOUNDERS AWARDS
MEDIA AWARDS
RESEARCH AWARDS
TECHNOLOGY AWARDS
TRIBUTE AWARDS

WORLD SPORTS AWARDS ARE ALSO PRESENTED
REGULARLY. EXAMPLE IN 2003 AN INTERNATIONAL
ORGANIZATION HANDED OUT THESE AWARDS.
SPORTSMAN CYCLIST LANCE ARMSTRONG
SPORTSWOMAN TENNIS PLAYER SERENA WILLIAMS
TEAM OF THE YEAR BRAZIL FOOTBALL [SOCCER]
TEAM

NATO :-NORTH ATLANTIC TREATY ORGANIZATION. THIS
IS AN INTERNATIONAL ORGANIZATION CREATED IN 1949
FOR PURPOSES OF COLLECTIVE SECURITY.
SOME MEMBERS OF NATO AND THEIR HEADS OF STATE
ARE :-

COUNTRY	HEAD OF STATE
BELGIUM	LE ROI ALBERT 2
BULGARIA	GEORGI PARVANOV
CANADA	QUEEN ELIZABETH 2
CZECH REPUBLIC	MR. VACLAV KLAUS
DENMARK	QUEEN MARGRETHE 2

ESTONIA	MR. ARNOLD RUUTEL
FRANCE	JACQUES CHIRAC
GERMANY	JOHANNES RAU
GREECE	MR. C STEPHANOPOULOS
HUNGARY	DR. FERENC MADL
ICELAND	MR. OLAFUR R GRIMSSON
ITALY	MR. CARLO A CIAMPI
LATVIA	DR. VAIRA VIKE – FREIBERGA
LITHUANIA	MR. ROLANDAS PAKSAS
LUXEMBOURG	LE GRAND DUC HENRI
NETHERLANDS	QUEEN BEATRIX
NORWAY	KING HARALD V
POLAND	MR. ALEKSANDER KWASNIEWSKI
PORTUGAL	DR. JORGE SAMPAIO
ROMANIA	MR. LON LLIESCU
SLOVAK REPUBLIC	MR. RUDOLF SCHUSTER
SLOVENIA	DR. JANEZ DRNOVSEK
SPAIN	KING JUAN CARLOS 1
TURKEY	MR. AHMET N SEZER
UNITED KINGDOM	QUEEN ELIZABETH 2
UNITED STATES OF AMERICA	MR. GEORGE W BUSH

MUSIC :-IS THE ART OF COMPOSING OR PERFORMING SONGS, SYMPHONIES ETC. THERE ARE MANY TYPES OF MUSIC SUCH AS :-

JAZZ
BLUES
DISCO
OLDIES
COUNTRY AND WESTERN
OPERA
GOSPEL
RAP
METAL
HEAVY METAL
R & B
ALTERNATIVE
CLASSICAL
SKA
HIP – HOP

REGGAE
NEW WAVE
ROCK N ROLL
EASY LISTENING

DANCE :-IS RHYTHMIC MOVEMENT TO MUSIC. SOME TYPES OF DANCES ARE :-
APACHE
BAMBA
BARN DANCES
BOOGIE WOOGIE
BUNNY HOP
CAN CAN
CHA CHA
CONGA
TANGO
COUNTRY DANCE
DIRTY DANCING
MERENGUE
FANDANGO
FOX TROT
FREESTYLE
WALTZ
HULA
HUSTLE
SWING HUSTLE
JIVE
MAMBO
MODERN DANCE
ONE STEP
QUICK STEP
ROCK N ROLL
ROUND DANCES
RUMBA
SALSA
SAMBA
SQUARE DANCE
SWING
TWIST
TWO STEP
ZAMBRA

BREAK DANCE
BALLET
TAP

SOME TOP VACATION – HOLIDAY RESORTS - STOPS IN THE WORLD ARE :-

[a] LAS VAGAS - CASINOS, FREMONT STREET, HOOVER DAM, RED ROCK CANYON.

[b] ORLANDO - WALT DISNEY WORLD RESORT, SEA WORLD, UNIVERSAL ORLANDO, HARRY P LEU GARDENS.

[c] HAWAII - ALOHA STATE STUNNING SITES, PEARL HARBOR, WAIMEA BAY, HALEAKALA CRATER, NA PALI COAST.

[d] NEW YORK CITY - KNOWN AS THE BIG APPLE; CENTRAL PARK, LITTLE ITALY, CHINA TOWN, LITTLE GUYANA, SOHO, TIMES SQUARE.

[e] SAN FRANCISCO - NAPA VALLEY, NORTH BEACH, HAIGHT ASHBURY, MARIN WOODS.

[f] THE CARIBBEAN - BARBADOS, PUERTO RICO, JAMAICA'S BLUE MOUNTAINS, MAGENS BAY OF ST. THOMAS, KAIETURE FALLS AND THE ESSEQUIBO ISLANDS OF GUYANA.

[g] MEXICO - CANCUN, ISLA MURJERES, LOS CABOS, PUERTO VALLARTA.

[h] LOS ANGELES - HOLLYWOOD, SANTA MONICA PIER, VENICE BEACH BOARDWALK, BEVERLY HILLS.

[I] DENVER - GOLDEN MINING HISTORY, ROCKY MOUNTAIN NATIONAL PARK, ASPEN, STREET MALL IN BOULDER.

[j] NEW ORLEANS - FRENCH QUARTER, GARDEN DISTRICT, MISSISSIPPI RIVER, WAREHOUSE DISTRICT.

CHAPTER 24.

CONSULATE :-A CONSULATE IS A DIPLOMATIC BUILDING THAT SERVES AS THE RESIDENCE OR WORKPLACE OF A CONSUL; RENDERING SERVICES TO CITIZENS OF THE COUNTRY OF THE CONSULATE. A CONSULATE IS THE REPRESENTATION OF THE PUBLIC ADMINISTRATION OF A COUNTRY IN A FOREIGN PLACE. IT IS RESPONSIBLE FOR ITS OWN FELLOW CITIZENS, LIVING OR TRAVELLING IN THE HOST COUNTRY. THE MOST IMPORTANT DUTIES OF A CONSULATE ARE :-

[a] TO ESTABLISH AND RENEW PASSPORTS AND OTHER OFFICIAL DOCUMENTS.

[b] TO REPORT BIRTHS, DEATHS, MARRIAGES, DIVORCES, ADOPTIONS ETC, THAT HAPPENED IN THE HOST COUNTRY TO THE COMPETENT AUTHORITIES HOME

[c] TO INFORM ITS OWN CITIZENS LIVING ABROAD ABOUT THE SOCIAL SECURITY SITUATION.

[d] TO HANDLE THE MILITARY FORMALITIES AND CONTROL FOR ITS OWN CITIZENS LIABLE TO MILITARY SERVICE.

[e] TO HELP ITS OWN CITIZENS IN DISTRESS OR OTHER EMERGENCY SITUATIONS.

[f] TO LOOK AFTER ITS OWN CITIZENS IN DETENTION OR ARREST AND TO WATCH OVER THE RULE OF LAW AND FAIR TRIALS.

[g] TO ESTABLISH ENTRY VISAS TO FOREIGN CITIZENS AND TO INFORM THEM ABOUT IMMIGRATION, RESIDENCE AND WORK PERMITS

EMBASSY :-AN EMBASSY IS THE DIPLOMATIC REPRESENTATION OF A COUNTRY'S GOVERNMENT IN ANOTHER COUNTRY. THE TASK OF AN EMBASSY ARE :-

[a] IT TRANSMITS MESSAGES OF ITS GOVERNMENT TO THE GOVERNMENT OF THE HOST COUNTRY AND VICE VERSA.

[b] IT INFORMS ITS HOME GOVERNMENT ABOUT IMPORTANT POLITICAL, SOCIAL, ECONOMICAL, MILITARY AND OTHER EVENTS HAPPENING IN THE HOST COUNTRY.

[c] IT PREPARES INTERNATIONAL TREATIES AND OFFICIAL STATE VISITS.

[d] IT PROMOTES ITS OWN HOME CULTURE, ECONOMY AND SCIENCE IN THE HOST COUNTRY.

[e] THE MILITARY ATTACHE IS RESPONSIBLE FOR CONTACTS BETWEEN THE TWO ARMED FORCES AND FOR ARMS BUSINESS.

[f] MANY EMBASSIES, ALSO HAVE A CONSULAR SECTION EXERCISING THE FUNCTIONS OF A CONSULATE.

THE DIPLOMATIC REPRESENTATION TO AN INTERNATIONAL ORGANIZATION SUCH AS THE UNITED NATIONS OR EUROPEAN UNION IS MOSTLY CALLED MISSION, PERMANENT MISSION OR DELEGATION.

A HIGH COMMISSION IS THE EMBASSY OF A MEMBER COUNTRY OF THE BRITISH COMMONWEALTH IN ANOTHER COMMONWEALTH COUNTRY.

A NUNCIATURE IS THE NAME OF THE EMBASSY OF THE STATE OF VATICAN.

WORLD CUSTOMS ORGANIZATIONS [WCO] WITH HEADQUARTERS IN BRUSSELS, BELGIUM IS CONCERNED WITH ASSESSMENT OF DUTIES AND TAXES ON IMPORTED GOODS – COMMODITIES. THE COUNTRIES ASSOCIATED WITH THE WORLD CUSTOMS ORGANIZATIONS ARE :-

ALBANIA
ALGERIA
ANDORRA
ARGENTINA

ARMENIA
AUSTRALIA
AUSTRIA
AZERBAIJAN
BAHAMAS
BAHRAIN
BANGLADESH
BARBADOS
BELARUS
BELGIUM
BENIN
BERMUDA
BHUTAN
BOLIVIA
BOTSWANA
BRAZIL
BRUNEI DARUSSALAM
BULGARIA
BURKINA FASO
BURUNDI
CAMBODIA
CAMEROON
CANADA
CAPE VERDE
CENTRAL AFRICAN REPUBLIC
CHILE
CHINA
COLOMBIA
COMOROS
CONGO, REPUBLIC OF THE
COSTA RICA
COTE D'LVOIRE
CROATIA
CUBA
CYPRUS
CZECH REPUBLIC
DEMOCRATIC REPUBLIC OF THE CONGO
DENMARK
ECUADOR
EGYPT
ERITREA

ESTONIA
ETHIOPIA
FIJI
FINLAND
FORMER YUGOSLAV REPUBLIC OF MACEDONIA
FRANCE
GABON
GAMBIA
GEORGIA
GERMANY
GHANA
GREECE
GUATEMALA
GUINEA
GUYANA
HAITI
HONG KONG
HUNGARY
ICELAND
INDIA
INDONESIA
IRAN
IRAQ
IRELAND
ISRAEL
ITALY
JAMAICA
JAPAN
JORDAN
KAZAKHSTAN
KENYA
KOREA
KUWAIT
KYRGYZSTAN
LATIVA
LEBANON
LESOTHO
LIBERIA
LIBYA
LITHUANIA
LUXEMBOURG

MACAU
MADAGASCAR
MALAWI
MALAYSIA
MALDIVES
MALI
MALTA
MAURITANIA
MAURITIUS
MEXICO
MOLDOVA
MONGOLIA
MOROCCO
MOZAMBIQUE
MYANMAR
NAMIBIA
NEPAL
NETHERLANDS
NETHERLANDS ANTILLES
NEW ZEALAND
NICARAGUA
NIGER
NIGERIA
NORWAY
OMAN
PAKISTAN
PANAMA
PAPUA NEW GUINEA
PARAGUAY
PERU
PHILIPPINES
POLAND
PORTUGAL
QATAR
ROMANIA
RUSSIAN FEDERATION
RWANDA
SAMOA
SAUDI ARABIA
SENEGAL
SERBIA AND MONTENEGRO

SEYCHELLES
SIERRA LEONE
SINGAPORE
SLOVAKIA
SLOVENIA
SOUTH AFRICA
SPAIN
SRI LANKA
SUDAN
SWAZILAND
SWEDEN
SWITZERLAND
SYRIA
TAJIKISTAN
TANZANIA
THAILAND
TIMOR – LESTE
TOGO
TRINIDAD AND TOBAGO
TUNISIA
TURKEY
TURKMENISTAN
UGANDA
UKRAINE
UNITED ARAB EMIRATES
UNITED KINGDOM
UNITED STATES OF AMERICA
URUGUAY
UZBEKISTAN
VENEZUELA
VIETNAM
YEMEN
ZAMBIA
ZIMBABWE

TYPES OF WORLD DISASTERS :-
AIRCRAFT
AVALANCHE
DAM
DROUGHT
EARTHQUAKE

EPIDEMIC
EXPLOSION
FIRE
FLOOD
HURRICANE
MARINE
SHIPWRECKS
MINE
OIL SPILL
RAILROAD
SUBMARINE
TERRORIST ATTACK
TORNADO
WINTER STORM
VOLCANIO
STORMS
DROUGHTS
HEAT WAVE
NUCLEAR POWER PLANT ACCIDENTS
SPACE ACCIDENTS
TIDAL WAVES
SPORTS DISASTERS
MISCELLANEOUS DISASTERS
FAMINE

SOCIAL SECURITY :-IS A SOCIAL WELFARE PROGRAM IN THE U.S AS WELL AS OTHER COUNTRIES OF THE WORLD. IT INCLUDES OLD AGE AND SURVIVORS INSURANCE AND SOME UNEMPLOYMENT INSURANCE AND OLD AGE ASSISTANCE.

IN THE U.S.A THE SOCIAL SECURITY ACT OF 1935 IS A SYSTEM OF FEDERAL OLD – AGE PENSIONS FOR PERSONS EMPLOYED; A PORTION OF THE PAYMENT IS DEDUCTED FROM THE EMPLOYEE'S SALARY AND AN EQUAL PORTION IS CONTRIBUTED BY THE EMPLOYER. BENEFITS ARE COMPUTED AND DISTRIBUTED IN SEVERAL WAYS AND FORMS TO ASSIST THOSE WHO QUALIFY AND ARE IN NEED OF ASSISTANCE. AREAS COVERED ARE SUCH AS :-

[a] GRANTS TO STATES FOR OLD AGE ASSISTANCE.

[b] FEDERAL OLD AGE BENEFITS.

[c] GRANTS TO STATES FOR UNEMPLOYMENT COMPENSATION ADMINISTRATION.

[d] GRANTS TO STATES FOR AID TO DEPENDENT CHILDREN.

[e] GRANTS TO STATES FOR MATERNAL AND CHILD WELFARE.

[f] PUBLIC HEALTH WORK.

[g] SOCIAL SECURITY BOARD.

[h] TAXES WITH RESPECT TO EMPLOYMENT.

[I] TAX ON EMPLOYERS.

[j] GRANTS TO STATES FOR AIDS TO THE BLIND.

[k] GENERAL PROVISIONS.

AMONG OTHER AREAS OF INTEREST.

FRANCHISE :-IS A BUSINESS WITH THE RIGHT TO PROVIDE PRODUCT OR SERVICE, USUALLY BOUGHT FOR FEES FROM A FOUNDER BUSINESS CONCERN. ACCORDING TO THE NEW NUMBERS FROM INTERNATIONAL FRANCHISE ASSOCIATION, FRANCHISING SPANS 1,500 CONCEPTS, FRANCHISE TYPES IN 75 INDUSTRIES, AND ITS 316,000 U.S UNITS REAP $ 1 TRILLION IN ANNUAL SALES.

THE GREAT DEPRESSION :-IS THE PERIOD OF HISTORY FROM 1929 TO 1942; THAT FOLLOWED BLACK THURSDAY. THE STOCK MARKET CRASH OF THURSDAY OCTOBER, 24 1929; CAUSED AN ACTUAL PANIC THAT BEGAN IN EARNEST ON BLACK TUESDAY, OCTOBER 29. THE EVENTS THAT TRIGGERED A WORLD WIDE DEPRESSION, WHICH LED TO DEFLATION AND A GREAT INCREASE IN UNEMPLOYMENT. ON THE GLOBAL – WORLD SCALE, THE MARKET CRASH IN THE U.S WAS A FINAL STRAW IN AN ALREADY SHAKY WORLD ECONOMIC SITUATION. GERMANY WAS SUFFERING FROM HYPERINFLATION OF CURRENCY AND MANY OF THE ALLIED VICTORS OF WORLD WAR 1 WERE HAVING SERIOUS PROBLEMS PAYING OFF HUGE WAR DEBTS. IN THE LATE 1920 THE AMERICAN ECONOMY AT FIRST SEEMED IMMUNE TO THE MOUNTING TROUBLES, BUT WITH THE START OF THE 1930'S IT CRASHED WITH STARTLING RAPIDITY.

WORLD COUNCIL OF CHURCHES OR [WCC] :-IS THE PRINCIPAL INTERNATIONAL CHRISTIAN ECUMENICAL ORGANIZATION BASED IN GENEVA, SWITZERLAND, IT HAS A MEMBERSHIP OF OVER A HUNDRED CHURCHES AND CHURCH ORGANIZATIONS.

THE WORLD ECONOMIC FORUM [WEF] :-IS AN ANNUAL MEETING AMONG CHIEF EXECUTIVES OF THE WORLD'S RICHEST CORPORATIONS, SOME NATIONAL POLITICAL LEADERS, PRESIDENTS, PRIME MINISTERS, AND OTHERS; AND SELECTED INTELLECTUALS AND JOURNALISTS, ABOUT 2000 PEOPLE IN ALL, USUALLY HELD IN DAVOS, SWITZERLAND; ALONG WITH RELATED REGIONAL MEETINGS BY WEF MEMBERS. IT WAS FOUNDED IN 1971.

AMNESTY INTERNATIONAL OR [AI] :-IS AN INTERNATIONAL NON – GOVERNMENTAL ORGANIZATION [NGO] THAT WORKS TO PROMOTE ALL THE HUMAN RIGHTS ENSHRINED IN THE UNIVERSAL DECLARATION OF HUMAN RIGHTS AND OTHER INTERNATIONAL STANDARDS. IN PARTICULAR, AMNESTY INTERNATIONAL CAMPAIGNS TO FREE ALL PRISONERS OF CONSCIENCE, ENSURE FAIR AND PROMPT TRIALS FOR POLITICAL PRISONERS, ABOLISH THE DEATH PENALTY, TORTURE AND OTHER CRUEL TREATMENT OF PRISONERS, END POLITICAL KILLINGS AND FORCED DISAPPEARANCES AND OPPOSE ALL HUMAN RIGHTS ABUSES, WHETHER BY GOVERNMENTS OR OPPOSITION GROUPS.

THE OLYMPIC GAMES :-IS AN EVENT THAT BRINGS PEOPLE TOGETHER IN PEACE TO RESPECT UNIVERSAL MORAL PRINCIPLES. THE GAMES FEATURE ATHLETES FROM ALL OVER THE WORLD; COMPETING FOR MEDALS AND PROMOTING THE SPIRIT OF UNITY IN THE WORLD. GREECE WAS THE BIRTHPLACE OF THE ANCIENT OLYMPIC GAMES. THE FIRST MODERN OLYMPIC GAMES WERE HELD IN ATHENS IN 1896.THE GAMES ARE BOTH SUMMER OLYMPICS AND WINTER OLYMPICS.
THE SUMMER OLYMPIC GAMES WERE HELD IN THE FOLLOWING CITIES OVER THE YEARS.
1896 ATHENS
1900 PARIS
1904 ST. LOUIS
1908 LONDON
1912 STOCKHOLM
1920 ANTWERP
1924 PARIS

1928 AMSTERDAM
1932 LOS ANGELES
1936 BERLIN
1948 LONDON
1952 HELSINKI
1956 MELBOURNE
1960 ROME
1964 TOKYO
1968 MEXICO CITY
1972 MUNICH
1976 MONTREAL
1980 MOSCOW
1984 LOS ANGELES
1988 SEOUL
1992 BARCELONA
1996 ATLANTA
2000 SYDNEY
PROJECTED TO BE HELD IN ATHENS IN 2004 AND IN BEIJING IN 2008

THE WINTER OLYMPIC GAMES WERE HELD IN THE FOLLOWING CITIES OVER THE YEARS :-
1924 CHAMONIX
1928 ST. MORITZ
1932 LAKE PLACID
1936 GARMISCH - PARTENKIRCHEN
1948 ST. MORITZ
1952 OSLO
1956 CORTINA D'AMPEZZO
1960 SQUAW VALLEY
1964 INNSBRUCK
1968 GRENOBLE
1972 SAPPORO
1976 INNSBRUCK
1980 LAKE PLACID
1984 SARAJEVO
1988 CALGARY
1992 ALBERTVILLE
1994 LILLEHAMMER
1998 NAGANO
2002 SALT LAKE CITY

PROJECTED TO BE HELD IN TORINO IN 2006 AND IN VANCOUVER IN 2010.

THERE IS ALSO THE PARALYMPIC GAMES [SPECIAL OLYMPICS] WHICH ARE ELITE SPORTS EVENTS FOR ATHLETES FROM DIFFERENT DISABILITY GROUPS. THE NUMBER OF ATHLETES PARTICIPATING IN THE SUMMER PARALYMPIC GAMES HAS INCREASED FROM 400 ATHLETES IN ROME IN 1960 TO 3,843 ATHLETES FROM 122 COUNTRIES IN SYDNEY, AUSTRALIA IN 2000.

WILLIAM SHAKESPEARE :-HAD A CAREER AS AN ACTOR, POET, AND PLAYWRIGHT FROM 1564 TO 1616. HE IS WIDELY ACCLAIMED AS A MAN OF GREAT REPUTE IN HIS FIELD OF WORK. HIS WORK INCLUDED WORKS IN HISTORY, TRAGEDY, COMEDIES, POETRY.

UNDER HISTORIES HIS WORK COVER :-
THE FIRST PART OF KING HENRY THE SIXTH
THE SECOND PART OF KING HENRY THE SIXTH
THE THIRD PART OF KING HENRY THE SIXTH
THE FIRST PART OF KING HENRY THE FOURTH
THE SECOND PART OF KING HENRY THE FOURTH
THE LIFE OF KING HENRY THE FIFTH
THE TRAGEDY OF KING RICHARD THE SECOND
THE TRAGEDY OF KING RICHARD THE THIRD
THE LIFE AND DEATH OF KING JOHN
THE FAMOUS HISTORY OF THE LIFE OF KING HENRY THE EIGHT

UNDER TRAGEDIES HIS WORK INCLUDE :-
TITUS ANDRONICUS
ROMEO AND JULIET
JULIUS CAESAR
HAMLET, THE PRINCE OF DENMARK
OTHELLO, THE MOOR OF VENICE
TIMON OF ATHENS
KING LEAR
MACBETH
ANTONY AND CLEOPATRA
CORIOLANUS

UNDER COMEDIES HIS WORK COVER :-
THE TWO GENTLEMEN OF VERONA
THE TAMING OF THE SHREW
THE COMEDY OF ERRORS
LOVE'S LABOR'S LOST
A MIDSUMMER NIGHT'S DREAM
THE MERCHANT OF VENICE
THE MERRY WIVES OF WINDSOR
MUCH ADO ABOUT NOTHING
AS YOU LIKE IT
TWELFTH NIGHT OR WHAT YOU WILL
TROILUS AND CRESSIDA
MEASURE FOR MEASURE
ALL'S WELL THAT ENDS WELL
PERICIES, PRINCE OF TYRE
THE WINTER'S TALE
CYMBELINE
THE TEMPEST

UNDER POETRY HIS WORK INCLUDES :-
THE SONNETS
A LOVER'S COMPLAINT
THE RAPE OF LUCRECE
VENUS AND ADONIS
FUNERAL ELEGY BY W.S

HOLLYWOOD :-IS THE MOVIE MAKING CENTER OF
THE WORLD. HOLLYWOOD IS GOVERNED UNDER SEVERAL
AREAS SUCH AS :-
HOLLYWOOD AWARDS
HOLLYWOOD NEWS
HOLLYWOOD FILM FESTIVAL
HOLLYWOOD WORLD AWARDS
HOLLYWOOD EUROPEAN AWARDS
HOLLYWOOD CONFERENCES
THESE WERE CREATED TO BRIDGE THE GAP BETWEEN
HOLLYWOOD AND THE GLOBAL CREATIVE COMMUNITY;
WHILE AT THE SAME TIME HONORING ESTABLISHED
HOLLYWOOD PROFESSIONALS.

ASPECTS OF MOVIE MAKING INCLUDE :-
DIRECTING
SCREEN – WRITING
CINEMATOGRAPHY
DIGITAL EDITING
PRODUCING
FILM EDUCATION
ACTING
AMONG OTHERS.

BROADWAY :-IS THE LEAGUE OF AMERICAN THEATRES AND PRODUCERS INC. BROADWAY IN NEW YORK CITY IS IN THE NEIGHBORHOOD OF TIMES SQUARE. THERE ARE CURRENTLY ABOUT 40 BROADWAY THEATRES IN OPERATION IN NEW YORK CITY.
NAMES OF A FEW BROADWAY THEATRES IN NEW YORK ARE :-
AMBASSADOR
BOOTH
BROADWAY
CIRCLE IN THE SQUARE
CORT
HELEN HAYES
IMPERIAL
MAJESTIC
MUSIC BOX
NEW AMSTERDAM
PALACE
ROYALE
VIRGINIA

RECENT TOP TEN BEST SELLERS SHOWS ARE :-
THE PRODUCERS
THE LION KING
MAMMA MIA
THE PHANTOM OF THE OPERA
WICKED
MOVING OUT
CHICAGO
HAIRSPRAY
42 ND STREET

BEAUTY AND THE BEAST

TOURING BROADWAY SHOWS VISIT AS MANY AS 140 CITIES EACH YEAR IN UNITED STATES OF AMERICA AND CANADA.

THE WORLD'S BEST AMUSEMENT PARKS ARE :-

BUSEH GARDENS IN WILLIAMSBURG VA AND TAMPA FLORIDA.

CEDAR POINT IN OHIO WHICH HAS SOME 15 COASTERS AND 68 RIDES

DISCOVERY COVE IN ORLANDO FLORIDA

EVERLAND IN SOUTH KOREA

HERSHEY PARK IN HERSEY PA

LEGO LAND IN CARLSBAD CALIFORNIA

PARC ASTERIX IN PLAILLY FRANCE

PARAMONT PARKS IN KINGS ISLAND CINNCINNATI OHIO

RATANGA JUNCTION IN CAPETOWN SOUTH AFRICA

SEAWORLD IN SAN DIEGO CALIFORNIA, SAN ANTONIO TEXAS, AND ORLANDO FLORIDA

SESAME PLACE IN SESAME ROAD LANGHORNE PA

UNIVERSAL STUDIOS IN ORLANDO FLORIDA AND UNIVERSAL CITY CALIFORNIA

DISNEY THEME PARKS AND RESORTS :-HAS FOUR LOCATIONS IN ANAHEIM CALIFORNIA, ORLANDO FLORIDA, TOKYO AND PARIS. ALL FOUR PARKS ARE STAGGERINGLY HUGE AND HAVE EVERYTHING FROM RIDES, GAMES, RESTAURANTS, ANIMALS AND WATER PARKS TO LEARNING CENTERS AND SPAS.

ZOO :-IS A PLACE WITH WILD ANIMALS ON EXHIBITION.

THE WORLD'S TOP ZOOS OF ANIMAL COLLECTIONS – BASED ON NUMBER OF SPECIES AND POPULATION ARE :-

BERLIN ZOO IN GERMANY

BERLIN TIERPARK ZOO IN GERMANY

BRONX ZOO IN NEW YORK U.S.A

SAN DIEGO ZOO IN CALIFORNIA U.S.A

ARTIS ZOO IN THE NETHERLANDS

FRANKFURT ZOO IN GERMANY

LONDON ZOO IN ENGLAND

NATIONAL ZOO IN SOUTH AFRICA
SAN ANTONIO ZOO IN TEXAS U.S.A
WILHELMA ZOO IN GERMANY

THE TOP CHILDREN'S ZOOS IN THE U.S.A BASED ON SIZE AND QUALITY ARE :-
BALTIMORE ZOO
BRONX ZOO
LOS ANGELES ZOO
HOUSTON ZOO
LINCOLN PARK ZOO
OGLEBAY'S GOOD CHILDREN'S ZOO
PHOENIX ZOO
SAN ANTONIO ZOO
SAN DIEGO ZOO
SAN FRANCISCO ZOO

ZOOLOGY :-IS THE SCIENCE OF ANIMAL LIFE.

THE ELEPHANT :-IS THE LARGEST ANIMAL THAT LIVES ON LAND. AMONG ALL THE ANIMALS ONLY SOME KINDS OF WHALES ARE LARGER. THE ELEPHANT IS THE SECOND TALLEST ANIMAL; ONLY THE GIRAFFE IS TALLER IN THE ANIMAL KINGDOM. ELEPHANTS ARE THE ONLY ANIMALS THAT HAVE A NOSE IN THE FORM OF A LONG TRUNK; WHICH THEY USE AS A HAND. ELEPHANTS HAVE LARGER EARS THAN ANY OTHER ANIMAL, AND THEIR TUSKS ARE THE LARGEST TEETH.

THE CAMEL :-IS A LARGE STRONG DESERT ANIMAL. CAMELS CAN TRAVEL GREAT DISTANCES ACROSS HOT, DRY DESERTS WITH LITTLE FOOD OR WATER FOR DAYS. A CAMEL CARRIES A BUILT – IN FOOD SUPPLY ON ITS BACK IN THE FORM OF A HUMP. THE HUMP IS A LARGE LUMP OF FAT THAT PROVIDES ENERGY FOR THE CAMEL IF FOOD IS SCARCE.

THE HEAVIEST ANIMAL BABIES EVER RECORDED ARE :-

WHALE
ELEPHANT

BELGIAN DRAFT HORSE
INDIAN RHINO
GIRAFFE

SOME OF THE WORLD'S RELIGIONS AND HOLY BOOKS
ARE :-

CHRISTIANITY - BIBLE.
ISLAM - QUAR'AN AND HADITH.
HINDUISM - THE VEDA.
BUDDHISM - THE TRIPITAKA.
TRIBAL RELIGIONS, ANIMISM - ORAL TRADITION.
JUDAISM - TORAH, TALMUD.
SIKHISM - GURU GRANTH   SAHIB.
SHAMANISTS - ORAL TRADITION.
CONFUCIANISM - LUN YU.
BAHA'I FAITH - MOST HOLY BOOK.
JANINISM - SIDDHANTA, PAKRIT.
SHINTO - KOJIKI, NOHON SHOKI.
ZOROASTRIANISM - AVESTA.
AMONG OTHERS .

NAMES OF RELIGIONS, THEIR PLACES OF WORSHIP, AND
TITLES OF THEIR LOCAL LEADERS :-

CHRISTIANITY	CHURCH, CATHEDRAL, TEMPLE,	
MISSION,	PASTOR, PRIEST, MINISTER.	
ISLAM	MOSQUE	IMAM.
HINDUISM	TEMPLE	PRIEST, PANDIT.
BUDDHISM	TEMPLE	PRIEST.
TRIBAL RELIGIONS, ANIMISM		IN NATURE
SHAMAN.		
JUDAISM	SYNAGOGUE	RABBI.
SIKHISM	GURDWARAS	GRANTHI.
SHAMANISTS	IN NATURE	SHAMAN.
CONFUCIANISM	TEMPLE, SHRINE, SEOWON	
ELDER.		
BAHA'I FAITH	HOUSE OF	
	WORSHIP	USUALLY A LAY
		LEADER.
JAINISM	TEMPLE	PRIEST, PANDIT.
SHINTO	TEMPLE	PRIEST.

| WICCA | CIRCLE, GROVE | PRIESTESS, PRIEST, WICCAN. |
| ZOROAST RIANISM | ATASH BEHRAM, AGIYARI, PRAYER ROOM | MOBED, DASTUR. |

AMONG OTHERS .

RELIGIONS :-ARE SUBDIVIDED INTO A TOTAL OF ABOUT 275 LARGE RELIGIOUS GROUPS AND MANY SMALLER ONES. 34,000 SEPARATE CHRISTIAN GROUPS HAVE BEEN IDENTIFIED IN THE WORLD.

RELIGIOUS ADHERENTS AS A PERCENT OF WORLD POPULATION :-

CHRISTIANS	33 %.
MUSLIMS	19.6 %.
HINDUS	13.4 %.
NON – RELIGIONS	12.7 %.
CHINESE FOLK	6.4 %.
BUDDHISTS	5.9 %.
SIKHS	.4 %.
ETHNO RELIGIONISTS	3.8 %.
JEWS	.2 %.
NEW RELIGIONISTS	1.7 %.
ATHEISTS	2.5 %

THOSE THAT DO NOT BELIEVE IN GOD.

| OTHERS | .4 %. |

THE TOTAL SUM OF ESTIMATED FATALITIES ON NATURAL DISASTERS THAT OCCURRED IN THE WORLD FROM JANUARY TO MID APRIL 2004 ARE AS FOLLOWS :-

AVALANCHES 63
EARTHQUAKES 718
EXTREME WEATHER HOT AND COLD 584
FLOODING 374
LANDSLIDES 111
STORMS 603
VOLCANIC ACTIVITY 1
WILD FIRES 5

WORLD WIDE NATURAL DISASTER OF 2004; WHEN, WHERE AND WHAT OCCURRED.

APRIL 22	JAVA LANDSLIDE 13 DEAD.
APRIL 14	BANGLADESH TORNADOES 65 DEAD, ONE THOUSAND INJURED.
APRIL 13	EASTERN AFRICA HEAVY RAINS 50 DEAD, THOUSANDS HOMELESS.
APRIL 6	MEXICO FLASH FLOOD 36 DEAD, 18 MISSING.
MARCH 26	SOUTH SULAWESI INDONESIA LANDSLIDES 32 DEAD.
MARCH 25	TURKEY 5.6 EARTHQUAKE 10 DEAD.
MARCH 14	KAZAKHSTAN LANDSLIDE 28 DEAD.
MARCH 7	MADAGASCAR CYCLONE GAFILO 198 DEAD, 166 MISSING, 50,000 HOMELESS.
MARCH 7	TURKEY FLOODS 11 DEAD.
FEBRUARY 24	MOROCCO 6.5 EARTHQUAKE 628 DEAD.
FEBRUARY 14	PAKISTAN TWIN EARTHQUAKE 24 DEAD.
FEBRUARY 12	MADAGASCAR CYCLONE ELITA 29 DEAD, 30,000 HOMELESS.
FEBRUARY 5	PAPAU NEW GUINEA 6.9 EARTHQUAKE 34 DEAD, 600 INJURED.
FEBRUARY 3	BRAZIL MUDSLIDES AND FLOODS 91 DEAD, 117,000 HOMELESS.
JANUARY 31	INDONESIA MUDSLIDE 15 DEAD.
JANUARY 27	BRAZIL MONTH LONG RAIN 56 DEAD.
JANUARY 26	MIDWEST AND EASTERN UNITED STATES SNOW AND FREEZING RAIN 25 DEAD.
JANUARY 23	SOUTHEASTERN EUROPE MASSIVE WIND AND SNOW STORM 10 DEAD.
JANUARY 17	BRAZIL HEAVY RAINS AND MUDSLIDES 11 DEAD.
JANUARY 3	CHINA LANDSLIDE 14 DEAD.
JANUARY 2	NEPAL THREE WEEK COLD SNAP 19 DEAD.
JANUARY 1	INDIA AND BANGLADESH THREE WEEKS COLD WAVE 324 DEAD.

BEST ACTS – PERFORMANCES ALL OVER THE WORLD ARE PERFORMED BY THE FOLLOWING RENOWNED AND POPULAR PERSONS OR GROUPS
DUO MILANY
DUO MOUVANCE
ZEBRAS
PERES BROTHERS
VICTOR KEE
ANTHONY GATTO
PETER SHUB
OLEG IZOSSIMOV
KIM AND LESS
ZEE DENECK
DUO BONDARENKO
ELENA BORANDINO
DANIEL AND REYNALD
FAN YANG
KRISTIAN KRISTOF
PATRICK JEAN
RODOLFO REYES
JACQUELINE ALVAREZ
ALEXIS BROTHERS
VANESSA ALVAREZ
CLOWNS LUFTMAN
GOLDEN POWER
DOUBLE FACE
MONGOLIAN
AURELA CATS
OLIVER GROSZER
STEPHEN BROTHERS
ROKASHKOV TRUPE
PELLEGRIM BROTHERS
TIMO FERREIRA

PHOBIA :-IS IRRATIONAL, PERSISTENT FEAR OF SOMETHING. SOME COMMON AND WELL KNOWN PHOBIAS PEOPLE SUFFER FROM ARE :-
ACHLUOPHOBIA THE FEAR OF DARKNESS.
ACROPHOBIA THE FEAR OF HEIGHTS.
ALTOPHOBIA THE FEAR OF HEIGHTS.
ARSONPHOBIA THE FEAR OF FIRE.

ATYCHIPHOBIA THE FEAR OF FAILURE.
AUTOPHOBIA THE FEAR OF BEING ALONE.
BRONTOPHOBIA THE FEAR OF THUNDER AND LIGHTNING.
COIMETROPHOBIA THE FEAR OF CEMETERIES.
DECIDOPHOBIA THE FEAR OF MAKING DECISIONS.
DENTOPHOBIA THE FEAR OF DENTISTS.
ELECTROPHOBIA THE FEAR OF ELECTRICITY.
GALEOPHOBIA OR GATOPHOBIA THE FEAR OF CATS.
GERASCOPHOBIA THE FEAR OF GROWING OLD.
GLOSSOPHOBIA THE FEAR OF SPEAKING IN PUBLIC.
HOPLOPHOBIA THE FEAR OF FIREARMS.
NOSOCOMEPHOBIA THE FEAR OF HOSPITALS.
ONEVIOPHOBIA THE FEAR OF DREAMS.
RADIOPHOBIA THE FEAR OF RADIATION, X-RAY.
SATANOPHOBIA THE FEAR OF SATAN.
SCOLIONO THE FEAR OF SCHOOL.
TACHOPHOBIA THE FEAR OF SPEED.
THALASSOPHOBIA THE FEAR OF THE SEA.
WICCAPHOBIA THE FEAR OF WITCHCRAFT.

CHAPTER 25.

GREAT CHESS PLAYERS OF THE WORLD ARE :-
FEDOROV A
FISCHER
KASPAROV
KARPOV
SPASSKY
LASKER
STEINITZ
EUWE
PETROSIAN
TAL
BOTVINVIK
CAPABLANCA
ALEKHINE
AMONG OTHERS.

SOME OF THE WORLD'S GREATEST BOXING CHAMPIONS
ARE :-
GEORGE FOREMAN
MUHAMMAD ALI
LENNOX LEWIS
MIKE TYSON
EVANDER HOLIFIELD
VITALI KLITSCHKO
BUSTER DOUGLAS
TOMMY HEARNS
MARVIN HAGLER

FRAZIER
SPINKS
ROY JONES JR
CHAVES
ROBERTO DURAN
SUGAR RAY LEONARD
FELIX TRINIDAD
OSCAR DE LA HOYA
MAYWEATHER
SHANE MOSLEY
JAMES TONEY
TERRENCE ALI
AMONG OTHERS.

SOME OF THE WORLD'S TOP CRICKETERS OVER THE YEARS ARE :-
ROHAN KANHAI
CLIVE LLOYD
ALVIN KALICHARRAN
LAWRENCE ROWE
VIVAN RICHARDS
GRAHAM GOOCH
POLLOCK
SMITH
COLIN COWDREY
IMRAN KHAN
ZAHEER ABBAS
MIANDAD
R S DRAVID
H H GIBBS
R T PONTING
A RANATUNGA
S CHANDERPAUL
S C GANGULY
L KLUSENER
A SYMONDS
A C GILCHRIST
G D MCGRATH
M MURALITHARAN
A A DONALD
C A WALSH

D W FLEMING
G I ALLOTT
AMONG OTHERS,

SOME OF THE TOP GOLF PLAYERS ARE :-
TIGER WOODS
VIJAY SINGH
JIM FURYK
ERNIE ELS
NICK PRICE
AMONG OTHERS.

SOME OF THE ALL TIME GREAT BASEBALL PLAYERS
ARE :-
BABE RUTH
JACKIE ROBINSON
DEREK JETER
CAL RIPKIN JR
YOGI BERRA
ALEX RODRIGUEZ
BARRY BONDS
ROGER CLEMENTS
NOLAN RYAN
MARK MCGWIRE
SAMMY SOSA
CHIPPER JONES
ANDREW JONES
AMONG OTHERS.

A FEW TOP SOCCER PLAYERS OVER THE YEARS ARE :-
RONALDO
BECKHAM
PELE
ROMARIO
ROBERTO BAGGIO
ZICO
MARADONA
MATTHIAS
CAFU
TOBIE BAYARD
CARLOS VALDERRAMA

ALI AKBARPOUR
DAVID AMSALEM
WARREN BARRETT
HATTORI HIRANO
CAMPOS
TARIBO WEST
RUBEN RUIZ
JACEK ZIELINSKI
AL DOSSARY SAMI
SPASOJE
ALEX BANELA
KIM BYUNG
KHALID
YURYII
M BALBOA
COBI JONES
C REYNA
J AGOOS
D BECKHAM
A SHEARER
J BARNES
AMONG OTHERS.

SOME TOP BASKETBALL PLAYERS OVER THE YEARS
ARE :-
MICHAEL JORDAN
SCOTTIE PIPPEN
MAGIC JOHNSON
LARRY BIRD
IVERSON
KUKOCH
ISIAH THOMAS
SHAQUEL ONEAL
COBY BRYAN
VINCE CARTER
ALAN HOUSTON
GRANT HILL
JASON KIDD
KARL MALONE
JERRY STACKHOUSE
BEN WALLACE

YAO MING
PATRICK EWING
ANTHONY CARMELO
BYRON JAMES
CHARLIE WARD
TIM DUNCAN
CHRIS WEBBER
KEVIN GARNETT
AMONG OTHERS.

SOME TOP WRESTLERS OVER THE YEARS ARE :-
HULK HOGAN
CHRIS BENOIR
EDDIE GUERRERO
BOOKER T
RIC FLAIR
SHAWN MICHAELS
STONE COLD
THE ROCK
TRIPLE H
UNDERTAKER
AMONG OTHERS.

SOME OF THE TOP HOCKEY PLAYERS ARE :-
MIKE RICHTER
POKEY REDDICK
KARI TAKKO
PETE PEETERS
JARI KURRI
MATT CULEM
MARK MESSIER
B HOLIK
J JAGR
A KOVALEV
T AMONTE
M BRODEUR
J BLAKE
D TARNSTROM
M NASLUND
M COOKE
BRIAN LEETCH

E BELFOUR
ERIC LINDROS
N LIDSTROM
C JOSEPH

SOME OF THE TOP FOOTBALL PLAYERS ARE :-
DREW BLEDSOE
JERRY RICE
MARSHALL FAULK
JUNIOR SEAU
JOE MONTANA
STEVE YOUNG
JESSIE ARMSTEAD
LAWRENCE TAYLOR
TIKI BARBER
MARK BRUNELL
DAUNTE CULPEPPER
IKE HILLARD
KEYSHAWN JOHNSON
DORSEY LEVENS
PEYTON MANNING
RANDY MOSS
PHIL SIMMS
JAKE PLUMMER
WARREN SAPP
JEREMY SHOCKEY
EMMITT SMITH
AMANI TOOMER
AMONG OTHERS :-

SOME OF THE TOP TENNIS PLAYERS ARE :-
ANDRE AGASSI
PETE SAMPRAS
MICHAEL CHANG
ALBERT COSTA
GORAN IVANISEVIC
ANDY RODDICK
STEPHAN EDBERG
VENUS WILLIAMS
SERENA WILLIAMS
BORIS BECKER

MONICA SELES
CHANDA RUBIN
LISA RAYMOND
LINSDAY DAVENPORT
MARY PIERCE
CONCHITA MARTINEZ
ANNA KOURNIKOVA
THOMAS BLAKE
JENNIFER CAPRIATI
STEFFI GRAFF
MARTINA NAVRATILOVA
CHRIS EVERT
JIMMY CONNORS
JOHN MCENROW
IVAN LENDLL
AMONG OTHERS :-

MAJOR HORSE RACES IN THE WORLD :-
KENTUCKY DERBY - IN KENTUCKY.
BREEDERS CUP CHAMPIONSHIP - LOCATIONS VARY.
BELMONT STAKES - IN NEW YORK.
ROYAL ASCOT - IN ENGLAND.
THE GRAND NATIONAL - IN ENGLAND.
PRIX DE L'ARC DE TRIOMPHE - IN FRANCE.
THE PREAKNESS STAKES - IN MARYLAND.
DUBAI WORLD CUP - IN THE UNITED ARAB EMIRATES.
MELBOURNE CUP IN AUSTRALIA.
HAMBLETONIAN STAKES IN NEW JERSEY.

XTREME SPORTS :-
THE FIRST XTREME GAMES WERE HELD IN 1995.
A LARGE NUMBER OF AMERICANS PARTICIPATE IN ROLLER SKATING AND IN LINE SKATING.
TONY HAWK WAS THE FIRST TO SUCCESSFULLY COMPLETE THE TRICK OF DOING A 900 IN COMPETITION.

CHAPTER 26.

SOME TYPES OF SHIPS ARE :-
CONTAINER
TANKER
CARGO
PASSENGER LINER
FISHING BOAT
CANOE
PONTOON
TUG
AMONG OTHERS.

SOME TYPES OF TRAINS ARE :-
EXPRESS
LOCAL
CARGO
ANIMALS
SHUTTLE
AMTRAK
AMONG OTHERS.

SUBURBAN TRAIN IS ONE THAT TRAVELS BETWEEN A BIG CITY AND ITS SUBURBS.

LOCAL TRAIN IS ONE THAT TRAVELS WITHIN A PARTICULAR AREA.

INTERCITY TRAIN IS ONE THAT TRAVELS WITHIN MANY AREAS.

INTERNATIONAL TRAIN IS ONE THAT TRAVELS BETWEEN TWO OR MORE COUNTRIES.

SOME TYPES OR MAKES OR MODELS OF CARS ARE :-
ACURA
AUDI
BENTLEY
BUICK
BMW
CADILLAC
CHEVROLET
CHRYSLER
DODGE
FERRARI
FORD
GMC
HONDA
HYUNDAI
JAGUAR
KIA
LEXUS
LINCOLN
MAZDA
MERCEDES – BENZ
MERCURY
MITSUBISHI
NISSAN
OLDSMOBILE
PONTIAC
PORSCHE
ROLLS – ROYCE
SAAB
SATURN
SUZUKI
TOYOTA
VOLKSWAGEN
VOLVO

SOME OF THE BIGGEST SHIPS OF THE WORLD ARE :-

NAME	LENGTH	GROSS REGISTER TONS
CARNIVAL DESTINY	893 FEET	101,000
TITANIC	882.5 FEET	46,329
GRAND PRINCESS	951 FEET	109,000

S/R MEDITERRANEAN	987 FEET	95,000
QUEEN ELIZABETH 2	963 FEET	70,327
QUEEN MARY	1019.5 FEET	81,237
ROYAL CARIBBEAN		
EAGLE CLASS SHIPS	1019 FEET	136,000
USS NIMITZ	1092 FEET	95,000
NORWAY	1035 FEET	70,049
JAHRE VIKING	1504 FEET	260,851

FLOWERS :-THE FLOWER IS A REPRODUCTIVE UNIT OF SOME PLANTS [ANGIOSPERMS]. PARTS OF THE FLOWER INCLUDE PETALS, SEPALS, ONE OR MORE CARPELS [THE FEMALE REPRODUCTIVE ORGANS] AND STAMENS [THE MALE REPRODUCTIVE ORGANS]. THE FLOWER ANATOMY - PARTS OF A FLOWER ARE :-

PETAL.
STIGMA.
STYLE.
OVARY
OVULE
PEDUNCLE
SEPAL
CALYX
FILAMENT
ANTHER
SOME CLASSIFICATION VARIETIES OF FLOWERS ARE :-
ROSES
ORCHIDS
HYDRANGEAS
MUMS
CACTI
DAISIES
LILIES
IRIS
TULIPS
DAHLIAS
CHRYSANTHEMUMS
DAFFODILS
WATER LILIES
RHODENDENDROUS
HYDRANGEAS

GLADIOLI

IT'S POSSIBLE TO LEARN TO DISTINGUISH BETWEEN THE DIFFERENT CLASSIFICATIONS OF FLOWERS BY HOW THEY GROW, THE PETALS, THE ROOT SYSTEM, THE COLOR, THE BLOSSOM IN BLOOM AND MANY OTHER FEATURES.

VEGETABLES :-IS DESCRIBED AS ANY HERBACEOUS [NON – WOODY] PLANT OR PLANT PART THAT IS EATEN WITH THE MAIN COURSE RATHER THAN AS A DESERT.
EXAMPLES OF SOME VEGETABLES ARE :-
BASIL
BROCCOLI
BRUSSEL SPROUTS
CABBAGE
CAULIFLOWER
CUCUMBER
EGGPLANT
LETTUCE
PARSLEY
PEPPER
TOMATO
BEAN
CARROT
CORN
DANDELION
GARLIC
GINGER
HERBS
MELONS
MINTS
MUSHROOM
OKRA
ONION
PUMPKIN
PIGEON PEA
IRISH POTATO
RADISH
SHALLOTS
SQUASH
SPINNACH

SWEET POTATO
TURNIP

FRUIT :-BOTANICALLY THE FRUIT IS THE DEVELOPED OVARY OF A SEED PLANT WITH ITS CONTENTS AND ACCESSORY PARTS; AS THE PEA POD, NUT, TOMATO, PINEAPPLE ETC ; OR THE EDIBLE PART OF A PLANT DEVELOPED FROM A FLOWER WITH ANY ACCESSORY TISSUES, SUCH AS THE PEACH, MULBERRY, BANANA ETC.

THE NAMES OF SOME FRUITS ARE :-
APPLE
CHERRY
AVOCADO
BETEL LEAF
BILIMBI
BLACK PEPPER
BREAD FRUIT
BREAD NUT
CACAO
CARAMBOLLA
GUAVA
GOOSEBERRY
FIG
STRAWBERRY
LEMON GRASS
PLUM
OLIVE
PASSION FRUIT
PAW PAW
SAPODILLA
GRAPE
LIME
STAR APPLE
SUGAR APPLE
TAMARIND
VANILLA

MEAT :-IS THE WORD USED FOR THE PARTS OF THE ANIMAL YOU CAN EAT.

SOME KINDS OF MEAT ARE :-
BEEF

PORK
LAMB
VEAL
GOAT
RABBIT
CAMEL
AGOUTI
ANT EATER
VENISON
AMONG OTHERS :-

POULTRY :-IS THE WORD USED FOR MEAT FROM BIRDS.
BIRD MEAT IS GOTTEN FROM :-
CHICKEN
DUCK
PHEASANT
PIGEON
GEESE
QUAIL
TURKEY
DOVE
COCKS
AMONG OTHERS :-

SEAFOOD :-IS THE WORD USED FOR THE ANIMALS FROM THE SEA.
SOME SEAFOOD ANIMALS ARE :-
CATFISH
CRAB
LOBSTER
SHRIMP
SHARK
OCTOPUS
SHELL FISH
WHALES
SEALS
AMONG OTHERS :-

PARTS OF A FISH ARE :-
MOUTH

TAIL
TAIL FIN
SCALES
FINS
GILLS
EYES

THERE ARE 20,000 PLUS SPECIES OF FISH. THE LARGEST FISH IS THE WHALE SHARK, THE SECOND LARGEST IS THE BASKING SHARK. THE SMALLEST FISH IS THE TINY GOBY. THE MOST COMMON OF FISHES ARE THE CYCLOTHONE SPECIES.

CHAPTER 27.

TRADEMARK :-A TRADEMARK [WHICH RELATES TO GOODS] AND A SERVICE MARK [WHICH RELATES TO SERVICES] CAN BE ANY WORD, NAME, SYMBOL, OR DEVICE, OR ANY COMBINATION, USED, OR INTENDED TO BE USED IN COMMERCE. TRADEMARKS, WHICH IS USUALLY THE TERM USED TO COLLECTIVELY REFER TO WHAT ARE TECHNICALLY TRADEMARKS AND SERVICE MARKS, SERVE TWO PRIMARY PURPOSES. FIRST, TRADEMARKS IDENTIFY AND DISTINGUISH EITHER THE GOODS OR SERVICES OF ONE MANUFACTURER OR SELLER FROM GOODS OR SERVICES MANUFACTURED OR SOLD BY OTHERS. SECOND, TRADEMARKS INDICATE THE SOURCE OF THE GOODS OR SERVICES. IN SHORT A TRADEMARK IS A BRAND NAME.

COPYRIGHT :-A COPYRIGHT IS A FORM OF INTELLECTUAL PROTECTION THAT IS PROVIDED TO THE AUTHORS OF ORIGINAL WORKS OF AUTHORSHIP. THE COPYRIGHT ACT STATES THAT AN ORIGINAL WORK OF AUTHORSHIP THAT IS ENTITLED TO COPYRIGHT PROTECTION INCLUDES LITERARY, DRAMATIC, MUSICAL, ARTISTIC AND CERTAIN OTHER INTELLECTUAL WORKS, REGARDLESS OF WHETHER THEY ARE PUBLISHED OR UNPUBLISHED.

PATENT :-A PATENT FOR AN INVENTION IS THE GRANT OF A PROPERTY RIGHT TO THE INVENTOR, ISSUED BY THE PATENT AND TRADEMARK OFFICE; IT'S FOR CERTAIN PERIOD OF TIME AND MAINTENANCE FEES HAVE TO BE PAID.

INTERNET :-AREAS LOOKED AT INCLUDE :-
CONSTITUTIONAL LAW
CYBERCRIMES
CYBERSQUATTING
DEFAMATION
E – COMMERCE
ENCRYPTION
HACKING
CRACKING AND VIRUS
HYPERLINKING
GOVERNANCE
IDENTITY THEFT
INTELLECTUAL PROPERTY
INTERNET GAMBLING
INTERNET PORNOGRAPHY
INVESTING
JURISDICTION
PATENTS
PRIVACY
SPAM
TAXATION

THE INTERNET GOT STARTED IN 1969 WHEN THE U.S. DEPARTMENT OF DEFENSE CARRIED OUT A STUDY THAT LED TO THE DEPLOYMENT OF AN EXPERIMENTAL PACKET – SWITCHED NETWORK [THE ARPANET] THAT EVENTUALLY EVOLVED INTO THE INTERNET.

IT WAS CREATED BECAUSE THE MILITARY THEORIZED THAT A DISTRIBUTED DATA NETWORK WOULD BE MORE FAULT – TOLERANT THAN A TELEPHONE NETWORK, WHICH COULD BE DISABLED SIMPLY BY ATTACKING ITS CENTRAL OFFICE. THE ARPANET WAS CREATED TO TEST THIS THEORY.

THE INITIAL CONTRACTOR TO CONSTRUCT THE ARPANET HARDWARE WAS BBN. IMPORTANT UNIX SOFTWARE DEVELOPMENT WAS DONE BY THE UNIVERSITY OF CALIFORNIA, BERKELEY.

THE ABBREVIATION HTTP STAND FOR, HYPERTEXT TRANSFER PROTOCOL.

THE ABBREVIATION URL STAND FOR UNIFORM RESOURCE LOCATOR.

TIM BERNERS LEE WAS CREDITED WITH INVENTING THE WORLD WIDE WEB.

TRADE SECRET :-A TRADE SECRET IS ANY VALUABLE BUSINESS INFORMATION THAT IS NOT GENERALLY KNOWN AND IS SUBJECT TO REASONABLE EFFORTS TO PRESERVE CONFIDENTIALITY. A TRADE SECRET WILL BE PROTECTED FROM EXPLOITATION BY THOSE WHO EITHER OBTAIN ACCESS THROUGH IMPROPER MEANS, THOSE WHO OBTAIN THE INFORMATION FROM ONE WHO THEY KNOW OR SHOULD HAVE KNOWN GAINED ACCESS THROUGH IMPROPER MEANS, OR THOSE WHO BREACH A PROMISE TO KEEP THE INFORMATION CONFIDENTIAL.

ENTERTAINMENT LAW :-CAN BE DEALING WITH COPYRIGHT ISSUES, LICENSING, PERSONAL SERVICES CONTRACT, RIGHTS OF PUBLICITY, TRADEMARKS OR ANY NUMBER OF OTHER SUBSTANTIVE LEGAL TOPICS.

ANTITRUST LAW :-APPLY TO VIRTUALLY ALL INDUSTRIES AND TO EVERY LEVEL OF BUSINESS, INCLUDING MANUFACTURING, TRANSPORTATION, DISTRIBUTION AND MARKETING. THEY PROHIBIT A VARIETY OF PRACTICES THAT RESTRAIN TRADE, SUCH AS PRICE FIXING CONSPIRACIES, CORPORATE MERGERS LIKELY TO REDUCE THE COMPETITIVE VIGOR OF PARTICULAR MARKETS, AND PREDATORY ACTS DESIGNED TO ACHIEVE OR MAINTAIN MONOPOLY POWER.

BRAND NAMES :-THE PURPOSES OF BRAND NAMES ON COMMODITIES ARE :-
[a] TO HAVE THE RIGHT NAME ON YOUR BRAND NAME PRODUCT; SO AS TO IDENTIFY IT.
[b] IT SPEAKS OF THE PERSONALITY, THE QUALITY, THE ESSENCE OF YOUR COMPANY, OR YOUR CREATIVE IDEAS AND THE PRODUCTS YOU PRODUCE.

[c] THE RIGHT NAME FOR YOUR BRAND PROVIDES AN UMBRELLA UNDER WHICH PRODUCTS AND SERVICES, DIVISIONS AND SUBSIDIARIES CAN BE A COHESIVE FAMILY.

[d] THE RIGHT NAME SETS YOU, YOUR IDEA, YOUR COMPANY, YOUR PRODUCTS AND SERVICES APART FROM THE REST.

REGISTRATION :-IS THE ACT OF ENROLLING. IT CAN BE REGISTERING A DOCUMENT CERTIFYING AN ACT OF REGISTRATION.

CONSTITUTION :-A CONSTITUTION EMBODIES THE FUNDAMENTAL PRINCIPLES OF A GOVERNMENT. A CONSTITUTION ADOPTED BY THE SOVEREIGN POWER, IS AMENDABLE BY THE CONTROLLING BODY ONLY. TO THE CONSTITUTION ALL LAWS, EXECUTIVE ACTIONS, AND JUDICIAL DECISIONS MUST CONFORM AS IT IS THE CREATOR OF THE POWERS EXERCISED BY THE DEPARTMENTS OF GOVERNMENT. THE GOVERNMENT OF ANY COUNTRY ONLY CAN POSSESS SUCH POWERS AS ARE SPECIFICALLY GRANTED TO IT BY THE CONSTITUTION. IT CONSTITUTES THE SUPREME LAW OF THE LAND.

THE UNITED STATES CONSTITUTION WAS ADOPTED IN 1787.

BILL OF RIGHTS :-THE UNITED STATES OF AMERICA BILL OF RIGHTS IS THE FIRST TEN AMENDMENTS TO THE CONSTITUTION. THE TEN AMENDMENTS CALLED THE BILL OF RIGHTS ARE :-
1 ST FREEDOM OF RELIGION, PRESS, EXPRESSION.
2 ND RIGHT TO BEAR ARMS.
3 RD QUARTERING OF SOLDIERS.
4 TH SEARCH AND SEIZURE.
5 TH TRIAL AND PUNISHMENT, COMPENSATION FOR TAKINGS.
6 TH RIGHT TO SPEEDY TRIAL, CONFRONTATION OF WITNESSES.
7 TH TRIAL BY JURY IN CIVIL CASES.
8 TH CRUEL AND UNUSUAL PUNISHMENT.

9 TH CONSTRUCTION OF CONSTITUTION.
10 TH POWERS OF THE STATES AND PEOPLE.

OTHER AMENDMENTS ARE :-
11 TH JUDICIAL LIMITS.
12 TH CHOOSING THE PRESIDENT, VICE PRESIDENT.
13 TH SLAVERY ABOLISHED.
14 TH CITIZENSHIP RIGHTS.
15 TH RACE NO BAR TO VOTE.
16 TH INCOME TAX AUTHORIZED.
17 TH SENATORS ELECTED BY POPULAR VOTE.
18 TH LIQUOR ABOLISHED.
19 TH WOMEN'S SUFFRAGE [RIGHT TO VOTE].
20 TH PRESIDENTIAL, CONGRESSIONAL TERMS.
21 ST AMENDMENT 18 TH REPEALED.
22 ND PRESIDENTIAL TERM LIMITS.
23 RD PRESIDENTIAL VOTE FOR DISTRICT OF COLUMBIA
24 TH POLL TAXES BARRED.
25 TH PRESIDENTIAL DISABILITY AND SUCCESSION.
26 TH VOTING AGE SET TO 18 YEARS.
27 TH CONGRESSIONAL PAY INCREASES.

THE LEGISLATIVE BRANCH OF GOVERNMENT :-
ALL LEGISLATIVE POWERS HEREIN GRANTED SHALL BE VESTED IN A CONGRESS OF THE UNITED STATES, WHICH SHALL CONSIST OF A SENATE AND HOUSE OF REPRESENTATIVES.

POWERS OF CONGRESS :-TO LAY AND COLLECT TAXES, DUTIES, IMPOSTS – TAX DUTY, AND EXCISES; TO PAY DEBTS AND PROVIDE FOR THE COMMON DEFENCE AND GENERAL WELFARE OF THE UNITED STATES; BUT ALL DUTIES, IMPOSTS – TAX DUTY AND EXCISES SHALL BE UNIFORM THROUGHOUT THE UNITED STATES.

EXCISE :-IS A TAX ON THE MANUFACTURE, SALE OR CONSUMPTION OF GOODS WITHIN A COUNTRY.

JURISDICTION :-IS THE POWER, RIGHT, OR AUTHORITY TO INTERPRET AND APPLY THE LAW; WITHIN THE LIMITS OR TERRITORY IN WHICH AUTHORITY MAY BE EXERCISED.

TREASON :-IS THE OFFENCE OF ATTEMPTING TO OVERTHROW THE GOVERNMENT OF ONE'S COUNTRY OR OF ASSISTING ITS ENEMIES IN WAR.

SOME TOPICS THAT ARE GOVERNED UNDER GOVERNMENT BENEFITS AND ASSISTANCE PROGRAMS ARE :-
VARIOUS AGENCIES.
ARRESTED OR IN PRISON.
CHILD SUPPORT.
CIVIL RIGHTS.
COLLEGE AID.
EMPLOYMENT AID.
FOOD STAMPS.
GOVERNMENT JOBS.
GRANTS.
LOANS.
HOUSING.
LEGAL AID.
MEDICARE.
PENSIONS.
SENIORS AID.
SOCIAL SECURITY.
UNEMPLOYMENT.
WELFARE.
ABUSE VICTIMS.
PEOPLE WITH DISABILITIES.
NON – PROFIT ORGANIZATION.
VETERANS.
WOMEN AND MINORITIES.

FAULTS OR FOLD OF THE EARTH :-THERE ARE FOUR MAIN TYPES OF FAULTS; NORMAL FAULTS, REVERSE FAULTS, THRUST FAULTS, AND LATERAL FAULTS. FAULTS OCCUR WHEN THE EARTH – ROCK IS COMPRESSED ENOUGH, IT BREAKS OR FAULTS. THE FACTORS THAT DECIDE IF A ROCK WILL FAULT OR FOLD ARE TEMPERATURE, PRESSURE, ROCK TYPE, AS WELL AS HOW THE STRESS IS APPLIED.

PLATE TECTONICS :-IS WHEN NEW ROCK IS BEING CREATED, FORCING OLD ROCK TO MOVE AND CAUSING ROCK PLATES TO COLLIDE, ONE PLATE IS SUCKED UNDER ANOTHER. THE EARTH IS DIVIDED INTO SEVEN MAJOR PLATES AND MANY MINOR ONES. THE MAJOR PLATES ARE :-

PACIFIC PLATE.
NORTH AMERICAN PLATE.
SOUTH AMERICAN PLATE.
EURASIAN PLATE.
AFRICAN PLATE.
INDO AUSTRALIAN PLATE.
ANTARCTIC PLATE.

LAYERS OF THE EARTH :-
INNER CORE.
OUTER CORE.
MANTLE.
CRUST.

BIOGRAPHY :-IS ONE'S LIFE STORY WRITTEN BY ANOTHER PERSON. THERE ARE NUNEROUS BIOGRAPHIES OF PEOPLE OF ALL WALKS OF LIFE :-
PRESIDENTS.
VICE PRESIDENTS.
PRIME MINISTERS.
SUPREME COURT JUSTICES.
BUSINESS LEADERS.
NOTABLE WOMEN.
WRITERS.
ENTERTAINERS.
ARCHITECTS.
EXPLORERS.
SCIENTISTS.
POETS.
FILMMAKERS.
ARTISTS.
AMONG OTHERS.

SOCIETY AND CULTURE :-ARE LOOKED AT UNDER VARIOUS HEADINGS SUCH AS :-
FAMILY TRENDS.
TRADITIONS.
EDUCATION.
GENDER ISSUES.
CALENDAR AND HOLIDAYS.
RACE AND ETHNICITY.
CRIME.
RELIGION.
POLITICAL PREFERENCES.
ENTERTAINMENT.
AREAS OF SPORTS IDENTITY.
AMONG OTHERS.

SOCIETY :-IS DEFINED AS A COMMUNITY OF PEOPLE.

CULTURE :-CAN BE SAID AS BEING THE CIVILIZATION OF A PEOPLE AS FAR AS THE TRAINING OF THE MIND, TASTE, PRACTICES IN LIFE, ETC ARE CONCERNED.

GLOBAL POLITICAL, ECONOMIC, AND SOCIAL FACTS :-

1 IN THE LAST TWO DECADES, POLITICAL AND CIVIL RIGHTS HAVE IMPROVED SUBSTANTIALLY THROUGHOUT THE WORLD; SINCE THE 1980'S SOME 80 PLUS COUNTRIES HAVE TAKEN SIGNIFICANT STEPS IN DEMOCRATIZATION, WITH OVER 33 MILITARY REGIMES REPLACED BY CIVILIAN GOVERNMENTS. BUT OF THESE ONLY SOME 47 ARE CONSIDERED FULLY DEMOCRACIES.

2 ONLY ABOUT 82 COUNTRIES REPRESENTING APPROXIMATELY 57 % OF THE WORLD'S POPULATION ARE FULLY DEMOCRATIC.

3 MULTIPARTY ELECTIONS ARE NOW HELD IN OVER 140 OF THE WORLD'S APPROXIMATE 200 COUNTRIES.

4 COUPS OVERTHREW SOME 46 ELECTED GOVERNMENTS IN THE SECOND HALF OF THE 20 TH CENTURY.

5 THE PROPORTION OF THE WORLD'S EXTREMELY POOR FELL FROM 29 % TO 23 % BY 1999.

6 JUST ABOUT 125 COUNTRIES, 62 % OF THE WORLD'S POPULATION HAVE A FREE OR PARTLY FREE PRESS – JOURNALISTS.

FACTS OF THE WORLD :-

[a] TOTAL AREA -510,072 MILLION SQUARE KILOMETERS OR 316.96 MILLION SQUARE MILES.
[b] LAND AREA 148.94 MILLION SQUARE KILOMETERS OR 92.55 MILLION SQUARE MILES.
[c] WATER AREA 361.132 MILLION SQUARE KILOMETERS OR 224.41 MILLION SQUARE MILES.
[d] COASTLINE 356,000 KILOMETERS OR 221,208 MILES.
[e] 70.8 % OF THE WORLD IS WATER.
[f] 29.2 % OF THE WORLD IS LAND.
[g] IRRIGATED LAND [GOOD WATER SUPPLY] 2,481,250 SQUARE KILOMETERS OR 1,541,849 SQUARE MILES.

LAND USE OF THE WORLD :-

1 ARABLE LAND [FIT FOR PLOWING] 10 %.
2 PERMANENT CROPS LESS THAN 5 %.
3 MEADOWS AND PASTURES 25 %.
4 FORESTS AND WOODLANDS 33 %.
5 OTHER ABOUT 27 %.

PEOPLE OF THE WORLD :-

[a] POPULATION -6,314,869,159.
[b] GROWTH RATE 1.23 %.
[c] BIRTH RATE 21 BIRTHS / 1000 POPULATION.
[d] DEATH RATE 9 DEATHS / 1000 POPULATION.
[e] LIFE EXPECTANCY AT BIRTH TOTAL POPULATION 64 YEARS. MALE 62 YEARS AND FEMALES 65 YEARS. WITH CONSTANT IMPROVEMENT IN MEDICAL TECHNOLOGY, LIFE EXPECTANCY IS EXPECTED TO CONSTANTLY RISE.
[f] SEX RATIO AT BIRTH 1.05 MALE / FEMALE.

[g] INFANT MORTALITY RATE 51 / 1000 LIVE BIRTHS.

[h] LITERACY RATE FOR AGE 15 AND OVER WHO CAN READ AND WRITE MALE 83 %, FEMALE 71 %, COMBINED 77 %.

NOTE THESE FIGURES ARE CONSTANTLY BEING CHANGE.

WORLD TYPES OF EPIDEMICS [DISEASE THAT SPREAD RAPIDLY].

MEASLES
YELLOW FEVER
INFLUENZA
SMALL POX
CHOLERA
TYPHUS
MALARIA
TYPHOID
AIDS
BILIOUS DISORDER
ASTHMA
CANCER
CHICKENPOX
DENQUE
DYSENTERY
EPILEPSY
LEPROSY
MENTAL DISORDERS
MUMPS
RABIES
SEXUAL DISEASES SUCH AS SYPHILIS, GONORRHE.
AMONG OTHERS. SOME OF THESE ARE HIGHLY COMMUNICABLE, WHILE OTHERS ARE NOT; HOWEVER, THEY ARE ALL SERIOUS DISEASES AND PEOPLE SHOULD TAKE EVERY PRECAUTION TO AVOID GETTING THEM.

NUCLEAR POWER PLANT ACCIDENTS :-
1952 DECEMBER 12 CHALK RIVER NEAR OTTAWA CANADA; MILLIONS OF GALLONS OF RADIOACTIVE WATER ACCUMULATED INSIDE THE REACTOR; HOWEVER THERE WERE NO INJURIES.

1957 LIVERPOOL ENGLAND. A GRAPHITE COOLED REACTOR SPEWED RADIATION OVER THE COUNTRY SIDE, CONTAMINATING A 200 SQUARE MILE AREA.

1957 SOUTH URAL MOUNTAINS RADIOACTIVE WASTES FORCED THE EVACUATION OF OVER 10,000 PEOPLE.

1976 EAST GERMANY RADIO ACTIVE CORE OF REACTOR IN THE LUBMIN NUCLEAR POWER PLANT NEARLY MELTED DOWN DUE TO THE FAILURE OF THE SAFETY SYSTEM DURING A FIRE.

1979 MARCH 28 THREE MILE ISLAND HARRISBURG PA ONE OF TWO REACTORS LOST ITS COOLANT, WHICH CAUSED OVERHEATING AND PARTIAL MELTDOWN OF ITS URANIUM CORE. SOME RADIOACTIVE WATER AND GASES WERE RELEASED.

1986 APRIL 26 CHERNOBYL KLEV UKRAINE. EXPLOSION AND FIRE 31 PEOPLE CLAIMED DEAD.

1999 SEPTEMBER 30 TOKAIMURA JAPAN HIGH LEVELS OF RADIOACTIVE GAS WAS SPEWED INTO THE AIR KILLING ONE WORKER AND SERIOUSLY INJURING TWO OTHERS.

RADIOACTIVE :-EMITTING RADIANT ENERGY BY THE DISINTEGRATION OF ATOMIC NUCLEI.

ATOMIC ENERGY :-IS ENERGY RELEASED FROM AN ATOM IN NUCLEAR REACTIONS.

NUCLEAR :-FORMATION OF A NUCLEUS OR NUCLEI.

REACTOR IS A DEVICE FOR PRODUCING ATOMIC ENERGY.

SPACE ACCIDENTS :-

1967 JANUARY 27 APOLLO 1 A FIRE ABOARD THE SPACE CAPSULE ON THE GROUND AT CAPE KENNEDY FLORIDA; KILLED THREE ASTRONAUTS.

1967 APRIL 23 – 24 SOYUZ VLADIMER   M. KOMAROV WAS KILLED WHEN HIS CRAFT CRASHED AFTER ITS PARACHUTE LINES RELEASED AT 23000 FEET FOR REENTRY SNARLED.

1971 JUNE 6 – 30 SOYUZ THREE COSMONAUTS FOUND DEAD IN THE CRAFT AFTER ITS AUTOMATIC LANDING. APPARENT CAUSE OF DEATH, WAS LOSS OF PRESSURIZATION

IN THE SPACE CRAFT DURING REENTRY INTO THE EARTH ATMOSPHERE.

1980 MARCH 18 U.S.S.R A VOSTOK ROCKET EXPLODED ON ITS LAUNCH PAD WHILE BEING REFUELED, KILLING 50 PEOPLE AT THE PLESETSK SPACE CENTER.

1986 JANUARY 28 CHALLENGER SPACE SHUTTLE EXPLODED 73 SECONDS AFTER LIFT OFF KILLING ALL SEVEN CREW MEMBERS. A BOOSTER LEAK IGNITED THE FUEL, CAUSING THE EXPLOSION.

2003 FEBRUARY 1 COLUMBIA SPACE SHUTTLE BROKE UP ON REENTERING EARTH'S ATMOSPHERE, KILLING ALL SEVEN CREW MEMBERS. FOAM INSULATION FELL FROM THE SHUTTLE DURING LAUNCH, DAMAGING THE LEFT WING. ON REENTRY HOT GASES ENTERED THE WING, LEADING TO THE DESTRUCTION OF THE SPACE CRAFT.

GENERAL TRUE FACTS NOT FICTION :-

1 ALL THE PLANETS IN OUR SOLAR SYSTEM ROTATE ANTICLOCKWISE, EXCEPT VENUS; IT IS THE ONLY PLANET THAT ROTATES CLOCKWISE

2 HUMMING BIRDS ARE THE ONLY ANIMAL THAT CAN ALSO FLY BACKWARDS.

3 INSECTS DO NOT MAKE NOISES WITH THEIR VOICES. THE NOISE OF BEES, MOSQUITOES, AND OTHER BUZZING INSECTS IS CAUSED BY RAPIDLY MOVING THEIR WINGS.

4 THE COCKROACH IS THE FASTEST ANIMAL ON SIX LEGS; COVERING A METER A SECOND.

5 THE ONLY TWO ANIMALS THAT CAN SEE BEHIND ITSELF, WITHOUT TURNING IT'S HEAD ARE THE RABBIT AND THE PARROT.

6 A JIFFY IS AN ACTUAL UNIT OF TIME FOR 1 / 100 TH OF A SECOND.

7 INDIA INVENTED THE NUMBER SYSTEM. ZERO WAS INVENTED BY ARYABHATTA.

8 THE WHIP MAKES A CRACKING SOUND BECAUSE ITS TIP MOVES FASTER THAN THE SPEED OF SOUND.

9 A HIPPOPOTAMUS CAN RUN FASTER THAN A MAN.

10 HIPPOPOTOMONSTROSESQUIPPEDALIOPHOBIA IS THE FEAR OF LONG WORDS.

11 IT IS IMPOSSIBLE TO LICK YOUR ELBOW.

12 A SNAIL CAN SLEEP FOR THREE YEARS.

13 THE NAMES OF THE CONTINENTS ALL END WITH THE SAME LETTER WITH WHICH THEY START.

14 ALMOST – IS THE LONGEST WORD IN THE ENGLISH LANGUAGE WITH ALL THE LETTERS IN ALPHABETICAL ORDER.

15 ELECTRICITY DOESN'T MOVE THROUGH A WIRE BUT THROUGH A FIELD AROUND THE WIRE

16 55% OF PEOPLE YAWN WITHIN 5 MINUTES OF SEEING SOMEONE ELSE YAWN.

17 THE MAJOR AIR – POLLUTING INDUSTRIES ARE IRON, STEEL, AND CEMENT.

18 EVERY YEAR SOME 50 MILLION CARS ARE ADDED TO THE WORLDS' ROADS. CAR MAKING IS NOW THE LARGEST MANUFACTURING INDUSTRY IN THE WORLD.

19 BUTTERFLIES AND MOTHS ARE FOUND ON ALL LAND MASSES EXCEPT ANTARCTICA.

20 THERE ARE BETWEEN 10 MILLION AND 30 MILLION SPECIES OF INSECTS IN THE WORLD, OF WHICH ONLY 1 MILLION ARE KNOWN TO SCIENCE.

21 THE METALLIC – COLORED WING COVERS OF SOME BEETLES ARE USED FOR JEWELRY.

22 THERE ARE MORE THAN 300,000 SPECIES OF BEETLES, MAKING THEM THE LARGEST ORDER OF INSECTS IN THE WORLD.

23 FLIES CAN TASTE WITH THEIR FEET.

24 THE FASTEST KNOWN INSECT IS A DRAGON FLY THAT HAS BEEN CLOCKED AT 58 KILOMETERS AN HOUR.

25 THE LONGEST INSECT IS A WALKING STICK THAT CAN REACH A LENGTH OF 33 CENTIMETERS.

26 THE HEAVIEST INSECT IN THE WORLD IS THE GOLIATH BEETLE FROM AFRICA. A BIG MALE CAN WEIGH UP TO 100 GRAMS.

27 OF THE 35,000 SPECIES OF SPIDERS, ONLY 27 SPECIES ARE KNOWN TO HAVE CAUSED HUMAN FATALITIES.

28 A FLEA CAN JUMP 130 TIMES ITS OWN HEIGHT.

29 SOME MOSQUITOES CAN BEAT THEIR WINGS 600 TIMES A SECOND OR IS IT A MINUTE.

30 ABOUT 10% OF THE WORLD'S POPULATION IS LEFT – HANDED.

31 A COW GIVES NEARLY 200,000 GLASSES OF MILK IN HER LIFETIME

32 THE FEMALE LION DOES MORE THAN 90 % OF THE HUNTING, WHILE THE MALE SIMPLY PREFERS TO REST.

33 A JELLYFISH IS 95 % WATER.

34 OF ALL THE WORDS IN THE ENGLISH LANGUAGE, THE WORD SET HAS THE MOST DEFINITIONS.

35 THE SUN IS 330,330 TIMES LARGER THAN THE EARTH.

36 A GIRAFFE CAN CLEAN ITS EARS WITH ITS 21 – INCH TONGUE.

37 A CROCODILE CANNOT STICK ITS TONGUE OUT.

38 A CAT'S JAWS CANNOT MOVE SIDEWAYS.

39 GO IS THE SHORTEST COMPLETE SENTENCE IN THE ENGLISH LANGUAGE.

40 THE AVERAGE PERSON WALKS THE EQUIVALENT OF TWICE AROUND THE WORLD IN A LIFETIME.

41 ALL POLAR BEARS ARE LEFT HANDED.

42 ANTS DON'T SLEEP.

43 THE SMALLEST BIRD IN THE WORLD IS THE HUMMING BIRD; IT WEIGHTS 1 OUNCE.

44 THE FASTEST HUMAN SWIMMER CAN SWIM SIX MILES PER HOUR.

45 THE FASTEST MAMMAL – THE DOLPHIN – CAN SWIM UP TO 35 MPH.

46 THE BIRD THAT CAN FLY THE FASTEST IS CALLED A WHITE. IT CAN FLY UP TO 95 MPH.

47 THE OLDEST LIVING THING ON EARTH IS 12,000 YEARS OLD. IT IS THE FLOWERING SHRUBS CALLED CREOSOTE BUSHES IN THE MOJAVE DESERT.

48 A PERSON CAN LIVE WITHOUT FOOD FOR ABOUT A MONTH.

49 A PERSON CAN LIVE WITHOUT WATER FOR ONLY ABOUT A WEEK.

50 IF THE AMOUNT OF WATER IN YOUR BODY IS REDUCED BY JUST 1 %, YOU'LL FEEL THIRSTY. IF IT'S REDUCED BY 10 % YOU'LL DIE.

51 THE AVERAGE LEAD PENCIL CAN DRAW A LINE THAT IS ALMOST 35 MILES LONG OR YOU CAN WRITE ALMOST 50,000 WORDS IN ENGLISH WITH JUST ONE PENCIL.

52 THE FIRST STEAM POWERED TRAIN WAS INVENTED BY ROBERT STEPHENSON. IT WAS CALLED THE ROCKET.

53 PEARLS ARE FOUND IN OYSTERS. THE LARGEST PEARL EVER FOUND WAS 620 CARATS.

54 THE SWORDTAIL IS THE FASTEST SWIMMER OF ALL THE FISH.

55 THE HUMAN BODY IS MADE UP OF TRILLIONS OF CELLS.

56 ABOUT 70 % OF THE HUMAN BODY WEIGHT IS WATER.

57 OBJECTS AND PEOPLE MOVE AND OBEY THREE BASIC LAWS OF MOTION; INERTIA, MASS AND FORCE, ACTION AND REACTION.

58 THE BLUE WHALE'S WHISTLE IS THE LOUDEST NOISE MADE BY AN ANIMAL.

59 THE OPPOSITE SIDES OF A DICE ALWAYS ADD UP TO SEVEN.

CHAPTER 28.

BRANCHES OF GOVERNMENT OF THE U.S.A :-

EXECUTIVE :- THIS IS COMPRISED OF THE PRESIDENT - THE LEADER OF THE COUNTRY AND HE ALSO COMMANDS THE MILITARY. THE VICE - PRESIDENT WHO IS THE PRESIDENT OF THE SENATE, AND HE BECOMES PRESIDENT IF THE PRESIDENT CAN NO LONGER DO THE JOB. DEPARTMENTS - DEPARTMENT HEADS ADVISE THE PRESIDENT ON ISSUES AND HELP CARRY OUT POLICIES. THEN THERE ARE THE INDEPENDENT AGENCIES, THEY HELP TO CARRY OUT POLICY OR PROVIDE SPECIAL SERVICES.

LEGISLATIVE :- IS MADE UP OF CONGRESS, THE HOUSE OF REPRESENTATIVES AND THE SENATE.

JUDICIAL :- IS MADE UP OF THE COURT SYSTEM. THE SUPREME COURT IS THE HIGHEST COURT IN THE LAND; ARTICLE 111 OF THE CONSTITUTION ESTABLISHED THIS COURT AND ALL OTHER FEDERAL COURTS WERE CREATED BY CONGRESS. COURTS DECIDE ARGUMENTS ABOUT THE MEANING OF LAWS, HOW THEY ARE APPLIED, AND WHETHER THEY BREAK THE RULES OF THE CONSTITUTION.

PARTS OF A BIRD :-
EYES.
CROWN
MOUSTACHE

BREAST
RUMP
FLANK
WINGS
FEET
TAIL

PARTS OF AN ELEPHANT :-
EYES
EARS
TAIL
LEGS
TRUNK
MOUTH
A PAIR OF TUSKS.
NOTE - THE TIP OF THE TRUNK HAS TWO FINGERS.
AN ELEPHANT AT 33 YEARS OF AGE WAS FOUND TO HAVE :-
EAR WIDTH [FRONT TO BACK] 2 FEET 10 INCHES.
EAR HEIGHT [TOP TO LOWEST PART ON BOTTOM] 3 FEET 10 INCHES
FRONT FOOT CIRCUMFERENCE 4 FEET 4 INCHES.
REAR FOOT CIRCUMFERENCE 4 FEET 1 INCHES.
HEIGHT TO SHOULDER 8 FEET 4 INCHES.
FOREHEAD TO BASE OF TAIL LENGTH 11 FEET 10 INCHES.
WEIGHT 9300 POUNDS.

INSECTS :-THERE ARE MORE KINDS OF INSECTS IN THE WORLD THAN ANY OTHER KINDS OF ANIMALS ADDED TOGETHER. THE PARTS OF AN INSECT ARE :-
HEAD
ANTENNAE
MOUTH PARTS
THORAX
WINGS
LEGS
ABDOMEN

SOME ANIMALS FOUND IN A ZOO ARE :-

DIFFERENT KINDS OF BIRDS - SUCH AS EAGLES, FLAMINGOS, PARROT, SWAN. ETC.
ALLIGATOR
CROCODILE
SNAKES
FROGS
LEOPARDS
TIGER
LION
ELEPHANT
MONKEYS
TURTLES
BABBON
CAMEL
GIRAFFE
GUINEA PIGS
HORSES
OTTER
RABBIT
SEAL
SEA LIONS
SQUIRREL
AMONG OTHERS .

ANIMALS COMPETITIONS :-THIS IS CARRIED OUT IN MANY COUNTRIES OF THE WORLD WHERE ANIMALS COMPETE IN VARIOUS CATEGORIES SUCH AS BEST GROOMED, BEST TRAINED ETC. SOME ANIMALS INVOLVED IN COMPETITIONS ARE :-
RABBITS.
POULTRY.
GUINEAS.
SHEEP.
GOATS.
CATS.
DOGS.

ANIMALS ARE ALSO INVOLVED IN RACES, WHERE THEY COMPETE IN RUNNING. SOME FORM OF ANIMALS RACES ARE :-
HORSES.

GOATS.
DOGS.
AMONG OTHERS.

SOME TYPES OF AIRCRAFTS :-
AIRBUS SUCH AS THE A-300, A-310, A-320, A-330, A-340.
AIRSPEED SUCH AS THE AMBASSADOR.
ANTONOV SUCH AS THE AN-2.
BRITISH AIRSPACE SUCH AS THE JETSTREAM 61.
BOEING SUCH AS THE B-247, B-377, B-707, B-717, B-727 ETC.
CURTIS WRIGHT SUCH AS THE CW-20.
LOCKHEED SUCH AS CONSTELLATION, ELECTRA.
SAAB SUCH AS THE 340.
SHORT SUCH AS THE 330, 360.
TUPOLEV SUCH AS THE TU-104, TU-134,TU-154, THE CONCORDE SST.

SOME AIRLINES IN THE WORLD ARE :-
AIR CANADA.
AIR NEW ZEALAND.
AIR ZIMBABWE
AMERICAN INTERNATIONAL AIRWAYS.
BRITISH AIRWAYS.
B.W.I.A
INTERNATIONAL CHINA
EASTERN
FLORIDA EXPRESS
MID PACIFIC AIR
MIDWEST EXPRESS
NORTH AMERICAN
NORTHWEST
TRANS CANADA
UNITED
SOUTHWEST
AMONG OTHERS.

ATOMS :- EVERYTHING AROUND US IS MADE OF ATOMS. SCIENTISTS SO FAR HAVE FOUND SOME 115 DIFFERENT KINDS OF ATOMS. EVERYTHING YOU SEE IS MADE OF DIFFERENT COMBINATIONS OF THESE ATOMS. IN THE

MIDDLE OF EACH ATOM IS A NUCLEUS; WHICH CONTAINS TWO KINDS OF TINY PARTICLES CALLED PROTONS AND NEUTRONS. ORBITING AROUND THE NUCLEUS ARE EVEN SMALLER PARTICLES CALLED ELECTRONS.

STIMULATION :- IN ORDER TO STIMULATE YOUR BRAIN AND ASSIST YOURSELF TO BECOME INVESTIGATIVE IN ACCOMPLISHING THINGS SO THAT IT CAN HELP TO MAKE YOU GAIN KNOWLEDGE AND INDEPENDENCE IN LIFE, HERE ARE SOME SIMPLE SCIENCE PROJECTS FOR YOU TO WORK ON; REMEMBER, YOU ARE TO HAVE FUN IN YOUR LEARNING EXERCISES AND EXPERIENCES.

[a] HOW DO I HEAR SOUNDS?
[b] WHY DO PEOPLE NEED EYEGLASSES?
[c] WHAT MAKES THE SEASONS?
[d] WHY DO THE DAYS GET SHORTER?
[e] WHAT IS A RAINBOW?
[f] WHY DO YOU BREATHE?
[g] HOW DO LIGHT BULBS WORK?
[h] WHAT IS PLASTIC?
[I] WHY DO YOU GET SICK?
[j] WHY DO LEAVES CHANGE COLOR?
[k] WHY IS THE SKY BLUE?
[l] HOW DO ANIMALS SPEND THE WINTER?
[m] HOW DO BOATS FLOAT?
[n] WHY ARE LEAVES GREEN?
[o] HOW DO REFRIGERATORS WORK?
[p] WHY IS ICE SLIPPERY?
[q] HOW DO BATTERIES WORK?
[r] HOW DO AIRPLANES FLY?
[s] WHAT ARE THE LAYERS OF THE EARTH?

BE SURE TO USE THE LIBRARY AND GET INFORMED ADULTS TO ASSIST YOU.

CRUISE :-IS TO TRAVEL ABOUT, AS BY SHIP. SOME NAMES OF SOME COMPANIES IN THE CRUISE LINER INDUSTRY ARE :-

AIRTOURS SUN.
CAPTAIN COOK CRUISES.
CARNIVAL

CELEBRITY
CRYSTAL
DISNEY CRUISE LINE.
HOLLAND AMERICA
ISLAND CRUISES
OCEAN VILLAGE
OCEANIA CRUISES
ORIENT LINES
PRINCESS
ROYAL CARIBBEAN
SEABOURNE
STAR CRUISES
VOYAGES OF DISCOVERY
WINDSTAR

SOME NAMES OF CRUISE SHIPS ARE :-
ADVENTURE OF THE SEAS.
AMSTERDAM
CALYPSO
CARIBBEAN PRINCESS
BRILLIANCE OF THE SEAS.
CARNIVAL DESTINY
CARNIVAL
GLORY
CARNIVAL LEGEND
CARNIVAL MIRACLE
CARNIVAL PRIDE
CORAL PRINCESS
CRYSTAL HARMONY
CRYSTAL SERENITY
DISNEY MAGIC
ECSTASY
FANTASY
GALAXY
GOLDEN PRINCESS
HOLIDAY HORIZON
MELODY
NORWEGIAN SEA
OCEANA
PACIFIC PRINCESS
PARADISE

ROYAL PRINCESS
SENSATION
SPLENDOUR OF THE SEAS
VOYAGER OF THE SEAS
ZENITH.

CRUISE SHIPS ARE BUILT WITH EVERY AMENITIES POSSIBLE; THEY HAVE EVERYTHING INCLUDING RESTAURANTS, SWIMMING POOLS, AND THEIR ACCOMMODATIONS ARE STRIKING TO BEHOLD; THEY ARE DECKED OUT WITH SUCH ACCOMMODATIONS AS :-
OWNER'S SUITE.
VISTA SUITE.
PENTHOUSE SUITE.
STATEROOM WITH VERANDA.
DELUXE OCEAN VIEW STATEROOM.
OCEAN VIEW STATEROOM.
INSIDE STATEROOM.
AMONG OTHERS .
THEY ALSO PROVIDE SERVICES OF ALL SORTS SUCH AS INTERNATIONAL CHEFS, BUTLER SERVICE.ETC.

SOME UNUSUAL ANIMALS OF THE WORLD ARE :-
BONGO -THIS IS AN ANTELOPE THAT IS FOUND IN AFRICA.
CAPYBARA -THIS IS A GUINEA PIG THAT IS FOUND IN SOUTH AMERICA.
CIVET -THIS IS A TYPE OF CAT THAT IS FOUND IN AFRICA AND ASIA
ECHIDNA -THIS IS AN EGG LAYING MAMMAL THAT IS FOUND IN AUSTRALIA, NEW GUINEA, AND TASMANIA.
JERBOA -THIS IS A RODENT THAT IS FOUND IN AFRICA AND ASIA.
KINKAJON -THIS IS A MAMMAL RELATED TO THE RACCOON THAT IS FOUND IN THE AMERICAS.
KIWI -IS A FLIGHTLESS BIRD FOUND IN NEW ZEALAND.
OKAPI -THIS ANIMAL IS SOMEWHAT PART ZEBRA AND PART GIRAFFE AND FOUND IN AFRICA.
PANGOLIN -IS A SHORT LEGGED MAMMAL FOUND IN AFRICA AND ASIA.

TARSIER -THIS IS A SQUIRREL SIZED PRIMATE THAT'S FOUND IN SOUTHEAST ASIA.

SIGNS AND SYMBOLS - BASICS IN MATHEMATICS :-
PLACE VALUE
ADDITION
SUBTRACTION
MULTIPLICATION
DIVISION
DECIMALS
INTEGERS
FRACTIONS
PERCENT
RATIOS
MEASUREMENTS
METRIC SYSTEM
GEOMETRY
PROBABILITY
ALGEBRA
STATISTICS
POLYNOMIALS
LINEAR EQUATIONS
MATRICES
EXPONENTS
IRRATIONAL NUMBERS
QUADRATIC EQUATIONS
COMPLEX NUMBERS
LOGARITHMS
TRIGONOMETRY
TIME AND TELLING TIME.
CALENDAR
MONEY
BUSINESS MATH
INVESTING
PERIMETER
CIRCUMFERENCE
DIAMETER
AREA
VOLUME
GRAPHS
SQUARE ROOTS

AMONG OTHERS .

FIGURES OF SPEECH :-

TROPES :- FIGURES WHICH CHANGE THE TYPICAL MEANING OF A WORD OR WORDS.

METAPLASMIC FIGURES :- ARE FIGURES WHICH MOVE THE LETTERS OR SYLLABLES OF A WORD FROM THEIR TYPICAL PLACES.

FIGURES OF OMISSION :- ARE FIGURES WHICH OMIT SOMETHING E.G WORD, WORDS, PHRASES, OR CLAUSES – FROM A SENTENCE.

FIGURES OF REPETITION [WORDS] FIGURES WHICH REPEAT ONE OR MORE WORDS.

FIGURES OF REPETITION [CLAUSES AND IDEAS] FIGURES WHICH REPEAT A PHRASE, A CLAUSE, OR AN IDEA.

FIGURES OF UNUSUAL WORD ORDER :- FIGURES WHICH ALTER THE ORDINARY ORDER OF WORDS OF SENTENCES.

FIGURES OF THOUGHT :- IS A MISCELLANEOUS GROUP OF FIGURES WHICH DEAL WITH EMOTIONAL APPEALS AND TECHNIQUES OF ARGUMENT.

LITERALLY :-IS PRECISE, EXACT, STRICT; THAT IS RESTRICTED TO ACTUAL FACTS.

FIGURATIVELY :-USING METAPHORS, SIMILES AS A VIVID EXPRESSION

SYMBOLICALLY :-USING OBJECTS, MARK, IDEAS ETC, TO REPRESENT WHAT YOU ARE PORTRAYING.

BANKS :-IS A BUSINESS HANDLING SAVINGS, LOANS ETC. TYPES OF BANKING SYSTEMS SERVICES INCLUDE SAVING ACCOUNTS, VARIOUS TYPES OF LOANS TRANSACTIONS, CURRENT ACCOUNTS, ESCROW, INTERNET BANKING, PAYMENT PROCESSING, MONEY MARKET ACCOUNTS, OFFSHORE BANKING; AMONG OTHERS. THE NAMES OF SOME BANKS ARE :-
WORLD BANK.
BANK OF ENGLAND.
FEDERAL RESERVE BANK.

BARCLAYS.
BANK OF AMERICA.
H.S.B.C
NORTH FOLK.
GREENPOINT.
FLEET.
JAMAICA BANK.
CITI BANK.
AND MANY OTHER BANKS ESTABLISHED ALL OVER THE WORLD.

OFFSHORE BANKING :-IS DOING YOUR BANKING BUSINESS IN A FOREIGN COUNTRY; HAVING GLOBAL BANKING SERVICES AT LOCATIONS AROUND THE WORLD. THE OFFSHORE WORLD IS THE PERFECT ENVIRONMENT FOR PROTECTING HARD – EARNED ASSETS AS WELL AS DOING BUSINESS, BANKING AND INVESTING IN A COMPLETELY CONFIDENTIAL MANNER. OFFSHORE BANKING SERVICES INCLUDE AMONG OTHERS :-
CASH MANAGEMENT.
FOREIGN EXCHANGE AND TREASURY SERVICES.
INTERNATIONAL TRADE IN AREAS OF LETTERS OF CREDIT.
DOCUMENTARY COLLECTIONS.
CROSS BORDER GUARANTEES.
RISK MANAGEMENT AND FOREIGN EXCHANGE.
INTEREST RATES AREAS OF CONCERN.
EQUITY AND ENERGY PRICE RISK MANAGEMENT TOOLS.
FINANCING.
PAYMENT, RECEIVABLES AND PAYROLL SOLUTIONS.
SELLING SOLUTIONS.
POINT OF SALE.
E – COMMERCE AND MERCHANT PROGRAMS.
SPECIALTY SOLUTIONS, SUCH AS DEALER, SHAREOWNER, AND FUND SERVICES.
EXPERTISE IN MATTERS SUCH AS ENERGY, AVIATION, SHIPPING, AND / OR REAL ESTATE.

THE OFFSHORE SECRECY LAWS :-OFFSHORE BANKING REFERRED TO AS TAX HAVENS, HAVE LAWS THE FORBID

FINANCIAL INSTITUTIONS SUCH AS BANKS, BROKERAGES, INSURANCE COMPANIES ETC. AND ADVISORS SUCH AS BROKERS, ACCOUNTANTS, ATTORNEYS, INVESTMENT ADVISORS ETC. FROM DIVULGING INFORMATION ABOUT CLIENTS OR ACCOUNTS TO ANY THIRD PARTY UNDER PENALTY OF LAW.

INTERNATIONAL TRADE AND FINANCE :-
NAFTA -MEANS NORTH AMERICAN FREE TRADE AGREEMENT.

THE DIFFERENCE BETWEEN A NATION'S TOTAL EXPORTS AND ITS TOTAL IMPORTS IS CALLED THE BALANCE OF TRADE.
GATT -ALLOWED MEMBER NATIONS TO PROTECT THEIR DOMESTIC INDUSTRIES FROM FOREIGN COMPETITION THROUGH TARIFFS. IN 1995, GATT WAS SUCCEEDED BY THE WORLD TRADE ORGANIZATION.

MERCOSUR -IS A FREE TRADE BLOCK OF SOUTH AMERICAN COUNTRIES.

IN 1976 THE INTERNATIONAL MONETARY FUND [IMF] STABILIZED THE WORLD'S MONETARY SYSTEM BY ALLOWING THE VALUE OF THE WORLD CURRENCIES TO BE DETERMINED BY THE MARKET.

HOTELS :-PLACE WITH ROOMS, FOOD ETC. FOR TRAVELERS. HOTELS ARE LOCATED ALL OVER THE WORLD. THE NAMES OF SOME RECOGNIZED HOTELS ARE :-
SKYLINE.
RAMADA PLAZA.
THE CARLTON.
BENTLEY.
HELMSLEY.
MILFORD PLAZA.
HILTON.
MARRIOTT MARQUIS.
RADISSON LEXINGTON.
CENTRAL PARK N.Y.
ROOSEVELT.

SHERATON.
HUDSON.
SOFITEL.
SALISBURY.
BENTLEY.
PLAZA FITTY.
PARIS LAS VAGAS.
CATHEDRAL HILL.
RAMADA INN.
NATIONAL HOTEL.
THE STRAND PALACE – LONDON.
LE MERIDIEN MONTPARNASSE – PARIS.
GRAND HOTEL DE LA MINERVE – ROME.
CASTLE MAUI BEACH – HAWAII.
LOS CABOS – MEXICO.
LA CABANA – ARUBA.
PANTAGES - TORONTO, CANADA.
AMONG OTHERS.

INN :-IS A HOTEL OR RESTAURANT.

MOTEL :-ROADSIDE HOTEL FOR MOTORISTS.

CARBON MONOXIDE :-IS A COLORLESS, ODORLESS, TASTELESS AND EXTREMELY POISONOUS GAS, BECAUSE IT HAS NO ODOR OR COLOR, PEOPLE BREATHING IT USUALLY FELL ASLEEP WITHOUT REALIZING THEY ARE BEING POISONED. CARBON MONOXIDE PREVENTS HEMOGLOBIN [THE OXYGEN – CARRYING SUBSTANCE IN THE BLOOD]FROM SUPPLYING OXYGEN TO THE BODY. WITHOUT OXYGEN PEOPLE AND ANIMALS SOON DIE.

SOME HIGHLIGHTS ON ROYALS AND RULERS

1 PRINCE WILLIAM FAIRLY RECENTLY GRADUATED FROM THE FAMOUS BRITISH SCHOOL NAME ETON.
2 PRINCE HARRY'S REAL NAME IS HENRY CHARLES ALBERT DAVID.
3 AS AN ECONOMY MEASURE, THE ROYAL FAMILY GAVE UP THEIR YACHT IN 1997, WHICH IS NAMED BRITANNIA.

4 PRINCESS DIANA IS BURIED AT AN ISLAND AT ALTHORP - THE SPENCER FAMILY ESTATE.

5 THE QUEEN'S MOTHER IS A PARTICULAR DEDICATED FAN OF THE HORSE RACING SPORT.

6 THE ROYAL WHO COMPETED IN THE OLYMPICS, IS PRINCESS ANNE IN HORSEBACK RIDING.

7 PRINCE CHARLES HAS BEEN CRITICIZED FOR CONDEMNING MODERN ARCHITECTURE.

SOME KNOWN ROYALTIES ARE :-
HER MAJESTY THE QUEEN.
HRH PRINCE PHILIP, DUKE OF EDINBURGH.
HRH THE PRINCE OF WALES.
HRH THE DUKE OF YORK.
TRH THE EARL AND COUNTESS OF WESSEX.
HRH THE PRINGESS ROYAL.
HRH PRINCESS ALICE, DUCHESS OF GLOUCESTER.
TRH THE DUKE AND DUCHESS OF GLOUCESTER.
TRH THE DUKE AND DUCHESS OF KENT.
TRH PRINCE AND PRINCESS MICHAEL OF KENT.
HRH PRINCESS ALEXANDRA.

IN HER ROLE AS HEAD OF STATE, THE QUEEN IS SUPPORTED BY MEMBERS OF THE ROYAL FAMILY; WHO CARRY OUT A WIDE RANGE OF PUBLIC AND OFFICIAL DUTIES. BIOGRAPHIES OF MEMBERS OF THE ROYAL FAMILY CONTAIN SECTIONAL INFORMATION ABOUT VARIOUS MEMBERS OF THE ROYAL FAMILY, INCLUDING THEIR EARLY LIFE AND EDUCATION, PROFESSIONAL CAREERS, OFFICIAL ROYAL WORK, INVOLVEMENT WITH CHARITIES AND OTHER ORGANIZATIONS, PERSONAL INTERESTS AND MORE.

ROYALTIES ARE SO PROCLAIMED IN MANY PARTS OF THE WORLD, INCLUDING :-
AFRICAN ROYALTY.
AMERICAN ROYALTY.
ASIAN ROYALTY.
EUROPEAN ROYALTY.
MIDDLE EASTERN ROYALTY.
OCEANIAN ROYALTY.
AMONG OTHERS.

SOME NOTABLE ROYALTIES AND RULERS THROUGH OUT THE WORLD WHO WERE KNOWN FOR ONE REASON OR ANOTHER ARE SUCH AS :-

BRITISH PRIME MINISTERS.
CANADIAN PRIME MINISTERS.
EGYPTIANS PHAROAHS.
ENGLISH MONARCHS.
GERMAN EMPERORS.
U.S PRESIDENTS.
YASSER ARAFAT.
NAPOLEON BONAPARTE.
AUGUSTUS CAESAR.
JULIUS CAESAR.
CHARLES DE GAULLE.
HAILE SELASSIE.
ADOLF HITLER.
LOUIS XIV OF FRANCE.
NELSON MANDELA.
BENITO MUSSOLINI.
JAWAHARLAL NEHRU.
ANWAR SADAT.
XERXES OF PERSIA.
ALEXANDER THE GREAT.
FORBES BURNHAM.
CHEDDI JAGAN.
MICHAEL MANLEY.
AMONG OTHERS.

SOME CHEMICAL ELEMENTS AND THEIR SYMBOLS ARE :-

ALUMINUM	Al.
ARGON	Ar.
CALCIUM	Ca.
CARBON	C.
CHLORINE	Cl.
COBALT	Co.
COPPER	Cu.
GOLD	Au.
HELIUM	He.

HYDROGEN	Ho.
IODINE	I.
LEAD	Pb.
MANGANESE	Mn.
MERCURY	Hg.
NEON	Ne.
NICKEL	Ni.
NITROGEN	N.
OXYGEN	O.
PLATINUM	Pt.
POTASSIUM	K.
RADIUM	Ra.
SILICON	Si.
SILVER	Ag.
SODIUM	Na.
SULFUR	S.
TIN	Sn.
TITANIUM	Ti.
URANIUM	U.
ZINC	Zn.

SPEED OF ANIMALS :-

MEASUREMENTS ARE FOR MAXIMUM SPEEDS OVER APPROXIMATELY QUARTER – MILE DISTANCES. IN SOME CASES A BURST OF SPEED IS MEASURED.

ANIMALS SPEED IN MILES PER HOUR.	
PEREGRINE FALCON	200.
CHEETAH	70.
PRONGHORN ANTELOPE	61.
WILDEBEEST	50.
LION	50.
THOMSON'S GAZELLE	50.
QUARTER HORSE	47.5.
ELK	45.
CAPE HUNTING DOG	45.
COYOTE	43.
GRAY FOX	42.
OSTRICH	40.
HYENA	40.

ZEBRA	40.
MONGOLIAN WILD ASS	40.
GREYHOUND	39.35.
WHIPPET	35.50.
RABBIT	35.
MULE DEER	35.
JACKAL	35.
REINDEER	32.
GIRAFFE	32.
KANGAROO	30.
GRIZZLY BEAR	30.
CAT	30.
HUMAN	27.89.
ELEPHANT	25.
SNAKE	20.
SQUIRREL	12.
PIG	11.
CHICKEN	9.
HOUSE MOUSE	8.
SPIDER	1.17.
TORTOISE	0.17.
THREE TOED SLOTH	0.15.
GARDEN SNAIL	0.03.

DROUGHT :-A DROUGHT IS CONSIDERED A PERIOD OF ABNORMALLY DRY WEATHER THAT CAUSES SERIOUS HYDROLOGICAL IMBALANCE IN THE AREA. THERE ARE THREE GENERAL TYPES OF DROUGHT.

1 A METEOROLOGICAL DROUGHT IS A LACK OF RAINFALL OVER A LONG PERIOD OF TIME.

2 A HYDROLOGICAL DROUGHT OCCURS WHEN THERE ARE CRITICALLY LOW GROUND WATER TABLES AND REDUCED RIVER AND STREAM FLOW.

3 AN AGRICULTURAL DROUGHT OCCURS WHEN EXTENDED DRY PERIODS AND GENERAL LACK OF RAINFALL RESULT IN A LACK OF MOISTURE IN THE ROOT ZONE OF THE SOIL, AFFECTING AGRICULTURE.

FLOOD :-A FLOOD OCCURS WHEN A BODY OF WATER RISES AND OVERFLOWS ONTO NORMAL DRY LAND. THE EFFECTS ARE BOTH BENEFICIAL [FOR THE SOIL] AND

DESTRUCTIVE TO PROPERTY AND LIVES. FLOODS HAVE BEEN RECORDED FOR AT LEAST 5,000 YEARS; SERVING THE BASIS FOR MYTH, RELIGIOUS BELIEFS, AND SCIENTIFIC STUDY. THE MOST POPULAR KNOWN FLOOD IS THE FLOOD OF THE BIBLE DURING NOAH'S TIME WHEN GOD BROUGHT THE WORLD TO AN END BY FLOOD. FLOOD IS CLASSIFIED AS COASTAL, RIVER, AND FLASH.

OIL SPILLS :-A FEW RECENT MAJOR OIL SPILLS THAT OCCURRED THAT ARE NOT GOOD FOR THE WORLD'S ECOLOGY ARE :-

1 JANUARY 18 2000, OFF RIO DE JANEIRO, PIPELINE OWNED BY GOVERNMENT OIL COMPANY PETROBRAS SPEWED 343,200 GALLONS OF HEAVY OIL INTO GUANABARA BAY.

2 NOVEMBER 28 2000, MISSISSIPPI RIVER – OIL TANKER WEST CHESTER DUMPED 567,000 GALLONS OF CRUDE OIL, THE SPILL WAS THE LARGEST SINCE THE EXXON VALDEZ DISASTER IN MARCH 1989.

3 DECEMBER 12 1999, FRENCH ATLANTIC COAST. TANKER ERIKA BROKE APART AND SANK OFF BRITANNY SPILLING THREE MILLION GALLONS OF HEAVY OIL INTO THE SEA.

4 FEBRUARY 15 1996, OFF WELSH COAST. SUPERTANKER SEA EMPRESS SPEWED OUT 70,000 TONS OF CRUDE OIL, IT CREATED A 25 MILE OIL SLICK.

5 SEPTEMBER 8 1994, RUSSIA, DAM BUILT TO CONTAIN OIL BURST AND SPILLED TWO MILLION BARRELS OF OIL.

6 AUGUST 10 1993, TAMPA BAY FLORIDA, 3 SHIPS COLLIDED, SPILLED AN ESTIMATED 336 GALLONS OF NO. 6 FUEL OIL INTO TAMPA BAY.

GENERAL INFORMATION :-

THE YOUNGEST FIRST LADY EVER IN THE WHITE HOUSE WAS FRANCES CLEVELAND; SHE WAS JUST 21 YEARS OLD AT THE TIME.

THE FIRST SUBWAY SYSTEM WAS BUILT IN LONDON.

IN A CANAL, LOCKS ARE AREAS WHERE A BOAT IS LOWERED OR RAISED FROM ONE WATER LEVEL TO ANOTHER.

FACTS ABOUT THE NEWEST COUNTRIES OF THE WORLD AS WELL AS OTHER INTERESTING OBSERVATIONS :-

1 THE REPUBLIC OF PALAU IS MADE UP OF 200 SMALL ISLANDS IN THE PACIFIC OCEAN SOME 500 MILES SOUTH OF THE PHILIPPINES.

2 THE NEW COUNTRY THAT IS ALSO SOMETIMES KNOWN AS WHITE RUSSIA IS BELARUS.

3 IN 1993 FORMER EASTERN EUROPEAN NATION CZECHOSLOVAKIA, BROKE UP TO FORM TWO NEW COUNTRIES SLOVAKIA AND CZECH REPUBLIC.

4 THE SUFFIX 'STAN' WHEN IT APPEARS IN THE NAME OF A NATION SUCH AS TURKMENISTAN MEAN LAND OF.

5 THE NEW NATION OF ERITREA BECAME INDEPENDENT FOLLOWING ONE OF THE LONGEST WAR IN HISTORY.

6 THE NEW NATION EAST TIMOR WAS ONCE RULED BY THE PORTUGUESE.

7 THE NEW COUNTRY SLOVENIA WAS ONCE THE MOST INDUSTRIALIZED PART OF YUGOSLAVIA.

8 GREECE HAS PROTESTED THE NAME OF THE NEW NATION MACEDONIA ON THE GROUNDS THAT ANCIENT MACEDONIA IS A PART OF GREECE.

9 SOUTH AFRICA ELECTED NELSON MANDELA A FORMER POLITICAL PRISONER THE COUNTRY'S FIRST BLACK PRESIDENT IN ELECTIONS HELD ON 29 APRIL 1994.

10 WHILE FLAGS OF MOST COUNTRIES ARE RECTANGULAR, THE FLAGS OF SWITZERLAND AND THE VATICAN CITY ARE SQUARE.

11 LIBYA'S FLAG IS SOLID GREEN WITH NO EMBLEM OR DESIGNS.

12 NEPAL'S FLAG IS NOT A QUADRILATERAL.

13 IN 1964 THE U.S CORPORATION MCDONALD REGISTERED A THREE DIMENSIONAL TRADEMARK THE GOLDEN ARCHES THAT IS NOW INTERNATIONALLY RECOGNIZABLE.

14 IN 1972, STANDARD OIL CHANGED ITS NAME TO EXXON.

15 THE FIRST TRADEMARK IN THE U.S WAS GRANTED TO AVERILL PAINTS.

16 IN 1999, FRANCE WAS THE TOP TOURIST DESTINATION IN THE WORLD.

17 THE BLACK FOREST IS IN GERMANY.

18 THE WORLD'S LARGEST SUBWAY SYSTEM, WHICH SPANS MORE THAN 390 KM, IS IN LONDON.

19 THE STATE OF MAINE IS THE EASTERNMOST POINT IN THE U.S.

20 RED IS THE MOST ATTENTION GETTING COLOR.

21 PURPLE IS THE COLOR OF ROYALTY.

THE AMAZON RIVER :-IS THE GREATEST RIVER IN THE WORLD; THE VOLUME OF WATER IT CARRIES TO THE SEA IS APPROXIMATELY 20 % OF ALL THE FRESH WATER DISCHARGE INTO THE OCEANS. THE AMAZON RIVER IS THE LONGEST IN THE WORLD, FOLLOWED BY THE NILE RIVER. THE AMAZON RIVER IS ANYWHERE BETWEEN 3, 903 MILES AND 4,195 MILES LONG. THE NILE RIVER IS AS LONG AS ANYWHERE BETWEEN 3,437 MILES AND 4,180 MILES LONG. IN AN AVERAGE DRY SEASON 110,000 SQUARE KILOMETERS OF LAND ARE WATER COVERED BY THE AMAZON RIVER, WHILE IN THE WET SEASON THE FLOODED AREA OF THE AMAZON BASIN RISES TO 350,000 SQUARE KILOMETERS. WHERE THE AMAZON RIVER OPENS AT ITS ESTUARY [MOUTH] THE RIVER IS OVER 202 MILES WIDE. THE AMAZON DRAINS THE ENTIRE NORTHERN HALF OF THE SOUTH AMERICAN CONTINENT WHICH IS APPROXIMATELY 40 % LANDMASS. THE AMAZON RIVER IS SO WIDE AND DEEP THAT OCEAN GOING SHIPS HAVE NAVIGATED ITS WATERS AND TRAVELED AS FAR INLAND AS TWO – THIRDS THE WAY UP THE ENTIRE LENGTH OF THE RIVER. MORE THAN 200 SMALLER RIVERS FLOW INTO THE AMAZON. NO BRIDGE CROSSES THE RIVER ALONG ITS ENTIRE LENGTH. THE AMAZON AND ITS TRIBUTARIES FLOW THROUGH THE COUNTRIES OF PERU, BOLIVIA, VENEZUELA, COLOMBIA, ECUADOR AND BRAZIL; BEFORE EMPTYING INTO THE ATLANTIC OCEAN.

THE NILE RIVER BASIN COMPRISES TEN COUNTRIES :- BURUNDI.

DEMOCRATIC REPUBLIC OF CONGO.
EGYPT.
ERITREA.
ETHIOPIA.
KENYA.
RWANDA.
SUDAN.
TANZANIA.
UGANDA.
THE NILE RIVER FINALLY FLOWS INTO THE MEDITERRANEAN SEA. LOTS OF PEOPLE ARE OF THE OPINION THAT THE NILE RIVER IS LONGER THAN THE AMAZON RIVER. I GUESS IT IS A VERY DEBATABLE SUBJECT.

DAM :-IS A BARRIER TO HOLD BACK FLOWING WATER. DAM IS USEFUL AS A SOURCE OF GENERATING HYDRO – ELECTRIC POWER; ALSO AS A SOURCE OF CONSERVATION OF WATER RESOURCES, FOR WATER SUPPLY, IRRIGATION, AND FLOOD PREVENTION. THERE IS AN INTERNATIONAL WORLD COMMISSION ON DAMS [WCD] AS WELL AS ENVIRONMENTAL MONITORING GROUPS; THAT LOOK AT COMMUNITIES AFFECTED BY DAMS.

FIRE :-IS BURNING THING, FLAME. FOR A FIRE TO BE IGNITED, THERE MUST BE THREE ELEMENTS PRESENT, THAT IS OXYGEN, HEAT, AND COMBUSTIBLE – FLAMMABLE MATERIALS. IT IS A WELL KNOWN FACT THAT FIRE CAN BE VERY DESTRUCTIVE TO LIVES AND PROPERTIES; BUT FIRE IS ALSO VERY ESSENTIAL IN EVERY DAY LIVING TO CARRY OUT FUNCTIONS SUCH AS COOKING. IT IS SAID, AND I AM SURE YOU WILL AGREE THAT FIRE IS A GOOD SERVANT BUT A BAD MASTER.

MINES :-IS A LARGE EXCAVATION FROM WHICH TO EXTRACT ORES, COALS ETC. THERE IS THE MINE SAFETY AND HEALTH ADMINISTRATION [MSHA] WHICH LOOKS INTO EMPLOYMENT, ACCIDENTS, INJURY, AND ILLNESS AMONG OTHER AREAS OF INTERESTS TO MINE WORKERS – OPERATORS. THERE ARE DIFFERENT TYPES OF MINING OPERATIONS SUCH AS :-
COAL.

NON – METAL.
SAND AND GRAVEL.
STONE.
METAL.

KINDS OF COAL MINING ARE ANTHRACITE, BITUMINOUS.

TYPES OF METAL MINING ARE SUCH AS :-
IRON ORE.
COPPER.
GOLD.
LEAD.
ZINC.
SILVER.
PLATINUM.
ALUMINUM.
OTHER METALS.

NON METAL MINING ARE SUCH AS :-
CLAY.
ROCK.
OTHER NON – METALS.

STONE MINING ARE SUCH AS :-
DIMENSION STONE.
CRUSHED STONE.
CEMENT.
LIME.

A MINE DISASTER IS AN ACCIDENT WITH FIVE OR MORE FATALITIES.

SUBMARINE :-IS A WARSHIP OPERATING UNDER WATER. HISTORY OF SUBMARINES DATE WAY BACK FOR EXAMPLE :-

IN 1923 THE USS S-35 [SS140] WAS COMMISSIONED.
IN 1931 THE USS R-15 [SS92] WAS DECOMMISSIONED.
IN 1943 THE KEEL [BOTTOM] WAS LAID FOR USS PINTADO [SS387].

THERE ARE DIFFERENT TYPES OF SUBMARINES SUCH AS THE GUIDED MISSILE SUBMARINES, EXAMPLES OF THESE ARE THE CHARLIE 11, PAPA, JULIET.

SUBMARINES ARE DIVIDED INTO WATER TIGHT COMPARTMENTS SUCH AS :-
THE FORWARD TORPEDO ROOM.
LIVING ACCOMMODATIONS FOR OFFICERS AND CREWS.
AREAS FOR BATTERIES.
THE MISSILE CONTROL ROOM.
THE CONTROL ROOM.
CREW BERTHING AND BATTERIES.
THE FORWARD ENGINE ROOM CONTAINING THE DIESELS AND GENERATORS.
THE AFTER ENGINE ROOM WITH THE ELECTRIC MOTORS.
THE AFTER TORPEDO ROOM.
AMONG OTHERS.

WORLD EXPOSITIONS OR EXHIBITIONS :-IS A TEEM FREQUENTLY APPLIED TO AN ORGANIZED PUBLIC FAIR OR DISPLAY OF INDUSTRIAL AND ARTISTIC PRODUCTIONS, DESIGNED USUALLY TO PROMOTE TRADE AND TO REFLECT CULTURAL PROGRESS. EXPOSITIONS HAVE ALSO BEEN IMPORTANT FOR THEIR EMPHASIS ON SCIENTIFIC AND TECHNOLOGICAL INNOVATIONS.
TO MAKE THE MOST OF EXPOSITIONS AND / OR EXHIBITIONS; THE FOLLOWING IS DONE TO ENHANCE THE SUCCESS OF THE EXPOSITION OR EXHIBITION. THE MESSAGE PORTRAYED IS OFTEN STRENGTHENED BY USE OF :-
DIAGRAMS.
MAPS.
PHOTOGRAPHS.
MODELS.
OTHER INTERPRETIVE MEDIA ARE INTERWOVEN TO PROVIDE A SATISFYING MESSAGE.
NAMES OF A FEW COMPANIES AND CORPORATIONS – INDUSTRIES THAT RUN OR CARRIED OUT RECENT EXHIBITIONS – TRADE FAIRS ARE

1 RESTAURATION DEMAIN IN PARIS, FRANCE FROM 14 TH TO THE 17 TH APRIL 2004.

2 AUSTROPHARM IN VIENNA, AUSTRIA CARRIED OUT A TRADE FAIR FOR PHARMACEUTICAL PRODUCTS FROM 16 TH TO 18 TH APRIL 2004.

3 HOREXPO IN LISBON, PORTUGAL HAD THEIR EXHIBITION FROM 17 TH TO 20 TH APRIL 2004.

4 SINGAPORE CONFERENCE IN SINGAPORE WAS RUN FROM 18 TH TO 20 TH APRIL 2004.

5 SPA AND RESORT EXPOSITION AND CONFERENCE IN NEW YORK U.S.A FROM 18 TH TO 19 TH APRIL 2004.

6 MEDICAL SPA EXPOSITION AND CONFERENCE IN NEW YORK U.S.A FROM 18 TH TO 19 TH APRIL 2004.

7 ITEC IN LONDON U.K HELD THEIR EXHIBITION FROM 20 TH TO 22 TH APRIL 2004.

8 INTERTOOL KIEV 2004 HELD THEIR 5 TH INTERNATIONAL TRADE FAIR FOR TOOLS, METAL WORKING AND MANUFACTURING TECHNOLOGIES ALONG WITH WELDING TECHNOLOGIES. THIS IS IN KIEV, UKRAINE FROM 20 TH TO 23 RD APRIL 2004.

9 INCENTIVE WORLD IN LONDON U.K HAD THEIR FAIR FROM 20 TH TO 22 ND APRIL 2004.

10 DP - DIGITAL PUBLISHING FAIR IN TOKYO, JAPAN FROM 22 ND TO 24 TH APRIL 2004.

11 TIBF OF TOKYO JAPAN, HAD THEIR BOOK FAIR FROM 22 ND TO 25 TH APRIL 2004.

12 VINOVA OF VIENNA, AUSTRIA HELD THEIR INTERNATIONAL WINE FAIR FROM 25 TH TO 28 TH APRIL 2004.

WORLD CULTURAL HERITAGE :-
THE WORLD CULTURAL HERITAGE BODY HAS ADOPTED A LIST IN WHICH THERE ARE 754 PROPERTIES ON ITS LIST; IT IS MADE UP OF 582 CULTURAL, 149 NATURAL, AND 23 MIXED PROPERTIES IN 129 STATES PARTIES. THIS NUMBER IS BEING CONSTANTLY ADDED TO.

EXAMPLES OF SOME OF THE PROPERTIES THAT ARE ON THE LIST ARE :-

[a] THE JESUIT MISSIONS OF THE GUARANIS IN ARGENTINA – BRAZIL.

[b] THE GREAT BARRIER REEF OF AUSTRALIA ADOPTED IN 1981.

[c] BELIZE BARRIER REEF ADOPTED TO THE LIST IN 1996.

[d] THE RESERVE SYSTEM IN BENIN IN 1985.

[e] ROYAL PALACES OF ABOMEY.

[f] BRASILIA OF BRAZIL IN 1987.

[g] CANADIAN ROCKY MOUNTAIN PARKS OF CANADA IN 1984.

[h] THE GREAT WALL OF CHINA IN CHINA IN 1987.

[I] MEMPHIS AND ITS NECROPOLIS – OF EGYPT IN 1979.

[j] THE PYRAMID FIELDS FROM GAZA.

[k] THE VATICAN CITY IN 1984.

[l] THE TAJ MAHAL OF INDIA WAS ADDED TO THE LIST IN 1983.

[m] THE OLD CITY OF JERUSALEM AND ITS WALLS IN JERUSALEM ADDED IN 1981.

[n] CENTRAL SURINAME NATURE RESERVE IN SURINAME IN 2000.

THE WORLD HERITAGE LIST IS ESTABLISHED AND REVIEWED UNDER THE TERMS OF THE CONVENTION AS FAR AS THE PROTECTION OF THE WORLD CULTURAL AND NATURAL HERITAGE IS CONCERNED; THIS WAS RATIFIED IN NOVEMBER 17 TH 1972 AT THE GENERAL CONFERENCE ON UNESCO.

WORLD BUSINESS COUNCIL [WBCSD] :-IS A COALITION OF SOME 170 INTERNATIONAL COMPANIES FROM ABOUT 35 COUNTRIES AND 20 MAJOR INDUSTRIAL SECTORS. THE AIMS OF THE COUNCIL ARE TO DEVELOP AREAS OF BUSINESS

LEADERSHIP, POLICY DEVELOPMENT, BEST PRACTICE, AND GLOBAL OUTREACH.

WORLD CONSERVATION UNION [IUCN] :-IS A UNIQUE UNION. ITS MEMBERS ARE FROM SOME 140 COUNTRIES AND INCLUDE OVER 70 STATES, 100 GOVERNMENT AGENCIES AND 750 PLUS NON – GOVERNMENTAL ORGANIZATIONS. MORE THAN 10,000 INTERNATIONALLY RECOGNIZED SCIENTISTS AND EXPERTS FROM MORE THAN 180 COUNTRIES, VOLUNTEER THEIR SERVICES TO ITS SIX GLOBAL COMMISSIONS. ITS 1000 STAFF MEMBERS IN OFFICES AROUND THE WORLD ARE WORKING ON SOME 500 PROJECTS. IT HAS GENERATED ENVIRONMENTAL CONVENTIONS, GLOBAL STANDARDS, SCIENTIFIC KNOWLEDGE AND INNOVATIVE LEADERSHIP. IT IS TRULY A WORLD FORCE FOR ENVIRONMENTAL GOVERNANCE. IT'S MISSION IS TO INFLUENCE, ENCOURAGE, AND ASSIST SOCIETIES THROUGH OUT THE WORLD TO CONSERVE THE INTEGRITY AND DIVERSITY OF NATURE AND TO ENSURE THAT ANY USE OF NATURAL RESOURCES IS EQUITABLE AND ECOLOGICALLY SUSTAINABLE.

CHAPTER 29.

PHOTOGRAPHY :-IS THE PROCESS OF PRODUCING IMAGES ON A SURFACE SENSITIVE TO LIGHT. THE NAME PHOTOGRAPHY WAS DERIVED BY SIR JOHN HERSCHEL IN 1839. IT COMES FROM THE GREEK WORDS FOR LIGHT AND WRITING. THERE ARE TWO DISTINCT SCIENTIFIC PROCESSES THAT COMBINE TO MAKE PHOTOGRAPHY POSSIBLE; THE FIRST PROCESS IS OPTICAL AND THE SECOND PROCESS IS CHEMICAL. PHOTOGRAPHY IS DONE IN MANY AREAS INCLUDING, ARCHITECTURAL, SOCIAL RECORD, TRAVEL, UNUSUAL VENTURES, WAR ETC.

PROCESSES, STYLES AND MOVEMENTS IN PHOTOGRAPHY ARE IN THE FOLLOWING AREAS :-

AMATEUR PHOTOGRAPHERS.
PROFESSIONAL PHOTOGRAPHERS.
ARCHITECTURAL PHOTOGRAPHY.
ARTISTS AND PHOTOGRAPHY.
CAMERA WORK.
DEVELOPMENT OF FILMS.
FILM.
IMPRESSIONISM.
LANDSCAPE PHOTOGRAPHY.
SIGHTSEEING PHOTOGRAPHY.
AMONG OTHERS.

VALLEY :-IS LOW LANDS BETWEEN HILLS AND MOUNTAINS.

HILLS :-IS A MOUND OF LAND.

MOUNTAIN :-IS A VERY HIGH RISE OF LAND ON EARTH'S SURFACE.

FURNITURE :-IS CHAIRS, BEDS ETC, THAT IS ANYTHING THAT IS USED FOR DIFFERENT PURPOSES IN A ROOM.
SOME TYPES OF FURNITURE ARE :-
INDOORS.
OUTDOORS.
GARDEN.
LIVING ROOM.
GENERAL USE.
BEDROOM.
DINNING ROOM.
KITCHEN.
OFFICE.
CHILDREN'S FURNITURE.
AMONG OTHERS.

THE NAMES OF SOME FURNITURE ARE :-
SOFA.
TABLE.
CHAIR.
BED SET.
OTTOMAN.
BENCH.
SOUND SYSTEM.
RECLINER.
DESK.
DESK STAND.
MASSAGE CHAIR.
COMPUTER DESK.
CLOCK.
SHELF.
FANS.
COUCH.
AMONG MANY NUMBERLESS OTHERS.

SOME POPULAR COMPUTER COMPANIES THAT SUPPLY COMPUTERS, PERIPHERAL UNITS [HARDWARE], SOFTWARE,

NETWORKS, SEMI – CONDUCTORS, AND OTHER COMPUTER – RELATED DATA, SERVICES AND PRODUCTS ARE :-

AOL.
ADOBE SYSTEMS.
APPLE.
BMC SOFTWARE.
3 COM.
CISCO SYSTEMS.
COMPAQ.
COMPUTER ASSOCIATES.
COMPU WARE.
DELL.
EDS.
EMC.
IBM.
INTC.
IOM.
LUCENT TECHNOLOGIES.
MICROSOFT.
ORACLE.
SUN MICROSYSTEMS.
XEROX.
AMONG OTHERS.

IMPORTANT STATISTICS :-

YOUR CHANCES OF BEING INVOLVED IN AN AIRCRAFT ACCIDENT ARE ABOUT ONE IN ELEVEN MILLION; ON THE OTHER HAND, YOUR CHANCES OF BEING INJURED IN AN AUTOMOBILE ACCIDENT ARE ONE IN FIVE THOUSAND.

AUTO RACING :-
THERE ARE MANY DIFFERENT KINDS OF MOTOR SPORTS - RACING SUCH AS :-
CART.
STOCK CAR.
DRAG RACING.
FORMULA 1.
NASCAR RACING.
INDIANPOLIS 500.

AVIATION MOTOR SPORTS.
FUNNY CARS MOTOR SPORTS.
TRUCK AND MONSTER TRUCKS MOTOR SPORTS.
MOTORCYCLE OFFROAD MOTOR SPORTS.
MOTOR CYCLE ONROAD MOTOR SPORTS.
OFFROAD CARS MOTOR SPORTS.
OPEN WHEEL CARS MOTOR SPORTS.
SPRINT CARS MOTOR SPORTS.
STOCK CARS MOTOR SPORTS.
SNOWMOBILE MOTOR SPORTS.
DIRT TRACK AUTO RACING.
BOAT MOTOR SPORTS.

THE NAMES OF SOME SANCTIONING BODIES AND CLUBS
FOR MOTOR SPORTS RACING ARE :-
FEDERATION INTERNATIONALE DE L'AUTOMOBILE.
FIA GLOBAL GT ENDURANCE SERIES.
INTERNATIONAL MOTOR CONTEST ASSOCIATION.
INDEPENDENT DIRT RACERS ASSOCIATION.
INDY RACING LEAGUE.
NASCAR.
PRO SPORTS CAR.
SCORE INTERNATIONAL.
VINTAGE AUTO RACING ASSOCIATION.

THE NAMES OF SOME RACE TEAMS AND SPONSORS
ARE :-
BUDWEISER.
FERRARI AND SHELL F1.
FIRESTONE INDY RACING.
GM GOODWRENCH MOTORSPORTS.
MOTOROLA / PAC WEST RACING.
VALVOLINE RACING.
TEAM RAHAL.
TOYOTA MOTORSPORTS.
TEXACO RACING.
WESTERN AUTO'S NASCAR.
WESTERN AUTO'S NHRA.
AMONG OTHERS.

SOME MOTOR SPORTS PUBLICATIONS ARE :-

AUTO RACING ANALYSIS.
CAR AND DRIVER.
CYBER CYCLE.
CYCLE NEWS.
DRAG NEWS.
INDY CAR RACING.
MOTORCYCLE WORLD.
SNOW RIDER.
U.S.A TODAY AUTO RACING.
AMONG OTHERS.

PROBATE AND ESTATE PLANNING :-

PROBATE :-IS TO ESTABLISH THE VALIDITY OF SUCH ACTION AS A WILL.
ESTATE :-IS ONE'S POSSESSIONS; A PIECE OF LAND WITH A RESIDENCE.
WILL :-IS A LEGAL DOCUMENT DISPOSING OF ONE'S PROPERTY AFTER DEATH.
TRUST :-IS TO HAVE YOUR PROPERTY PUT IN CARE OF ANOTHER.

OVER 60 % OF PEOPLE IN THE WORLD DO NOT CURRENTLY HAVE A WILL OR TRUST. IT IS IMPORTANT TO UNDERSTAND THAT NOT UNDERTAKING ESTATE PLANNING NOW, DURING YOUR LIFE TIME IN TERMS OF LEAVING A WILL AND OR TRUST WILL INEVITABLE LEAVE YOUR FAMILY AND RELATIVES WITH THE RESPONSIBILITY OF FINANCIAL AND TAX CONSEQUENCES IN THE FUTURE. IT IS ALWAYS BEST IN THE INTEREST OF ALL CONCERNED TO HAVE A GOOD AND PROPER WILL IN PLACE. LEARN WHAT HAPPENS IF A PERSON DIES WITHOUT A WILL. KNOW THE LEGAL REQUIREMENTS FOR A VALID WILL; UNDERSTAND ABOUT CHANGING, REVOKING AND CONTESTING WILLS. LEARN ABOUT TRUSTS, LEARN THE MEANING OF TRUSTS AND HOW THEY WORK; KNOW THE ADVANTAGES AND DISADVANTAGES OF TRUSTS. TRANSFERRING OF PROPERTY, LEARN ABOUT JOINT TENANCY, FIND OUT ABOUT PUTTING YOUR PROPERTY IN JOINT TENANCY WITH YOUR CHILDREN. LEARN ABOUT WAYS TO DEAL WITH PROBATE.

RELATED AGRICULTURAL TOPICS. AGRICULTURE:-IS FARMING; USING THE LAND TO RAISE CROPS AND ANIMALS. RELATED TOPICS TO THE SUCCESS OF AGRICULTURAL FARMING, ARE AS FOLLOWS :-

FARM LOAN PROGRAMS.
MARKETING ASSISTANCE.
OUTREACH PROGRAM.
PRICE SUPPORT.
RISK MANAGEMENT.
DATA AND STATISTICS.
WEATHER AND CLIMATE.
LIVESTOCK PROMOTIONS.
ENERGY PROGRAM.
DISASTER ASSISTANCE.
CROP INSURANCE.
COOPERATIVES.
CONSERVATION.
BIOTECHNOLOGY.
AQUACULTURE.
ANIMAL HEALTH – VETERINARIAN SUPPORT.
AMONG OTHERS.

IT IS IMPORTANT FOR AGRICULTURE TO BE A STRIVING BUSINESS, FOR LAWS AND REGULATIONS – FARM BILLS TO HAVE FUNDAMENTAL INTENTS IN PLACE TO SUPPORT AND COMPLEMENT EXISTING PROGRAMS ENHANCING THE STEWARDSHIP OF THE NATURAL RESOURCES OF WORKING AGRICULTURAL LANDS. SOME SUBJECTS OF INTEREST WOULD BE :-

BIOTECHNOLOGY.
COMMODITY REPORTS.
INSPECTIONS.
DRAINAGE AND IRRIGATION.
POWER SUPPLY.
FOOD PROGRAM POLICIES.
FOOD DISTRIBUTION SYSTEM.
RISK MANAGEMENT.
DEVELOPMENTAL PROGRAMS.
SPECIFICATIONS AND STANDARDS.
TECHNICAL SERVICES.
TELECOMMUNICATION.

WATER AND ENVIRONMENT.
TRADE POLICIES.
ADMINISTRATIVE PROCEDURES.
AMONG OTHERS.

FOOD AND NUTRITION :-THIS IS A VITAL AREA OF ANY NATION; IF IT IS TO HAVE A STRONG AND VIBRANT PEOPLE GEARED FOR DEVELOPMENT AND IMPROVEMENT OF THE COUNTRY; FOR THE BENEFIT OF ALL THE PEOPLE. THERE ARE TO BE FOOD SAFETY AND SECURITY GUIDELINES FOR CONSUMERS; WITH DIETARY ASSESSMENT TOOLS IN PLACE TO PROVIDE DIET QUALITY, RELATED NUTRITION INFORMATION; HAVING INTEGRATED FOOD PROGRAMS IN RESEARCH AND EDUCATION ACTIVITIES THAT WILL REACH AND BENEFIT THE HEALTH AND WELFARE OF ALL THE PEOPLE FOR THE GOOD OF ALL.

AREAS LOOKED INTO AS FAR AS QUALITY FOOD AND NUTRITION ARE CONCERNED OUGHT TO BE SUCH AS :-
FOOD QUALITY.
FOOD SAFETY.
FOOD TECHNOLOGY.
LABELING AND CORRECT INFORMATION GIVEN ABOUT RESPECTIVE PRODUCTS.
KNOWLEDGE OF THE FOOD GUIDE PYRAMID.
DIETARY GUIDELINES.
FOOD ASSISTANCE PROGRAMS.
FOOD BORNE ILLNESSES.
NUTRITION EDUCATION.
AMONG OTHERS.

AS FAR AS NATURAL RESOURCES AND ENVIRONMENT ARE TO BE LOOKED AT, IT IS IMPORTANT THAT CONSERVATION AND PROTECTION PROGRAMS ALWAYS BE IN PLACE TO KEEP THE DESIRED BALANCE OF THE ECOLOGY OF THE WORLD ORDER. CONSERVING AND PROTECTING SOIL, WATER AND WILDLIFE SHOULD BE THE COMMITMENT OF EVERYONE. AREAS OF INTEREST TO THE ENVIRONMENT WOULD BE SUCH AS :-
AIR.
WATER.
SOIL.

BIO DIVERSITY.
DISASTER ASSISTANCE.
ENERGY.
FIRE SAFETY AND EDUCATION.
FOREST AND FOREST PRODUCTS.
CULTIVATING A HEALTHY AND BALANCED ENVIRONMENT.
LAND CONSERVATION.
RESEARCH.
WILDLIFE.
PROTECTION OF ENDANGERED SPECIES.
AMONG OTHERS.

MARKETING AND TRADE :-BALANCE OF PAYMENT IS OF GREAT CONCERN TO ALL NATIONS. EXPORTS AND IMPORTS ARE AREAS OF GREAT CONCERN AND SHOULD ALWAYS BE ADDRESSED IN THE BEST WAY POSSIBLE TO AVOID A COUNTRY BEING IN UNNECESSARY DEBT PROBLEMS; WHICH ALWAYS HAVE FAR REACHING CONSEQUENCES TO THE ECONOMY AS A WHOLE. RELATED AREAS OF MARKETING AND TRADE WOULD COVER :-
IMPORTATION.
EXPORTATION.
MARKETING ANALYSIS.
MARKET AND TRADE NEWS AND DEVELOPMENTS.
PRICING AS A RESULT OF SUPPLY AND DEMAND.
REPORTS AND STATISTICS.
TRADE POLICY AGREEMENTS.
COMMUNITY TREATIES.
CONTRACTUAL AGREEMENTS.
TRANSPORTATION.
AMONG OTHERS.

HOSPITALS :-IS A PLACE OF MEDICAL CARE FOR SICK AND INJURED.
HOSPITALS CAN BE OF VARYING TYPES SUCH AS TEACHING HOSPITALS, COMMERCIAL HOSPITALS, AND NON PROFIT COMMUNITY HOSPITAL. KNOWING WHETHER A HOSPITAL OFFERS SPECIALIZED OR GENERAL CARE, WHETHER THE HOSPITAL IS A TEACHING HOSPITAL, OR WHETHER IT IS NON – PROFIT OR FOR – PROFIT INSTITUTION

CAN MEAN DIFFERENT LEVELS OF CARE AND ATTENTION AND ULTIMATELY COMPETENCY.

TEACHING HOSPITALS ARE ALMOST ALWAYS AFFILIATED WITH A MEDICAL SCHOOL. THIS CAN MEAN ACCESS TO HIGHLY SKILLED SPECIALISTS WHO TEACH AT THE SCHOOL AND ARE THE BEST AND BRIGHTEST IN THEIR SPECIALTY. IT COULD ALSO MEAN YOU WILL BE TREATED BY STUDENT DOCTORS WITH VARYING LEVELS OF EXPERIENCE AND TALENT.

COMMERCIAL HOSPITALS ARE PROFIT MAKING BUSINESSES. ALSO KNOWN AS, PROPRIETARY HOSPITALS AND ARE USUALLY OWNED BY CORPORATIONS OR MEDICAL PARTNERSHIPS. SOME CONSUMER ADVOCATES HAVE ARGUED THAT THESE TYPES OF BUSINESS MODELS ARE MORE PRONE TO SUBSTANDARD CARE SUCH AS PREMATURE DISCHARGE OF A PATIENT OR THE FAILURE TO ORDER COSTLY MEDICAL TESTING.

NON – PROFIT COMMUNITY HOSPITALS OPERATE UNDER A RELIGIOUS AFFILIATION OR UNDER SOME OTHER FORM OF VOLUNTARY SUPPORT. ULTIMATELY RESPONSIBILITY FOR THE CARE GIVEN RESTS WITH A BOARD OF TRUSTEES, WHO USUALLY ARE APPOINTED AND SERVE WITHOUT PAY.

IN THE MEDICAL FIELD, WORKING IN HOSPITALS AND OTHER INSTITUTIONS, CLINICS ETC ; ARE MEDICAL WORKERS IN VARIOUS FIELDS OF OCCUPATION SUCH AS DOCTORS IN DIFFERENT FIELDS AND EXPERTISE SUCH AS GENERAL MEDICINE, SURGEONS, THERE ARE SUPERVISORS, REGISTERED NURSES AND LICENSED PRACTICAL NURSES, NURSING ASSISTANTS, X-RAY TECHNICIANS, THERAPISTS ETC. OF ALL THE PEOPLE INVOLVED IN PATIENT CARE, THE NURSING ASSISTANT AND THE L.P.N ARE THE ONES WHO HAVE MORE OVERALL CONTACT WITH PATIENTS OR RESIDENTS AS FAR AS PERSONAL CARE AND ATTENTION ARE CONCERNED. EXAMPLES OF THE FUNCTIONS OF THE NURSING ASSISTANT ARE AS FOLLOWS :-

[a] FUNCTION AS A NURSING ASSISTANT WITHIN THE LEGAL AND ETHNICAL STANDARDS DESCRIBED IN THEIR JOB DESCRIPTION.

[b] DEMONSTRATE THE USE OF EFFECTIVE COMMUNICATION SKILLS AS AN INTEGRAL FUNCTION OF THE NURSING ASSISTANT.

[c] APPLY THE BASIC PRINCIPLES OF INFECTION CONTROL.

[d] DEMONSTRATE THE APPLICATION OF CONCEPTS OF BASIC EMERGENCY PROCEDURES.

[e] DESCRIBE THE BEHAVIOR INVOLVED IN PROVIDING / MAINTAINING THE RIGHTS OF THE RESIDENT / PATIENT.

[f] DEMONSTRATE BEHAVIOR AND SKILLS THAT PROMOTE THE RESIDENT'S INDEPENDENCE.

[g] DESCRIBE THE RESPONSIBILITIES OF THE NURSING ASSISTANT IN ADDRESSING THE NUTRITIONAL NEEDS OF THE RESIDENT.

[h] OBSERVE FOR ABNORMAL SIGNS AND SYMPTOMS OF COMMON DISEASES AND CONDITIONS.

[I] PROVIDE FOR A SAFE, CLEAN ENVIRONMENT.

[j] DEMONSTRATE BASIC NURSING SKILLS NEEDED TO MEET THE RESIDENT'S HEALTH AND PERSONAL CARE REQUIREMENTS.

[k] PROVIDE CARE TO THE PATIENT WHEN DEATH IS IMMINENT.

[l] DEMONSTRATE CARE AND SKILLS THAT INCORPORATE PRINCIPLES OF RESTORATIVE CARE UNDER THE DIRECTION OF THE L.P.N,. R.N, THERAPISTS, DOCTORS, AND ALL CONCERNED WITH THE SUPERVISION OF NURSING ASSISTANTS IN THE CARRYING OUT OF THEIR DUTIES EFFICIENTLY AND EFFECTIVELY.

AS CAN BE SEEN FROM THE ABOVE DESCRIPTION OF A NURSING ASSISTANT'S RESPONSIBILITY, IT IS IMPORTANT FOR THE WHOLE MEDICAL TEAM INCLUDING THOSE AT THE BOTTOM OF THE LADDER TO HAVE A GOOD, PROPER AND EFFECTIVE WORKING RELATIONSHIP IN THE BEST INTEREST OF THE RESIDENT / PATIENT AND ALL CONCERNED.

LICENSED PRACTICAL NURSE [LPN], CARE FOR THE SICK, INJURED AND DISABLED UNDER THE DIRECTION

OF PHYSICIANS AND REGISTERED NURSES [RN]. MOST LPN'S PROVIDE BASIC BEDSIDE CARE, THEY TAKE VITAL SIGNS; TEMPERATURE, BLOOD   PRESSURE, PULSE, AND RESPIRATION. LPN'S OBSERVE PATIENTS AND REPORT ADVERSE REACTIONS TO MEDICATIONS OR TREATMENTS. THEY COLLECT SAMPLES FOR TESTING, PERFORM ROUTINE LABORATORY TESTS, FEED PATIENTS, AND RECORD FOOD AND FLUID INTAKE AND OUTPUT. EXPERIENCED NURSING ASSISTANTS ASSIST THE LPN'S IN WAYS THEY CAN AND ARE SUPERVISED IN CARRYING OUT THEIR FUNCTIONS. LPN'S REPORT TO RN'S, WHO IN TURN GO TO THE CHARGE NURSE AND THEN TO THE SUPERVISOR AND THEN ON TO THE DOCTORS AND OTHERS INVOLVED IN MAKING DECISIONS CONCERNING PATIENTS AND THEIR TREATMENT AND CARE. IN SHORT, THE MEDICAL PROFESSION INVOLVES COOPERATIVE EFFICIENT AND EFFECTIVE TEAMWORK.

AS IS THE CASE IN THE MEDICAL FIELD, THERE ARE PERSONNEL IN MANY AREAS OF PATIENT CARE SUCH AS PHYSICAL THERAPIST, OCCUPATIONAL THERAPIST, X – RAY TECHNICIANS; AMONG OTHERS.

X – RAY TECHNICIANS AS AN EXAMPLE OF THE MEDICAL TEAM, PLAY AN IMPORTANT ROLE AS A MEMBER OF THE HEALTH CARE TEAM IN A PHYSICIAN'S CLINIC OR HOSPITAL. FOR THE SUCCESS OF THE X –RAY TECHNICIAN, HE OR SHE HAS TO BE VERSED IN LEARNING AND PRACTICING THE FUNDAMENTALS OF ANATOMY AND PHYSIOLOGY.

THERE ARE NUMEROUS MEDICAL PROGRAMS THAT PEOPLE PURSUE IN THE MEDICAL FIELD SUCH AS :-
DENTAL.
HOSPITAL UNIT COORDINATOR.
HOSPITAL ADMINISTRATOR.
MASSAGE THERAPY.
MEDICAL BILLING AND CODING.
PHARMACY TECHNICIAN.
SURGICAL TECHNOLOGIST.
AMONG OTHERS.

CAMERA :-IS A DEVICE FOR TAKING PHOTOGRAPHS. THE CAMERA IS USED TO PROJECT AN IMAGE. THE IDEA OF THE CAMERA IS SAID TO DATE BACK TO ARISTOTLE THOUGH THE CAMERA WAS NOT INVENTED UNTIL 1267 AD. A TINKER NAMED BACON WAS THE FIRST TO BRING TO LIFE ARISTOTLE'S IDEAS. THERE ARE MANY DIFFERENT VIEWS AS TO WHY BACON INVENTED THE CAMERA, THE MOST RECOGNIZED BY SCHOLARS IS THE FIRST USE OF THE CAMERA WAS TO OBSERVE THE SUN AND SOLAR ECLIPSES. IT WAS NOT UNTIL THE RENAISSANCE THE CAMERA WAS USED FOR PICTURES AND ART. AFTER THE RENAISSANCE THE CAMERA'S POPULARITY GREW. PEOPLE DISCOVERED THAT THE CAMERA COULD ALSO BE USED IN ART. DEVINCI WAS ONE OF THE FIRST TO USE THE CAMERA TO HELP HIM DRAW AND UNDERSTAND LIGHT PATTERNS.

SOCIAL EVENTS :-IS THE COMING–GATHERING TOGETHER OF PEOPLE FOR A COMMON CAUSE SUCH AS A PARTY. SOME SOCIAL EVENTS – OCCASIONS ARE :-
PRIVATE ORGANIZATION PARTY.
OPEN HOUSE PARTY.
PRIVATE HOUSE PARTY.
PERSONAL PARTY.
APARTMENT PARTY.
WEEKENDS PARTY.
HOUSE SENIOR BANQUETS.
FUND RAISING.
WEDDINGS.
BIRTHDAYS.
BACHELOR PARTY.
BABY SHOWERS.
ANNIVERSARY.
SOCIAL LUNCHEON.
DINNER CONFERENCE.
TOURS.
BRUNCH.
COCKTAIL.
AMONG OTHERS.

CIRCUS :-IS A SHOW WITH ACROBATS, ANIMALS, CLOWNS ETC.

CIRCUSES ARE CITED BY THE RELEVANT AUTHORITY ON NUMEROUS OCCASIONS FOR FAILING TO PROVIDE PROPER VETERINARY CARE, PROPER HANDLING, NUTRITIOUS FOOD AND CLEAN WATER, SHELTER FROM THE ELEMENTS, AND EXERCISE AND FOR INADEQUATE AND UNSAFE ENCLOSURES. INCIDENTS OCCUR FROM TIME TO TIME THAT DEMAND CLOSE ATTENTION TO CIRCUS SHOW BUSINESS AS A WHOLE

THE PETA ORGANIZATION LOOKS INTO THE WELFARE OF ANIMALS INVOLVED IN CIRCUS ACTS. EXAMPLES OF SOME INCIDENTS OR ACCIDENTS THAT HAVE TAKEN PLACE IN THE CIRCUS ENVIRONMENT OVER THE YEARS AND WHICH HAVE BEEN DOCUMENTED ARE AS FOLLOWS :-

MARCH 2, 2003 : A 9,000 POUND AFRICAN ELEPHANT PERFORMING WITH JORDAN WORLD CIRCUS AT THE SHRINE CIRCUS IN MUSKEGON, MICHIGAN; ESCAPED FROM A TENT SHORTLY BEFORE A PERFORMANCE AND WAS RECAPTURED 15 MINUTES LATER IN A BUSY DOWNTOWN AREA.

FEBRUARY 11, 2000 :THE ALBUQUERQUE JOURNAL REPORTED THAT A CIRCUS LEASED AN ELEPHANT NAMED MISTY FROM HAWTHORN CORPORATION FOR A SHRINE CIRCUS. ON JULY 24, 1983, MISTY KILLED A HANDLER IN RIVERSIDE COUNTY, CALIFORNIA. IN A 1996 INCIDENT, MISTY ATTACKED HER TRAINER WHILE GIVING RIDES TO CHILDREN.

OCTOBER 7, 1999 : THE USDA CITED A CIRCUS FOR USING A POORLY VENTILATED TRAILER TO TRANSPORT A CAMEL.

DECEMBER 9, 1998 : THE USDA ALSO CITED A CIRCUS FOR GIVING DIRTY DRINKING WATER TO THE ANIMALS, HAVING FILTHY ENCLOSURES, AND FAILURE TO MAINTAIN CORRALS AND THE TRANSPORT TRAILER.

JULY 29, 1998 : THE USDA CITED A CIRCUS FOR FAILURE TO PROVIDE ADEQUATE VETERINARY CARE. A TIGER NAMED

DUTCHESS WAS LIMPING, AND THERE WAS NO VETERINARY EVALUATION OR TREATMENT PLAN.

JULY 1998 : A CIRCUS WAS FINED $ 2,475 FOR IMPROPER HANDLING AND VETERINARY CARE.

MARCH 16, 1996 : A CIRCUS WAS CITED FOR IMPROPER FOOD STORAGE.

IN FEBRUARY, 1980 : THE MONTE CARLO INTERNATIONAL CIRCUS WAS CHARGED WITH FAILING TO CONFORM WITH MINIMUM CAGE REQUIREMENTS.

IN 1983, THE DIRECTOR OF CIRCUS STARTIME, LATER CIRCUS SANTOS WAS FOUND GUILTY OF FAILING TO CONFORM WITH CAGING REGULATIONS, AND A BEAR TRAINER FROM EDGLEY'S WORLD'S GREATEST CIRCUS SPECTACULAR PLEADED GUILTY TO A CHARGE OF OVERCROWDING.

IN JUNE 1992, IN ST. MARYS [NSW] A TIGER BELONGING TO ROBINSON'S FAMILY CIRCUS WAS SHOT DEAD AFTER ESCAPING FROM ITS CAGE.

CIRCUSES ARE SCHEDULED FOR SHOWS AROUND THE WORLD FOR LENGTHY PERIOD OF TIMES; SOMETIMES AS MUCH AS A YEAR IN ADVANCE. EXAMPLES OF SCHEDULED CIRCUSES ARE AS FOLLOWS.

THE CARSON AND BARNES CIRCUS IN DUE TO SHOW IN ONTARIO, CA. IN MAY, 2004. IT IS ALSO DUE TO PERFORM IN OAKLAND, CA. IN JUNE, 2004 AS WELL AS NUMEROUS OTHER SCHEDULED DATES IN VARIOUS CITIES.

CIRCUS ROYALE IS DUE TO BE IN FENNIMORE W.I. AT INDUSTRIAL PARK IN AUGUST 2004.

RINGLING BROS. AND BARNUM AND BAILEY CIRCUS IS DUE TO BE IN SEVERAL AREAS DURING 2004; FOR EXAMPLE THEY WILL BE IN HARTFORD CT. AT THE HARTFORD CIVIC CENTER IN MAY. ALSO THEY WILL BE IN ROCHESTER N.Y.

AT THE BLUE CROSS ARENA IN MAY. THEY ARE ALSO SCHEDULED FOR LITTLE ROCK, AR. AT THE ALLTEL ARENA IN JUNE; AMONG MANY OTHER PLACES.

ROYAL HANNEFORD CIRCUS WILL BE IN W. VALLEY CITY UT. AT THE EAST CENTER IN MAY, 2004.

A CIRCUS IS ALSO DUE IN BIRMINGHAM AL IN ALABAMA STATE FAIRGROUNDS IN SEPTEMBER, 2004.

A CIRCUS WILL BE IN DETROIT, MI AT THE CHENE PARK IN SEPTEMBER, 2004.

ALSO A CIRCUS IS SCHEDULED FOR CHICAGO, IL AT WASHINGTON PARK IN SEPTEMBER, 2004.

THERE WILL BE A CIRCUS SHOW IN ST. LOUIS, MO AT THE NORTHLAND SHOPPING CENTER IN OCTOBER, 2004.

A CIRCUS SHOW IS PLANNED FOR JACKSON, MS AT THE TBA IN NOVEMBER, 2004.

MAGICIAN :-ONE WHO DOES MAGIC; USING OF SLEIGHT OF HANDS, CHARMS, SPELLS ETC. MAGICIANS ARE VERY SKILLFUL AND DO PERFORMANCES IN AREAS SUCH AS :-
ACROBATS.
AERIALISTS.
ARTISTS.
BALLOON MODELLERS.
CABARET.
CARICATURE ARTISTS.
CLOWNS.
COMEDIANS.
COMPERES.
CONTORTIONISTS.
DANCERS.
DRUMMERS.
FACE PAINTERS.
FAKIR.
FAMILY ENTERTAINMENT.
FIRE PERFORMERS.

HAND BALANCERS.
HOT AIR BALLOONS.
INSTALLATIONS.
JUGGLERS.
LOOKALIKES.
MIME ARTISTS.
PUPPETEERS.
ROBOTS.
ROPE WALKERS.
SIGN PERFORMERS.
STATUES.
STILT WALKERS.
STREET SHOWS.
SWORD SWALLOWERS.
TRAMPOLINE SHOWS.
UNICYCLISTS.

MAGICIANS AND OTHER PERFORMERS ARE ENGAGED IN SHOWS AT PLACES OF RELAXATION GET – TOGETHER ENTERTAINMENT AND CELEBRATION SUCH AS :-
ANNIVERSARY.
BACHELOR PARTIES.
BACHELORETTE – SPINSTER PARTIES.
BAPTISM.
BABY SHOWER.
SCHOOL PROM / ORDINATION.
BAR MITZVAH.
CONFIRMATION.
CORPORATE EVENTS.
ENGAGEMENT.
WEDDING.
SCHOOL REUNION.
PICNIC.
FAMILY REUNION.
BIRTHDAYS.
AMONG OTHERS.

HARRY HOUDINI :-THE MOST FAMOUS MAGICIAN OF ALL TIME. HOUDINI'S ACTUAL NAME WAS EHRICH WEISS. HE WAS BORN ON MARCH 24 TH 1874. AT EIGHT YEARS OF AGE HE WORKED SELLING NEWSPAPER AND AS A SHOE SHINE

437

BOY. AT AGE 13 HE MOVED TO NEW YORK CITY; WHERE HE TURNED TO MAGIC. HE WAS VERY ATHLETIC AND WON AWARDS IN SWIMMING AND TRACK. HE WOULD USE HIS ATHLETIC AND SWIMMING TALENTS TO GREAT USE IN HIS FUTURE AS AN ESCAPE ARTIST. IN NEW YORK FOR A PERIOD OF TIME HE WORKED AS A MESSENGER, AND AS A CUTTER IN A GARMENT CENTER SHOP; A TIE FACTORY. INFLUENCED BY THE INTERNATIONALLY KNOWN ROBERT HOUDIN, HE CHANGED HIS NAME TO HOUDINI. HOUDINI'S FIRST MAGIC SHOWS CONSISTED OF CARD TRICKS AND OTHER SIMPLE MAGIC. HOUDINI EARLY ON CALLED HIMSELF THE KING OF CARDS. HOUDINI SOON EXPERIENCED WHAT IT WAS LIKE TO EXPERIMENT WITH HANDCUFFS AND STARTED USING THEM IN ACTS. HIS YOUNGER BROTHER THEO WERE INVOLVED WITH HIM IN HIS ACTS. THEY PERFORMED AT AMUSEMENT PARKS, BEER HALLS, DIME MUSEUMS, AND AT FAIRS. IN 1894, HOUDINI MET WILHELMINA BEATRICE RAHNER, WHO WAS A SINGER AND DANCER. AFTER TWO WEEKS THEY WERE MARRIED AND SHE BECAME HIS ACTING PARTNER. HE TRAVELED THROUGHOUT THE U.S.A AND THE WORLD FOR THE NEXT 33 YEARS; HE ESCAPED FROM HANDCUFFS, LEG IRONS, STRAIGHT JACKETS, JAILS AND PRISON CELLS, A MAIL POUCH, PACKING CRATES, A GIANT PAPER BAG, WITHOUT TEARING THE BAG, A GIANT FOOTBALL, AN IRON BOILER, MILK CANS, COFFINS, AND THE FAMOUS WATER TORTURE CELL. HE PURCHASED A BUILDING IN NEW YORK CITY ON 113 TH STREET THAT WAS TO BECOME HIS RESIDENCE FOR THE REST OF HIS LIFE. HOUDINI INVENTED THE UNDERWATER PACKING BOX ESCAPE AS A FABULOUS PUBLICITY STUNT THAT WAS COPIED BY MANY OTHERS; HE WAS THE FIRST PERSON TO DO THE STRAIGHT JACKET ESCAPE AS WELL. HE WAS THE FIRST PERSON TO FLY A PLANE IN AUSTRALIA. HOUDINI HAD GREAT STRENGTH AND AGILITY THAT HE USED TO HELP HIM IN HIS MAGICAL STUNTS. HOUDINI ALSO SPENT MANY HOURS STUDYING, PRACTICING, AND CONDITIONING. IN 1916 HOUDINI BEGAN A FILM CAREER; HE MADE FIVE MAJOR FILMS UP UNTIL 1923. HIS FILMS INCLUDED THE MASTER MYSTERY, THE GRIM GAME, TERROR ISLAND, AND THE MAN FROM BEYOND. HOUDINI WAS GIVEN ONE OF THE FIRST STARS ON THE HOLLYWOOD WALK OF FAME FOR HIS CONTRIBUTION TO

THE FILM INDUSTRY. HE ALSO WROTE MANY BOOKS AND ARTICLES THROUGHOUT HIS CAREER; SUCH AS THE RIGHT WAY TO DO WRONG, A MAGICIAN AMONG THE SPIRITS. HOUDINI DID NOT DIE IN AN ESCAPE OR FAIL IN SOME FINAL ESCAPE AS MANY BELIEVE; HE DIED ON OCTOBER 31, 1926 DUE TO AN ILLNESS HE SUFFERED.

TIDAL WAVES :-ALSO CALLED TSUNAMIS. THE WORD TSUNAMI COMES FROM THE JAPANESE TSU [HARBOR] AND NAMI [WAVE]. IT IS APPROPRIATE NAMING BECAUSE SOME 80 % OF ALL TIDAL WAVES OCCUR IN THE PACIFIC OCEAN AND JAPAN HAS SUFFERED MANY, SOME COMING FROM AS FAR AWAY AS SOUTH AMERICA. TSUNAMIS ARE OFTEN INCORRECTLY CALLED TIDAL WAVES, BUT TIDES HAVE NOTHING TO DO WITH THEM [THOUGH THE DAMAGE MAY BE WORSE IF A TSUNAMI HITS AT HIGH TIDE]. A TSUNAMI IS A WAVE TRAIN, OR SERIES OF WAVES, GENERATED IN A BODY OF WATER BY AN IMPULSIVE DISTURBANCE THAT VERTICALLY DISPLACES THE WATER COLUMN. EARTHQUAKES, LANDSLIDES, VOLCANIC ERUPTIONS, EXPLOSIONS, AND EVEN THE IMPACT OF COSMIC BODIES, SUCH AS METEORITES, CAN GENERATE TSUNAMIS. TSUNAMIS CAN SAVAGELY ATTACK COASTLINES, CAUSING DEVASTATING PROPERTY DAMAGE AND LOSS OF LIFE. TSUNAMIS CAN BE GENERATED WHEN THE SEA FLOOR ABRUPTLY DEFORMS AND VERTICALLY DISPLACES THE OVERLYING WATER. AROUND THE MARGINS OF THE PACIFIC OCEAN, FOR EXAMPLE, DENSER OCEANIC PLATES SLIP UNDER CONTINENTAL PLATES IN A PROCESS KNOWN AS SUBDUCTION. THIS CAUSES EARTHQUAKES WHICH ARE PARTICULARLY EFFECTIVE IN GENERATING TSUNAMIS.

ONE OF THE WORST TSUNAMI DISASTERS ENGULFED WHOLE VILLAGES ALONG SANRIKU, JAPAN, IN 1896. A WAVE MORE THAN 7 STORIES TALL DROWNED SOME 26,000 PEOPLE. MORE THAN 30,000 PEOPLE DIED IN JAVA FROM A TSUNAMI CAUSE BY A VOLCANIC ERUPTION. SOME RECENT TSUNAMIS WHICH OCCURRED ARE :-

[a] 1946 : AN EARTHQUAKE IN THE ALEUTIAN ISLANDS SENT A TSUNAMI TO HAWAII, KILLING 159 PEOPLE HOWEVER ONLY 5 DIED IN ALASKA.

[b] 1964 : AN ALASKAN EARTHQUAKE TRIGGERED A TSUNAMI UP TO 20 FEET TALL THAT KILLED 11 PEOPLE AS FAR AWAY AS CRESCENT CITY, CALIFORNIA AND CAUSED MORE THAN 120 DEATHS IN ALL.

[c] 1983 : 104 PEOPLE IN WESTERN JAPAN WERE KILLED BY TSUNAMI WHICH SPAWNED FROM A NEARBY EARTHQUAKE.

[d] ON JULY 17 TH, 1998 : A PAPUA NEW GUINEA TSUNAMI KILLED ROUGHLY 3,000 PEOPLE. A 7.1 MAGNITUDE EARTHQUAKE 15 MILES OFF SHORE WAS FOLLOWED WITHIN 10 MINUTES BY A WAVE SOME 40 FEET TALL. THE VILLAGES OF AROP AND WARAPU WERE DESTROYED.

ABOUT 8,000 YEARS AGO, A MASSIVE UNDERSEA LANDSLIDE OFF THE COAST OF NORWAY SENT A 30 – FT. WALL OF WATER - A TSUNAMI WAVE - BARRELING INTO THE NORTHERN COAST OF EUROPE; IF THIS WERE TO OCCUR TODAY, AS SCIENTISTS SAY IT COULD, ALMOST ANYWHERE IN THE WORLD, IT WOULD COST BILLIONS IF NOT TENS OF BILLIONS OF DOLLARS TO REPAIR THE DAMAGE TO COASTAL CITIES, AND THE COST IN LIVES COULD BE VERY, VERY HIGH.

TSUNAMIS ARE TIDAL WAVES FORMED BY UNDERWATER EARTHQUAKES. THEY ARE PRODUCED BY UNDER SEA EARTHQUAKE OR MUCH LESS FREQUENTLY BY VOLCANIC ERUPTIONS – METEOR IMPACTS - OR UNDERWATER LANDSLIDES; THERE ARE THOSE THAT CAN EXCEED 400 MILES PER HOUR IN THE DEEP OCEAN. IN DEEP WATER A TSUNAMI MAY ONLY BE INCHES OR A FEW FEET HIGH; BUT WHEN IT REACHES A SHORELINE, IT CAN ENERGIZE ITSELF INTO A WALL OF WATER THAT CAN BE A MILE HIGH.

SINCE 1990, THERE HAVE BEEN 82 TSUNAMIS ON RECORD, OUT OF WHICH 10 HAVE CLAIMED MORE THAN

AT LEAST 4 LIVES. THE MOST RECENT, AND BY FAR THE MOST DESTRUCTIVE, WAS ON JULY 17, 1998 THE ONE THAT STRUCK PAPUA NEW GUINEA'S NORTH COAST.

UP UNTIL NOW, THE AVERAGE TSUNAMIS PER DECADE HAS BEEN 57. THE INCREASE IN TSUNAMIS REPORTED IN DUE TO THE IMPROVED GLOBAL COMMUNICATIONS; THE HIGH DEATH ARE PARTLY DUE TO INCREASES IN COASTAL POPULATIONS.

AVALANCHE :-GREAT FALL OF ROCK, SNOW ETC, DOWN A HILL. AVALANCHES ARE POWERFUL AND UNPREDICTABLE DISASTERS, A DANGER TO ALL WINTER RECREATIONISTS IN MOUNTAINOUS TERRAIN. THESE CATASTROPHIC EVENTS RARELY HAPPEN BY ACCIDENT; MOST FATAL AVALANCHES ARE TRIGGERED BY PEOPLE; AND THEIR PRESENCE IS USUALLY BY CHOICE, NOT CHANCE, AS THEY SEEK OUT THE BEST SNOW FOR THEIR WINTER SPORTS. WARM ATLANTIC AIR AND COLD ARCTIC AIR HAVE ALTERNATELY INVADED THE ALPS DURING WINTER; THIS CAUSES THE TOP LAYERS OF SNOW TO THAW AND FREEZE. THEY BECOME MORE COMPACT AND HEAVY THAN THE POWDERY SNOW INSULATED BENEATH. THIS ARRANGEMENT OF HEAVY LAYERS ON LIGHTER LAYERS IS UNSTABLE AND MAKE AVALANCHES EASIER TO TRIGGER. EVERY YEAR OVER ONE MILLION AVALANCHES HAPPEN. SLAB AVALANCHES ARE THE MOST DANGEROUS KIND, WHERE A WHOLE LAYER SLIPS OFF A MOUNTAINSIDE AS ONE THUNDERING MASS. THIS CAN BE TRIGGERED BY THE WIND OR A LOUD NOISE AND PULL IN SURROUNDING ROCKS AND STONES. SOMETIMES THE START OF THE AVALANCHE IS MARKED BY THE SOUND OF SNOW CRACKING, SOMETHING LIKE A GUNSHOT. AVALANCHES OF LOOSER, POWDERY SNOW START AT A SINGLE POINT AND EVENTUALLY EXPAND OUT TO FORM AN UPSIDE DOWN V – SHAPE. SOME SKI PATROLS USE LARGE GUNS TO SHOOT EXPLOSIVES AT THE MOUNTAINS WHEN FRESH SNOW HAS FALLEN; THIS CAUSES SMALL AVALANCHES WHEN NO ONE ELSE IS AROUND, AND MAKES THE RISK OF A BIG AVALANCHE LESS LIKELY. PEOPLE ALSO CONTROL AVALANCHES BY PLANTING TREES OR BUILDING LARGE SNOW FENCES IN LIKELY STARTING

ZONES. AVALANCHES MAINLY KILL PEOPLE SKIING OUTSIDE OFFICIAL BOUNDARIES, WHERE THE SNOW BUILD UP HAS NOT BEEN CONTROLLED.

SURVIVING AN AVALANCHE :-

[a] NEVER COUNT ON YOUR ABILITY TO OUT RUN AN AVALANCHE.

[b] DO NOT PANIC, YOU NEED TO CONSERVE OXYGEN.

[c] MAKE SWIMMING MOTIONS AND TRY TO STAY ON TOP OF THE SNOW; WORK YOUR WAY TO THE SIDE OF THE FALL.

[d] AS THE SNOW SETTLES, CLEAR BREATHING SPACE WITH YOUR HANDS.

[e] IF YOU WITNESS AN AVALANCHE, MARK THE PLACE YOU LAST SAW VICTIMS.

WORLD TRADE - MOST FAVORED NATIONS :-

MOST FAVORED NATION [MFN] WAS PROVIDED FOR IN A COMMERCIAL TREATY BINDING THE SIGNATORIES TO EXTEND TRADING BENEFITS EQUAL TO THOSE ACCORDED ANY THIRD STATE. THE CLAUSE ENSURES EQUAL COMMERCIAL OPPORTUNITIES, ESPECIALLY CONCERNING IMPORT DUTIES AND FREEDOM OF INVESTMENT. GENERALLY RECIPROCAL, IN THE LATE 19 TH AND EARLY 20 TH CENTURY. UNILATERAL MFN CLAUSES WERE IMPOSED ON ASIAN NATIONS BY THE MORE POWERFUL WESTERN COUNTRIES. IN THE LATE 20 TH CENTURY, TARIFF AND TRADE AGREEMENTS WERE NEGOTIATED SIMULTANEOUSLY BY ALL INTERESTED PARTIES THROUGH THE GENERAL AGREEMENT ON TARIFF AND TRADE [GATT], WHICH ULTIMATELY RESULTED IN THE WORLD TRADE ORGANIZATION. SUCH A WIDE EXCHANGE OF CONCESSIONS IS INTENDED TO PROMOTE FREE TRADE, ALTHOUGH THERE HAS BEEN CRITICISM OF THE PRINCIPLE OF EQUAL TRADING OPPORTUNITIES ON THE GROUNDS THAT FREER TRADE BENEFITS THE ECONOMICALLY STRONGEST COUNTRIES. WORLD TRADE ORGANIZATION MEMBERS, FORMERLY GATT, RECOGNIZED IN PRINCIPLE THAT THE MFN RULE SHOULD BE RELAXED TO ACCOMMODATE THE NEEDS OF DEVELOPING COUNTRIES, AND THE UNITED NATIONS CONFERENCE ON TRADE AND DEVELOPMENT WHICH WAS ESTABLISHED IN 1964,

HAS SOUGHT TO EXTEND PREFERENTIAL TREATMENT TO THE EXPORTS OF THE DEVELOPING COUNTRIES. ANOTHER CHALLENGE TO THE MFN PRINCIPLE HAS BEEN POSED BY REGIONAL TRADING GROUPS SUCH AS THE EUROPEAN UNION, WHICH HAVE LOWERED OR ELIMINATED TARIFFS AMONG THE MEMBERS WHILE MAINTAINING TARIFF WALLS BETWEEN MEMBER NATIONS AND THE REST OF THE WORLD. IN THE 1990'S CONTINUED MFN STATUS FOR CHINA SPARKED U.S. CONTROVERSY BECAUSE OF ITS SALES OF SENSITIVE MILITARY TECHNOLOGY AND ITS USE OF PRISON LABOR, AND ITS MFN STATUS WAS ONLY MADE PERMANENT IN 2000. ALL OF THE FORMER SOVIET STATES, INCLUDING RUSSIA, WERE GRANTED MFN STATUS IN 1992.

TRADING COMPANIES :-THE NAMES OF SOME COMPANIES INVOLVED IN THE STOCK TRADING BUSINESS ESPECIALLY AS ONLINE TRADERS ARE :-
AMERITRADE.
SHAREBUILDER.
HARRIS DIRECT.
T.D.WATERHOUSE.
POWER E*TRADE.
JANUS.

AMONG OTHERS. OTHER COMPANIES INVOLVED IN STOCK AND OTHER FORMS OF TRADING ARE :-
MERRYL LYNCH.
STANLEY MORGAN DEAN WITTER.
BARONS.
BERKSHIRE HATHAWAY.
CHARLES SCHWAB.
T. ROWE PRICE.
SMITH BARNEY.
PAYNE WEBBER.
FIDELITY.
DEYFUS.
GALAXY.
VANGUARD.
RUSSELL.
TEMPLETON.
DIRECT TRADE.

TRADE. COM.
YORK SECURITIES.
AMONG OTHERS.

WORLD CYCLING CHAMPIONSHIPS :-
THE FIRST PROFESSIONAL WORLD CYCLING CHAMPIONSHIP TOOK PLACE IN 1927 AT THE NURBURGRING IN GERMANY AND WAS WON BY ALFREDO BINDA OF ITALY. THE EVENT IS A MASSED START ROAD RACE, WITH THE WINNER THE FIRST ACROSS THE LINE AT THE COMPLETION OF THE FULL RACE DISTANCE. THERE ARE ALSO WORLD CYCLING CHAMPIONSHIPS FOR TRACK CYCLING AND INDIVIDUAL TIME TRIAL DISCIPLINES, AMONG OTHERS. THE WORLD CYCLING CHAMPIONSHIP, ALONG WITH THE TOUR DE FRANCE WHICH IS AN ANNUAL EVENT THAT IS VERY POPULAR AND REALLY TESTS THE STAMINA AND ENDURANCE OF CYCLISTS; COMBINED WITH THE GIRO D'LTALIA MAKE UP THE TRIPLE CROWN OF CYCLING. SOME OF THE WORLD CYCLING CHAMPIONS WHO IS CROWNED ANNUALLY OVER THE YEARS HAVE BEEN :-
1927 - ALFREDO BINDA, ITALY.
1983 - GREG LEMOND, U.S.A.
1984 - CLAUDE CRIQUIELION, BELGIUM.
1985 - JOOP ZOETEMELK, NETHERLANDS.
1986 - MORENO ARGENTIN, ITALY.
1987 - STEPHEN ROCHE, IRELAND.
1988 - MAURIZIO FONDRIEST, ITALY.
1989 - GREG LEMOND, U.S.A.
1990 - RUDY DHAENENS, BELGIUM.
1991 - GIANNI BUGNO, ITALY.
1992 - GIANNI BUGNO, ITALY.
1993 - LANCE ARMSTRONG, U.S.A.
1994 - LUC LEBLANC, FRANCE.
1995 - ABRAHAM OLANO, SPAIN.
1996 - JOHAN MUSEEUW, BELGIUM.
1997 - LAURENT BROCHARD, FRANCE.
1998 - OSKAR CAMENZIND, SWITZERLAND.
1999 - OSCAR FREIRE, SPAIN.
2000 - ROMANS VAINSTEINS, LATIVA.
2001 - OSCAR FREIRE, SPAIN.
2002 - MARIO CIPOLLINI, ITALY.

2003 - IGOR ASTARLOA, SPAIN.

CHAPTER 30.

ART :-IS SKILLED WORK IN FIELDS SUCH AS PAINTING, SCULPTURE, MUSIC ETC. ARTS COME IN MANY FORMS; HERE ARE SOME IMPORTANT AND POPULAR ART FORMS :

TOILET MAKE UP AND USE OF BEAUTIFYING AGENTS.
PAINTING THE BODY AND COLORING THE NAILS, HAIR ETC.
ART OF HAIR DRESSING.
ART OF DRESSING.
PROPER MATCHING OF DECORATIONS AND JEWELRY.
ART OF MUSIC AND DANCING.
SINGING.
PLAYING ON MUSICAL INSTRUMENTS.
ACTING.
GOOD MANNERS AND ETIQUETTE.
KNOWLEDGE OF DIFFERENT LANGUAGES AND DIALECTS.
ART OF CRITICISM OF DRAMAS.
ANALYSIS OF STORIES.
ART OF COOKING.
PREPARATION OF DIFFERENT BEVERAGES, SWEET AND ACID DRINKS, CHUTNEYS ETC.
SEWING AND NEEDLE WORK.
SKILL IN DIFFERENT SPORTS.
PUZZLES AND THEIR SOLUTIONS.
ART OF ENTERTAINING.
ART OF MAGIC, CREATING ILLUSIONS.

MIMICRY OR IMITATION OF VOICE OR SOUND.
PAINTING IN COLORS.
FLORAL DECORATIONS.
CLAY MOLDING, MAKING FIGURES AND IMAGES.
MAKING BIRDS, FLOWERS ETC. OF THREAD YARN.
PREPARATION OF EARRINGS, CHAINS ETC. OF SHELL, IVORY ETC.
ART OF TRAINING PET ANIMALS SUCH AS PARROTS, DOGS ETC.
GARDENING AND AGRICULTURE.
PREPARATION OF PERFUMERY.
MAKING FURNITURE FROM CANES AND REEDS.
WOOD ENGRAVING.
CARPENTRY.
KNOWLEDGE OF MACHINERY.
CONSTRUCTION OF BUILDING, ARCHITECTURE.
FLOOR DECORATIONS AND COLORED STONES.
KNOWLEDGE OF METALS.
KNOWLEDGE OF GEMS AND JEWELS.
COLORING PRECIOUS STONES.
ART OF WAR.
KNOWLEDGE OF CODE WORDS.
SIGNALS FOR CONVEYING MESSAGES.
AMONG OTHERS.

CRAFTS :-IS SKILL, ART IN WORKMAN OR CRAFTSMANSHIP. AREAS IN WHICH CRAFT WORKS ARE DONE ARE SUCH AS :-

ANGELS MAKING.
BASKETS.
ANIMALS SUCH AS BEAR, RABBIT ETC.
HOME DÉCOR.
JEWELRY.
KITCHEN.
LAMPS AND LIGHTING.
CANDLES.
LINENS.
PAINTINGS.
CERAMICS.
PAPER PRODUCTS.

PATTERNS.
CLOTHING.
QUILTING AND SEWING.
CRAFT RESOURCES.
RUBBER STAMPING.
DOLLS.
SCRAP BOOKING.
FLORAL AND GARDEN.
GAMES.
TOYS.
WOOD ITEMS.
AMONG OTHERS.

ARTS AND CRAFTS ARE INTER – RELATED AND CLOSELY ASSOCIATED WITH EACH OTHER.

BUSINESS INDUSTRY SECTORS ARE DIVIDED INTO INDUSTRIAL CATEGORIES SUCH AS :-

[a] MANUFACTURING INDUSTRIES.
[b] RESOURCES INDUSTRIES.
[c] SERVICES INDUSTRIES.
[d] TECHNOLOGICAL INDUSTRIES.
[e] MISCELLANEOUS INDUSTRIES.

THE FOLLOWING ARE UNDER THE HEADING OF MANUFACTURING INDUSTRIES :-

AEROSPACE AND DEFENSE.
AGRICULTURE.
APPAREL.
ASSISTANCE DEVICES.
AUTOMOTIVE.
RECREATIONAL BOATS.
BUILDING PRODUCTS - WOOD AND METAL.
CHEMICALS.
COMMERCIAL PRINTING.
INFORMATION AND COMMUNICATION EQUIPMENT.
ELECTRICAL POWER EQUIPMENT.
FABRICATED METAL PRODUCTS.
FOOD.

BEVERAGES.
TOBACCO.
FOOTWEAR.
FOREST INDUSTRIES.
FURNITURE.
GIFTWARE AND CRAFTS.
HOUSEHOLD APPLIANCES.
MEDICAL DEVICES.
MICRO ELECTRONICS.
NON – METALLIC MINERAL.
PRODUCT MANUFACTURING.
OPTICAL NETWORKING.
OIL AND GAS.
PHARMACEUTICALS.
PLASTICS.
PRIMARY METALS.
RAILWAY EQUIPMENT MANUFACTURING.
RUBBER.
SHIPBUILDING AND INDUSTRIAL MARINE.
SPORTING GOODS.
TELECOMMUNICATIONS EQUIPMENT.
TEXTILES.

RESOURCE INDUSTRIES ARE SUCH AS :-

AGRICULTURE.
FISHERIES.
MINES.
METALS AND MINERALS.
FORESTRY.

SERVICE INDUSTRIES ARE SUCH AS :-

ACCOUNTING.
ADVERTISING.
ARCHITECTURAL.
COMMERCIAL.
EDUCATION AND TRAINING.
CONSTRUCTION - CONTRACTING.
CONSULTING ENGINEERING.
CUSTOMS BROKERS.

DEVELOPERS - REAL ESTATE.
DESIGN - INDUSTRIAL, GRAPHIC, INTERIOR.
ELECTRIC POWER.
ELECTRONIC COMMERCE.
ELECTRONIC MANUFACTURING.
ENVIRONMENTAL INDUSTRY.
FRANCHISING.
FREIGHT FORWARDERS.
HEALTH SERVICES.
SECURITY SERVICES.
INFORMATION SERVICES.
LANGUAGE INDUSTRIES.
LEGAL SERVICES.
LOGISTICS.
MANAGEMENT CONSULTING.
MARKETING SERVICES.
MULTIMEDIA INDUSTRY.
NON – STORE RETAIL.
OIL AND GAS.
RAILWAY SERVICES.
RETAIL TRADE.
RETAIL - INTERNET.
SOFTWARE.
TELECOMMUNICATIONS.
TOURISM.
TRADING HOUSES.
WHOLESALE.
TRANSLATION OF LANGUAGES SERVICES.
TRUCKING SERVICES.
URBAN PLANNING.
WAREHOUSE SERVICES.
WIRELESS.

TECHNOLOGICAL SECTOR – INDUSTRIES ARE SUCH AS :-

BIOTECHNOLOGY.
ADVANCED MATERIALS.
ENVIRONMENTAL INDUSTRY.
INFORMATION AND COMMUNICATION TECHNOLOGIES.
INTELLIGENT SYSTEMS.

INTELLIGENT TRANSPORTATION SYSTEM – INFORMATION AND COMMUNICATIONS.
CELESTIAL RESEARCH TECHNOLOGIES.
TERRESTRIAL RESEARCH TECHNOLOGIES.
OCEAN TECHNOLOGIES.
OPTICAL TECHNOLOGY.
MEDICAL HEALTH TECHNOLOGIES.
WIRELESS COMMUNICATIONS TECHNOLOGIES.

UNDER MISCELLANEOUS INDUSTRY SECTORS WOULD BE AREAS SUCH AS :-

ENVIRONMENTAL.
HEALTH.
AMONG OTHERS.

NOTE :-IN QUITE A FEW OF THESE SECTOR – INDUSTRIES CERTAIN ASPECTS OF THEIR BUSINESSES FALL UNDER THE DIFFERENT HEADINGS, AND AS SUCH ARE ACCOUNTED AS FALLING UNDER MORE THAN ONE TYPE OF INDUSTRY – SECTOR BRANCH. EXAMPLES OF THIS WOULD BE AGRICULTURE, HEALTH, AND ENVIRONMENTAL.

SOME OF THE WORLD'S WORST TRAIN – RAIL DISASTERS OCCURRED AS FOLLOWS :-

2004, IRAN, NEARLY 300 PEOPLE KILLED; WHEN A TRAIN DERAILED AND CAUGHT FIRE.
2002, TANZANIA, NEARLY 300 PEOPLE DIED, WHEN A PASSENGER TRAIN CARRYING MORE THAN 1200 PEOPLE LOSSES POWER AND ROLLS BACK INTO A FREIGHT TRAIN AT HIGH SPEED.
2002, EGYPT, A TRAIN CAUGHT FIRE AFTER LEAVING CAIRO FOR LUXOR, KILLING 373 PEOPLE.
1999, INDIA, AS MANY AS 285 WERE KILLED WHEN TRAINS COLLIDED HEAD ON.
1998, INDIA, 201 PASSENGERS KILLED; AFTER A TRAIN DERAILED AND WAS HIT BY ANOTHER TRAIN TRAVELLING IN THE OPPOSITE DIRECTION.
1995, INDIA, AROUND 300 PEOPLE DIED AND 400 PEOPLE GOT INJURED WHEN TWO EXPRESS TRAINS COLLIDED.

1989, RUSSIA, ABOUT 400 PEOPLE KILLED NEAR THE TOWN OF UFA, WHEN A GAS EXPLOSION ERUPTED BENEATH TWO TRAINS CARRYING MORE THAN 1200 PEOPLE.

1981, INDIA, 800 PEOPLE WERE KILLED WHEN A CYCLONE BLEW A TRAIN INTO A RIVER.

SOME SHIP DISASTERS THAT OCCURRED ARE SUCH AS THE FOLLOWING :-

1 THE PASSENGER LINER VOLTURNO SANK IN OCTOBER, 1913 IN THE NORTH ATLANTIC, BETWEEN ROTTERDAM AND HALIFAX.

2 THE BRITISH - INDIA STEAM NAVIGATION COMPANY'S PASSENGER LINER DARA SANK ON APRIL 9, 1961 IN THE PERSIAN GULF.

3 THE LUXURY LINER, PRINDENDAM, CAUGHT FIRE ON OCTOBER 4, 1980 AND HAD TO BE ABANDONED NEAR YAKUTAT, ALASKA.

4 THE ORE CARRIER, EDMUND FITZGERALD, SUBJECT OF A POPULAR BALLAD WAS LOST ON NOVEMBER 10, 1975 IN LAKE SUPERIOR.

5 THE VEHICLE / PASSENGER FERRY, ESTONIA WAS LOST ON A STORMY DAY OF SEPTEMBER 29, 1994 IN THE BALTIC SEA.

6 THE COLLISION BETWEEN THE STOCKHOLM AND THE ANDREA DORIA TOOK PLACE NEAR NANTUCKET, MASSACHUSETTS, U.S.A.

7 THE WELL KNOWN AND DOCUMENTED STORY OF THE TITANIC IS SAID TO HAVE SANK ON 15 TH APRIL, 1912 AT APPROXIMATELY 2:20 A.M.

AIRLINES ACCIDENTS - DISASTERS THAT OCCURRED IN RECENT TIMES ARE AS FOLLOWS :-

1 ON 10 TH FEBRUARY, 2004 IN SHARJAH, UNITED ARAB EMIRATES THE AIRCRAFT FOKKER F-50 OF THE KISH AIRLINES CRASHED ON APPROACH TO LAND 2 MILES SHORT OF THE RUNWAY WHILE ATTEMPTING AN EMERGENCY LANDING. THE PLANE CRASHED MIDWAY BETWEEN TWO RESIDENTIAL COMPOUNDS. OF THE 46 PEOPLE ABOARD, 43 DIED.

2 ON 17 TH JANUARY, 2004 IN PELEE ISLAND, ONTARIO, CANADA; THE AIRCRAFT CESSNA 208 B GRAND CARAVAN OF THE GEORGIA EXPRESS AIRLINE CRASHED WHEN THE PILOT REPORTED HAVING TROUBLE SHORTLY AFTER TAKING OFF FROM PELEE ISLAND. THE SINGLE ENGINE PLANE CRASHED INTO LAKE ERIE ONE THIRD OF A MILE WEST OF PELEE ISLAND IN SNOW SHOWERS AND FREEZING RAIN; OF THE 10 PEOPLE ABOARD, NO ONE SURVIVED.

3 ON 13 TH JANUARY 2004, THE AIRCRAFT YAKOVLEV YAK-40 OF THE UZBEKISTAN AIRWAYS; CRASHED WHILE ATTEMPTING TO LAND IN HEAVY FOG. THE AIRCRAFT STRUCK A STANCHION OF APPROACH LIGHTS AND FLIPPED OVER, HITTING THE OUTSIDE OF A WALL SURROUNDING THE LANDING AREA. OF THE 37 PEOPLE ON BOARD, ALL WERE FATAL.

4 ON 3 RD JANUARY 2004, THE AIRCRAFT BOEING 737-300 OF THE AIRLINE FLASH AIR, CRASHED SHORTLY AFTER TAKING OFF INTO THE RED SEA 7 MILES SOUTH OF THE AIRPORT. THERE WERE FRENCH TOURISTS ON BOARD HEADING HOME FOR THE HOLIDAYS; ALL 148 ON BOARD WERE FATALITIES.

5 ON 25 TH DECEMBER 2003, AIRCRAFT BOEING 727-200 OF THE UNION DES TRANSPORTS AERIENS DE GUINEE [UTA]. THE AIRPLANE WAS BARELY ABLE TO CLIMB AFTER TAKING OFF FROM COTONOU AIRPORT. THE LANDING GEAR STRUCK A BUILDING HOUSING ELECTRONICS, CRASHED THROUGH THE BARRIER FENCE AND BROKE UP ALONG THE SHORELINE ADJACENT TO THE AIRPORT. OF THE 161 PEOPLE INVOLVED, 140 DIED.

6 ON 26 TH OCTOBER 2003, THE AIRCRAFT FAIRCHILD HILLER FH-227 B OF THE CATA LINEA AEREA AIRLINE, CRASHED WHEN 3 MINUTES AFTER TAKING OFF FROM BUENOS AIRES AIRPORT, THE CREW REPORTED A TECHNICAL PROBLEM AND ASKED TO TURN AROUND. THEY WERE CLEARED TO LAND ON RUNWAY 17 BUT CRASHED 30 KM SOUTHWEST OF BUENOS AIRES. ALL 5 PEOPLE ON BOARD DIED.

7 ON 20 TH SEPTEMBER 2003, AIRCRAFT AEROSPATIALE AS350BA OF A-STAR TOUR AIRLINE, CRASHED; THE SIGHTSEEING HELICOPTER, HEADED FOR THE BOTTOM OF THE GRAND CANYON, HIT THE FACE OF A CLIFF AND

CRASHED IN RUGGED TERRAIN KILLING ALL ABOARD. TOURISTS WERE SUPPOSED TO BOARD A PONTOON BOAT WHEN THE ACCIDENT OCCURRED 2 / 3 OF THE WAY DOWN THE CANYON. TOTAL CASUALTIES 7.

8 ON 11 TH SEPTEMBER 2003, THE AIRCRAFT CESSANA 208 B GRAND CARAVAN OF WASAYA AIRWAYS CRASHED 10 KM NORTHWEST OF SUMMER BEAVER CANADA ONE HOUR AFTER LEAVING PICKLE LAKE AIRPORT. THUNDERSTORM ACTIVITY WAS REPORTED ALONG THE ROUTE. ALL 8 PERSONS ON BOARD DIED.

9 ON 24 TH OF AUGUST 2003, AIRCRAFT LET 420 UVP-E OF TROPICAL AIRWAYS AIRLINE CRASHED SHORTLY AFTER TAKING OFF FROM CAP HAITIEN AIRPORT IN HAITI. THE PLANE NOSE DIVED INTO A SUGARCANE FIELD AND EXPLODED. ALL 21 PEOPLE ABOARD DIED.

10 ON 20 TH OF AUGUST 2003, THE AIRCRAFT MI-8 HELICOPTER OF THE KHALATYRKA AIRLINE CRASHED. IT WAS REPORTED THAT THE HELICOPTER WAS FLYING AT A 13 – METER HEIGHT WHEN THE PILOT PULLED UP ITS NOSE IN AN ATTEMPT TO AVOID A CLOSE OBSTACLE. THE MANEUVER CAUSED THE HELICOPTER'S ROTOR BLADES TO SWING BACK, SLICING ITS TAIL, CAUSING THE CRASH. SAKHALIN GOVERNOR, IGOR FARKHUTDINOV, WAS AMONG THE CASUALTIES. THIS WAS IN RUSSIA; ALL 20 ON BOARD DIED.

11 ON 23 TH OF JULY 2003, AIRCRAFT BELL 206 B – HELICOPTER OF AIRLINE JACK HARTER HELICOPTERS COLLIDED WITH TERRAIN WHILE MANEUVERING IN THE WAIALEALE CRATER, KAUAI, HAWAII. THE HELICOPTER IMPACTED STEEP UPSLOPING TERRAIN ON THE NORTHWESTERN INSIDE CRATER WALL AND WAS DESTROYED. IT WAS BECAUSE OF LOST OF ENGINE POWER. ALL 5 PERSONS ON BOARD DIED.

12 ON 19 TH JULY 2003, AIRCRAFT SWEARINGEN SA-226T METRO 11 OF THE AIRLINE RYAN BLAKE AIR CHARTER, CRASHED INTO THE EASTERN SLOPES OF MOUNT KENYA IN KENYA AT AN ALTITUDE OF 16,355 FEET AS IT ATTEMPTED TO FLY AROUND LENANA PEAK AND LAND IN SAMBURU NATIONAL PARK. 10 AMERICAN TOURISTS AND 2 PILOTS WERE KILLED WHEN THE PLANE HIT THE MOUNTAIN 450 FEET BELOW THE SNOW COVERED PEAK

AND DISINTEGRATED UPON IMPACT. POOR VISIBILITY MAY HAVE BEEN A FACTOR. ALL ON BOARD DIED.

13 ON 13 TH OF JULY 2003, AIRCRAFT LET 410UVP-E OF THE RUIBAN AND DURAN COMPANIA AEREA AIRLINE IN VENEZUELA CRASHED ATOP A HILL IN CHORRO DEL INDIO NATIONAL PARK DURING DESCENT TO SAN CRISTOBAL. OF THE 10 PEOPLE ON BOARD, 4 DIED.

14 ON 8 TH JULY 2003, AIRCRAFT BOEING 737 200 C OF THE AIRLINE SUDAN AIRWAYS CRASHED AFTER THE CREW REPORTED TECHNICAL DIFFICULTIES 10 MINUTES AFTER TAKING OFF FROM PORT SUDAN AIRPORT IN SUDAN. THE PLANE CRASHED INTO A HILLSIDE, 3 MILES FROM THE AIRPORT AS THE CREW TRIED TO RETURN AND MAKE EMERGENCY LANDING. A THREE – YEAR OLD BOY WAS THE ONLY SURVIVOR. 116 OF THE 117 PERISHED.

15 ON 22 ND OF JUNE 2003, THE AIRCRAFT CANADAIR CRJ-100 ER OF THE BRIT AIR AIRLINE IN FRANCE CRASHED ONTO A ROAD AND CAUGHT FIRE 1 KM FROM BREST-GUIPAVAS AIRPORT IN FRANCE'S BRITTANY REGION, KILLING THE PILOT AND INJURING 3 OTHERS. THERE WERE THUNDERSTORMS IN THE AREA WITH 800 METERS VISIBILITY AT THE TIME THE ACCIDENT TOOK PLACE. OF THE 24 PEOPLE ON BOARD, ONLY THE PILOT WAS KILLED.

16 ON 15 TH OF JUNE 2003, AIRCRAFT MCDONNELL DOUGLAS 369 D [HELICOPTER] OF THE PARADISE TOUR HELICOPTERS, IMPACTED A LAVA FIELD ON THE PULAMA PALI IN THE VOLCANOES NATIONAL PARK, VOLCANO HAWAII. ALL 4 PERSONS ON BOARD DIED.

17 ON 6 TH OF JUNE 2003, AIRCRAFT PIPER PA-31-350 NAVAJO CHIEFTAIN OF THE AIRLINE CHARTER – AIR ADVENTURES NEW ZEALAND LTD; CRASHED SHORT OF THE RUNWAY IN FOG WHILE ON APPROACH TO CHRISTCHURCH AIRPORT IN NEW ZEALAND. THE PLANE CRASHED 2 KM FROM THE AIRPORT, HITTING A FARM HEDGE AND SLIDING ACROSS A PADDOCK BEFORE SMASHING INTO A ROW OF TREES. OF THE 10 PEOPLE ON BOARD, 8 DIED.

18 ON 28 TH OF MAY 2003, AIRCRAFT CESSNA 185 OF MCKINLEY AIR SERVICE – AIR TAXI AIRLINE; WAS DESTROYED DURING A COLLISION WITH A SNOW – COVERED GLACIAL TERRAIN FOLLOWING A LOSS OF CONTROL DURING

CRUISE FLIGHT, ABOUT 40 MILES NORTH – NORTHWEST OF TALKEETNA, ALASKA. ALL 4 PERSONS ON BOARD DIED.

19 ON 26 TH MAY 2003, AIRCRAFT YAKOVLEV 42 D OF THE UKRANIAN – MEDITERRANEAN AIRLINES IN TURKEY STRUCK THE SIDE OF A STEEP MOUNTAIN IN HEAVY FOG ON ITS THIRD ATTEMPT TO LAND AT TRABZON TO REFUEL. THE PILOT REPORTED NOT BEING ABLE TO SEE THE RUNWAY ON THE FIRST TWO ATTEMPTS. THE AIRCRAFT CHARTER WAS CARRYING SPANISH PEACEKEEPING FORCES BACK TO ZARAGOZA. ALL 75 PEOPLE ON BOARD DIED.

20 ON 8 TH MAY 2003, AIRCRAFT LLLYUSHIN 11-76 OF AIRLINE UKRAINIAN CARGO AIRLINES - CONGOLESE ARMY CHARTER, A LARGE NUMBER OF MILITARY PERSONNEL AND THEIR FAMILY MEMBERS WERE SUCKED OUT OF THE PLANE AFTER THE AIRCRAFT'S BACK RAMP ACCIDENTALLY DROPPED OPEN IN FLIGHT. THE RAMP OPENED AS THE PRESSURE SYSTEM BROKE DOWN. THE CREW MANAGED TO CONTROL THE PLANE AND TURN IT AROUND AND LAND AT KINSHASA AIRPORT CONGO, FOLLOWING THE ACCIDENT, WHICH TOOK PLACE 45 MINUTES INTO THE FLIGHT. THERE IS A WIDE DISCREPANCY IN THE NUMBER KILLED RANGING FROM 0 TO 250.

21 ON 27 OF MARCH 2003, AIRCRAFT DE HAVILLAND CANADA DHC-6 TWIN OTTER, OF THE AIRLINE PT AIR REGIONAL; INDONESIA, CRASHED INTO A 7,000 FEET MOUNTAIN MOMENTS AFTER TAKING OFF. KILLING 4 OF THE 16 PERSONS ON BOARD.

22 ON 6 TH OF MARCH 2003, AIRCRAFT BOEING 737-200, OF THE AIRLINE AIR ALGERIE OF ALGERIA, HAD A MISHAP WHEN THE STARBOARD ENGINE CAUGHT FIRE AND FAILED WHILE THE PLANE WAS ATTEMPTING TO TAKE OF. THE AIRCRAFT CONTINUED 2,000 FEET PAST THE END OF THE RUNWAY AND CRASHED KILLING 102 OF THE 103 PERSONS ON BOARD.

23 ON 20 TH OF FEBRUARY 2003, AIRCRAFT FOKKER F-27 FRIENDSHIP 200 OF THE MILITARY – PAKISTAN AIR FORCE AIRLINE; CRASHED INTO A MOUNTAINSIDE IN A REMOTE REGION NEAR THE TOWN OF KOHAT, ABOUT 250 KM NORTHWEST OF ISLAMABAD PAKISTAN. AMONG THOSE KILLED WAS AIR FORCE CHIEF MUSHAF ALI MIR. ALL 17 PERSONS ON BOARD DIED.

24 ON 19 TH OF FEBRUARY 2003, AIRCRAFT LLYUSHIN 11-76 MD OF THE MILITARY AIRLINE ISLAMIC REVOLUTION'S GUARD CORPS, CRASHED INTO A 11,500 FEET MOUNTAIN IN POOR WEATHER, ABOUT 20 MILES FROM ITS DESTINATION OF KERMAN, IRAN. BESIDES THE 18 CREW MEMBERS, THE VICTIMS INCLUDED IRAN'S REVOLUTIONARY GUARD. ALL 276 PEOPLE ON BOARD DIED.

25 ON 16 TH OF FEBRUARY 2003, THE AIRCRAFT CESSNA 421, OF THE AIRLINE AIR TAXI, WAS DESTROYED DURING A COLLISION WITH TREES AND TERRAIN IN FERGUSON, KENTUCKY, WHILE ON AN INSTRUMENT APPROACH TO SOMERSET – PULASKI COUNTY AIRPORT.

26 ON 24 TH OF JANUARY 2003, AIRCRAFT GRUMMAN G-159 GULFSTREAM 1 OF AFRICAN COMMUTER SERVICES AIRLINE, KENYA ENCOUNTERED TROUBLE WHEN THE PLANE FAILED TO GAIN ALTITUDE DURING TAKEOFF, IT HIT POWER LINES AND CRASHED INVERTED INTO A HOUSE. KENYAN LABOR MINISTER, AHMED KHALIF AND THE TWO PILOTS WERE KILLED. THE PLANE WAS GROSSLY OVERLOADED. THE PLANE WHICH WEIGHED 16 TONS, WAS TAKING OFF FROM AN AIRSTRIP DESIGNED FOR AIRCRAFT WEIGHING LESS THAN 5.7 TONS. FATALITIES WAS 3 OF 13 PERSONS.

27 ON 9 TH OF JANUARY 2003, AIRCRAFT FOKKER F –28 FELLOWSHIP 1000, OF TANS AIRLINES PERU; DISAPPEARED OFF RADAR AFTER TRANSMITTING A DISTRESS CALL, THREE MINUTES FROM LANDING AT THE JUNGLE CITY OF CHACHAPOYAS. ALL 46 PEOPLE ON BOARD DIED.

28 ON 8 TH OF JANUARY 2003, AIRCRAFT BEECHCRAFT 1900 D OF AIRLINE AIR MIDWEST [MESA AIR GROUP] [US AIRWAYS EXPRESS], ENCOUNTERED PROBLEMS AND THE COMMUTER PLANE WAS NOT ABLE TO MAINTAIN ALTITUDE AFTER TAKING OFF FROM CHARLOTTE – DOUGLAS INTERNATIONAL AIRPORT IN NORTH CAROLINA, AND CRASHED INTO THE SIDE OF A HANGER AND BURST INTO FLAMES. THE WEATHER WAS CLEAR, COLD AND WINDY, WITH GREATER THAN 10 MILES VISIBILITY AT THE TIME OF THE ACCIDENT. ALL 21 PERSONS WERE CASUALTIES.

29 ON 8 TH OF JANUARY 2003, AIRCRAFT BRITISH AEROSPACE AVRO RJ – 100 OF THE TURKISH AIRLINES [THY] TURKEY, CRASHED 130 FEET SHORT OF THE RUNWAY THRESHOLD WHILE ATTEMPTING TO LAND IN HEAVY FOG;

VISIBILITY WAS LESS THAN 200 FEET. 75 OF THE 80 PEOPLE ON BOARD DIED.

ANTIQUES :-IS THINGS SUCH AS FURNITURE, ART, COINS AND CURRENCY, COLLECTIBLES, ESTATE ITEMS ETC. FROM A FORMER PERIOD; EARLIER TIMES. ALONG WITH THESE ITEMS MENTIONED ARE OTHERS SUCH AS :-
PORCELAIN.
POTTERY.
GLASS.
BOOKS.
CLOCKS.
JEWELRY.
LIGHTING DEVICES.
PHOTOGRAPHY.
SILVERWARE.
TEXTILES – SEWING.
WATCHES.
PAINTINGS.
INSTRUMENTS.
BOTTLES.
CARDS – VARYING TYPES.
SCULPTURE.
STAMPS.
TOOLS.
DOLLS.
DRAWINGS.
MUSIC.
AMONG OTHERS.

THERE ARE DEALERS AND COLLECTORS ALL OVER THE WORLD WHO ARE ENGAGED IN THIS MANNER OF BUSINESS. ANTIQUES ARE A VERY LUCRATIVE BUSINESS; WITH PEOPLE ALWAYS VYING FOR THE COLLECTION OF RARE AND HISTORIC ITEMS. THERE ARE REGULAR ANTIQUE SHOWS WHERE APPRAISERS DETERMINE THE VALUE OF ITEMS BASED ON SEVERAL VARYING FACTORS SUCH AS HOW ANCIENT THE ITEM IS, HOW UNIQUE AN ITEM HAPPENS TO BE ETC.

A LIST OF SOME DEALERS IN THE WORLD ARE AS FOLLOWS :-

ABIDING FINE ART IN VANCOUVER.
ACCURATE ANTIQUES AND APPRAISALS IN SPOKANE.
ANGLO – MANCHURIA TRADING LTD IN SHANGHAI.
ANTIQUES AND OLD WORLD CHARMS IN ELIZABETH.
ANTIQUES PROVENCAL IN JERSEY CITY.
ARCHITECTURAL GARDEN ANTIQUES IN NORTH HOLLYWOOD.
B4 IN NEW YORK.
CLARY AND CO. ANTIQUES LTD. IN NEW YORK.
D AND S ANTIQUES IN VIENNA.
FRENCH TREASURES IN YARDLEY.
INTERIEURS DE FRANCE IN LEVALLOIS – PERRET.
JACKSON HILL ANTIQUES IN PENSACOLA.
JOHN J GREDLER WORKS OF ART INC. IN NEW YORK.
JUNE AND TONY STONE IN LONDON.
JUST ART POTTERY IN PEORIA.

GIFTS :IS A GIVING OF PRESENTS. THERE ARE GIFTS OF GREAT SELECTION FOR EVERY TASTE, AGE, OCCASION, AND BUDGET. GIFTS ARE CONSTANTLY COMING OUT IN THE MARKET WITH MORE AND MORE CREATIVE IDEAS. GIFTS ARE GIVEN FOR A GREAT NUMBER OF OCCASIONS SUCH AS :-

HOLIDAYS.
BABY SHOWER.
WEDDING.
ANNIVERSARY.
BIRTHDAY.
MOTHER'S DAY.
FATHER'S DAY.
GRADUATION.
ROMANTIC.
ENGAGEMENT.
BUSINESS.
GARDEN.
SPORTS.
COMPETITION OF VARIOUS SORTS.

A POPULAR WAY OF GIVING A GIFT, IS TO GIVE A GIFT CERTIFICATE; SO THAT THE RECIPIENT CAN BE ABLE TO OBTAIN A GIFT OF HIS OR HER NEED AND CHOOSING.

BLOOD :-IS THE RED FLUID IN THE ARTERIES AND VEINS. BLOOD IS THE RIVER OF LIFE THAT FLOWS THROUGH THE HUMAN BODY. WE CANNOT LIVE WITHOUT IT. THE HEART PUMPS BLOOD TO ALL OUR BODY CELLS, SUPPLYING THEM WITH OXYGEN AND FOOD. AT THE SAME TIME BLOOD CARRIES CARBON DIOXIDE AND OTHER WASTE PRODUCTS FROM THE CELLS. BLOOD ALSO FIGHTS INFECTION, KEEP OUR TEMPERATURE STEADY, AND CARRIES CHEMICALS THAT REGULATE MANY BODY FUNCTIONS. BLOOD EVEN HAS SUBSTANCES THAT PLUG BROKEN BLOOD VESSELS AND SO PREVENT US FROM BLEEDING TO DEATH. THE AMOUNT OF BLOOD IN YOUR BODY DEPENDS ON YOUR SIZE AND THE ALTITUDE AT WHICH YOU LIVE. AN ADULT WHO WEIGHS 160 POUNDS OR 73 KILOGRAMS HAS ABOUT 5 QUARTS OR 4.7 LITERS OF BLOOD. AN 80 POUND OR 36 KILOGRAM CHILD HAS ABOUT HALF THAT AMOUNT, AND AN 8 POUND OR 3.6 KILOGRAM INFANT HAS ABOUT 8.5 OUNCES OR 250 MILLILITERS.

THE COMPOSITION OF THE BLOOD IS MADE UP OF :-
PLASMA.
RED BLOOD CELLS.
WHITE BLOOD CELLS.
PLATELETS.

MEDICAL USES OF BLOOD ARE FOR :-
BLOOD TRANSFUSIONS.
BLOOD TESTS.
SCREENING TESTS.
DIAGNOSTIC TESTS.

BLOOD DISORDERS ARE :-
ANEMIA.
WHITE – CELL.
ABNORMALITIES.
BLEEDING DISORDERS.

INFECTIONS.

THE SIGNIFICANCE OF BLOOD GROUPS; BLOOD GROUP CLASSIFICATIONS HAVE EXTREME IMPORTANCE IN CERTAIN MEDICAL PROCEDURES, INFORMATION ABOUT BLOOD GROUPS HAS ALSO BEEN USED IN LAW AND ANTHROPOLOGY.

TYPES OF BLOOD GROUPS ARE :-
A.
B.
AB.
O.
YOU CAN ALSO HAVE POSITIVE OR NEGATIVE GROUP TYPES.

DISK :-IS A THIN, FLAT, CIRCULAR PLATE FOR STORING DATA; IT'S A ROUND PLATE ON WHICH DATA CAN BE ENCODED. THERE ARE TWO BASIC TYPES OF DISKS; MAGNETIC DISKS AND OPTICAL DISKS. ON MAGNETIC DISKS, DATA IS ENCODED AS MICROSCOPIC MAGNETIZED NEEDLES ON THE DISK'S SURFACE. YOU CAN RECORD AND ERASE DATA ON A MAGNETIC DISK ANY NUMBER OF TIMES, JUST AS YOU CAN WITH A CASSETTE TAPE. MAGNETIC DISKS COME IN A NUMBER OF DIFFERENT FORMS.
[a] FLOPPY DISK : A TYPICAL 5 ¼ - INCH FLOPPY DISK CAN HOLD 360 K OR 1.2 MB [MEGABYTES]. 3 ½ - INCH FLOPPIES NORMALLY STORE 720 K, 1.2 MB OR 1.44 MB OF DATA.
[b] HARD DISK :-HARD DISK CAN STORE ANYWHERE FROM 20 MB TO MORE THAN 10 GB. HARD DISK ARE ALSO FROM 10 TO 100 TIMES FASTER THAN FLOPPY DISKS.
[c] REMOVABLE CARTRIDGE :-REMOVABLE CARTRIDGES ARE HARD DISKS ENCASED IN A METAL OR PLASTIC CARTRIDGE, SO YOU CAN REMOVE THEM JUST LIKE A FLOPPY DISK. REMOVABLE CARTRIDGES
ARE VERY FAST, THOUGH USUALLY NOT AS FAST AS FIXED HARD DISKS.

OPTICAL DISKS RECORD DATA BY BURNING MICROSCOPIC HOLES IN THE SURFACE OF THE DISK WITH A LASER.

TO READ THE DISK, ANOTHER LASER BEAM SHINES ON THE DISK AND DETECTS THE HOLES BY CHANGES IN THE REFLECTION PATTERN.

OPTICAL DISKS COME IN THREE BASIC FORMS :-
[a] CD – ROM -MOST OPTICAL DISKS ARE READ ONLY. WHEN YOU PURCHASE THEM, THEY ARE ALREADY FILLED WITH DATA. YOU CAN READ THE DATA FROM A CD – ROM, BUT YOU CANNOT MODIFY, DELETE, OR WRITE NEW DATA.
[b] WORM -STANDS FOR WRITE ONCE, READ MANY. WORM DISKS CAN BE WRITTEN ON ONCE AND THEN READ ANY NUMBER OF TIMES; HOWEVER, YOU NEED A SPECIAL WORM DISK DRIVE TO WRITE DATA ONTO A WORM DISK.
[c] ERASABLE OPTICAL [EO] :-EO DISKS CAN BE READ TO, WRITTEN TO, AND ERASED JUST LIKE MAGNETIC DISKS.

THE MACHINE THAT SPINS A DISK IS CALLED A DISK DRIVE. WITHIN EACH DISK DRIVE IS ONE OR MORE HEADS [OFTEN CALLED READ / WRITE HEADS] THAT ACTUALLY READ AND WRITE DATA.

ACCESSING DATA FROM A DISK IS NOT AS FAST AS ACCESSING DATA FROM MAIN MEMORY, BUT DISKS ARE MUCH CHEAPER; AND UNLIKE RAM, DISKS HOLD ON TO DATA EVEN WHEN THE COMPUTER IS TURNED OFF. CONSEQUENTLY, DISKS ARE THE STORAGE MEDIUM OF CHOICE FOR MOST TYPES OF DATA. ANOTHER STORAGE MEDIUM IS MAGNETIC TAPE. BUT TAPES ARE USED ONLY FOR BACKUP AND ARCHIVING BECAUSE THEY ARE SEQUENTIAL ACCESS DEVICES [TO ACCESS DATA IN THE MIDDLE OF A TAPE, THE TAPE DRIVE MUST PASS THROUGH ALL THE PRECEDING DATA].
A NEW DISK, CALLED A BLANK DISK, HAS NO DATA ON IT. BEFORE YOU CAN STORE DATA ON A BLANK DISK, HOWEVER, YOU MUST FORMAT IT.

FOOD AND DRUG ADMINISTRATION [FDA] :-

THE ORIGINS OF THE FDA CAN BE TRACED BACK TO 1862 WHEN PRESIDENT LINCOLN APPOINTED CHEMIST CHARLES M WETHERILL TO HEAD THE CHEMICAL DIVISION IN THE THEN NEW U.S DEPARTMENT OF AGRICULTURE. DURING THE COURSE OF TIME, VARIOUS SELECTED FOOD, DRUG, COSMETIC AND DEVICE LAWS WERE IMPLEMENTED. SOME OF THESE LAWS ARE :-

NAME OF LAW	DATE IN FORCE.
VACCINE ACT	FEBRUARY, 27 TH 1813
DRUG IMPORTATION ACT	JUNE, 26 TH 1848.
TEA IMPORTATION ACT	MARCH, 3 RD 1883.
FOOD AND DRUG IMPORTATION ACT	AUGUST, 30 TH 1890.
FOOD IMPORTATION ACT	MARCH, 1 ST 1899.
BIOLOGICS CONTROL ACT	JULY, 1 ST 1902.
PURE FOOD AND DRUGS ACT	JUNE, 30 TH 1906.
MEAT INSPECTION ACT	JUNE, 30 TH 1906.
CHILD PROTECTION ACT	NOVEMBER, 3 RD 1966
FOOD AND DRUG MODERNIZATION ACT	NOVEMBER, 21 ST 1997

THE FDA USES PRINCIPLES AND TECHNOLOGIES TO REDUCE DELAYS AND COSTS RELATED TO PRODUCT APPROVALS, AND WILL OVERHAUL AND UPDATE HOW MEDICAL PRODUCTS ARE MANUFACTURED; BETTER STRATEGIES FOR FOOD IMPORTS AND FOOD SAFETY ALSO WILL BE IMPLEMENTED, ALONG WITH CIVIL CRIMINAL ENFORCEMENT RELATED TO SALES OF ILLEGAL DRUGS ONLINE AND TO FALSE AND MISLEADING PRODUCT CLAIMS. THE FDA IS THE GOVERNING BODY THAT APPROVES PRODUCTS. THEY LOOK TO HAVE CLARIFYING STANDARDS AND EXPECTATIONS FOR PRODUCTS FOR CONSIDERATION FOR SUITABILITY OF CONSUMER USE.

WINTER STORMS -
WINTER STORMS ARE AMONG NATURE'S MOST IMPRESSIVE WEATHER SPECTACLES. THEIR COMBINATION OF HEAVY SNOW, FREEZING RAIN, AND HIGH WINDS CAN TOTALLY DISRUPT MODERN CIVILIZATION; CLOSING DOWN AIRPORTS AND ROADS, CREATING POWER OUTAGES, AND

DOWNING TELEPHONE LINES. WINTER STORMS REMIND US OF HOW VULNERABLE WE ARE TO NATURE'S AWESOME POWERS.

WINTER STORMS DERIVE THEIR ENERGY FROM THE CLASH OF TWO AIR MASSES OF SUBSTANTIALLY DIFFERENT TEMPERATURE AND MOISTURE LEVEL. AN AIR MASS IS A LARGE [1,000 TO 5,000 KM IN DIAMETER] REGION ABOVE THE EARTH THAT HAS A FAIRLY UNIFORM TEMPERATURE AND MOISTURE LEVEL. IN NORTH AMERICA, WINTER STORMS TYPICALLY FORM WHEN AN AIR MASS OF COLD, DRY CANADIAN AIR MOVES SOUTH AND INTERACTS WITH A WARM, MOIST AIR MASS MOVING NORTH FROM THE GULF OF MEXICO. THE POINT WHERE THESE TWO AIR MASSES MEET IS CALLED A FRONT. IF COLD AIR IS ADVANCING AND PUSHING AWAY THE WARM AIR, THE FRONT IS CALLED A COLD FRONT. IF THE WARM AIR IS ADVANCING, IT RIDES UP OVER THE COLD AIR MASS [SINCE WARM AIR IS LESS DENSE THAN COLD AIR], AND THE FRONT IS CALLED A WARM FRONT. IF NEITHER AIR MASS IS ADVANCING, THE FRONT IS CALLED A STATIONARY FRONT.

IT IS ALONG A STATIONARY FRONT THAT A WINTER STORM WILL TYPICALLY BEGIN. AN AREA OF LOWER PRESSURE WILL DEVELOP ALONG THE FRONT AS THE ATMOSPHERE TRIES TO EVEN OUT THE PRESSURE DIFFERENCE. THIS CREATES WIND, WHICH ALWAYS BLOWS FROM HIGH PRESSURE TOWARDS LOW PRESSURE, IN AN ATTEMPT TO MOVE ENOUGH AIR TO EVEN OUT THE PRESSURE DIFFERENCE.

AS THE AIR MOVES TOWARD THE CENTER OF THE LOW PRESSURE AREA, IT HAS NOWHERE TO GO BUT UP INTO THE COLDER REGIONS OF THE UPPER ATMOSPHERE. THIS CAUSES THE WATER VAPOR IN THE AIR TO CONDENSE. TO THE NORTH OF THE STORM, WHERE THE TEMPERATURES ARE COLDER, THIS CONDENSED WATER FALLS AS SNOW. TO THE SOUTH, IF THE TEMPERATURES ARE WARM ENOUGH, IT CAN FALL AS HEAVY RAIN IN THUNDERSTORMS.

OVER NORTH AMERICA, STRONG WINDS BLOWING FROM WEST TO EAST USUALLY MOVE A WINTER STORM

QUICKLY ACROSS THE CONTINENT. THAT'S WHY A WINTER STORM RARELY LASTS MORE THAN A DAY IN ONE AREA. ONE EXCEPTION TO THIS RULE OCCURS DOWNWIND OF MAJOR BODIES OF WATER LIKE THE GREAT LAKES. IF A STRONG, COLD WIND BLOWS OVER A GREAT LENGTH OF UNFROZEN WATER, THE AIR CAN ACQUIRE A SUBSTANTIAL AMOUNT OF MOISTURE; THIS MOISTURE TURNS INTO HEAVY SNOW WHEN IT REACHES LAND. THESE LAKE – EFFECT SNOWSTORMS CAN LAST FOR MANY DAYS AND DUMP HUGE AMOUNTS OF SNOW.

HEAT WAVES :-
HEAT CAN KILL BY PUSHING THE HUMAN BODY BEYOND ITS LIMITS. UNDER NORMAL CONDITIONS, THE BODY'S INTERNAL THERMOSTAT PRODUCES PERSPIRATION THAT EVAPORATES AND COOLS THE BODY. HOWEVER, IN EXTREME HEAT AND HIGH HUMIDITY, EVAPORATION IS SLOWED AND THE BODY MUST WORK EXTRA HARD TO MAINTAIN A NORMAL TEMPERATURE. ELDERLY PEOPLE, YOUNG CHILDREN, AND THOSE WHO ARE SICK OR OVERWEIGHT ARE MORE LIKELY TO BECOME VICTIMS OF EXTREME HEAT. BECAUSE MEN SWEAT MORE THAN WOMEN THEY ARE MORE SUSCEPTIBLE TO HEAT ILLNESS BECAUSE THEY BECOME MORE QUICKLY DEHYDRATED.

HEAT AWARENESS INFORMATION :-
[a] HEAT WAVE - IS A PROLONGED PERIOD OF EXCESSIVE HEAT, OFTEN COMBINED WITH EXCESSIVE HUMIDITY.
[b] HEAT INDEX - A NUMBER IN DEGREES FAHRENHEIT [F] THAT TELLS HOW HOT IT REALLY FEELS WHEN RELATIVE HUMIDITY IS ADDED TO THE ACTUAL AIR TEMPERATURE. EXPOSURE TO FULL SUNSHINE CAN INCREASE THE HEAT INDEX BY 15 DEGREES.
[c] HEAT CRAMPS - ARE MUSCULAR PAINS AND SPASMS DUE TO HEAVY EXERTION. ALTHOUGH HEAT CRAMPS ARE THE LESS SEVERE, THEY ARE OFTEN THE FIRST SIGNAL THAT THE BODY IS HAVING TROUBLE WITH THE HEAT.
[d] HEAT EXHAUSTION - TYPICALLY OCCURS WHEN PEOPLE EXERCISE HEAVILY OR WORK IN A HOT, HUMID PLACE WHERE BODY FLUIDS ARE LOST THROUGH HEAVY SWEATING. BLOOD FLOW TO THE SKIN INCREASES, CAUSING

BLOOD FLOW TO DECREASE TO THE VITAL ORGANS. THIS RESULTS IN A FORM OF MILD SHOCK. IF NOT TREATED, THE VICTIM'S CONDITION WILL WORSEN. BODY TEMPERATURE WILL KEEP RISING AND THE VICTIM MAY SUFFER HEAT STROKE.

[e] HEAT STROKE :- IS LIFE THREATENING. THE VICTIM'S TEMPERATURE CONTROL SYSTEM, WHICH PRODUCES SWEATING TO COOL THE BODY, STOPS WORKING. THE BODY TEMPERATURE CAN RISE SO HIGH THAT BRAIN DAMAGE AND DEATH MAY RESULT IF THE BODY IN NOT COOLED QUICKLY.

[f] SUNSTROKE - IS ANOTHER TERM FOR HEAT STROKE.

SIGNALS OF HEAT EXHAUSTION ARE :-COOL, MOIST, PALE, OR FLUSHED SKIN; HEAVY SWEATING, HEADACHES, NAUSEA OR VOMITING, DIZZINESS, AND EXHAUSTION. BODY TEMPERATURE MAY BE NORMAL OR IS LIKELY TO BE RISING.

SIGNALS OF HEAT STROKE ARE :-HOT, RED SKIN, CHANGES IN CONSCIOUSNESS, RAPID – WEAK PULSE, AND RAPID SHALLOW BREATHING. BODY TEMPERATURE CAN BE VERY HIGH; SOMETIMES AS HIGH AS 104 DEGREES F.

DURING TIMES OF EXTREME HEAT, IT IS ADVISABLE TO WEAR LIGHTWEIGHT, LIGHT – COLORED CLOTHING. LIGHT COLORS WILL REFLECT AWAY THE SUN'S RAYS MORE THAN DARK COLORS, WHICH ABSORB THE SUN'S RAYS.

DURING HEAT WAVE IT IS ALWAYS GOOD TO HAVE ADDITIONAL SUPPLY OF WATER AND A BASIC FIRST – AID DISASTER SUPPLIES KIT.

PROTECTION OF PROPERTY IN TIMES OF HEAT WAVES:-

INSTALL WINDOW AIR CONDITIONERS SNUGLY.
MAKE SURE YOUR HOME IS PROPERLY INSULATED.
DURING A DROUGHT, APPLY WATER CONSERVATION SENSIBLY.

CONSIDER KEEPING STORM WINDOWS INSTALLED THROUGHOUT THE YEAR, IT KEEPS THE HEAT OUT JUST AS IT KEEPS THE COLD OUT IN WINTER.

CHECK AIR CONDITIONING DUCTS FOR PROPER INSULATION.

PROTECT WINDOWS, HANG SHADES, DRAPERIES, AWNINGS, OR LOUVERS ON WINDOWS THAT RECEIVE MORNING OR AFTERNOON SUN. OUTDOOR AWNINGS OR LOUVERS CAN REDUCE THE HEAT ENTERING THE HOUSE BY AS MUCH AS 80 %.

USE FANS -IT HELPS TO KEEP THE HOME COOL.

DURING TIMES OF SEVERE HEAT WAVES, IT IS BEST TO OBSERVE THE FOLLOWING METHODS OF DEALING AND COPING WITH THE EXISTING CONDITION :-

1 SLOW DOWN, AVOID STRENUOUS ACTIVITIES.

2 AVOID TOO MUCH SUNSHINE.

3 POSTPONE OUTDOORS GAMES AND ACTIVITIES.

4 AVOID EXTREME TEMPERATURE CHANGES.

5 STAY INDOORS AS MUCH AS POSSIBLE.

6 KEEP HEAT OUTSIDE AND COOL AIR INSIDE.

7 CONSERVE ELECTRICITY NOT NEEDED TO KEEP YOU COOL.

8 VACUUM AIR CONDITIONER FILTERS REGULARLY DURING PERIODS OF HIGH USE.

9 DRESS APPROPRIATELY.

10 DRINK PLENTY OF FLUIDS, EVEN IF YOU DO NOT FEEL THIRSTY.

11 AVOID DRINKS WITH ALCOHOL OR CAFFEINE IN THEM.

12 EAT SMALL MEALS AND EAT MORE OFTEN.

13 NEVER LEAVE CHILDREN OR PETS ALONE IN CLOSED VEHICLES.

WORLD CLIMATES :-

CLIMATE IS THE CHARACTERISTIC CONDITION OF THE ATMOSPHERE NEAR THE EARTH'S SURFACE AT A CERTAIN PLACE ON EARTH. IT IS THE LONG TERM WEATHER OF THAT AREA [AT LEAST 35 YEARS]. THIS INCLUDES THE REGION'S GENERAL PATTERN OF WEATHER CONDITIONS, SEASONS AND WEATHER EXTREMES LIKE HURRICANES,

DROUGHTS, OR RAINY PERIODS. TWO OF THE MOST IMPORTANT FACTORS DETERMINING AN AREA'S CLIMATE ARE AIR TEMPERATURE AND PRECIPITATION.

HAVE YOU EVER WONDERED WHY ONE AREA OF THE WORLD IS A DESERT, ANOTHER A GRASSLAND, AND ANOTHER A RAINFOREST? WHY ARE THERE DIFFERENT FORESTS AND DESERTS, AND WHY ARE THERE DIFFERENT TYPES OF LIFE IN EACH AREA? WELL MY FRIEND THE ANSWER IS CLIMATE.

SOME FACTS ABOUT CLIMATE ARE :-
1 THE SUN'S RAYS HIT THE EQUATOR AT A DIRECT ANGLE BETWEEN 23 DEGREES NORTH AND 23 DEGREES SOUTH LATITUDE. RADIATION THAT REACHES THE ATMOSPHERE HERE IS AT ITS MOST INTENSE.
2 IN ALL OTHER CASES, THE RAYS ARRIVE AT AN ANGLE TO THE SURFACE AND ARE LESS INTENSE. THE CLOSER A PLACE IS TO THE POLES, THE SMALLER THE ANGLE AND THEREFORE THE LESS INTENSE THE RADIATION.
3 OUR CLIMATE SYSTEM IS BASED ON THE LOCATION OF THESE HOT AND COLD AIR – MASS REGIONS AND THE ATMOSPHERIC CIRCULATION CREATED BY THE TRADE WINDS AND WESTERLIES.

SEASONS :-
THE EARTH ROTATES ABOUT ITS AXIS, WHICH IS TILTED AT 23.5 DEGREES. THIS TILT AND THE SUN'S RADIATION RESULT IN THE EARTH'S SEASONS. THE SUN EMITS RAYS THAT HIT THE EARTH'S SURFACE AT DIFFERENT ANGLES. THESE RAYS TRANSMIT THE HIGHEST LEVEL OF ENERGY WHEN THEY STRIKE THE EARTH AT A RIGHT ANGLE [90 DEGREES]. TEMPERATURES IN THESE AREAS TEND TO BE THE HOTTEST PLACES ON EARTH. OTHER LOCATIONS, WHERE THE SUN'S RAYS HIT AT LESSER ANGLES, TEND TO BE COOLER.

AS THE EARTH ROTATES ON IT'S TILTED AXIS AROUND THE SUN, DIFFERENT PARTS OF THE EARTH RECEIVE HIGHER AND LOWER LEVELS OF RADIANT ENERGY. THIS CREATES THE SEASONS.

THERE IS A SYSTEM CALLED THE KOPPEN CLIMATE CLASSIFICATION SYSTEM WHICH RECOGNIZES FIVE MAJOR CLIMATE TYPES BASED ON THE ANNUAL AND MONTHLY AVERAGES OF TEMPERATURE AND PRECIPITATION. THE FIVE TYPES ARE DESIGNATED A, B, C, D, AND E.

THERE ARE THREE BASIC CLIMATE GROUPS WHICH SHOW THE DOMINANCE OF SPECIAL COMBINATIONS OF AIR – MASS SOURCE REGIONS. THESE ARE :-

GROUP 1 :-LOW LATITUDE CLIMATES :-THESE CLIMATES ARE CONTROLLED BY EQUATORIAL – TROPICAL AIR MASSES. UNDER GROUP 1 ARE :-

TROPICAL MOIST CLIMATES – RAINFOREST.
WET – DRY TROPICAL CLIMATES – SAVANNA.
DRY TROPICAL CLIMATE – DESERT BIOME.

GROUP 11 :-MID – LATITUDE CLIMATES, SUCH AS :-
DRY MID – LATITUDE CLIMATES – STEPPE.
MEDITERRANEAN CLIMATE – CHAPARRAL BIOME.
DRY MID-LATITUDE CLIMATES – GRASSLANDS BIOME.
MOIST CONTINENTAL CLIMATE – DECIDUOUS FOREST BIOME.

GROUP 111 :-HIGH LATITUDE CLIMATES, SUCH AS :-
BOREAL FOREST CLIMATE – TAIGA BIOME.
TUNDRA CLIMATE – TUNDRA BIOME.
HIGHLAND CLIMATE – ALPINE BIOME.

WINDS :-IS AIR IN MOTION.

THE TRADE WINDS :-THE AIR AT DOLDRUMS RISES HIGH OVER THE EARTH, RECIRCULATES POLEWARD, AND SINKS BACK TOWARD THE EARTH'S SURFACE IN THE REGION OF HORSE LATITUDE, AND CONVERGE NEAR THE SURFACE OF THE DOLDRUMS. SURFACE AIR FROM THE HORSE LATITUDES THAT MOVES BACK TOWARDS THE EQUATOR AND IS DEFLECTED BY THE CORIOLIS FORCE, CAUSING THE WINDS TO BLOW FROM THE NORTH EAST IN THE

NORTHERN HEMISPHERE AND FROM THE SOUTH EAST IN THE SOUTHERN HEMISPHERE IS CALLED TRADE WINDS. IT MEANS THAT IN BOTH HEMISPHERES, THEY TEND TO BLOW FROM THE EAST TO THE WEST AND TOWARDS THE EQUATOR. TRADE WINDS NORTH OF THE EQUATOR BLOW FROM THE NORTHEAST. SOUTH OF THE EQUATOR, THEY BLOW FROM THE SOUTHEAST. THE TRADE WINDS OF THE TWO HEMISPHERES MEET NEAR THE EQUATOR, CAUSING THE AIR TO RISE. AS THE RISING AIR COOLS, CLOUDS AND RAIN DEVELOP. THE RESULTING BANDS OF CLOUDY AND RAINY WEATHER NEAR THE EQUATOR CREATE TROPICAL CONDITIONS.

WESTERLIES :-BLOW FROM THE SOUTHWEST ON THE NORTHERN HEMISPHERE AND FROM THE NORTHWEST IN THE SOUTHERN HEMISPHERE. WESTERLIES STEER STORMS FROM WEST TO EAST ACROSS MIDDLE LATITUDES.

BOTH WESTERLIES AND TRADE WINDS BLOW AWAY FROM THE 30 DEGREES LATITUDE BELT; OVER LARGE AREAS CENTERED AT 30 DEGREES LATITUDE, SURFACE WINDS ARE LIGHT. AIR SLOWLY DESCENDS TO REPLACE THE AIR THAT BLOWS AWAY. ANY MOISTURE THE AIR CONTAINS EVAPORATES IN THE INTENSE HEAT. THE TROPICAL DESERTS, SUCH AS THE SAHARA OF AFRICA AND THE SONORAN OF MEXICO, EXIST UNDER THESE REGIONS

MONSOONS :-WIND BRINGING RAINY SEASON. A MONSOON CIRCULATION IS DETERMINING THE DIFFERENT HEAT CAPACITY CHANGE OF CONTINENTS AND OCEANS, E.G SEA / LAND BREEZE, EXCEPT THAT OVER A MUCH LARGER AREA. IN FACT WINDS USUALLY FLOW FROM THE VERY LAND, CAUSING HEAVY RAINS IN LANDS IN WINTER, THE WINDS USUALLY REVERSE THE FLOW FROM THE LAND TO THE SEA IN DRY CONDITIONS. THE WORD MONSOON IS DERIVED FROM THE ARABIC WORD MAUSIM WHICH IS USED TO DESCRIBE A SYSTEM OF WINDS WHICH BLOW PERSISTENTLY NORTHEAST DURING THE NORTHERNLIES FROM THE OPPOSITE DIRECTION, TO SOUTHWEST, DURING THE NORHERNLIES. THUS, THE TERM MONSOON ACTIVITIES

ARE DUE SOLELY TO A SEASONAL WIND SHIFTING
PRECIPITATION.

EVEN THOUGH THE TERM MONSOON WAS ORIGINALLY
DEFINED FOR THE INDIAN SUBCONTINENT, MONSOON
CIRCULATION EXIST IN OTHER LOCATIONS OF THE WORLD
AS WELL, SUCH AS IN EUROPE, AFRICA, AUSTRALIA, AND
THE WEST COASTS OF CHILE AND THE UNITED STATES.
APPROXIMATELY 65 % OF THE WORLD'S POPULATION LIVES
WITHIN MONSOON REGIONS. THE MOST FAMOUS MONSOON
CIRCULATION OCCURS OVER INDIA AND SOUTHEAST ASIA.
DURING THE SUMMER, THE AIR OVER THE CONTINENT
BECOMES MUCH WARMER THAN THE WATER SURFACE,
SO THE SURFACE AIR MOVES FROM THE WATER TO THE
LAND. THE HUMID AIR FROM THE WATER CONVERGES WITH
DRY AIR FROM OVER THE CONTINENT AND PRODUCES
PRECIPITATION OVER THE REGION. ADDITIONAL LIFTING
FROM HILLS AND MOUNTAINS CAUSES COPIOUS AMOUNTS
OF PRECIPITATION TO OCCUR, OVER 400 INCHES AT SOME
LOCATIONS. DURING THE WINTER THE FLOW REVERSES
AND THE DOMINANT SURFACE FLOW MOVES FROM THE
LAND TO THE WATER.

THE INDIAN SUMMER MONSOON TYPICALLY LASTS
FROM JUNE THROUGH SEPTEMBER. DURING THIS PERIOD
LARGE AREAS OF WESTERN AND CENTRAL INDIA RECEIVE
MORE THAN 90 % OF THEIR TOTAL ANNUAL RAINFALL,
WHILE SOUTHERN AND NORTHWESTERN INDIA RECEIVE
50 % – 75 % OF THEIR TOTAL ANNUAL RAINFALL. OVERALL,
MONTHLY RAINFALL TOTALS AVERAGE 200 – 300 MM, WITH
THE LARGEST VALUES OBSERVED DURING THE HEART OF
THE MONSOON SEASON IN JULY AND AUGUST.

RAINFALL ACROSS SOUTHEASTERN ASIA IS ALSO
MONSOON IN NATURE, WITH THE LARGEST TYPICALLY
OBSERVED DURING MAY – SEPTEMBER. SEASONAL TOTALS
OF 1000 MM IS COMMONLY OBSERVED.

PRECIPITATION :-IS THE AMOUNT OF RAIN, SNOW ETC.

CHAPTER 31.

PRINT OUTS :-

ILLUSTRATIONS.

MORSE CODE :-EITHER OF TWO CODES CONSISTING OF DOT – AND – DASH SIGNALS, AND USED TO TRANSMIT MESSAGES. THE CODES ARE NAMED FOR SAMUEL F B MORSE, WHO DEVELOPED THE SYSTEM OF SIGNALS THAT FORMS THE BASIS FOR THE PRESENT CODES. THE INTERNATIONAL, OR CONTINENTAL, MORSE CODE IS THE STANDARD CODE FOR ALL COMMUNICATIONS TRANSMITTED BY RADIO TELEGRAPHY AND FOR NAVAL COMMUNICATIONS TRANSMITTED BY FLASHING LIGHT. THE AMERICAN MORSE CODE, WHICH IS NOW LARGELY OBSOLETE, IS SOMETIMES USED IN TELEGRAPHY IN THE UNITED STATES AND CANADA. THE CODES TRANSMIT LETTERS OF THE ALPHABET, NUMERALS, PUNCTUATION, AND CERTAIN CONVENTIONAL PHRASES. MORSE MESSAGES ARE BASED ON A SYSTEM OF DOTS, DASHES, AND PAUSES. MORSE CODE HAS BEEN LARGELY REPLACED IN TELEGRAPHY BY THE USE OF FACSIMILE MACHINES AND TELETYPEWRITERS.

THE MORSE CODE [ILLUSTRATION 1 PAGE]

DEAF :-IS BEING UNABLE TO HEAR.
DEAF – MUTE :-IS A DEAF PERSON WHO HAS NOT LEARNED SPEECH.

DEAFNESS :-AFFECTS FUNCTION IN SOCIETY FOR THE HEARING – IMPAIRED PERSON. IN THE UNITED STATES ALONE; APPROXIMATELY 17 MILLION U.S CITIZENS HAVE A HEARING IMPAIRMENT. THIS CONDITION AFFECTS ALL AGE GROUPS, AND ITS CONSEQUENCES RANGE FROM MINOR TO SEVERE. OF THESE 17 MILLION PERSONS, MORE THAN 2 MILLION ARE CONSIDERED PROFOUNDLY DEAF; THAT IS, THEY HAVE A HEARING LOSS SO SEVERE THAT THEY CANNOT BENEFIT FROM MECHANICAL AMPLIFICATION, WHEREAS HARD – OF – HEARING PERSONS OFTEN CAN BENEFIT, TO VARYING DEGREES, FROM THE USE OF SUCH AMPLIFICATION. THERE ARE FOUR TYPES OF HEARING LOSS :-
CONDUCTIVE HEARING LOSS.
SENSORINEURAL HEARING LOSS.
MIXED HEARING LOSS.
CENTRAL HEARING LOSS.

DEAFNESS IS GENERALLY CAUSED BY ILLNESS OR ACCIDENT, OR IT MAY BE INHERITED. CONTINUOUS OR FREQUENT EXPOSURE TO NOISE LEVELS ABOVE 85 DB CAN CAUSE A PROGRESSIVE AND EVENTUALLY SEVERE SENSORINEURAL HEARING LOSS. A SPANISH BENEDICTINE MONK, PEDRO DE PONCE IS CONSIDERED THE FIRST TEACHER OF DEAF STUDENTS; AND IN 1620 JUAN PAULO BONET, ANOTHER SPANIARD, WROTE THE FIRST BOOK ON EDUCATING DEAF PERSONS. THE BOOK CONTAINED A MANUAL ALPHABET SIMILAR TO THE ONE IN USE TODAY. THE FIRST U.S SCHOOL FOR DEAF CHILDREN, STILL IN EXISTENCE WAS ESTABLISHED IN 1817 BY THOMAS HOPKINS GALLAUDET, LAURENT CLERC, MASON F COGSWELL AND A GROUP OF OTHER CONCERNED PERSONS. INCREASINGLY, THE PHILOSOPHY OF TOTAL COMMUNICATION IS BEING USED IN SCHOOLS AND CLASSES FOR DEAF CHILDREN. THIS PHILOSOPHY ENCOURAGES THE COMBINED USE OF WHATEVER COMMUNICATION METHODS ARE APPROPRIATE TO THE DEAF CHILD, INCLUDING :-

SPEECH.
LIP READING.
AMERICAN SIGN LANGUAGE.

MANUALLY CODED ENGLISH.
CUED SPEECH.
FINGER SPELLING.
ART.
ELECTRONIC MEDIA.
MIME.
GESTURE.
READING AND WRITING.

FINGER SPELLING IS A SYSTEM IN WHICH HAND SHAPES AND POSITIONS CORRESPOND TO THE LETTERS OF THE WRITTEN ALPHABET; ALLOWING THE DEAF PERSON TO BE ABLE TO READ AND UNDERSTAND THE MESSAGE BEING COMMUNICATED; THIS IS PRACTICED IN DEAF SCHOOLS, CHURCHES AND OTHER INSTITUTIONS.

THE SIGN LANGUAGE ALPHABET USED BY THE DEAF.
[ILLUSTRATION 1 PAGE]

FLAG :-SIMPLY PUT IS CLOTH WITH COLORS OR DESIGNS, USED AS A NATIONAL SYMBOL ETC. IT'S USUALLY LIGHT PIECES OF CLOTH; PRIMARILY RECTANGULAR IN SHARE; BUT VARYING IN SIZE, COLOR, AND DESIGN; AND INTENDED FOR USE AS AN EMBLEM OR AS A KIND OF SIGNALING DEVICE. FLAGS SOMETIMES REFERRED TO AS BANNERS, ENSIGNS, OR STANDARDS, ARE MOST COMMONLY DISPLAYED HANGING FREE FROM A FLAG – POLE, FLAG – STAFF, OR ROPE; TO WHICH THEY ARE ATTACHED ALONG ONE EDGE. FLAGS ARE USED FOR IDENTIFICATION SUCH AS :-
COUNTRY FLAG.
GOVERNMENTAL SUBDIVISIONS.
OFFICIALS.
AGENCIES.
SPORTS TEAMS.
CORPORATIONS.
SERVICES.
MILITARY UNITS.
CLASSES OF YACHTS.
SHIPS.
CLUBS.
ORGANIZATIONS.
INSTITUTIONS.

STATES.
COUNTIES
AMONG OTHERS .

NATIONAL WORLD FLAGS ARE FLAGS DISTINCTIVELY DESIGNED TO SERVE AS THE EMBLEM OF A PARTICULAR NATION OR COUNTRY.

FLAGS OF THE WORLD [ILLUSTRATIONS 5 PAGES].

FLAGS OF THE STATES AND TERRITORIES OF THE UNITED STATES.

[ILLUSTRATIONS OF U.S.A FLAGS 2 PAGES]
[NUMBERED PAGES 6 AND 7]

ANATOMY :-IS THE BRANCH OF NATURAL SCIENCE DEALING WITH THE STRUCTURAL ORGANIZATION OF LIVING THINGS. THE STUDY OF ANATOMY IS DIVIDED INTO SEVERAL BROAD FIELDS. THESE INCLUDE
1 COMPARATIVE ANATOMY :-THIS IS THE STUDY OF THE SIMILARITIES AND DIFFERENCES BETWEEN THE STRUCTURES OF MAN AND ANIMALS.
2 HISTOLOGY OR MICROSCOPIC ANATOMY :-THIS DEALS WITH THE STUDY OF THE CELLS THAT MAKE UP AN ORGAN OR TISSUE.
3 GROSS ANATOMY :-THIS IS THE STUDY OF THE STRUCTURES VISIBLE TO THE UNAIDED EYE.
4 EMBRYOLOGY :-THIS IS THE STUDY OF THE DEVELOPMENT OF THE STRUCTURE OF AN ORGANISM FROM ITS EARLIEST STAGE TO ITS MATURE FORM.
5 PATHOLOGICAL ANATOMY :-THIS IS THE STUDY OF THE EFFECTS OF DISEASES ON BODY TISSUES.

IN ADDITION, THERE ARE VARIOUS BRANCHES DEALING WITH SPECIFIC ORGANS OR TYPES OF ORGANS. THESE INCLUDE NEUROLOGY [NERVE ANATOMY], OSTEOLOGY [BONES], MYOLOGY [MUSCLES], DESMOLOGY [LIGAMENTS AND SINEWS], SPLANCHNOLOGY [INTERNAL ORGANS], ANGIOLOGY [BLOOD VESSELS AND LYMPHATIC SYSTEM], AND DERMATOLOGY.

THE SYSTEMS OF THE BODY – ANATOMY WERE DISCUSSED IN AN EARLIER CHAPTER.

[ILLUSTRATIONS RELATING TO THE HUMAN ANATOMY 4 PAGES]

CHAPTER 32.

TEST YOURSELF :-   PRACTICE EXERCISES :-
BE SURE TO KNOW WHY THE ANSWER IS WHAT IT IS.

QUESTIONS :-
STATE THE PLURAL OF :-
1 LOAF
2 PIANO
3 ECHO
4 LIFE
5 WOLF
6 HOOF
7 CARGO
8 BY - WAY
9 MAID – OF - HONOR
10 CLOTH

ANSWERS :-
1 LOAVES
2 PIANOS
3 ECHOES
4 LIVES
5 WOLVES
6 HOOFS, HOOVES
7 CARGOES
8 BY - WAYS
9 MAIDS – OF - HONOR
10 CLOTHS, CLOTHES

QUESTIONS :- GIVE THE SINGULAR OF :-
1 KNIVES
2 CLOTHES
3 TROUT
4 MICE
5 MEN
6 LADIES
7 THIEVES
8 BOXES
9 GEESE
10 MAIDS – OF - HONOR

ANSWERS :-
1 KNIFE
2 CLOTH
3 TROUT
4 MOUSE
5 MAN
6 LADY
7 THIEF
8 BOX
9 GOOSE
10 MAID – OF - HONOR

FILL IN THE BLANK SPACES WITH THE SINGULAR OR PLURAL FORM – AS REQUIRED.
1 FLIES
2 ROOF
3 CHILDREN
4 SHELF
5 WOMEN
6 LADY
7 POTATO
8 DEER
9 COD
10 DOZEN
11 SHEEP

ANSWERS :-
1 FLY

2 ROOFS
3 CHILD
4 SHELVES
5 WOMAN
6 LADIES
7 POTATOES
8 DEER
9 COD
10 DOZEN
11 SHEEP

CHANGE ALL SINGULAR INTO PLURALS :-
1 THE CHILD CRIED BECAUSE HE WAS SICK.
2 THE HORSE IS IN THE FIELD.
3 THE BOY TAKES THE EGG FROM THE BIRD'S NEST.
4 THE BOY'S BOOK IS ON THE TABLE.
5 THE MAN CAUGHT A TROUT.
6 THE SHIP IS AT THE DOCK.
7 THE MOUSE RAN INTO THE HOLE.
8 MY HAND TROUBLED ME.
9 THE CAT RUNS FROM THE DOG.
10 THE MAN SPOKE TO THE BOY.

ANSWERS :-
1 THE CHILDREN CRIED BECAUSE THEY WERE SICK.
2 THE HORSES ARE IN THE FIELDS.
3 THE BOYS TAKE THE EGGS FROM THE BIRDS' NESTS.
4 THE BOYS' BOOKS ARE ON THE TABLES
5 THE MEN CAUGHT SOME TROUT.
6 THE SHIPS ARE AT THE DOCKS.
7 THE MICE RAN INTO THE HOLES.
8 THEIR HANDS TROUBLED THEM.
9 THE CATS RUN FROM THE DOGS.
10 THE MEN SPOKE TO THE BOYS.

CHANGE THE VERBS INTO THE PAST TENSE.
1 THE BOY WEARS A BLUE HAT.
2 THE MAN SWIMS IN THE POOL.
3 HE HAS A HAMMER.
4 HE TAKES HER BOOK.

5 THE LADY SITS IN THE HAMMOCK.
6 THE GIRL WALKS TO SCHOOL.
7 THE DOG RUNS AFTER THE CAT.
8 THE GOATS RUN IN THE FIELDS.
9 THE GIRL STEALS THE PEN.
10 THE RAT IS EATING THE CHEESE.
11 THE LADY WRITES HER NAME.

ANSWERS :-
1 WORE
2 SWAM
3 HAD
4 TOOK
5 SAT
6 WALKED
7 RAN
8 RAN
9 STOLE
10 WAS
11 WROTE

GIVE THE FEMININE OF :-
1 NEPHEW
2 WAITER
3 SIR
4 HERO
5 POET
6 PRINCE
7 MALE
8 MR.
9 EXECUTOR
10 FATHER
11 DUKE
12 ACTOR

ANSWERS :-
1 NIECE
2 WAITRESS
3 MADAM
4 HEROINE
5 POETESS

6 PRINCESS
7 FEMALE
8 MRS.
9 EXECUTRIX
10 MOTHER
11 DUCHESS
12 ACTRESS

GIVE THE MASCULINE OF :-
1 COW
2 HEN
3 FILLY
4 BITCH
5 DUCK
6 GOOSE
7 EWE
8 MARE
9 HEIFER
10 AUNT
11 WITCH

ANSWERS :-
1 BULL
2 COCK
3 COLT
4 DOG
5 DRAKE
6 GANDER
7 RAM
8 STALLION
9 STEER
10 UNCLE
11 WIZARD

CHANGE ALL MASCULINE INTO CORRESPONDING FEMININE.:-
1 THE LANDLORD IS A WIDOWER.
2 THE DUKE TALKED TO THE BOY.
3 THE PRINCE WENT TO SEE THE WIZARD.
4 "YES SIR," THE MAN SAID.
5 "HE IS A DEAD HERO," SAID THE KING.

6 THE HOST WAS BOTHERED BY THE MEN.
7 GEORGE HAS A BROTHER, WHO IS A BOY SCOUT.

ANSWERS :-
1 THE LANDLADY IS A WIDOW.
2 THE DUCHESS TALKED TO THE GIRL.
3 THE PRINCESS WENT TO SEE THE WITCH.
4 "YES MADAM," THE WOMAN SAID.
5 "SHE IS A DEAD HEROINE," SAID THE QUEEN.
6 THE HOSTESS WAS BOTHERED BY THE WOMEN.
7 GEORGINA HAS A SISTER, WHO IS A GIRL GUIDE.

STATE THE GENDER OF THE FOLLOWING :-
1 PEN
2 BROTHER
3 FRIEND
4 MISTRESS
5 COUSIN
6 CHILDREN
7 TABLE
8 GIRL
9 MAN
10 GLASS
11 PAPER

ANSWERS :-
1 NEUTER
2 MASCULINE
3 COMMON
4 FEMININE
5 COMMON
6 COMMON
7 NEUTER
8 FEMININE
9 MASCULINE
10 NEUTER
11 NEUTER

GIVE THE CORRESPONDING FEMININE OF THE FOLLOWING NAMES :-
1 JOHN

2 JOSEPH
3 PATRICK
4 OLIVER
5 PAUL
6 ROBERT
7 VICTOR
8 CLARENCE
9 ALEXANDER
10 CHARLES

ANSWERS :-
1 JOAN
2 JOSEPHINE
3 PATRICIA
4 OLIVE
5 PAULINE
6 ROBERTA
7 VICTORIA
8 CLARA
9 ALEXANDRA
10 CHARLOTTE

NAME THE YOUNG OF :-
1 COW
2 DEER
3 SWAN
4 HEN
5 DOG
6 DUCK
7 EAGLE
8 GOOSE
9 LION
10 BEE
11 BIRD
12 BUTTERFLY

ANSWERS :-
1 CALF
2 FAWN
3 CYGNET
4 CHICKEN

5 PUP
6 DUCKLING
7 EAGLET
8 GOSLING
9 CUB
10 GRUB
11 NESTLING
12 CATERPILLAR

NAME THE PARENT OF :-
1 PARR
2 TADPOLE
3 FRY
4 ELVER
5 FOAL
6 LAMB
7 OWLER
8 KITTEN
9 KID
10 PIGLET
11 RACK

ANSWERS :-
1 SALMON
2 FROG, TOAD
3 TROUT
4 EEL
5 STALLION
6 SHEEP
7 OWL
8 CAT
9 GOAT
10 PIG
11 RABBIT

NAME THE HOMES OF :-
1 CONVICT
2 ESKIMO
3 KING
4 MAN
5 NUN

6 SOLDIER
7 TINKER
8 VICAR
9 GIPSY
10 LUMBER - MAN
11 MONK
12 PIONEER

ANSWERS :-
1 PRISON
2 IGLOO
3 PALACE
4 HOUSE
5 CONVENT
6 BARRACKS, CAMP
7 TENT
8 VICARAGE
9 CARAVAN
10 LOG - CABIN
11 MONASTERY
12 WAGON

NAME THE HOMES OF THE FOLLOWING CREATURES :-
1 SHEEP
2 SNAIL
3 BEE
4 BIRD
5 COW
6 DOG
7 FOWL
8 HORSE
9 LION
10 MOUSE
11 PIG
12 SPIDER

ANSWERS :-
1 PEN, FOLD
2 SHELL
3 HIVE
4 NEST

5 BYRE
6 KENNEL
7 COOP
8 STABLE
9 DEN, LAIR
10 HOLE, NEST
11 STY
12 WEB

WHAT NAME IS GIVEN TO A NUMBER OF :-
1 CATS
2 RUNNERS
3 SPARROWS
4 KITTENS
5 LEOPARDS
6 MICE
7 ASSES
8 DUCKS
9 POLICEMEN
10 LIONS
11 HORSES
12 GOATS
13 PAPERS
14 SHOTS
15 STARS
16 ISLANDS
17 BANANAS
18 MACHINE - GUNS
19 ARROWS
20 CATTLE
21 THIEVES
22 SHEEP
23 SINGERS
24 CHICKENS
25 SERVANTS

ANSWERS :-
1 CLOWDER
2 FIELD
3 HOST
4 KINDLE

5 LEAP

6 NEST

7 PACE

8 PADDLING

9 POSSE

10 PRIDE

11 STRING

12 TRIBE

13 BUDGET

14 FUSILLADE

15 GALAXY

16 GROUP

17 BUNCH

18 NEST

19 SHEAF

20 HERD

21 GANG

22 FLOCK

23 CHOIR

24 BROOD

25 STAFF

GIVE ONE WORD FOR A NUMBER OF PEOPLE :-

1 IN A RIOT.

2 IN CHURCH.

3 AT A FOOTBALL MATCH.

4 AT A CONCERT.

5 IN THE STREET.

ANSWERS :-

1 MOB

2 CONGREGATION

3 SPECTATORS

4 AUDIENCE

5 CROWD, THRONG

SUPPLY THE MISSING WORDS IN THE FOLLOWING SIMILES :-

1 AS FAST AS A -

2 AS FAT AS A -

3 AS FEEBLE AS A -

4 AS FIERCE AS A -
5 AS GENTLE AS A -
6 AS GRACEFUL AS A -
7 AS HAPPY AS A -
8 AS HARMLESS AS A -
9 AS HEAVY AS AN -
10 AS HUNGRY AS A -
11 AS MEEK AS A -
12 AS PLAYFUL AS A -
13 AS PROUD AS A -
14 AS QUIET AS A -
15 AS SICK AS A -
16 AS SLOW AS A -
17 AS SOBER AS A -
18 AS STRONG AS A -
19 AS SWIFT AS A -
20 AS WISE AS AN -

ANSWERS :-
1 DEER, HARE
2 PIG
3 CHILD
4 LION
5 DOVE, LAMB
6 SWAN
7 KING, LARK
8 DOVE
9 ELEPHANT
10 HUNTER, WOLF
11 LAMB
12 KITTEN, PUPPY
13 PEACOCK
14 MOUSE
15 DOG
16 SNAIL, TORTOISE
17 JUDGE
18 HORSE, OX
19 DEER, HARE, HAWK
20 OWL, SOLOMON

PICK OUT BY UNDERLINING THE BEST SIMILE IN THE FOLLOWING :-

1 AS GREEN AS [DAISY, A ROCK, A LARK, GRASS]

2 AS GOOD AS [SOLOMON, STEEL, GOLD, WOOL]

3 AS FLAT AS [A ROCK, A PANCAKE, HERRING, A BOX]

4 AS WEAK AS [JOB, SNOW, WATER, HONEY]

5 AS FAST AS [A MAN, A RABBIT, A SERPENT, A DEER]

6 AS UGLY AS [A CLOWN, A KETTLE, SIN, FIRE]

7 AS TALL AS [A GIANT, A SHEPHERD, A KING, A MONKEY]

8 AS STRONG AS [A HAWK, A GAZELLE, A HORSE, A FOX]

ANSWERS :-

1 GRASS

2 GOLD

3 A PANCAKE

4 WATER

5 A DEER

6 SIN

7 A GIANT

8 A HORSE

WRITE THE NAMES OF THE CREATURES :-

1 THE   PURRS.

2 THE   LOWS.

3 THE   BELLS.

4 THE   BRAYS.

5 THE   TRUMPETS

6 THE   CROAKS.

7 THE   NEIGHS.

8 THE   BLEATS.

9 THE   ROARS.

10 THE   GRUNTS.

11 THE   SQUEALS.

12 THE   HISSES.

13 THE   WHISTLES.

14 THE   CAWS.

15 THE   HOOTS.

ANSWERS :-

1 CAT.

2 COW.

3 DEER

4 DONKEY

5 ELEPHANT

6 FROG

7 HORSE

8 LAMB

9 LION

10 PIG

11 RABBIT

12 SERPENT

13 BIRD

14 CROW

15 OWL

DESCRIBE THE MOVEMENTS OF THE FOLLOWING :-

1 THE LION

2 THE MONKEY

3 A PERSON

4 A MOUSE

5 A SERPENT

6 A RABBIT

7 A PIG

8 A BEE

9 A BULL

10 A COW

11 A CAT

12 A DOG

13 AN ELEPHANT

14 A FROG

15 A HORSE

16 A LAMB

17 A BIRD

18 A DUCK

19 AN EAGLE

20 A HEN

21 AN OWL

22 AN APE

23 AN ASS

24 A BEAR

25 A DEER

ANSWERS :-
1 PROWLS
2 CLIMBS
3 WALKS
4 SCAMPERS
5 GLIDES
6 LEAPS
7 TROTS
8 FLITS
9 CHARGES
10 WANDERS
11 STEALS
12 RUNS
13 AMBLES
14 LEAPS
15 GALLOPS
16 FRISKS
17 FLIES
18 WADDLES
19 SWOOPS
20 STRUTS
21 FLITS
22 SWINGS
23 JOGS
24 LUMBERS
25 BOUNDS

VARIOUS ANIMAL SOUNDS :-
COMPLETE THE FOLLOWING :-
1 A HYENA
2 AN APE
3 A BEAR
4 A BEE
5 A BEETLE
6 A MONKEY
7 A MOUSE
8 A RABBIT
9 A WOLF
10 A CROW

ANSWERS :-
1 SCREAMS
2 GIBBERS
3 GROWLS
4 HUMS
5 DRONES
6 CHATTERS
7 SQUEAKS
8 SQUEALS
9 HOWLS
10 CAWS

EXPLAIN THE FOLLOWING WORDS IN THE SENTENCES :-

1 THE THIEF STALKED WITH FELINE STEPS.
2 THE WOMAN STAMPED IN ELEPHANTINE FASHION.
3 SHE HAD THE APPEARANCE OF FERINE WAYS.
4 HE EATS IN A PORCINE FORM.
5 THE MAN HAS AQUILINE LOOKING EYES.
6 THE LADY SWIMS IN PISCINE MODE.
7 THE BOY COWERS IN OVINE WAY FROM THE HITS.
8 THE ATHLETE RUNS IN EQUINE STRIDES.
9 THE GIRL HAS SHARP CANINE TEETH.
10 HE CHEWS HIS FOOD IN BOVINE REGULARITY.

ANSWERS :-
1 LIKE A CAT.
THE THIEF STALKED WITH CAT LIKE STEPS.
2 LIKE AN ELEPHANT.
THE WOMAN STAMPED LIKE AN ELEPHANT.
3 LIKE A WILD BEAST.
SHE HAD THE APPEARANCE OF A WILD BEAST.
4 LIKE A PIG.
HE EATS LIKE A PIG.
5 LIKE AN EAGLE.
THE MAN HAS EYES LIKE AN EAGLE.
6 LIKE A FISH.
THE LADY SWIMS LIKE A FISH.
7 LIKE A SHEEP.
THE BOY COWERS LIKE A SHEEP FROM THE HITS.

8 LIKE A HORSE.
THE ATHLETE RUNS LIKE A HORSE.
9 LIKE A DOG.
THE GIRL HAS SHARP TEETH LIKE A DOG.
10 LIKE A COW
HE CHEWS HIS FOOD ALL THE TIME LIKE A COW.

WHAT IS MEANT BY CALLING A PERSON :-
1 AN ASS.
2 A BEAR
3 A BEE
4 A BULL
5 A DOG
6 A DONKEY
7 A LAMB
8 A MONKEY
9 A PIG
10 A PIGEON
11 A TURKEY
12 A CAT

ANSWERS :-
1 STUPID
2 CLUMSY
3 BUSY
4 ANGRY
5 FAITHFUL
6 OBSTINATE
7 GENTLE
8 AGILE
9 FAT
10 GENTLE
11 PLUMP
12 SLEEK

WHICH CREATURES ARE YOU THINKING OF WHEN YOU
SAY :-
1 THEY WERE   STUNG   BY HER WORDS.
2 THE BOY   BELLOWS   WITH ANGER.
3 DON'T CROW SO OFTEN.
4 THE SOLDIER BARKED AN ORDER.

5 THE CHILDREN WERE CHATTERING IN SCHOOL.

6 THE BOY WAS GALLOPING IN THE PARK.

7 WHY ARE YOU SCAMPERING ABOUT LIKE THAT?

8 THE WOMAN GROWLS HER ANSWER.

9 HE WHISTLES ON HIS WAY HOME FROM WORK.

10 WHY ARE YOU GOBBLING UP THE FOOD SO QUICKLY?

ANSWERS :-

1 BEE

2 BULL

3 COCK

4 DOG

5 MONKEY

6 HORSE

7 MOUSE

8 BEAR

9 BIRD

10 TURKEY

INSERT THE SUITABLE SOUND IN THE FOLLOWING SENTENCES :-

1 THE   OF A DRUM.

2 THE   OF AN EXPLOSION.

3 THE   OF WATER.

4 THE   OF A SAW.

5 THE   OF A CLOCK.

6 THE   OF A COIN.

7 THE   OF A WHIP.

8 THE   OF A HINGE.

9 THE   OF PAPER.

10 THE   OF STEAM.

11 THE   OF THE WIND.

12 THE   OF COINS.

13 THE   OF FEET, RAIN.

14 THE   OF DISHES.

15 THE   OF A TRAIN.

ANSWERS :-

1 BEAT

2 BLAST
3 DRIPPING, BUBBLING, LAPPING.
4 BUZZ
5 CHIME
6 CLINK
7 CRACK
8 CREAK
9 CRINKLE
10 HISSING
11 HOWLING
12 JINGLE
13 PATTER
14 RATTLING
15 RUMBLE

SUPPLY THE MISSING WORDS :-
1 THE BLARE OF A
2 THE RING OF A
3 THE CHUG OF AN
4 THE CLANKING OF
5 THE CLATTER OF
6 THE CRACKLING OF
7 THE GRINDING OR SCREECHING OF
8 THE HOOT OF A
9 THE POPPING OF
10 THE RUSTLING OF
11 THE SHRIEK OF A
12 THE WAIL OF A

ANSWERS :-
1 TRUMPET
2 TELEPHONE
3 ENGINE
4 CHAINS
5 HOOFS, HOOVES
6 WOOD
7 BRAKES
8 HORN
9 CORKS
10 LEAVES
11 WHISTLE

12 SIREN

STATE THE TWO WORDS IN THE BRACKETS WHICH ARE CLOSELY ASSOCIATED WITH THE FIRST WORD.
1 HEAD [RUNNING, LISTENING, ACHE, NODDING, GRIN].
2 MOUTH [LASHES, SWINGING, TASTING, NOTICED, CHEWING].
3 NOSE [LAUGHED, GRIN, ODOR, SNIFFED, STRODE].
4 HANDS [WRITING, CLASP, WINK, LASHES, DANCING].
5 EYE [SMILED, LASHES, GRIN, BLINKED, ROARED]
6 ARMS [WAVING, FOLDED, GLANCING, SNIFFED, WINK]
7 LEGS [FINGERED, MUTTERED, CROSSED, RUNNING, WAVING]
8 EAR [LISTENING, DEAFNESS, WALKED,WINK, SMILED]
9 FACE [FOLDED, SANG, SMILE, GRIN, FLYING]
10 FEET [WAVING, KICKING, DANCING, FOLDED, TALKING]

ANSWERS :-
1 ACHE, NODDING.
2 TASTING, CHEWING.
3 ODOR, SNIFFED.
4 WRITING, CLASP.
5 LASHES, BLINKED.
6 WAVING, FOLDED.
7 CROSSED, RUNNING.
8 LISTENING, DEAFNESS.
9 SMILE, GRIN.
10 KICKING, DANCING.

WHAT DO THE FOLLOWING ABBREVIATIONS MEAN :-
1 DR.
2 N.B
3 P.C
4 P.S
5 P.T.O
6 R.S.V.P
7 MR.
8 MRS.
9 P.M
10 C.O.D

11 E.G
12 ETC

ANSWERS :-
1 DOCTOR
2 NOTE WELL
3 POST CARD
4 WRITTEN AFTER
5 PLEASE TURN OVER
6 REPLY IF YOU PLEASE
7 MISTER
8 MISTRESS
9 AFTERNOON
10 CASH ON DELIVERY
11 FOR EXAMPLE
12 AND THE OTHER THINGS

GIVE THE OPPOSITES OF THE FOLLOWING :-
1 CAREFUL
2 ASCEND
3 ENCOURAGE
4 IMPORT
5 INFERIOR
6 INTERNAL
7 DECREASE
8 INSIDE
9 SOUTH
10 EAST
11 ENTRANCE
12 ROUGH
13 PEDESTRIAN
14 GUILTY
15 ENEMY
16 SENIOR
17 BITTER

ANSWERS :-
1 CARELESS
2 DECEND
3 DISCOURAGE
4 EXPORT

5 EXTERIOR
6 EXTERNAL
7 INCREASE
8 OUTSIDE
9 NORTH
10 WEST
11 EXIT
12 SMOOTH
13 MOTORIST
14 INNOCENT
15 FRIEND, FOE
16 JUNIOR
17 SWEET

PRINCIPLES OF CLASSIFICATION :-
STRIKE OUT THE ODD WORD THAT DOESN'T FIT OR BELONG IN THE FOLLOWING SENTENCES.
[a] EYES COLOR :-
HAZEL, BROWN, BLUE, BLACK, FAR – SIGHTED.
[b] PURSE :-
WALLET, LEATHER, PLASTIC, FABRIC, BOUGHT.
[c] SCHOOL :-
ENJOY, LIKE, ATTEND, LESSONS, AFTERNOON.
[d] ANIMALS :-
BOOK, CAT, DOG, BIRD, LION.
[e] ACTIVITIES :-
WALKING, TIRED, RUNNING, CLAPPING, SWIMMING.

ANSWERS :-
[a] FARSIGHTED.
[b] BOUGHT.
[c] AFTERNOON.
[d] BOOK.
[e] TIRED.

GIVE THE OPPOSITES OF THE ADJECTIVES IN THE FOLLOWING PHRASES.:-

1 A	TAME	HORSE.
2 A	CALM	DAY.
3 A	DULL	BOY.
4 A	TRUE	GIFT.

5 A	STORMY	SEA.
6 A	DULL	LIGHT.
7 A	STORMY	MEETING.
8 A	BRIGHT	COLOR.

ANSWERS :-

1 A	WILD	HORSE.
2 A	STORMY	DAY.
3 A	BRIGHT	BOY.
4 A	TRUE	GIFT.
5 A	CALM	SEA.
6 A	BRIGHT	LIGHT.
7 A	QUIET	MEETING.
8 A	DARK	COLOR.

REWRITE THE FOLLOWING SENTENCES; GIVING THE OPPOSITES.

1 THE BOY IS GOING UP NORTH.

2 THE HERO WAS PRAISED FOR HIS BRAVERY.

3 THE BIG BOX IS HEAVY.

4 LOSS ON INFERIOR MATERIALS MADE HIM POOR.

5 HE GAVE AN INTELLIGENT ANSWER.

6 THE SEA IS ROUGH.

7 IN THE AFTERNOON THE SUN SETS IN THE WEST.

ANSWERS :-

1 THE GIRL IS GOING DOWN SOUTH.

2 THE COWARD WAS CONDEMNED FOR HIS COWARDICE.

3 THE SMALL BOX IS LIGHT.

4 PROFITS ON SUPERIOR MATERIALS MADE HIM RICH.

5 SHE GAVE A DUMB ANSWER.

6 THE SEA IS CALM.

7 IN THE MORNING THE SUN RISES IN THE EAST.

PRINCIPLES OF CLASSIFICATION :-

STRIKE OUT THE ODD WORD THAT DOESN'T FIT OR BELONG IN THE FOLLOWING SENTENCES.

[a] EYES COLOR.

HAZEL, BROWN, BLUE, BLACK, FAR – SIGHTED.

[b] PURSE.

WALLET, LEATHER, PLASTIC, FABRIC, BOUGHT.
[c] SCHOOL.
ENJOY, LIKE, ATTEND, LESSONS, AFTERNOON.
[d] ANIMALS.
BOOK, CAT, DOG, BIRD, LION.
[e] ACTIVITIES.
WALKING, TIRED, RUNNING, CLAPPING, SWIMMING.

ANSWERS :-
[a] FAR – SIGHTED.
[b] BOUGHT.
[c] AFTERNOON.
[d] BOOK.
[e] TIRED.

GIVE WORDS SIMILAR IN MEANING TO THE FOLLOWING :-

1 REGRET
2 MAD
3 ANCIENT
4 MODERN
5 HIGH
6 WICKED
7 WITHDRAW
8 WRETCHED
9 WRATH
10 VANQUISH
11 SURRENDER
12 STERN
13 SHRINE
14 ROAM
15 MOISTURE
16 MUTE
17 ODOR
18 OPTION
19 PROFIT
20 PROMPT
21 PURCHASE
22 REMEDY
23 LOYAL
24 COMPREHEND

25 AID

ANSWERS :-
1 SORROW
2 INSANE
3 OLD
4 NEW
5 LOFTY
6 SINFUL
7 RETIRE
8 MISERABLE
9 ANGER
10 DEFEAT
11 YIELD
12 STRICK
13 TOMB
14 WANDER
15 DAMPNESS
16 DUMB
17 SMELL
18 CHOICE
19 GAIN
20 QUICK
21 BUY
22 CURE
23 TRUE
24 UNDERSTAND
25 HELP

SCORE OUT THE WRONG WORD :-
1 THE BOY HAD TO [WAIT, WEIGHT] TILL ONE O'CLOCK.
2 THE SICK MAN UTTERED A LOUD [GROWN, GROAN].
3 [THEIR, THERE] CLOTHES ARE AT THE LAUNDRY.
4 WE FOLLOWED THE [COURSE, COARSE] SHOWN ON THE MAP.
5 THE CARPENTER [BOARD, BORED] A BIG [HOLE, WHOLE] IN THE [WOULD, WOOD].
6 THE GIRL ATE THE [STAKE, STEAK].
7 THE CAR IS FOR [SALE, SAIL].
8 THE [WHOLE, HOLE] FOOTBALL TEAM PLAYED WELL.

9 THE LADY IS EXPERIENCING [PANE, PAIN] IN HER LEG.

10 THE WOMAN USED [FLOUR, FLOWER] TO COOK.

ANSWERS :-
1 WEIGHT.
2 GROWN
3 THERE
4 COARSE
5 BOARD, WHOLE, WOULD.
6 STAKE
7 SAIL
8 HOLE
9 PANE
10 FLOWER

GIVE THE PAST TENSE OF THE FOLLOWING PRESENT TENSE WORDS
1 SHAKE
2 SING
3 AM
4 BEAR
5 SEND
6 SPEAK
7 DRIVE
8 DRINK
9 BUY
10 CATCH
11 CHOOSE
12 DIG
13 DO
14 SAY
15 LEAVE
16 MAKE
17 MEET
18 BRING
19 COME
20 DRAW
21 FALL
22 FIGHT
23 FLY

24 BEAT
25 HEAR

ANSWERS :-
1 SHOOK
2 SANG
3 WAS
4 BORE
5 SENT
6 SPOKE
7 DROVE
8 DRANK
9 BOUGHT
10 CAUGHT
11 CHOSE
12 DUG
13 DID
14 SAID
15 LEFT
16 MADE
17 MET
18 BROUGHT
19 CAME
20 DREW
21 FELL
22 FOUGHT
23 FLEW
24 BEAT
25 HEARD

GIVE THE PAST PARTICIPLE OF THE FOLLOWING PRESENT TENSE WORDS :-
1 HIDE
2 BEND
3 BITE
4 CHOOSE
5 COME
6 CUT
7 DO
8 EAT
9 FLY

10 SPEAK

11 SAY

12 FALL

13 SWIM

14 TEAR

15 RING

16 SHAKE

17 DRAW

18 BEAR

19 AM

20 BEGIN

ANSWERS :-

1 HIDDEN

2 BENT

3 BITTEN

4 CHOSEN

5 COME

6 CUT

7 DONE

8 EATEN

9 FLOWN

10 SPOKEN

11 SAID

12 FALLEN

13 SWUM

14 TORN

15 RUNG

16 SHAKEN

17 DRAWN

18 BORNE

19 BEEN

20 BEGUN

IN EACH OF THE SENTENCES BELOW THERE ARE GROUPS OF TWO WORDS WITHIN BRACKETS. ONE OF THE TWO WORDS IS CORRECT, THE OTHER WRONG. CHOOSE THE CORRECT WORD.

1 SHE [BEGUN, BEGAN] TO LOOK FOR THE TOY WHICH SHE HAD [GAVE, GIVEN] TO THE CHILD.

2 THE THIEF HAD [THROWN, THREW] AWAY THE PURSE WHICH WAS [STOLE, STOLEN] FROM THE OLD MAN.

3 AFTER THEY HAD [EATEN, ATE] THEIR LUNCH, THEY WENT TO THE LAKE WHICH WAS [FROZE, FROZEN] OVER.

4 THE ART WAS [DRAWN, DREW] BY THE WELL KNOWN ARTIST WHO HAD [ROSE, RISEN] TO FAME.

5 THE OLD OAK TREE HAD [FELL, FALLEN] ACROSS THE LAWN AND MANY OF ITS BRANCHES WERE [BROKEN, BROKE].

ANSWERS :-
1 BEGAN, GIVEN.
2 THROWN, STOLEN.
3 EATEN, FROZEN.
4 DRAWN, RISEN.
5 FALLEN, BROKEN.

PICK OUT THE ADJECTIVES IN THE FOLLOWING SENTENCES.
1 THE LITTLE GIRL WORE A PURPLE HAT.
2 THE TALL BOY HAS A BLACK BALL.
3 THE BLUE SKY HAD LOTS OF WHITE CLOUDS.
4 THE OLD LADY WAS A DELICATE LADY WITH PALE SKIN.
5 THE UGLY DUCKLING GREW INTO A BEAUTIFUL SWAN.

ANSWERS :-
1 LITTLE, PURPLE.
2 TALL, BLACK.
3 BLUE, WHITE.
4 OLD, DELICATE, PALE.
5 UGLY, BEAUTIFUL.

WRITE THE COMPARATIVES AND SUPERLATIVES FROM THESE POSITIVES.
1 SMALL
2 BAD
3 GOOD
4 LITTLE

5 MUCH
6 MANY
7 BEAUTIFUL

ANSWERS :-
1 SMALLER, SMALLEST.
2 WORSE, WORST.
3 BETTER, BEST.
4 LESS, LEAST.
5 MORE, MOST.
6 MORE, MOST.
7 MORE BEAUTIFUL, MOST BEAUTIFUL.

STATE WHETHER THE FOLLOWING WORDS ARE POSITIVE, COMPARATIVE OR SUPERLATIVE.
1 WORSE
2 GREATEST
3 BETTER
4 MANY
5 MUCH
6 WONDERFUL
7 FASTER
8 GREAT
9 LONGEST
10 BAD
11 MOST
12 LATER
13 TALL
14 MOST GENEROUS
15 MORE HANDSOME

ANSWERS :-
1 COMPARATIVE
2 SUPERLATIVE
3 COMPARATIVE
4 POSITIVE
5 POSITIVE
6 POSITIVE
7 COMPARATIVE
8 POSITIVE
9 SUPERLATIVE

10 POSITIVE
11 SUPERLATIVE
12 COMPARATIVE
13 POSITIVE
14 SUPERLATIVE
15 COMPARATIVE

CORRECT THE FOLLOWING SENTENCES :-
1 THE BEST TEAM WON THE BASKETBALL GAME.
2 RODNEY WAS THE BIGGEST OF THE TWINS.
3 JENNY WAS THE MOST LATE OF ALL THE STUDENTS
4 WHO IS THE SMALLEST JOSHUA OR DALLAS?
5 OF THE TWO, I LIKE ALAN BEST.
6 A BADDER PERSON I HAVE NEVER KNOWN.
7 THE BOY SCOUT LIFTED THE THINNEST END OF THE ROPE.
8 THE SOLDIER MADE THE WONDERFULEST RECOVERY.
9 GARY PROVED TO BE THE HANDSOMEST BOY AT THE PARTY.
10 WHO IS THE GREATEST ANN OR SALLY?

ANSWERS :-
1 BETTER
2 BIGGER
3 LATEST
4 SMALLER
5 BETTER
6 WORSE
7 THINNER
8 MOST WONDERFUL
9 MOST HANDSOME
10 GREATER

ADD ANY SUITABLE ADVERB TO THE FOLLOWING SENTENCES.
1 THE BULL CHARGES
2 THE TIGER WALKS
3 THE BABY SLEEPS
4 THE CHOIR SINGS
5 THE ACTOR ACTS

6 THE SOLDIER FIGHTS
7 THE SUN SHINES
8 THE DOG BARKS

ANSWERS :-
1 WILDLY
2 QUIETLY
3 SOUNDLY
4 SWEETLY
5 WONDERFULLY
6 BRAVELY
7 BRIGHTLY
8 LOUDLY

COMPLETE THE FOLLOWING COMPOUND WORDS :-
1 GRAND
2 BOOK
3 CUP
4 BALL
5 POST
6 STOOL
7 TOOTH
8 LAMP
9 BOARD
10 HAT

ANSWERS :-
1 MOTHER
2 SHELF
3 FUL
4 BASE
5 DOOR
6 BAR
7 ACHE
8 POST
9 CUP
10 STAND

IN THE FOLLOWING SENTENCES ARE TWO WORDS WITHIN BRACKETS. ONE OF THE WORDS IS CORRECT, THE OTHER WRONG. CHOOSE THE CORRECT WORD.

1 YOU ARE QUITE RIGHT [AS FAR AS, WHERE] I CAN SEE.

2 [AFTER, UNLESS] THEY ARRIVED, THEY HAD FOOD TO EAT.

3 HE READ A BOOK [WHILE, THAT] I COOK SOME FOOD.

4 THE FAITHFUL DOG FOLLOWED THE BOY [SINCE, WHEREVER]HE WENT.

5 YOU ASK HIM [THEN, SINCE] YOU ARE FRIENDS.

6 WE WILL GO [LEST, EVEN IF] IT RAINS.

7 I WAS AFRAID TO TALK [LEST, BECAUSE] HE SHOULD TELL.

8 LESLIE PUT ON THE LIGHT [AFTER, SO THAT] HE CAN WRITE.

9 JANE RAN QUICKLY [SO THAT, WHILE] SHE WAS IN TIME FOR SCHOOL.

10 ALAN WAITED [WHILE, UNTIL] HIS BROTHER RETURNED.

ANSWERS :-
1 AS FAR AS
2 AFTER
3 WHILE
4 WHEREVER
5 SINCE
6 EVEN IF
7 LEST
8 SO THAT
9 SO THAT
10 UNTIL

USE THE CORRECT PREPOSITIONS IN THE BLANK SPACES :-

1 ARNOLD MUST APOLOGIZE THE OLD MAN.
2 THE WOMAN IS AN AUTHORITY COOKING.
3 THE MOTHER WAS PLEASED HER SON'S RESULTS.
4 ROYO PUT THE BALL THE TABLE.
5 TRICIA PUT THE BOOK THE DRAWER.
6 THE BALL WENT THE DOORWAY.
7 ANGEL TAKES GREAT PRIDE HER APPEARANCE.
8 GORDON RAN THE AVENUE.

9 HER OPINION DIFFERS MINE.
10 THERE IS ALWAYS EXCEPTION THE RULE.

ANSWERS :-
1 TO
2 WITH
3 WITH
4 ON
5 IN
6 INTO
7 WITH
8 DOWN
9 FROM
10 TO

PUT THE FOLLOWING WORDS IN THE SENTENCES BEST SUITED TO THEIR USE :-
CONCLUDED, STOPPED, COMPLETED, ENDED, CLOSED, FINISHED.
1 THE MEETING AFTER THE CASTING OF VOTES.
2 THE TAILOR HAS THE ALTERATIONS.
3 HAVING ENOUGH SHARES THEY THE FUND.
4 HER WATCH AT ONE O'CLOCK.
5 I REMEMBER HOW THE STORY
6 I HAVE MY HOMEWORK.

ANSWERS :-
1 CONCLUDED.
2 FINISHED
3 CLOSED
4 STOPPED
5 ENDED
6 COMPLETED

PLACED THE FOLLOWING WORDS IN THE SENTENCES BEST SUITED TO THEIR USE :-
LISTENED, FROWNED, SMILED, SANG, MUMBLED, BOWED, CHUCKLED, WHISPERED.
1 HE   HUMBLY.
2 SHE   INDISTINCTLY.
3 HE   BROADLY.

4 SHE   GLEEFULLY.
5 SHE   TUNEFULLY.
6 HE   ANGRILY.
7 SHE   SOFTLY.
8 HE   ATTENTIVELY.

ANSWERS :-
1 BOWED.
2 WHISPERED.
3 SMILED.
4 CHUCKLED.
5 SANG.
6 FROWNED.
7 MUMBLED.
8 LISTENED.

PLACE THE FOLLOWING WORDS IN THE SENTENCES BEST SUITED TO THEIR USE.
EXPLAINED, WHISPERED, PLEADED, MUTTERED, SHOUTED, EXCLAIMED, SAID, ANSWERED.
1 SHE THAT SHE WOULD COME.
2 THE MAN WHY HE WAS LATE.
3 THE CONVICT FOR MERCY.
4 HE QUIETLY TO HIS WIFE.
5 JENNY WITH JOY.
6 "LOOK ! "SHE
7 THE GIRL UNDER HER BREATH.
8 "THAT IS SO, "SHE .

ANSWERS :-
1 SAID.
2 EXPLAINED.
3 PLEADED.
4 WHISPERED.
5 SHOUTED.
6 EXCLAIMED.
7 MUTTERED.
8 ANSWERED.

PUT THE RIGHT WORDS OF :- ANY, NO, NEVER, NOT, NONE, IN THE FOLLOWING SENTENCES.

1, HE IS WELL ENOUGH TO EAT CANDIES.

2, OF THE GIRLS KNEW THE ANSWERS.

3, THEY ARE GOING THERE MORE.

4, THANK YOU I DRINK.

5, DID YOU NOTICE RELATIVES THERE.

6, HAVE I SEEN SUCH AN ACT BEFORE.

7, WE HAVE RECEIVED OF THE TOYS.

ANSWERS :-

1 NO, NOT, ANY.

2 NONE.

3 NOT, ANY.

4 NO, NEVER.

5 ANY.

6 NEVER.

7 NOT, ANY

IN THE GIVEN SENTENCES REPLACE THE WORD "WALKED "BY A MORE SUITABLE WORD FROM THE FOLLOWING LIST.

STROLLED, PACED, RAMBLED, TRAMPED, STRODE, STAMPED, HOBBLED, MARCHED, LIMPED, PROWLED, SHUFFLED.

1 THE LAME BOY WALKED ACROSS THE LOBBY.

2 THE OLD LADY WALKED DOWN THE WALK – WAY.

3 THE ANGRY MAN WALKED INTO THE STUDIO.

4 THE PROUD GIRL WALKED UP AND DOWN THE FLOOR.

5 THE VISITORS WALKED THROUGH THE MUSEUM.

6 THE SOLDIERS WALKED TO THEIR CAMP.

7 THE CUNNING THIEF WALKED INTO THE BEDROOM.

8 THE HUSBAND AND WIFE WALKED THROUGH THE PARK.

9 THE SICK PATIENT WALKED TO HIS BED.

10 THE DISAGREEABLE GIRL WALKED INTO HER OFFICE.

11 THE HIKERS WALKED A LONG WAY.

ANSWERS :-

1 LIMPED.

2 HOBBLED

3 STAMPED

4 PACED

5 SHUFFLED

6 MARCHED

7 PROWLED

8 STROLLED

9 RAMBLED

10 TRAMPED

11 STRODE

REPLACE THE SEPARATED WORDS BY A SINGLE WORD :-

1 THE SOLDIERS WENT FORWARD TOWARDS THE VILLAGE.

2 THE MAN WAS SORRY FOR HIS HASTY WORDS.

3 SHE WISHED TO SEE HER AT ONCE.

4 THE MOVIE WAS PUT OFF FOR A WEEK.

5 THE GUARD RAN AWAY FROM HIS POST.

6 THE FUND RAISING IS HELD ONCE EVERY YEAR.

7 THE MOON WENT OUT OF SIGHT BEHIND THE CLOUDS

8 THE PEOPLE WHO LIVE NEXT DOOR ARE VERY NICE.

9 THEY MADE UP THEIR MINDS TO PLAY THE GAME.

10 THE LADY IS ALWAYS ON TIME.

ANSWERS :-

1 MARCHED

2 REGRET

3 IMMEDIATELY

4 RESCHEDULE

5 DESERTED

6 ANNUALLY

7 DISAPPEARED

8 NEIGHBORS.

9 DECIDED.

10 PUNCTUAL.

QUESTIONS :-

1 HOW MANY PEOPLE DIED WHEN THE TITANIC SANK?

2 WHAT WAS THE GREATEST NUMBER OF PEOPLE SAVED IN A SEA RESCUE?

3 WHAT 1622 SHIPWRECK WAS DISCOVERED IN 1985?

4 WHAT WAS THE GREATEST LOSS OF LIFE IN SHIPWRECK IN THIS CENTURY?

5 HOW MANY PEOPLE ARE ATTACKED BY SHARKS EACH YEAR?

6 DO SHARKS LIKE THE TASTE OF HUMANS?

7 WHAT RECENT HURRICANE CAUSED THE GREATEST MONETARY DAMAGE?

8 WHAT TROPICAL CYCLONE OR HURRICANE PRODUCED THE HIGHEST STORM SURGE?

ANSWERS :-

1 1,522 OUT OF THE 2,223 PASSENGERS PERISHED IN FREEZING WATER

2 1,660 PEOPLE WERE SAVED FROM THE ANDREA DORIA IN 1956.

3 THE SPANISH ATOCHA WAS DISCOVERED CONTAINING 40 TONS OF GOLD AND SILVER.

4 7,000 TO 8,000 PEOPLE PERISHED WHEN A GERMAN OCEAN LINER SANK IN 1945.

5 70 - 100 PEOPLE ARE ATTACKED BY SHARKS.

6 NO. THEY USUALLY BITE ONCE AND DON'T RETURN.

7 IN 1992, HURRICANE ANDREW CAUSED THIRTY BILLION DOLLARS IN DAMAGE.

8 IN 1899, A HURRICANE PRODUCED A FORTY THREE FOOT SURGE IN BATHHURST BAY, AUSTRALIA.

QUESTIONS :-

1 WHICH PRESIDENT OF THE USSR ENCOURAGED THE POLICY OF GLASSNOST?

2 WHAT IS THE WORLD'S LARGEST DESERT?

3 WHAT IS THE LAST LETTER OF THE GREEK ALPHABET?

4 WHAT MONUMENT OCCUPIES CENTER STAGE IN TRAFALGAR SQUARE?

5 WHAT WAS THE CLASSICAL STANDARD LANGUAGE OF ANCIENT INDIA?

6 NAME THE THREE TYPES OF CLASSICAL ARCHITECTURAL COLUMN?

7 BENEATH WHICH PARIS MONUMENT IN THE TOMB OF FRANCE'S UNKNOWN SOLDIER?

8 WHICH DRUG IS BEST KNOWN FOR ITS USE IN PREVENTING MALARIA?

9 WHICH SEA IS SO NAMED BECAUSE IT IS TOO SALTY TO MAINTAIN LIFE?

10 WHAT IS THE MOST INDISPENSABLE INSTRUMENT IN ASTRONOMY?

ANSWERS :-
1 MR. CHECKHOV
2 THE SAHARA
3 OMEGA
4 NELSON'S COLUMS
5 SANSKRIT
6 DORIC, IONIC, AND CONINTHIAN
7 ARC DE TRIOMPHE
8 QUININE
9 DEAD SEA
10 TELESCOPE

QUESTIONS :-
1 WHICH INDEPENDENT ISLAND IS AUSTRALIA'S NEAREST NEIGHBOR TO THE WEST?

2 AT THE END OF SHAKESPEARE'S ROMEO AND JULIET, WHICH OF THE PRINCIPLES ARE DEAD?

3 NAME A STATE OF THE U.S.A BEGINNING WITH B?

4 WHAT WAS THE FIRST EVENT DECIDED AT THE 1896 OLYMPICS?

5 WHICH IS THE ONLY CONTINENT OCCUPIED BY ONE NATION?

6 WHAT IS GOD CALLED BY THE ISLAMIC OR MUSLIM FAITH?

7 IN WHICH AMERICAN CITY WAS THE WORLD'S FIRST SKYSCRAPER BUILT IN 1885?

8 WHAT IS THE CHRISTIAN NAME OF WEBSTER, WHO PUBLISHED A DICTIONARY STILL USED TODAY?

9 OUTSIDE OF THE PRESIDENCY, WHAT IS THE HIGHEST AMERICAN POLITICAL OFFICE?

10 NAME THE ONLY BOXER TO KNOCK OUT MOHAMMED ALI?

11 ON WHAT DATE DO AMERICANS CELEBRATE THEIR INDEPENDENCE DAY?

12 IF YOU CELEBRATING YOUR DIAMOND ANNIVERSARY, HOW MANY YEARS HAVE YOU BEEN MARRIED?

13 IN WHAT DECADE OF THIS CENTURY WAS IT DECIDED U.S.A PRESIDENTS WOULD BE RESTRICTED TO TWO TERMS?

14 WHAT WAS THE GIVEN NAME OF STALIN'S DAUGHTER WHO DEFECTED TO THE U.S.A IN 1967?

15 NAME THE SOUTH AFRICAN SURGEON WHO CARRIED OUT THE FIRST HEART TRANSPLANT OPERATION?

16 WHAT WAS THE FIRST SHIP TO REACH THE TITANIC AFTER THE DISASTER?

ANSWERS :-

1 MAURITIUS

2 BOTH ROMEO AND JULIET

3 THERE IS NONE

4 TRIPLE JUMP

5 AUSTRALIA

6 ALLAH

7 CHICAGO

8 NOAH

9 PRESIDENT OF THE UNITED STATES SENATE

10 LARRY HOLMES IN 1980

11 JULY 4 TH

12 SIXTY

13 THE 6 TH, 1951

14 SVETLANA

15 DR. CHRISTIAN BARNARD

16 THE CARPARTHIA

QUESTIONS :-

1 WHERE WERE THE 1960 SUMMER OLYMPICS HELD?

2 NAME THE MAIN ORE OF IRON?

3 WHAT IS THE STUDY OF HEREDITY CALLED?

4 WHAT ANCIENT UNIT OF MEASUREMENT IS SUPPOSEDLY THE DISTANCE FROM THE ELBOW TO THE TIP OF THE INDEX FINGER?

5 WHAT IS THE OFFICIAL LANGUAGE OF EGYPT?

6 ON WHICH CONTINENT IS VINCON MASSIF THE HIGHEST PEAK?

7 WHERE DID JOHN F KENNEDY, LEE HARVEY OSWALD, AND JACK RUBY ALL DIE?

8 WHAT IS THE LAST BOOK OF THE BIBLE?

9 WHAT IS THE ALTERNATIVE NAME FOR A BEEKEEPER?

10 HOW MANY BOOKS COMPRISE THE OLD AND NEW TESTAMENTS?

11 AT WHAT ANGLE ABOVE THE HORIZON MUST THE SUN BE TO CREATE A RAINBOW?

ANSWERS :-

1 ROME

2 HEMATITE

3 GENETICS

4 THE CUBIT

5 ARABIC

6 ANTARCTICA

7 PARKLAND MEMORIAL HOSPITAL, DALLAS, TEXAS, U.S.A

8 REVELATION

9 APIARIST

10 39 IN THE OLD TESTAMENT AND 27 IN THE NEW TESTAMENT

11 40 DEGREES

QUESTIONS :-

1 WHAT IS THE HEBREW NAME OF CALVARY, WHERE JESUS CHRIST WAS CRUCIFIED?

2 WHICH NUMBER ON A ROULETTE WHEEL IS COLORED GREEN?

3 HOW MANY CANNONS ARE INVOLVED IN A ROYAL SALUTE?

4 WHICH ISLAND IS 50 TIMES LARGER THAN ITS MOTHER COUNTRY, DENMARK?

5 WHO WAS THE FIRST WHITE MAN TO CLIMB MT. KOSCIUSKO?

6 WHAT NAME IS GIVEN TO THE POPE'S PONTIFICIAL RING?

7 WHAT WAS THE NAME OF THE FIRST PATENTED CONTRACEPTIVE PILL?

8 WHAT NAME IS GIVEN COLLECTIVELY TO THE FIRST FIVE BOOKS OF THE BIBLE?

9 IN WHAT YEAR DID JAPAN BOMB PEARL HARBOR?

ROY NOLAN

10 WHAT NUMBER DID MICHAEL JORDAN MAKE FAMOUS DURING HIS CAREER WITH THE CHICAGO BULLS?

11 HOW MANY SIDES DOES A RHOMBUS HAVE?

12 UNTIL THE END OF THE 20 TH CENTURY, WHAT WAS THE MOST POPULAR NAME ADOPTED BY THE POPES?

13 WHAT NAME IS GIVEN TO THE STAR THAT APPEARS ON THE FLAG OF ISRAEL?

14 K IS THE CHEMICAL SYMBOL FOR WHAT?

ANSWERS :-
1 GOLGOTHA
2 ZERO
3 TWENTY - ONE
4 GREENLAND
5 PAUL STRZLECKI
6 THE FISHERMAN'S RING
7 ENOVID
8 THE PENTALEUCH, TORAH
9 1941
10 23
11 FOUR
12 JOHN
13 THE STAR OF DAVID
14 POTASSIUM

QUESTIONS :-
1 WHICH AMERICAN PRESIDENT WAS ASSASSINATED BY LEON CZOLGOSZ?

2 TO WHICH PEOPLE DID DELILAH PASS ON THE SECRET OF SAMSON'S STRENGTH?

3 WHO WROTE THE SHORTEST OF THE GOSPELS?

4 NAME THE FIRST WOMAN IN SPACE?

5 WHO WAS CONVICTED OF SHOOTING AND KILLING JOHN F KENNEDY?

6 THE SOUND OF MUSIC IS SET IN WHICH EUROPEAN COUNTRY?

7 WHICH PLANET HAS THE LONGEST YEAR?

8 IN EARTH TERMS, HOW LONG IS THAT YEAR?

9 WHAT IS THE HIGHEST MOUNTAIN IN NEW ZEALAND?

10 WHAT TERM IS USED TO DESCRIBE THE WOOL CUT FROM AROUND A SHEEP'S EYES?

11 WHAT TYPE OF CREATURE IS A BEAGLE?

12 IN WHAT ASIAN NATION WOULD YOU FIND THE STATE OF PUNJAB?

13 Ra IS THE CHEMICAL SYMBOL FOR WHICH ELEMENT?

14 HOW MANY METERS MAKE A KILOMETER?

15 WHO FOUNDED THE KENTUCKY FRIED CHICKEN RESTAURANT CHAIN?

ANSWERS :-

1 WILLIAM McKINLEY

2 THE PHILISTINES

3 MARK

4 VALENTINA TERESKOAVA

5 LEE HARVEY OSWALD

6 AUSTRIA

7 PLUTO

8 247 YEARS, 255 DAYS

9 MT. COOK

10 EYECLIP

11 DOG

12 INDIA

13 RADIUM

14 1000

15 COLONEL HARLAN SANDERS

QUESTIONS :-

1 IN WHICH YEAR DID FRED ASTAIR DIE?

2 WHO WAS THE 3 RD MAN ON THE MOON?

3 WHO WAS THE LAST PERSON TO BE EXECUTED IN THE TOWER OF LONDON?

4 WHAT IS THE WORLD'S LARGEST BIRD OF PREY?

5 NEAR WHICH ISRAELI CITY WOULD YOU FIND THE MOUNT OF OLIVES?

6 WHAT COLOR ARE THE THE TOWERS OF SAN FRANCISCO'S GOLDEN GATE BRIDGE?

7 HOW MANY YEARS OF MARRIAGE ARE CELEBRATED BY A GOLDEN WEDDING ANNIVERSARY?

8 WHAT NAME IS GIVEN TO THE PUNCTUATION MARK WITH A DOT DIRECTLY ABOVE A COMMA?

9 WHO DISCOVERED OXYGEN IN 1774?

10 HOW MANY EARTH YEARS DOES IT TAKE PLUTO TO ORBIT THE SUN?

11 WHAT NAME IS GIVEN TO THE CENTRAL PART OF A FLESHY FRUIT, CONTAINING THE SEEDS?

12 WHAT IS IT THAT MAKES SODA WATER FIZZ?

ANSWERS :-

1 1987

2 CHARLES CONRAD

3 JOSEF JAKOBS

4 CALIFORNIAN CONDOR

5 JERUSALEM

6 RED

7 50

8 SEMI - COLON

9 JOSEPH PRIESTLY

10 248

11 THE CORE

12 CARBON DIOXIDE

QUESTIONS :-

1 NAME FOUR TYPES OF ANGLES?

2 NAME THREE GROUPS WHICH ARE VERTEBRATE ANIMALS?

3 THE ANIMAL KINGDOM IS DIVIDED INTO WHAT TWO GROUPS?

4 WHO WAS THE EXPLORER THAT FIRST REACHED THE NORTH POLE?

5 HOW MANY PLANETS ARE THERE?

6 NAME FIVE PLANETS?

7 THE ZODIAC IS MADE UP OF A BELT OF HOW MANY CONSTELLATION?

8 NAME FIVE OF THE ZODIAC CONSTELLATION?

9 WHAT ARE ENGLISH NAMES FOR AQUARIUS, CANCER, AND LEO RESPECTIVELY?

10 NAME TWO PHASES OF THE MOON?

11 NAME FOUR COLORS OF THE STARS?

12 WHERE IS GREENWICH MEAN TIME LOCATED AND RECKONED FROM?

13 WHO INVENTED THE SEWING MACHINE?

14 WHO INVENTED THE AIRPLANE?

ANSWERS :-

1 RIGHT, ACUTE, OBTUSE, COMPLEMENTARY.

2 BIRDS, MAMMALS, FISHES.

3 INVERTEBRATES, VERTEBRATES.

4 ROBERT E PEARY OF THE U.S.A.IN 1909.

5 NINE

6 EARTH, MARS, PLUTO, VENUS, JUPITER.

7 12

8 AQUARIUS, PISCES, GEMINI, LEO, CANCER.

9 WATER CARRIER, CRAB, LION.

10 NEW MOON, FULL MOON.

11 WHITE, YELLOW, ORANGE, RED.

12 IN THE UNITED KINGDOM.

13 BARTHELEMY THIMONNIER OF FRANCE IN 1830

14 WILBUR AND ORVILLE WRIGHT OF U.S.A IN 1903

QUESTIONS :-

1 NAME THREE MINERALS THAT ARE EFFECTIVE AS ABRASIVES?

2 WHICH SCALE LIST MINERALS IN ORDER OF HARDNESS?

3 WHAT ARE THE FOUR OBSERVABLE SIGNS THAT MAKE UP THE VITAL SIGNS IN PATIENTS

4 NAME FOUR STATES IN THE U.S.A THAT STARTS WITH A?

5 NAME TWO OUTLYING AREAS OF THE U.S.A?

6 WHERE IS THE HEADQUARTERS OF THE UNITED NATIONS ESTABLISHED?

7 WHAT IS THE IMO ORGANIZATION?

8 WHAT IS THE WMO ORGANIZATION?

9 WHAT IS THE WHO ORGANIZATION?

10 WHAT IS THE FAO ORGANIZATION?

11 NAME FIVE MEMBER STATES OF THE UNITED NATIONS?

12 NAME THREE FORMER PRESIDENTS OF THE UNITED STATES?

ANSWERS :-

1 QUARTZ, TOPAZ, DIAMOND.

2 MOHS.

3 TEMPERATURE, PULSE, RESPIRATION RATE, AND BLOOD PRESSURE.

4 ALABAMA, ALASKA, ARIZONA, ARKANSAS.

5 PUERTO RICO, VIRGIN ISLANDS.

6 IN NEW YORK, U.S.A.

7 INTERNATIONAL MARITIME ORGANIZATION.

8 WORLD METEOROLOGICAL ORGANIZATION.

9 WORLD HEALTH ORGANIZATION.

10 FOOD AND AGRICULTURE ORGANIZATION.

11 AUSTRALIA, BARBADOS, CAMBODIA, MEXICO, PHILIPPINES.

12 RICHARD NIXON, RONALD REGAN, BILL CLINTON.

QUESTIONS :-

1 NAME FIVE MIDDLE EASTERN COUNTRIES?

2 NAME THREE ETHNIC GROUPS OF THE MIDDLE EAST?

3 NAME FIVE COUNTRIES OF LATIN AMERICA?

4 NAME FIVE MAMMALS?

5 NAME FOUR BRANCHES OF MATHEMATICS?

6 NAME FOUR MINERALS?

7 NAME THREE PLANTS BELONGING TO THE MINT FAMILY?

8 NAME THREE OF THE HIGHEST MOUNTAINS IN THE WORLD?

9 NAME FIVE MUSICAL INSTRUMENTS?

10 COMPLETE THE FABLE : UNITED WE STAND

11 NAME FIVE COUNTRIES OF AFRICA?

12 NAME FOUR PRINCIPAL ALLOYS.?

ANSWERS :-

1 ISRAEL, IRAQ, IRAN, SAUDI ARABIA, EGYPT.

2 ARABS, JEWS, PERSIANS.

3 BRAZIL, CUBA, DOMINICA, HAITI, GUYANA.

4 MAN, MONKEY, DOG, SHEEP, WHALE.

5 ARITHMETIC, ALGEBRA, GEOMETRY, TRIGONOMETRY.

6 GOLD, COPPER, QUARTZ, BERYL.

7 THYME, HYSSOP, LAVENDER.

8 EVEREST, ANDES, KENYA.

9 DRUM, CYMBAL, GUITAR, PIANO, VIOLIN.

10 DIVIDED WE FALL.

11 ANGOLA, GHANA, LIBERIA, NIGERIA, SOUTH AFRICA.

12 BRONZE, ALUMINUM, IRON, LEAD.

QUESTIONS :-

1 WHEN DID SADDAM HUSSEIN BECOME PRESIDENT OF IRAQ?

2 WHO THOUGHT OF DAYLIGHT SAVING TIME?

3 WHAT IS THE SMALLEST REPUBLIC IN THE WORLD?

4 WHO CAME UP WITH COCO COLA?

5 WHAT IS THE FIRST KNOWN MATHEMATICAL PUZZLE?

6 WHO INVENTED THE KALEIDOSCOPE?

7 WHAT IS THE LARGEST FISH?

8 WHAT IS THE WORLD'S SMALLEST PRIMATE?

9 WHO WAS THE FIRST SECRETARY GENERAL OF THE UNITED NATIONS?

10 WHAT WAS THE DISTRESS SIGNAL BEFORE S.O.S WAS ADOPTED IN 1908?

11 WHAT IS THE LONGEST POSSIBLE COMPUTER – DOMAIN NAME?

12 WHICH IS SAID TO BE THE DEEPEST LAKE?

13 WHAT IS SAID TO BE THE HIGHEST WIND GUST EVER RECORDED?

14 WHEN DID DECEMBER, 25 BECOME CHRISTMAS?

15 HOW FAST HAS ANYONE EVER TRAVELED ON LAND?

16 WHO INVENTED THE SLIDE RULE?

17 WHO INVENTED ICE CREAM?

18 WHO INVENTED THE STETHOSCOPE?

19 WHO DISCOVERED PENICILLIN?

ANSWERS :-

1 JULY 17, 1979

2 BENJAMIN FRANKLIN WHILE IN PARIS IN 1784

3 NAURU

VATICAN CITY AND MONACO ARE SMALLER, BUT ARE NOT REPUBLICS.

4 JOHN PEMBERTON IN 1886

5 THE RHIND PAPYRUS AN EGYPTIAN SCROLL WRITTEN AROUND 1650 BC.

6 IT WAS INVENTED BY SIR DAVID BREWSTER OF SCOTLAND IN 1816

7 THE WHALE SHARK

8 LESSER MOUSE LEMUR

9 TRYGUE LIE OF NORWAY 1946 - 1952

10 CQD

11 67 CHARACTERS, INCLUDING THE .COM

12 LAKE BAIKAL IN RUSSIA 5,134 FEET.

13 231 MILES PER HOUR ON TOP OF MT. WASHINGTON, NEW HAMPSHIRE 11 APRIL, 1934

14 IN 354 THE CHURCH IN ROME DECLARED THE BIRTHDAY OF JESUS CHRIST.

15 763. 035 MILES PER HOUR, FASTER THAN THE SPEED OF SOUND, OCTOBER, 13, 1977 BY ANDY GREEN.

16 WILLIAM OUGHTRED, IN 1630

17 THE CHINESE ABOUT 2000 BC

18 RENE THEOPHILE HYACINTHE LAENNEC IN 1816

19 ALEXANDER FLEMING IN 1928

QUESTIONS :-

1 NAME FOUR MODES OF TRANSPORTATION?

2 NAME THREE OF THE TOP UNIVERSITIES OF THE WORLD?

3 WHO IS THE RICHEST PERSON IN THE WORLD?

4 WHO IS ONE OF THE RICHEST WOMAN IN THE WORLD?

5 NAME FOUR POWERFUL WOMEN IN THE WORLD?

6 NAME FIVE COMPANIES OF WHICH MINORITIES MAKE UP A LARGE PERCENTAGE OF THE WORK FORCE?

7 NAME THE COUNTRY WHICH HAS THE MOST BILLIONAIRES?

8 WHAT IS FLORA REFERRED TO?

9 WHAT IS FAUNA REFERRED TO?

10 NAME FOUR OF THE WORLD'S REGIONS?

11 WHICH ARE THE TWO RICHEST COUNTRIES OF THE WORLD?

12 WHICH ARE THE THREE POOREST COUNTRIES OF THE WORLD?

13 NAME FIVE BUSINESS INDUSTRIES?

14 NAME THE TOP SIX OIL PRODUCING COUNTRIES OF THE WORLD?

15 NAME THREE COUNTRIES OF THE OECD?

ANSWERS :-

1 CAR, TRAIN, SHIP, AIRPLANE.

2 HARVARD, OXFORD, YALE.

3 WILLIAM [BILL] GATES OF MICROSOFT U.S.A

4 ALICE L WALTON OF WAL – MART U.S.A

5 OPRAH WINFREY, MARJORIE MAGNER, ANDREA JUNG, MEG WHITMAN.

6 McDONALDS, FANNIE MAE, U.S POSTAL SERVICE, U.P.S., VERIZON COMMUNICATIONS.

7 UNITED STATES OF AMERICA.

8 PLANT LIFE.

9 ANIMAL LIFE.

10 CARIBBEAN, OCEANIA, AFRICA, NORTH AMERICA.

11 LUXEMBOURG, U.S.A.

12 EAST TUMOR, SOMALIA, SIERRA LEONE.

13 AIRLINES, BANKS, CONSUMER SERVICES, ENERGY, FOOD.

14 SAUDI ARABIA, U.S.A, RUSSIA, MEXICO, CHINA, IRAN.

15 CANADA, FRANCE, ITALY.

QUESTIONS :-

1 WHAT DIVIDES THE EARTH INTO TWO HEMISPHERES?

2 NAME THREE TYPES OF LIBRARIES?

3 NAME FOUR TYPES OF TIMBER – LUMBER?

4 NAME FOUR MEANS OF TRANSACTION – EXCHANGE USE AS MONEY?

5 NAME SIX TYPES OF RELIGION THAT IS PRACTICE IN THE WORLD?

6 WHAT SCALE IS EARTHQUAKE MEASURED ON?

7 WHAT SCALE IS TORNADO SPEED ESTIMATED ON?

8 NAME FOUR SCALES USED IN EVERYDAY LIFE?

9 NAME TWO KINDS OF MONITORING MACHINES?

10 NAME THREE FIELDS OF CHEMISTRY STUDIES?

11 NAME THREE FIELDS OF PHYSICS STUDIES?

12 NAME FOUR IMPORTANT INTERNATIONAL ORGANIZATIONS?

13 NAME THREE OF THE HIGHEST WATERFALLS IN THE WORLD?

ANSWERS :-

1 EQUATOR

2 PUBLIC, SCHOOL, SCIENCE.

3 MAHOGANY, GREENHEART, PULPWOOD, EBONY.

4 GOLD, SILVER, PAPER MONEY, COINS.

5 CHRISTIAN, JUDAISM, ISLAM, HINDUISM, SIKH, BUDDHISM.

6 RICHTER MAGNITUDE SCALE.

7 THE FUJITA SCALE.

8 JEWELRY SCALE, KITCHEN SCALE, SHIPPING SCALE, BATHROOM SCALE.

9 BLOOD PRESSURE MONITOR, HEART RATE MONITOR.

10 CHEMICAL ENGINEERING, CHEMICAL PHYSICS, GEO CHEMISTRY.

11 ATOMIC PHYSICS, PLASMA PHYSICS, THEORETICAL PHYSICS.

12 UNITED NATIONS, WORLD BANK, GLOBAL MARKETS, INTERNATIONAL MONETARY FUND.

13 ANGEL IN VENEZUELA, TUGELA IN SOUTH AFRICA, UTIGORD IN NORWAY.

QUESTIONS :-

1 WHAT CAN THE NATURE OF ANATOMY BE DIVIDED AND CLASSIFIED AS?

2 NAME FOUR SYSTEMS UNDER HUMAN ANATOMY?

3 ABOUT HOW MANY POUNDS THE HUMAN BRAIN WEIGHS?

4 NAME THREE AREAS OF THE BODY COMMONLY DISTURBED BY CANCEROUS ATTACKS?

5 NAME FOUR FIELDS OF PRACTICE IN WHICH DOCTORS WORK?

6 NAME THREE TYPES OF DEADLY DISEASES?

7 HOW MANY CONTINENTS ARE IN THE WORLD?

8 NAME FIVE OF THE WORLD'S CONTINENTS?

9 WHICH IS THE LARGEST OF THE WORLD'S SEVEN CONTINENTS?

10 NAME FIVE COUNTRIES OF ASIA?

11 NAME THREE OF THE COUNTRIES OF CENTRAL AMERICA?

12 NAME FIVE STATES OF THE U.S.S.R?

13 WHAT DO THE ABBREVIATIONS B.A, M.A, B.Sc STAND FOR RESPECTIVELY?

ANSWERS :-

1 ANIMAL ANATOMY AND PLANT ANATOMY.

2 NERVOUS SYSTEM, SKELETAL SYSTEM, CIRCULATORY SYSTEM, DIGESTIVE SYSTEM.

3 ABOUT THREE POUNDS.

4 COLON, BREASTS, PROSTATE GLAND.

5 NEUROLOGY, GENERAL MEDICINE, PEDIATRICS, GERIATRICS.

6 HEART DISEASE, AIDS, STROKE.

7 SEVEN.

8 ASIA, EUROPE, AFRICA, SOUTH AMERICA, NORTH AMERICA.

9 ASIA.

10 BANGLADESH, TAIWAN, INDIA, PAKISTAN, TURKEY.

11 COSTA RICA, BELIZE, PANAMA.

12 LITHUANIA, BELARUS, UKRAINE, ARMENIA, KYRGYZSTAN.

13 BACHELOR OF ARTS, MASTER OF ARTS, BACHELOR OF SCIENCE.

QUESTIONS :-

1 WHAT IS THE COLOR OF THE BLACK BOX THAT HOUSES AN AIRPLANE'S VOICE RECORDER?

2 NAMES OF THE TWO LIONS GUARDING THE STEPS OF THE NEW YORK PUBLIC LIBRARY?

3 WHAT IS THE MAKE OF CAR THAT WAS NAMED FOR A CHIEF OF THE OTTAWA INDIANS?

4 HOW MANY ELECTORAL VOTES ARE REQUIRED TO WIN THE PRESIDENCY OF THE UNITED STATES OF AMERICA?

5 WHAT IS THE NUMBER OF CHRISTMAS LIGHTS THAT ADORN THE FAMOUS ROCKEFELLER CENTER TREE?

6 WHAT IS THE NUMBER OF STEPS LEADING TO THE TOP OF THE LEANING TOWER OF PISA?

7 WHAT WAS THE ORIGINAL BARBIE DOLL SOLD FOR?

8 WHEN WAS THE FIRST TELEPHONE DIRECTORY PUBLISHED?

9 WHO WAS THE FIRST BLACK WOMAN TO BE EDUCATED AS A DOCTOR IN THE UNITED STATES OF AMERICA?

10 WHO WAS THE DOCTOR THAT DEVELOPED A TEST FOR DETECTING SYPHILIS?

11 IN 1973 THE FIRST BLACK OTOLARYNGOLOGIST – EAR, THROAT, AND NOSE SPECIALIST WAS?

12 WHO IS THE AFRICAN AMERICAN WOMAN WHO INVENTED THE IRONING BOARD AND RECEIVED A PATENT IN 1892?

13 WHO INVENTED THE AUTHOMATIC TRAFFIC SIGNAL?

14 THE FIRST AFRICAN AMERICAN IN SPACE ON CHALLENGER IN AUGUST, 1983 WAS?

15 THE FIRST AFRICAN AMERICAN TO RECEIVE A DEGREE IN COMPUTER SCIENCE IS?

ANSWERS :-

1 ORANGE

2 PATIENCE AND FORTITUDE

3 PONTIAC

4 270

5 26000

6 296

7 THREE DOLLARS

8 IT WAS PUBLISHED IN NEW HAVEN, CONNECTICUT, FEBRUARY 21, 1878.

9 REBECCA LEE - CRUMPLER

10 WILLIAM A HINTON

11 WILLIAM H BARNES

12 SARAH BOONE

13 GARRETT A MORGAN

14 COLONEL GUION GUY BLUFORD

15 CLARENCE ELLIS

QUESTIONS :-

1 WHEN DID HORSE RACING BECOME AMERICA'S FIRST ORGANIZED SPORT?

2 WHICH COUNTRY CONSUMES THE MOST COCA COLA?

3 WHO DISCOVERED INSULIN?

4 WHO WAS THE U.S.A PRESIDENT TO BE BORN IN A LOG CABIN?

5 WHICH MONTH OF THE YEAR THE EARTH IS CLOSEST TO THE SUN, BETWEEN THE 1 ST AND 4 TH, WHEN THE EARTH IS 91.4 MILLION MILES FROM THE SUN; THIS POINT IS KNOWN AS PERIHELION.

6 WHICH IS THE ONLY SNAKE THAT BUILDS A NEST FOR ITS EGGS?

7 WHICH IS THE LARGEST LAKE IN CENTRAL AMERICA?

8 WHICH IS THE LARGEST FRESH WATER LAKE IN THE WORLD?

9 WHICH IS THE ONLY COUNTRY IN THE MIDDLE EAST THAT DOES NOT HAVE A DESERT?

10 WHICH COUNTRY HAS A GREEN SINGLE COLORED FLAG?

11 WHAT IS THE WORLD'S MOST POPULAR BRAND OF CIGARETTE?

13 HOW OLD WAS NOAH, WHEN THE RAINS – THE GREAT FLOOD CAME?

14 WHAT IS THE NUMBER OF RECORDINGS SOLD FOR A SINGLE RECORD TO BE CONSIDERED PLATINUM?

ANSWERS :-

1 1664

2 ICELAND – PER CAPITA

3 CHARLES BEST AND FREDRICK BANTING

4 ANDREW JACKSON

5 JANUARY

6 KING COBRA

7 LAKE NICARAGUA

8 LAKE SUPERIOR

9 LEBANON

10 LIBYA

11 MARLBORO

12 CINDY NICHOLAS

13 NOAH WAS 600 YEARS, 2 MONTHS, 17 DAYS OLD.

14 1 MILLION

QUESTIONS :-

1 WHO WAS THE FIRST FEMALE VOCALIST TO ACHIEVE 7 CONSECUTIVE TRIPLE – PLATINUM ALBUMS?

2 WHAT WAS FRANKLIN D ROOSEVELT'S ALLIED CODE NAME DURING WORLD WAR 2?

3 WHO WAS THE FIRST U.S.A PRESIDENT TO BE BORN IN A HOSPITAL?

4 WHICH FOOD GETS ITS NAME FROM THE AZTEC WORD XOCATL MEANING BITTER WATER?

5 WHICH OUTFIT LAUNCHED THE FIRST CLONE OF AN IBM PERSONAL COMPUTER IN 1982?

6 WHO WAS THE FIRST PRESIDENT TO LIVE IN THE WHITE HOUSE?

7 HOW MANY PEOPLE VISIT THE GRAND CANYON EACH YEAR?

8 WHEN WAS D – DAY?

9 HOW MANY U.S.A PRESIDENTS GOT ASSASSINATED WHILE IN OFFICE?

10 WHEN WAS THE FIRST AIRPLANE FLOWN?

11 WHICH WAS THE FIRST APOLLO MISSION TO CARRY A COLOR T.V CAMERA TO THE MOON?

12 WHEN DID THE BEATLES U.S. ALBUM DEBUT?

13 WHAT IS THE C.I.A.'S HIGHEST HONOR FOR BRAVERY?

14 WHAT IS THE ENGLISH NAME FOR CHECKERS?

15 WHO WAS THE YOUNGEST BRITISH MONARCH, BECOMING KING AT THE AGE OF 8 MONTHS?

ANSWERS :-
1 MARIAH CAREY
2 CARGO
3 JIMMY CARTER
4 CHOCOLATE
5 COMPAC
6 JOHN ADAMS AND HIS WIFE ABIGAIL
7 OVER 5 MILLION
8 JUNE,6 TH,1944
9 FOUR – ABRAHAM LINCOLN, JAMES A GARFIELD, WILLIAM MCKINLEY, JOHN F KENNEDY.
10 DECEMBER, 17 TH 1903 THE WRIGHT BROTHERS; ORVILLE AND WILBUR.
11 APOLLO X11
12 1964
13 THE DISTINGUISHED INTELLIGENCE CROSS.
14 DRAUGHTS
15 HENRY V1

QUESTIONS :-
1 NAME FIVE GEMS?
2 NAME FOUR FIELDS OF STUDIES IN GEOLOGY?
3 HOW MANY QUARTS EQUAL TO ONE GALLON?
4 HOW MANY POUNDS EQUAL TO ONE HUNDREDWEIGHT?
5 HOW MANY POUNDS EQUAL TO ONE TON?

6 HOW MANY CHAINS EQUAL TO ONE MILE?

7 HOW MANY METERS EQUAL TO ONE NAUTICAL MILE?

8 HOW MANY DEGREES EQUAL TO ONE CIRCLE?

9 HOW MANY KILOGRAMS EQUAL TO ONE METRIC TON?

10 NAME FIVE COUNTRIES OF THE WEST INDIES?

11 NAME FIVE COUNTRIES OF THE CARIBBEAN?

12 NAME FIVE CARICOM MEMBER STATES?

13 NAME THREE OF THE LARGEST COUNTRIES OF THE WORLD?

14 NAME THREE OF THE LARGEST ISLANDS OF THE WORLD?

15 WHAT SCALE IS WIND SPEED MEASURED ON?

16 NAME FIVE KINDS OF PESTS?

17 NAME TWO OF THE LARGEST CANALS OF THE WORLD?

18 NAME THE COLORS OF THE RAINBOW?

ANSWERS :-

1 EMERALDS, RUBIES, DIAMONDS, TOPAZ, JASPER.

2 GEOPHYSICS, GEOCHEMISTRY, ENGINEERING GEOLOGY, ECONOMIC GEOLOGY.

3 4

4 100

5 2240 LBS

6 80

7 1852

8 360

9 1000

10 ST. LUCIA, ST KITTS – NEVIS, MARTINQUE, GUADELOUPE, TURKS AND CAICOS ISLANDS.

11 ARUBA, CUBA, GRENADA, HAITI, ST. VINCENT AND THE GRENADINES.

12 BELIZE, BAHAMAS, DOMINICA, SURINAME, MONTSERRAT

13 RUSSIA, CANADA, CHINA.

14 GREENLAND, NEW GUINEA, BORNEO

15 BEAUFORT

16 COCKROACH, MOSQUITO, LOUSE, TERMITE, FLEA.

17 PANAMA, SUEZ

18 RED, ORANGE, YELLOW, GREEN, BLUE, VIOLET.

QUESTIONS :-

1 NAME FOUR TYPES OF ATHLETIC EVENTS?

2 NAME SIX TYPES OF SPORTING EVENTS?

3 NAME THREE INDOORS SPORTING EVENTS?

4 HOW DO FISHES BREATHE?

5 NAME THREE TYPES OF DOMESTIC BIRDS?

6 NAME FOUR HOLIDAYS KNOWN THROUGH OUT THE WORLD?

7 NAME FIVE RECIPIENTS OF THE NOBEL PEACE PRIZE?

8 WHAT IS THE ROMAN NUMERALS FOR 5, 10, 50, 100, 1000 RESPECTIVELY?

9 NAME THREE OCEANS OF THE WORLD?

10 NAME FOUR COUNTRIES OF OCEANIA?

11 NAME TWO OF THE LARGEST SEAS OF THE WORLD?

12 NAME TWO OF THE LARGEST LAKES OF THE WORLD?

13 NAME FOUR KINDS OF KNOTS?

14 NAME SEVEN LANGUAGES SPOKEN IN THE WORLD?

ANSWERS :-

1 100 METERS, 110 METERS HURDLES, HIGH JUMP, DECATHION.

2 BASKETBALL, FOOTBALL, SOCCER, HOCKEY, ICE SKATING, CRICKET.

3 CHESS, CARDS, POOLS

4 THROUGH GILLS.

5 DUCKS, GEESE, PIGEON

6 MOTHERS' DAY, FATHERS' DAY, VALENTINE'S DAY, CHRISTMAS

7 ANWAR SADAT [EGYPT], MOTHER TERESA [INDIA], DALAI LAMA [TIBET], NELSON MANDELA [AFRICA], JIMMY CARTER [U.S.A]

8 V, X, L, C, M

9 PACIFIC, ATLANTIC, INDIAN

10 NEW ZEALAND, TAIWAN, JAPAN, INDONESIA

11 MEDITERRANEAN SEA, CARIBBEAN SEA

12 LAKE SUPERIOR, LAKE HURON

13 BOWLINE, FIGURE OF EIGHT, REEF KNOT, SHEEPSHANK

14 ENGLISH, FRENCH, SPANISH, RUSSIAN, ARABIC, HINDI, GREEK, ITALIAN, PORTUGUESE.

QUESTIONS :-

1 NAME SIX COMMONWEALTH NATIONS?

2 NAME TWO THINGS CIGARETTE SMOKING MAY CAUSE?

3 NAME THREE EFFECTS ALCHOLICS SUFFER FROM?

4 NAME FIVE FIELDS OF SCIENCE?

5 NAME TWO TYPES OF SOIL OF THE EARTH?

6 NAME SEVEN COUNTRIES OF SOUTH AMERICA?

7 WHICH SOUTH AMERICAN COUNTRY SPEAKS DUTCH?

8 WHICH SOUTH AMERICAN COUNTRY SPEAKS FRENCH?

9 WHICH SOUTH AMERICAN COUNTRY SPEAKS ENGLISH?

10 WHAT ARE THREE RECOGNIZED STROKES OF SWIMMING?

11 WHAT SIZE OF POOL IS RECOGNIZED FOR SWIMMING IN INTERNATIONAL COMPETITION?

12 NAME THREE FORMS OF TAXATION?

13 NAME THREE TYPES OF TEETH?

14 WHAT IS THE THERMOMETER USED FOR?

ANSWERS :-

1 JAMAICA, MALAYSIA, IRELAND, PAPUA NEW GUINEA, GHANA, BERMUDA.

2 LUNG CANCER, HEART DISEASE

3 TREMORS, STRESS, CONVULSIONS

4 PHYSICS, CHEMISTRY, ZOOLOGY, BOTANY, ANATOMY

5 OXISOL, VERTISOL

6 BRAZIL, COLOMBIA, ECUADOR, PERU, ARGENTINA, FRENCH GUIANA, PARAGUAY.

7 SURINAME

8 FRENCH GUIANA

9 GUYANA

10 FREESTYLE, BACKSTROKE, BUTTERFLY

11 50 METERS

12 INCOME TAX, IMPORT DUTIES, EXCISES TAXES.

13 INCISORS, BICUSPIDS, MOLARS.

14 TO MEASURE TEMPERATURE.

QUESTIONS :-

1 NAME FIVE AREAS OF LAW?

2 IN WHICH COUNTRY IS THE INTERNATIONAL COURT OF JUSTICE?

3 NAME SEVEN HEADINGS THAT QUANTITIES ARE MEASURED UNDER?

4 NAME SEVEN INTERESTING FIELDS OF STUDIES?

5 NAME THREE AREAS THAT WORLD AGRICULTURE COVER?

6 NAME SIX CHEMICAL ELEMENTS?

7 NAME SIX MINERALS?

8 NAME SEVEN COUNTRIES OF EUROPE?

9 NAME THREE AIR POLLUTANTS?

10 NAME TWO SOURCES OF ENERGY?

11 NAME THREE TYPES OF GASES?

12 NAME FIVE COUNTIES OF ENGLAND?

ANSWERS :-

1   BUSINESS, BANKRUPTCY, CRIMINAL, LABOR, MALPRACTICE.

2 THE HAGUE – NETHERLANDS.

3   LENGTH, MASS, TIME, VOLUME, AREA, DENSITY, PRESSURE.

4 ART, CHEMISTRY, PHYSICS, LAW, COMPUTER SCIENCE, MEDICINE, BUSINESS.

5   LIVESTOCK FARMING, DIARY FARMING, FOREST EXPLORATION.

6   CHLORINE, IODINE, MERCURY, NITROGEN, OXYGEN, SODIUM.

7 SILVER, GOLD, LEAD, ZINC, DIAMOND, BAUXITE.

8   DENMARK, FRANCE, SPAIN, YUGOSLAVIA, SWEDEN, POLAND, GREECE.

9 CARBON DIOXIDE, CARBON MONOXIDE, ETHANE.

10 GAS, ELECTRICITY.

11 HYDROGEN, NITROGEN, OXYGEN.

12   ESSEX, HAMPSHIRE, MANCHESTER, SURREY, WARWICKSHIRE.

QUESTIONS :-

1 WHO WAS THE U.S.A RUNNER THAT ONCE SET FIVE WORLD RECORDS AND TIED A SIXTH IN LESS THAN SIXTY MINUTES?

2 WHO INVENTED FRANCHISING?

3 WHO WAS THE FIRST TENNIS PLAYER TO WEAR SHORT PANTS ON THE COURT?

4 WHAT WAS THE LOWEST THE DOW JONES INDEX REACHED DURING THE DEPRESSION?

5 WHAT IS THE LONGEST WORD IN THE ENGLISH LANGUAGE THAT CONTAINS JUST ONE VOWEL?

6 WHAT IS THE ONLY ANIMAL THAT CAN SEE ULTRA – VIOLET AND INFRA – RED LIGHT?

7 WHO WAS THE FIRST PILOT TO LAND A PLANE ON A SHIP?

8 WHAT IS THE ONLY CITY IN THE U.S.A THAT IS SPELLED USING ONLY VOWELS?

9 WHO WAS THE ONLY VICE – PRESIDENT OF THE U.S.A WHO WASN'T WHITE?

10 HOW MANY COUNTRIES HAVE SPECIAL OLYMPICS ATHLETES?

11 WHAT IS THE ONLY NATURAL SUBSTANCE THAT CAN BE RESTORED TO ITS ORIGINAL ROCKLIKE STATE BY ADDING WATER?

ANSWERS :-

1 JESSE OWENS

2 MARTHA MATILDA HARPER IN 1888, WITH HARPER HAIR DRESSING SALONS.

3 HENRY WILFRED "BUNNY" AUSTIN

4 41. 22 ON JULY 8, 1932

5 STRENGTHS

6 GOLDFISH

7 EUGENE B ELY IN 1911 ONTO THE USS PENNSYLVANIA

8 AIEA, IN HAWAII

9 CHARLES CURTIS, A KAW INDIAN WAS VICE PRESIDENT UNDER HERBERT HOOVER.

10 OVER 150 COUNTRIES ALL OVER THE WORLD.

11 GYPSUM

QUESTIONS :-
1 WHAT WAS ELVIS PRESLEY'S LIFE LIKE?
2 WHO WAS THE FIRST AMERICAN TO MAKE $100 MILLION A YEAR?
3 WHO DEVISED AND USED THE FIRST ELECTRIC STOCK QUOTATION BOARD?
4 WHICH WAS THE SLOWEST TRADING DAY IN THE NEW YORK STOCK EXCHANGE HISTORY?
5 WHAT COMPANY WAS FIRST TO EARN ONE BILLION DOLLARS IN ONE YEAR?
6 WHO WAS AMERICA'S FIRST BILLIONAIRE?
7 WHAT HAPPENED TO THE DOW JONES INDUSTRIAL AVERAGE DURING WORLD WAR 2?
8 WHAT IS THE BUSIEST TIME OF THE DAY FOR BUSINESS CALLING?
9 WHAT IS THE MOST EXPENSIVE WRIST WATCH?
10 WHAT IS THE WORLD'S LARGEST OIL CONCERN?

ANSWERS :-
1 ELVIS PRESLEY HAD 114 SINGLES CHART, TOP 10 SINGLES 38 TIMES, NO 1 POSITION 80 TIMES AND HE ALSO MADE 33 MOVIES.
2 AL CAPONE
3 SUTRO AND CO. MADE IT IN 1929
4 MARCH 31 ST 1830, ONLY 31 SHARES TRADED FOR THE DAY.
5 GENERAL MOTORS
6 HENRY FORD
7 IT RALLIED FROM A LOW 92. 70 IN EARLY 1942 TO 213. 40 BY THE END OF THE WAR.
8 IT IS FROM 11 : 00 AM TO NOON EASTERN TIME.
9 VACHERON CONSTANTIN'S KALLISTA WATCH WAS SOLD FOR $ 9 MILLIOM IN 1977 ; IT FEATURES 118 DIAMONDS, WEIGHING 130 CARATS.
10 EXXON MOBILE WITH A MARKET CAPITALIZATION OF ABOUT 250 BILLION DOLLARS.

QUESTIONS :
1 RONALD REGAN'S LAST ACTING ROLE BEFORE ENTERING POLITICS WAS IN WHICH FILM?

2 WHO WAS THE FIRST BLACK ACTOR TO WIN AN OSCAR?

3 WHICH FILM WAS WILL SMITH'S FIRST BIG SCREEN ROLE?

4 WHO IS BRAD PITT MARRIED TO, AS OF 2002?

5 WHAT'S THE MIDDLE NAME OF ELIZABETH TAYLOR?

6 WHAT THE DERIVATION SCUBA, PUT A SOCK IN IT, RED TAPE, HIP HIP HOORAY, BURY THE HATCHET, SCOT FREE MEAN RESPECTIVELY?

7 WHO INVENTED THE COMPUTER LANGUAGE OF THE INTERNET?

8 WHO WAS THE FIRST WOMAN TO RUN FOR THE U.S.A PRESIDENCY?

9 WHAT PERCENTAGE OF DRIVERS OF THE HIGHWAY CANNOT READ ROAD SIGNS?

10 IF YOU HAVE TRISKAIDEKAPHOPIA, WHAT DO YOU FEAR?

ANSWERS :-

1 THE KILLERS

2 SIDNEY POITIER

3 WHERE THE DAY TAKES YOU

4 JENNIFER ANISTON

5 ROSEMOND

6 DIVING, SHUT UP, BUREAUCRACY, THREE CHEERS, AGREE TO STOP ARGUING, ESCAPE WITHOUT PUNISHMENT.

7 TIM BERNERS – LEE CREATED HYPER TEXT MARKUP LANGUAGE [HTML] AT SWITZERLAND'S CERN LABS.

8 VICTORIA CLAFLIN WOODHULL IN 1872

9 TEN PERCENT

10 THE NUMBER 13

QUESTIONS :-

1 WHAT IS A MUSEUM?

2 NAME THREE STOCK EXCHANGES?

3 NAME THREE SEAPORTS?

4 NAME TWO TREATIES?

5 NAME FIVE WARS?

6 NAME THE SIX COUNTRIES WITH THE MOST POPULATION?

7 NAME THREE TYPES OF CLOUDS?

8 NAME FOUR HEAD OF STATE?
9 HOW MANY DAYS IN A LEAP YEAR?
10 NAME SEVEN FAMOUS ACTORS?
11 NAME SEVEN FAMOUS ACTRESS?

ANSWERS :-
1 A PLACE FOR DISPLAYING ARTISTIC, HISTORICAL, OR SCIENTIFIC OBJECTS.
2 NEW YORK STOCK EXCHANGE, BOMBAY STOCK EXCHANGE, NIGERIA STOCK EXCHANGE.
3 PORT OF GEORGETOWN GUYANA, PORT OF MONTREAL CANADA, PORT OF OSAKA JAPAN.
4 NAFTA AND GATT.
5 AMERICAN CIVIL WAR, GULF WAR, KOREAN WAR, WORLD WAR 1, WORLD WAR 2.
6 CHINA, INDIA, U.S.A, INDONESIA, BRAZIL, PAKISTAN.
7 STRATUS, CUMULUS, CIRRUS.
8 PRESIDENT GEORGE W BUSH OF U.S.A, PRIME MINISTER TONY BLAIR OF U.K, PRIME MINISTER JOHN HOWARD OF AUSTRALIA, PRIME MINISTER JEAN CHRETIEN OF CANADA.
9 366
10 TOM CRUISE, CLINT EASTWOOD, EDDIE MURPHY, AL PACINO, ROBERT DE NIRO, DENZIL WASHINGTON, JACK NICHOLSON, DHARMENDRA.
11 JULIA ROBERTS, WHOOPI GOLDBERG, ELIZABETH TAYLOR, KIM BASINGER, JESSICA LANGE, HEMA MALINI.

QUESTIONS :-
1 WHAT ARE THE ACADEMY AWARDS AFFECTIONATELY KNOWN AS?
2 NAME TEN RECENT WINNERS OF THE ACADEMY AWARDS?
3 NAME TWO WINNERS OF RECENT MUSIC AWARDS?
4 NAME SEVEN TYPES OF MUSIC?
5 NAME SEVEN TYPES OF DANCE?
6 NAME TWO PLACES WHERE PEOPLE FROM FOREIGN COUNTRIES ARE REPRESENTED IN THE HOST COUNTRY?
7 WHAT IS THE WCO?
8 NAME SEVEN TYPES OF WORLD DISASTERS.
9 WHAT IS THE WCC?

10 WHAT IS THE WEF?

11 WHAT IS THE AMNESTY INTERNATIONAL ORGANIZATION'S MAIN FUNCTION?

12 NAME FIVE CLICHES – FIGURE OF SPEECH SAYINGS?

13 WHERE WAS THE 2000 OLYMPIC GAMES HELD?

14 HOW MANY COUNTRIES PARTICIPATED IN THE PARALYMPIC GAMES – SPECIAL OLYMPICS IN SYDNEY, AUSTRALIA IN 2002?

15 NAME SEVEN OF WILLIAM SHAKESPEARE'S WORK – WRITINGS?

16 NAME TWO MUSICAL ARTISTS WHO HAVE BEEN AFFECTIONATELY CALLED KINGS BY THEIR FANS?

ANSWERS :-

1 THE OSCARS

2 KEVIN KOSTNER, MERYL STREEP, TOMMY LEE JONES, GENE HACKMAN, TOM CRUISE, MICHAEL CAINE, ANGELINA JOLIE, SEAN PENN, BEN KINGSLEY, HALLE BERRY.

3 ARTIST 50 CENT AND THE POP GROUP T.A.T.U

4 JAZZ, DISCO, COUNTRY AND WESTERN, RAP, R & B, REGGAE, INDIAN

5 TANGO, FOX TROT, FREESTYLE, TAP, INDIAN, BALLET, WALTZ.

6 CONSULATE, EMBASSY.

7 WORLD CUSTOMS ORGANIZATIONS.

8 AIRCRAFT, DROUGHT, FLOOD, HURRICANE, SHIPWRECKS, FIRE, FAMINE.

9 WORLD COUNCIL OF CHURCHES.

10 WORLD ECONOMIC FORUM.

11 TO PROMOTE HUMAN RIGHTS.

12 THERE'S NO PLACE LIKE HOME, LIKE FATHER LIKE SON, ALL IN DUE TIME, CALL IT A DAY, RAINING CATS AND DOGS.

13 SYDNEY, AUSTRALIA.

14 122 COUNTRIES.

15 ROMEO AND JULIET, JULIUS CAESAR, MACBETH, THE TAMING OF THE SHREW, A MIDSUMMER NIGHT'S DREAM, ALL'S WELL THAT ENDS WELL, AS YOU LIKE IT.

16 MICHAEL JACKSON AND ELVIS PRESLEY.

QUESTIONS :-

1 WHICH ANIMAL HAS THE LONGEST LIFE SPAN?
2 WHICH ANIMAL HAS THE SHORTEST LIFE SPAN?
3 HOW LONG DOES A HOUSE FLY LIVE?
4 HOW MUCH DOES THE HEAVIEST ELEPHANT WEIGH?
5 WHAT IS THE SPEED OF A FALLING RAINDROP?
6 DOES THE SUN HAVE MAGNETIC POLES?
7 WHICH ANIMAL HAS THE BIGGEST EYE?
8 WHY DO PEOPLE HAVE FIVE FINGERS?
9 WHAT IS THE DRIEST DESERT ON EARTH?
10 WHAT ANIMAL LAYS THE HEAVIEST EGG?
11 WHAT ANIMAL HAS THE HEAVIEST BRAIN?
12 DO INSECTS BREATHE?
13 CAN YOU CATCH AIDS FROM A MOSQUITO BITE?
14 NEXT TO HUMANS, WHAT ANIMAL IS SMARTEST?

ANSWERS :-

1 THE GIANT TORTOISE LIVES THE LONGEST 177 YEARS IN CAPTIVITY

2 THE GASTROTRICH WHICH IS A MINUTE AQUATIC ANIMAL LIVES AS SHORT AS THREE DAYS.

3 THE HOUSE FLY HAS ONE OF THE SHORTEST CYCLES KNOWN 20 TO 30 DAYS.

4 A MALE AFRICAN BUSH ELEPHANT IN ANGOLA ON NOVEMBER, 7 TH 1974 WEIGHED 13.5 TONS; AS MUCH AS NINE AVERAGE SIZE CARS IN THE U.S.A.

5 IT DEPENDS ON THE SIZE AND WEIGHT OF THE RAINDROP HOW FAST IT FALLS; THE HEAVIER THE FASTER.

6 YES, AND THEY FLIP ABOUT EVERY 11 YEARS.

7 THE GIANT SQUID HAS EYES ABOUT 10 INCHES; IS AS LARGE AS A HUMAN HEAD AND TEN TIMES THE SIZE OF THE HUMAN EYE.

8 IT'S NOT JUST PEOPLE. MAMMALS, BIRDS, AND REPTILES ALL HAVE NO MORE THAN 5 DIGITS IN THEIR FOREARMS.

9 THAT'S DEBATABLE, SOME SAY THE ATACAMA OF NORTHERN CHILE; OTHERS THE LUT DESERT IN EASTERN IRAN.

10 THE WORLD'S LARGEST LIVING BIRD, THE OSTRICH.

11 THE SPERM WHALE ABOUT 17.2 LBS.

12 YES, LIKE HUMANS ALL INSECTS REQUIRE OXYGEN TO SURVIVE.

13 NO, BUT YOU GET OTHER THINGS LIKE MALARIA.

14 PROBABLY THE CHIMPANZEE IS THE NEXT SMARTEST, BONOBOS ARE CLOSE CONTENDERS, PARROTS ARE ALSO ADEPT AT USING TOOLS AND SOLVING PROBLEMS.

TRUE AND FALSE QUESTIONS AND ANSWERS :-
QUESTIONS :-

1 THE ONLY EVEN PRIME NUMBER IS 2.

2 OUR NOSE, EYES AND EARS NEVER STOP GROWING UNTIL THE DAY WE DIE.

3 THE WHITE PART OF THE FINGER NAIL IS CALLED LUNA.

4 YOU CAN ONLY SEE A RAINBOW WITH YOUR BACK TO THE SUN.

5 A JIFFY IS AN ACTUAL UNIT OF TIME.

6 ISAAC NEWTON WAS AN ANGLICAN DECON.

7 MARK TWAIN'S REAL NAME WAS SAMUEL CLEMENTINE.

8 THE MOST COMMON FIRST NAME IN THE WORLD IS MOHAMMED.

9 THE WORD GIRL APPEARS IN THE BIBLE ONLY THREE TIMES.

10 IN WRITTEN ENGLISH, ONE OUT OF EVERY 8 LETTERS IS AN E.

11 NO WORD IN THE ENGLISH LANGUAGE HAS 5 CONSECUTIVE LETTERS THAT ARE VOWELS.

12 IT TAKES MORE THAN 1 HOUR TO COMPLETELY BOIL AN OSTRICH EGG.

13 A FULL GROWN BEAR CAN RUN AS FAST AS A HORSE.

14 TIGERS HAVE STRIPED SKIN AS WELL AS STRIPED FUR.

15 OTHER THAN HUMANS THE ONLY PRIMATE THAT CAN HAVE BLUE EYES IS THE BLACK LEMUR.

16 IF A MONTH STARTS ON A SUNDAY IT WILL ALWAYS CONTAIN FRIDAY 13 TH.

17 THERE ARE ONLY 25 COUNTRIES WORLD – WIDE IN WHICH PEOPLE DRIVE ON THE LEFT HAND SIDE OF THE ROAD.

18 THERE IS ONLY ONE COIN DENOMINATION IN VIETNAMESE DONGS

19 WHAT ANIMAL HOLDS THE RECORD FOR THE TALLEST ANIMAL.?

20 DO FISH SEE IN COLOR?

ANSWERS :-

1 TRUE
2 FALSE
3 FALSE
4 FALSE
5 TRUE
6 TRUE
7 FALSE
8 TRUE
9 FALSE
10 TRUE
11 FALSE
12 FALSE
13 TRUE
14 TRUE
15 FALSE
16 TRUE
17 FALSE
18 FALSE
19 THE GIRAFFE – UP TO 18 FEET
20 MOST FISH SEE IN COLOR.

QUESTIONS :-

1 THE YOUNGEST EVER POPE WAS ONLY 10 YEARS OLD.

2 IF YOU MULTIPLY 111,111,111 BY ITSELF, THE ANSWER IS 12,345,687,987,654,321.

3 THE ORIGINAL COLOR OF COCA COLA WAS GREEN.

4 A CAT HAS MORE THAN DOUBLE THE AMOUNT OF VERTEBRAE IN THEIR SPINE THAN A HUMAN,

5 DIAMOND IS THE HARDEST NATURALLY OCCURRING SUBSTANCE ON EARTH.

6 ALL ZEBRAS ARE WHITE WITH BLACK STRIPES.

7 A MAN'S HEART BEATS FASTER THAN A WOMAN'S ON AVERAGE.

8 FINGERNAILS GROW FASTER THAN TOE NAILS.

9 THE FIRST SHIP TO USE THE SOS SIGNAL WAS THE TITANIC.

10 THE BONES OF A PIGEON ARE SO LIGHT THAT THEY WEIGH LESS THAN ITS FEATHERS.

11 THE SHORTEST WAR IN HISTORY LASTED JUST OVER AN HOUR.

12 NATURAL PROPANE GAS HAS NO ODOR.

13 THE HIGHEST MEASUREMENT POSSIBLE ON THE RICHTER SCALE IS 10.

14 THE EXACT MIDDLE OF THE YEAR IS JUNE 30 TH.

15 THE PHRASE THE BLIND LEADING THE BLIND COMES FROM THE BIBLE.

16 ALL SPECIES OF SPIDERS DON'T GET CAUGHT IN THEIR OWN WEBS BECAUSE THEIR LEGS HAVE A SPECIAL NON – STICK FLUID ON THEM.

17 MORE THAN 1.5 MILLION PEOPLE DIE EACH YEAR FROM MALARIA.

ANSWERS :-

1 FALSE HE WAS ACTUALLY 11 YEARS OLD.

2 TRUE

3 FALSE

4 FALSE THE CAT HAS 60 VERTEBRAE AND HUMANS 34

5 TRUE

6 FALSE IT CAN ALSO BE THE OTHER WAY AROUND.

7 FALSE ACTUALLY IT'S THE OTHER WAY AROUND.

8 TRUE

9 FALSE

10 TRUE

11 FALSE IT LASTED JUST 10 MINUTES.

12 TRUE ODOR IS ADDED TO IT.

13 FALSE

14 FALSE IT IS 2 ND JULY AND 1 ST JULY IN A LEAP YEAR.

15 TRUE

16 FALSE

17 TRUE

QUESTIONS :-

1 IT IS IMPOSSIBLE TO GET A MCDONALD'S HAPPY MEAL IN NEW DELHI INDIA.

2 WOMEN ATHLETES COMPETED WITH MALES ATHLETES IN THE ANCIENT GREEK OLYMPIC GAMES.

3 ADULTS HAVE MORE BONES THAN BABIES DO.

4 THE BIGGEST KNOWN VOLCANO IN THE SOLAR SYSTEM IS ON MARS.

5 ON JULY 20 TH 1969 AMERICAN ASTRONAUT ALAN SHEPPHERD MADE THE FIRST FOOTSTEPS EVER ON THE SURFACE OF THE MOON.

6 JOSHUA SLOCUM WAS THE FIRST PERSON TO SAIL AROUND THE WORLD SINGLE HANDED.

7 A BABY CANNOT BLUSH.

8 THE WHALE, THE WORLD'S LARGEST CREATURE HAS THE BIGGEST EYE IN THE ANIMAL KINGDOM.

9 THE MARTIAL ART OF TAE KWON DO ORIGINATES FROM JAPAN.

10 THE TRANS–SIBERIAN RAILWAY LINE IS THE LONGEST IN THE WORLD.

11 THE BIRTHSTONE FOR SEPTEMBER IS THE SAPPHIRE.

ANSWERS :-

1 FALSE

2 FALSE

3 FALSE WHEN WE ARE BORN WE HAVE OVER 300 BONES. BY THE TIME AGE 20; SOME OF THEM HAVE GROWN TOGETHER MAKING OUR SKELETONS STRONGER. AS ADULTS WE HAVE ABOUT 206 BONES.

4 TRUE OLYMPUS MONS ON MARS IS THE TALLEST AND WIDEST KNOWN VOLCANO.

5 FALSE IT WAS NEIL ARMSTRONG WHO WAS THE FIRST.

6 TRUE

7 TRUE

8 FALSE

9 FALSE IT IS KOREA

10 TRUE

11 TRUE

QUESTIONS :-

1 A FEW FIBERS OF A FIBER OPTIC CABLE IS ENOUGH TO CARRY OVER 100,000 PHONE CALLS, IT CAN FIT THROUGH THE EYE OF A NEEDLE.

2 IN 1882 HENRY SEELY INVENTED THE FIRST ELECTRIC IRON.

3 THERE IS NO SUCH THING AS A FLYING FISH.

4 THE LARGE INTESTINE IS 4 TIMES LONGER THAN THE SMALL INTESTINE.

5 AIRPLANE TIRES ARE FILLED WITH NITROGEN INSTEAD OF REGULAR AIR LIKE A CAR TIRE.

6 THE FLAVOR SENSING CELLS IN YOUR MOUTH THAT MAKE UP YOUR TASTE BUDS LAST FOR A LIFE TIME.

7 A GALLON OF PURE WATER WEIGHS 10 OUNCES.

8 IT IS IMPOSSIBLE TO SNEEZE AND KEEP YOUR EYES OPEN AT THE SAME TIME.

9 BENJAMIN FRANKLIN INVENTED THE DIGITAL CLOCK IN 1777

ANSWERS :-

1 TRUE

2 TRUE

3 FALSE

4 FALSE IT IS THE OTHER WAY AROUND; THE SMALL INTESTINE IS 20 FEET LONG AND THE LARGE INTESTINE IS 5 FEET LONG.

5 TRUE IN ORDER THAT THE TIRES DO NOT CATCH FIRE ON THE RUNWAY.

6 FALSE

7 FALSE IT IS 10 POUNDS

8 TRUE

9 FALSE

QUESTIONS :-

1 TORONTO IS THE CAPITAL OF CANADA

2 IN TENNIS THE AUSTRALIAN OPEN IS ONE OF THE FOUR TOURNAMENT MAKING UP THE GRAND SLAM.

3 BEFORE BECOMING GOVENOR OF TEXAS, GEORGE W BUSH WAS CO – OWNER OF A PROFESSIONAL BASEBALL TEAM.

4 AN ELEPHANT CAN SMELL WATER UP TO 3 MILES AWAY.

5 DENNIS THE MENACE'S FAVORITE BEVERAGE IS MILK.

6 THE PREFIX GIGA MEANS A MILLION.

7 MOUNT ACONCAGUA IS THE TALLEST MOUNTAIN IN THE AMERICA

8 LEIT ERICSON WAS THE FIRST PERSON TO CROSS THE ATLANTIC.9

9 FBI MEANS FEDERAL BUREAU OF INVESTIGATIONS.

10 THERE IS SUCH A COUNTRY KNOWN AS BENIN.

ANSWERS :-

1 FALSE OTTAWA IS THE CAPITAL OF CANADA. TORONTO IS THE CAPITAL OF ONTARIO.

2 TRUE THE OTHER THREE ARE THE FRENCH OPEN, WIMBLEDON, AND THE U.S OPEN.

3 TRUE THE TEXAS RANGERS.

4 TRUE

5 FALSE IT IS ROOT BEER.

6 FALSE IT IS A BILLION.

7 TRUE IT IS OVER 22,000 FEET HIGH.

8 FALSE

9 TRUE

10 TRUE IT IS WEST OF NIGERIA

QUESTIONS :-

1 STRAWBERRIES HAVE MORE VITAMIN C THAN ORANGES.

2 NIAGARA FALLS IS THE HIGHEST WATERFALL IN THE WORLD.

3 BOWLING WAS FIRST PLAYED IN ITALY.

4 THE LOS ANGELES ZOO HAS THE LARGEST COLLECTION OF ANIMALS.

5 HARVARD IS THE OLDEST COLLEGE IN THE U.S.A

6 ON AVERAGE THE EYE MUSCLES MOVE 300,000 TIMES A DAY.

7 THE BULLET PROOF VEST WAS CREATED BY A WOMAN.

8 THE LEOPARD IS THE FASTEST MAMMAL ON EARTH.

9 COWS HAVE FOUR – CHAMBERED STOMACHS.

10 MOMENTUM IS VELOCITY MULTIPLY BY FORCE.

11 THE FIRE ESCAPE WAS CREATED BY A WOMAN.

ANSWERS :-

1 TRUE

2 FALSE ANGEL FALLS IN VENEZUELA IS THE HIGHEST.

3 FALSE IT WAS GERMANY.

4 FALSE IT IS THE SAN DIEGO ZOO.

5 TRUE

6 FALSE IT IS ABOUT 100,000 TIMES A DAY

7 TRUE

8 FALSE IT IS THE CHEETAH

9 TRUE

10 FALSE MOMENTUM IS VELOCITY MULTIPLY BY MASS.

11 TRUE

QUESTIONS :-

1 IN MEXICO BULLFIGHTS ARE TRADITIONALLY HELD ON SUNDAYS.

2 THERE ARE 36 BLACK KEYS ON A STANDARD PIANO.

3 WALT DISNEY'S MIDDLE NAME WAS ENOCH.

4 IN THE PAST GUITARS USED TO HAVE 7 STRINGS.

5 IN THE GULF WAR 84 AMERICAN SOLDIERS DIED.

6 A STANDARD GUITAR HAS 5 STRINGS.

7 GUATEMALA IS LOCATED IN SOUTH AMERICA.

8 APR MEANS ANNUAL PERCENTAGE RATIO.

9 THE AVERAGE NUMBER OF PEOPLE WHO WILL GET CANCER AT SOME POINT IN THEIR LIVES IS 15 IN 100.

ANSWERS :-

1 TRUE

2 TRUE THERE ARE 52 OF ANOTHER COLOR.

3 FALSE IT WAS ELIAS.

4 TRUE

5 FALSE THE NUMBER WAS 79.

6 FALSE IT IS 6 STRINGS.

7 FALSE IT IS IN CENTRAL AMERICA.

8 FALSE IT MEANS ANNUAL PERCENTAGE RATE.

10 FALSE IT IS ALMOST 30 IN 100. SMOKING, OBESITY, HEREDITY; LACK OF EXERCISE, AND POOR DIET ALL

GREATLY INCREASE THE RISK ASSOCIATED WITH GETTING CANCER.

QUESTIONS :-
1 AT ONE TIME GEORGE W BUSH DECLARED JUNE 10 TO BE JESUS DAY.
2 IF YOU SWALLOW CHEWING GUM IT DOESN'T DIGEST NORMALLY.
3 FRYER WAS THE NAME GIVEN TO THE WRIGHT BROTHER'S AIRPLANE.
4 THERE ARE MORE LEFT HANDED WOMEN THAN MEN.
5 THE LARGEST NATURALLY – MADE OBJECT WAS THE GREAT WALL OF CHINA.
6 WORLD WAR 2 LASTED FROM 1939 TO 1945 IN EUROPE.
7 FRENCH FRIES ARE THE MOST ORDERED ITEM IN AMERICAN RESTAURANTS.
8 OLIVES ARE A VEGETABLE.
9 AN ITALIAN DECK OF CARDS HAS NO JACKS.
10 KETCHUP WAS ONCE SOLD AS MEDICINE.
11 RABBITS AND HORSES CAN'T VOMIT.
12 QUEEN BEES ONLY STING WORKER BEES.

ANSWERS :-
1 TRUE
2 FALSE IT DIGESTS JUST AS ANY OTHER PRODUCT.
3 FALSE
4 FALSE
5 FALSE IT IS THE BIGGEST MAN – MADE OBJECT.
6 TRUE
7 TRUE
8 FALSE IT IS A FRUIT.
9 FALSE IT HAS NO QUEENS.
10 TRUE
11 TRUE
12 FALSE THEY ONLY STING OTHER QUEEN BEES.

QUESTIONS :-
1 JOHANN GUTENBERG INVENTED THE PRINTING PRESS IN THE 14 CENTURY.

2 IF YOU HANG THE POLISH FLAG UPSIDE DOWN YOU WILL GET THE INDONESIAN FLAG.

3 THE LENGTH OF THE SUEZ CANAL IS 100 KM.

4 IN MORSE CODE FIVE DOTS MEANS I MADE A MISTAKE.

5 IN ANCIENT EGYPT THE KINGS SOMETIMES MARRIED THEIR SISTERS

6 VITAMIN C IS ALSO KNOWN AS FOLIC ACID.

7 RATS CAN'T FLEE FROM SINKING SHIPS BECAUSE THEY CAN'T SWIM.

8 THE DISTANCE BETWEEN THE RED SEA AND THE MEDITERRANEAN SEA IS 120 KM.

9 A MEGAWATT POWERS ABOUT 200 HOMES.

10 JUAN PONCE DE LEON DISCOVERED FLORIDA IN 1513.

ANSWERS :-

1 FALSE IT WAS THE 15 CENTURY IN 1445.

2 TRUE

3 FALSE IT IS 168 KM LONG.

4 FALSE IT IS 8 DOTS.

5 TRUE

6 FALSE IT IS ASCORBIC ACID.

7 FALSE THEY CAN SWIM.

8 TRUE

9 TRUE

10 TRUE

QUESTIONS :-

1 A RAT CAN LAST LONGER WITHOUT WATER THAN A CAMEL.

2 DURING WORLD WAR 2 THE OSCARS WERE MADE OF PLASTER.

3 THERE ARE NO KNOWN WORDS THAT RHYME WITH ORANGE, PURPLE, SILVER AND BROWN.

4 THE 1988 WINTER OLYMPICS WERE HELD IN CALGARY, CANADA.

5 ELVIS PRESLEY HAD A KARATE BLACK BELT.

6 A VIPER CAN BE A CAR OR A SNAKE.

7 LAS VEGAS IS CALLED THE BIG EASY.

8 WHALES BREATHE AIR JUST AS HUMANS DO.

ANSWERS :-

1 TRUE

2 TRUE BECAUSE OF A SCARCITY OF METAL

3 FALSE

4 TRUE

5 TRUE

6 TRUE

7 FALSE

8 TRUE

QUESTIONS :-

1 ALEXANDER THE GREAT WAS ALSO KNOWN AS ALEXANDER OF MACEDONIA.

2 DIAGONALS THAT BISECT EACH OTHER ARE A FEATURE OF ALL RECTANGLES.

3 ONLY THE CHINESE TIGER IS AN ENDANGERED TIGER.

4 THE LUMBAR CURVE IS LOCATED IN THE LEG ON THE HUMAN BODY.

5 IN THE ENGLISH VERSION OF THE GAME MONOPOLY OLD KENT ROAD IS THE HIGHEST SELLING PROPERTY.

6 AMETHYST GEMSTONE IS THE BIRTHSTONE OF AUGUST.

7 WALT DISNEY HAD A JOB ON A RAILROAD.

8 GABRIEL AND MICHAEL WERE THE TWO ANGELS MENTIONED BY NAME IN THE BIBLE.

9 SELACHOPHOBIA IS THE FEAR OF LIGHT FLASHES.

10 SELAPHOBIA IS THE FEAR OF SHARKS.

ANSWERS :-

1 TRUE

2 TRUE

3 FALSE

4 FALSE IT IS IN THE TORSO REGION.

5 FALSE IT IS THE CHEAPEST, THE MAYFAIR IS HIGHEST.

6 FALSE IT IS FEBRUARY.

7 TRUE

8 THERE WERE ALSO RAPHAEL AND LUCIFER.

9 FALSE IT IS THE FEAR OF SHARKS.

10 FALSE IT IS THE FEAR OF LIGHT FLASHES

CHAPTER 33.

DO YOU KNOW?

QUESTIONS :-

1 WINSTON CHURCHILL WAS BORN IN A LADIES ROOM.

2 THE AVERAGE EYELASH LIVES APPROXIMATELY 90 DAYS BEFORE IT FALLS OUT

3 MAGELLAN WAS THE FIRST MAN TO TRAVEL AROUND THE EARTH.

4 IF YOU HAVE AN I.Q ABOVE 140 YOU ARE CONSIDERED A GENIUS.

5 IF YOU HAVE AN I.Q BELOW 25 YOU ARE CONSIDERED AN IDIOT.

6 ABSOLUTE ZERO IS -459.69 DEGREES F OR -273.16 DEGREES C.

7 THE PLANET PLUTO WAS DISCOVERED IN 1928.

8 THE TOWER OF LONDON IS ON THE SOUTH BANK OF THE RIVER THAMES.

9 THE ONLY MAN MADE STRUCTURE THAT CAN BE SEEN FROM OUTER SPACE ARE THE GREAT PYRAMIDS.

10 THE UNITED NATIONS WAS ORIGINALLY HEADQUARTERED IN SAN FRANCISCO.

11 THE UNITED NATIONS NOW IS HEADQUARTERED IN NEW YORK.

12 A CYGNET IS A BABY DOLPHIN.

13 N.A.T.O IS AN ACRONYM FOR NORTH AMERICAN TREATY ORGANIZATION.

ANSWERS :-

1 TRUE

2 FALSE IT IS ABOUT 150 DAYS.

3 FALSE MAGELLAN DIED BEFORE HE COULD HAVE ACCOMPLISHED THAT, IT WAS MAGELLAN'S FIRST MATE DEL CANO WHO WAS THE FIRST MAN TO TRAVEL AROUND THE EARTH.

4 TRUE

5 TRUE

6 TRUE

7 FALSE IT WAS IN 1930

8 FALSE IT IS ON THE NORTH BANK NOT THE SOUTH BANK.

9 FALSE IT IS THE GREAT WALLS OF CHINA.

10 TRUE

11 TRUE

12 FALSE IT IS A BABY SWAN

13 FALSE IT IS NORTH ATLANTIC TREATY ORGANIZATION.

QUESTIONS :-

1 IN THE 1890'S HARVARD AND ARMY WERE THE FIRST COLLEGES TO ADOPT ANIMAL MASCOTS.

2 THE LONGEST NAME IN THE BIBLE IS MAHERSHALALHASHBAZ.

3 THE AFRICAN RHINOCEROS HAS 2 HORNS ON ITS HEAD.

4 THE FEAR OF EXTREME COLD, ICE OR FROST IS CALLED CRYSTALLOPHOBIA.

5 THE FEAR OF GLASS OR CRYSTAL IS CALLED CRYOPHOBIA.

6 THE EARTH ROTATES ON ITS AXIS FROM EAST TO WEST.

7 GAUL WAS THE ANCIENT NAME OF FRANCE.

8 THERE ARE 25 SHEETS OF PAPER IN A QUIRE.

9 NEW AMSTERDAM WAS THE ORIGINAL NAME OF NEW YORK

10 CREAM IS HEAVIER THAN MILK.

11 SACCHARINE IS DERIVED FROM COAL.

12 THE HAGUE IS IN HOLLAND – NETHERLANDS.

13 A TINE IS THE PRONG OF A FORK.

14 A LUTHIER IS A VIOLIN MAKER.

15 SULPHURIC ACID IS ANOTHER NAME FOR VITRIOL.

16 THE GAME OF KINGS IS HORSE RACING.

17 THE SPORT OF KINGS IS CHESS.

ANSWERS :-

1 FALSE THE TWO COLLEGES WERE YALE AND NAVY. YALE'S MASCOT WAS A BULLDOG NAMED HANDSOME DAN AND NAVY'S MASCOT WAS A GOAT NAMED NATURALLY BILLY.

2 TRUE

3 TRUE

4 FALSE THE FEAR OF EXTREME COLD IS CRYOPHOBIA

5 FALSE THE FEAR OF GLASS OR CRYSTAL IS CRYSTALLOPHOBIA.

6 FALSE IT IS FROM WEST TO EAST.

7 TRUE

8 TRUE

9 TRUE

10 FALSE

11 TRUE

12 TRUE

13 TRUE

14 TRUE

15 TRUE

16 FALSE IT IS CHESS.

17 FALSE IT IS HORSE RACING.

QUESTIONS :-

1 IN THE BIBLE NOAH'S 3 SONS ARE HAM, SHEM, AND JEHOSHAPHAT

2 PETER FINCH WAS THE FIRST ACTOR TO BE NOMINATED FOR AN OSCAR POSTHUMOUSLY.

3 IF I AM LOOKING AT A PARLIAMENT OF ANIMALS, I AM LOOKING AT A GROUP OF PEACOCKS.

4 JOHN TRAVOLTA'S MOTHER WAS IN THE MOVIE SATURDAY NIGHT FEVER STARING JOHN TRAVOLTA.

5 ON INAUGURATION DAY, WHEN THE PRESIDENT OF THE U.S.A TAKES THE OATH OF OFFICE, THE BIBLE IS OPENED IN THE BOOK OF ACTS.

6 SNOW WHITE WAS WALT DISNEY'S FAVORITE ANIMATED HEROINE.

7 AFTER 5 NOMINATIONS ALFRED HITCHCOCK FINALLY WON AN ACADEMY AWARD FOR BEST DIRECTOR FOR DIRECTING PSYCHO.

8 PAUL NEWMAN DROPPED OUT OF HIGH SCHOOL.

ANSWERS :-

1 FALSE THE NAMES WERE SHEM, HAM, AND JAPETH.

2 FALSE JAMES DEAN WAS THE FIRST.

3 FALSE IT IS CALLED A MUSTER OR OSTENTATION; IT IS A PARLIAMENT OF OWLS.

4 TRUE

5 IF THE PRESIDENT HAS A FAVORITE PASSAGE OR VERSE, THE BIBLE IS OPEN TO IT; IF NOT HE PLACES HIS HAND ON A CLOSED BIBLE.

6 FALSE IT IS CINDERALLA.

7 FALSE ALFRED HITCHCOCK NEVER WON AN ACADEMY AWARD EVEN THOUGH HE WAS NOMINATED FOR REBECCA, LIFEBOAT, SPELL BOUND, REAR WINDOW, AND PSYCHO. HE WAS PRESENTED THE IRVING G THALBERG AWARD IN 1967.

8 FALSE HE GRADUATED FROM YALE IN 1954.

QUESTIONS :-

1 THE VOICE OF DONALD DUCK IS PROVIDED BY JIM JOHNSON.

2 JIMMY CARTER'S CAMPAIGN JET WAS NAMED THE BIG PEANUT.

3 THE FIRST PROFESSIONAL BASEBALL TEAM WAS THE RIVER CITY BATS.

4 THE WINDS OF A HURRICANE CAN REACH UP TO 200 MILES PER HOUR.

5 TROPICAL RAINSTORMS CLAIM MORE LIVES THAN ANY OTHER TYPE OF STORM.

6 MOUNT VESUVIUS IS AN ACTIVE VOLCANO.

7 THE SAN ANDREAS FAULT IS 900 MILES LONG.

8 IN THE CONOZOIC ERA, ICE SHEETS COVERED MOST OF NORTH AMERICA.

9 90 % OF CANADIANS LIVE WITHIN 600 KM OF THE U.S BORDER.

10 DRINKING COFFEE CANNOT HELP YOU SOBER UP.

11 OVER 3000 PEOPLE DIE EACH DAY FROM SMOKING CIGARETTES.

12 WHO HOLDS THE RECORD FOR THE HIGHEST CRICKET TEST SCORE

ANSWERS :-

1 FALSE IT IS BY CLARENCE NASH.

2 FALSE IT WAS PEANUT ONE.

3 FALSE IT WAS THE CINCINNATI RED STOCKINGS.

4 TRUE

5 FALSE HURRICANES CLAIM MORE LIVES.

6 TRUE

7 FALSE IT IS 800 MILES LONG.

8 TRUE

9 TRUE

10 TRUE

11 FALSE THE FIGURE IS OVER 1000 PEOPLE.

12 BRIAN LARA OF TRINIDAD AND TOBAGO WEST INDIES 400 RUNS NOT OUT.

QUESTIONS :-

1 FRANCIS SCOTT KEY, WRITER OF THE STAR SPANGLED BANNER WAS A SUPPORTER OF THE WAR OF 1812.

2 THE TRAGEDY OF THE BOSTON MASSACRE WAS THAT THE AMERICAN COLONISTS WERE COMPLETELY UNARMED.

3 HERBERT HOOVER CALLED PROHIBITION A NOBLE EXPERIMENT.

4 THE CREATION OF A NATIONAL FLAG WAS VERY IMPORTANT TO CONGRESS TO REPRESENT THE UNITED STATES INDEPENDENCE.

5 AFTER 7 MAY, 1992, THERE ARE 11 AMENDMENTS IN THE BILL OF RIGHTS.

6 HERBERT HOOVER WAS A MEMBER OF STANFORD'S FIRST GRADUATING CLASS.

7 PENNY STOCKS SOMETIMES TRADE OVER $5.

8 EBAY WAS FOUNDED BY PIERRE OMIDYAR.

ANSWERS :-
1 FALSE KEY CALLED IT AN ABOMINABLE WAR AND A LUMP OF WICKEDNESS.

2 FALSE THEY WERE ARMED WITH ROCKS AND CLUBS; THEY STARTED THE FIGHTING WITH THE REDCOATS.

3 FALSE HE SAID OUR NATION HAS DELIBERATELY TAKEN A GREAT SOCIAL AND ECONOMIC EXPERIMENT, NOBLE IN MOTIVE AND FAR REACHING IN PURPOSE.

4 FALSE

5 FALSE

6 TRUE IN THE YEAR 1895

7 FALSE THEY ALWAYS TRADE UNDER $5.

8 TRUE IN THE YEAR 1995.

QUESTIONS :-
1 GOLDEN RETRIEVERS ARE THE WORLD'S MOST POPULAR BREED OF DOG.

2 STALACTITES COME UP FROM THE GROUND.

3 EUROPE WON THE YEAR 2000 PRESIDENT'S CUP.

4 THE MOST WIDELY USED LANGUAGE IN THE WORLD IS ENGLISH.

5 BILL GATES IS THE CEO OF DELL COMPUTERS.

6 THE CONTRABASSOON IS A PERCUSSION INSTRUMENT.

7 WOOD FROM ONE MAHOGANY TREE CAN PRODUCE $220,000 OF FURNITURE.

8 RUSSIA IS GROWING AS A WORLD OIL POWER AND IS TAKING PRECIOUS MARKET SHARE FROM O.P.E.C

ANSWERS :-
1 FALSE THE LABRADOR RETRIEVERS ARE MOST POPULAR.

2 FALSE IT IS STALAGMITES.

3 FALSE THE U.S WON IN 2000.

4 FALSE IT IS CHINESE.

5 FALSE MICHAEL DELL IS THE CEO OF DELL COMPUTERS; BILL GATES IS CEO OF MICROSOFT.

6 FALSE

7 FALSE IT IS ABOUT $130,000 OF FURNITURE. MAHOGANY IS KNOWN AS THE GREEN GOLD OF THE AMAZON.

8 TRUE

QUESTIONS :-

1 LATER IN LIFE BENJAMIN FRANKLIN KEPT A TAMED BEAR AS A PET. EVERYONE CALLED THE BEAR GENTLE BEN

2 GEORGE ELIOT IS THE MAN WHO WROTE THE BOOKS SILAS MARNER, AND MIDDLEMARCH.

3 IDENTICAL TWINS HAVE THE SAME FINGER PRINTS.

4 THE FIRST ELEVATOR WAS ERECTED IN 1743 IN THE PALACE OF VERSAILLES.

5 SATURN IS THE THIRD LARGEST PLANET AFTER JUPITER AND NEPTUNE.

6 THE WORLD'S SHORTEST BUILDING IS THE LEGO BUILDING IN DOWNTOWN HOUSTON, TEXAS.

7 JOHN LANGDON WAS THE FIRST PERSON TO SIGN THE CONSTITUTION OF THE U.S.

8 THE POET, SHEL SILVERSTEIN, ALSO WROTE THE SONG A BOY NAMED SUE RECORDED BY JOHNNY CASH.

9 THE BATTLE OF BARNET IN THE ENGLISH WARS OF THE ROSES WAS FOUGHT ON EASTER DAY 1471.

10 THE LAST RECORDED WORDS OF THE CAPTAIN ON THE TITANIC BEFORE IT SANK WERE IF WE DON'T TELL ANYONE, NOBODY WILL KNOW, WILL THEY?

11 HALLEY'S COMET IS NAMED AFTER THE ENGLISH ASTRONOMER EDMOND HALLEY.

12 THE COUNTRY OF ISRAEL WAS CREATED ON MARCH 12, 1948.

13 MAHATMA GANDHI WAS ASSASSINATED ON MARCH 12, 1948.

14 THE DEPLETION OF THE OZONE LAYER IS HEAVILY BLAMED ON SOCIETY'S EMISSION OF CHC GASES INTO THE ATMOSPHERE.

15 CARBON MONOXIDE IN THE ATMOSPHERE IS ALLEGEDLY THE CAUSE OF GLOBAL WARMING AND THE SO – CALLED GREENHOUSE EFFECT.

16 SCIENTISTS HAVE NOT YET PROVED THAT INTELLIGENT LIFE EXISTS ANYWHERE IN OUR SOLAR SYSTEM.

ROY NOLAN

ANSWERS :-

1 FALSE
2 FALSE
3 FALSE
4 TRUE
5 FALSE
6 FALSE
7 TRUE
8 TRUE
9 TRUE
10 FALSE THE TITANIC SANK APRIL 14 – 15 1912; LOSS OF APPROXIMATELY 1500 LIVES.
11 TRUE
12 FALSE IT WAS ON MAY 14 1948.
13 FALSE HE WAS ASSASSINATED ON 30 JANUARY 1948; HE WAS BORN ON 2 OCTOBER 1869.
14 FALSE
15 FALSE
16 FALSE THERE IS INTELLIGENT LIFE ON EARTH.

QUESTIONS :-

1 THE 2 ND AMENDMENT OF THE U.S. CONSTITUTION GIVES AMERICANS THE RIGHT TO ASSEMBLE.
2 THE OAK TREE IS CLASSIFIED AS A SOFTWOOD.
3 A PENTADECAGON IS A 2 – D SHAPE WITH 15 SIDES.
4 TO PRODUCE A BLUE COLOR IN FIRE WORKS, YOU WOULD HEAT COMPOUNDS OF BARIUM.
5 FORMER GOVENOR JESSE VENTURA APPEARED IN THE 1997 MOVIE BATMAN AND ROBIN.
6 HANS CHRISTIAN ANDERSEN IS THE AUTHOR OF THE UGLY DUCKLING.
7 TORNADOES SELDOM MOVE AT SPEEDS GREATER THAN 40 MILES PER HOUR.
8 COLORADO IS THE BIGGEST ROCKY MOUNTAIN STATE.
9 TOMATOES ARE CONSIDERED VEGETABLES.
10 THE SEA OF TRANQUILITY IS A SMALL SEA IN WEST AFRICA.
11 LARGE KANGAROOS CAN COVER OVER 60 FEET IN ONE JUMP.

12 EATING TOO MUCH CARROTS CAN CAUSE A PERSON TO TURN ORANGE.

13 THE FIRST MINIMUM WAGE IN THE U.S.A WAS 25 CENTS PER HOUR

ANSWERS :-

1 FALSE IT IS THE 1 ST AMENDMENT. THE 2 ND AMENDMENT IS THE RIGHT TO BEAR ARMS.

2 FALSE IT IS CLASSIFIED AS HARDWOOD. PINE AND CEDAR ARE CLASSIFIED AS SOFTWOOD.

3 TRUE PENTA MEANS 5 AND DECA MEANS 10.

4 FALSE YOU WOULD HEAT COPPER.

5 TRUE

6 TRUE HE ALSO WROTE THE LITTLE MERMAID.

7 TRUE

8 FALSE MONTANA IS THE BIGGEST, COLORADO IS THE 2 ND BIGGEST.

9 FALSE ANY EDIBLE FOOD OF A PLANT THAT HAS NOTICEABLE SEEDS; IS A FRUIT.

10 FALSE IT IS ON THE MOON.

11 FALSE.

12 TRUE

13 TRUE.

QUESTIONS :-

1 THE CUBAN REVOLUTION TOOK PLACE IN JUNE OF 1959.

2 RIO DE JANEIRO IS ARGENTINA'S CAPITAL CITY.

3 LIGHTNING ALWAYS PRECEDES THUNDER.

4 IT'S ILLEGAL FOR ANY SOCCER PLAYER TO TOUCH THE BALL WITH HIS OR HER HANDS DURING THE GAME.

5 ERNESTO CHE GUEVARA WAS CUBAN.

6 THE CD PLAYER WAS INVENTED BY SONY.

7 THE FAMOUS PAINTING GUERNICA WAS PAINTED BY JOAN MIRO.

8 YOU CAN SEE THE LIGHT OF A STAR THAT IS ALREADY DEAD.

9 CENTIPEDES HAVE 50 PAIRS OF LEGS.

10 THE MOON IS LARGER THAN THE UNITED STATES.

11 NO ANIMALS EAT BEES.

12 THE SHOCK OF AN ELECTRIC EEL CAN KNOCK A MAN DOWN.

13 PEARLS MELT IN VINEGAR.

ANSWERS :-

1 FALSE IT WAS IN JULY OF 1959.

2 FALSE THE CAPITAL IS BUENOS AIRES.

3 TRUE BECAUSE LIGHT TRAVELS FASTER THAN SOUND.

4 FALSE GOALKEEPERS CAN.

5 FALSE HE WAS ARGENTINIAN.

6 FALSE IT WAS PHILIPS; SONY INVENTED THE WALKMAN.

7 FALSE IT WAS BY PABLO PICASSO

8 TRUE

9 FALSE

10 FALSE

11 FALSE SKUNKS EAT BEES.

12 TRUE THE ELECTRIC EEL OF SOUTH AMERICA CAN GENERATE 600 VOLTS AND CAN PARALYZE A HORSE.

13 TRUE A PULVERIZED–CRUSHED PEARL WILL DISSOLVE IN STRONG VINEGAR IN ABOUT 3 HOURS.

QUESTIONS :-

1 IN SOCCER THERE IS A FOUL CALLED DANGEROUS PLAY.

2 ANTS HAVE A BETTER SENSE OF SMELL THAN DOGS.

3 IN THE STATE OF MAINE THERE ARE MORE THAN 100 LIGHTHOUSES

4 IF YOU KEEP A GOLD FISH IN A DARK ROOM, IT WILL TURN WHITE IN A FEW DAYS.

5 DRAGON FLIES HAVE BEEN KNOWN TO FLY 80 TO 90 MILES PER HOUR.

6 THE RINGS OF SATURN ALWAYS MOVE WITH THE EQUATOR OF THE PLANET.

7 THE CLOCK IN LONDON TOWER IS NAMED BIG BEN.

8 THE CAPE OF GOOD HOPE IS THE SOUTHERN MOST TIP OF SOUTH AFRICA.

ANSWERS :-

1 TRUE

2 TRUE

3 FALSE THERE ARE ONLY 62.

4 TRUE

5 FALSE IT IS 50 TO 60 MILES PER HOUR; SOME CARRY A WING SPAN OF UP TO 2 FEET 6 INCHES.

6 TRUE THE RINGS OF SATURN ARE MADE UP OF BILLIONS OF PIECES OF ICE.

7 FALSE BIG BEN IS THE NAME OF THE 13.5 TON BELL IN THE ST. STEPHEN'S TOWER OF THE HOUSES OF PARLIAMENT IN LONDON.

8 FALSE IT IS THE CAPE AGULHAS.

QUESTIONS :-

1 THE ENCYCLOPEDIA BRITTANICA IS BRITISH.

2 CHINESE CHECKERS DID NOT ORIGINATE IN CHINA.

3 TURKEY IS THE TERM USED TO INDICATE THREE CONSECUTIVE STRIKES IN BOWLING.

4 COFFEE IS NOT THE ONLY BEVERAGE EVER TO RECEIVE THE PAPAL SEAL OF APPROVAL.

5 THE CHINESE INVENTED POP CORN.

6 YOU HAVE TO BE SINGLE TO EARN A BACHELOR OF ARTS OR SCIENCE DEGREE.

7 THE LETTER E IS THE MOST COMMON LETTER IN THE ENGLISH LANGUAGE.

8 THE PRIMARY COLORS OF PIGMENT; SOMETIMES CALLED THE SUBTRACTIVE PRIMARY COLORS ARE RED, YELLOW, BLUE.

9 ZERO IS BOTH AN EVEN NUMBER AND AN ODD NUMBER.

10 IN THE ENGLISH LANGUAGE IT IS NEVER GRAMMATICALLY CORRECT TO START A SENTENCE WITH THE WORD BECAUSE.

11 THE NORTH POLE IS THE ONLY PLACE ON EARTH FROM WHICH IT IS POSSIBLE TO WALK 50 MILES SOUTH 50 MILES EAST AND 50 MILES NORTH AND END BACK WHERE YOU STARTED.

12 THERE IS ACTUALLY A PAINTING CALLED RED SQUARE CONSISTING OF A PLAIN RED SQUARE.

ANSWERS :-
1 FALSE IT IS AMERICAN.
2 TRUE
3 TRUE
4 FALSE IT IS COFFEE ONLY.
5 FALSE IT WAS THE AMERICAN INDIANS.
6 FALSE
7 TRUE
8 FALSE THE COLORS ARE CYAN, YELLOW, MAGENTA.
9 FALSE
10 FALSE
11 FALSE
12 TRUE

QUESTIONS :-
1 A LUNAR ECLIPSE TAKES PLACE WHEN THE EARTH IS DIRECTLY BETWEEN THE SUN AND THE MOON. IT CAUSES THE MOON TO TURN A DARK REDDISH COLOR.

2 THERE IS AN ISLAND CALLED BIKINI ATOLL WHERE THE U.S TESTED NUCLEAR BOMBS.

3 THE ERIE CANAL WAS 363 MILES LONG WHEN FINISHED.

4 WHO SANG SINGING IN THE RAIN WHILE DANCING IN THE STREETS IN THIS MOVIE MUSICAL.

5 WHAT COLOR IS THE RAIN ACCORDING TO PRINCE.

6 WHAT COLOR IS THE RAIN ACCORDING TO PETER GABRIEL.

7 IF THE RAIN COMES THEY RUN AND HIDE THEIR HEADS. THEY MIGHT AS WELL BE DEAD. IF THE RAIN COMES, IF THE RAIN COMES WHO SANG THIS?

8 WHO WROTE BLUE EYES CRYING IN THE RAIN.?

9 WHAT TOWN WAS IT RAINING IN WHEN HARRY PICKED UP SUE IN HARRY CHAPIN'S SONG TAXI.

10 ALBERT HAMMOND SAYS IT NEVER RAINS IN THE SOUTHERN PART OF THIS U.S STATE; NAME IT.

11 ON WHAT BEATLES ALBUM COVER ARE THEY HOLDING UMBRELLAS.

12 IT'S RAINING THIS ACCORDING TO THE WEATHER GIRLS.

13 WHAT WAS LEFT OUT IN THE RAIN ACCORDING TO JIMMY WEBB'S MAC ARTHUR PARK.

14 RAINY DAYS AND MONDAYS GET WHAT GROUP DOWN.

15 WHERE IS THE RAIN LOCATED ACCORDING TO ELIZA DOOLITTLE IN MY FAIR LADY.

16 THIS BAND WANTED TO KNOW WHO'LL STOP THE RAIN.

17 WHO SAID BUT MY WORDS LIKE SILENT RAINDROPS FILL AND ECHOED IN THE WELLS OF SILENCE.

18 THIS BAND SAID IT FELT GOOD TO BE OUT OF THE RAIN MAINLY BECAUSE THEY'D JUST BEEN THROUGH THE DESERT WHILE RIDING A STRANGE HORSE. NAME THE BAND.

ANSWERS :-
1 TRUE
2 TRUE
3 TRUE
4 GENE KELLY
5 PURPLE
6 RED
7 THE BEATLES
8 WILLIE NELSON
9 SAN FRANCISCO
10 CALIFORNIA
11 BEATLES 65
12 MEN
13 CAKE
14 CARPENTERS
15 SPAIN
16 CREEDENCE CLEARWATER REVIVAL
17 SIMON AND GARFUNKEL
18 AMERICA

QUESTIONS :-
1 AN IRONMONGER WORKS WHERE?
2 FROM WHAT WERE THE U.S PENNIES MADE IN 1943?
3 YOU'VE REALLY GOT ME NOW, WHICH BAND PRODUCED THIS SONG.
4 IF YOU ARE A GOLD BRICKER WHAT ARE YOU LIKELY TO BE DOING?

5 WHICH METAL IS NOT FOUND IN SEAWATER IN THE HIGHEST CONCENTRATION.

6 THE WEIGHT OF AN ELECTRON IS 1.6 * 10 ^ -19 KGS.

7 ATOMIC WEIGHT IS EXPRESSED IN WHAT?

8 WHAT PRINCIPLE STATES THE ORBITALS OF LOWER ENERGY ARE FILLED FIRST THAN THOSE OF HIGHER ENERGY.

9 HALF AND FULL FILLED ORBITALS ARE MORE STABLE THAN OTHERS.

10 PRINCIPAL QUANTUM NUMBER IS DENOTED BY WHAT?

11 WHICH ORBITAL IS SPHERICAL IN SHAPE?

12 AN ELECTRON HAS HOW MANY QUANTUM NUMBERS?

ANSWERS :-
1 HARDWARE STORE.
2 STEEL
3 THE KINKS
4 AS LITTLE AS POSSIBLE.
5 MANGANESE
6 FALSE IT IS 9.1 * 10 ^ - 31 KGS.
7 ATOMIC MASS UNITS [AMU].
8 AUFBAU
9 TRUE
10 N
11 S
12 4

QUESTIONS :-
1 WHAT DO YOU MEAN BY SAYING CHEERS?
2 WHAT DO YOU MEAN BY THANKS ME OLD MUCKER?
3 YOU ARE HAVING A BUBBLE; WHAT ARE YOU DOING?
4 YOU ARE CALLED A SPANNER.
5 SOMEONE SAYS HE WANTS A PLASTER.
6 ASKED IF YOU HAVE A COTTON BUD.
7 ASKED IF YOU WOULD LIKE SOME PICKLE IN YOUR SANDWICH,
8 IN AMERICA IT IS CALLED A BISCUIT. WHAT DO THE BRITISH CALL IT?
9 IN AMERICA IT IS CALLED COTTON CANDY. WHAT DO THE BRITISH CALL IT?

ANSWERS :-

1 THANKING SOMEONE FOR A NOBLE GESTURE.

2 THANK YOU MY FRIEND.

3 YOU ARE HAVING A LAUGH, PULLING SOMEONE'S LEG.

4 YOU ARE AN IDIOT.

5 HE WANTS A BAND – AID.

6 IT MEANS A Q – TIP.

7 A SWEET CHUTNEY

8 SCONE

9 CANDY FLOSS.

QUESTIONS :-

1 WHERE AND WHEN WAS WINSTON CHURCHILL BORN?

2 WHERE DID CHURCHILL CONTINUE HIS EDUCATION AFTER LEAVING HARROW?

3 WHEN DID CHURCHILL FIRST BECOME A MEMBER OF THE BRITISH PARLIAMENT?

4 DURING WORLD WAR 1 CHURCHILL CAME TO BE ASSOCIATED WITH A MILITARY DISASTER; WHAT WAS IT?

5 WHEN DID CHURCHILL START HIS WARNINGS ABOUT NAZI GERMANY?

6 WHEN DID CHURCHILL FIRST BECOME PRIME MINISTER?

7 IN THE SECOND HALF OF THE 1940'S CHURCHILL FAVORED EUROPEAN INTEGRATION.

8 WHEN DID CHURCHILL DIE?

9 WHERE IS HE BURIED?

ANSWERS :-

1 WOODSTOCK, OXFORDSHIRE 1874

2 ROYAL MILITARY ACADEMY, SANDHURST.

3 1900

4 THE DARDENELLES.

5 1934

6 MAY 1940

7 TRUE

8 24 JANUARY 1965.

9 BLADON, OXFORDSHIRE.

QUESTIONS :-

1 WHICH GREEK HISTORIAN WROTE A UNIVERSAL HISTORY OF ROME'S RISE TO HEGEMONY [DOMINANCE OF ONE NATION OVER OTHERS] OVER THE WHOLE WORLD?

2 WHICH KING LEFT HIS COUNTRY IN A WILL TO ROME IN 133 BC?

3 WHICH FAMOUS ROMAN GENERAL EVENTUALLY WON THE JUGURTHINE WAR 112 – 105 BC FOR ROME?

4 IN WHAT YEAR WAS JULIUS CAESAR'S FIRST INVASION OF BRITAIN

ANSWERS :-
1 POLYBIUS
2 ATTALUS 111
3 MARIUS
4 55 BC

QUESTIONS REGARDING PAST PRESIDENTS OF THE U.S.A :-
1 HE WAS ONLY PRESIDENT FOR 4 MONTHS.
2 HE WAS SHERIFF, MAYOR AND GOVERNOR.
3 HE SERVED IN THE CIVIL WAR.
4 HE WAS KNOWN FOR COLD FOOT BATHS AS HIS SECRET TO LONGEVITY.
5 WAS A MAILROOM CLERK AND FARMER.
6 HE MISSED BEING ASSASSINATED 2 TIMES.
7 HE SPOKE 7 LANGUAGES.
8 HIS PARENTS BELONGED TO A FUNDAMENTALIST RELIGIOUS SECT CALLED THE RIVER BRETHREN.
9 HE CREATED THE CONSTITUTION OF THE COMMONWEALTH OF MASSECHUSETTES.
10 HE WAS A LAWYER.

ANSWERS :-
1 JAMES A GARFIELD
2 GROVER CLEVELAND
3 WILLIAM MCKINLEY
4 THOMAS JEFFERSON
5 HARRY S TRUMAN
6 ANDREW JACKSON
7 JOHN QUINCY ADAMS
8 DWIGHT EISENHOWER

9 JOHN ADAMS

10 JAMES BUCHANAN

QUESTIONS :-

1 KING CANUTE OF ENGLAND WAS ALSO KING OF TWO OTHER COUNTRIES.

2 WHO WAS THE ONLY WOMAN TO HAVE BEEN QUEEN OF ENGLAND AND QUEEN OF FRANCE?

3 WHICH SPANISH KING PROCLAIMED HIMSELF EMPEROR OF HISPANIA IN 1056?

4 MARY STUART WAS QUEEN OF SCOTLAND IN HER OWN RIGHT BUT SHE WAS ALSO QUEEN – CONSORT OF FRANCE. TO WHICH KING WAS SHE MARRIED?

5 WHICH PRUSSIAN KING BECAME EMPEROR OF GERMANY IN 1871?

6 YING ZHENG WAS THE RULER OF WHICH CHINESE KINGDOM BEFORE BECOMING THE FIRST EMPEROR TO UNITE THE WHOLE OF CHINA?

7 VICTOR EMMANUEL 11 WAS THE FIRST KING OF ITALY. OF WHICH KINGDOM HAD HE BEEN THE RULER PRIOR TO THIS?

8 BETWEEN 1707 AND 1837 THE KINGS OF GREAT BRITAIN AND IRELAND WERE ALSO MONARCHS OF WHICH GERMAN KINGDOM?

9 KING LUDWIK 1 OF POLAND, KING WENCELAS 111 OF BOHEMIA AND KING CHARLES 111 OF NAPLES ALL HELD WHICH ADDITIONAL TITLE AT SOME POINT IN THEIR CAREERS?

ANSWERS :-

1 DENMARK AND NORWAY.

2 ELEANOR OF ACQUITAINE

3 FERDINAND 1 OF CASTILE.

4 FRANCIS 11

5 WILLIAM 1

6 QIN

7 SARDINIA

8 HANOVER

9 KING OF HUNGARY.

QUESTIONS :-

1 WHAT IS AN SCBA USED FOR?

2 WHAT DOES THE ACRONYM SCBA STAND FOR?

3 A BLEVE IS A USEFUL TOOL FOR A HAZARDOUS MATERIALS TECHNICIAN.

4 WHICH IS A DANGEROUS RADIO ACTIVE PARTICLE DURING AN INCIDENT?

5 A SPECIFIC GRAVITY OF LESS THAN ONE MEANS THAT A MATERIAL WILL BEHAVE IN WHICH MANNER WHEN RELEASED IN WATER?

6 WHAT DOES THE NOTATION LC – 50 INDICATE?

7 WATER HAS A PH VALUE OF 7.

8 WHAT IS SUBLIMATION?

9 DECONTAMINATION OF PERSONNEL SHOULD TAKE PLACE IN THE WHAT ZONE?

10 IF YOU ARE NEAR A HAZARDOUS MATERIALS RELEASE INCIDENT, YOU SHOULD IMMEDIATELY POSITION YOURSELF UPWIND AND DOWNHILL FROM THE INCIDENT LOCATION?

ANSWERS :-

1 BREATHING FRESH AIR IN A TOXIC ENVIRONMENT.

2 SELF CONTAINED BREATHING APPARATUS.

3 FALSE

4 GAMMA

5 IT WILL FLOAT.

6 LETHAL CONCENTRATION 50 %.

7 TRUE.

8 PROCESS BY WHICH A SOLID TURNS TO A VAPOR WITHOUT GOING THROUGH A LIQUID STATE.

9 WARM ZONE.

10 FALSE .

CHAPTER 34.

CAN YOU SAY.

QUESTIONS :-

1 ISOBARS ARE AN IMPORTANT FEATURE SHOWN ON WEATHER MAPS. THEY JOIN UP POINTS WHICH HAVE EQUAL VALUES OF WHAT?

2 THE AIR IN A LARGE PAPER BAG IS HEATED. THE BAG THEN RISES THROUGH THE SURROUNDING COLD AIR. THIS IS BECAUSE HEAT ALWAYS RISES.

3 WHICH IS A POOR CONDUCTOR OF ELECTRICITY?

4 THE MOTION OF THE MOLECULES OF TWO GASES CAUSES THEM TO MIX. WHAT IS THIS MIXING CALLED?

5 THE RANGE OF AUDIBLE FREQUENCIES OF HEARING FOR A YOUNG PERSON IS FROM 20 HZ TO 2000 HZ.

6 WHEN A PLASTIC ROD IS CHARGED POSITIVELY BY FRICTION, WHAT HAPPENS?

7 WHICH QUANTITY CAN BE MEASURED IN UNITS OF JOULE / COULOMB?

ANSWERS :-

1 PRESSURE

2 NO. THE AIR EXPANDS WHEN IT IS HEATED AND BECOMES LESS DENSE.

3 A VACUUM. A VACUUM CANNOT CONDUCT HEAT ENERGY SINCE IT HAS NO PARTICLES FOR CONDUCTION.

4 DIFFUSION

5 NO. THE AUDIBLE FREQUENCIES IS 20 HZ TO 20,000 HZ.

6 IT LOSES ELECTRONS.

7 POTENTIAL DIFFERENCE.

QUESTIONS :-

1 WHO ARE THE 5 PERSONS WHO PLAYED JAMES BOND?

2 WHAT IS THE REAL NAME OF THE LEAD SINGER FROM U2; OTHERWISE KNOWN AS BONO?

3 ELTON JOHN USED PART OF HIS REAL NAME IN AN ALBUM TITLE. WHAT IS HIS REAL NAME?

4 CHER IS AN ICON WHO ONLY NEEDS ONE NAME, BUT WHAT NAME WAS SHE BORN WITH?

5 GEORGE MICHAEL TOOK A STAGE NAME EASIER FOR HIS FANS TO PRONOUNCE. WHAT IS HIS REAL NAME?

6 WHAT IS SINGER MACY GRAY ALSO KNOWN AS?

ANSWERS :-

1 SEAN CONNERY, ROGER MOORE, GEORGE LAZENBY, TIMOTHY DALTON, PIERCE BROSNAN.

2 PAUL HEWSON

3 REGINALD KENNETH DWIGHT

4 CHERILYN SARKISIAN LA PIERE.

5 GEORGIOS PANAYIOTON

6 NATALIE MCINTYRE

QUESTIONS :-

1 WHAT IS THE LEGAL MINIMUM AGE TO CONSUME ALCOHOL IN THE UNITED STATES?

2 WHAT IS THE LEGAL MINIMUM AGE TO CONSUME ALCOHOL IN AUSTRALIA?

3 WHAT IS THE LEGAL MINIMUM AGE TO CONSUME ALCOHOL IN CHINA?

4 WHAT IS THE LEGAL MINIMUM AGE TO CONSUME ALCOHOL IN GERMANY?

5 WHAT IS THE LEGAL MINIMUM AGE TO CONSUME ALCOHOL IN JAPAN?

6 WHAT IS THE AGE LIMIT AT HOME WITH PARENT CONSENT IN THE UNITED KINGDOM?

7 WHAT IS THE LEGAL MINIMUM AGE TO CONSUME ALCOHOL IN SPAIN AND ITALY?

8 WHICH COUNTRY DOES NOT HAVE A LEGALLY SPECIFIED DRINKING AGE?

9 WHAT AGE DO YOU HAVE TO ATTAIN BEFORE YOU CAN PURCHASE ALCOHOL IN DENMARK?

10 WHAT IS THE LEGAL MINIMUM AGE TO CONSUME ALCOHOL IN MEXICO?

ANSWERS :-

1 21

2 18

3 THERE IS NO LEGAL AGE LIMIT.

4 16 FOR BEER AND 18 FOR SPIRITS.

5 20

6 5

7 16

8 THAILAND

9 15

10 18

QUESTIONS :-

1 WHEN WAS THOMAS EDISON BORN?

2 WHAT IS THOMAS EDISON'S MIDDLE NAME?

3 WHAT DID THOMAS EDISON DISCOVER OR HELP TO IMPROVE?

4 WHEN DID THOMAS EDISON DIE?

5 AT WHAT AGE DID THOMAS EDISON BECOME A TELEGRAPH OPERATOR?

6 IN 1876 THOMAS EDISON BUILT HIS FAMOUS LABORATORY IN MENLO PARK. IN WHICH U.S STATE IS THAT?

7 IN 1879 THOMAS EDISON SUCCESSFULLY TESTED THE INCANDESCENT LIGHT. WHAT DID HE USE FOR A FILAMENT?

8 WHAT IS THE NAME OF THOMAS EDISON'S MOTION PICTURE INVENTION?

9 WHEN DID THOMAS EDISON MARRY HIS FIRST WIFE MARY STILWELL?

10 THOMAS EDISON'S SECOND WIFE MINA MILLER HAD 3 KIDS WITH HIM; MADELEINE, CHARLES, AND THEODORE. WHICH OF THESE CHILDREN BECAME THE MOST FAMOUS?

ANSWERS :-
1 FEBRUARY 11 1847.
2 ALVA
3 PHONOGRAPH, LIGHT BULB, TELEPHONE.
4 OCTOBER 18 1931.
5 15
6 NEW JERSEY.
7 BURNED SEWING THREAD.
8 KIMETOSCOPE.
9 DECEMBER 25 1871.
10 CHARLES; HE WAS A SECRETARY OF THE U.S NAVY AND GOVERNOR OF NEW JERSEY.

QUESTIONS :-
1 WHAT PROPERTY APPLIES TO THE X – RAYS, GAMMA RAYS, INFRA – RED, ULTRA – VIOLET AND VISIBLE LIGHT?
2 A COPPER PLATE IS HEATED TO 100 DEGREES CENTIGRADE. IT COOLS BY EMITTING WHAT?
3 FROM WHICH MATERIAL SHOULD A BOX FOR STORING RADIOACTIVE SUBSTANCE BE MADE
4 MANY HOUSES HAVE AN ELECTRICITY METER THAT IS READ SO THAT THE COST OF THE ELECTRICITY USED BY THE CUSTOMER CAN BE CALCULATED. WHAT DOES THE ELECTRIC METER RECORDS?
5 WHICH PROPERTY OF A BODY IS AFFECTED BY A CHANGE IN THE GRAVITATIONAL FIELD?
6 WHICH MATERIAL IS THE BEST ABSORBER OF INFRA – RED RADIATION?
7 WHAT CAUSES A MOVING BODY TO RESIST A CHANGE IN ITS STATE OF MOTION?

ANSWERS :-
1 THEY ALL TRAVEL WITH THE SAME SPEED IN A VACUUM. THEY ARE ALL ELECTROMAGNETIC WAVES.
2 INFRA – RED RADIATION.
3 LEAD.
4 ENERGY
5 WEIGHT
6 DARK ANIMAL FUR.
7 INERTIA

QUESTIONS :-

1 WHAT SPORT IS PLAYED ON BILLY WILLIAM'S CABBAGE PATCH?

2 WHAT DO JANE SHORE, NELL GWYN AND LILLIE LANGTRY HAVE IN COMMON?

3 THE ACT OF UNION OF 1536 INVOLVED WHICH 2 COUNTRIES?

4 WHAT IS THE NAME OF THE ONLY PRIVATE ARMY IN BRITAIN?

5 SARAH GAMP WAS A CHARACTER IN WHICH CHARLES DICKENS NOVEL?

6 HENRY V11 WAS RESPONSIBLE FOR BRINGING WHAT TO ENGLAND?

7 WHO ENTRUSTED HENRY 11 WITH CAPTURING IRELAND?

8 QUEEN ELIZABETH 1 REIGNED FOR HOW MANY YEARS?

9 HENRY 1'S TWO LEGITIMATE SONS DIED IN WHICH TRAGEDY?

10 WHO WAS THE LAST STUART MONARCH?

11 WHO WAS THE LAST REIGNING MONARCH TO LEAD HIS SUBJECTS ON THE FIELD OF BATTLE?

12 HOW MANY PRIME MINISTERS DID BRITAIN HAVE DURING QUEEN VICTORIA'S REIGN?

ANSWERS :-

1 RUGBY.

2 THEY WERE ROYAL MISTRESSES.

3 ENGLAND AND WALES.

4 THE ATHOLL HIGHLANDERS.

5 MARTIN CHUZZLEWITT.

6 THE RENAISSANCE.

7 POPE ADRIAN 1V.

8 44.

9 THE WHITE SHIP.

10 QUEEN ANNE.

11 GEORGE 11.

12 10.

QUESTIONS :-

1 IF YOU ARE A COWARD, YOU MAY BE CALLED WHAT COLOR?

2 WILLIAM III OF ENGLAND WAS OF THE HOUSE OF ORANGE.

3 WHICH IS THE LARGEST MAMMAL?

4 IN WHICH YEAR WAS GREENPEACE SET UP?

5 INDIGO IS THE NAME OF A BLUE PIGMENT.

6 GOD GAVE NOAH AND MANKIND THE FIRST RAINBOW AFTER THE FLOOD. HOW LONG DID THE FLOOD LAST?

7 SOUTH AFRICA IS KNOWN AS THE RAINBOW NATION.

8 YOU CAN GO UNDER A RAINBOW'S ARCH AND COME OUT THE OTHER SIDE.

ANSWERS :-

1 YELLOW.

2 TRUE.

3 BLUE WHALE.

4 1971.

5 TRUE.

6 40 DAYS AND 40 NIGHTS. THE RAINBOW WAS GIVEN AS A SIGN THAT SUCH A GREAT FLOOD WOULD NEVER HAPPEN AGAIN.

7 TRUE.

8 FALSE.

QUESTIONS :-

1 WHAT IS THE NAME OF THE LARGEST LAKE IN HONDURAS?

2 WHICH HURRICANE DEVASTATED HONDURAS IN 1998, KILLING SOME 5,600 PEOPLE?

3 AT 2,870 METERS TALL, THIS MOUNTAIN IS THE HIGHEST POINT IN HONDURAS. WHAT IS THE NAME OF THE MOUNTAIN?

4 ON WHAT DATE DID HONDURAS BECOME INDEPENDENT FROM SPAIN?

5 OVER 50 % OF THE HONDURAN PEOPLE ARE LIVING BELOW THE POVERTY LINE.

ANSWERS :-

1 CAGO DE YOJOA.

2 HURRICANE MITCH; ALSO ONE BILLION DOLLARS [1,000,000,000,000] WORTH OF DAMAGE OCCURRED.

3 CERRO LAS MINAS.

4 SEPTEMBER 15 1821.

5 TRUE.

QUESTIONS ON HEBREW :-

1 WHAT DOES THE NAME SHAI MEAN?

2 MICHAEL OR MICHAL FOR GIRLS MEANS SHE OR HE WHO IS LIKE GOD.

3 WHAT DOES THE NAME MATANYA MEAN?

4 WHAT DOES THE NAME ADAM MEAN?

5 DAVID MEANS BELOVED.

6 WHICH ANIMAL DOES THE HEBREW ZE'EV MEAN?

7 WHAT DOES NISSAN MEAN?

8 WHAT DOES SHEM MEAN?

ANSWERS :-

1 A GIFT.

2 TRUE.

3 GIFT OF GOD.

4 EARTH.

5 TRUE.

6 WOLF.

7 A MIRACLE.

8 NAME.

QUESTIONS :-

1 WHICH CLASS OF ANIMALS ARE SO CALLED BECAUSE THEIR STOMACH IS CLOSE TO THEIR FOOT?

2 WHICH GROUP OF 320 ISLANDS WAS DISCOVERED BY ABEL TASMAN IN 1643 AND CEDED TO BRITAIN IN 1874?

3 COMPACT DISCS [CD'S] ARE MADE FROM WHICH METAL?

4 WHAT IS POLYTETRAFLUOROETHYLENE MORE COMMONLY CALLED?

5 WHICH PLAY BY WILLIAM SHAKESPEARE REQUIRES A DOG TO APPEAR ON STAGE?

6 INZVAR KAMPRAD WAS THE FOUNDER OF WHICH COMPANY OF HOME FURNISHING RETAIL CHAIN IN 1943?

7 APPROXIMATELY HOW MANY STRINGS HAS THE MUSICAL INSTRUMENT CALLED A SITAR?

8 WHO WAS THE FAMOUS BRITISH VICTORIAN EXPLORER WHO SPOKE AT LEAST 29 DIFFERENT LANGUAGES?

9 HOW DID MARGARET MITCHELL, THE AUTHOR OF GONE WITH THE WIND DIE?

ANSWERS :-

1 GASTROPOD.

2 FIJI.

3 ALUMINIUM.

4 TEFLON.

5 THE TWO GENTLEMEN OF VERONA.

6 IKEA.

7 17.

8 SIR RICHARD BURTON.

9 SHE WAS STRUCK BY AN AUTOMOBILE.

QUESTIONS :-

1 THIS SMALL CRUSTACEAN LIVES ON THE PACIFIC SHORES OF NORTH AMERICA; GROWS TO ABOUT 2 INCHES IN LENGTH, AND LIVES ON ALGAE AND DEAD ANIMALS. WHAT IS IT?

2 THIS FISH FILLS ITS BODY WITH WATER; SO IT BECOMES TOO BIG FOR A PREDATOR TO SWALLOW. IT IS ALSO COVERED WITH SHARP SPINES. WHAT FISH IS IT?

3 THIS WORM LIVES UNDER ROCKS; REACHES UP TO 6 INCHES IN LENGTH AND IT DELIVERS PAINFUL STINGS. WHAT WORM IS IT?

4 THIS SPONGE IS VERY COMMON IN THE PACIFIC OCEAN. IT GROWS IN COLONIES AND IS NAMED FOR ITS STRIKING COLOR.

5 THIS SYMBIOTIC CREATURE REMOVES PARASITES AND DEAD SCALES FROM FISH.

6 THIS LOBSTER DIGS THROUGH THE SAND TO FIND ITS FOOD.

7 THIS IS THE LARGEST OF THE SEA TURTLES.

8 SHARKS ARE GENERALLY DANGEROUS TO HUMANS.

9 THIS IS TRUE OF OCTOPUSES.

10 HOW DID THE RIGHT WHALE GET ITS NAME?

ANSWERS :-
1 PURPLE SHORE CRAB.
2 PORCUPINE FISH.
3 ORANGE FIREWORM.
4 YELLOW SPONGE.
5 CLEANER SHRIMP.
6 SLIPPER LOBSTER.
7 LEATHERBACK SEA TURTLE.
8 FALSE.
9 OCTOPUSES HAVE POOR EYESIGHT.
10 IT WAS CONSIDERED TO BE THE BEST WHALE TO HUNT.

QUESTIONS :-
1 HOW DID PEPSI – COLA GET ITS NAME?
2 WHY DID DR. PEPPER ONCE HAVE 10 – 2 – 4 ON ITS BOTTLES?
3 WHICH AMERICAN PRESIDENT GAVE US THE MAXWELL HOUSE COFFEE SLOGAN?
4 WHAT DID ANHENSER AND BUSCH NAME BUDWEISER BEER AFTER?
5 MERCEDES – BENZ IS NAMED FOR CARL BENZ'S WIFE.
6 WHERE DID THE CHEVROLET CROSS ORIGINATE?
7 A CAR BRAND NAME WAS ONCE USED TO SELL LIGHT BULBS.
8 NAME THE NATIONALITY OF THE FOUNDER OF BRIDGESTONE TIRES
9 WHERE DID H.J. HEINZ GET HIS 57 VARIETIES SLOGAN FROM?
10 WHERE DID PARAMOUNT PICTURES GET ITS NAME FROM?
11 THE EXXON LOGO WAS ONCE USED IN A MYSTERY STORY.

ANSWERS :-
1 IT ONCE CLAIMED TO CONTAIN PEPSIN.
2 THEY WERE THE TIMES OF THE DAY TO DRINK IT.
3 THEODORE ROOSEVELT.

ROY NOLAN

4 A CZECH TOWN.
5 FALSE.
6 FROM A HOTEL WALLPAPER.
7 TRUE.
8 JAPANESE.
9 A SHOE AD.
10 A NEW YORK APARTMENT HOUSE.
11 TRUE.

QUESTIONS :-
1 WHICH IS A SCALAR QUANTITY?
2 A FORCE OF FRICTION IS NECESSARY IN.
3 WHAT IS EMITTED BY THE HOT METAL FILAMENT IN THE CATHODE RAY TUBE?
4 WHICH FUSE SHOULD BE USED FOR A 750 WATT ELECTRIC IRON CONNECTED TO A 240 VOLT SUPPLY?
5 ON WHAT DOES THE QUALITY – TIMBRE OF A SOUND WAVE DEPEND?
6 WATT – SECOND CAN BE USED AS A UNIT OF ENERGY.

ANSWERS :-
1 THE HEAT NEEDED TO BOIL SOME WATER.
2 THE ACCELERATION OF A CAR.
3 ELECTRONS.
4 5A.
5 THE SHAPE OF THE WAVE.
6 YES.

QUESTIONS :-
1 NAME 4 GREAT CRICKETERS?
2 NAME 4 GREAT CRICKET BOWLERS?
3 NAME 4 ALL ROUNDERS IN CRICKET?
4 NAME 3 WICKET KEEPERS IN CRICKET?
5 NAME 4 OPENING BATSMEN IN CRICKET?
6 HOW MANY CHAPPELL BROTHERS HAVE PLAYED TEST CRICKET FOR AUSTRALIA?
7 FORMER ENGLAND BATSMAN GRAEME HICK WAS BORN IN WHICH COUNTRY?
8 HE PLAYED TEST CRICKET FOR BOTH SOUTH AFRICA AND ZIMBABWE.

9 THIS ENGLISH BOWLER WAS THE FIRST TO TAKE 10 WICKETS IN AN INNINGS.

10 THIS BOWLER BECAME ONLY THE 2 ND MAN TO TAKE 10 WICKETS IN AN INNINGS.

11 WHAT WAS SIR DONALD BRADMAN'S BATTING AVERAGE?

ANSWERS :-

1 GARY SOBERS, BRIAN LARA, SASHIN TENDULKAR, ALAN BORDER.

2 JOHN SNOW, DENNIS LILLIE, LANCE GIBBS, BISHAN SINGH BEDI.

3 IAN BOTHAM, CARL HOOPER, STEVE WAUGH, KAPIL DEV.

4 ALAN KNOT, JEFFREY DUJON, DERRICK MURRAY.

5 GEOFFREY BOYCOTT, GORDON GREENIDGE, DESMOND HAYNES, SUNIL GAVASKAR.

6 3 IAN, GREG, TREVOR.

7 ZIMBABWE.

8 JOHN TRAICOS.

9 JIM LAKER.

10 ANIL KUMBLE.

11 NEARLY 100.

QUESTIONS :-

1 WHAT WAS THE TITLE OF THE NOVEL WRITTEN BY H G WELLS IN 1895?

2 WHAT TYPE OF CLOCK IS A REGULATOR?

3 IN CHILDHOOD WHAT COMMON PLANT WAS USED TO TELL THE TIME?

4 WHAT DOES GMT STAND FOR?

ANSWERS :-

1 THE TIME MACHINE.

2 A PENDULUM CLOCK.

3 DANDELION.

4 GREENWICH MEAN TIME.

QUESTIONS :-

1 WHAT IS THE MOST COMMON BIRD SPECIES IN THE WORLD?

2 THE U.S FIVE CENT PIECE IS COMMONLY REFERRED TO AS A NICKEL. BUT HOW MUCH ACTUAL NICKEL – METAL IS THERE IN A NICKEL?

3 WHICH WEIGHS MORE ASSUMING EQUAL VOLUME; A CUP OF WATER, A CUP OF HEAVY CREAM, OR A CUP OF MOTOR OIL?

4 WHAT IS THE SHORTEST VERSE IN THE BIBLE?

5 WHAT IS THE LONGEST VERSE IN THE BIBLE?

6 WHICH NATION HAS THE HIGHEST PER CAPITA WINE CONSUMPTION

7 IF YOU WORK FOR WAGES IN THE U.S, WHAT PERCENTAGE OF YOUR SALARY WILL BE HELD FOR SOCIAL SECURITY AND MEDICARE TAXES?

8 A SEMI POSTAL STAMP IS ONE WHICH.

9 WHICH WAS THE FIRST U.S STATE TO ABOLISH CAPITAL PUNISHMENT?

ANSWERS :-

1 RED – BILLED QUELEA.

2 25 %.

3 WATER.

4 JOHN 11:35 JESUS WEPT.

5 ESTER 8:9 IT CONTAINS 78 WORDS ACCORDING TO SOME BIBLE VERSIONS.

6 LUXEMBOURG

7 7.65 %.

8 HAS A SURCHARGE ADDED IN ADDITION TO THE POSTAGE COST.

9 MICHIGAN.

QUESTIONS :-

1 RUBBER BANDS LAST LONGER WHEN REFRIGERATED.

2 THERE ARE 293 WAYS TO MAKE CHANGE FOR A DOLLAR.

3 THE AVERAGE PERSON'S LEFT HAND DOES 56 % OF THE TYPING.

4 A SHARK IS THE ONLY FISH THAT CAN BLINK WITH BOTH EYES.

5 THERE ARE MORE CHICKENS THAN PEOPLE IN THE WORLD.

6 TWO – THIRDS OF THE WORLD'S EGGPLANTS ARE GROWN IN NEW JERSEY.

7 THE LONGEST ONE – SYLLABLE WORD IN THE ENGLISH LANGUAGE IS SCREECHED.

8 NO WORD IN THE ENGLISH LANGUAGE RHYMES WITH MONTH, ORANGE, OR PURPLE.

9 DREAMT IS THE ONLY ENGLISH WORD THAT ENDS IN MT.

10 ALMONDS ARE A MEMBER OF THE PEACH FAMILY.

ANSWERS :-
1 TRUE.
2 TRUE.
3 TRUE.
4 TRUE.
5 TRUE.
6 FALSE.
7 TRUE.
8 TRUE.
9 TRUE.
10 TRUE.

QUESTIONS :-
1 MAINE IS THE ONLY STATE WHOSE NAME IS JUST ONE SYLLABLE.

2 THERE ARE ONLY 4 WORDS IN THE ENGLISH LANGUAGE WHICH END IN DOUS.

3 A CAT HAS 32 MUSCLES IN EACH EAR.

4 AN OSTRICH'S EYE IS BIGGER THAN ITS BRAIN.

5 A DRAGONFLY HAS A LIFE SPAN OF 24 HOURS.

6 A GOLDFISH HAS A MEMORY OF 3 SECONDS.

ANSWERS :-
1 TRUE.
2 YES AND THEY ARE TREMENDOUS, HORRENDOUS, STUPENDOUS, HAZARDOUS.
3 TRUE.
4 TRUE.
5 TRUE.
6 TRUE.

QUESTIONS :-

1 IN WHAT BOOK OF THE BIBLE IS EASTER MENTIONED?

2 WHICH WOMAN IS MENTIONED IN EACH OF THE 4 GOSPELS OF THE BIBLE AS COMING TO THE TOMB OF JESUS CHRIST?

3 WHICH BOOK OF THE BIBLE TELLS US THE STONE ON JESUS CHRIST'S TOMB WAS SEALED?

4 WHO REQUESTED THE TOMB TO BE SEALED?

5 HOW MANY ANGELS WERE IN THE TOMB OF JESUS CHRIST?

6 WHAT DAY OF THE WEEK DID JESUS RISE?

7 WHAT WERE JESUS' FIRST RECORDED WORDS AFTER THE RESURRECTION?

8 WHO ROLLED THE STONE AWAY FROM THE FRONT OF THE TOMB?

9 WHAT TIME OF DAY DID THE WOMEN COME TO THE TOMB TO ANNOINT THE BODY OF JESUS?

10 WHAT DID JESUS FIRST EAT AFTER THE RESURRECTION?

ANSWERS :-

1 ACTS.

2 MARY MAGDALENE.

3 MATTHEW.

4 CHIEF PRIESTS AND PHARISEES.

5 2.

6 THE FIRST DAY.

7 WOMAN, WHY WEEPEST THOU.

8 THE ANGEL OF THE LORD.

9 VERY EARLY IN THE MORNING.

10 FISH AND HONEYCOMB.

QUESTIONS :-

1 THE DOMINICAN REPUBLIC BORDERS ONLY ONE OTHER NATION. WHICH IS IT?

2 THIS IS THE SECOND LARGEST COUNTRY BY AREA IN THE WORLD; YET IT ONLY BORDERS ONE OTHER COUNTRY. WHICH BIG COUNTRY HAS ONLY ONE NEIGHBOR?

3 WHICH OF SPAIN'S NEIGHBOR'S HAS A BORDER WITH SPAIN ONLY?

4 WHAT IS GAMBIA'S ONLY CONTIGUOUS – BEING IN CONTACT WITH NEIGHBOR?

5 WHICH IS THE UNITED KINGDOM'S ONLY LAND NEIGHBOR?

6 WHICH LANDLOCKED COUNTRY IS ENTIRELY SURROUNDED BY SOUTH AFRICA?

7 SAN MARINO IS ENTIRELY LANDLOCKED BY WHICH COUNTRY?

8 WHICH OF THESE ASIAN COUNTRIES HAS ONLY ONE CONTIGUOUS – BEING IN CONTACT WITH NEIGHBOR?

ANSWERS :-
1 HAITI.
2 CANADA.
3 PORTUGAL.
4 SENEGAL.
5 IRELAND AND EIRE AND REPUBLIC OF IRELAND.
6 LESOTHO.
7 ITALY.
8 BRUNEI.

QUESTION WHAT ARE THE OFFICIAL NAMES GIVEN TO THE FOLLOWING COUNTRIES?
1 MEXICO.
2 BRITAIN.
3 VIETNAM.
4 SOUTH AFRICA.
5 NORTH KOREA.
6 GERMANY.
7 RUSSIA.
8 ISRAEL.
9 BOLIVIA.
10 IRAN.
11 MALAYSIA.
12 SWITZERLAND.
13 BANGLADESH.
14 TANZANIA.
15 PAKISTAN.
16 EGYPT.
17 TURKEY.
18 MICRONESIA.
19 OMAN.
20 THE BAHAMAS.

21 NAMIBIA.

22 NIGERIA.

23 KYRGYZSTAN.

24 LAOS.

25 SWEDEN.

ANSWERS :-

1 UNITED MEXICAN STATES.

2 UNITED KINGDOM OF GREAT BRITAIN AND NORTHERN IRELAND.

3 SOCIALIST REPUBLIC OF VIETNAM.

4 REPUBLIC OF SOUTH AFRICA.

5 DEMOCRATIC PEOPLE'S REPUBLIC OF KOREA.

6 FEDERAL REPUBLIC OF GERMANY.

7 RUSSIAN FEDERATION.

8 STATE OF ISRAEL.

9 REPUBLIC OF BOLIVIA.

10 ISLAMIC REPUBLIC OF IRAN.

11 IT'S THE SAME MALAYSIA.

12 SWISS CONFEDERATION.

13 PEOPLE'S REPUBLIC OF BANGLADESH.

14 UNITED REPUBLIC OF TANZANIA.

15 ISLAMIC REPUBLIC OF PAKISTAN.

16 ARAB REPUBLIC OF EGYPT.

17 REPUBLIC OF TURKEY.

18 FEDERATED STATES OF MICRONESIA.

19 SULTANATE OF OMAN.

20 COMMONWEALTH OF THE BAHAMAS.

21 REPUBLIC OF NAMIBIA.

22 FEDERAL REPUBLIC OF NIGERIA.

23 KYRGYZ REPUBLIC.

24 LAOS PEOPLE'S DEMOCRATIC REPUBLIC.

25 KINGDOM OF SWEDEN.

EPILOGUE :-

YES MY FRIEND, THEY WHO DO BUSINESS IN THE DEEP; SEE THE GLORY OF GOD AS IT RELATES TO ALL AREAS OF LIFE IN THIS WORLD. DO NOT BE TOSSED TO AND FRO IN LIFE AS THE WAVES OF THE SEA; BE STABLE AND ASSURED OF YOURSELF AND GOD SHALL ESTABLISH YOU WITH KNOWLEDGE AND POWER AND BLESS YOU BEYOND MEASURE; HERE IN THIS LIFE AS WELL AS FOR ALL ETERNITY. PEOPLE SUFFER AND ARE DESTROYED FOR LACK OF KNOWLEDGE. WITH EFFECTIVE AND EFFICIENT ACCUMULATED KNOWLEDGE, YOU ARE ABLE TO MAKE INFORMED DECISIONS IN LIFE; MAKING INTELLIGENT CHOICES; FOR THE CHOICES YOU MAKE ULTIMATELY DETERMINE YOUR DESTINY IN LIFE. IN ORDER TO BE A POWERFUL AND SUCCESSFULLY SECURE PERSON, IT'S ABSOLUTELY ESSENTIAL AND NECESSARY TO HAVE BASIC KNOWLEDGE OF THE WORLD IN WHICH YOU LIVE; IN THE VARIOUS SUBJECT MATTERS. IN THIS BOOK "KNOWLEDGE IS POWER", IT HELPS YOU THROUGH INFORMED KNOWLEDGE TO OOZE WITH CONFIDENCE AND COMPETENCE WHICH ARE OF GREAT VALUE TO YOUR WELL BEING IN ACHIEVING SUCCESS IN LIFE. IN THIS BOOK YOU HAVE THE WORLD IN YOUR HANDS. IT GIVES SO MUCH USEFUL INFORMATION, IT AMAZES YOU. THERE IS A LARGE ARRAY – SECTION THAT DEALS WITH NUMBERLESS QUESTION WITH THE ACCOMPANYING ANSWERS. FROM THE KNOWLEDGE DISPENSE IN THIS BOOK, YOU WILL COVER A VAST NUMBER OF SELECTED SUBJECT MATTERS AND AREAS;

ALL FOR YOUR EDIFICATION AND GLORIFIED UPLIFTING IN LIFE; AS YOU LIVE YOUR LIFE ON A DAY TO DAY BASIS, BEING ABLE TO MAKE BETTER INFORMED DECISIONS AND CHOICES REGARDING THE WAY YOU LIVE YOUR LIFE. AS YOU KNOW, KNOWLEDGE IS POWER, APPLY KNOWLEDGE YOU HAVE GAINED TO YOU LIFE AND BECOME A POWERFUL PERSON IN THIS WORLD OF OURS; ENRICH YOUR LIFE AND BE A VALUABLE ALL ROUND PERSON OF DIVERSIFIED KNOWLEDGE; AND SO BE A SHINING EXAMPLE OF A LIFE WELL LIVED IN THE SOCIETY OF HUMANITY. THIS BOOK IS KNOWLEDGEABLE TO ALL PERSONS; OF ALL AGE GROUPS, OF ALL WALKS – AREAS OF LIFE. YOU WILL BE SURE TO WANT YOUR FAMILY, CHILDREN, RELATIVES, FRIENDS AND ACQUAINTANCES TO BE ONES TO GET THIS INDISPENSABLE TEACHING OF KNOWLEDGE; SO THAT IT CAN ENRICH AND BENEFIT THEIR LIVES ALSO. IT IS ROY NOLAN'S TRUST THAT YOU WILL HAVE BENEFITED IMMENSELY FROM THE MATERIALS CONTAINED IN THIS BOOK "KNOWLEDGE IS POWER" LEARN AND YOU WILL KNOW AND BECOME POWERFUL IN KNOWLEDGE, IT WILL LEAD YOU TOWARDS HAVING A PRESTIGIOUS LIFE. IT CAN CERTAINLY HELP YOU TO MAKE YOUR LIFE A SUCCESS; GIVING MEANING AND SATISFACTION TO YOUR LIFE AS YOU DWELL HERE ON THIS EARTH. BE WORTHY OF WHO YOU ARE, A CHILD OF GOD; IN GAINING KNOWLEDGE, THE SPIRIT OF THE LORD SHALL REST UPON YOU AND LEAD YOU INTO ALL TRUTH; YOU SHALL WITH THE HELP OF GOD THROUGH THE HOLY SPIRIT, HAVE THE SPIRIT OF WISDOM OF KNOWLEDGE; AND UNDERSTANDING AND BE BLESSED WITH A LIFE OF MEEKNESS AND RIGHTEOUSNESS AND NO SITUATION OR CIRCUMSTANCE OF LIFE WILL BE ABLE TO OVERWHELM YOU. YOU CAN AND WILL GO FORWARD CONQUERING ON TO CONQUER. THEREFORE, BE FILLED OF THE KNOWLEDGE OF THE WORLD AS IT RELATES TO EVERY ASPECT OF GOD'S CREATION AND DISPENSATION OF KNOWLEDGE IN THE VARIOUS FIELDS OF ENDEAVOR IN LIFE. INCREASE IN KNOWLEDGE FOR ONE DAY YOU WILL HAVE TO GIVE AN ACCOUNT TO GOD FOR THE LIFE YOU LIVE HERE ON EARTH, IN THIS WORLD. I AM SURE YOU WILL WANT TO HEAR GOD SAYS "WELL DONE". SO DO WELL, THIS BOOK "KNOWLEDGE IS POWER", CAN ENLIGHTEN AND ENLIVEN

YOU AS YOU TAKE YOUR LIFE TO A HIGHER LEVEL; BECOME A POWERFUL PERSON OF SUBSTANCE AND VALUE IN LIFE. BECOME KNOWLEDGEABLE AND YOU SHALL FIND FAVOR AND GOOD UNDERSTANDING IN THE SIGHT OF GOD AND ALL PERSONS.

ROY NOLAN CAN BE CONTACTED AT :-
ROYNET123@AOL.COM

ABOUT THE AUTHOR

Roy Nolan: Author, Master Mariner, Oceanographer, University Graduate, Spiritual Counselor, Social Director and lecturer is the author of several books. His books are so realistically forceful and counseling; he engages the attention of a wide cross section of readers in all age groups.

His mission is to be very informative and edifying. He writes on various subject matters; and as always, his works are enlivening and increases and widens your scope of knowledge.

He lays out for the basic educational knowledge foundation in all areas of life. In this book, Knowledge is Power, you have a valuable gem which is priceless in the form of the entire world in your hands. It will enrivh your life beyond measure; making you a more successful and happy person so you too can become and *"BE AS A QUIET WHISPER IN THE WIND."*

Lightning Source UK Ltd.
Milton Keynes UK
UKOW05f2232040814

236350UK00001B/185/P